POLITICAL THOUGHT SINCE WORLD WAR II

Critical and Interpretive Essays

POLITICAL THOUGHT SINCE WORLD WAR II

Edited by W. J. Stankiewicz

The Free Press of Glencoe
Collier-Macmillan Limited, London

To my students in Political Theory—
Docendo discimus

CONTRIBUTORS

RAYMOND ARON (born 1905): Professor of Sociology at the Sorbonne; Editor of *Figaro* since 1947; Author of *L'introduction à la Philosophie de l'Histoire*, 1938 (English edition 1961), *L'opium des Intellectuels*, 1955 (American edition 1957, 1962), *Paix et Guerre entre les Nations*, 1962, and other books.

DANIEL BELL (born 1919): Professor of Sociology at Columbia University; Author of *History of Marxian Socialism in the U.S.*, 1952, *Work and its Discontents: the Cult of Efficiency in America*, 1956, and *The End of Ideology*, 1959.

ERNST BIERI (born 1920): Political Editor, *Neue Zürcher Zeitung;* Author of *Gotteswerk und menschliche Verantwortung im Glauben*, 1946.

ZBIGNIEW K. BRZEZINSKI (born 1928): Professor of Government at Columbia University; Author of *The Permanent Purge—Politics in Soviet Totalitarianism*, 1956, *The Soviet Bloc: Unity and Conflict*, 1960, *Ideology and Power in Soviet Politics*, 1962.

WILLIAM GRAVES CARLETON (born 1903): Professor Emeritus of Political Science at the University of Florida; Author of *The Revolution in American Foreign Policy*, 1954, 1963.

LLOYD GORDON CHURCHWARD (born 1919): Senior Lecturer in Political Science at the University of Melbourne; Joint author (with T. H. Rigby) of *Policy-Making in the U.S.S.R., 1953–1961*, 1962.

ARTHUR A. COHEN (born 1923): A student of Chinese affairs; Preparing a book on Mao Tse-tung and the Communist doctrine.

FRANCIS W. COKER (born 1878): Professor Emeritus of Political Science at Yale University; Author of *Organismic Theories of the State*, 1910, *Recent Political Thought*, 1934.

LEWIS A. COSER (born 1913): Professor of Sociology at Brandeis University; Author of *The Functions of Social Conflict*, 1956; Joint author (with Bernard Rosenberg) of *Sociological Theory*, 1957, and (with Irving Howe) *The American Communist Party: A Critical History (1919–1957)*, 1957.

W. Y. ELLIOTT (born 1896): Leroy B. Williams Professor of History and Political Science at Harvard University; Author of *The Pragmatic Revolt in Politics*, 1926, *The Need for Constitutional Reform*, 1935, *Political Economy of the Foreign Policy of the U.S.*, 1955, and other books.

RUPERT EMERSON (born 1899): Professor of Political Science at

Harvard University; Author of *Malaysia*, 1937, *Representative Govern-ment in Southeast Asia*, 1955, *From Empire to Nation*, 1960, and other books.

CARL J. FRIEDRICH (born 1901): Eaton Professor of the Science of Government at Harvard University and Professor of Political Science at the University of Heidelberg; Author of *Constitutional Government and Democracy*, 1941, 1951, *Inevitable Peace*, 1947, *Philosophy of Law in Historical Perspective*, 1958, and other books.

MORRIS GINSBERG (born 1889): Professor Emeritus of Sociology at the University of London; Author of *Studies in Sociology*, 1932, *Moral Progress*, 1944, *Essays in Sociology and Social Philosophy* (3 volumes), 1956–1961, and other books.

ALAN P. GRIMES (born 1919): Professor of Political Science at Michigan State University; Author of *The Political Liberalism of the New York Nation 1865–1932*, 1953, *American Political Thought*, 1955.

SIDNEY HOOK (born 1902): Professor of Philosophy at New York University; Author of *Heresy, Yes—Conspiracy, No*, 1953, *From Hegel to Marx*, 1950, 1962, *Political Power and Personal Freedom*, 1959, and other books.

IRVING HOWE (born 1920): Professor of English at Stanford Uni-versity; Author of *Sherwood Anderson: A Critical Biography*, 1951, *William Faulkner: A Critical Study*, 1952, 1962, *Politics and the Novel*, 1957.

SAMUEL P. HUNTINGTON (born 1927): Associate Professor of Govern-ment at Columbia University; Author of *The Soldier and the State: The Theory and Politics of Civil-Military Relations*, 1957, *The Common De-fense: Strategic Programs in National Politics*, 1961, *Changing Patterns of Military Politics*, 1962.

Z. A. JORDAN (born 1911): Philosopher; Senior Fellow at the Russian Institute, Columbia University, during 1962–1964; Author of *Mathematical Foundations of Plato's System* (in Polish), 1937, *The Development of Mathematical Logic and of Logical Positivism in Poland between the Wars*, 1945, *Philosophy and Ideology: the Development of Philosophy and Marxism-Leninism in Poland since the Second World War*, 1963.

HANS KELSEN (born 1881): Professor Emeritus at the University of California (Berkeley); Author of *General Theory of Law and State*, 1945, *The Political Theory of Bolshevism*, 1948, *Principles of Interna-tional Law*, 1952, and other books.

KENNETH K. KROGH (born 1921): Director of the International Trade Fairs Division of the U.S. Department of Agriculture.

LEOPOLD LABEDZ (born 1920): Associate Editor of the British magazine *Survey;* Visiting Senior Fellow at Columbia University during 1962–1963.

GORDON K. LEWIS (born 1919): Associate Professor at the College of Social Sciences, University of Puerto Rico; Author of *Puerto Rico: Freedom and Power in the Caribbean*, 1962.

FRED WARNER NEAL (born 1915): Professor of International Relations and Government at Claremont Graduate School; Author of *Titoism in Action*, 1958, *War and Peace and Germany*, 1962; Joint author (with George W. Hoffman) of *Yugoslavia and the New Communism*, 1962.

ENRICO OPOCHER (born 1914): Professor of Philosophy of Law at the University of Padua; Author of *G. A. Fichte e il problema dell' individualità*, 1944, *Il valore dell' esperienza giuridica*, 1947, *Lezioni di storia delle doctrine politiche*, 1955, and other books.

Z. A. PELCZYNSKI (born 1925): Fellow and Tutor in Politics at Pembroke College, Oxford; Joint author (with T. M. Knox) of *Hegel as a Political Writer*, in press.

GEORGE S. PETTEE (born 1904): Chairman of the Advanced Research and Planning Staff at Research Analysis Corporation, Washington, D.C.; Author of *The Progress of Revolution*, 1938, *The Future of American Secret Intelligence*, 1946.

DAVID J. SAPOSS (born 1886): Professorial Lecturer at the School for International Service, American University, Washington, D.C.; Author of *Left Wing Unionism*, 1926, *The Labor Movement of Post-War France*, 1931, *Communism in American Politics*, 1960.

FRANCIS G. WILSON (born 1901): Professor of Political Science at the University of Illinois; Author of *Elements of Modern Politics*, 1936, *Case for Conservatism*, 1951, *A Theory of Public Opinion*, 1962, and other books.

BERTRAM D. WOLFE (born 1896): Historian and political scientist; At present Visiting Professor of Russian History at the University of California (Davis); Author of *Three Who Made a Revolution*, 1948, *Khrushchev and Stalin's Ghost*, 1956, *Communist Totalitarianism: Keys to the Soviet System*, 1961, and other books.

RICHARD WOLLHEIM (born 1923): Reader in Philosophy at the University of London; Author of *F. H. Bradley*, 1959, *Socialism and Culture*, 1961.

DONALD S. ZAGORIA (born 1928): Member of the Social Science Department of the Rand Corporation; Visiting Fellow at Columbia University during 1962–1963; Author of *The Sino-Soviet Conflict 1956–1961*, 1962.

EDITOR

W. J. STANKIEWICZ (born 1922): Associate Professor of Political Science at the University of British Columbia; Author of *Politics and Religion in Seventeenth-Century France*, 1960; Joint author (with J. M. Montias) of *Institutional Changes in the Postwar Economy of Poland*, 1955.

CONTENTS

PART THREE   MARXISM AND COMMUNISM

PART FOUR   VARIETIES OF DEMOCRATIC IDEOLOGIES

PART FIVE NATIONALISM

POSTSCRIPT

INTRODUCTION

Books on modern political thought do not as a rule carry the discussion of ideologies up to the present day; in nearly all of them, the "last chapter" is missing. Although they discuss main doctrines, they are not concerned with the temper of *current* political thought from which future political ideologies will emerge. Modern ideologies tend to be discussed on an abstract level as static "models," without due regard to the modifying process to which they are continually subjected.

The purpose of this book is to present a number of interpretive essays reflecting the current state of discussion on the traditional issues of political ideologies. The selection is not exhaustive. It is not a compendium of all the ideologies that have some adherents today, but only of those that have been specifically formulated (or reformulated) within the existing political systems whose fabrics they permeate. For example, this book does not include a selection on fascism because no significant addition has been made to its original conceptual basis, even though the fascist ideology has survived in neofascist movements in Germany and Italy.

The organization of this book reflects the existence of two conflicting ways of life—the totalitarian and the democratic. Hence the focus on ideological tensions. Hence the attempts to find a definition of the word "ideology" which will encompass such differences; to account for the significance of the diffusion of political ideologies; and to determine the role played by ideologies in the "East-West" conflict. The question of the nature of these ideologies' impact on the conflict is familiar, and the answers are well known. Ideologies, we are told, help to build psychological resistance and strengthen morale. They also offer an effective means of combating an opponent. But what impact does the conflict between East and West have on ideologies? Certainly the main ideologies now current have in some way or other been affected by it.

Under conditions of tension and conflict, ideologies are provided with their "tests of survival" (W. Y. Elliott analyzes this process in terms of power, economic adequacy, hold on man's soul, etc.), and become subject to accelerated change, restatement, and revision. This is true of all the principal ideologies existing within the broad framework of the two opposing ways of life—for example, democracy, totalitarianism, the various brands of revisionism, the new American conservatism, democratic socialism, and liberalism. Consequently, this book will attempt to examine the present state of these ideologies.

The editor has tried to avoid that affliction from which many books of readings suffer: trying to say too much. Some books form a mosaic in which snippets, minute excerpts, and heavily edited pieces vie with each other for priority. Aristotle rubs shoulders with John Doe, and the biographical data of both are dutifully recorded in footnotes. Unfortunately, the obscure and second-rate do not gain stature when placed in the company of the great; their presence serves merely to detract.

The criteria for including the selections here were their degree of emphasis on philosophical aspects and their contribution to an understanding of the state of current debate. No collection of this type can claim evenness, and not all articles in this book are equally critical; but it is hoped that in varying degree these demands have been met and that papers of only transitory interest have been omitted.

No discussion of ideologies can be significant to political science unless it has philosophical roots. Political ideologies provide a meeting ground for political science and philosophy because they contain elements of both. Like systematic political theory (a component of political philosophy), ideologies bear with them systems of values in the ideas or the "myths" they provide. Like political science, ideologies are also positive. They are concerned with facts and the sphere of action, and political science—which is concerned with the analysis of actual political behavior—cannot ignore them. In Carl Friedrich's terms, "the ideological potential . . . does not detract, but rather heightens the significance of political philosophy for political science." Political philosophy must serve as a source of concepts which are relevant to the discussion of ideological trends.

The general picture of current debate on ideologies is one of confusion. The content of various ideologies has often been described with such fuzziness and lack of discrimination that the reader must fail to grasp the essentials. Furthermore, the habitual, unthinking, and almost automatic use of political labels has clouded the issue. As Sartori puts it in his *Democratic Theory:* "To make of thought a matter of discussing whether it is progressive or conservative is for the most part a way of concealing bad thinking and of cheating with good thinking." [1] The most valuable contribution can come only from those whose writings are free of meaningless ideological labels.

Together with the unsatisfactory research on ideology, one must note that political scientists have not recognized their responsibility for the systematic study of ideologies. Since ideologies are the ground upon which political science and philosophy meet, an effort by political scientists to probe the importance of ideologies to their discipline may foster a rapprochement between "institutionalists" and "behavioralists." Both fields should be urged to concentrate on the area in which cooperation seems feasible, rather than follow their separate paths and

1. Giovanni Sartori, *Democratic Theory,* Wayne State University Press, Detroit, 1962, p. 460.

deepen the existing rift. The major obstacle to reconciliation is the perpetuation of the schism within the discipline caused by each scholar's commitment to his approach, which tends to acquire a quasi-ideological character.

Needless to say, this selection of readings does not attempt to include all authors who have made a significant contribution to critical political thought. The politician who writes on contemporary ideologies will not be found here; his writings, if they have any value, are documents rather than critical analyses. Nor will we find the scholar, however eminent, who spins a web of his own esoteric theories, arresting though these theories may be.

A book of readings can never be a homogeneous treatise. It must be regarded as a "workshop" that offers some insight into an evolving process, and helps those who study this process to participate in another activity—that of speculative thinking and generalizing anew.

Inevitably, the various chapters of this book represent a simplified approach to trends and concepts which in reality are not simple. There is a constant interplay of ideas among different political ideologies; for this reason, it is often not helpful to label a particular current of thought as purely socialist, liberal, democratic, or conservative. Certain old labels have lost their meanings; others have acquired new ones; all are in a state of flux. In recent years, for example, fascism has been nearly eliminated, totalitarianism confined to one major area, Marxism subjected to "revision," American conservatism and liberalism strangely intermingled, and democratic principles exposed to scrutiny in the search for "foundations." Like other concepts, nationalism needs a more meaningful label—perhaps several. It is the need to redefine and reclassify that determines the trend of current political thought.

Sincere thanks are due to my friends Professor George Krzywicki-Herburt, of Queens College of the City University of New York, on whom I have repeatedly called for advice, Professor Marketa Goetz of the University of British Columbia for her cooperation throughout the various stages of this project, and Mr. Ronald C. Cooke of Toronto and Dr. Edwin R. Black of UBC for their interest in the same, as well as to the Social Science Research Institute at UBC for financial assistance.

W. J. Stankiewicz

University of British Columbia
August 1963

PART ONE

THE PROBLEM OF IDEOLOGY

INTRODUCTORY NOTE

Current ideologies—the sets of norms and values that dominate each society—cover a broad range, delimited by the positions of the United States and the Soviet Union. The first inculcates its ideology in a loose, haphazard, and indirect fashion, relying largely on an economic offensive and a glorification of its way of life. The other side, neglecting some tenets of its official doctrine, concentrates on political propaganda and spreads its gospel abroad, while treating it in a rather flexible fashion at home.

Representatives of the American point of view refuse to be committed to *any* set of ideological values; they like to imagine themselves free of them because they consider commitment to an ideology unbecoming to citizens of a democracy. In contrast, representatives of the Soviet point of view constantly invoke the ideology within which their action has to be accommodated. They have to justify their actions dialectically and to accept the Party's most recent interpretation of dialectics. The result is ideological hegemony in theory, and Party hegemony in practice.

If the representatives of one camp are wary of committing themselves to any ideology, those of the opposing camp are apprehensive of any noncommitted action. This difference alone indicates the degree of ideological acceptance and diffusion in the two societies, and accounts for the prevailing Western skepticism about the power of ideologies.

This power is being habitually ignored in the West. In some countries, the barriers put up by ignorance are particularly high; habitual empiricism in practice, pragmatism in philosophy, great confidence in the values of one's own system (perhaps a substitute for ideology) contribute to inflexibility in judging the aspirations of other societies which *are* susceptible to the call of ideology. Mental inertia, unwillingness to go beyond the established frame of reference, wishful thinking that all people are basically alike, reluctance to accept a more informed point of view on the ground that it is mere opinion—all this makes it extremely hard for people so oriented to grasp clearly the world in which they live.

On the other side, facing this soft, amorphous society whose ignorance is largely self-imposed, there is another society—a society which is hardboiled, indoctrinated by an ideology, and dedicated to its goals. This other world, although torn by a desperate reaction against the abuses of the system, and often cynical about its dialectical jargon, is proud of its achievements and is developing a feeling of superiority over the West, a feeling for which ideology has been largely responsible.

[2]

These attitudes betray some profound differences between the two sets of ideologies. Do they differ in degree or in kind? One could perhaps suggest that their differences in degree go so far as to become differences in kind. If so, would it be possible to find a single, comprehensive definition of "ideology" applicable to both systems? The issue is more complicated, for the theoretical component of democracy seems to be nonideological in the sense that it is free of rigid norms, even though the present democratic systems tend to develop their own democratic ideologies. It is the totalitarian regimes that most definitions of "ideology" fit best. Not only is totalitarian behavior clearly ideology-oriented, but also, as Marxists maintain, an ideology can serve as an efficient tool of analysis only when it reflects the total socio-political structure of a (totalitarian) state. In such a situation, an ideology can also, to quote Sartre, "interpret and surpass experience in the unity of rational and technical projections."

Today even non-Marxist political science cannot escape the predicament of having to cope with ideologies as systems of action-oriented values. This concern may finally lead to a comprehensive theory of ideology. No attempt has yet been made to treat the whole concept of ideology systematically and to relate it to modern political systems. A partial exception is a book on totalitarian ideology by Carl J. Friedrich and Zbigniew K. Brzezinski, *Totalitarian Dictatorship and Autocracy,* from which two excerpts have been included in this symposium.

Little progress has been made since the pioneer study by Arne Naess and associates, entitled *Democracy, Ideology and Objectivity* (1956), despite pleas such as Léon Dion's to make political ideology "a useful tool of socio-political analysis." [1] Only too often have ideologies been discussed in a loose and unrelated fashion, which adds to the general confusion. The purpose of the four papers (by Aron, Pettee, Coser and Howe, and Elliott) reproduced in this Part is not, of course, to make a systematic, analytical scrutiny, but to indicate possible working definitions and to establish a framework for discussing modern ideological trends, a discussion which constitutes the subject matter of the remaining Parts of this book.

NOTE

1. Léon Dion, "Political Ideology as a Tool of Functional Analysis in Socio-Political Dynamics," *The Canadian Journal of Economics and Political Science,* Vol. 25, No. 1, February 1959, pp. 47-59.

THE DIFFUSION OF IDEOLOGIES

Raymond Aron

. . . It is hardly possible to define the term "ideology" in such a way as to limit its application. On the philosophical level, one can distinguish between "idea" and "ideology" and use the latter term for a certain distortion of ideas. But the political observer or the sociologist, who is interested in ideas as they are thought or lived by individuals or groups, could hardly adopt such a distinction. Any idea or body of ideas, in the lives of men or of collectivities, loses its intrinsic qualities of exactness or demonstrable truth. The modern concept of the heliocentric system may be true, and the Ptolemaic system false: the masses who adhere to the former, after having abandoned the latter, do not proceed psychologically from an ideology to an idea, but change ideologies. A scientific truth, accepted by millions of men, no longer differs psychologically or socially from an accustomed mythological concept. We shall, therefore, call "ideologies" all ideas or bodies of ideas accepted by individuals or peoples, without regard to their origin or nature.

If we give the term "ideology" this broad meaning, it follows that the *methods of diffusion* and the *conditions of acceptance* will be infinitely varied. The first phrase covers all media, from scientific journals to radio, by which, in any period of history, ideas pass from one mind to another or from one region to another. The second applies to all aspects of social reality, for the correlation of the various elements of a society is such that the conditions which determine the acceptance or the non-acceptance of ideas include all the phenomena, demographic, economic, spiritual, and the history of the group under consideration. . . .

I

The facts which have struck observers are universally known. I shall formulate them as follows: An ideology, whose creator was the son of

Reprinted from *Confluence*, vol. 2, no. 1 (March, 1953), 3-12. By permission of the author and the publisher.

[4]

a middle-class Jewish family from the Rhineland, a refugee in London in the middle of the last century, has become the official doctrine first of a country of two hundred million people, then of a country of four hundred million, rich in the oldest, perhaps the highest, culture in the world. On the Gold Coast, on the other hand, parliamentary institutions modeled on those of Great Britain have sprung up, and in South Korea democratic institutions patterned after those of the United States. In a series of countries in Asia and the Near East, ideas of Western democracy (elections, parties, parliaments, unions) have been introduced, as if they represented the normal way men must govern themselves.

This phenomenon presents, it seems to me, several original features in comparison with phenomena of the same type observed in the past. The diffusion of ideologies is accompanied by the transmission of institutions, the most important institutions in the lives of collectivities, namely those which establish the relationships between government and governed, and define the methods by which officials will be chosen. The ideology which is spreading in one part or another of the world is linked, in men's minds, with one or the other of the great powers. Its diffusion is associated with the hegemony exercised, or supposedly exercised, by the Soviet Union or the United States. The ideologies which are being disseminated all originate in Western societies; their spread is accompanied by more or less violent reactions against the West. The two main ideologies currently in process of dissemination appear in the form of an antithesis, often employing the same words and related symbols, but manifesting irreconcilable hatred for each other.

All these remarks are commonplace, and are presented as such. Their aim is simply to indicate a working principle. Although our topic fits into a larger framework, that of the spread of ideologies, of which the expansion of Christianity, Islam, Protestantism, and democracy are familiar examples, it assumes in these times a peculiar urgency. At the present moment, the same ideology (or at least apparently the same) is spreading in Western societies against legal governments and in societies which are fundamentally different from those of the West. The same institutions (or at least apparently the same) are developing in countries whose economic and social structures are as dissimilar as possible. The adaptation of political regimes to the economic and social substructure, which was fundamentally the common basis of most political doctrines of the last century, is belied by the facts.

The most varied methods of diffusion—from class to class, from civilization to civilization, by military conquest, apparently without the intervention of force, by the action of the few, by the action of masses—are thus found in the case of the diffusion of the so-called Western ideologies as well as in that of the so-called Communist ideologies. In both cases, likewise, the diffusion of ideologies tends toward the diffusion of institutions. In both cases one can observe the individuals and the peoples who are the bearers of the new ideologies, and one ought to be able to analyze the social origins and the recruiting of these groups, as well as their relations with the privileged groups of the old social structure.

These specific characteristics of the spread of ideologies in the twentieth century cannot be the direct object of inquiry. But, in drawing the lines of our discussion, we must keep these characteristics in mind, so that as a group they may furnish answers to the questions which dominate the subject as a whole. What factors explain the global dissemination of the Western ideologies in our times? What is the precise role of ideologies in this spread of the forms of civilization? How are the ideas and the institutions which have ripened in Western societies implanted in untilled soil?

II

Let us examine as one aspect of the general problem the diffusion of ideologies through Point Four. Point Four, or the extension of Western skills and technical resources to so-called underdeveloped countries, has within the space of a few years become one of the officially recognized and proclaimed objectives of American policy. If there are differences of opinion as to the amounts which the United States can devote to Point Four, there is hardly any controversy, it seems to me, over the effectiveness of that assistance in the world struggle against Communism. It is an article of faith with American opinion that fortunate peoples, that is, those with a high standard of living, are hostile to Communism, as to any other form of despotism. The best barrier against Communism, so the argument goes, is prosperity or, at least, economic progress.

It is not my intention to question the guiding ideas of American policy. The spread of Western techniques seems to me both inevitable and, from a humanitarian standpoint, desirable. To be sure, the expression "underdeveloped countries" is shocking to the historian. Indeed, this concept takes in the black tribes of Central Africa and some of the highest cultures humanity has ever known (in China or the Indies). The only common feature of these underdeveloped countries is, of course, their backwardness in the ways of industrial civilization, which is of Western origin. But, at the present moment, a rejection of that civilization would not insure the preservation of values which are perhaps incompatible with science and Western technology; it would instead condemn those countries, with their ancient cultures, to helplessness and dismemberment.

The following remarks, which are not a dogmatic pronouncement but an introduction to a concerted investigation, are intended to call attention to a fundamental question: In what political circumstances is the extension of technical skills and resources possible? What will the probable results of that assistance be, as determined by the methods employed and by the ideological and political atmosphere?

Out of a hundred articles concerning Point Four which have appeared in the American press, I do not believe that one can be found which analyzes its political conditions. And yet, is it not obvious that the rationalizing of an economy presupposes a certain judicial and political environment? Everyone knows that the exportation of the most modern machines serves no practical purpose if the factory in which these machines are installed is not managed in a spirit similar to that of the Western economies. The spread of technological methods within enterprises carries with it that of modes of thought and organization. What conditions must be fulfilled in order that private capital will be prepared to invest in a given territory? What guarantees must the leaders of underdeveloped countries give that government capital invested in them will produce satisfactory results (*a*) on the economic level and (*b*) on the political level?

These questions are very broad, but our inquiry bears particularly on *the urgent need to study them.*

We have witnessed for a century what is probably the most extraordinary spread of political ideologies and institutions in history. European civilization, with its North American extension, has circled the globe and compelled recognition of its superiority (in control over nature and men, at least) by the peoples of other continents. Chinese, Hindus, Moslems have been subjugated, humiliated, and exploited by the makers of machines. Prestige goes with power. The institutions of the conquering country seem endowed with singular virtues. English fortunes in the nineteenth century contributed to the diffusion of parliamentary institutions. European fortunes gave democratic ideas and representative institutions such a luster that the five continents sought to imitate them. The idea of democracy and the creation of elected parliaments passed for models of modern political science.

We have no thought of inviting a discussion of the merits and demerits of democracy, but only of recalling the problematical element in its expansion. In Europe, democracy was the term of a long evolution; the states were strong, the nations unified by centuries of community life, before the exercise of power was constitutionalized and the executive itself finally chosen by electoral process. The introduction of a parliamentary democracy in the former Dutch empire, baptized Indonesia, is a much more hazardous venture.

My second question would be expressed therefore in the following terms: May it not be time for the political scientist to make it understood that a parliamentary democracy, like any other regime, must be adapted to environment and traditions, that it cannot be implanted just anywhere, that it is not an absolute value, but one form of government among others, whose diffusion may be desirable everywhere but is not possible everywhere?

III

The expansion of the political ideologies and institutions of the West appears at the moment in the form of an irreconcilable conflict between Western democracy and Russian Communism. American power and prestige tend more and more to link Western democracy to American influence. American and Soviet ideologies are both revolutionary, directed against European domination of the peoples of Africa and Asia (a domination discredited by the word "colonialism"), against the traditional caste systems and the inequitable distribution of wealth. Both ideologies promise happiness in this world by the application of science and technology to production, by the overthrow of despotic governments, by the liberation of peoples or masses or proletariats. Despite their rivalry (perhaps we should say *because* of it), they appear in the Near East and in Asia, it would seem, as two forms of the same Western industrial civilization, which, although of European origin, is represented especially today by the two heir-states.

The American ideology as such is moderate. It recommends reforms, does not promise the Kingdom of God on earth, and is concerned with political liberties and personal rights as much as with production. But in its institutional embodiment it is radically hostile to authority— as long as the Communist menace does not incline it toward conservatism—since it grants the new masters (the elected governments) only limited and precarious powers. The Communist ideology as such is extremist, since it promises a paradise on earth and in the meantime demands death for those who obstruct the path which leads to that paradise. But, translated into institutions, it immediately helps replace the destroyed state, the old order, with a new state and a new caste system. The new masters are all-powerful, and bring with them a technique of enrollment of the masses and a justifying belief in the state.

In other words, American influence tends to overthrow the old structure of societies and states, and, by way of constructive accomplishment, brings personal liberties. Soviet influence is revolutionary, but it immediately fills the void with institutions which we consider despotic but which work.

Does not the error lie in forgetting that freedoms (personal, electoral, the right of labor to organize, etc.), desirable as they may be, do not create the state and can not flourish in simply *any* environment? Is that not the explanation of the fact, so often observed, that American influence, incapable of supporting leaders in accord with the true American ideology, is reduced to supporting any available *de facto* potentate (whom the leftist intellectuals and the fellow travelers hasten to denounce as feudal or fascist)?

American opinion has a tendency to explain these reverses in terms of the poverty of the country or the inadequacy of economic aid. Overpopulation, the ineffectiveness of agricultural methods, and poverty, as well as the sapping of traditions, are, as a matter of fact, at the bottom of the crisis which the societies of the Near East and Asia are experiencing. The question is to what extent these disturbances can be quelled merely by improvement of the economic situation. One can hardly risk a generalization in the matter in view of the different circumstances of each country.

It can be noted, however, that Communist action, despite party doctrine, gives pre-eminence to political considerations, whereas American action is often taken as though the pre-eminence of economics were an accepted fact. The Communists direct their efforts to the seizure of power, and once in power they think first of all of consolidating the state and industrial and military strength; improvement of the standard of living is postponed until a subsequent phase. The American ambition, laudable from a humanitarian point of view, seems to be to cure the revolutionary virus by the active improvement of living conditions. But is this improvement possible everywhere? Is it possible without the establishment of a firm power and an effective administration? Even in those cases where this improvement is possible, will it be enough to calm revolutionary ardor?

Certain applications of Point Four (improvement of agricultural methods, land reforms, etc.) have perhaps an immediate soothing influence. The same is not true of other applications, the construction of industries, for example. The workers in the first factories, even with a higher standard of living, are often more rebellious than peasants integrated in traditional communities. It has long been recognized that the first phases of industrialization tend to inaugurate a period of disturbances.

The strength of Communism lies in creating, for this dangerous period, the tyrannical apparatus of the party. The weakness of the Western democracies lies in entrusting to representative institutions the task of presiding over these painful transformations. The question would take somewhat this form: Is it possible to spread simultaneously the economic and the political institutions of the Western democracies? Is it not necessary at least, for this simultaneous introduction to be possible, that the hierarchy and beliefs of the old regime should not be shaken too much? In those cases where the traditions and beliefs of the past remain more or less intact, representative institutions could be introduced gradually along with specific liberties.

The old democracies of Europe have difficulty in achieving a practical reconciliation of the socialistic tendency toward equality and leveling and the preservation of personal and political liberties. Does not this reconciliation exceed even more the means of underdeveloped countries, that is, of countries which are only at the beginning of both their democratic and their industrial careers?

IV

We must obviously not form judgments in advance or emphasize one aspect of our problem unduly. It seems proper, however, to suggest a few guiding ideas. The particular part played by ideas in effecting political change cannot be the object of investigation: the distinction between ideas, organizations, institutions, is too nebulous. If the introduction of ideas does not always carry with it immediately the introduction of institutions, the diffusion of these latter never occurs without a transformation of modes of thought. The question therefore is much less one of succeeding in determining the particular role of ideas as opposed to that of force, of organization of institutions, or of economic conditions, than it is of determining the precise way in which this dissemination is wrought in our times.

As to the practical consequences which could eventually be drawn from such inquiries, hardly any effort of imagination is needed to discern them. The obsession of our Western societies with economics has led international bodies to spend millions of dollars on analyses of the conditions of economic progress. It does not seem as though anyone has realized that economic progress (in the sense in which we understand it) is possible only under certain political conditions. The finest products of industrialization are vain if governments do not create the atmosphere in which those projects may be carried out. To what extent may the transmission of Western political institutions go hand in hand with the transmission of economic institutions? To such a question this inquiry may well bring the beginning of a reply.

IDEOLOGY IN AMERICA

George S. Pettee

It is well that the nature of ideologies has been made a topic of discussion at an early stage in an enterprise which seeks better understanding among men of different nations. For ideology, if properly defined and examined, is a topic favorable for the meeting of minds, and ideology, omitted from overt discussion, can more obfuscate and frustrate than almost any other matter.

Raymond Aron, not unexpectedly to those who know him, has dealt with the subject with logical pertinacity and at the same time with tact. The burden of his argument, as read by the present writer, is, first and foremost, that America has little understanding of ideologies in general, of its own ideology in particular, and of how to conduct affairs with a recognition of the nature and functioning of ideologies in life. He reminds us that ideologies take institutional form when diffused or transmitted, and that they are expressed in action as well as in ideas and institutions.

He also points out what America is most inclined to hide from itself, that the two great positions taken in the modern struggle, Americanism and Communism, both take quite different turns in action and in institutions from the simple or literal implications of their verbally expressed ideas. For America, under Point Four, seeks to proselytize for modern science and technology while ignoring the need for an institutional system that might be conducive to this in recipient countries. And while advocating a doctrine of political moderation we nevertheless transmit ideas that are "radically hostile to authority." At the same time, Communism, as he is right in insisting, talks the language of extremism against authority and property, but sets up a most powerful and tyrannical state. And America talks the language of political freedom yet clearly assumes the preeminence of the economic factors, while Communism professes its concern for the economic yet assumes the preeminence of the political.

Reprinted from *Confluence*, vol. 2, no. 2 (June, 1953), 69-80. By permission of the author and the publisher.

I

A good paradox or group of paradoxes often makes a good beginning of discussion, and here is paradox enough to be most promising. Surely, given the validity of the paradoxical observations, we cannot clear up the matter without arriving at sharpened comprehension. The questions are begged; what is an ideology, how does it function, and how does its functioning relate to the understanding of those who hold it?

It was tactful, almost kind, of Aron to leave the argument not quite finished. He did not explicate to the last degree of positiveness the point that America has illusions about its own ideology and about its conduct of ideological affairs (or call it ideological warfare). For the remedies must be taken by Americans; it is even essential to the best in American ideology that it be compatible with clear perception by Americans of the problems presented, and that correction could not be accomplished by, nor require, didactic admonition.

The proposition which brings an ideology in its verbal or literal form into juxtaposition with its institutional expression, and with its expression in action, presents a direct challenge to prevailing attitudes. It is still at this date far more common to regard an ideology as a set of abstract ideas, self-contained, having its own rules of change and development. It is easy to find any desired number of illustrations of the tendency to think about ideology as if an ideology were a separate and independent thing, and also to find plenty of illustrations that reflect the other point of view, that ideology is related to institutions, to action, and, in short, to the culture.[1] The observer who is addicted to the position which holds that ideas are eternal and immutable will naturally regard an ideology as a self-contained body of ideas, related by internal logic, valid or invalid on general grounds, capable of causing effects in action perhaps, but, so to speak, immune to effects derived in turn from action. The opposed position will take an ideology as the verbal expression of something deeper in consciousness, revealed by action as well or better than by words, expressed in macrocosmic form in the culture, including institutions, and in microcosmic form in personality. This latter position is characteristic of sociology; it is the attitude toward ideology taken by Mannheim, by Lévy-Bruhl, by Horney, by Pareto, by Parsons, and, within limits, by the Marxists themselves for all ideologies except Marxism. It is implied in the approach taken by Aron.

The application of the approach which I am calling sociological to the discussion of ideologies can be taken, and is taken by some, to have something like a corrosive effect. It certainly is congenial to a skeptical and critical approach. It has its eyes wide open to faults of logic in an ideology, and finds evidence of such faults in action and institutions as well as in the structure of ideas. However, there are at least good examples to show that it is compatible with a position of belief in the essentials of an ideology. Latourette in his *History of the Expansion of Christianity* poses fully modern questions at the start, yet never draws the conclusion that there is no core of basic truth beneath the crust of *ad hoc* custom. He asks how Christianity expanded, what effect it had upon the societies which received it, what means and methods were employed, what effect the means and methods had upon Christianity itself, and what other interactions occurred, with no thought that Christianity was immune to such mutual interaction, and without fear that this admission need open Pandora's box for the escape of the demons of destructive criticism.

II

All of the attitudes dealt with so far are present in American life today, and it would be foolish to discuss our attitudes about our own or other ideologies without regard for this fact. Also, without doubt, the attitude that is related to philosophical idealism is observably more prevalent than the sociological. This is altogether natural, for the modern sociological observations are recent as intellectual history goes in terms of time, have been spread only to a restricted class of persons through books and education, and have by no means taken solid hold, nor have they become the consensus of more than small and special groups. Nevertheless, the conduct of American ideological affairs might be consistent if any one group happened to dominate such conduct. There are two good reasons why this could not occur up to the present, and may not occur for some time in the future. (This aside from the question of whether it *should* occur.) *First,* American affairs related to ideological matters are conducted by amateurs. *Second,* the professionals, although they may have individually consistent positions, have no well-integrated common position.

Before elaborating upon these statements, it would be well to indicate what we mean by *the conduct of ideological affairs.* We mean by this the encouragement of others to accept our basic ideas. We mean also the presentation to the world of a rationale in justification of our policies and actions, and the aid given to those who are willing to endeavor to accept and implement some of our ideas, or some of our techniques. And we mean the demonstration in action of the principles which guide our action. But we also mean the criticism of other societies as faulty by our standards, for we Americans have been free to apply such criticism to regimes, to policies, to programs, and to customs, in other countries, ranging from our former enemies to our dearest allies, Korea, France, Italy, Britain, the China of the first postwar years, the colonies and non-industrial countries, or the British Dominions.

This, the conduct of ideological affairs by America, is carried on by our statesmen, our soldiers, our journalists, our scholars, and others. What is meant by the statement that it is nevertheless conducted by amateurs is that these men, however expert at something or at several things, are generally amateurs at the conduct of ideological affairs. The statesman speaking for America may be master of the economic or political reasons for our policy, without being in any way master of the sociological implications. The journalist or historian who criticizes a foreign regime may be expert in his knowledge of the country concerned, but far from expert in the analysis of ideological matters. Even the sociological student of ideology may be expert in this, but not in the general situation of a country upon which he presumes to comment.

The approach to ideological problems by the sociological students is, moreover, far from consistent. In general they do agree that an ideology interacts with, or is in relations of interdependence with, all the other elements in a culture. But what relations are most direct, what ones produce consequences in what time, what are the short-run and long-run consequences, and what is the most efficacious line of action for results that are desired—these questions can be, and most often are, subject to controversy rather than agreement.

III

So far we can go on accepting, confirming, and explaining what Aron has suggested; that our conduct of ideological affairs falls short of being masterful. There are some other factors present in the American system of ideas which also bear on the problem, and which result from our ideology, or from elements in it, and not directly from the lack of an accepted science about ideologies in general.

We share with true believers in all faiths the tendency to regard our own faith as self-evident and valid. This is seldom stated, but constantly demonstrated in a number of different ways.

An outstanding way in which we show that we assume our own ideas to be self-evident is in the attitude we take to alternative systems of ideas. To simplify for brevity's sake, we have two positions on such ideas: *first*, that the other system of ideas is wrong, wicked, and stubborn only because wickedness is stubborn; *second*, the other system may be socially conditioned, may reflect obscurely some of the truths that are manifest to us, and may need only a little patience and correction.

Thus, if our ideas will spread to others who have not yet received them, it will be with but little overt effort on our part. Exposition may be needed, but exposition should suffice. It would not be possible for us to seek to propagate our ideology without concern for institutions and action, as we tend to do, if we went at it with any other preconceptions than these.

Our long-time reluctance to undertake anything that might be called propaganda is part and parcel of this same position. This reluctance makes sense if, and only if, our ideas are essentially common sense, universal reason, and apparent to all men of good will and right mind. It relates to the concept that our ideas are in point of fact not an ideology at all. This implies no lack of conviction. The deepest of all states of conviction may be the one which holds it unnecessary to state a proposition because it is so obviously true.

Is this not, in fact, a point of view from which many of the most perplexing of American positions become more explicable? Our refusal to cooperate effectively in the League of Nations was not so much because we were against it as because our cooperation should be unnecessary if men on other continents had good sense, or because the institutionalized form of international virtue could be taken as an inevitably corrupt expression of the ideals it professed to implement. The American attitude toward world affairs in general, and toward war in particular, concerning which Walter Lippmann has given so much thought and had so much to say for many years, is cut from the same cloth. The failure of other nations to preserve the peace when the preservation of peace has been so obviously good has seemed to us to prove malice or sin in others, an occasion not so much for propaganda as for excision of the evil.

Now there is still some mystery here. Any reader who knows American thought in this century must have been ready before reaching this point to raise objection to what may have seemed some over-simple formulations. American thought is not all of the stripe that has been described. The conduct of ideological affairs at home has been in contrast, historically, to the conduct of such affairs abroad. We have taken the deed as well as the word for evidence in domestic affairs, and have taken the institution as well as the lip service as essential to the fulfillment of ideals. The question is apparent, how could such a contrast occur?

The answer in brief is that the ideology we apply at home and the ideology which we apply abroad are not the same. The mechanism for this disparity is simple. We have been trained, so to speak, to think of our ideology as common sense, and as if it were not in fact an ideology. We conduct our home affairs by a complex of principles, including ideas of freedom and ideas of order, ideas concerning popular will and ideas concerning the rights of minorities and individuals against the popular will. We have, well instituted and well guarded by active and capable persons and groups, different sets of ideas or principles, and of institutions and patterns of action to implement the ideas, which constitute our system. But few of us are concerned for the whole, and we have specialized the task of care for the various parts. At home we maintain the constitutional side of our system by sociologically well-rooted means. Though our emphasis and attention shift from time to time between that side of our ideology and our general system which embodies order and that side which embodies freedom, we do have both and our passing emphasis on one is generally required by the fact that the other is strongly established. Yet when asked, explicitly and from without, what is the system of ideas by which we live, we are quite apt to answer from one side only, and to cite the side of liberty and equality without qualification or reservation.

This is most apparent in the semi-cult which has flourished for the past two decades, which has taken Paine, Jefferson, Jackson, Whitman, and others, and their expressions on one side of the argument, as central and exact expressions of American ideas. This was in part a reaction against a period in which one of our Supreme Court Justices found it necessary to object to the idea that our constitutional law should implement a doctrine of social statics. Perhaps we had too much emphasis on order and not enough on freedom and dynamics at one period, and no doubt, if this was so, it was natural and proper to react in the other direction. This certainly happened in our style of expression, and in the consciousness of many of those who have thought themselves to be most concerned to know what is best in American thought.

The consequence is direct. When we are now called upon to express to the world the essentials of our highly successful way of life the answer comes from this specially conditioned emphasis on one side of our thought, and the results have the paradoxical character upon which Aron comments, that while we and others know that our true position is moderate, the ideas we put forth have extremist and anti-authoritarian impact.

IV

The division of our ideology into two parts, with different priesthoods charged with the care of each and with recurrent shifts of dominance or subordination in our regard for one or the other in different periods, could go far to explain the distortion of effect we get when we turn to the world and give out a one-sided version. There is another deeper factor, and this is the distorted effect of the Civil War upon the expression of American ideas and upon American historical judgment.

Bernard de Voto in *Harper's Magazine*, in 1946, first put forward the thesis that the American historians have reduced the Civil War to an absurdity. In 1949 Arthur Schlesinger, Jr., wrote a commentary and concurrence upon this thesis. Neither de Voto nor Schlesinger made any attempt to relate this to the peculiarities of the American interpretation of the two World Wars, which have been the objects of Lippmann's critical attention; but it is clear that the relation between the interpretation of the Civil War by historians and of the World Wars by contemporary political leaders and public opinion have much in common. Both interpretations seek the cause of war in the malice aforethought of a responsible villain. Both evade the sociological problem of war. To treat the Civil War as basically unnecessary, or as made necessary only by the wrong-headed extremism of abolitionists, results in wholly evading the issue of the structure of the Republic. It ignores the issue as stated by Stephen Douglas at Bellair, Ohio, in 1861, when he argued that the economic freedom of the great central area of the United States would be destroyed by successful secession.

The question is open: why have the historians dealt so strangely with one of the great crises of American history? There are many reasons, including the development of a rationalistic liberalism which could give no rational account of *any* war. More important for our purpose, however, is the fact that the victory of the North secured the federal principle beyond the need for argument, and that the "road to reunion" was most easily traversed in the absence of fundamental discussion between victor and vanquished. Thus there was a special reason why it was useful in America to de-emphasize and even to forget one of the most solidly established principles of the Republic.

To carry this trait of intentional silence on the essential nature of the Civil War from the context in which it had practical usefulness in the internal affairs of the United States in the last three decades of the 19th Century, over into the field of American action in the 20th Century world, relates directly to the separation of the American ideology into parts, of which one part is predominant in verbal argument because the other part is instituted and is taken for granted. We do not argue now, in the United States, about the right of states to secede. We do argue about the rights of labor and farmers to greater political influence than they had before the great depression, and about their rights to a greater or lesser share in welfare out of the general economic product of the nation. Therefore when we now set out to tell others what ideas we live by and what makes our system work we purvey the narrow and special version that was appropriate to our own most recent past, and little if any of the other great fundamentals which we have established so firmly that we have forgotten them.

This can be related further to Aron's other main point, that we firmly believe that economic welfare is incompatible with Communism. The tragic feature of this, of which Aron is certainly aware, is that there is a very long and hard row to hoe in any "backward" country before welfare in the American manner can be had by any but a very few. The slow creation of a national capital so productive that welfare through distributive leveling is welfare for all instead of misery for all, and is compatible with a high continuing rate of capital formation, contains a complex of factors of which we are ourselves naively unconscious when we urge and encourage welfare in a wholly different context from our own.

Here we have broadened the discussion specifically to include economic institutions and ideas as well as the political. For it is true that the American ideology presented to the world includes Point Four, and that the purpose of Point Four is primarily focused upon economic welfare, through technological means, as a counter to Communism. And here again, while Aron is quite correct in pointing out that we seem to offer Point Four to the world without concern for the political prerequisites, it remains true also that we can look within America to find, instituted and in action, the necessary ideas to complete a sane ideological and political relationship.

In short, it behooves us to take account of stock and to array our ideology properly before our own eyes if we are to present it to others. The American intellectuals who have been concerned to concentrate their attention and emotions on that fraction of it which most needed renewed and heightened emphasis at home should turn much more of their attention to a balance-sheet approach. We must seek the means, institutional and organized, to present to the world our whole ideology, as the ideas by which we live and in whose value for the future we believe, and not just the half or less emphasized in our own passing fad or fashion. We must rediscover the value of order as the condition of freedom, and discover for this age a more lucid rationale of this than any we inherited. We must not talk to the world as if welfare without productivity, or productivity without capital, were as easy as a New Year's resolution. We must not talk as if free enterprise were easily maintained with high productivity in a small market or without some of the great system of regulatory techniques which have given American free enterprise a new lease on life in this century. We must not sell disorder when we mean to sell freedom, and thus sell the world to Communism when we mean to accomplish the opposite.

The situation would not be so serious if it were not also so urgent. The task of reassessment of national principles and the bringing of the parts into balance is a task which must always be undertaken by any nation moving to the center of the stage of history. Others have faced this task before us, with or without success. Britain and France, after the Renaissance, faced it as the emergent leading powers of the world at that time. They faced it well for several centuries, which is no great failure surely. Changes in the scales of power have made the United States responsible now, as they were formerly, and have done so with far greater suddenness than was true for them. The crisis in the national consciousness is in one aspect a crisis in our own view of our own ideology, and in our conduct of ideological affairs. To turn from conducting such affairs only for our own internal purposes to conducting them with responsibility for the consequences in the world calls for a vastly different point of view, and poses a very great intellectual task.

In this discussion I have said far more about the faults in the conduct of ideological affairs by America, and about the underlying reasons for those faults, than about the greatness of our system. This should be permissible. The entire situation proclaims the greatness of our system, not least when the flaws in our system contribute most to tragic consequences. For only in a great system could flaws be tragic. Most tragic of all may be the habituated lethargy of American intellectuals toward the new task which should command their greatest efforts, not to redesign our system of principles but to retool it, to reassess it, and to mobilize it, so to speak, for new applications.

NOTE

1. This involves directly a fundamental but seldom mentioned fact of life in this period. Before the Michelson-Morley experiment, Western philosophy was a mixture of schools and systems, with many of idealist type on the one hand and of realist or pragmatic type on the other. The crisis of philosophy which began in the 1890s, and which was hailed by Pearson and by Henry Adams with quick perception of its importance, has since then made creeping progress towards reconstruction of Western philosophy, if it has made any progress at all. Philosophical attitudes are present in the thinking of all, and not only of philosophers, and condition the thinking we do about ideologies as well as on other matters. It is not necessary for the present purpose that we settle the issues involved. But it is essential that we note the disorder imposed upon discussion of ideology by the disorder of premises present in the discussion.

THE ROLE OF IDEOLOGY

Lewis Coser and Irving Howe

"A political party," wrote Edmund Burke at the dawn of the nation-state, "is a body of men united for promoting by their joint endeavours the national interest, upon some particular principle in which they are all agreed." [1]

This description no longer holds fully for any political party, but least of all for Stalinism. And not merely because the Communist parties have no genuine stake in the national interest, but more important, because they are not united upon "some particular principle." The totalitarian party is "unprincipled" in the root sense of the term. All parties may violate their principles, yet the act of violation implies a certain recognition of norms. By contrast, the totalitarian party cannot, in any precise sense, be said to violate its principles: it can be described by its structure, its characteristics, its power goals, but not by any stable ideology

Reprinted from Lewis Coser and Irving Howe, *The American Communist Party* (Boston: Beacon Press, 1957), pp. 542-548. By permission of the authors and the publisher. © 1957 by Irving Howe and Lewis Coser.

or group of ideas. *The movement exists far less for the ideology than the ideology for the movement.*[2]

Though the ideological spokesmen of Stalinism advanced claims in regard to its ultimate ends that might seem similar to those of classical socialist thought, such pronouncements were manipulative, hortatory and self-deceptive—generally a mixture of the three. For these statements of ultimate ends had no controlling or restraining influence on the actual behavior of the Stalinist movement; the claim it made to the heritage of socialism could not in itself lead to a softening of the cruelties in the Siberian labor camps, though a shrewd political expediency might. In the life of the totalitarian movement, the instrumental swallows up the ideological.

Or almost. For if the above is a usable description of the objective workings of the Stalinist movement, it is not sufficient for grasping the subjective processes of Stalinist thought. Many individual Stalinists were obviously entangled with ideology as no one else in our time. They felt that their version of "Marxism" provided them with omniscient knowledge of the course of History—knowledge so complete as to constitute a *possession* of History; that it made possible a finished program and a final answer; and that the decisions of the party were the means for realizing the decrees of History. Yet it is no contradiction to say that in a movement for which ideology has become a device there were many people whose submission to ideology was total, fanatical and ruthless. On the contrary: the existence of such people was a precondition for such a movement.

Beliefs concerning the nature of History are here important in so far as they support the Stalinist myth, yet they cannot in themselves serve as guides to political or moral courses of action. History as such cannot provide values, though it may help and permit valuation. Moral and political principles, however, are based on choices among opposing possibilities; hence, an acceptance of or identification with the supposed decrees of History, simply because they are supposed decrees of History, is an amoral act, leading more often than not to color-blindness in the choice of values. It is here, in its reliance upon History, that Stalinism came closest to being an ideology. If, however, we mean by a genuine ideology a pattern of ideal norms that guide policy, something very different controlled the Stalinist movement. In the Communist parties ideologies were conceived as instruments of power, manipulable according to the needs of a given moment and very seldom serving as either check or standard for behavior.[3]

Further qualifications are necessary, however, for in the relation between the Stalinist movement and the tradition of Marxism we face a highly complex and perhaps unprecedented problem. Stalinism, it is true, manipulated and exploited Marxist concepts and terms—but to say this is not yet fully to describe the relationship. Recognizing how deeply the Marxist mode of thought has seeped into the modern mind, the

Stalinist movement stressed its claim to being the true receptacle of Marxism with a vigor second only to its claim to being true to the tradition of the October revolution. Particularly in so far as they were uncritically or even enthusiastically honored by most of its opponents, these claims constituted a major source of Stalinist power and prestige. Yet it would clearly have been impossible for the Stalinist movement to keep reiterating these claims without, in some way, coming to give them a certain credence itself.

Stalinism grew out of, even as it destroyed, a movement that had been deeply attached to the letter of Marxism. The older leaders of the Stalinist movement, who had once known what it meant to live in a non-totalitarian atmosphere, were trained in a school of exegetics that sharpened wits through prolonged polemics over the meaning of Marxist doctrine. In the world of their youth, a ready capacity to cite Marxist classics, and to cite them with some relevance, could bring prestige and political preferment. But the new Stalinist functionaries, those who were themselves products of Stalinism and had never lived in any other milieu, showed very little interest in Marxist or any other form of speculative thought. They no longer needed to engage in debates with brilliant opposition leaders, as Stalin had once done.

Priding themselves on being practical men, they attached very little prestige to intellectual work and betrayed no desire to emulate Stalin's pretensions as a political theoretician. They looked upon Marxism as a vocabulary useful in controlling followers abroad, a group of symbols that helped cement social loyalty at home, and a body of dogmatics to be guarded by professional scholiasts, who in turn were themselves to be guarded. As Stalinism grew older, its relationship to Marxist doctrine became more manipulative, though seldom to the point of being entirely free of self-deception.

Fascinated as they now were by the mechanics of power, the Stalinist leaders, if they read Marxist works at all, were likely to turn to those dealing with political strategy and tactics rather than those concerned with ultimate goals or values. Lenin's *What Is to Be Done?* or *Left Wing Communism* might still be read by them with a certain interest, for while the topics of these pamphlets were not immediately relevant to the problems of Stalinism, they could be regarded as manuals of political warfare rich in suggestion to political strategists of almost any kind. By contrast, Marx's philosophical and economic studies were likely to be neglected by most Stalinist leaders—even though the need to validate their claim to the Marxist heritage, as well as to give themselves satisfactions akin to those felt by patrons of scholarship, prompted the Communist parties to publish these works.

Like one of the dark heretical cults of the Middle Ages which celebrated the devil through the ritual and imagery of Christ, Stalinism missed no occasion for proclaiming its Marxist orthodoxy. It defiled the intentions of Marx, his ethical passion and humanistic prophecy, but it clothed a rejection of his vision in the very language through which he had expressed it. Not for the first time in history, the vocabulary of a great thinker was turned against him, to corrupt his ideas and mock his values. Unlike other totalitarian and quasi-totalitarian movements, Stalinism was unable or unwilling to develop its own vocabulary, being an ideologically "dependent" system, an aftermath rather than a beginning.

Yet it would be an error to suppose that this dependence on the trappings of Marx's system was a mere useless survival. For many Stalinists it provided an indispensable means of reassurance: as long as the old words remained it was easier to evade the fact that new ideas had taken over. For the party, it facilitated the strategy of political access. The Stalinist claim to the Marxist tradition enabled it to compete for the allegiance of European workers who had been brought up in the socialist movements, particularly those who were taught to suspect the Social Democratic parties as reformist. To have surrendered the signs and symbols it had appropriated from Marxism would have meant to face the enormously difficult task of trying to establish itself in the labor movement through a new vocabulary and what it would have had to acknowledge as a new set of ideas. Strategically, it proved far more advantageous to appear as the defender of orthodox Marxism even while ruthlessly emasculating it. The humanist elements in Marxism were discarded, the passion for man that animates Marx's writing eliminated, and instead those aspects of Marx's thought were emphasized which might be said to be most tainted by the Hegelian *hubris* of claiming to know what the future *must* be.

So understood, Marxism could provide a feeling of having reached a "total view" which permits one to identify with History and act in accordance with its inner rhythm. The "essence" of History having been grasped, it then became possible to proclaim the primacy of *praxis*. From that point on, since there need be no further desire to question the underlying principle of social existence, strategy and tactics became all-important. The uncritical acceptance of a metaphysical assumption proved in practice to be a shield against any further assaults by metaphysical doubt or contemplative temptations. It was through works that the faith was to be manifested and tested. Theory, even while ritually celebrated, became an object of contempt.

This mixture of knowingness and a pragmatic rejection of abstract thought—a remarkable reflection, by the way, of the profoundly ambiguous feeling of the modern world toward the intellectual vocation —provided the Stalinist leaders and intellectuals with a sense of certainty in a time of doubt. And for the intellectuals it offered the sanction of doing, or seeming to do, something "real."

The elements in Marxism that have proved most attractive to the Stalinists were those most intimately tied to the 19th-century progressivism, a mode of thought still powerful in the life of the European "Left." Appearing before the world as fellow progressives—*fellow pro-*

gressives in a hurry—the Stalinists were able to utilize many aspects of the liberal tradition and to claim that far from being enemies of Western humanism—as, by contrast, many Nazi ideologues openly declared themselves—they were actually its true heirs.

Precisely to the extent that the left tradition in the West did adhere indiscriminately to a simple optimistic theory of progress, it became most vulnerable to Stalinist infiltration. For if all change tends to be impelled by the Logic of History in a progressive direction, those who seemed to stand for the most change would also seem to be the greatest progressives. Put so crudely, the "progressivist" ideology comes close to intellectual caricature; but so, often enough, does political life itself. No Stalinoid intellectual in Paris would have been so unsophisticated as to accept the formula as we have reduced it here, but in the subtle writings of many a Stalinoid intellectual in Paris there was buried exactly this deification of "progress."

And precisely to the extent that modern progressivism committed itself to what might be called technological optimism—the notion that the growth of a society's productive forces automatically renders it "progressive"—did it, in turn, become most vulnerable to Stalinist influence. For the technological optimist, Dnieperstroy is an irrefutable argument.

Ideology in the Stalinist movement was both exalted and degraded as in no other movement: exalted in that it was constantly put to work and accorded formal honor, degraded in that it was never allowed any status in its own right but came to be regarded as a weapon in the struggle for power.

This relationship between Stalinism and its ideology followed from a fundamental attiude of totalitarian movements toward social and personal reality. The most terrifying assumption of the totalitarian mind is that, given the control of terror, anything is possible. In Orwell's *1984* and Milosz's *The Captive Mind* this idea is reiterated again and again, out of a despairing conviction that almost anyone can say the words but almost no one can apprehend their full significance. Given modern technology, total state control, the means of terror and a rationalized contempt for moral values, you can do anything with men, anything with the past.

Reality is not something one recognizes or experiences; reality is something one manufactures, sometimes in anticipation, sometimes in retrospect. One day Beria is a hero of the Soviet Union, the next day a villain—which is neither bad nor unusual. What is new is that by the third day *he does not exist*. His past has been destroyed, his name removed from the records. Many political movements have claimed to control the present, and others the future; totalitarianism was the first, however, which systematically proceeded to remake the past.

To do this, it was necessary to regard words and ideas as instrumentalities that could be put to any use. Nothing in thought or language need impose any limit. As Milosz wrote: *"What is not expressed does not exist.* Therefore if one forbids men to explore the depths of human nature, one destroys in them the urge to make such explorations; and the depths in themselves slowly become unreal."[4] And Orwell, in describing the totalitarian attitude to thought and language, pushed everything to an extreme which helped make the reality all the clearer:

To know and not to know, to be conscious of complete truthfulness while telling carefully constructed lies, to hold simultaneously two opinions which cancelled out, knowing them to be contradictory and believing in both of them, to use logic, to repudiate morality while laying claim to it, to believe that democracy was impossible and that the Party was the guardian of democracy, to forget whatever it was necessary to forget, then to draw it back into memory again at the moment when it was needed, and then promptly to forget it again, and above all, to apply the same process to the process itself—this was the ultimate subtlety: consciously to induce unconsciousness and then, once again, to become unconscious of the act of hypnosis you had just performed. Even to understand the word "doublethink" involved the use of doublethink.[5]

NOTES

1. *Thoughts on the Cause of the Present Discontent,* page 96.

2. In Ignazio Silone's novel *The Seed Beneath the Snow,* a fascist orator, true in his comic fashion to the totalitarian ethos, asks the rhetorical question, Is the handkerchief for the nose or the nose for the handkerchief? and answers that every good fascist understands that the nose is for the handkerchief.

3. The notion that the Stalinist leaders were fanatical ideologists who could not take a political step without measuring it against their dogmas seems to us an error. It is sometimes said, in defense of this notion, that in those countries where Stalinist parties have taken power they have shown their ideological rigidity by risking the most severe opposition from the peasants rather than relax their insistence upon nationalization of the land. In fact, however, the Stalinists have shown a capacity for making temporary compromises with peasant ownership; and their general drive toward the abolition of private farms seems based far less on dogma than on the correct insight that as a ruling group which derives its power from total control of a statified economy, they must regard *any* property-owning class as a potential threat.

4. *The Captive Mind,* page 215.

5. Quoted from George Orwell's *Nineteen Eighty-Four.* By permission of Harcourt, Brace & World, Inc., and Secker & Warburg. [Editor's Note.]

IDEAS AND IDEOLOGIES

W. Y. Elliott

. . . What is an ideology? How is it related to what are called, since Plato, political "myths"? How does it differ from theology? Is it a "scientific" construct, capable of useful definition and rigid application? Is it a "magic formula" for manipulating human beings—and to what end? Is Coca-Cola an ideology? Or even an ideological symbol? Then what of champagne, wine, vodka, or Scotch whiskey? They are symbols perhaps, but they are also matters of taste and fashion, depending on the willingness of the recipients to accept them in these latter terms. One is reminded of Dr. Samuel Johnson's crusty aphorism: "Rome did not spread upon the world, Sir. The world spread upon Rome."

I

The word *ideology* was not discovered by Mannheim, nor the idea by Karl Marx. It is an idea older, surely, than Hobbes or David Hume —but Hume's cold Scot's mind gave it its most effective early formulation. In essence, an ideology, in Hume's sense, is a system of belief rationalized by men's total faculties (including what we call reason) but *produced* by the more fundamental causes of what we have come to call cultural determinism. For Hume, social habits and customs produced beliefs which were impressed on societies in much the same way that necessary experience wrote, through the sensate perceptions, on the individual mind. There is an *organic* character to an ideology so conceived. It is set apart by the confines of some other type of group, religious or familial, which can stamp authoritatively its own members with the imprint of common institutions (i.e., social customs and habits), based on common beliefs.

For Hume, this causality was complex but essentially *natural,* and therefore *determined.* Ideas were not produced *ex nihilo;* therefore

Reprinted from *Confluence*, vol. 2, No. 3 (September, 1953), 130-138. By permission of the author and the publisher.

social formulations were not ideas with a creative role, but systems of beliefs which had been stamped out of total environment—in short, they were ideologies. Their truth could not be tested by the usual references to coherence and correspondence; as ideologies they were what they were because they were socially produced facts, each inevitable for its own cultural context.

Marx developed this by speaking of all political and economic systems (except his own) as superstructures, erected on the foundation of materialism and the necessary laws of economic development in the control over the instruments of production. Of course, to speak of "control" was to introduce a political and not an economic force. This inner contradiction becomes even clearer when the idea of class war and the nature of the dictatorship of the proletariat proved to be the "magic formula" which in due course was to free men from necessity. Generally speaking, ideology, since the time of Marx, has come to mean a collection of rationalized concepts claiming to unlock the meaning of history or alternatively to supply a "magic formula" for the control of history.

The essence of ideology, then, from Hume's contribution on through various schools of cultural determinists in sociology and anthropology, is that ideas are produced by some historical forces of which the ideas are not themselves a creative part. They are reactions rather than actions. They are determined by context. They are ideologies—systems of beliefs political, economic, theological, whose pretense to sufficient rationality is illusory and essentially pathetic self-deception. They are products of some "law" of history.

Freedom, on the other hand, in its very nature and by almost any definition assumes that the test of ideas is their truth, and that the ability to seek truth, by the eternal tension between doubt and affirmation through testing, is a creative process that can change environment, produce dynamism in cultures, and is not, as a process, in a mechanistic straitjacket of external forces. It acknowledges habits, institutions, myths, and constructs what Lippmann called "stereotypes." But it refuses to play Procrustes, or to be treated as were his guests. Free systems are the natural enemies of ideologies in the traditional use of the word.

This may account for the difficulty . . . in accepting the rather generalized use of the term "ideology" which is proposed by Raymond Aron. In Aron's view, if I understand it, an ideology may embrace things as diverse as those scientific constructs of the time which are broadly accepted, as much as it does religious concepts. Indeed, they often tend, as he says, to become interchangeable—an accustomed "mythological concept." But to use the word "ideology" as he does as meaning "all ideas or bodies of ideas accepted by individuals or peoples, without regard to their origin or nature" gives the term so broad a meaning that it perhaps accounts for the diffuseness which has marked the discussion of ideological diffusion.

In any case, we in the West pride ourselves on not having an ideology in the sense of a "magic formula," and it is certainly doubtful if a deep analysis of American beliefs would find that they really assume, as Pettee summarizes Aron's analysis, the "pre-eminence of economic factors." The underlying American assumption is rather that the economic factors themselves can be brought into line with man's conscious control through his powers of invention and management: economic factors themselves may express freedom, but it is assumed to reside ultimately in individual responsibility and energy and in voluntary groups rather than in the planned collective action assumed to be necessary in both Socialism and Communism.

What perhaps is not adequately appreciated by any of the protagonists in the symposium is that so long as there exists real political freedom beliefs are under constant revision, and are never shared, even by the effective majority of the population, in such a form as to be unchallengeable or monolithic. Heresy is never ruled out and for that reason free systems do not offer the systematic completeness of an ideology that demands "party line" development and application and indoctrination, by purges and terror. Even the sociological approach to ideology, which Pettee identifies as including the Marxians' attitude towards all other ideologies except their own, is relative to the particular formula for cultural interpretation which is stressed by the sociologists, and very naturally produces what Pettee calls a "corrosive effect."

As opposed to this, the ideologies of the totalitarian systems become, as Aron has noted . . . a matter of religion quite as much as a matter of rationalized ideology. From this characteristic flow the attractions of Communism to people who have not lived under it, but from it comes also the need for enforced orthodoxy. . . .

II

If ideologies are to be diffused, they must first be created and sustained. Accepting the broader definition of ideology that Aron has proposed, all ideologies must meet the test of survival on at least five major points:

1. Ideologies must meet, first of all, the test of creating institutions adequate to insure their domestic survival in the group of origin. Ideologies, in Hume's sense of opinion as resting on embedded social habits, exist in all systems (free and totalitarian) as institutions. They are relatively rigid in totalitarian systems. They are as subject to revision in the United States as elsewhere, even including the venerable Constitution. Can the revision keep pace with the need?

The logic of power, when unchecked by moral criticism or built-in political balances, is ruthless. It creates a single center, a one-party elite, a terror, an all-pervasive and controlling espionage system, and periodic purges. The ideology *is* the system. It makes the institutions work to fit it. George Orwell's *1984* is no fantasy. It is logically deducible, and, in its major outlines, from inescapable premises. That is why $2 + 2 = 4$ becomes (as Orwell notes) the most dangerous heresy to the system. It can blow up the whole theology of totalitarian conditioning of the mind to the myth—unless it be totally suppressed and its outside seepage into the system dammed off.

2. Institutions depend in turn on ideas—rigid for totalitarian myths, revisable for the free societies. George Pettee has admirably shown the reaction, in the "ideology" of the Supreme Court, of so-called "rationalist liberalism" (taking Paine, Jefferson [revised], and Walt Whitman as prophets) against the previous period which was typified by the supremacy of the judiciary. Represented by John Adams, Alexander Hamilton, and John Marshall, this older conservative constitutionalism stood for an emphasis on centralized order, sovereignty, control, and balance through legal and political power to the rich, who by a sort of natural law were supposed to be the best. This was the aristocratic brake against the "excesses of democracy" noted by our founding fathers. The rationalistic reaction of the "liberals" against Hamilton produced some bizarre and utopian ideas, which tended to become enough of an ideology to be easily exploitable by Communists to create fellow-travelers.

Our national life has indeed responded to great tidal phases connected with the nineteenth century. It found the surge of extreme democracy washing over the old barriers: universal suffrage, direct election of senators, a direct federal income tax, a welfare state that on the one side tried to legislate morality in the use of alcohol and on the other pushed social legislation much farther in the protection of the masses from unemployment, poverty, and disease than is generally realized in Europe. All this, together with two world wars, had cataclysmic effects on American beliefs. Extreme liberalism became the fashion and brought about the conviction that our democracy could be exported along with our somewhat misnamed but nevertheless basically "free" enterprise system.

Totalitarian ideas, too, change. But they have in their power to change all the ambivalence noted by Aron. And when they fail as "magic formulas" they may change into religions. Into that realm we shall pursue them later.

3. Yet ideologies have another aspect and one contradictory to the moral homilies of, for example, the Kellogg Pact. They must meet the test of survival not only in terms of truth, but in those of power, i.e., in conflict with other systems. Even after the smugness of Bryan's attitude of world peace by treaty, and after the magic-formula aspects of "one-worldism" and "world federalism" had begun to fade before the stubborn facts of totalitarian realities, it was still possible for Americans to hope that peace might be bought by foreign aid. Or it was possible to rely on our superiority as a system of production for war, *and* the atomic supremacy with which the combination of European pure science and American technology had endowed us. Our institutions, our energy, our freedom, our "prosperity" had given us this lead. It was comfortably hoped that they would maintain it.

The impact of the threat of atomic destruction that will shortly become possible against the United States, and against the remainder of the world, has not yet made itself fully recognized and deeply felt. What will be its ideological effect? Whose political warfare will it help or hurt? What will be its psychological impact on the West? To speed up the still possible application of now technically possible defenses, but at what cost? Or to run away from the bad dream and make a settlement, as the aged and ailing Mr. Churchill seems to feel we must, "while there is still time"? What sort of settlement? How guaranteed? Of what value? At the sacrifice of what portions of humanity to continued slavery? Or will cataclysm produce apocalypse?

There is little enough recognition of this new factor, which is certainly of no mean order of magnitude, in the discussions in *Confluence* on the diffusion of ideologies. But it is obvious that a sufficiently ruthless regime, armed with the atomic weapon *and its sole effective possessor*, might not be unduly troubled about the slower methods of diffusion. For the crucial period of establishing world supremacy it would not need to bother too much about whether its ideology were pleasing to those it could and would terrorize, with weapons of mass terror beyond those available even to Genghis Khan. Or does the risk of the counterstroke, and the diffusion of bases for its delivery, present too great a threat of ending the regime of Moscow by destroying its power centers and permitting the devastating rise of men with weapons in their hands, instead of the "stones against tanks" risings as in East Berlin and the like?

4. The fourth test which every ideology must meet is economic adequacy in the broadest sense of the word "economic." Indeed, this is the test by which Communism condemns its rivals and tests its own superiority. It poses the supreme test of so perfect an economic system, brought about by the suppression of all classes and class war and the control of the instruments of production in the hands of the dictatorship of the proletariat, that the state can then wither away and the economic order will be carried on with anarchic freedom. It is scarcely worth while stressing again the historic naivete of the "law" of economic development which underlies this ideology. It may furnish the religious element of the ideology in Bolshevik theory, but it has certainly disappeared from any prospect of Russian reality. The state and all the elements of the urge to dominate seem to grow with each success, as the horrid appetite does with feeding.

On the other hand, the "capitalistic system" has no magic formula that dispenses with social discipline or with a sufficient control of fiscal and economic systems. It clearly will be facing a crisis when confronted with the prospect of such wars as are outlined above. The military and security factors of economic policy become dominant. But capitalistic systems, on the test simply of the distribution of more goods to consumers who are free to express their wants, still stand in no need of fear of comparison with the Soviet system of total control. Its weakness lies, as all the contributors to the symposium have in some measure admitted, in not being able to force the pace of savings and capital investments in backward societies which have cut off the international flow of capital by an exacerbated nationalism, often produced as a reaction against colonialism.

The point made . . . in some measure by Aron needs to be understood: the free systems of the West must find some more effective measure of control over the economic area of the world which is still available to them before the complete disintegration of colonialism. Were the U.N. capable of genuine trusteeship, a middle ground and some limitations of the past doctrinaire attitude which considered nothing except "rights of the natives" might emerge. It is surely the weak point of the West and one on which such honest analysis as this symposium has produced may tend to reverse the clichés of liberalism that far exceeded any ideas even of John Stuart Mill in the matter of representative government for native populations.

5. *But the final and ultimate test of any ideology is its hold on men's souls.* Is it too much to say that the basic values of the West, the values of human freedom, are grounded in religion? There is a common ground in the beliefs of all basic world religions against the religion of Communism, if it may be called that. Whereas Communism proposes no other end or goal for human freedom than "to each according to his needs," every great religion concludes that "man does not live by bread alone." In this matter it is Communism against the field, against Judaism *and* Christianity, against the Moslem faith as well as the Hindu.

It would be folly to refuse to recognize the strength of Communism in appealing to the uprooted, and the lonely, and those lost in modern society, or its ability to fill the hopeless with some hope, however illusory, and the weak with a sense of collective power. It has skilled practitioners of confusion to spread its "gospel," as Burnham shows. But Burnham, like a good Machiavellian and with all the insights of his past, nevertheless misses, as Machiavelli did, the weakness of *mere technique*, which Eastern European satellites are now proving. On the evidence, Communism does not inspire a faith that continues the past of men's hopes and prayers, since Communist ideology and practice destroy his wholeness as a human being, along with love, friendship, trust, family—indeed all the things that make for his moral responsibility and growth. Already the signs of inner dry rot where Communism has been in power for some time are not lacking. On the other side, the West too is being forced to find that doubt, though creative, is not enough without affirmation, and that if it is not to rely on magic it must resort to the truth of prayer, the core of man's relation to the divine principle of the universe: "not *my* will, but *Thy* will, be done."

With all due deference to both sociology and history, we do all hold in our hearts that *magna est veritas, et praevalebit.* And we believe, if we are not complete moral relativists, that the totalitarian has to impose his myth, his rigid ideology, by force, because it cannot survive criticism. His ideology is in this sense *absolutely morally wrong.* He must condition men to its acceptance by destroying in them the distinctively human, i.e., free, reason.

PART TWO

TOTALITARIANISM
AND DEMOCRACY

INTRODUCTORY NOTE

During the last decade or two the opposition between totalitarianism and democracy has been very sharply reasserted. Both concepts have acquired new dimensions. On the theoretical plane, democracy has become concerned with values—the vogue of linguistic analysis notwithstanding. Any theoretical probing must lead to a greater awareness of the relativism that is inherent in democracy. Relativism is at once democracy's strength and weakness. There are many frustrations in a democracy because one cannot prove the validity of many of its basic statements, nor can one consider the system to be identical with absolute truth. Yet, while democracy's advocates must resist any attempt to justify their system by proof (which would be to succumb to totalitarian habits of thought and to philosophical absolutism), they can sharpen their awareness of the particular beliefs on which the system rests, as well as constantly redefine the system's relationship with ethics, religion, and economics.

Democracy as a system has become more "ideological," rigid, and conservative—in spite of the fact that its champions are aware of the disparity between professed values and existing institutions—democracy has been exposed to indirect influences from nationalist and internationalist movements. The direct challenge, however, has come from totalitarianism, which seems to have had the best of the debate so far.

Perhaps the most complete definition of totalitarianism is that given by Friedrich and Brzezinski in an excerpt quoted in Section I of this Part. These authors isolate five attributes which they consider to be essential to totalitarianism: (1) an official ideology, (2) a single mass party, (3) a system of terroristic police control, (4) a technologically-conditioned, near-complete monopoly of control of all means of effective mass communication and effective armed combat, and (5) a central control and direction of the entire economy. In a later book, *Ideology and Power in Soviet Politics* (1962), Brzezinski adds the attribute of (6) an all-permeating "institutionalized revolutionary zeal" as a necessary attribute of the above "syndrome."

Over the last decade totalitarianism has been given a more systematic, analytical treatment than it received earlier. Originally discussed mainly with reference to fascism, it is now scrutinized as a phenomenon particularly evident in the communist system. But although it has become a respectable term in the vocabulary of political science, no unanimity has been reached with regard to its meaning. However, suggestions have been made about the necessity of distinguishing between the two types of totalitariansm: the harsh, Stalinistic brand and the milder bureaucratized type (see, for example, Alfred G. Meyer's *Communism* [1960]). Also, the question has been posed as to whether a totalitarian society can gradually evolve "into a relatively democratized bureaucratic collectivism," as Sidney Hook puts it.

Hence the interest in discussing the mutual interpenetration of totalitarianism and democracy and their resemblance to each other in some features. What is already common knowledge in the sphere of economics—that the two opposing systems are becoming more alike— is far fetched in the realm of politics. Yet preoccupation with the idea of mutual interpenetration cannot be overlooked. This preoccupation embraces the Talmonian concept of totalitarian democracy (discussed in this symposium by Z. A. Pelczynski), the discussion of certain quasi-democratic features of communist totalitarianism, and the concern with the question of whether totalitarianism can be generated by democratic societies (as Enrico Opocher suggests in Section II of this Part).

A direct restatement of democratic theory has resulted from this preoccupation; however, it has not been too successful. The unsatisfactory state of contemporary democratic theory is linked with defective "democratic consciousness"—the decline of faith in the effective power of reason and therefore in rational political behavior. Such democratic ideologies as liberalism and socialism have suffered a heavy decline in prestige; their moral foundations have been shaken, and the formulation of clear-cut programs is now proving difficult.

But the difficulties are not necessarily inherent in the subject. Some are also artificially induced by political scientists, many of whom have become positivists to whom "grand theorizing" seems futile. The decline in ideological thought does not mean that ideologies have become less important, but merely that the theoreticians are now less interested in them. On the whole, democratic ideologies happen to be peripheral to the interest of model-builders and behavioralists. Political scientists in this category dismiss ideologies as "literature," as nonmeasurable collections of concepts that escape precise analysis and therefore lie outside the sphere of research. Thus, these men operate within a "closed system" of their own making and foster a new scholasticism (whose chief preoccupation is with the continuous sharpening of tools and the addition of new methodological refinements), instead of inquiring into real issues and objectives and seeking solutions to problems. So long as the "quantifiers" strive for the front stage of political analysis, micro-politics will be popular and the atomistic viewpoint will predominate, while the "generalizers" will be looked upon with suspicion as nonscientific *littérateurs*. Such overspecialization and parochial scholasticism increase the difficulty of providing a systematic analysis of the warring ideologies.

Hans Kelsen's and Richard Wollheim's individual papers on democracy, reprinted here, survey the content of modern concepts of democracy. Wollheim, from a philosopher's point of view, deals with the anatomy of Anglo-American democracy, pointing to the four main subjects of contemporary discussions on democracy: its meaning, its conditions, its justification, and its relation to other political concepts and principles.

Kelsen, a leading positivist jurist, separates the substance of democracy, which is virtually unchanging, from its symbols, which are subject to change. His basic democratic truths include government by the people, civil liberties, principles of majority and equality, and the inherent connection between democracy and discussion, as well as between democracy and liberalism. He asserts that participation in the government must be considered the essential characteristic of democracy.

THE GENERAL CHARACTERISTICS OF
TOTALITARIAN DICTATORSHIP

Carl J. Friedrich and Zbigniew K. Brzezinski

Everybody talks about totalitarian dictatorships and about totalitarianism. They are said to be tyrannies, despotisms, absolutisms. And yet, the greatest uncertainty surrounds the most elementary aspects of this form of government. One flatters it, actually, when one calls a dictatorship of this kind a tyranny or a despotism. The autocratic regimes of the past were not nearly as ghastly as the totalitarian dictatorships of our time. Yet, one also maligns totalitarian dictatorship by these descriptions, for, whereas tyranny was conducted, according to the definition of Aristotle, for the benefit of the tyrant, it is not very realistic to make that kind of egoism the basis of an interpretation of totalitarian dictatorship.

The truth of the matter seems to be that totalitarian dictatorship is a logical extension of certain traits of our modern industrial society (oftentimes called "capitalism"). It is our purpose in this introductory chapter to trace the main aspects of this novel kind of government and thereby lay out the pattern for the later more detailed treatment. We also propose to indicate by way of contrast how and why totalitarian dictatorships differ from autocracies of the past. Though actually neither a tyranny nor a despotism, totalitarian dictatorship is apparently linked to both in certain important ways, or at least there are significant similarities which justify putting all of these regimes into one common category. This category might properly be suggested to be that of "autocracy."

There have been many types of autocracy in the history of government. The several forms of despotism, often associated with the deification of the ruler characteristic of the Orient, the tyranny of the Greek cities and their replicas in Renaissance Italy, and the absolutist monarchies of modern Europe, are among the more familiar patterns of autocracy. In all these systems, the truly distinguishing feature is that the ruler is not responsible to anyone else for what he does; he is the *autos*, who himself wields power; that is to say, he makes the decisions and reaps the fruits of them. The logical opposite of autocracy, therefore, would be any rule in which another, an *heteros*, shared the power through the fact that the ruler is responsible to him or them. In the modern West, it has become customary to speak of such systems as responsible or constitutional governments.* Among these, constitutional democracy has become the predominant type, though there have been constitutional monarchies, aristocracies, and theocracies in the past.

Since any pattern of responsibility must be expressed in rules of some kind, which together constitute the "constitution," and, as rules are properly speaking a kind of legal norm, it has been customary since Plato and Aristotle to stress the role of law and to distinguish political systems according to whether or not they are characterized by the subordination of the political rulers to law. From this viewpoint, an autocracy is any political system in which the rulers are insufficiently, or not at all, subject to antecedent and enforceable rules of law— enforceable, that is, by other authorities who share the government and who have sufficient power to compel the lawbreaking rulers to submit to the law.

This problem of the control of the rulers by the law must be distinguished from the problem of the role of law in a given society. All human societies, communities, and groups of any sort have some kind of law, and the totalitarian dictatorships of our time are characterized by a vast amount of "legislation," necessitated by the requirements of a technically industrialized economy and of the masses of dependent operators involved in such a society.[1] Similarly the Roman empire saw an increase, not a decline, in the detailed complexity of its legal system during the very period when it was becoming more and more autocratic. This autocracy eventually reached the point of deifying the emperor, while the detailed development of the legal system continued. Long before this time, all enforceable control of the ruler had vanished and the responsibility of which the Republic had been so proud had completely disappeared. The will of the emperor was the ultimate source of all law. This conception was expressed in a number of celebrated phrases which eventually became the basis of the doctrine of sovereignty that provided the rationalization for the autocracy of absolute monarchs in the seventeenth century.

---

* The term *heterocracy* has never been suggested though as it is the genuine logical alternative to *autocracy* there is something to be said for it, in order to escape the common connotations surrounding the term "constitutional government."

Autocratic legalism, however, must not be confused with the totalitarian distortion of the notion of law in what is spoken of as the "laws of movement." These are presumably "laws of nature" or "laws of history" (but history understood as a part of nature); they contain an existential, rather than a normative, judgment. The interrelation of existential and normative law has been a central problem in the long history of the law of nature.[2] The totalitarian ideology tends to dissolve the normative in the existential realm, and to consider all ordinary laws merely as expressions of laws of nature and history. "All history is the history of class struggles," for example, would be such a law in terms of which the positive legal order must be structured; it provides the standard by which to measure positive laws, to interpret and if necessary to alter and break them. All laws become fluid when they are treated merely as the emanation of such laws of movement, and their very multiplicity testifies to their normative weakness.[3] Such fluidity makes them incapable of serving as standards of responsible conduct, since every violation can be argued away by the rulers as merely an adaptation to the higher laws of movement. A similar difficulty attached to the law of nature when it was to serve as a restraint upon absolute rulers, who in the past were allowed to contravene it in case "reason of state" required it.

Thus, as far as this characteristic absence of responsibility is concerned, totalitarian dictatorship resembles earlier forms of autocracy. But it is our contention in this volume that totalitarian dictatorship is historically unique and *sui generis*. It is also our conclusion from all the facts available to us that fascist and communist totalitarian dictatorships are basically alike, or at any rate more nearly like each other than like any other system of government, including earlier forms of autocracy. These two theses are closely linked and must be examined together. They are also linked to a third, that totalitarian dictatorship as it actually developed was not intended by those who created it—Mussolini talked of it, but meant something different—but resulted from the political situations in which the anticonstitutionalist and antidemocratic revolutionary movements and their leaders found themselves. Let us take the third of these points first, treating the second and first afterward.

The fascist and communist systems evolved in response to a series of unprecedented crises, and they have shown a continuous, though intermittent, tendency to become more "totalitarian." There is no present reason to conclude that the existing totalitarian systems will disappear as a result of internal evolution, though this possibility cannot be excluded. The two totalitarian governments which have perished thus far have perished as the result of wars in which they had become involved with outside powers, but this does not mean that the Soviet Union necessarily will. We do not presuppose that totalitarian societies are fixed and static entities, but, on the contrary, that they have undergone and continue to undergo a steady evolution, presumably involving both growth and deterioration.

In terms of historical perspective, three points might be added. First, certain autocracies in the past have shown extraordinary capacity for survival. Not only the Roman but also several Oriental empires lasted for hundreds of years, at least as systems they did, though the dynasties changed.[4] By contrast, the tyrannies of the Greek city states were usually short-lived, as Aristotle noted. Second, such autocracies have as a rule perished in consequence of foreign invasions. Third, their autocratic features have usually been intensified over long periods, the reason being that violence is readily available for dealing with the tensions and break-downs that occur. In short, some of these autocracies were not stable, but lasting.

To the uncertainties about the end correspond the controversies about the beginning of totalitarian dictatorship. The debate about the causes or origins of totalitarianism has run all the way from a primitive bad-man theory [5] to the "moral crisis of our time" kind of argument. A detailed inspection of the available evidence suggests that virtually every one of the factors which has been offered by itself as an explanation of the origin of totalitarian dictatorship has played its role. For example, in the case of Germany—Hitler's moral and personal defects, weaknesses in the German constitutional tradition, certain traits involved in the German "national character," the Versailles Treaty and its aftermath, the economic crisis and the "contradictions" of an aging capitalism, the "threat" of communism, the decline of Christianity and of such other spiritual moorings as the belief in the reason and the reasonableness of man—all have played a role in the total configuration of factors contributing to the over-all result. As in the case of other broad developments in history, only a multiple-factor analysis will do. But at the present time, we cannot fully explain the rise of totalitarian dictatorship. All we can do is to explain it partially by identifying some of the antecedent and concomitant conditions. Broadly speaking, totalitarian dictatorship is a new development; there has never been anything quite like it before.

Now concerning the second point, it is very important to explain somewhat at the outset why the totalitarian dictatorships, communist and fascist, are *basically alike*. What does this mean? In the first place, it means that they are *not wholly alike*. Popular and journalistic interpretation has oscillated between two extremes; some have said that the communist and fascist dictatorships are wholly alike, others that they are not at all alike. The latter view was the prevailing one during the popular-front days in Europe as well as in "liberal" circles in the United States. It was even more popular during the Second World War, especially among Allied propagandists. Besides, it was and is the official Soviet and Hitler party line. It is only natural that these regimes, conceiving of themselves as bitter enemies, dedicated to the task of liquidating each other, should take the view that they have nothing in common. This has happened before in history. When the Protestants and Catholics were fighting each other during the religious wars of the sixteenth and seventeenth centuries, they very commonly denied to each other the name of "Christians," and argued about each other that they were not "true churches." Actually, and from the viewpoint of the sectarians whom they both persecuted, they were indeed that.

The other view, that communist and fascist dictatorships are wholly alike, is presently favored in the United States and in Western Europe to an increasing extent. Yet they are obviously not wholly alike. For example, they differ in their proclaimed purposes and intentions. Everyone knows that the communists say they seek the world revolution of the proletariat, while the fascists proclaimed their determination to establish the world dominance of a particular nation or people, or at least their imperial predominance in a region, as in the case of the Italian Fascists. The communist and fascist dictatorships differ also in their historical antecedents: the fascist movements have arisen in reaction to the communist challenge and have offered themselves to a frightened middle class as the saviors from the communist danger. As we shall have occasion to show in the chapters which follow, there are many other differences which do not allow us to speak of the communist and fascist totalitarian dictatorships as wholly alike, but which suggest that they are sufficiently alike to class them together and contrast them not only with constitutional systems, but also with former types of autocracy.

Before we turn to these common features, however, there is another difference which used to be emphasized by many who wanted "to do business with Hitler" or who admired Mussolini and therefore argued that, far from being wholly like the communist dictatorship, the fascist regimes must really be seen as merely authoritarian forms of constitutional systems. It is indeed true that more of the institutions of the preceding liberal and constitutional society survived in the Italian Fascist than in the Russian Communist society. But this is due in part to the fact that no liberal, constitutional society preceded Soviet Communism. The promising period of the Duma came to naught as a result of the war and the disintegration of tsarism, while the Kerensky interlude was far too brief and too superficial to become meaningful for the future. In Czechoslovakia and in the Soviet Zone of Germany (German Democratic Republic) we find precisely such institutions as universities, churches, and schools surviving. It is likely that, were a communist dictatorship to be established in Great Britain or France, the situation would be similar, and that here even more such institutions of the liberal era would continue to operate for a considerable initial period at least. Precisely this argument has been advanced by such British radicals as Sidney and Beatrice Webb. The tendency of isolated fragments of the preceding state of society to survive has been a significant source of misinterpretation of the fascist totalitarian society, especially in the case of Italy. In the twenties, Italian totalitarianism was very commonly misinterpreted as being "merely" an authoritarian form of middle class rule, with the trains running on time, and the beggars off the street.[6] In the case of Germany, this sort of misinterpretation took a slightly different form. In the thirties, various authors tried to interpret German totalitarianism as either "the end phase of capitalism" or as "militarist imperialism." [7] These interpretations stress the continuance of a "capitalist" economy whose leaders are represented as dominating the regime. The facts as we know them do not correspond to this view. For one who sympathized with socialism or communism it was very tempting to try and depict the totalitarian dictatorship of Hitler as nothing but a capitalist society and therefore totally at variance with the "new civilization" that was arising in the Soviet Union. These few remarks have suggested, it is hoped, why it may be wrong to consider the totalitarian dictatorships under discussion as either wholly alike or basically different. Why they are basically alike remains to be shown, and to this key argument we now turn.

The basic features or traits which we suggest as generally recognized to be common to totalitarian dictatorships are six in number. The "syndrome," or pattern of interrelated traits, of the totalitarian dictatorship consists of an ideology, a single party typically led by one man, a terroristic police, a communications monopoly, a weapons monopoly, and a centrally directed economy. Of these, the last two are also found in constitutional systems: Socialist Britain had a centrally directed economy, and all modern states possess a weapons monopoly. Whether these latter suggest a "trend" toward totalitarianism is a question which will be discussed in our last chapter.

These six basic features, which we think constitute the character of totalitarian dictatorship, form a cluster of interrelated traits, intertwined and mutually supporting each other, as usual in "organic" systems.[8] They should therefore not be considered in isolation or be made the focal point of comparisons, such as "Caesar developed a terroristic secret police, therefore he was the first totalitarian dictatorship," or "the Catholic Church has practised ideological thought control, therefore . . ."

The totalitarian dictatorships all possess the following:

1. An official ideology, consisting of an official body of doctrine covering all vital aspects of man's existence to which everyone living in that society is supposed to adhere, at least passively; this ideology is characteristically focused and projected toward a perfect final state of mankind, that is to say, it contains a chiliastic claim, based upon a radical rejection of the existing society and conquest of the world for the new one;

2. A single mass party led typically by one man, the "dictator," and consisting of a relatively small percentage of the total population (up to 10 per cent) of men and women, a hard core of them passionately and unquestioningly dedicated to the ideology and prepared to assist in every way in promoting its general acceptance, such a party being hierarchically, oligarchically organized, and typically either superior to, or completely intertwined with the bureaucratic government organization;

3. A system of terroristic police control, supporting but also supervising the party for its leaders, and characteristically directed not only against demonstrable "enemies" of the regime, but against arbitrarily selected classes of the population; the terror of the secret police systematically exploiting modern science, and more especially scientific psychology;

4. A technologically conditioned near-complete monopoly of control, in the hands of the party and its subservient cadres, of all means of effective mass communication, such as the press, radio, motion pictures;

5. A similarly technologically conditioned near-complete monopoly of control (in the same hands) of all means of effective armed combat;

6. A central control and direction of the entire economy through the bureaucratic co-ordination of its formerly independent corporate entities, typically including most other associations and group activities.

The enumeration of these six traits or trait clusters is not meant to suggest that there might not be others, now insufficiently recognized, but that these are universally acknowledged to be the features of totalitarian dictatorship to which the writings of students of the most varied backgrounds, including totalitarian writers, bear witness.

Within this broad pattern of similarities, there are many significant variations to which the analysis of this book will give detailed attention. To offer a few random illustrations, at present the party zealots play less of a role in the Soviet Union than the party bureaucrats, as contrasted with an earlier stage; the ideology of the Soviet Union is more specifically committed to certain assumptions, because of its Marx-Engels bible, than that of Italian or German fascism, where ideology was formulated by the leader of the party himself; the corporate entities of the fascist economy remained in private hands, as far as property claims are concerned, whereas they become public property in the Soviet Union.

Let us now turn to our first point, namely, that these systems are historically "unique"; that is to say, that no government like totalitarian dictatorship has ever before existed, even though it bears a resemblance to autocracies of the past. It may be interesting to consider briefly some data which show that the six traits we have just identified are to a large extent lacking in historically known autocratic regimes.* Neither the Oriental despotisms of the more remote past, nor the absolute monarchies of modern Europe, neither the tyrannies of the ancient Greek cities, nor the Roman Empire, nor yet the tyrannies of the city states of the Italian Renaissance and the Bonapartist military dictatorships of the last century exhibit this design, this combination of features, though they may possess one or another of its constituent traits. For example, efforts have often been made to organize some kind of secret police, but they have not been even horse-and-buggy affairs compared with the terror

---

* Autocratic regimes, as defined above, should be clearly distinguished from the broader category of "authoritarian" regimes of which some of them form a subdivision. Thus both monarchy and tyranny may be said to have been authoritarian, but the difference has long been decisive.

of the Gestapo or of the OGPU (MVD today). Similarly, there have been both military and propagandistic concentrations of power and control, but the limits of technology prevented any thoroughgoing development along totalitarian lines. It is very evident, we trust, that the six distinctive features here sketched, and to be developed in what follows, sharply differentiate contemporary totalitarian dictatorships from past autocratic regimes. Certainly neither the Roman emperor nor the absolute monarch sought or needed a party to support him nor an ideology in the modern party sense, and the same is obviously true of oriental despots. The tyrants of Greece and Italy may have had a party —that of the Medicis in Florence was called *lo stato*—but they had no ideology to speak of. And, of course, all of these autocratic regimes were far removed from the very distinctive features which are rooted in modern technology, from the terror to the centrally directed economy.

Something more should perhaps be added on the subject of technology. This technological aspect of totalitarianism is, of course, particularly striking in the matter of weapons and communications, but it is involved also in the secret police terror, depending as it does upon technically enhanced possibilities of supervision and control of the movement of persons. In addition, the centrally directed economy presupposes the reporting, cataloging, and calculating devices provided by modern technology. In short, four of the six traits are technologically conditioned. To envisage what this technological advance means in terms of political control, one has to think only of the weapons field. The Constitution of the United States guarantees to every citizen the "right to bear arms" (Fourth Amendment). In the days of the minutemen, this was a very important right, and the freedom of the citizen was indeed symbolized by the gun over the hearth, as it is in Switzerland to this day. But who can "bear" such arms as a tank, a bomber, or a flame-thrower, let alone an atom bomb? The citizen as an individual, and indeed in larger groups, is simply defenseless against the overwhelming technological superiority of those who can centralize in their hands the means with which to wield these modern arms and thereby physically to coerce the mass of the citizenry. Similar observations are easy to make regarding the press, the radio, and so forth. "Freedom" does not have the same potential, resting as it did upon individual effort, which it had a hundred and fifty years ago. With few exceptions, the trend of technological advance implies the trend toward greater and greater size of organization. In the perspective of these four traits, therefore, totalitarian societies appear to be merely exaggerations, but nonetheless logical exaggerations, of the technological state of modern society.

The same cannot be said with respect to the first two distinctive features of totalitarian dictatorships, for neither ideology nor party have any significant relation to the state of technology. (This may not be strictly true, since the mass conversion continually attempted by totalitarian propaganda through its effective use of the communications monopoly could not be carried through without it.) However, the party, its leader(s), and the ideology link the totalitarian dictatorship to modern democracy. It is the perversion of democracy. Not only did Hitler, Mussolini, and Lenin build typical parties within a constitutional, if not a democratic, context but the connection is plain between the stress on ideology and the role which platforms and other types of ideological goal-formation play in democratic parties. To be sure, totalitarian parties developed a pronounced authoritarian pattern while organizing themselves into effective revolutionary instruments of action; but, at the same time, its leaders, beginning with Marx and Engels, saw themselves as constituting the vanguard of the democratic movement of their day, and Stalin always talked of the Soviet totalitarian society as the "perfect democracy"; Hitler and Mussolini [9] made similar statements. Both the world brotherhood of the proletariat and the folk community were conceived of as supplanting the class divisions of past societies by a complete harmony—the classless society of the socialist tradition.

Not only the party but also its ideology harkens back to the democratic context within which the totalitarian movements arose. Ideology generally, but more especially totalitarian ideology, involves a high degree of convictional certainty. As has been indicated, totalitarian ideology consists of an official doctrine which radically rejects the pre-existing society in terms of a chiliastic proposal for a new one. As such it contains strongly utopian elements, some kind of notion of a paradise on earth. This utopian and chiliastic outlook of totalitarian ideologies gives them a pseudoreligious quality. In fact, they often elicit in the less critical followers a depth of conviction and a fervor of devotion usually found only among persons inspired by a transcendent faith. Whether these aspects of totalitarian ideologies bear some sort of relationship to the religions which they seek to replace is arguable. Marx denounced religion as "the opium of the people." It would seem that this is rather an appropriate way of describing totalitarian ideologies. In place of the more or less sane platforms of regular political parties, critical of the existing state of affairs, in a limited way, totalitarian ideologies are perversions of such programs. They substitute faith for reason, magic exhortation for scientific knowledge. And yet, it must be recognized that there is enough of these same elements in the operations of democratic parties to attest to the relation between them and their perverted descendants, the totalitarian movements. That is why these movements must be seen and analyzed in their relationship to the democracy which they seek to supplant. . . .

NOTES

1. Fraenkel, Ernst, *The Dual State—A Contribution to the Theory of Dictatorship,* New York, 1941, *passim.*
2. Friedrich, C. J., *Die Philosophie des Rechts in historischer Perspektive,* Heidelberg, 1955, chapter 8.
3. Hannah Arendt, "Ideology and Terror: A Novel Form of Government," *Review of Politics,* 15:309ff (1953). The antecedents in earlier discussions of the

law of nature are inadequately recognized, since Miss Arendt takes only the normative (scholastic) law of nature into account.

4. *Ibid.*, pp. 303ff. In this interesting paper, Miss Arendt advances the thesis that it is not merely the utopian nature of the ideology, but its alleged logicality, that leads to the terror. Based on a "scientific" law of movement, these ideologies are "literally the logic of an idea" which is carried through with "ice-cold reasoning."

5. Bullock, Alan, *Hitler—A Study in Tyranny*, London, 1952, *passim*.

6. Borgese, G. A., *Goliath, The March of Fascism*, New York, 1937, pp. 271-344. For a bitter criticism of this tendency, see Emil Ludwig's *Mussolini*, Berlin, 1932, p. 231.

7. Neumann, Franz, *Behemoth*, New York, 1942. Also, Maxine B. Sweezey, *The Structure of the Nazi Economy*, Cambridge, Mass., 1941, and R. A. Brady, *The Spirit and Structure of German Fascism*, New York, 1937. Neumann's analysis is much the ablest of the three. The "imperialist" interpretation ties in with Thorstein Veblen's earlier analysis of German and Japanese militarism and imperialism.

8. Bertalanffy, Livon, *General System Theory: A New Approach to the Unity of Science*, 1951. A system is characterized by three features: it consists of several parts that are quite distinct and different from each other; these parts bear a defined functional relation to each other; and typically the destruction of some of these parts (the essential ones) entails the destruction of the system as a whole. Such systems may be composed of physical entities, of animated beings, or of thoughts. A social or cultural or political system is typically a combination of all three.

9. Tasca, A., *Nascita e avvento del Fascismo*, Rome, 1950. Mussolini's attitude toward democracy was ambivalent. Fascist theory was much more frankly elitist than Nazi ideology.

TYPES OF TOTALITARIAN IDEOLOGY

Carl J. Friedrich and Zbigniew K. Brzezinski

"Ideas are weapons," in the view of many. But are they only weapons? The cynic answers "yes," because the truth has no meaning for him. Totalitarians tend to be such cynics. Yet they are fanatics when it comes to maintaining their own ideas. They seem to believe passionately in *their* truth. But are passionate belief and fanaticism signs of the strength of one's conviction? One does not argue violently with a man,

Reprinted from Carl J. Friedrich and Zbigniew K. Brzezinski, *Totalitarian Dictatorship and Autocracy* (Cambridge, Mass.: Harvard University Press, 1956), pp. 71-79. Copyright by the President and Fellows of Harvard College. By permission of the authors and the publisher.

let alone assault him, because he refuses to agree that two and two make four. Nor is the Christian who is firm in his belief intolerant of the man who cannot see the truth of his beliefs. The history of religion, as indeed the history of ideas generally, shows that periods of witch-hunting are periods of declining faith, of doubt, uncertainty, and anxiety. Ideas become weapons when they are no longer firmly seen as true.

Marx and Engels described the whole range of ideas as "super-structure." Religion, law, and other value systems were seen by them as nothing but camouflage, surrounding the bare and brute facts of economic controls, the "control of the means of production." They served as weapons in the class struggle, by which the ruling class buttressed its position of power. Thus Marx wrote: "The ruling ideas of each age have ever been the ideas of its ruling class,"[1] and again: ". . . every historical period has laws of its own, . . . as soon as society has outlived a given period of development, and is passing over from one given stage to another, it begins to be subject to other laws."[2] Clearly, according to them, the prevailing ideology of any particular epoch was both the outward rationalization of that epoch's economic organization and also the tool used by the dominant class to stop history from continuing on its inevitable path. For, as Marx and Engels saw it, history was a perpetual progress through time, propelled irresistibly by the class struggle, though at varying rates of advance. The struggle produced the historical momentum and established the economically dominant classes in a position of power and then toppled them from it. "All history is the history of class struggles," the *Communist Manifesto* declared. Throughout this unfolding pattern of dialectical change, combining revolution and evolution, ideology served both to mask and then to unmask "objective reality."

Though we can readily see that this communist approach to history and the ideas at work in it was the product of a specific historical period, Marx and his followers believed its unique quality to be that it was more than an ideology. To them, their thought embodied the science of history, and as such constituted an unprecedented insight into the true course of development. As such, it provided those who fully grasped it with a key for understanding not only the past and the present, but also the future. And because its view of the future was said to be scientifically accurate, and because it asserted that the future would be better than the present, it readily became a compelling call to action. The future, thus clearly perceived and rightly valued, must be hastened; its advent must be assisted with all available means. Dialectical material-ism (or *Diamat,* in current Soviet parlance) offers, according to the communists, not only an infallible perception of the meaning of the interrelationship of social forces, but also a clear guide to the character of inevitable social change. It combines moral indignation against the Today with a fiercely fanatic conviction that the Tomorrow, which is bound to come, will be a higher, indeed a near perfect, state of society.[3]

Marx and Engels, by making ideas depend upon the economic system, raised the issue of what has come to be known as the "sociology of knowledge"—or, the study of the social conditioning which causes and thereby explains the rise and growth of ideas, of notions regarding values, of scientific discoveries, and of practical programs of social reform. By claiming that all such knowledge is essentially superstructure, of which the substructure is the system of economic controls, the Marxist makes knowledge a dependent variable which changes with the economic system. This is a sweeping sociological generalization and it was natural that not only scholars should question it and ask in turn: how true is this proposition? To what extent is the economic system primary, the first cause of all other changes in the intellectual field? Indeed, the obvious query suggested itself: is this true of the Marxist system itself?

We are not now going to go into this vast problem of intellectual creativity and its relation to environmental conditioning, but wish to make quite clear at the outset that these issues are involved in the problem of ideology and its role in the totalitarian dictatorships of our time. The Soviet dictatorship, more particularly, rests upon this belief in the instrumental nature of ideas and ideology. Far from reducing the role of ideology, this conviction has led to its explicit cultivation and to the large-scale indoctrination of the masses. An intense concern with ideological conformity is the paradoxical consequence of the doctrine that ideas are nothing but weapons.

But before we further elaborate a typology of totalitarian ideologies it is necessary to define the term. The problem of totalitarian ideology must be seen within the more general context of the role of ideology in the political community. Some would define it as "a general system of beliefs held in common by the members of a collectivity, i.e., a society, or a subcollectivity of one—including a movement deviant from the main culture of the society—a system of ideas which is oriented to the evaluative integration of the collectivity and of the situation in which it is placed, the processes by which it has developed to its given state, the goals toward which its members are collectively oriented, and their relation to the future course of events." [4] Such a definition makes an ideology a characteristic feature of any politically organized community, equivalent in function to a rationalization in an individual, and serving the purpose of integration. The wisdom of so broad a definition of the term ideology may well be doubted. Ideologies are of much less general and more recent significance. They arise in connection with parties and movements maintaining explicit systems of thought; they are a product of the age of mass communication.

Even more dubious is another definition which would sharply contrast ideology and utopia. Deriving their thought from Karl Mannheim's well-known work,[5] these writers would maintain that ideology serves as the "political myth," which is further defined as the "pattern of basic political symbols." It is the function of this political myth "to preserve the social structure." It should be clearly distinguished from an "utopia" whose function it is "to destroy the social structure." [6] As a consequence, it is then argued that, "with the seizure of power, utopian symbols become ideologies." This contrasting and juxtaposing of ideology and utopia is confusing, to say the least. It obstructs an understanding of the actualities of totalitarian politics.* And it has the further inconvenience that the same set of ideas are at some fixed point in time changed from an utopia into an ideology, when as a matter of fact they serve as both, before and after the seizure of power. This may be manageable in a case like the Soviet Union, but it is perplexing in the case of Hitler's *Mein Kampf*, which would be an utopia before, and an ideology after, January 30, 1933. Actually, *Mein Kampf* contains the utopian ideology of the German Fascist movement both before and after that date.

It would seem best, in the light of all the facts, to restrict the term ideology to that of a set of *literate ideas*. An ideology thus defined is a reasonably coherent body of ideas concerning practical means of how to change and reform a society, based upon a more or less elaborate criticism of what is wrong with the existing, or antecedent, society. And a totalitarian ideology would then be one which is concerned with total destruction and total reconstruction, involving typically an ideological acceptance of violence as the only practicable means for such total destruction. It might accordingly be defined as "a reasonably coherent body of ideas concerning practical means of how totally to change and reconstruct a society by force, or violence, based upon an all-inclusive or total criticism of what is wrong with an existing or antecedent society." This total change and reconstruction in its very nature constitutes an "utopia" and hence totalitarian ideologies are typically utopian in nature.[7] Totalitarian ideologies, in this perspective, are a radical form of a development which, although there are precedents, is typically modern; they must not be confused with traditional notions, beliefs, and customs prevalent in older traditional societies.

Consequently, we also reject the suggestion of Mannheim that we speak of an ideology as "total" when "we are concerned with the characteristics and composition of the total structure of the mind of this epoch, or of this group." [8] He informs us that the idea of a total ideology is "intended to designate the outlook inevitably associated with a given historical and social situation, and the *Weltanschauung* and style of thought bound up with it." [9] Mannheim would contrast with this total ideology "particular" ideologies, which would include "all those utterances, the falsity of which is due to an intentional or unintentional, conscious, semiconscious, or unconscious deluding of oneself or of others, taking place on a psychological level and structurally resembling lies." [10] This dichotomy of two kinds of ideologies, total and par-

---

* In a special discussion on conservatism Karl Mannheim argued (*Essays on Sociology and Social Psychology*, London, 1953) the point involved in Lasswell's generalization, by particular reference to the Italian Fascists. Actually, the "conservative" note in Italian fascism turned up soon after 1919, long before the March on Rome. Mr. Germino suggests that one might even argue that fascism was conservative before and utopian after the attainment of power.

ticular, which is based upon psychological and moral aspects shared as a matter of fact by all systems of ideas, is quite unfortunate.* It is therefore not surprising that Mannheim in the later sections of his work drops the "total ideology" as a valid conception, observing that "we shall, as far as possible, avoid the use of the term 'ideology,' *because of its moral connotation,* and shall instead speak of the 'perspective' of a thinker." This "perspective" Mannheim considers the proper subject of the "sociology of knowledge." [11] What remains as Mannheim's notion of ideologies is that they are "utterances" and that they "structurally resemble lies." But the "structure" of a lie is typically that of a statement which does not correspond to what can be known as a true statement, such as "all men are created equal." While such an utterance is undoubtedly part of democratic ideology, it receives its "ideological" significance from the fact that it carries the implication that hereditary privileges are bad and should be abolished and that a society without such privileges is good and should be so constructed.

In short, ideologies are essentially action-related systems of ideas. They typically contain a program and a strategy for its realization and their essential purpose is to unite organizations which are built around them.[12]

The rise and development of such ideologies appears to be a feature of the democratic age, as we have said, and seems to be associated with the development of parties. Parties of reform especially tend to develop such ideologies, which they propose to put into practice upon their assumption of power. In this process, adaptations take place and some of the more utopian aspects of the ideology are eliminated as a concession to reality.[13] Totalitarian parties are an extreme instance of this general trend. By their elimination of all rivals they monopolize the field and convert their group ideology into a governmental one. But the process of adaptation to "reality" still takes place even though a persistent effort is made to maintain the myth that the ideology is intact, and that the concessions are temporary. Thus Hitler found himself obliged to compromise with big business and indeed to strengthen its position of monopolistic control in the German economy, although his ideology called for "socialism" in the sense of the state protecting the interests of the lower middle classes and the workers. By mobilizing the idea of "leadership" and by making the factory owner or manager the "leader" of the enterprise, he tried to straddle the ideological conflict.

Similarly in the Soviet Union the regime had to face the problem of adjusting the hallowed concept of "withering away of the state" to the new "socialist realities." This concept, highly utopian in its appeal, had been repeatedly stressed in Lenin's writings, in which he quoted Marx and Engels as his authority and emphasized himself that "the

---

* When seen as creations of finite minds, all ideas are limiting in scope, selecting aspects of an infinitely complex reality, and hence may be described as "deluding one's self and others."

proletariat needs only a state which is withering away, i.e., a state so constituted that it begins to wither away immediately, and cannot but wither away." [14]

The abyss between this statement and current Soviety reality is obvious, and the Soviet leaders have not been blind to it. The concept has consequently been redefined to suit the imperatives of power without prima facie invalidating it. Stalin merely stated that

[the concept] is correct but only on one of two conditions: (1) *if* we study the socialist state only from the angle of internal development of the country, abstracting ourselves in advance from the international factor, isolating, for the convenience of investigation, the country and state from the international situation; or (2) *if* we assume that *socialism* is already victorious in all countries, or in the majority of countries, that a Socialist encirclement exists instead of a *capitalist encirclement,* that there is no more danger of foreign attack, and that there is no more need to strength the army and the state.[15]

These illustrations serve to show that an ideology can be more or less "rational" in its elaboration. The Soviet ideology, based as it is upon the allegedly "scientific" findings of Karl Marx and Friedrich Engels, as elaborated by N. Lenin and others, appears to be decidedly more rational than either that of Fascist Italy or Hitler Germany. In the last two instances, the ideology was distinctly "personal," resting, in the case of Mussolini, upon his journalistic writings and more especially his article on fascism in the *Encyclopedia Italiana* (1932) [16]; in the case of Hitler, upon *Mein Kampf* [17] written in 1923-24 during his sojourn in jail, and maintained ever after as the gospel of National Socialism. An analysis in terms of antecedent intellectual influences and the like would incline one to differentiate further and call Mussolini's creed more rational than that of Hitler. The degree of "rationality" here involved is that of a rationality of means, rather than ends. For the values in all three ideologies are of a highly emotional sort. This may not make much difference to the skeptic who considers all value judgments beyond rational discourse, but in any case there are differences of degree, and it is certainly permissible to assert that the value judgments at the base of Thomism, Confucianism, and modern constitutionalism are more rational than those of the totalitarian creeds, even if they are not wholly rational.

These totalitarian ideologies can also be classified according to their ultimate values, and this is the more usual and conventional procedure. We then arrive at the very well-known differentiation between the Soviet ideology which is universal in its appeal—"Workers of all the world, unite!"—and the fascist ideologies—which address themselves to a particular people in terms of their grandeur, power, and historical role. In the Soviet ideology, the place of the national group is taken by the proletariat, which is invested with the historical role of liberating mankind from the shackles of industrial capitalism, but Marx and Engels make it very clear that this proletariat, by overthrowing the existing class structure, ultimately eliminates itself and ceases to exist as a proletariat. From this standpoint, social justice appears to be the ultimate value, unless it be the classless society which is its essential condition; for the fascist, this ultimate or highest value is dominion, eventually world dominion, and the strong and pure nation-race is *its* essential condition, as seen by its ideology. Since there are many nations and races, there can theoretically be as many fascisms, and this has actually proven to be the case. Wherever fascism has raised its head, whether in France, England, or the United States, the strength and the purification of the particular nation involved has been in the center of ideological attention. This aspect is an element of weakness in fascist ideologies, as contrasted with the communist ones. The latter have the advantage of an inherent universalism and the consequent ability to cope more readily with the extension of power to other nations (the Soviet Union vis-à-vis Poland, Czechoslovakia, Germany, and so forth, China vis-à-vis Korea, Indochina, and so forth).

It is precisely this doctrinal catholicism which makes communism an effective weapon of combat, not only between nations, but also, and generally unlike fascism, within nations. Fascism, when a spontaneous product of local combustion, by necessity tended to accentuate national distinctiveness and national sovereignty. It emphasized frequently the biological superiority of the given community. Fascism, when imposed on several nations, produced, as it did during World War II, the most vigorous reactions from those nations which it enveloped. Universality based on a restricted nationalist appeal is a contradiction in terms. Actually, Italian Fascism had a good deal of appeal beyond Italy. Similar movements cropped up in Austria, Hungary, Rumania, Spain, France, and Great Britain, and one must not forget that Italian Fascism was, after all, the inspiration for many of Hitler's followers as well as for Hitler himself. Peron also followed the basic line of Italian Fascism. There is a very interesting item in the Italian Fascist catechism, used in the youth organizations: "Question: Is Fascism exclusively an Italian phenomenon? Answer: Fascism, as far as its ideas, doctrines and realizations are concerned, is *universal*, because it is in the position of saying to all civilized people *the word of truth without which there cannot be lasting peace in the world; therefore it is the sustainer and creator of a new civilization.*" It should be noted, however, that with this kind of "universalism," while it may be able to arouse imitators, each of the resulting fascist movements will itself seek world, or regional, dominion, and hence be creating obstacles to the extension of effective control by the "creator." Presumably, a fascist France or England would have been at least as vigorous a rival of Italian aspirations to dominion in the Mediterranean as the democratic regimes of these countries were.[18]

Communism, on the other hand, has been markedly successful in operating on the national base for the sake of supranational goals. For communism, unlike fascism, operates simultaneously on two levels: one is the universal, "orthodox," and philosophical plane, which at this time is still the private domain of Soviet leadership, notwithstanding some modest contributions of Mao Tse-Tung to the concept of the revolution. The other level is the practical, the tactical. On this level communism may vary, temporarily, at least, from country to country. Thus the nature of the communist appeal is markedly different in, let us say, France from that in India. Similarly, even in the captive nations of Eastern Europe and in China, great stress was laid on the distinct nature of their communist development. In Poland, for instance, in the immediate post-war years, the official party declarations stressed the fact that communism in Poland was to be implemented in "the Polish way." [19] Indeed, it became the standard weapon of the parlor communist in Eastern Europe to emphasize the distinctive, allegedly more democratic, character of the development of a communist society in Eastern Europe as contrasted with past Soviet history.

Such an attitude, at that time, was not heresy. It was merely an acknowledgment of the "fact" that history moves by stages, which according to Marxism are contradictory to one another, and that the Soviet Union at the given moment was operating on a higher plane of social development. The Tito affair, however, soon forced the Soviet leadership into the rigorous affirmation that past Soviet experience is binding on all communist parties, notwithstanding their local circumstances. The theoretical journal of the Soviet Communist Party, *Bolshevik*, stated in this connection that:

The assertion that every country advances towards Socialism along its own specific path cannot be recognized as correct, as well as the contention that there are as many roads in this direction as there are countries. To utter this means to deny the international portent of the Bolshevik experience. The general laws of transition from capitalism to Socialism, discovered by Marx and Engels, and tested, put to concrete use and developed by Lenin and Stalin on the basis of the experience of the Bolshevik Party and the Soviet State, are binding upon all countries.[20]

Nevertheless, significant local variations of a practical nature are to this day evident, as for instance in the treatment of the Catholic Church or the farmers in Poland, or the redefinition of the concept of the elite in China. The crucial determinant of ideological loyalty is the ultimate implication of the local variation: if it serves to further the over-all goals of the universal ideology, without fragmenting the power bloc on which the ideology rests, the practical deviation is tolerated. If not, it is excised.

NOTES

1. Marx, Karl and Friedrich Engels, *Die Deutsche Ideologie,* Berlin, 1953, pp. 35-36 and elsewhere.

2. Marx, Karl, *Das Kapital,* Hamburg, 1867, Vol. I., pp. 23-24.

3. Plamenatz, John P., *German Marxism and Russian Communism,* London, 1954, pp. 8-36, points out that the communist emphasis on *Diamat* is often merely lip-service. What communists refer to as dialectical materialism is not that at all, but historical materialism. Genuine dialectics has little to do with it.

4. Parson, Talcott, *The Social System* [New York: The Free Press of Glencoe], 1951, p. 349.

5. Mannheim, Karl, *Ideology and Utopia: An Introduction to the Sociology of Knowledge,* Oxford, 1936, 1950, *passim.*

6. Lasswell, Harold D. and Abraham Kaplan, *Power and Society,* New Haven, 1950. para. 3.1, 6.1, and 6.3.

7. [See] Karl Wittfogel, "The Historical Position of Communist China: Doctrine and Reality," *Review of Politics,* 16:463ff (1954), for further detail.

8. Mannheim, Karl, *Ideology and Utopia,* p. 50.

9. *Ibid.,* p. 111.

10. *Ibid.,* p. 238.

11. *Ibid.,* p. 239.

12. Leites, Nathan C., *A Study of Bolshevism* [New York: The Free Press of Glencoe], 1953, p. 24. "The party aims at a radical transformation of the world." The study is based upon such a concept of ideology, or rather that aspect of it which Leites calls its "operational code."

13. Aron, Raymond, *L'Opium des Intellectuels,* Paris, 1955, pp. 315ff. The author argues this case with persuasive insistence for the French Left, whose ideology, or myths, he compares with that of the Right, asking finally whether the age of ideologies is coming to an end.

14. Lenin, V. I., *Selected Works,* New York, 1943. "State and Revolution," Vol. VII, p. 24.

15. Stalin, J. V., *Problems of Leninism,* Moscow, 1940, pp. 659-699.

16. Oakeshott, Michael, *The Social and Political Doctrines of Contemporary Europe,* Cambridge, 1939. [See] pp. 164ff for reprint of this.

17. Hitler, Adolf, *Mein Kampf,* München, 1925-1927.

18. Germino, Dante, "The Party as an Instrument of Totalitarian Rule: The Partito Nazionale Fascista," Ph.D. thesis, Harvard University, 1956, p. 71.

19. *Nowe Drogi,* January 1947; the Secretary-General of the Party, Wladyslaw Gomulka (subsequently purged), went as far as to claim that there was no need of a dictatorship of the proletariat in Poland as communism in Poland would arrive through an evolutionary process.

20. *Bol'shevik,* no. 17 (1948), p. 51.

"TOTALITARIAN DEMOCRACY"

CAN DEMOCRACY BE TOTALITARIAN?

Z. A. Pelczynski

One hundred and fifty years ago "democracy" was a comparatively rare and unimportant word. One met it most frequently, if not exclusively, in books on political science, where it had been stock-in-trade since Aristotle's famous classification. It was the French Revolution and its aftermath that popularized the term. The revolutionaries might have talked more of "republic" than "democracy," but the latter word took root in political discussion and propaganda, and in due course has produced a rich crop of meanings and uses. However slow and uneven was the extension of political rights, more and more groups and classes were becoming reconciled to the term and finding it a handy ideological weapon. Distinctions, qualifications and subdivisions soon became necessary. Some time after the middle of the 19th century the radicals lost the monopoly of "democracy"; the word acquired respectability among the upper classes, was christened "tory" and "liberal," and the radicals were forced to adopt some such adjective as "social" to protect their own brand. "Christian democracy" was born when Catholicism and popular government were reconciled with each other, and the conversion of the U.S.S.R. to the term has been responsible for the adjectives "bourgeois," "capitalist," "proletarian," "Western," "Eastern," "soviet," and "people's." Meanwhile the political scientists have not been idle and have managed to add a few distinctions of their own such as "direct" and "representative" or "political" and "industrial."

The number of adjectives, which the politician, aided and abetted by the political scientist, has thus applied to "democracy," must be very large, and it is surprising that nobody has yet attempted to collect and

Reprinted from *Occidente*, vol. X, no. 5 (September-October, 1954), pp. 429-435. By permission of the author and the publisher.

This article [was] broadcast on the Third Programme of the B.B.C., on Sunday 24th October, 1954.

classify them. Nor does the ingenuity of one or the other show any signs of decreasing. Perhaps the latest, the least familiar and the most puzzling addition to this rich "democratic" vocabulary is the term "totalitarian democracy." Neither its parentage nor its date of birth is exactly known, but its sophisticated, paradoxical appearance suggests an academic rather than a propagandist origin, and the 1930's seem a probable time. Bertrand de Jouvenel used it to describe a corruption of liberal democracy in a book written during the last war, and published in Britain after the war under the title *Power—The Natural History of its Growth.*

More recently there appeared a book wholly devoted to the concept of "totalitarian democracy," whose influence on political thinking cannot probably be overestimated. J. L. Talmon, the author of *The Origins of Totalitarian Democracy*, puts forward the thesis that during the French Revolution the ideas of Rousseau and some other 18th century thinkers crystallized into a peculiar type of democracy, which he calls "totalitarian" and contrasts with the more familiar "liberal" type, represented, say, by Tocqueville or John Stuart Mill. According to Talmon "totalitarian democracy" was originally a way of feeling and acting in politics, a pattern of beliefs and values akin to religion; it became the ideology of a number of revolutionary movements in the 19th century, including marxism, and finally has found its institutional embodiment in the political and social system of the U.S.S.R.

We are not concerned here with the validity of the philosophical or historical analysis underlying Talmon's concept, but rather with the logical merits and implications of the term "totalitarian democracy" considered against the background of our established political terminology. And it cannot be denied that at first sight the term seems paradoxical, not to say absurd. "Democracy" and "totalitarianism," whether used in popular or academic language, are anything but precise and unambiguous terms, but to the majority of people in the West they stand for two distinct and opposed political systems.

"Democracy" generally means a political system in which the masses of the people, through periodical elections and universal franchise, are able to control or at least considerably influence the government of their country. The power of a single individual over the government is everywhere infinitesimal, but in a democracy he can add his vote to those of like-minded individuals, and help to put one party or particular combination of parties into office for a period of time. Hence democracy is thought to imply, as its necessary feature, the presence of at least two parties, the effective legal right to organize parties and conduct political propaganda, the possibility of opposing the party in power by constitutional means, and the liberty of holding different views about politics, expressing them in public and criticizing political opponents including the government. Democracy further implies respect for the existing rights of individuals and organized groups on the part of the agents of the government, and their alteration only according to a generally accepted procedure. Some of these rights—certain personal liberties of the individual or the autonomy of some associations—are universally held to be sacrosanct, and no interference with them is as a rule tolerated except in extreme national emergencies.

"Totalitarianism" and "totalitarian" are newer and rather less definite words. Often they are used in a vague, sloppy way to describe any system or action which arbitrarily overrides the wishes of individuals subject to it. In my opinion "totalitarianism" best applies to a political system in which one party or group of politicians is permanently in power, and uses governmental and extragovernmental means to suppress all potential rivals. Freedom of political criticism and discussion is confined within the narrow bounds of the official ideology and day-to-day party line, and political activity is permitted only within the framework of organizations controlled by the party in power. While the population thus has no effective constitutional means of controlling the government, the government has an almost unlimited power of influencing the opinions of its subjects and interfering with the individual and social life of the country. It is the sole master over the constitution and can at any time alter its provisions; it can legislate away any right when it obstructs or incommodes policy or permit the administration to ignore it in practice; more than that, it can, when necessary, secure the manifestations of popular support for its personnel, measures, ideology and the whole institutional system on which its own power is based.

Before we dismiss the term "totalitarian democracy" as a contradiction in terms, however, let us see if there is not, after all, some way of making it meaningful. The two political systems are complex wholes of structures; each has more than one characteristic feature and in fact combines several distinct, if interconnected, elements. Though hardly any of the elements are the same in both, some seem to differ in degree rather than kind. Can there be a hybrid of the two systems, to which the term might legitimately be applied? It is well known that in modern democratic countries the government controls a great and growing section of national life and performs for the individual an increasing number of services. Let us imagine a situation in which the process has gone much further, and a degree of state control and activity comparable to that found in Communist countries has been accepted by the electorate. The state would concern itself with all the aspects of economic, technical, scientific and cultural life of the country, establish and maintain appropriate institutions, raise and supply the funds, select the personnel, give them general directions, and so on. The situation is not so fantastic as it appears at first sight; did not Great Britain, during the last war, approximate to it, and might not another war push the process much further? Nevertheless it is doubtful if such a state could correctly be called "totalitarian democracy." What seems essential to totalitarianism is not so much the mere *extent* of governmental activity as the *method* by which it was arrived at and is maintained. In the hypothetical situation just considered the basic features of democracy—some correspondence between the laws of the country and the wishes of the population, and the absence of arbitrary infringement of existing rights—are still present, however much the laws and the rights themselves have changed in substance. People are still free to criticise the government and the system, free to oppose it by constitutional means, free to organize themselves for the purpose of influencing, modifying or altering the extent and direction of state activity, free to try to "put the clock back" by voting for a suitable party.

Let us, however, go further and assume a state of affairs, in which the population has voluntarily accepted the rule of a single organized political élite and periodically renews its mandate because it has spontaneously acquired an almost unanimous consensus about the ends and means of government, and an unshakable confidence in the wisdom and efficiency of the élite. Could one then not talk of "totalitarian democracy" without self-contradiction? The question is theoretically exciting, but of extremely limited practical importance. The hypothetical case just mentioned assumes away the very conditions in which democracy and totalitarianism, as we know them, are possible and make sense. Both political systems presuppose the absence of complete agreement on political issues among politicians and ordinary citizens, as well as the natural distrust of the ruled towards their rulers, but they deal in different ways with the problem. In democracy political disagreement is legalized within definite but fairly wide limits, and the people's faith in the government is put to a periodical test of a general election. I may be disappointed by the result and attempt to turn the other party out at the next election, but in the meantime there is nothing but tolerance—and criticism—left. In totalitarianism a facade of complete agreement and approval among politicians and the people is erected, and behind it steps are taken to minimize and stifle opposition. When all the enemies of the official ideology and the party line have been eliminated and the masses intimidated or imbued with a temporary enthusiasm, a vote of confidence from the electorate is perfectly safe and expedient. It seems that we are bound to conclude that "totalitarian democracy" is a practical impossibility and an unrealizable ideal in addition to being bad logic. It is, in the true sense of the word, a utopia, a gigantic political day-dream—or nightmare, according to one's point of view. As an *ideal* it may, of course, exercise profound influence on thought and action. Talmon has shown this strikingly in the case of the Jacobins and the Babouvists, and we sometimes catch glimpses of it in the writings and speeches of recent totalitarian politicians.

But there is yet another line, along which one could attempt to salvage the term. "Democracy," as it has been used so far, includes many things beside universal suffrage and periodical election, e.g. constitutionalism and the rule of law. Often, however, we use it in a narrow sense, meaning a form of organization where decisions concerning a group are taken by majority vote of the members of the group. The opposite of "democratic" in this sense is not "totalitarian" but

"aristocratic," "oligarchic," "monarchical" or "autocratic." What we normally call "democracy" is certainly "democratic" in one very important
respect, namely the decision as to which of the competing parties
shall form the government; but many other politically significant decisions in a democracy are not really "democratically" arrived at. For
example, the selection of party leaders or the determination of party
programmes may be "oligarchic" or even "autocratic," and very often is.
Thus a democracy can be more or less "democratic"; but so can a
totalitarianism. We seem to have reached the paradox that while it is
impossible for democracy to be totalitarian, it is possible for totalitarianism to be democratic.

Since in totalitarian countries governing is the monopoly of one
party, its composition and structure are of crucial importance. If its
membership is widely based and the rank and file have some share in
policy-making or the choice of leaders, the wishes of the population
have perhaps some chance of being taken into account by the government, and the latter's policy might, however faintly, reflect them. This
will tend to diminish in proportion as the composition and structure of
the party become oligarchic or autocratic. One can even conceive a
political system which was perfectly totalitarian in the relations of the
government to the people but maintained democracy *within* the ruling
class. Here pre-war Italy and Germany seem to have differed significantly
from Soviet Russia and the countries which have followed her in the
last few years. Fascism and Nazism not only were totalitarian; they
positively gloried in the name of totalitarianism. Democratic ideals and
institutions were openly despised; the principles stressed and exalted
were those of élite rather than egalitarianism, appointment from above
rather than election from below, unquestioned acclamation rather than
discussion. The Communist countries present a somewhat different
picture. First of all they insist on being called "democracies" though
with some such adjective as "soviet" or "people's" to distinguish them
from capitalist countries. Their formal constitutional structure is almost
unimpeachably democratic. The principle of "democratic centralism"
underlies the organization of the party. But much more important
than forms and phrases is the undeniable fact that the Communist
countries have succeeded in drawing the masses into politics to an
unprecedented extent. The total of man-hours annually spent on political
activity of one kind or another is not only greater than it was in Germany
or Italy; it is probably far greater than in the most advanced Western
democracies today. There are endless election campaigns, congresses,
conferences and mass meetings where countless speeches are made,
issues discussed and resolutions passed. The controlled press and radio
retail the proceedings to the ordinary man in the street at the expense
of other topics, thus forcibly turning his attention to politics the whole
time. We shouldn't be too hard on a man from Mars or an ancient Greek
or a modern peasant from Afghanistan if he therefore came to the conclusion that the East was really more democratic than the West!

All this political activity seems to us quite meaningless—a mere form of control without substance. For all its apparent ferocity the Eastern demos is a dog that barks a lot but never bites. But it would be wrong and dangerous to dismiss such activity as unimportant. There is a vast difference between the Communist countries and the old-fashioned autocratic or oligarchic régimes where a narrow, privileged and distant group lords it over a passive, politically inert populace. Public discussion of political issues and elections, even when wholly manipulated by the party in power, must tend to stimulate the population to greater effort, make unpleasant decisions more palatable, produce what the sociologists call an attitude of "collective commitment" and in general help to attach the masses to the régime and its policies. They may also, especially in countries where politics have in the past been the privilege of the few, immunize the people against the influence of any other type of democracy.

Thus the search after the meaning of "totalitarian democracy" has not been wholly unprofitable although the case against keeping it as a useful or necessary political term still stands. The distinction between "totalitarianism" and "democracy" is reasonably clear and well-established, and to blur it is to court confusion. But those who have invented and used the phrase have nevertheless performed a valuable service in drawing our attention to certain features of modern totalitarianism which are frequently overlooked. For this we must be grateful to them.

GENESIS OF TOTALITARIANISM IN DEMOCRATIC SOCIETIES

Enrico Opocher

The democratic system, by definition, involves an incessant battle against one of the most deeply-rooted traits of the human psyche: the spirit of intolerance. It would be a mistake, however, to conclude that modern totalitarianism is no more than a transient episode in this fight. The totalitarianism of today is, in fact, characterized not so much by a

Reprinted from *Confluence*, vol. 1, no. 3 (September, 1952), 47-53. By permission of the author and the publisher.

relapse into intolerance as by a paradoxical pretense of erecting this intolerance into a system of political organization, of giving a positive, even socially constructive, meaning to an attitude which had been considered by generation after generation as shameful for the individual and harmful to society. It is difficult to denounce such a pretense on an abstract moral plane as nothing more than the "wicked idea of wicked men"; and, on a philosophical plane, it is impossible to believe that this "wicked idea" could have found concrete historical expression without profound causes. Not only the politician, the sociologist, or the philosopher, but also the man in the street is confronted with the following problem at every moment of his difficult existence: Why did modern society, at the time when democratic progress seemed most secure, give birth to the paradox of totalitarianism?

The very question naturally arouses the suspicion that totalitarianism is really the most typical, if most violent expression of a possibility contained in the very logic of the democratic system, and that the conflict between democracy and totalitarianism conceals a relationship of growth towards some synthesis in the Hegelian sense. For this reason, it has seemed to me of some interest to choose, among the various points of view from which the genesis of totalitarianism can be studied, that which can be summed up in this proposition: Does the logic of the democratic system itself foster the transition to the totalitarian system?

I

As soon as we go beyond the purely psychological term of their antithesis and attempt to analyze what lies behind the democratic and totalitarian attitudes, we see that these two attitudes spring from profoundly differing beliefs about the nature of truth, from "Weltanschauungen" far transcending the purely political terms of the question. Democratic ideology conceives truth as something to be achieved through the conflict of freely expressed opinion and the test of every possible experiment; totalitarian ideology treats truth as revealed, as dogma which, even in the political sphere, excludes disagreement and the lessons of experiment. They can be crudely contrasted as the open political system and the closed political system, empiricism and dogmaticism. It is significant that the modern democratic system, which has so laboriously been established on the ruins of the medieval universalism of continental Europe, found its most complete and lasting expression in the empirical genius of the Anglo-Saxon peoples; and that the totalitarian system was readily accepted by nations which are most liable to dogmatism—the Germans and the Russians with their profound tendency to metaphysics, and the Italians with their quickly fired emotionality and their tradition of authoritarian Catholicism. How is it possible then to pass from the political empiricism of the democratic system to the dogmatism of the totalitarian system?

Democratic empiricism continuously oscillates between two tendencies which are fundamentally opposed: the spiritual, personalistic tendency, which is of Christian derivation, and the relativistic tendency, deeply akin to the laic humanism of the Renaissance. In the personalistic tendency, democratic empiricism and the "openness" of the political system rest on the "internalization" of the idea of truth. It depends on the presupposition that truth is inseparable from freedom as the expression of the spiritual process by which the "person" realizes, through responsible, concrete effort, the absolute values which he carries within him. In the relativistic tendency, democratic empiricism derives from the typically Renaissance thesis of the autonomy of politics, of its independence of any absolute values, and therefore on the identification of political truth with the opinion of the majority; its anti-dogmatism involves a relativism pure and simple. In the first instance, democracy is a system of tolerance because it is based on a faith in the absolute value of personal autonomy and hence in the value of every man's contribution to the attainment of truth; in the second, it is a system of tolerance for technical reasons because its relativistic presuppositions make it impossible to distinguish between different opinions, and, in fact, deny the spiritual value of freedom.

In this very oscillation of the democratic "Weltanschauung" lies the threat to democracy. When the democratic system is divested of its spiritual function, it loses its political effectiveness, it becomes a formal mechanism and the most contradictory of political systems. Its empiricism takes on, in its relativistic bias, a clearly dogmatic nature; there is no worse dogmatism than that which denies the very existence of truth. When a democratic system rejects as a vestige of metaphysics the idea that political opinion is but a means towards spiritual ends, it destroys at the same time the objective limits to intolerance. The contingency of opinion may after all be used as well to justify submission to any ideology.

If we examine totalitarian "dogmatism" more closely, we see that the "truth" which determines the "closing," and therefore the intolerance of the totalitarian system, is nothing but "opinion" which has been raised to the status of absolute truth. Blondel, with his usual acumen, noted this fact: there is no totalitarian ideology which does not pretend to impose as absolute some partial point of view. Whether the instances be "racist," "classist," or "nationalist," these ideologies always involve the substitution of the "partial" for the "entire," or "universal,"—the myth for the truth. Totalitarian "truth" and the intolerance which derives from it is always a means of dividing men. Totalitarian "dogmatism" develops out of the relativistic tendency of the democratic system because man has need of values to justify his endeavor. If he loses sight of them, he turns with his sense of the absolute toward "idols." The denial of the existence of "truth" involves not freedom, but its opposite. When the democratic system swings too far towards relativism, there comes the hour of that most modern form of idolatry, totalitarianism.

II

This can be more readily observed in the institutional aspect of political organization. Here, too, the idea that the totalitarian system has its roots in the democratic system might seem at first glance paradoxical. The principles of the single-party system and that of the plurality of parties would appear to be irreconcilable. The single-party system implies subordination of the state to the ideology of the party; the system of a plurality of parties involves profound distinctions between the organs and functions of the parties and those of the state and the subordination of individual political ideologies to the common goals of the state. Nevertheless, in almost all the democracies of western Europe, a phenomenon called "partocracy" has appeared; it represents on the institutional plane the transition from the system of the plurality of parties to that of the single party—from the subordination of parties to the state to the subordination of the state to a dominant party. This means, in general terms, that the parties have assumed a monopoly of political power, that the "center of sovereignty" has been transferred from the will of the people to the will of the "elites" in control of the parties. In more specific terms, it means that public opinion has not succeeded in expressing itself politically—and in influencing the actions of the state—except by rigidly organizing itself under the aegis of some party, or by adapting itself in some measure to the rigid schemes of some preconstituted ideology. Partocracy reverses the classical relationship between public opinion and party; it is no longer public opinion which in its fluctuations determines the organization of parties; it is the parties, which have become "closed," which organize opinion into the obligatory schemes of their own ideologies.

Partocracy, then, is one of the stages, on the institutional plane, of the transition from democratic relativism to totalitarian dogmatism. It seems clear that partocracy has its roots in the relativistic tendency of the democratic system. The technical exigencies which today condition political action, and the role now played in politics by propaganda, no doubt facilitate its rise. However, technology and propaganda can succeed in reversing the relation between public opinion and parties only when political ideologies have become ends in themselves—not merely means to higher ends. The very act of commitment to a "closed" party involves, objectively if not subjectively, an acceptance of the ideology of that party as unconditionally true and the denial of any limitations except those of political expediency. It presupposes that "raising of opinion to the status of absolute truth" which we saw to be the logical development of democratic relativism.

To be sure, as long as none of the parties in the arena prevails, the transformation of politics brought about by partocracy does not touch the formal structure of the state. But this state of affairs is deceptive and at best only temporary. Each party already constitutes, at least po-

tentially, a kind of "state within the state" and acts through agencies
entirely analogous to those of the state. Individuals not connected with
any party do not possess an outlet for the expression of their opinions,
and democratic control loses strength proportionately. More important,
effective power has already passed into the hands of the agencies of
the parties which control the government. In such a situation the
plurality of parties and the formal distinction between their agencies
and those of the state have purely negative significance; they are the
expression of a balance of forces which, in spite of its instability, none
of the parties dares disturb until it is sure of victory. This does not
mean, however, that the parties do not aim at a step which, given their
definitive ideological and organizational "closing," would only be logical:
the conquest of the state and the suppression of the other parties. As
soon as conditions favorable to this decisive step occur, the favored
party does not hesitate to profit by them: it happened yesterday, and
it could happen tomorrow.

III

On the sociological plane, the derivation of totalitarianism from the
relativistic tendency of the democratic system can be observed in an
even more advanced stage which, moreover, permits us to discern the
by now obvious distinction between the "totalitarianism of the right"
(fascism) and the "totalitarianism of the left" (communism). It is on
the sociological plane that democracy shows all of its truly revolutionary
power: it is the one system in which the more retarded social classes
can express themselves in the modern state. From this point of view,
the historical importance of the democratic system goes far beyond the
framework of its bourgeois beginnings. But democracy, for this very
reason, cuts so deeply into the social structure as to endanger its own
existence. And here the opposition between the personalistic and relativistic tendencies of democracy becomes very important.

In its personalistic tendency, democracy presupposes that a process
of material and cultural elevation accompany the extension of political
power to the masses so as to provide a moral justification for so violent
a change. In its relativistic tendency, on the other hand, it is more
concerned with the form of political organization than its substance. By
emphasizing the extension of political power at the expense of its social
and cultural base, it puts a premium on the formulation of political
programs as abstract ideologies, and the more abstract the greater the
social inequalities—as Marx quite accurately remarked. Democratic relativism fosters within its own system, then, its greatest contradiction: it
offers the means of political expression to masses which because of
their social position cannot enter into the democratic process except by
setting forth their demands in terms of ideologies; in other words by
identifying political "truth" with a dogma which although humanly

understandable is clearly of totalitarian character. The totalitarian degeneration of democratic relativism begins with the formation of marxist parties—the earliest examples of "closed" parties. But before such a move on the part of the lower classes, the dominating classes also tend to unite and to unify their own "open" ideologies in a single "closed" ideology which represents their line of defense on the social plane. The marxists have accurately described the social content and the primarily bourgeois frame of action of the totalitarianism of the right.

Democratic relativism, then, inevitably shifts the political contest to the social plane, and brings about the "closing" of political ideologies and organizations along just those lines which more than any others make "tolerance" difficult—the class lines. In this manner, democracy ends by being attacked from two sides. There is no totalitarianism which has no social program, be it totalitarianism of the "right" or of the "left," and it is always the logical outcome of the actions, on the social plane, of democratic relativism. Totalitarianism is the typical form through which the social struggle finds expression in democratic societies of the relativistic type.

It is time to come to a conclusion. The genesis of totalitarianism can be seen as the logical development of democracy based on relativistic premises. The question raised at the beginning of this discussion must be answered in the affirmative. I do not need to add that this does not mean, as the advocates of totalitarianism claim, that the democratic system is now obsolete. It means rather that we must honestly recognize that the problem of totalitarianism is in reality only one among the problems of democracy and that only by giving concrete expression to developing its personalistic premises can democracy hope to overcome the danger of totalitarianism.

Section III

DEMOCRACY

FOUNDATIONS OF DEMOCRACY [1]

Hans Kelsen

I. DEMOCRACY AND PHILOSOPHY

Democracy as "Government by the People": A Political Procedure
The political idea of the nineteenth century, born in the American and
French revolutions of the eighteenth century, was democracy. To be
sure, there were also in Western civilization remarkable forces working
for the maintenance of the autocracy principle. But its representatives
were stigmatized as reactionaries. The future belonged to a government
by the people. This was the hope of everybody who believed in progress, who stood up for higher standards of social life. It was, above all,
the young, rising bourgeoisie which fought for this idea.

In the twentieth century, however, the intellectual and political
situation has changed. The immediate effect of the First World War—
it is true—seemed to be a victory of the democratic principle. The
newly erected states adopted democratic constitutions. The German
Reich, the most powerful bastion of monarchy, became a republic. But
the ink on the peace document of Versailles was not yet dry when in
Italy the Fascist government came into power and in Germany the
National Socialist party began its victorious drive. Together with them a
new political doctrine was advocated, passionately opposed to democracy and proclaiming a new way of political salvation: dictatorship.
There should be no doubt about the great attraction which the new
idol exerted over the bourgeois intelligentsia, not only in Italy and
Germany, but everywhere in the Western world. And although fascism
and national socialism have been destroyed as political realities in the
Second World War, their ideologies have not disappeared and still
directly, or indirectly, counteract the democratic creed.

Reprinted from *Ethics,* vol. LXVI, no. 1, Part II (October, 1955), 1-67. By
permission of the author and the publisher.

[64]

A more dangerous adversary than fascism and national socialism is Soviet communism, which is fighting the democratic idea under the disguise of a democratic terminology. It seems that the symbol of democracy has assumed such a generally recognized value that the substance of democracy cannot be abandoned without maintaining the symbol. Well-known is the cynical statement: If fascism should come to the United States it would be called democracy.[2] Hence the symbol must change its meaning so radically that it can be used to designate the very contrary: In Soviet political theory the dictatorship of the Communist party, pretending to be the dictatorship of the proletariat, is presented as democracy. It is of the greatest importance to disclose the conceptual device through which this distortion of the symbol could be achieved.

The original meaning of the term "democracy," coined in the political theory of ancient Greece, was: government by the people (*demos* = people, *kratein* = govern). The essence of the political phenomenon designated by the term was the participation of the governed in the government, the principle of freedom in the sense of political self-determination; and this was the meaning with which the term has been taken over by the political theory of Western civilization. It stands to reason that in antiquity as well as in our time a government by the people is desired because such a government is supposed to be a government for the people. A government "for the people" means a government acting in the interest of the people. But the question as to what is the interest of the people may be answered in different ways, and what the people themselves believe to be their interest is not necessarily the only possible answer. It may even be doubted whether there is such a thing as an opinion of the people about their own interest and a will of the people directed at its realization. Hence a government may consider itself to be a government for the people—and as a matter of fact every government does so—although it may not be a government by the people at all. Already in ancient Greece adversaries of democracy, like Plato and Aristotle, pointed out that a government by the people as a government, by men inexperienced in governmental practice and without the necessary knowledge of the facts and problems of political life may be not at all in the interest of the people and thus may prove to be a government against the people. Again and again, political writers tried to demonstrate that autocracy, be it hereditary monarchy or leader-dictatorship, is a better government for the people than a government by the people, i.e., democracy. That there is something true in this argument and that "government for the people" is not identical with "government by the people" cannot be denied. Since not only democracy but also its very contrary, autocracy, may be a government for the people, this quality cannot be an element of the definition of democracy. This is also the reason why the doctrine that democracy presupposes the belief that there exists an objectively ascertainable common good and that the people are able to know it and therefore to make it the content of their will is erroneous. If it were correct, democracy would not be possible. For it is easy to show that there is no such thing as an objectively ascertainable common good, that the question as to what is the common good can be answered only by subjective value judgments which may differ essentially from each other; and that even if it existed, the average man, and hence the people, would hardly be able to know it. It cannot be denied that the people as a mass of individuals of different economic and cultural standards have no uniform will, that only the individual human being has a real will, that the so-called "will of the people" is a figure of speech and not a reality. But the form of government which is defined as "government by the people" does not presuppose a will of the people directed at the realization of that which, according to the opinion of the people, is the common good. The term designates a government in which the people directly or indirectly participate, that is to say, a government exercised by majority decisions of a popular assembly or of a body or bodies of individuals or even by a single individual elected by the people. The individuals elected by the people are called its representatives. This representation of the people means the relationship, constituted by election, between the electorate and the elected. By "people" all the adult individuals are to be understood who are subject to the government exercised directly by the assembly of these individuals or indirectly by the elected representatives. Democratic elections are those which are based on universal, equal, free, and secret suffrage. According to the extent to which these requirements, especially the universality of suffrage, are fulfilled, the democratic principle may be realized in different degrees. It has considerably increased during the twentieth century by the fact that the right of voting, restricted during the nineteenth century to taxpaying people and to the male sex, has been extended to nontaxpaying wage earners and to women. Democracy became a mass democracy. Whether the government of an unrestricted democracy realizes to a greater extent than the government of a restricted democracy the problematic opinion or the no less problematic will of people or the mysterious common good according to the opinion and the will of the people is another question. However that question may be answered, no answer whatsoever justifies rejecting the concept of democracy as government by the people and replacing it by another concept, especially by the concept of a government for the people.

Hence, participation in the government, and that means in the creation and application of the general and individual norms of the social order constituting the community, must be considered as the essential characteristic of democracy. Whether this participation is direct or indirect, that is to say, whether there is a direct or a representative democracy, it is in both cases a *procedure*, a specific method of creating and applying the social order constituting the community, which is the criterion of that political system which is properly called democracy. It is not a specific content of the social order insofar as the procedure in question is not itself a content of, that is to say, regulated by, this order. The method of creating the order is always regulated by the order itself if the order is a legal order. For it is characteristic of the law that it regulates its own creation and application.[3] To be sure, the modern concept of democracy prevailing in Western civilization is not quite identical with the original, the antique, concept, insofar as the latter has been modified by political liberalism, the tendency of which is to restrict the power of government in the interest of the freedom of the individual. Under this influence guaranties for certain intellectual freedoms, especially freedom of conscience, have been included in the concept of democracy, so that a social order which does not contain such a guaranty would not be considered democratic, even if the procedure for its creation and application guarantees the participation of the governed in the government. However, the liberal or modern democracy is only a special type of democracy. It is of importance to be aware that the principle of democracy and that of liberalism are not identical, that there exists even a certain antagonism between them. For according to the principle of democracy the power of the people is unrestricted, or as the French Declaration of the Rights of Men and Citizens formulates it: "The principle of all sovereignty resides essentially in the nation." This is the idea of the sovereignty of the people. Liberalism, however, means restriction of governmental power, whatever form the government may assume. It means also restriction of democratic power. Hence democracy is essentially a government *by* the people. The procedural element remains in the foreground, the liberal element—as a particular content of the social order —being of secondary importance. Even the liberal democracy is in the first place a specific procedure.

It has been said that democracy as a political method, that is to say, as a certain type of institutional arrangement for arriving at political, legislative, and administrative decisions, is "incapable of being an end in itself irrespective of what decisions it will produce under given historical conditions";[4] and that as a mere method it cannot "necessarily, always and everywhere, serve certain interests or ideals for which we do mean to fight and die unconditionally"; that "the democratic method does not necessarily guarantee a greater amount of individual freedom than another political method would permit in similar circumstances";[5] and, in particular, that democracy cannot "always safeguard freedom of conscience better than autocracy."[6] This inference from the procedural character of democracy is not quite correct. If we define democracy as a political method by which the social order is created and applied by those subject to the order, so that political freedom, in the sense of self-determination, is secured, then democracy necessarily, always and everywhere, serves this ideal of political freedom. And if we include in our definition the idea that the social order, created in the way just indicated, in order to be democratic, must guarantee certain intellectual freedoms, such as freedom of conscience, freedom of press, etc., then democracy necessarily, always and everywhere, serves also this ideal of intellectual freedom. If in a concrete case the social order is not created in a way corresponding to the definition, or does not contain the guaranties of freedom, it is not democracy which does not serve the ideals. The ideals are not served because democracy has been abandoned. This critique confuses the idea of democracy with a political reality which wrongly interprets itself as democracy, although it does not correspond to the idea.

It further confuses the question as to whether democracy can necessarily serve a certain ideal with the question as to whether democracy can be itself an absolute ideal. It seems that the author infers from the negative answer he gives to the first question a negative answer to the second one. But although the answer to the first question has certainly to be in the affirmative, the answer to the second question may be in the negative. The ideal of freedom—as any social ideal—is from the point of view of political science only a relative ideal. But it may be from the point of view of emotional evaluation the highest, the supreme, ideal of an individual, a value which the individual prefers to any other value conflicting with the former. I may fight and die unconditionally for the freedom democracy is able to realize, although I may admit that from the point of view of rational science my ideal is only a relative one. Schumpeter quite correctly says: "To realize the relative validity of one's convictions and yet stand for them unflinchingly is what distinguishes a civilized man from a barbarian." [7]

As a method or procedure, democracy is a "form" of government. For the procedure by which a social order is created and applied is considered to be formal, in contradistinction to the content of the order as a material or substantial element. If, however, democracy is primarily a form, a form of a state or a form of government, it must be kept in mind that the antagonism of form and substance or form and content is only a relative one, that one and the same thing may appear from one point of view as form and from another as substance or content. There is, in particular, no objective principle that constitutes a difference between the value of the one and that of the other. In some respects the form, in others the content or substance, may be of greater importance. The argument of "formalism," frequently used in order to disparage a certain train of thought and especially a political scheme, is mostly a device for the purpose of hiding an antagonistic interest which is the true reason of the opposition. There is therefore no better means to obstruct the movement for democracy, to pave the way for autocracy, to dissuade the people from their desire for participation in government, than to depreciate the definition of democracy as a procedure by the argument that it is "formalistic," to make the people believe that their desire is fulfilled if the government acts in their interest, that they have achieved the longed for democracy if they have a government for the people. The political doctrine which furnishes the appropriate ideology for such a tendency emphasizes the point that the essence of democracy is a government in the interest of the mass of the people, that the participation of the people in the government is of secondary importance. If a government is for the people, that is to say, if it acts in the interest of the people, it realizes the will of the people, and hence it is also a government by the people. For what everybody "wills" is his interest; and if a government realizes the interest of the people, it is the will of the people and hence the people who govern, even if the govenment is not elected by the people on the basis of a universal, equal, free, and secret suffrage or is not elected at all or elected on the basis of an electoral system which does not allow everybody to express freely his political will. The objection that in such a case the interest which the government tries to realize may not be what the people themselves consider to be their interest is rejected by the argument that the people may be in error about their "true" interest, and if the government realizes the true interest of the people, it represents also the true will of the people and thus is to be considered as a "true" democracy—in contradistinction to a merely formal or sham democracy. In such a "true" democracy the people may be "represented" by an elite, an *avant garde,* or even by a charismatic leader. All that is necessary to do is to shift in the definition of democracy the accent from "government by the people" to "government for the people."

The Soviet Doctrine of Democracy This shift is a characteristic feature of the Soviet doctrine according to which the dictatorship of the Communist party is democracy.[8] The tendency to put in the foreground of the political ideology the interest of the masses appears already in the *Communist Manifesto,* where the establishment of the dictatorship of the proletariat, the immediate goal of the socialist movement, is presented as the victory of democracy. "The first step in the revolution by the working class" is "to win the battle of democracy." The "proletarian movement" is characterized as "the self-conscious, independent movement of the immense majority, in the interest of the immense majority." Following this line of thought, Lenin declares that the dictatorship of the proletariat, i.e., the "organization of the vanguard of the oppressed," is "an immense expansion of democracy, for it becomes democracy for the poor, *democracy for the people,* and not [as the bourgeois democracy] democracy for the rich."[9] The essential characteristic of this democracy is that it "leads to the extension of the actual enjoyment of democracy to those who are oppressed by capitalism, to the toiling classes, to a degree hitherto unprecedented in world history."[10] What is decisive is not the formalistic criterion of representative institutions but the material realization of the interests of the masses. Hence Lenin declared that "socialist democracy is not contradictory to individual management and dictatorship in any way, that the will of a class may sometimes be carried out by a dictator, who at times may do more alone and who is frequently more necessary."[11] "Lenin taught us," wrote *Pravda,* "that the dictatorship of the proletariat in a class society represents the interest of the majority and is *therefore* a form of proletarian democracy." [12]

But the democracy of the dictatorship of the proletariat is not the last step in the development of socialist democracy. "Democracy means equality," but bourgeois democracy means only "formal" equality, whereas the socialist democracy is "going beyond formal equality to real equality, i.e., to applying the rule: from each according to his ability, to each according to his needs." [13] This is the Marxian formula for justice in the Communist stateless society of the future. In this democracy the people have no share in the government, for there is no government at all.

This perversion of the concept of democracy from a government by the people, and that can mean in a modern state only by representatives elected by the people, to a political regime in the interest of the people is not only theoretically inadmissible because of a misuse of terminology, but it is also politically most problematical. For it substitutes as the criterion of the form of government defined as democracy a highly subjective value judgment—the interest of the people—for the objectively ascertainable fact of representation by elected organs. Every government may—and, as pointed out, actually every government does—assert that it is acting in the interest of the people. Since there is no objective criterion for what is called the interest of the people, the phrase "government for the people" is an empty formula apt to be used for an ideological justification of any government whatsoever.[14] It is highly significant that as long as the ideologists of the National Socialist party did not dare turn openly against democracy, they used exactly the same device as the ideologists of the Communist party. They disparaged the democratic political system of Germany as plutocracy, as a merely "formal" democracy which in reality guaranteed a minority of the rich to govern over the majority of the poor, and asserted that the Nazi party as an elite of the German people intended to realize the true will of this people: the greatness and glory of the German race.

A New Doctrine of Representation The perversion of the concept of democracy which has just been characterized is not restricted to the Soviet or the National Socialist political doctrine. A quite similar pattern of thought has recently been presented as the theory of representation advocated by a "new science of politics." [15] The author distinguishes between a merely "elemental" and an "existential" type of representation, just as the Soviet theorists distinguish between a merely "formal" and a "real" democracy. By elemental type of representation is understood that representation in which "the members of the legislative assembly hold their membership by virtue of popular election." The author further characterizes it by referring to "the American election of a chief executive by the people," to "the English system of a committee of the parliamentary majority as the ministry," to "the Swiss system of having the executive elected by the two houses in common session," and even to a monarchical government "as long as the monarch can act only with the countersignature of a responsible minister"; by emphasizing that the representative must be elected "by all persons of age who are resident in a territorial district," that the elections shall be "reasonably frequent," and that political parties may be "the organizers and mediators of the election procedure." [16] The "elemental" type of representation is more or less identical with that called in Soviet political theory the merely "formal" democracy of the bourgeois states. This elemental type of representation, or—as it is also called—representation in a merely "constitutional sense," [17] is according to the new science of politics theoretically a concept of little "cognitive value." [18] It is "elemental" because it refers only to the "external existence of society," [19] "to simple data of the external world." [20] But society as an aggregate of interhuman relations can exist only in the external world, and consequently representation as a social phenomenon can only refer to data of the external world. As a matter of fact, the "existential" representation, which the new science of politics tries to substitute for the merely elemental representation, refers, as we shall see, to exactly the same external existence of society as the latter. . . .

Whether a government, which always represents the state, represents also the people of the state, that is to say, whether it is a democratic government, depends only and exclusively on the answer to the question whether or not it is established in a democratic way, that is to say, elected on the basis of universal and free suffrage. Hence it is impossible to differentiate the democratic type of representation from any other type of representation by the criterion of effectiveness.

This is just what the new science of politics endeavors to do when it deprecates the democratic type of representation as "elemental" because it does not—as does the existential type—imply the elment of effectiveness. Only by obliterating the difference between representation of the state and representation of the people can the new science of politics maintain that there exists a difference of cognitive value between the democratic representation as merely an "elemental" representation and the representation of the state as an "existential" representation. By obliterating this difference, by avoiding the term "representation of the state," by using the ambiguous formula "representation of society," the new science of politics creates the impression that only that concept of representation which includes the element of effectiveness is the correct one, and that this type of representation always implies, in some way, representation of the people. "Obviously," says the author, "the representative ruler of an articulated society cannot represent it as a whole without standing in some sort of relationship to the other members of the society." [21] By "the other members of the society" only the people can be understood:

Under pressure of the democratic symbolism, the resistance to distinguishing between the two relations terminologically has become so strong that it has also affected political theory. . . . The government represents the people, and

the symbol "people" has absorbed the two meanings which, in medieval
language, for instance, could be distinguished without emotional resistance
as the "realm" and the "subjects." [22]

The "two relations" which under the pressure of democratic symbolism are not distinguished are: the relationship of the ruler to the society
as a whole, and the relationship of the ruler to "the other members of
the society." The statement that the government in a democracy represents the people as subject to the government means that the government by representing the people as the society not including the
members of the government, the "other members of the society," represents the society as a whole because the members of the government
belong to the people as subject to the government. They at the same
time govern and are subject to the government. As members of the
government they are not—as is the ruler in an autocracy—exempt from
the government. It is just for this reason that only in a democracy the
government represents the society as a whole, because it represents the
society including the members of the government. But it is very likely
that the new science of politics understands by "society as a whole" the
state. For this term supposedly has the same meaning as the medieval
term "realm," in contradistinction to the term "subjects." This terminology
corresponds to the modern distinction between "state" and "people." The
statement that a democratic government represents the people does,
indeed, mean that the government by representing the people represents
the state. Again we ask: Why does the new science of politics refrain
from using the modern term "state," which is much less ambiguous than
the medieval term "realm," which literally means "kingdom"? Why does
it speak of "society as a whole," when it really means state? Evidently because representation of "the society as a whole" implies necessarily
representation of the "other members of the society," because the
existential representative of the state has to be considered as representing
also the people. "The representative ruler of an articulated society" can
only be a ruler who effectively represents the society; and if he effectively
represents the society, he represents it "as a whole," especially if
"society as a whole" means the "state." It can only be the "society as a
whole" which a ruler in the existential sense, an existential ruler,
represents; and by the "representative of an articulated society" referred
to in the above-quoted statement, obviously an "existential" ruler is
meant. But every government—whether democratic or autocratic—is
a ruler in the existential sense, an "existential" ruler. And now the new
science of politics declares that the representative ruler of an articulated
society cannot represent it as a whole—and that probably means, cannot
represent the state—without standing in some sort of relationship to the
other members of the society, that is to say, to the people. That he stands
in a relationship to the people can only mean that he represents the
people, for representation of the people is one of the two relations

terminologically not distinguished under the pressure of democratic symbolism. The ruler must stand "in some sort" of relationship to the other members of the society, that is, to the people, but not necessarily in that sort of relationship which is constituted by elections on the basis of universal, equal, free, and secret suffrage. For this sort of relationship is only "elemental," not "existential."

The Soviet government, as the new science of politics asserts, represents the Soviet society "as a political society" in the most effective way, because "the legislative and administrative acts of the Soviet government are domestically effective in the sense that the governmental commands find obedience with the people," and "the Soviet government can effectively operate an enormous military machine fed by the human and material resources of the Soviet society"; [23] and that can only mean that the Soviet government represents the Soviet society "as a whole," especially if "society as a whole" means the state. Hence the Soviet government is the ideal type of an existential ruler, a "representative ruler of an articulated society" represented as a whole by the ruler. If a representative ruler of an articulated society cannot represent it as a whole without standing in some relation to the other members of the society, that is to say, without representing in some way the people, then the Soviet government, which is certainly no democratic government, represents the Soviet people. This, of course, is not expressly maintained by the new science of politics. But it is clearly implied in its doctrine of representation with its tendency to belittle the importance of the democratic type of representation as merely elemental, to put in the foreground the existential type of representation in which the element of effectiveness is emphasized.

As a result of this doctrine of representation the new science of politics conveys the warning: "If a government is nothing but representative in the constitutional sense, a representative ruler in the existential sense will sooner or later make an end of it; and quite possibly the new existential ruler will not be too representative in the constitutional sense." [24] The representative ruler in the "existential sense," we remember, cannot represent the society as a whole "without standing in some sort of relationship to the other members of the society," that is to say, to the people. He too represents, somehow, the people, although he may not be too "representative" in the democratic sense, but a ruler who represents the people in a fascistic sense—"Fuehrer" or a "Duce" who effectively organizes the mass of the people for action and may claim to realize democracy.

Our analysis of the theory of representation advocated by the new science of politics shows that it is of the utmost importance to maintain as strictly as possible just that concept of representation which this science disparages as merely "elemental," or what amounts to the same, the concept of democracy as the concept of a government representing the people in a merely "constitutional" sense, and to reject its replacement by a concept of "existential" representation, which only obscures the fundamental antagonism between democracy and autocracy and thus obstructs objective understanding of the essence of democracy.

To achieve this understanding it does not suffice to describe the typical structures of the two antagonistic systems of organization. For if we recognize that the entire history of human society is a never-ending struggle between the will to power of a vigorous personality who tries to subject the multitude and to suppress their resistance against domination by the will of another, that is, their desire for self-determination, and if we admit that in the history of human thought the controversy about the value of autocracy and democracy is just as undecided as the conflict of the two political regimes in reality, that there too the fight never ends but is lost for the one and won for the other over and over again, we may assume that there is much more at stake than a problem of social technique, the choice between two different types of organization, and look for the roots of the antagonism in opposite views of the world: we may try to find out the connection which exists between politics and philosophy.

In the following sections I intend to show that there exists, indeed, not only an external parallelism but an inner relationship between the antagonism of autocracy and democracy, on the one hand, and philosophical absolutism and relativism, on the other, that autocracy as political absolutism is co-ordinated with philosophical absolutism and democracy as political relativism with philosophical relativism.[25]

Philosophical Absolutism and Relativism Since the time Aristotle presented his *Politics* as the second part of a treatise of which the first one was his *Ethics*, it is a truism that political theory and that part of philosophy which is called "ethics" have been in close connection. But there exists also a certain affinity, less generally recognized, between theory of politics and other parts of philosophy, such as epistemology, that is, the theory of cognition, and the theory of values. The main problem of political theory is the relationship between the subject and the object of domination; the main problem of epistemology is the relationship between the subject and the object of cognition. The process of domination is not so different from that of cognition by which the subject tries to be master of his object by bringing some order into the chaos of sensual perceptions; and it is not too far from the process of evaluation by which the subject declares an object as good or evil and thus sits in judgment upon the object. It is just within epistemology and theory of values that the antagonism between philosophical absolutism and philosophical relativism has its seat, which—as I shall try to show—is analogous to the antagonism between autocracy and democracy as they represent political absolutism, on the one hand, and political relativism, on the other, respectively.

In order to avoid misunderstandings with respect to the meaning of this analogy some preliminary remarks are necessary. Since, as pointed out, the center of politics and the theories of cognition and value is the relationship of subject and object, the character of the politicizing and philosophizing subject, his original disposition must be of decisive influence on the formation of the views about his relation to the object of domination as well as of cognition and evaluation. The common root of political creed and philosophical conviction remains always the mentality of the politician and philosopher, the nature of his ego that is to say, the way in which this ego experiences itself in its relation to the other who claims to be an ego himself and to the thing which makes no such claim. Only if we recognize that the formation of the political and philosophical systems is determined, in the last analysis, by peculiarities of the human mind may we explain why the antagonism between these systems is so insurmountable, why mutual understanding is so difficult, if not impossible, why there are such exasperated passions involved in the conflict, even if it takes place only in the intellectual sphere as a difference of opinion, and yet is not a clash in the struggle for power. A typology of political and philosophical doctrines must finally result in a characterology, or at least the former must try to combine its results with that of the latter. Because it is the same human being who tries to interpret his relations to his fellow-men and the order of these relations as well as his relation to the world at large, we may assume that a definite political creed is co-ordinated with a definite view of the world. But just because it is within the soul of the empirical human being and not within a sphere of pure reason that politics and philosophy originate, we must not expect that a definite political view will always and everywhere be combined with the philosophical system which logically corresponds to it. In the history of political and philosophical theories their connection can be demonstrated by an analysis of the works of the most representative thinkers. But it would be a great mistake to ignore the very effective forces of the human mind which may abolish this connection and prevent political attitudes to associate with the corresponding philosophical views, and vice versa. The human mind is not completely dominated by reason, and hence not always logical. The emotional forces may divert man's thinking from its original direction. It is necessary to take into consideration the external circumstances by which—though philosophical speculation may not be restricted—the freedom of political opinion is abolished. It is further to be noticed that political judgments, and especially the decision in favor of democracy or autocracy, are frequently based neither on a thorough investigation of facts nor on a conscientious self-examination but are the outcome of a momentary situation or a transient mood. Also, one must not underestimate the fact that every political regime is inevitably calling for an opposition, and thus those who, for some reason or another, are dissatisfied in a democracy will probably be for autocracy, and those who, for some reason or another, are disappointed in an autocracy will turn to democracy. Sometimes it is the same malcontents—and perhaps for good reason malcontent—who are always against the actually established and for the not yet or no longer established regime. Many who under a democratic government attribute all possible evils to democracy would be convinced democrats under a Fascist government and would probably be in favor of fascism if a democratic government were long enough in power to provoke considerable opposition. But these are only the small fry, who do not count very much for the solution of our problem. As far as the prominent people, especially the great thinkers, are concerned, the connection between their political and philosophical views is sometimes not demonstrable because the philosopher has not developed a political theory and the politician or political theorist has not yet reached the stage of consciously posing the philosophical problem. Only with these reservations can the relationship between politics and philosophy be maintained.

Philosophical absolutism is the metaphysical view that there is an absolute reality, i.e., a reality that exists independently of human cognition. Hence its existence is beyond space and time, to which human cognition is restricted. Philosophical relativism, on the other hand, advocates the empirical doctrine that reality exists only within human cognition, and that, as the object of cognition, reality is relative to the knowing subject. The absolute, the thing in itself, is beyond human experience; it is inaccessible to human knowledge and therefore unknowable.

To the assumption of absolute existence corresponds the possibility of absolute truth and absolute values, denied by philosophical relativism, which recognizes only relative truth and relative values. Only if the judgments about reality refer ultimately to an absolute existence may they aim at absolute truth, that is to say, claim to be true not only in relation to the human beings as the judging subjects, i.e., from the point of view of human reason, but also from the point of view of a superhuman, a divine, the absolute reason. If there is an absolute reality, it must coincide with absolute value. The absolute necessarily implies perfection. Absolute existence is identical with absolute authority as the source of absolute values. The personification of the absolute, its presentation as the omnipotent and absolutely just creator of the universe, whose will is the law of nature as well as of man, is the inevitable consequence of philosophical absolutism. Its metaphysics shows an irresistible tendency toward monotheistic religion. It is essentially connected with the view that value is immanent in reality as a creation or emanation of the absolute good. This metaphysics has the tendency to identify truth, that is, conformity with reality, with justice, meaning conformity with a value. Hence a judgment about what is just or unjust can be as absolute as a judgment about what is true or false. Value judgments can claim to be valid for everybody, always and everywhere, and not only in relation to the judging subject, if they refer to values inherent in an absolute reality or, what amounts to the same, are established by an absolute authority. Philosophical relativism, on the other hand, as antimetaphysical empiricism (or positivism), insists upon a clear separation of reality and value and distinguishes between propositions about reality and genuine value judgments, which, in the last analysis, are not based on a rational cognition of reality but on the emotional factors of human consciousness, on man's wishes and fears. Since they do not refer to values immanent in an absolute reality, they cannot establish absolute, but only relative, values. A relativistic philosophy is decidedly empiristic and rationalistic and consequently has an outspoken inclination to skepticism.

The hypothesis of philosophical absolutism that there is an absolute existence independent of human knowledge leads to the assumption that the function of knowledge is merely to reflect, like a mirror, the objects existing in themselves; whereas relativistic epistemology, in its most consistent presentation by Kant, interprets the process of cognition as the creation of its object. This view implies that the human subject of knowledge is—epistemologically—the creator of his world, a world which is constituted in and by his knowledge. This, of course, does not mean that the process of cognition has an arbitrary character. The constitution of the object of cognition by the process of cognition does not mean that the subject creates the object as God creates the world. There is a correlation between the subject and the object of cognition. There are normative laws determining this process. In complying with these norms, rational cognition of reality—in contradistinction to the expression of subjective emotions, the basis of value judgments—is objective. But these norms originate in the human mind, the subject of cognition being the autonomous lawgiver. Hence, freedom of the knowing subject—not the metaphysical freedom of will but freedom of cognition in the sense of self-determination—is a fundamental prerequisite of the relativistic theory of knowledge. Philosophical absolutism, on the other hand, if consistent, must conceive of the subject of knowledge as completely determined by heteronomous laws immanent in objective reality and as subject to the absolute, especially if the absolute is imagined as a personal being and superhuman authority.

The specific character of the relativistic theory of knowledge involves two perils. The one is a paradoxical solipsism; that is, the assumption that the ego as the subject of knowledge is the only existent reality, the impossibility of recognizing the simultaneous existence of other egos, the egotistic negation of the *tu*. Such assumption would involve a relativistic epistemology in a self-contradiction. For if the ego is the only existent reality, it must be an absolute reality. Uncompromised solipsism, too, is philosophical absolutism. The other danger is a no less paradoxical pluralism. Since the world exists only in the knowledge of the subject according to this view, the ego is, so to speak, the center of his own world. If, however, the existence of many egos must be admitted, the consequence seems to be inevitable that there are as many worlds as there are knowing subjects. Philosophical relativism deliberately avoids solipsism as well as pluralism. Taking into consideration—as true relativism—the mutual relations among the various subjects of knowledge, this theory compensates its inability to secure the objective existence of the one and same world for all subjects by the assumption that the individuals, as subjects of knowledge, are equal. This assumption implies also that the various processes of rational cognition in the minds of the subjects are—in contradistinction to their emotional reactions—equal; and thus the further assumption becomes possible that the objects of knowledge, as the results of these individual processes, are in conformity with one another, an assumption confirmed by the external behavior of the individuals. To be sure, there is an undeniable conflict between absolute freedom and equality. But the subject of cognition is not absolutely, he is only relatively, free, free under the laws of rational cognition; and this freedom is not incompatible with the equality of all the subjects of cognition. The restriction of freedom by a law under which all subjects are equal is essential to philosophical relativism. From the point of view of philosophical absolutism, on the other hand, it is not the equality of the subjects which is essential but, on the contrary, their fundamental inequality in relation to the absolute and supreme being.

·   ·   ·

The Majority Vote Principle If the principle of majority for the development of the social order is accepted, the idea of natural freedom can no longer be completely realized; only an approximation to this idea is possible. That democracy is still considered as self-determination, that its freedom still means that everybody is subject only to his own will, although the will of the majority is binding, is a further step in the metamorphosis of the idea of freedom.

Even the individual who votes with the majority is not subject only to his own will. He becomes immediately aware of this fact when he changes the will expressed in his vote. The fact that such change of his individual will is legally irrelevant shows clearly that he is subject to a foreign will or, formulated without the use of a metaphor, to the objective validity of the social order.[26] He is again free in the sense of being subject exclusively to his own will only if the change of his will is confirmed by a majority. This concordance of the will of the individual with the social order that may be changed by the will of the majority is all the more difficult, this guaranty of individual freedom all the more reduced, the more qualified the majority is that is required for a change of the established order, of the so-called will of the state. If unanimity is required, this guaranty is practically abolished. A strange ambivalence of the political mechanism becomes here manifest. The same principle which in the first establishment of the social order protects individual freedom now destroys it if it is no longer possible to withdraw from this order. Original creation of social order does not occur in the reality of our social experience. The individual is always born into an already established social order and normally also into a pre-existent state in the creation of which he did not participate. Only the change, the development, of this order is practically in question. In this respect the principle of a simple, not a qualified, majority constitutes the relatively greatest approximation to the idea of freedom. According to this principle, among the subjects of the social order the number of those who approve the order will always be larger than the number of those who —entirely or in part—disapprove but remain bound by the order. At the moment when the number of those who disapprove the order, or one of its norms, becomes greater than the number of those who approve, a change is possible by which a situation is re-established in which the order is in concordance with a number of subjects which is greater than the number of subjects with whom it is in discordance. The idea underlying the principle of majority is that the social order shall be in concordance with as many subjects as possible and in discordance with as few as possible.

Political freedom means agreement between the individual will and the collective will expressed in the social order. Consequently it is the principle of simple majority which secures the highest degree of political freedom that is possible within society. If an order could not be changed by the will of a simple majority of the subjects but only by the will of all (that means, unanimously), or by the will of a qualified majority (for instance, by a two-thirds or a three-fourths majority vote), then one single individual, or a minority of individuals, could prevent a change of the order. And then the order could be in discordance with a number of subjects which would be greater than the number of those with whose will it is in concordance.

The principle of majority, the greatest possible approximation to the idea of freedom in political reality, presupposes as an essential condition the principle of equality. For the view that the degree of freedom in society is proportionate to the number of free individuals implies that all individuals are of equal political value and that everybody has the same claim to freedom, that is, the same claim that the collective will be in concordance with his individual will. Only if it is irrelevant whether the one or the other is free in this sense (because the one is politically equal to the other) is the postulate justified that as many as possible shall be free, that the mere number of free individuals is decisive. This synthesis of freedom and equality is at the basis of the democratic idea concerning the relationship between the social order (as the collective will) and the individual will, between the subject and the object of domination, just as the synthesis of freedom and equality is at the basis of the relativistic idea concerning the relationship between the subject and the object of cognition.

Democratic Type of Personality From a psychological point of view the synthesis of freedom and equality, the essential characteristic of democracy, means that the individual, the ego, wants freedom not only for himself but also for the others, for the *tu*. And this is possible only if the ego experiences itself not as something unique, incomparable and unreproducible, but, at least in principle, as equal with the *tu*. Only if the individual considers the undeniable differences which exist between himself and the others as not essential, only if the ego- or self-consciousness is reduced to some extent by the feeling to be equal with others, can the ego honor the claim of the *tu* to be also an ego. This is just the intellectual situation of a relativistic philosophy. The personality whose desire for freedom is modified by his feeling of equality recognizes himself in the other. He represents the altruistic type, for he does not experience the other as his enemy but is inclined to see in his fellow-man his friend. He is the sympathizing, peace-loving kind of man whose tendency toward aggression is diverted from its original direction against others to himself and thus is manifested in the tendency toward self-criticism and an increased disposition of a feeling of guilt and a strong consciousness of responsibility. It is not as paradoxical as it may seem on first sight that it is just to the type of relatively lowered self-consciousness that a form of government corresponds, a form which is characterized as self-determination, meaning minimization of government. For the attitude of the individual toward the problem of government is essentially determined by the intensity of the will to power within the individual. And the individual, even as subject to government, is inclined, if living under a form of government which he approves, to identify himself with the government.

The stronger the will to power, the less the appreciation of freedom. The total negation of the value of freedom, the maximization of domination—this is the idea of autocracy, the principle of political absolutism. It is characterized by the fact that the whole power of the state is concentrated in one single individual, the ruler. Its idea is well formulated in the famous words attributed to Louis XIV, *l'état c'est moi*, in direct opposition to democracy, the motto of which is, *l'état c'est nous*. The ruler's and not the people's will is the law. For the people are subject to the ruler without participating in his power, which for this reason is unrestricted and has an inherent tendency toward totalitarianism. In this sense political absolutism means for the ruled the complete renunciation of self-determination. It is incompatible with the idea of equality because justifiable only by the assumption of an essential difference between the ruled and the ruler.

The parallelism which exists between philosophical and political absolutism is evident. The relationship between the object of knowledge, the absolute, and the subject of knowledge, the individual human being, is quite similar to that between an absolute government and its subjects. The unlimited power of such government is beyond any influence on the part of its subjects, who are bound to obey the laws without participating in their creation; similarly, the absolute is beyond our experience, and the object of knowledge, in the theory of philosophical absolutism, is independent of the subject of knowledge, totally determined in his cognition by heteronomous laws. Philosophical absolutism may very well be characterized as epistemological totalitarianism. According to this view, the constitution of the universe is certainly not a democracy. The creature does not participate in the creation.

There exists not only an external parallelism between political and philosophical absolutism; the former has in fact the unmistakable tendency to use the latter as an ideological instrument. To justify his un-limited power and the unconditional submission of all the others, the ruler must present himself, directly or indirectly, as authorized by the only true absolute, the supreme superhuman being, as his descendant or deputy or as inspired by him in a mystical way. Where the political ideology of an autocratic and totalitarian government does not permit recourse to the absolute of a historic religion, as in National Socialism or Bolshevism, it shows an unconcealed disposition to assume a religious character itself by absolutizing its basic value: the idea of the nation, the idea of socialism.

Psychologically, political absolutism corresponds to a type of exag-gerated ego-consciousness. The incapacity or disinclination of the indi-vidual to recognize and to respect his fellow-man as another ego, as an entity of the same kind as his own originally experienced ego, prevents this sort of man from accepting equality as a social ideal, just as his ardent urge of aggression and intensive will to power preclude freedom and peace as political values. It is a characteristic fact that the indi-vidual raises his self-consciousness by identifying himself with his superego, the ideal ego, and that the dictator endowed with unlimited power represents to himself the ideal ego. Hence it is not at all a con-tradiction but, from a psychological point of view, quite consistent to say that it is just this type of man who favors strict discipline, even blind obedience, and, indeed, finds happiness in obeying no less than in commanding. Identification with authority—that is the secret of obedience.

The Principle of Tolerance Since the principle of freedom and equality tends toward a minimization of domination, democracy can-not be an absolute domination, not even an absolute domination of the majority. For domination by the majority of the people distinguishes itself from any other domination by the fact that it not only presupposes by definition an opposition, namely, the minority, but also politically recognizes its existence and protects its rights. Nothing shows more clearly the misuse of terminology in Soviet political theory than the fact that it defines the democracy which the dictatorship of the pro-letariat pretends to be, the democracy for the majority of the poor and not for the minority of the rich, as an organization of violence for the suppression of this minority. "The dictatorship of the proletariat"— the true democracy—says Lenin,[27] "imposes a series of restrictions on the freedom of the oppressors, the exploiters, the capitalists," who under the dictatorship of the proletariat are no longer oppressors, exploiters, and capitalists, who could be only former oppressors, exploiters, and capitalists and are, if they still exist, simply the minority of the people. Among all the facts which deprive the Soviet state of the right to call itself a democracy, it is above all the fact that it considers as its main task the suppression by violence of the minority.

It is of the greatest importance to note that the transformation of the idea of natural freedom, as the idea of absence of government, into the idea of political freedom, as the idea of participation in government, does not imply a complete abandonment of the former. What remains is the principle of a certain restriction of the power of the government, the fundamental principle of political liberalism. Modern democracy cannot be separated from political liberalism. Its principle is that the government must not interfere with certain spheres of interests of the individual, which are to be protected by law as fundamental human rights or freedoms. It is by the respect of these rights that minorities are safeguarded against arbitrary rule by majorities. Because the permanent tension between majority and minority, government and opposition, results in the dialectical process so characteristic of the democratic formation of the will of the state, that one rightly may say: democracy is discussion. Consequently the will of the state, that is to say, the content of the legal order, may be the result of a compromise.[28] Because this type of government guarantees internal peace, it is preferred by the peace-loving, nonaggressive type of character. Hence freedom of religion, freedom of opinion and press, belong to the essence of democracy; and above all belongs freedom of science, based on the belief in the possibility of objective cognition. The appreciation of rational science and the tendency to keep it free from any intrusion by metaphysical or religious speculations are significant features of modern democracy such as it has been formed under the influence of political liberalism. The idea of freedom which is at the basis of political liberalism not only implies the postulate that the external behavior of the individual in relation to other individuals shall be subject—as far as this is possible —to his own will, and if to the will of the state, this can be only a will in the establishment of which his own will participates, but also the postulate that the internal behavior of the individual, his thinking, shall be subject only to his own reason and not to a transcendental authority existing or supposed to exist beyond his reason, an authority in which his reason has no share because it is not accessible to his reason. The liberalism inherent in modern democracy means not only political but also intellectual autonomy of the individual, autonomy of reason, which is the very essence of rationalism.

This attitude, especially the respect for science, corresponds perfectly to that kind of person which we have described as specifically democratic. In the great dilemma between volition and cognition, between the wish to dominate the world and that to understand it, the pendulum swings more in the direction of cognition than volition, more toward understanding than dominating, just because with this type of character the will to power, the intensity of the ego-experience, is relatively reduced and self-criticism relatively strengthened; hence, belief in critical, and thus objective, science is secured.

In an autocracy, on the other hand, no opposition is tolerated. There exists no discussion, no compromise; there is only dictate. Hence there is no freedom of religion or opinion. If volition prevails over cognition, justice prevails over truth. But the question as to what is just is to be decided exclusively by the authority of the state to which not only the will but also the opinion of the citizens are subject, so that nonconformity with this authority is not only an error but at the same time a punishable crime. It stands to reason that under such a political regime there can be no freedom of science, which is tolerated only as a pliant instrument of the government. Nothing is more significant of a turn to an intellectual attitude more or less in favor of autocracy than the abandonment of the belief in the possibility of an objective science, that is, a science which is independent from political interests and hence worthy of freedom. The existence of democracy is endangered if the ideal of objective cognition is placed behind other ideals. Such an intellectual movement goes usually hand in hand with the tendency to attribute to the irrational a higher value than to the rational. In the conflict between religion and science the former prevails over the latter.

The Rationalistic Character of Democracy The rationalistic character of democracy manifests itself especially in the tendency to establish the legal order of the state as a system of general norms created by a procedure well organized for this purpose. There is a clear intention of determining, by a pre-established law, the individual acts of the courts and administrative organs in order to make them—as far as possible—calculable. There exists an outspoken need for rationalizing the process in which the power of the state is displayed. This is the reason why legislation is considered to be the basis of the other functions of the state. The ideal of legality plays a decisive role: it is assumed that the individual acts of state may be justified by their conformity with the general norms of the law. Legal security rather than absolute justice is in the foreground of legal consciousness. Autocracy, on the other hand, disdains such rationalization of power. It avoids, as far as possible, any determination of the acts of state, especially of the acts of an autocratic ruler, by pre-established general norms, which could imply a restriction of discretion. As supreme legislator the autocrat is considered not to be bound by the laws issued by himself: *princeps legibus solutus est.* In Plato's ideal state, which is the archetype of an autocracy, there are no general rules of law at all. The "royal judges" have an unlimited power of discretion in deciding concrete cases. This, of course, is possible only because Plato's state is a very small community. In a state of an average size the autocrat is not able to perform all the necessary administrative and judicial acts and has to appoint subordinate organs. In order to have his intentions realized by these organs, he may bind them by laws determining their activities. But he retains for himself the absolute right to grant in every case any exemption from the laws that he thinks appropriate. Hence there can be no legal security in an autocracy. Nevertheless each manifestation of state power claims to be the realization of justice. And this justice refuses to express itself in general principles; it defies, by its very nature, any definition. It reveals itself only in individual decisions perfectly adapted to the particularities of the concrete case. The secret of justice is in the exclusive possession of the ruler; it is his personal virtue, his divine capacity, implanted in him by divine grace; it is the legitimation of his dictatorial power. Consequently an autocratic regime, in contradistinction to a democratic one, refuses to make public its aims by promulgating a program. And if it is pressed to do so, the program is either a series of empty phrases or promises, the fulfilment of most contradictory wishes. Against criticsm one argues that the program does not and cannot contain the essential achievements to be performed by the regime. Pulsating life can neither be grasped nor regulated by general rules. Everything depends on the concrete action, on the mystery of the creative *Kairós*.

Since in a democracy legal security, legality, and calculability of the functions of state are required, institutions for the purpose of controlling these functions in order to guarantee their lawfulness are established. As a consequence the principle of publicity prevails. The tendency to unveil the facts is specifically democratic; and this tendency leads a superficial and malevolent interpretation of this form of government to the unfounded judgment that corruption is more frequent in democracy than in autocracy, whereas—in truth—corruption only remains invisible in the latter, since there the contrary principle prevails. In an autocratic regime, there are no measures of control, which are supposed only to diminish the effectiveness of the government, and no publicity; there is only the intensive endeavor to veil everything that could be harmful to the authority of the government and undermine the discipline of the officials and the obedience of the citizens.

As pointed out, the rationalistic and critical attitudes of democracy manifest themselves also in a certain aversion to the religious, metaphysical ideologies which autocracy utilizes in order to maintain its power. The struggle in which democracy overcomes autocracy is to a great part conducted in the name of critical reason against ideologies which appeal to the irrational forces of the human soul. However, since no government seems to be able to act without the help of certain justifying ideologies, democratic governments too make use of them. But, as a rule, democratic ideologies are more rationalistic, nearer to reality, and hence less effective than those used by autocratic governments. Since the hold on the subjects by autocratic governments is more intense, they need a more dense veil to cover their true nature. To be sure, occasionally in a democracy the same religious, metaphysical ideologies are used to which autocratic governments owe or are supposed to owe their success, as, for instance, the idea that the popular government realizes the will of God. But the slogan *vox populi vox dei* has never been taken too seriously. The halo of an inspired monarch who pretends to hold his office by the grace of God or the charisma of a leader who claims to be inspired by supernatural forces can hardly be attributed to the people, to Mr. and Mrs. America. A democracy which tries to justify itself in this way would come suspiciously near to the fable of the ass in the skin of a lion.

The Problem of Leadership The antagonism between democracy and autocracy appears also in the different ways in which rulership is interpreted. In the ideology of autocracy the ruler represents an absolute value. Being of divine origin or endowed with supernatural forces, he is not considered an organ which is or can be created by the community. He is imagined as an authority that stands outside the community, which is constituted and held together by him. Therefore origin and creation of the ruler are not problems that could be solved by rational cognition. The political reality, namely, the inevitable usurpation of rulership, is assiduously veiled by the myth of the leader. In a democracy, on the other hand, the question of how to appoint the magistrates stands in the bright light of rational consideration. Rulership represents not an absolute but only a relative value. All the organs of the community are elected only for a short period. Even the chief executive is a "leader" only for a certain time and only in certain respects, since not only his term of office but also his competence is limited. He is, even in his capacity as the head of the state, a citizen like all the others and is subject to criticism. From the fact that the ruler in an autocracy is transcendent to, and in a democracy immanent in, the community follows that in the first case the man who exercises this function is considered to stand above the social order and consequently not responsible to the community constituted by it or—as it is ideologically formulated—responsible only to God and himself, whereas in the second case he stands under the social order and hence responsible to it. Since in democracy rulership has no supernatural quality, and the ruler is created by a rational, publicly controllable procedure, rulership cannot be the permanent monopoly of a single person. Publicity, criticism, and responsibility make it impossible that a ruler becomes irremovable. Democracy is characterized by a more or less quick change of rulership. It has, in this respect, a dynamic nature. A steady rise from the community of the ruled to the position of ruler takes place. Autocracy, on the other hand, shows an outspoken static character: the relationship between ruler and ruled has the tendency of being frozen.

On the whole, democracy has no ground which is favorable to the principle of authority in general and to the Fuehrer-ideal in particular. Insofar as the father is the archetype of authority, because the original experience of all authority, democracy is, according to its idea, a fatherless society. It is intended to be a community of equals. Its principle is co-ordination; its most primitive form is a mother-right organization, where men living together are brothers, the sons of the same mother. The trinity of the French Revolution, liberty, equality, and fraternity, is its true symbol. Autocracy, on the other hand, is by its very nature a paternal community. The child-father relationship is its corresponding category. Super- and sub-ordination, not co-ordination; i.e., hierarchical articulation, is its structure. It is just for this reason that one might attribute to it rather than to democracy a better chance to survive. And, indeed, it seems as if in history autocracies fill much greater spaces of time than democracies, which appear—so to speak—only in the entr'actes of the drama of mankind. Democracy seems to have less power of resistance than autocracy, which without any consideration destroys every opponent, whereas democracy, with its principle of legality, freedom of opinion, protection of minorities, tolerance, directly favors its enemy. It is a paradoxical privilege of this form of government, a doubtful advantage which it has over autocracy that it may, by its own specific methods of forming the will of the state, abolish itself. But the fact that in an autocracy there is no constitutional way of smoothing down the conflicts of interests, which after all exist here too, constitutes a serious danger. From the point of view of psycho-political technique, the mechanism of democratic institutions aims at raising the political emotions of the masses and especially the opposition parties above the threshold of social consciousness in order to let them "abreagieren" (abreact). The social equilibrium in the autocracy, on the other hand, is based on the repression of the political emotions in a sphere which could be compared with that of the unconscious. We shall leave undecided which technique is more appropriate to safeguard the government against revolutionary overthrow.

Among the attempts, mentioned before, to obscure the antagonism between democracy and autocracy, the tendency to present the problem of democracy as a problem of leadership is of an importance which should not be underestimated. It has been evoked by the undeniable success which fascism and nationalism had during a certain time. It aims at a new doctrine of democracy which, in opposition to the old one, emphasizes the necessity of efficient leadership. Its result is the concept of an authoritarian democracy, which, of course, is a contradiction in terms. But it enabled the followers of this doctrine to recognize fascism as democracy.[29] "Fascism," declared Mussolini, "is opposed to democracy, which equates the nation to the majority, lowering it to the level of that majority; nevertheless it is the *purest form of democracy* if the nation is conceived, as it should be, qualitatively and not quantitatively, as the most powerful ideal (most powerful because most moral, most coherent, most true) which acts within the nation as the conscience and the will of a few, even of one, which ideal tends to become active within the conscience and the will of all, that is to say, of all those who rightly constitute a nation. . . ."[30]

It cannot, of course, be denied that within a democratic state there is such a thing as leadership, that the democratic form of government does not prevent, although it does not favor, the coming into existence of powerful leaders who may obtain the enthusiastic support of the masses. Nor can it be denied that the rise of such a personality may result in the abolishment of this form of government and its replacement by an open autocracy or a dictatorship which pretends to be democracy. It is also true that constitutional measures such as the institution of recall, that is, the procedure by which a public official may be removed from office by a vote of the people, or those intended to prevent ostracism, as in antique democracy, have proved to be not very effective. But these facts do not justify the identification of the problem of democracy with that of leadership. The problem of democracy is not the problem of the most effective government; others may be more effective. It is the problem of a government guaranteeing the greatest possible amount of individual freedom. Consequently, the wish for effective government, or what is supposed to be an effective government, does not justify the substitution in place of the definition of democracy as government by the people a definition from which the people as an active power are eliminated and maintained only as a passive factor insofar as their approval of the leader expressed in some way or another is required. Such definitions have only the effect—if not the intention—of covering the retreat from the democratic position by a democratic terminology.

Democracy and Peace The pattern of internal policy just described corresponds to a definite standard of external policy. The democratic type is decidedly inclined to cherish a pacifistic ideal, whereas the autocratic type shows unmistakable symptoms of imperialism. Of course democracies too have waged wars of conquest. But the readiness for such actions is here much weaker, the inner political inhibitions to overcome much stronger, than in an autocracy. Consequently, there exists a clear tendency to justify foreign policy by a rationalistic, pacifistic ideology. It is necessary to present the war which one wages or intends to wage as a war of defense imposed upon the peace-loving government by the enemy—a measure which an autocracy with its heroic ideology does not need. Or the aim of the war is declared to be the final pacification of the world, or a part of it, through an international organization, which shows all the characteristics of a democracy—a community of states with equal rights under a kind of government composed of elected representatives and a world court competent to settle international conflicts—as the first step toward the development of a world state. This is an idea which from the point of view of an autocratic-imperialistic conviction not only does not represent any value at all but is decidedly rejected as a leveling mania, which ultimately must lead to the destruction of civilization, the progress of which depends on the struggle for life and the survival of the fittest.

Democracy and the Theory of the State The different ideas of the relationship which exists or should exist between one's own state and other states are closely connected with the theories of the nature of the state which are congenial, respectively, to the democratic and to the autocratic types of personality. The latter, with his hypertrophic self-consciousness based on his identification with a powerful autocrat, is predestined to advocate the doctrine that the state is an entity different from the mass of individual human beings, a superindividual, somehow a collective reality, a mystic organism, and, as such, a supreme authority, the realization of absolute value. It is the concept of sovereignty which accomplishes the absolutization, the divinization, of the state, represented in its totality by the divine ruler. Philosophical absolutism, as pointed out, may result from a view which, in its attempt to conceive the world, starts from the ego but ignores the *tu*, refuses to recognize its claim to be an ego too, and thus leads to an absolutization of the unique, sovereign ego within whose conception and will the whole universe together with all the others who in vain claim to be egos is comprised. In just the same way political absolutism starts in its interpretation of international relations from the interpreter's own sovereign state. It is a significant consequence of the doctrine of the absolute sovereignty of the state that the sovereignty of one state excludes the sovereignty of the others, that the state which is the starting point of this interpretation must be considered as the only sovereign state. Consequently the legal existence of other communities as states and the validity of the normative order regulating the conduct of the sovereign state in its relations with these states must be based on the recognition, and thus the will, of the sovereign state, which is the starting point of this interpretation. Since the legal existence of such states and the application of international law to their relationships with the sovereign state depend on this recognition, these states cannot be considered as sovereign in the absolute sense of the term. From this point of view the international legal order appears not as a normative order superior to the state or, what amounts to the same thing, to the national legal order, but—if as a legal order at all—as part of the legal order of the sovereign state which recognizes the validity of the international legal order itself. Thus the entire world of the law is conceived of as implied in the will of the absolute state-ego, the sovereign state.

Diametrically opposed to this view of the state and its relations with other states is the theory according to which the state is not a mysterious substance different from its members, i.e., the human beings forming the state, and hence a transcendental reality beyond rational, empirical cognition but a specific normative order regulating the mutual behavior of men. This doctrine refuses to look for the existence of the state in a sphere beyond or above; it finds this existence in the validity and efficacy of a normative order and consequently in the minds of the human beings who are the subjects of the obligations and rights stipulated by this order. This political theory is not directed at an absolutization but, on the contrary, at a relativization of the state. It denounces the concept of sovereignty as the ideology of a definite power policy and hence denies that this concept is applicable in a scientific description of political or legal reality. By demonstrating that absolute sovereignty is not and cannot be an essential quality of the state existing side by side with other states, it removes one of the most stubborn prejudices which prevent political and legal science from recognizing the possibility of an international legal order constituting an international community of which the state is a member, just as corporations are members of the state. This theory shows that the state as a legal community is an intermediate stage in a series of legal phenomena which leads from the universal international community of states, over particular international organizations, to the individual state and from the individual state to the associations incorporated in the state, ending finally with the individual human being as the legal subject.

It follows from all that has been said before that this anti-ideological, rationalistic, and relativistic political theory corresponds to that intellectual type which has been described as democratic. It is a scientific theory of political and legal reality to which the autocratic type prefers a metaphysical-theological interpretation of social phenomena in general and of the state in particular. Only the democratic type will allow an objective analysis of the different forms of government, the democratic form included. Nobody who believes in political absolutism will examine democracy on an equal footing with autocracy without a value judgment implied in his examination. To evaluate and hence to approve or to disapprove political reality is more important to him than value-free cognition. If the antagonism between democracy and autocracy can be reduced to a difference in the inner habitus of men, then the antagonism between a scientific attitude oriented toward the value of cognition and a political attitude oriented toward another, the social, value may also be brought in connection with the antagonism between political relativism and political absolutism. Then it is quite understandable why a genuine science of politics prospers better within a democracy where its freedom, its independence from the government, is guaranteed than within an autocracy where only political ideologies can be developed, and why the one who prefers democracy to autocracy has a stronger disposition for a scientific cognition of society in general, and state and law in particular, than the one whom his character pushes toward autocracy and thereby to an ideological attitude.

. . .

Democracy as Political Relativism It was a disciple of Hegel who, in the fight against the democratic movement in Germany during the nineteenth century, formulated the catchword: Authority, not majority! And, indeed, if one believes in the existence of the absolute, and consequently in absolute values, in the absolute good—to use Plato's terminology—is it not meaningless to let a majority vote decide what is politically good? To legislate, and that means to determine the contents of a social order, not according to what objectively is the best for the individuals subject to this order, but according to what these individuals, or their majority, rightly or wrongly believe to be their best—this consequence of the democratic principles of freedom and equality is justifiable only if there is no absolute answer to the question as to what is the best, if there is no such a thing as an absolute good. To let a majority of ignorant men decide instead of reserving the decision to the only one who, in virtue of his divine origin or inspiration, has the exclusive knowledge of the absolute good—this is not the most absurd method if it is believed that such knowledge is impossible and that, consequently, no single individual has the right to enforce his will upon the others. That value judgments have only relative validity—one of the basic principles of philosophical relativism—implies that opposite value judgments are neither logically nor morally excluded. One of the fundamental principles of democracy is that everybody has to respect the political opinion of everybody else, since all are equal and free. Tolerance, minority rights, freedom of speech, and freedom of thought, so characteristic of democracy, have no place within a political system based on the belief in absolute values. This brief irresistibly leads —and has always led—to a situation in which the one who assumes to possess the secret of the absolute good claims to have the right to impose his opinion as well as his will upon the others, who, if they do not agree, are in error. And to be in error is, according to this view, to be wrong, and hence punishable. If, however, it is recognized that only relative values are accessible to human knowledge and human will, then it is justifiable to enforce a social order against reluctant individuals only if this order is in harmony with the greatest possible number of equal individuals, that is to say, with the will of the majority. It may be that the opinion of the minority, and not the opinion of the majority, is correct. Solely because of this possibility, which only philosophical relativism can admit—that what is right today may be wrong tomorrow— the minority must have a chance to express freely their opinion and must have full opportunity of becoming the majority. Only if it is not possible to decide in an absolute way what is right and what is wrong is it advisable to discuss the issue and, after discussion, to submit to a compromise.[31]

This is the true meaning of the political system which we call democracy and which we may oppose to political absolutism only because it is political relativism.[32]

•   •   •

II. DEMOCRACY AND RELIGION

Democracy as a Problem of Justice The foregoing examination of the philosophical foundation of democracy is not and cannot be directed at an absolute justification of this type of political organization; it does not and cannot intend to prove that democracy is the best form of government. It is a scientific, and that means an objective, analysis of a social phenomenon and not its evaluation in the sense that it presupposes a definite social value as unconditionally valid and demonstrates democracy as the realization of this value. Such a justification is not possible from the point of view of a political science which cannot recognize a definite social value to the exclusion of another but can only ascertain that in social reality different and contradictory social values are recognized and examine the appropriate means for their realization. For the relationship between means and end is a relationship between cause and effect, objectively ascertainable by science, whereas the recognition of an end as an ultimate value, which is itself not the means for a further end, lies beyond scientific cognition. Hence a scientific theory of democracy can only maintain that this form of government tries to realize freedom together with equality of the individual and that *if* these values are to be realized, democracy is the appropriate means; which implies that if social values other than freedom and equality of the individual members of the community are to be realized, as for instance, the power of the nation, democracy may not be the appropriate form of government. This, of course, is—if a justification at all—only a conditional justification of democracy, the only justification a relativistic philosophy based on science and not on metaphysics or religion can afford. It leaves the decision about the social value to be realized to the individual acting in political reality. It does not and cannot take the burden of this grave responsibility off his shoulders.

This is, in the last analysis, the reason why a relativistic philosophy of value meets with such passionate resistance. For many people are not able, and not willing, to accept the responsibility for the decision about the social value to be realized, especially in a situation in which their decision may have fatal consequences for their personal welfare. Therefore they try to shift it from their own conscience to an outside authority competent to tell them what is right and wrong, to answer their question, what is justice?—seeking for an unconditional justification in terms of which they long to appease their conscience. Such an authority they find in religion. This fact explains the steadily increasing intellectual movement directed against rationalistic positivism and relativism toward religious metaphysics and natural law so characteristic of our time of high political tensions. Christian theology, leading this movement, offers a vindication of democracy which promises to be more effective than the problematical, because conditional, justification implied in a merely scientific theory of legal and political positivism. From the point of view of Christian theology the problem of democracy is presented and supposedly solved as a problem of divine, and that means of absolute, justice or, what amounts to the same, of Christian natural law. Most significant products of recent democratic theology are the writings of two outstanding Protestant theologians: the Swiss Emil Brunner's *Gerechtigkeit: Eine Lehre von den Grundgesetzen der Gesellschaftsordnung*,[1] and the American Reinhold Niebuhr's *The Children of Light and the Children of Darkness: A Vindication of Democracy and a Critique of Its Traditional Defense*.[2] A characteristic representative of modern Catholic political philosophy is the French thinker Jacques Maritain, who in his book *Christianisme et démocratie*[3] tries to prove an essential connection between democracy and religion from the Catholic point of view. I intend to present in the following a critical analysis of the main ideas of these writers, not only in order to demonstrate that Christian theology, too, can justify democracy only as a relative value, but also—and in the first place—to examine the claim of theology that it furnishes a foundation for democracy which it attempts to verify by showing that there is an essential connection between democracy and Christian religion.

Brunner as well as Niebuhr start their crusade against relativistic positivism or skeptical secularism, as Niebuhr puts it, with the accusation that this intellectual attitude is responsible for totalitarianism, especially National Socialism. This is an argument which plays a very important part in the antirelativistic movement and is used not only by theologians in favor of religion, but also by thinkers, not connected with a particular historic religion, in favor of metaphysical speculation in general. Hence it deserves careful consideration.

Relativistic Positivism Responsible for Totalitarianism Brunner writes, "The whole world is crying out for justice," [4] and this desire for justice "is a constant factor in all human history." [5] The vague sense of just and unjust, which everyone has, must be transformed into clear thought, into the principle of justice; and this principle is implied in the "conception of the Christian law of nature. It is the conception of justice as eternal, supernatural and absolutely valid;" [6] "it was the Western conception of justice for two thousand years." But it has disintegrated. It was "the positivism of the nineteenth century, with its denial of the metaphysical and superhuman, which dissolved the idea of justice by proclaiming the relativity of all views of justice. Thereby the idea of justice was stripped of all divine dignity and law abandoned to the vagaries of human will. The view that justice is of its nature relative became the dogma of the jurists." [7] As a consequence of this disintegration of the idea of justice, Brunner declares:

It was only to be expected that one day a political power devoid of all religious scruples should discard the last vestiges of the traditional idea of justice and proclaim the will of the ruling power as the sole canon of appeal in matters of law. The totalitarian State is simply and solely legal positivism in political practice, the abrogation in actual fact of the classical and Christian idea of a divine "law of nature." If there is no divine standard of justice, there is no criterion for the legal system set up by a State. If there is no justice transcending the State, then the State can declare anything it likes to be law; there is no limit set to its arbitrariness save its actual power to give force to its will. If it does so in the form of a logically coherent system, it thereby fulfils the one condition to which the legality of law is bound in the formalistic view of law. The totalitarian State is the inevitable result of the slow disintegration of the idea of justice in the Western world. [8]

The totalitarian state, this "monster of injustice," [9] is not "the invention of a handful of criminals in the grand style," but "the ineluctable consequence" of a "positivism void of faith and inimical to metaphysics and religion," "the inevitable result of man's loss of faith in a *divine* law, in an eternal justice. Yet the alternative stands clearly revealed. Either there is a valid criterion, a justice which stands above us all, a challenge presented *to* us, not *by* us, a standard rule of justice binding on every State and every system of law, or there is no justice, but only power organized in one fashion or another and setting itself up as law." [10] This means: If there is no absolute justice there is no justice at all. Justice is by its very nature an absolute value, and only a value posited by God can be absolute.

The consequence of this view—opposed to relativistic positivism— would be that there can be only one, the absolute divine, and not also another, merely relative, justice. If justice is, by its very nature as a divine value, absolute, a relative justice is a contradiction in terms. Only if theology accepts this consequence can it reject relativistic positivism in general and a relativistic theory of democracy in particular. However, Brunner recognizes, in addition to the absolute divine justice, a relative justice, the human justice of positive law. He says, "It is true that all social systems which we human beings create are only relatively just." [11] Positive law is only relatively just because its attempt to be just can never reach its goal. For it is absolute justice

which the best of human laws strive to express, though they never reach their goal in the attempt. Hence it is the element of perpetual ferment in all human systems. Yet it is foolish and wrong to maintain that justice is a relative thing because no human system can fully express this law of justice. That is as unreasonable as to maintain that the notion of the straight line is a relative one because no human being has yet been able to draw a straight line. It is just *because* we can conceive an absolutely straight line that we can say that no man has ever drawn a straight line. It is just because we have knowledge of the law of absolute justice that we can say that all human laws are mere approximations to the truly just.[12]

Hence there are, according to this theology, two justices: an absolute divine and a relative human justice.

The argument set forth against relativistic positivism, that this philosophy makes the totalitarian state possible, that "if the positivistic theory of law is right, there is no possibility of waging war against the totalitarian State as a monster of injustice," [13] is a political argument, and as such, even if it were true, could prove nothing against relativism as an epistemological principle. The proposition that only relative values are accessible to human cognition cannot be disproved by the proposition that there are evils in this world, especially social evils, that is to say, facts which some people condemn as evil, whereas others—as in the case of the totalitarian state—praise them as good, even as realization of a higher justice. A statement may be true although the belief in its truth may have effects which from some point of view or another may be considered as evil, just as a statement may be false although the erroneous belief in its truth may have consequences which from some point of view or another may be considered as good. Hence Plato's famous doctrine of the useful lies. Besides, Brunner's assertion that relativism is responsible for the totalitarian state is in open contradiction to the undeniable fact that the classical justification of the totalitarian state, as pointed out earlier, is furnished just by that philosophy which more than any other has rejected relativism and emphatically asserted the transcendental existence of absolute values—Plato's doctrine of the ideas on the basis of which he outlined the constitution of his ideal state, which in every respect is a totalitarian autocracy. Totalitarian ideologists, therefore, have always referred to Plato's philosophical absolutism and recognized in the Platonic state the model for their political schemes. Brunner is not very consistent in this respect. For in another connection he makes the church responsible for the totalitarian state. He says:

The Church, which to-day protests, and rightly so, against the oppression it suffers at the hands of the totalitarian State, would do well to remember who first set the State the bad example of religious intolerance by using the secular arm to safeguard by force what can only spring from a free act of the will. The Church should always bethink itself with shame that it was the first teacher of the totalitarian State at nearly every point.[14]

The Church gave an example to the totalitarian State by using the State to intervene in the inner life—inquisition, moral police, monopoly of propaganda, persecution of dissidents and compulsory uniformity must largely be lad to its charge.[15]

This is true. But the church could be "the teacher of the totalitarian state in nearly every point," not because she represented "a positivism void of faith and inimical to metaphysics and religion," but because she taught just the contrary: the belief in absolute justice.

Brunner's assertion that we may not infer from the imperfect, and in this sense only relative, justice of the positive law, that there exists only a relative and not an absolute justice, is based on a false analogy. One cannot compare the idea of absolute justice with the notion of a straight line and the merely relatively just positive law with an actually drawn straight line. For absolute justice is the idea of a value, whereas a straight line is a notion of geometry, i.e., a science directed at reality. This notion is thinkable and can be defined in a rational, unambiguous way, although a straight line which completely corresponds to the definition cannot actually be drawn. The idea of absolute justice, however, as the essence of God, is beyond human cognition; it is not thinkable and rationally definable, and hence it is also not defined by Brunner, who only asserts to know of it. But he cannot prove that what he —according to his assertion—knows of absolute justice forms the content of God's will. What he presents as his knowledge of absolute justice is very contradictory and far from the "clear thought" into which everybody's vague sense of just and unjust has to be transformed according to Brunner's own suggestion. He misinterprets relativistic positivism by attributing to this philosophy the consideration that positive law is only relatively just because it does not completely correspond to absolute justice. Such consideration would, indeed, presuppose the existence of an absolute justice. Relativistic positivism considers positive law as only relatively just because it assumes that an absolute justice is unknowable, that one may, religiously, believe in the absolute, and that means in God, but that one cannot comprehend it; that it is by its very nature beyond human cognition and consequently no possible object of science, which can have nothing to do with the absolute in general and absolute justice in particular.

. . .

The View of Reinhold Niebuhr: Religion is the Necessary Basis of Democracy Like the Swiss theologian Brunner, the American theologian Reinhold Niebuhr makes a positivistic, that is to say, an areligious philosophy responsible for totalitarianism. He speaks of "secularism which attempts to achieve cultural unity" within a society split into opposite groups of material and intellectual interests "through the disavowal of traditional historical religions," [16] and which, in its more sophisticated form, "represents a form of scepticism which is conscious of the relativity of all human perspectives. In this form it stands on the abyss of moral nihilism and threatens the whole of life with a sense of meaninglessness. Thus it creates a spiritual vacuum into which demonic religions easily rush." [17] By "demonic religions" he means, in the first place, National Socialism and other forms of extravagant nationalism.[18] It is the same idea which he expresses in the statement: "A consistent pessimism in regard to man's rational capacity for justice invariably leads to absolutistic political theories; for they prompt the conviction that only preponderant power can coerce the various vitalities of a community into a working harmony." [19] Furthermore: "The most effective opponents of tyrannical government are today, as they have been in the past, men who can say, 'We must obey God rather than man.' Their resolution is possible because they have a vantage point from which they can discount the pretensions of demonic Caesars and from which they can defy malignant power as embodied in a given government." [20] If this statement means that Christian theology does and always did effectively resist tyrannical governments, its truth is not beyond doubt. For the source from which Christian theology takes the argument that "we must obey God rather than man" furnishes also the argument: all governments are given their powers from God; this argument has been formulated by St. Paul for the very purpose of being used in favor of a demonic Caesar, and since then has been again and again used to support tyrannical rulers such as Ivan the Terrible of Russia, Louis XIV of France, or Frederick II of Prussia. Also Mussolini and even Hitler found Christian theologians who justified their governments. Christian theology cannot claim to be recognized as an advocate of a definite political regime, because it can and actually did justify contrary regimes, just as it can and actually did defend as well as attack the distribution of property, as Niebuhr's excellent chapter on "The Community and Property" shows.[21] "The final resource against idolatrous national communities . . . must be found in the recognition of universal law by individuals, who have a source of moral insight beyond the partial and particular national communities." [22] Religion is, according to Niebuhr, the source of this insight. "Religious ideas and traditions may not be directly involved in the organization of a community. But they are the ultimate sources of the moral standards from which political principles are derived. In any case both the foundation and the pinnacle of any cultural structure are religious; for any scheme of values is finally determined by the ultimate answer which is given to the ultimate question about the meaning of life." [23] Modern democracy requires a religious basis.[24] Consequently, Christian theology can vindicate the democratic political system more effectively than skeptic secularism, hampered by its disavowal of religion and its pessimism in regard to man's capacity for justice.

Niebuhr's critique of traditional democratic philosophy is not very consistent. On the one hand he blames this philosophy for its pessimism in regard to man's rational capacity for justice. "A free society," he says, "requires some confidence in the ability of men to reach tentative and tolerable adjustments between their competing interests and to arrive at some common notions of justice which transcend all partial interests." [25] To expect only "tentative and tolerable" adjustments between the competing interests is the characteristic result of that pessimistic view according to which human reason is not able to reach perfect, that is, absolutely just, solutions for human conflicts. Niebuhr does not say that the "common notions of justice," to which he here refers, are to be understood as notions of an absolute justice, although his recourse to religion seems to point in this direction. He does not, in contradistinction to Brunner, expressly require that our political value judgments be guided by the idea of an absolute justice, because he is quite aware of the limitations of human nature, whose achievements are, as he says, "infected with sinful corruption." [26] Consequently he arrives, as we shall see, at a completely relativistic justification of democracy. On the other hand, he sees the reason for the insufficiency of the traditional justification of democracy "by the liberal culture" in the "excessively optimistic estimates of human nature and of human history with which the democratic credo has been historically associated." [27] Pessimism in regard to man's rational capacity for justice is not quite compatible with excessively optimistic estimates of human nature. Liberalism is not necessarily combined with an optimistic over-estimation of human nature and certainly not with "a too great reliance upon the human capacity for transcendence over self-interest." [28] There are many representatives of liberalism, especially liberal economists, who take into full account man's egoistic tendencies, and none of the leading liberal philosophers, in his confidence in human nature, went so far as to consider a coercive order as superfluous. It was just because he had no confidence in human nature that one of the outstanding representatives of political liberalism, Wilhelm von Humboldt, in spite of his racial individualism, recognized the state as a "necessary evil." [29] Niebuhr, who reproaches the liberal democratic theory with its "general confidence of an identity between self-interest and the commonweal," [30] must admit that if there were not a possibility of a harmony between self-interest and the commonweal, "any form of social harmony among men would be impossible; and certainly a democratic version of such harmony would be quite unthinkable." [31] He emphasizes that "the same man who displays this capacity" of transcending his self-interest "also reveals varying degrees of the power of self-interest and of the subservience of the mind to these interests." [32] No liberal philosopher has ignored this fact. Niebuhr's critique is directed against an imaginary opponent, constructed for this purpose. He believes "that a Christian view of human nature is more adequate for the development of a democratic society" [33] than the liberal view. But there is not only the pessimistic Christian view of man as "infected with sinful corruption" but also a Christian belief in man as the image of God, which is certainly more optimistic than any liberal view of human nature could be.

"The consistent optimism of our liberal culture," says Niebuhr, "has prevented modern democratic societies both from gauging the perils of freedom accurately and from appreciating democracy fully as the only alternative to injustice and oppression." [34] Hence his task is to show that democracy is the only alternative to injustice, and that means the realization of absolute justice. For if democracy is demonstrated as relatively just only, it cannot be the "only" alternative to injustice. This is the decisive difference between an absolute and a merely relative justice: that only the former, but not the latter, excludes the possibility of another justice. The judgment that a norm or social institution is relatively just means that it is just only under definite conditions; consequently the judgment implies that under other conditions the norm or institution may not be just, and another, even an opposite norm or institution, may be just. Only the judgment that something is absolutely, that is to say, under all conditions, just excludes such a possibility. However, the political philosophy of Niebuhr, based on "religious and theological convictions," [35] is far from fulfilling this task. It is not even in a position to recognize this task. For it is in open contradiction to the very nature of its religious-theological basis, since it is an unmistakable form of political relativism.

Religious Relativism At first sight it might seem that Niebuhr, as a consequence of his religious-theological convictions, rejects relativism. He assumes that the "use of restrictive power" by the rulers and the community would be "purely arbitrary if it were not informed by some general principles of justice, which define the right order of life in a community." These "general principles of justice" are, as he expressly declares, the "natural law." He refers to the fact "that there are no living communities which do not have some notions of justice, beyond their historic laws, by which they seek to gauge the justice of their legislative enactments." He ascertains, evidently with regret, "that in the present stage of liberal democratic thought, moral theory has become too relativistic to make appeal to natural law as plausible as in other centuries," and again emphasizes that "every human society does have something like a natural-law concept; for it assumes that there are more immutable and purer principles of justice than those actually embodied in its obviously relative laws." [36] "The final question to confront the proponent of a democratic and free society," he asserts, "is whether the freedom of a society should extend to the point of allowing these principles to be called into question." He asks: "Should they not stand above criticism or amendment? If they are themselves subjected to the democratic process and if they are made dependent upon the moods and vagaries of various communities and epochs, have we not sacrificed the final criterion of justice and order, by which we might set bounds to what is inordinate in both individual and collective impulses?" [37] The answer to these questions can be only in the affirmative. For if the principles of justice or natural law are subjected to criticism and the democratic process, very different and even contradictory ideas about what is just become possible, and then the "final" criterion of justice is indeed sacrificed. Hence the principles of justice must be declared to be not accessible to critical reason, to be derivable only from religious belief. This is what Niebuhr seems to maintain. He says: "Every society needs working principles of justice, as criteria for its positive law and system of restraints. The profoundest of these actually transcend reason and lie rooted in religious conceptions of the meaning of existence." [38] This means that Niebuhr believes in the existence of a natural law as the criterion of justice for positive law and that this natural law has its source in religion. Since he identifies religion with Christianity, religion means the belief in an absolutely just God. Hence a natural law based on Christian religion necessarily claims to represent absolute justice. Only as an absolute justice can it be that criterion for positive law which Niebuhr has in mind. In order to be such a criterion, natural law must differ from positive law, and the difference consists in nothing else but in the fact that natural law is or pretends to be absolutely just, whereas positive law is only relatively just; and every positive law is relatively just, that is to say, just under a definite condition, under the condition that some social value is presupposed which the law claims to realize, but without being able to claim that this value is absolutely supreme and hence the only one to be realized if in conflict with another. If natural law, too, is only relatively just, if a system of natural law cannot be presented with the claim of being the only possible natural law, if there are various and even contradictory systems of natural law, then the question arises which of the different systems of natural law should be the criterion for the positive law; and to this question a relativistic natural law doctrine has no answer. Thus natural law has no advantage over positive law. For then the difference between a system of norms which is presented as natural law and a system of norms which has the character of positive law is exactly the same as the difference between two systems of positive law, and that means that there is no absolute reason to prefer the one to the other, because the decisive question as to the supreme value to be realized by the law remains unanswered. A relative natural law is a contradiction in terms.

It is just such a relative natural law to which Niebuhr refers as the necessary criterion for positive law. For, although he insists on the belief in a natural law based on the Christian religion as the criterion for positive law, he, in the last analysis, does not accept the consequence that the principles of natural law must not be subjected to criticism and hence not to the democratic process, that is to say, he cannot deny the possibility of different ideas about the content of natural law without a possibility of deciding which is the right one, excluding the others. For he admits "that there is no historical reality, whether it be church or government, whether it be the reason of wise men or specialists, which is not involved in the flux and relativity of human existence; which is not subject to error and sin, and which is not tempted to exaggerate its errors and sins when they are made immune to criticism." [39] Hence "every historical statement" of the "principles of justice" is "subject to amendment. If it becomes fixed it will destroy some of the potentialities of a higher justice, which the mind of one generation is unable to anticipate in the life of subsequent eras." [40] However, the principles of justice or natural law exist only in "historical statements." We know nothing about these principles but that which is expressed in "historical statements"; and if these statements refer only to a relative justice, we can have no knowledge of an absolute justice or natural law in the true sense of the term and are not entitled to maintain the existence of such justice or natural law. There is then no reason to assume that the justice which the mind of one generation is able to reach is "higher" than that of another generation. Besides, the principles of justice, formulated in historical statements, change not only from one generation to another but also from one society to another within the same generation and from one group to another within the same society.

Niebuhr carefully avoids referring to an absolute justice. He does not speak of the justice of natural law in its relation to positive law in terms of superlatives. He says only that the principles of natural law are "more immutable and purer" than those embodied in the "obviously relative" positive law. But if natural law is only "more" immutable than positive law and hence mutable and not absolutely immutable, then it is relative too. And if both are mutable, then the question arises why the one is more and the other less mutable or pure; and to this question there is no answer in a relativistic philosophy of justice such as that presented by Niebuhr. If the only principles of justice or natural law known by man and hence applicable in social reality are those expressed in historical statements, and if these statements are subject to amendment because subject to error and sin, and hence cannot claim to represent an absolute but only a relative justice, then there is no difference between Niebuhr's philosophy of justice and the relativistic moral theory which he rejects for the reason that it does not appeal to natural law as a plausible criterion for positive law. For this relativistic moral theory asserts exactly the same thing as Niebuhr emphasizes: that the ideas men have of justice represent only relative, not absolute, values. He says:

Natural-law theories which derive absolutely valid principles of morals and politics from reason invariably introduce contingent practical applications into the definition of the principle.[41]

The principles of poltical morality, being inherently more relative than those of pure morality, cannot be stated without the introduction of relative and contingent factors.[42]

If a natural-law theory insists that absolute equality is a possibility of society, it becomes an ideology of some rebellious group which does not recognize that functional inequalities are necessary in all societies, however excessive they may be in the society which is under attack. If on the other hand functional inequalities are exactly defined, the definitions are bound to contain dubious justifications of some functional privileges, possessed by the dominant classes of the culture which hazards the definition.[43]

Even if natural-law concepts do not contain the ideological taint of a particular class or nation, they are bound to express the limited imagination of a particular epoch, which failed to take new historical possibilities into consideration. This alone would justify the ultimate freedom of a democratic society, in which not even the moral presuppositions upon which the society rests are withdrawn from constant scrutiny and re-examination. Only through such freedom can the premature arrest of new vitalities in history be prevented.[44]

A society which exempts ultimate principles from criticisms will find difficulty in dealing with the historical forces which have appropriated these truths as their special possession.[45]

These are statements to which the most radical relativist may wholeheartedly subscribe.

But Niebuhr makes the hopeless attempt to soften somehow the impression of his antiabsolutistic philosophy of justice by relativising its relativism. He thinks there are different degrees, "a descending scale of relativity." "The moral principle may be more valid than the political principles which are derived from it. The political principles may have greater validity than the specific applications by which they are made relevant to a particular situation."[46] Relativity is not a quality, like heat, which can have different degrees. The relativity of a value consists in its conditional character, and there is no possibility of being more or less conditioned. A moral or political value is conditioned or unconditioned. There are no intermediate stages between the one and the other. And the same applies to the concept of validity. That a norm referring to a certain human behavior is valid means that man ought to behave in this way and that he ought not to behave in the opposite way. There are no intermediate stages between the two situations. A general norm may be more or less effective, that is to say, in more or less cases obeyed or not obeyed. But its validity is not identical with its effectiveness. Even if it is not obeyed, and hence not effective in a concrete case, it is valid, and only if it is valid can it be disobeyed. The doctrine of a relative relativism is as untenable as the doctrine of a relative absolutism, that is, the doctrine of a relative natural law.

Tolerance on a Religious Basis Niebuhr quite correctly points out that one of the essential conditions of democracy is tolerance, and he does not ignore the fact that tolerance presupposes relativism. He says: "Democratic life requires a spirit of tolerant cooperation between individuals and groups. . . . Democracy may be challenged from without. . . . But its internal peril lies in the conflict of various schools and classes of idealists, who profess different ideals but exhibit a common conviction that their own ideals are perfect." [47] That an ideal is perfect means that it represents an absolute value. Referring to democracy he says: "Every absolute devotion to relative political ends (and all political ends are relative) is a threat to communal peace." [48] This means that democracy presupposes relativism. But he cherishes the illusion—and as a theologian he has probably no other choice—that political relativism can be based on religion. However, religion is by its very nature belief in an absolute value, in an ideal which is perfect, because it is belief in God, who is the personification of perfectness, the absolute par excellence. A religious belief which admits that the object of the belief constitutes not an absolute but only a relative value, that it represents not an absolute but only a relative truth, and that, consequently, another religion, the belief in another God, another value, another truth, is not excluded and must therefore be tolerated is a contradiction in terms. It is on this contradiction that Niebuhr's relativistic theology is based.

He quite correctly sees the decisive problem in the need of maintaining social harmony, that is, freedom and peace, in spite of religious and other cultural diversities. He says that the solution of this problem "requires a very high form of religious commitment. It demands that each religion, or each version of a single faith, seek to proclaim its highest insights while yet preserving an humble and contrite recognition of the fact that all actual expressions of religious faith are subject to historical contingency and relativity. Such a recognition creates a spirit of tolerance and makes any religious or cultural movement hesitant to claim official validity for its form of religion or to demand an official monopoly for its cult." [49] He does not go so far as to say that religious faith refers only to a relative value or relative truth. He restricts relativity to the expression of the faith. He points to "the difference between divine majesty and human creatureliness; between the unconditioned character of the divine and the conditioned character of all human enterprise." [50] The "unconditioned" character of the divine is the absoluteness of God, which is the very object of religious faith. It is only the "expression" of religious faith which, as a human enterprise, is declared by Niebuhr as conditioned, and that means as relative. But the very meaning of the expression of the faith in God is that the truth or value expressed is absolute. The absolute or relative character of a symbol—as the expression of an idea—depends on the meaning of the symbol. It is not the psychological act of expressing an idea, it is the meaning of this act which has an absolute or relative character. The expression of an idea is absolute if by this expression an absolute truth or value is meant, and it is relative if only a relative truth or value is intended or expressed. Hence if the object to which the expression refers is supposed to be absolute—and the object to which the expression of religious faith refers, God, is *the* absolute—the expression cannot be characterized as relative. Niebuhr says: "Religious faith ought . . . to encourage men to moderate their natural pride and to achieve some decent consciousness of the relativity of their own statement of even the most ultimate truth." [51] An "ultimate truth" is evidently the "ultimate answer which is given to the ultimate question about the meaning of life," and which finally determines "any scheme of values." [52] The ultimate answer to an ultimate question about the meaning of life can only be an absolute truth. But to admit that the statement about a religious truth has only a relative character means that the truth to which the statement refers is only a relative—not an ultimate, i.e., absolute—and, hence, not a religious truth, in the specific sense of this term. Niebuhr says: Religious faith ought to teach men "that their religion is most certainly true if it recognizes the element of error and sin, of finiteness and contingency which creeps into the statement of even the sublimest truth." [53] To assert that a statement is certainly true if it must be admitted that this statement is possibly erroneous is a rather paradoxical contradiction. If the content of man's faith is founded upon statements or expressions of ultimate truth made by other men, and if human expression of faith is always only relatively true, no faith can claim to be in possession of an absolute truth; and then no faith exists that can claim a really religious character. For what a religious faith distinguishes from secular opinions is just its claim to refer to the absolute. If, however, a Christian believes that his religious faith is based on revelation, that is to say, on statements or expressions made by God or by His son, then he cannot admit that "the element of error and sin, of finiteness and contingency" may creep into these statements or expressions. Niebuhr's distinction between a religious faith in the absolute and a merely relative, because human, expression of this faith is meaningful only under the presupposition that God, i.e., absolute truth and absolute value, in His transcendence, is so far beyond man that neither his rational cognition nor his irrational faith is able to reach Him, and that consequently whatever may be expressed as his faith is subject to error and hence can claim only a relative truth. The inevitable consequence of this assumption, that God as the absolute is not accessible to man, is that man cannot make any statement about His qualities or functions, His will or intentions. The theology of such a transcendent God can have no social impact at all. The will of a God absolutely unknown and unknowable to men cannot apply to human society.

Niebuhr's fundamental error is that he thinks he can base relativism on "religious humility." "The real point of contact between democracy and profound religion is in the spirit of humility which democracy requires and which must be one of the fruits of religion." [54] "According to Christian faith," he says, "the pride, which seeks to hide the conditioned and finite character of all human endeavour, is the very quintessence of sin." [55] But the Christian religion is, according to its own meaning, not a human but a divine endeavor; it is revealed by God and implanted by Him in man's heart. Even the most exaggerated pride a man takes in this religion does not and cannot constitute a sin, because this pride does not at all seek to hide the conditioned and finite character of a human endeavor. It is the natural pride of a man who is certain of an absolute, a divine truth. And this pride is compatible with, because the compensation for, the most sincere humility which manifests itself in the unconditional submission to this absolute truth. Religious humility is an emotion much too ambivalent to form the basis of a decision between democracy and autocracy.

Tolerance presupposes the relativity of the truth maintained or the value postulated; and the relativity of a truth or value implies that the opposite truth or value is not entirely excluded. This is the reason why the expression of an opposite truth or propaganda for the opposite value must not be suppressed. If men who share a definite religious belief, in their capacity as members of the government of a state, adopt a policy of tolerance toward other religions, their decision is not determined by their religious, irrational belief in the absolute but by a highly rational wish to maintain peace together with freedom within the community. In the conflict between their religious and their political views, the latter prevails. That they tolerate a religion which is in opposition to their own, that their policy presupposes relativism, whereas their religion absolutism, is inconsistent. Niebuhr quotes Chesterton's statement that "tolerance is the virtue of people who do not believe anything." [56] This statement is certainly an exaggeration. Tolerance is rather the virtue of people whose religious conviction is not strong enough to overcome their political proclivity, to prevent them from the inconsistency of recognizing the possibility and legitimacy of other religious convictions. It is just on such an inconsistency that a religious ideology of democracy is based. But it must be admitted that it is not necessarily the most consistent ideology which is the most effective one.

Since Niebuhr is in favor of democratic tolerance which presupposes a relativistic view, he has recourse to the contradictory construction of religious relativism, because as a Christian theologian he cannot accept the relativism of a rationalistic, antimetaphysical, areligious, skeptical philosophy. He refers to such a philosophy, in the already quoted statement, as "secularism which attempts to achieve cultural unity through the disavowal of traditional historical religions," [57] and he asserts that "in its more sophisticated form secularism represents a form of scepticism which is conscious of the relativity of all human perspectives." [58] But

Niebuhr's religious relativism, which insists upon the relativity of all human enterprise, seems to be not very different from this sophisticated skepticism. According to Niebuhr, the difference consists in the fact that this skeptical secularism "stands on the abyss of moral nihilism and threatens the whole of life with a sense of meaninglessness. Thus it creates a spiritual vacuum into which demonic religions easily rush." By demonic religions—as pointed out—he means, in the first place, National Socialism. But a thinker who is so deeply involved in a relativistic view of social reality as to consider even religious faith as compatible with relativism should not share the traditional misinterpretation of positivistic philosophy by dogmatic metaphysics. Skepticism does not mean that cognition is impossible. That all truth is relative does not mean that there is no truth, just as the opinion that all moral values are only relative values does not mean that there are no moral values at all; and life is not meaningless to him who admits that others may attribute to life another meaning than he can find in it. The fact that a rationalistic philosophy refuses to fill the transcendental sphere beyond human experience with the products of an imagination nourished by man's wishes and fears is not at all responsible for the rise of demonic religions. To prevent the coming into existence of such religions is not the task of a positivistic philosophy, which holds itself aloof from any kind of religion. It is the very task of the religion which claims to be the true religion. The spiritual vacuum which a "demonic religion" can fill is just within the transcendental sphere to which positivistic philosophy has no claim, but which is the specific realm of Christian religion. If there was a spiritual vacuum into which the Nazi religion rushed, it was left by Christianity. It amounts to an inadmissible shift of responsibility to ask why positivistic philosophy, and not to ask why Christianity, has failed to prevent National Socialism from filling a spiritual vacuum. And if relativism is the answer to this question, it is rather the relativism of a religion, a religious relativism, such as advocated by Niebuhr, that should be made responsible for the victory of another religion, which in its demonism maintains the illusion of absolutism. But the Nazi religion is only the ideological superstructure of a real movement which has its causes in economic and political facts and not in the insufficiency of a philosophical or religious system. And this movement has been brought to an end, not by an improved philosophy or religion, but by hard facts.

Jacques Maritain's Philosophy of Democracy A most remarkable attempt at connecting democracy with Christian religion was made by the Catholic philosopher Jacques Maritain in his book *Christianisme et démocratie.* He asserts that the democratic ideal has its origin in evangelical inspiration,[59] that is to say, in the teaching of the Gospel, that the democratic principles have been formed in the profane conscience by the action of the evangelical ferment.[60] He goes even so far as to maintain that democracy has not yet been realized. Bourgeois democracy, that is, atheistic democracy, is not the true democracy because it denies the Gospel, because the principle of democracy and the principle of Christianity have been separated. In order to become a "real" democracy, democracy must become entirely human, and it can become entirely human only by becoming Christian. Thus, only by becoming Christian can the very essence of democracy be realized.[61]

This is a device somewhat similar to that used by the Soviet doctrine of democracy, which also declares that in order to become a "real" democracy, the merely formal bourgeois democracy must turn into a democracy entirely human. The difference consists only in the fact that according to the Soviet doctrine democracy becomes entirely human, not by becoming Christian, but by becoming socialist.

Although Maritain emphasizes that the essence of democracy is Christianity, he must, on the other hand, admit that Christianity as a religious belief is indifferent with respect to political life. He says:

It is clear that Christianity and the Christian faith cannot be made subservient to any political system whatever, and hence not to democracy as a form of government or to democracy as a philosophy of human life and politics. This results from the fundamental distinction introduced by Christ between the things that belong to Caesar and the things that belong to God. . . . No doctrine or opinion of simply human origin, as true as it might be, only things revealed by God are imposed on the faith of the Christian soul. One may be a Christian and seek salvation in fighting for any political regime whatever, under the condition that it does not violate the natural law and the law of God. One can be a Christian and seek salvation by defending a political philosophy other than the democratic philosophy, just as one could be a Christian at the time of the Roman empire while accepting the social regime of slavery or, in the seventeenth century, while adhering to the political regime of the absolute monarchy.[62]

It is difficult to understand how the very essence of democracy can be Christianity if Christianity as a religion is indifferent to political systems in accordance with Christ's distinction between political and religious matters, if a man can be a good Christian without being a democrat, and even adhering to the autocratic ideal. Maritain cannot deny that the Catholic church, in the name of Christian religion, has supported autocratic regimes and opposed democratic movements as long as they were not successful. He frankly admits:

We have seen the directing forces of the Christian social strata fight during a century against the democratic aspirations in the name of religion.[63]

It was not for the believers entirely faithful to the Catholic dogma, it was for rationalists to proclaim in France the rights of man and citizen.[64]

Neither Locke nor Jean Jacques Rousseau nor the Encyclopedists can be considered as thinkers faithfully maintaining the integrity of the Christian treasure.[65]

Maritain explains this fact as follows: it is not Christianity as a religious creed and a way to eternal life to which he refers when asserting an essential relationship between democracy and Christianity; it is Christianity as ferment of the social and political life of the people and as bearer of the temporal hope of man. It is not Christianity as treasury of divine truth, maintained and propagated by the church, it is Christianity as a historic energy at work in the world. It is not at the heights of theology but in the depths of profane conscience and profane existence that Christianity works,[66] that is to say, that Christianity becomes an essential element of democracy, that it constitutes a "real" democracy. But Christianity is by its very nature a religious creed; it can be a ferment of political life, a historic energy at work in the world only insofar as the Christian religious creed, its faith in a divine truth and its hope of eternal life, ferment the political life, as this creed becomes a historic energy working in the world. But if Christianity as religious creed is politically indifferent, it cannot ferment political life and cannot become a historic energy at work in the world; consequently there cannot be an essential connection between Christianity and any political system. Maritain speaks of a "secularized Christianity," [67] but this is a contradiction in terms.

It is perhaps possible to maintain—though it is difficult to prove—that a democratic government is more efficient when Christianity is the predominant religion of the people than if there is another religion or no religion at all prevailing, just as one may maintain that a democratic government is more efficient when it guarantees a capitalist rather than a socialist economic system, or vice versa. Maritain, who wrote his book during the Second World War, says: the Western democracies can win the peace after having won the war only "if the Christian inspiration and the democratic inspiration recognize each other and are reconciled." [68] This may be true; but even if true, it does not demonstrate an essential connection between democracy and Christianity. The question of the essence of democracy should not be confused with the question of the efficiency of democratic government. In the third part of this essay I shall show that it is not possible to demonstrate a connection between the essence of democracy and a definite economic system, even if it were possible to prove that democracy works better if associated with this than with another economic system. The same is true with respect to the relationship between democracy and religion: one cannot maintain that there exists a connection between the essence of democracy and a definite religious system because this system guarantees to democratic government a higher degree of efficiency than any other religious system. The antique democracy was connected with a religion totally different from Christianity, and there is no reason to assume that a people who have another than a Christian religion should not be able to establish a true democracy. There are, as a matter of fact, at the present time democratic states within the non-Christian part of humanity, such as Mohammedan, Jewish, Hindu democracies. What Maritain actually tries to show is not exactly an essential relationship between democracy and Christian religion, but a relationship between democracy and certain moral-political principles which he supposes to have the character of natural law and which he—without sufficient reason—identifies, or considers to be in harmony, with the evangelical law (*"loi évangélique"*) [69] as the specific Christian morality. There is, however, only one principle of morality which is specifically Christian because it is enunciated by Christ and embraced by no other moral system: to give up retribution, not to requite good with good and evil with evil, but to requite evil with good, to love not only our neighbor but also our enemy, which means not punishing the evildoer but forgiving him. This is the new principle of Christian justice, the principle of love. But this principle is inapplicable in political reality; it is incompatible with any state as an order providing for coercive acts to be directed against the lawbreaker. The other principles of Christian morality are not specifically Christian or evangelic; they are proclaimed also—and have been proclaimed prior to the Gospel—by other moral systems and are applicable within any society and not only in a democratically organized community.

For a confirmation of his thesis of the evangelical character of democracy Maritain refers to the statement of the French philosopher Henri Bergson: "Democracy is by its very nature evangelical, its moving force is love." [70] If love, the love of Christ, were really the moving force of democracy, then and only then could it be maintained that democracy is essentially connected with Christianity. But it is evident that this is not and cannot be the case. Bergson's statement is but a hyperbolic expression of the fact to which I have referred in the first part of this essay, that the democratic form of government corresponds rather to the peace-loving than to the aggressive type of character. But the love of peace within a political society is something quite different from the evangelical love, and the fact that democracy is congenial to the peace-loving type of man does not mean that the principle of democracy can be deduced from love of peace and certainly not that it can be realized only on the basis of the love of God taught by Christ.

Democracy and the Gospel How does Maritain demonstrate that the democratic ideal has its origin in the teaching of the Gospel, that it has been formed in the profane conscience by the action of the evangelical ferment, that it is a temporal manifestation of the evangelical inspiration? He says that through the mysterious force of evangelical inspiration the profane conscience has comprehended that the authority of the government "can be exercised only with the consent of the governed," [71] that the government acts only as "delegate or representative" of the people.[72] This is indeed the most important principle of democracy. But it is hardly possible to derive it from the Gospel. The teaching of Christ did not refer to any form of government. From what He said we can only infer that He was in favor of no government whatsoever, that He was far from justifying any government. If we accept the traditional interpretation of His saying, "render to God what belongs to God, and to Caesar what belongs to Caesar," He did not directly deny the right of an absolute monarch to be exercised in this aeon, that is to say, prior to the coming of the Kingdom of God. His concern was this Kingdom of God, which He considered as imminent and of which He believed that it would bring to an end all earthly governments. Consequently the question as to the just form of earthly government did not exist for Him at all. St. Paul, on the other hand, was very much concerned with the relationship of the followers of Christ to the earthly government. And his teaching is in direct opposition to that which Maritain presents as the result of evangelic inspiration. St. Paul did not teach that the authority of the government can be exercised only with the consent of the governed, which implies that an autocratic government has no authority to be respected by a Christian, that such a government is unjust or unlawful. Instead he admonished the followers of Christ to consider the authority of any established government, including governments exercised without the consent of the governed, as ordained by God; and thus he justified any form of an established government.

In complete conformity with the teaching of St. Paul, the Christian church—Catholic as well as Protestant—has supported the authority of every established government, autocratic or democratic. To be sure, the Catholic as well as the Protestant churches were, for obvious reasons, more in favor of an autocratic than a democratic government. They furnished absolute monarchy with its most effective ideology: the doctrine that the monarch has his authority by the grace of God, that he is in temporal matters the delegate or representative of God, not of the people. But when a democratic government was firmly established, the Catholic as well as the Protestant churches were willing to support such a government too. It is true that they gave their approval only on the condition that the government did not prevent or restrict the practice of the Christian religion. This, however, did not mean that the church required religious tolerance. The Catholic church had nothing against the suppression by the government of the Protestant, and the Protestant church nothing against the suppression of the Catholic religion. The Crusades against the Moslems, the believers in the faith established by Mohammed, who were significantly called the infidels, were initiated by the Christian church, and could much more easily be based on evangelical inspiration than on the democratic principles of political self-determination and tolerance of any religious or political creed.

Maritain ascribes the democratic principle of equality to evangelical inspiration by referring to the teaching of the Gospel that all men are the children of God and created in His image.[73] But the idea that men are equal before God applies much better to autocracy than to democracy. For it is based on the absolute inequality which exists in the relation between the ruler and the ruled. Men are equal before God, although God has created them as different personalities, because all their differences are irrelevant in view of the fundamental difference which exists in the relation between men and God. Democratic equality, on the other hand, implies the equality that is supposed to exist in the relation between those who exercise the government and those who are subject to that government, because the governed participate in the government, because democracy as political self-determination means identity of the ruled with the rulers. Hence there is an essential difference between the democratic and the evangelic equality.

Maritain considers dignity [74] of the human personality as a democratic principle and assumes that it is also an element of the teaching of the Gospel. That is true. But it is not specifically evangelical, since it is advocated also by philosophies and religions which are independent of the Gospel. There is no sufficient reason to attribute this ideal to evangelical inspiration. It is even doubtful whether the dignity of the human personality is not seriously impaired by the Christian obligation of unconditional obedience to the will of God, by the absoluteness of the divine government to which man is subject. As a matter of fact, it is precisely an antireligious rationalistic philosophy which emphasizes the value of the individual in opposition to a superindividual authority, be it state or God. There can be no doubt that the dignity of the human personality is respected within a social order which guarantees to this personality political autonomy to a much higher degree than within a religious order which is based on the principle of heteronomy, that is to say, on the principle that a religious man is subject to a divine law in the establishment of which he has no share at all. In order to neutralize that principle and to save the dignity of the human personality, Christian theology has introduced the doctrine of the freedom of will. But this doctrine cannot be supported by the teaching of the Gospel and is hardly compatible with the assumption of an omnipotent, all-determining will of God, the consequence of which is the belief in predestination.

Maritain says: "It is in its radical opposition to the philosophy of slavery (*philosophie esclavagiste*) that we can see most clearly the essential characteristics of the democratic philosophy of man and society." [75] This is not quite correct, since slavery was a legal institution of the antique democracy, and the American democracy abolished slavery long after the Declaration of Independence. It is, however, true that a state which does not recognize slavery, if it is a government by the people, is in a higher degree democratic than a government by the people under which slavery is permitted. Just as the exclusion of women from political rights is not democratic, and, nevertheless, we will not deny that Switzerland is a democracy although women there have no right to vote. However that may be, the condemnation of slavery is certainly not due to evangelical inspiration. Christ did not reject it, and St. Paul decidedly recognized it:

Slaves, be obedient to those who are your earthly masters, with fear and trembling, in singleness of heart, as to Christ; not in the way of eye service as men—pleasers, but as servants of Christ, doing the will of God from the heart, rendering service with a good will as to the Lord and not to men, knowing that whatever good any one does, he will receive the same again from the Lord, whether he is a slave or free.[76]

Let all who are under the yoke of slavery regard their masters as worthy of all honor, so that the name of God and the teaching may not be defamed. Those who have believing masters must not be disrespectful on the ground that they are brethren; rather they must serve all the better since those who benefit by their service are believers and beloved.[77]

To serve as a slave means to fulfil the will of God; evangelical brotherhood is perfectly compatible with slavery. This, and not opposition to slavery, is evangelical inspiration.

NOTES

I. Democracy and Philosophy

1. This paper was first presented as public lectures under the Charles R. Walgreen Foundation for the Study of American Institutions at the University of Chicago in April, 1954.

2. Cf. Ithiel de Sola Pool, *Symbols of Democracy* ("Hoover Institute Studies"; Stanford: Stanford University Press, 1952), p. 2.

3. Cf. my *General Theory of Law and State* (Cambridge: Harvard University Press, 1945), pp. 113 ff.

4. Joseph A. Schumpeter, *Capitalism, Socialism and Democracy* (New York and London: Harper & Bros., 1942), p. 242.

5. *Ibid.*, p. 271.

6. *Ibid.*, p. 243, note.

7. *Ibid.*, p. 243.

8. Cf. N. S. Timasheff, "The Soviet Concept of Democracy," *Review of Politics,* XII (1950), 506 ff.

9. Lenin, "State and Revolution," in *Selected Works,* ed. J. Fineburg (New York: International Publishers, 1935-38), VII, 80. Italics supplied.

10. Lenin, "Bourgeois Democracy and Proletarian Dictatorship" *[loc. cit.]*, p. 231.

11. Lenin, "Speech to the 9th Congress of CPSU" (March 31, 1920) *[loc. cit.]*, VIII, 222.

12. *Pravda*, August, 1945. Italics supplied.

13. Lenin, "State and Revolution," *op. cit.*, p. 91.

14. If one accepts the Marxian doctrine that the so-called dictatorship of the proletariat is true democracy, one may arrive at the concept of a "totalitarian democracy." J. L. Talmon, *The Rise of Totalitarian Democracy* (Boston: Beacon Press, 1952), tries to show "that concurrently with the liberal type of democracy there emerged from the same premises in the eighteenth century a trend towards what we propose to call the totalitarian type of democracy. . . . The tension between them has constituted an important chapter in modern history, and has now become the most vital issue of our time" (p. 1). Liberal democracy is, according to Talmon, characterized by the idea of freedom defined as "spontaneity and the absence of coercion," whereas totalitarian democracy is based on the belief that "freedom is to be realized only in the pursuit and attainment of an absolute collective purpose." The final aims of liberal democracy "are conceived in rather negative terms, and the use of force for their realization is considered as an evil." Totalitarian democracy "aims at the maximum of social justice and security," its "purpose" is thought "to constitute the fullest satisfaction of his [man's] true interest, and to be the guar-

antee of his freedom" (p. 2). "Modern totalitarian democracy is a dictatorship resting on popular enthusiasm completely different from absolute power wielded by a divine king or by a usurping tyrant" (p. 6). If "popular enthusiasm" cannot manifest itself through an electoral system based on universal, equal, free, and secret suffrage, its existence is more than problematical. It is not an objectively ascertainable fact, but an unproved assumption which may be, and actually has been, used for the ideological justification of every—even the most tyrannical—government. The "divine-right kings" have always maintained that their government is based on the love of their people; and there is no essential difference between the "love" and the "enthusiasm" of the people. If popular enthusiasm is the criterion of democracy, then the dictatorship of the National Socialist party is just as much a democracy as the dictatorship of the Communist party. If democracy can be a dictatorship, then the concept of democracy has lost its specific meaning, and there is no difference between democracy and autocracy. The antagonism which Talmon describes as tension between liberal and totalitarian democracy is in truth the antagonism between liberalism and socialism and not between two types of democracy. There are, indeed, two types of democracy, a democracy with restricted, and a democracy with unrestricted, power of government; the latter is the older, the original type, which, however, did not rise as late as in the eighteenth century but had already come into existence in antiquity. The common element of both, the criterion according to which the restricted, as well as the unrestricted, government is a democracy, is the fact that the government is exercised either directly by a popular assembly or by representatives elected on the basis of universal, equal, free, and secret suffrage. It is by ignoring this essential fact that Talmon—like the Soviet theory—can present a dictatorship as a democracy.

15. Eric Voegelin, *The New Science of Politics* (Chicago: University of Chicago Press, 1952), pp. 27 ff.

16. *Ibid.*, p. 32.

17. *Ibid.*, p. 49.

18. *Ibid.*, p. 32.

19. *Ibid.*, p. 31.

20. *Ibid.*, p. 33.

21. *Ibid.*, p. 38.

22. *Ibid.*

23. *Ibid.*, p. 36.

24. *Ibid.*, p. 49.

25. Cf. my *Vom Wesen und Wert der Demokratie* (2d ed.; Tübingen: J. C. B. Mohr [P. Siebeck], 1929) and *Staatsform und Weltanschauung* (Tübingen: J. C. B. Mohr [P. Siebeck], 1933).

26. John H. Hallowell, *The Moral Foundation of Democracy* (Chicago: University of Chicago Press, 1954), p. 120, says: "What is demanded by the democratic form of government is not submission to the will of the majority because that will is numerically superior but rather submission to the reasoned judgment of the majority." According to this author, the principle of majority rule does not demand "that we abandon all qualitative judgments in favor of a quantitative method." If this is true the question arises as to who is competent to decide whether the judgment of the majority is or is not "reasoned." The decision could be made only by the individual obligated to submit to the decision of the majority. Then submission to the decision of the majority depends in the last analysis on the discretion of the individual, which means anarchy, not democracy.

27. Lenin, "State and Revolution," *op. cit.*, pp. 81, 246.

28. The relativistic philosophy of values makes compromise possible, but compromise is not the essence or the "animating principle" of democracy. (Cf. Hallowell, *op. cit.*, pp. 27 f.) The essence or the animating principle of democracy is freedom combined with equality.

29. A typical representative of this doctrine is the one expounded by Carl Schmitt, who enjoyed temporary success as ideologist for National Socialism. In

his *Verfassungslehre* (Munich and Leipzig: Duncker & Humblot, 1928), he tried to obliterate the difference between democracy and dictatorship. He admitted that the rule of the Soviets in Russia and of the Fascists in Italy were dictatorships (pp. 81 f.). And dictatorship, he said, is characterized by the fact "that the competence of the dictator is not precisely determined by general norms but that the extent and content of his authorization depends on his own discretion" (p. 237). He further maintained that the principle of majority-vote decision was not specifically democratic but liberal (p. 82). The "will of the people" may be expressed in "irresistible acclamations and an uncontested public opinion" which "have nothing to do with the procedure of secret voting and statistical ascertainment of majority. In such a case it is even not certain that a subsequent secret voting will confirm the spontaneous eruption and expression of the will of the people. For the public opinion, as a rule, is produced only by an active politically interested minority of the people, whereas the overwhelming majority of the enfranchised citizens are not necessarily politically interested. Hence it is not at all democratic, and would be a strange political principle, that those who have no political will should have the power to decide against the others who have such a will" (p. 279). Consequently, Schmitt declares, "dictatorship is possible only on a democratic basis" (p. 237).

30. Benito Mussolini, "La Dottrina de Fascismo," *Enciclopedia Italiana*, XIV (1932), 847-51.

31. It is a gross misinterpretation of the relativistic value theory of positivism to assume—as does, e.g., John H. Hallowell—that it implies the view that there are no values at all, that "there is no moral law or moral order" (*op. cit.*, p. 76), that democracy is a mere "fiction" and that consequently the struggle against autocracy (or tyranny) "is both meaningless and futile," and that "we had best now surrender to the inevitable" (p. 21). Positivistic relativism means only that value judgments in general—without which human actions are not possible—and in particular the judgment that democracy is a good or the best form of government, cannot be proved by means of rational, scientific cognition to be absolute, that is to say, excluding the possibility of a contrary value judgment. Democracy, if actually established, is also from the point of view of a relativistic value theory the realization of a value and in this sense, though the value is only a relative one, a reality and not a mere fiction. If somebody prefers democracy to autocracy because freedom is to him the highest value, nothing can be more meaningful to him than to struggle for democracy and against autocracy, and that means to create for him and those who share his political ideal the social conditions which they consider to be the best. If those who prefer democracy are numerous enough, their struggle is not futile at all but may be highly successful. Hence they have not the slightest reason to accept autocracy as inevitable. The only consequence of a relativistic theory of values is: not to force democracy upon those who prefer another form of government, to remain aware in the struggle for one's own political ideal that the opponents, too, may be fighting for an ideal, and that this fight should be conducted in the spirit of tolerance.

A relativistic value theory does not deny the existence of a moral order and, therefore, is not—as it is sometimes maintained—incompatible with moral or legal responsibility. It denies that there exists only one such order that alone may claim to be recognized as valid and, hence, as universally applicable. It asserts that there are several moral orders quite different from one another, and that consequently a choice must be made among them. Thus relativism imposes upon the individual the difficult task of deciding for himself what is right and what is wrong. This, of course, implies a very serious responsibility, the most serious moral responsibility a man can assume. Positivistic relativism means: moral autonomy.

The assumption that there exist absolute values and that these values can be deduced from reality by means of rational cognition presupposes the view that value is immanent in reality. Hallowell formulates this assumption as a principle of what he calls "classical realism," "that being and goodness belong together. Through knowledge of what we are, we obtain knowledge of what we ought to do. To know what man is, is to know what he should be and do" (p. 25). This principle is based on a logical fallacy. It is the typical fallacy of the natural law doctrine. There is no rational possibility of inferring from that what is that what ought to be or to be done. As goodness is not thinkable without badness, not only being and goodness but also being and badness belong together. Since being in itself does not contain a criterion to distinguish the good from the bad—the good is not more or less "being" than the bad—it is not possible to obtain knowledge of what we ought to do through knowledge of what we are; we "are" good as well as bad. From the fact that men are and always have been waging war, thus demonstrating that war cannot be incompatible with human nature, it does not follow either that war ought to be or that war ought not to be. Hence it is not possible to deduce from our knowledge of what is in general and what we are in particular "universally applicable principles in terms of which we can guide our individual and social life toward the perfection of that which is distinctively human" (pp. 25-26), meaning moral principles constituting absolute social values. As a matter of fact, the most contradictory principles have been presented as being obtained through knowledge of "what we are" or, what amounts to the same thing, as deduced from human nature.

The principle "that being and goodness belong together" and that through knowledge of what is we obtain knowledge of what ought to be done can be maintained only on a religious basis, that is, on the basis of the belief that the existing world is created by God and thus is the realization of His absolutely good will; that man is formed in the image of God and hence human reason is somehow connected with divine reason. It is just this belief to which Hallowell, quite consistently, appeals. "We must recover," he emphasizes, "the belief in man as a unique being whose reason is a reflection of the image of God" and must recover "the theological foundations upon which the belief in natural law rests" (p. 83). If, abandoning the realm of science, we recover this belief and the theological foundations of natural law, a moral—and that means under these conditions a religious—foundation of democracy becomes more than problematical. It was precisely on the basis of a theological natural law doctrine that Robert Filmer rejected democracy as contrary to human nature and thus not in conformity with the will of God. As to the relationship between democracy and religion, I refer to the second part of this study.

32. J. L. Stocks, *Reason and Intuition* (London and New York: Oxford University Press, 1939), p. 143, says: "There is a close natural connection between the prevalence of democratic ideals in politics and the practice of methodical empiricism in science and other fields of thought . . . it is striking to observe that those countries in which the empirical tendency in thought has been most persistent are also those countries in which democracy has struck deepest root. It is surely no accident that among the Great Powers of Europe, France and England are at once the most democratic and the most empirical in their outlook on the world, while Germany which is the least democratic, is the most friendly to ambitious metaphysical systems." Sidney Hook in an article "The Philosophical Presuppositions of Democracy," *Ethics*, LII (1942), 275-96, maintains "that there is no necessary logical connection between a theory of being or becoming and any particular theory of ethics or politics. Stated more accurately, it seems to me demonstrable that no system of metaphysics univocally determines a system of ethics or politics" (p. 284). However, he admits: "The evidence seems to me to be overwhelming that there is a definite historical connection between the social movement of a period and its metaphysical teachings; further, I am prepared to defend as a historically true proposition that systems of idealistic metaphysics, because of the semi-official roles they have played in their respective cultures, have been more generally employed to bolster antidemocratic social movements than systems of empirical or materialistic metaphysics" (pp. 283-84). He also states: "If empiricism be a generic term for the philosophic attitude which submits *all* claims of fact and value to test by experience, then empiricism as a philosophy is more congenial to a democratic than to an antidemocratic com-

munity, for it brings into open light of criticism the interests in which moral values and social institutions are rooted" (p. 280). Hook distinguishes two kinds of metaphysics as theory of being and becoming, an "idealistic" and an "empirical or materialistic" metaphysics, and he assumes, it seems, that the idealistic metaphysics goes hand in hand with belief in supernatural religious truths (cf. p. 280). I am using the term metaphysics only in the latter sense. I, too, do not maintain that there exists a "necessary logical" connection between democracy and empirical relativism, on the one hand, and autocracy and metaphysical absolutism, on the other. The relationship which I assume to exist between the two political and the corresponding philosophical systems may very well be characterized as "congeniality." But Hook does not take into consideration the relationship between philosophical absolutism, essentially connected with "idealistic" metaphysics, and political absolutism, i.e., autocracy, on the one hand, and philosophical relativism, essentially connected with empiricism, and democracy, on the other. It is just this relationship which seems to me to be of the greatest importance.

II. Democracy and Religion

1. Emil Brunner, *Gerechtigkeit: Eine Lehre von den Grundgesetzen der Gesellschaftsordnung* (Zürich: Zwingli Verlag, 1943). English translation: *Justice and the Social Order*, trans. Mary Hottinger (London and Redhill: Lutterworth Press; New York: Harper & Bros., 1945). Quotations used by permission of Harper & Bros.
2. Reinhold Niebuhr, *The Children of Light and the Children of Darkness: A Vindication of Democracy and a Critique of Its Traditional Defense* (New York: Charles Scribner's Sons, 1950). Copyrighted by Charles Scribner's Sons. Reprinted by permission of the publisher.
3. Jacques Maritain, *Christianisme et démocratie* (Paris: P. Hartmann, 1943).
4. Brunner, *op. cit.*, p. 13.
5. *Ibid.*, p. 14.
6. *Ibid.*, p. 15.
7. *Ibid.*
8. *Ibid.*, pp. 15 ff.
9. *Ibid.*, p. 17.
10. *Ibid.*, p. 16.
11. *Ibid.*, p. 17.
12. *Ibid.*, pp. 27 ff.
13. *Ibid.*, p. 17.
14. *Ibid.*, p. 57.
15. *Ibid.*, p. 235.
16. Niebuhr, *op. cit.*, p. 126.
17. *Ibid.*, p. 133.
18. *Ibid.*, p. 134.
19. *Ibid.*, pp. x ff.
20. *Ibid.*, p. 82.
21. *Ibid.*, pp. 86 ff.
22. *Ibid.*, p. 82.
23. *Ibid.*, p. 125.
24. *Ibid.*, p. xi.
25. *Ibid.*, p. x.
26. *Ibid.*, p. 189.
27. *Ibid.*, p. x.
28. *Ibid.*, p. 39.
29. Wilhelm von Humboldt, "Ideen zu einem Versuch die Gränzen der Wirksamkeit des Staats zu bestimmen," *Gesammelte Werke*, Bd. VII (Berlin: Georg Reimer, 1852).
30. Niebuhr, *op. cit.*, p. 28.

31. *Ibid.*, p. 39.
32. *Ibid.*, pp. 39 ff.
33. *Ibid.*, p. xiii.
34. *Ibid.*, p. xii.
35. *Ibid.*
36. *Ibid.*, pp. 67 ff.
37. *Ibid.*, p. 68.
38. *Ibid.*, p. 71.
39. *Ibid.*, pp. 70 ff.
40. *Ibid.*, p. 71.
41. *Ibid.*, p. 72.
42. *Ibid.*, p. 73.
43. *Ibid.*, p. 74.
44. *Ibid.*
45. *Ibid.*, p. 75.
46. *Ibid.*, pp. 74 ff.
47. *Ibid.*, pp. 151 ff.
48. *Ibid.*, p. 151.
49. *Ibid.*, pp. 134 ff.
50. *Ibid.*, p. 135.
51. *Ibid.*
52. *Ibid.*, p. 125.
53. *Ibid.*, p. 135.
54. *Ibid.*, p. 151.
55. *Ibid.*, p. 135.
56. *Ibid.*, p. 130.
57. *Ibid.*, p. 126.
58. *Ibid.*, p. 133.
59. Jacques Maritain, *op. cit.*, p. 33.
60. *Ibid.*, p. 65.
61. *Ibid.*, pp. 31 ff., 36.
62. *Ibid.*, pp. 42 ff.
63. *Ibid.*, p. 33.
64. *Ibid.*, p. 44.
65. *Ibid.*, p. 47.
66. *Ibid.*, pp. 43 ff.
67. *Ibid.*, p. 49.
68. *Ibid.*, p. 35.
69. He says that "political life shall conform to natural law and, according to the conditions of its temporal object, to the evangelical law itself" (*ibid.*, p. 60).
70. Henri Bergson, *Les deux sources de la morale et de la religion* (Paris: F. Alcan, 1932), p. 304; Maritain, *op. cit.*, p. 78.
71. Maritain, *op. cit.*, p. 57.
72. *Ibid.*, p. 58.
73. *Ibid.*, p. 51.
74. *Ibid.*, p. 54.
75. *Ibid.*, p. 76.
76. Eph. 6:5-8.
77. Tim. 6:1-2.

DEMOCRACY *

Richard Wollheim

. . . Contemporary discussions of Democracy may be brought under four rough headings: the *meaning* of Democracy, the *conditions* of Democracy, the *justification* of Democracy, and the *relation of Democracy to other political concepts and principles.*

1. The problem of the meaning of Democracy arises as soon as one considers with any degree of literalness the word itself: *democracy,* the "rule of the people." For contrast this with other similar words, such as *pluto-cracy,* "rule of the rich," and *theo-cracy,* the "rule of the priests." [1] Immediately two questions assert themselves. In the first place, how can the people rule in the way in which the rich or the priests clearly can? For surely there are too many of them for it to be a practical possibility. And secondly, if the people rule, who is there left to be ruled? (It is to be observed that in the classical world neither of these two questions arose with the force that they do for us. For in the first place, the City State was generally small enough to permit the people to participate directly in government. Secondly, to most classical thinkers the word "demos" meant the people in the sense of "the common people" or "the ordinary man," or, more simply, "the poor," not in the modern sense of "the people as a whole," or "every member of society": in conse-

* This article was prepared in cooperation with the project of a "Dictionary of Fundamental Terms of Philosophy and Political Thought" sponsored by the International Council for Philosophy and Humanistic Studies and planned and carried out with the assistance of UNESCO. [Editor's Note: The plan of the Dictionary is to inquire into the divergent meanings of terms in different cultural traditions and therefore five essays in five different languages (French, German, Italian, Spanish, and English) are planned to trace the history of each concept from the common classical background to the peculiar development attached to the term in the language and cultural tradition of the author. The work is directed by an international editorial committee made up of Professors A. J. Ayer (Great Britain), Hans Barth (Switzerland), G. Calogero (Italy), R. Klibansky (Canada), A. Koyré (France), E. Garcia Maynez (Mexico), R. McKeon (United States), and J. Wahl (France.]
Reprinted from *Journal of the History of Ideas,* vol. XIX, no. 2 (April, 1958), 233-242. By permission of the author and the publisher.

quence if the demos ruled, this left the rich and the noble to be ruled over.)

Two traditions of democratic thought can be identified by the way in which they treat this problem. One tradition, stemming ultimately from Rousseau, insists on taking this problem very literally and proposing to it a radical and peculiar solution. To begin with, all the members of society are said to possess two wills or selves: a "true" or "real" self, and an "arbitrary" or "fitful" self. All the true selves in any community are harmonious in their demands, whereas it is a mark of the arbitrary selves that they are discordant. In terms of this para-psychological assumption the two questions outlined above—or the "paradox of self-government," as a thinker of this school, Bernard Bosanquet called it—are readily solved. For to the first question, how can the people rule, being so many and so diverse?, the reply comes that it is their better selves that rule, and these selves, though naturally diverse, are necessarily harmonious. Secondly, to the question, who remains to be ruled if everyone rules?, the answer is given that though in a Democracy the ruled are certainly different from the rulers as much as they are in a plutocracy or in a theocracy, they are however different, not in being different people, but in being different parts of the same people—that is, the ruled are the arbitrary or fitful selves of those whose real or true selves are the rulers.[2]

This tradition of thought, for all its metaphysical neatness, would appear to raise as many problems as it solves; and these further problems to be debarred of solution. For no empirical method is suggested whereby we can recognize or pick out the dictates of the true or real selves as opposed to those of the arbitrary selves. Indeed, when, as usually happens in this tradition of thought, the true self is further identified with the moral self, it is clear that no such method could be provided without falling into the errors of ethical Naturalism. From all this one might well assume that this "idealist" tradition of democratic thought would lead to a total and barren scepticism about democratic practice. In fact the result has been rather different. Idealist thinkers have been led to support the notion of a supreme legislator or leader who would be able to penetrate the surface of conflicting individual desires and intuit the underlying rational and harmonious will of the community. Such a conception has been called "Totalitarian Democracy."[3] If in Anglo-American political thought, little or no attention has ever been paid by "idealist" thinkers to this very difficult problem of the practical interpretation of their theory, such self-denial, though saying something for their political wisdom, scarcely redounds to their intellectual credit.

A different answer to this problem is provided by a school of thought, more empiricist in outlook, which seeks to remove the so-called paradox at an earlier stage. On this view, though in a Democracy the people rule, they do not rule in the sense in which the rich might rule in a plutocracy or the priests in a theocracy; that is to say, they do not rule in the sense of holding in their own hands and wielding directly the supreme legislative and executive powers. They rule in a modified sense in that they exercise some control over the use of these powers. And in this sense of ruling, the argument continues, there can be no difficulty in seeing how the people, many of them though there may be, can rule. Equally, on this view, there is no difficulty in seeing how the people can at once rule and be ruled. For the supreme legislative and executive powers, like any other external force or instrument, can be controlled *by* a group of people and yet also exercised *over* that group. This empiricist solution differs from the idealist solution above in that the paradox that is supposed to arise from the fact that the rulers and the ruled are in a Democracy identical, is disposed of, not by any dialectical legerdemain leading to a radical reinterpretation of political experience, but by an analysis which seeks to understand the concept of "rule" or "government" as it appears in the context of democratic thought, without in any way altering it.

However, it would be a mistake to assume that this empiricist view does not also give rise to further problems. For though it may answer the difficulties connected with the size or vastness of the ruling group in a Democracy, it still leaves unsettled those which arise or are alleged to arise out of its diversities and disharmonies. If the people do not agree upon how the supreme legislative and executive powers of the community are to be used—as they most likely will not —how can they control the use of these powers? Such difficulties certainly exist. It is, however, error to regard these as metaphysical or logical, rather than practical, difficulties. For there is no absurdity or inconsistency or self-contradiction in supposing the people to exert control over policy even when the policy pursued is not to the taste of all. The only issue is whether the method employed for selecting policy by aggregating tastes is "reasonable" or "fair," and this issue is practical.

In Anglo-Saxon countries the usual method employed for ensuring popular control is that of representative institutions with a composition determined by specific electoral procedures, and these methods have over the years been found to satisfy the natural or intuitive demands of "reasonableness" and "fairness." However, it needs to be emphasized that all these devices are no more than well-tried means of securing democratic control: none of them logically guarantees such control.

Though much of the criticism levelled at representative institutions is grossly exaggerated in that it assimilates the abuses of the system to its necessary concomitants, it does provide certain healthy reminders of how the system can go wrong. These may be brought under four headings:

a. The society may be so sunk in apathy or swept away by hysteria that the majority vote is untypical of the considered ideas and desires of the majority of the society. To guard against apathy certain democratic countries have introduced compulsory voting (Australia, Belgium, Switzerland, etc.). In spite of the arguments that can be put forward in favor of this measure—most of which were raised in the debates in the Australian Parliament on its introduction in 1924—it has generally been regarded as "undemocratic" in itself. Against mass hysteria no plausible constitutional safeguard has yet been proposed.

b. The society may be entirely reasonable and balanced in its voting habits, and yet, through some technical aspect of the electoral procedure, it may be impossible to arrive at a decision that can properly be said to represent the wishes of the majority. The limiting case which arises for any electoral procedure is where each of the alternatives voted upon attracts an equal number of voters, for then no decision whatsoever is forthcoming. A more difficult case is where a decision is forthcoming, but this clearly does not tally with what ordinarily or intuitively would be thought to be the majority will. It can be demonstrated that for every known "reasonable" method of voting if the alternatives are three or more there is a situation in which this is bound to happen.[4] The only absolutely foolproof system is where every elector votes in turn on every pair of alternatives—a scarcely practical method.[5] (Proportional representation, often at this stage recommended as a panacea, merely transfers these difficulties from the electoral stage to the legislative stage.)

c. The society may know its own mind, express it unequivocally through the electoral procedure, and then the majority so established may enforce its policy with a complete disregard for the desires, interests or rights of the minority. Fears of the "tyranny of the majority" were a constant theme in the nineteenth century, the great age of democratic thought. In the twentieth century, the great age of democratic practice, these fears have not on the whole been realized—though, significantly, where they have been, the reality has been on a scale far exceeding the worst envisaged. It would seem that the problem here is sociological rather than political, in that social conditioning is more likely to be an effective remedy than a system of constitutional checks and balances.

d. The majority may know its own mind; express it through the electoral mechanism, and the majority so constituted so far from tyrannizing over the minority, may fail even to exert rule over it. For power can fall into the hands of a minority within the majority. Some thinkers have indeed claimed that any machinery of majority rule is bound to put effective control into the hands of a minority. But this would seem to be exaggeration. Since the end of the last century, increasing attention has, however, been paid to the oligarchic tendencies implicit in democratic machinery: in particular, those relating to party organization and program construction.

Perhaps the most important single lesson to be learned from these objections is that Democracy cannot be self-guaranteeing. It is exposed to risks, in the first place, from the mechanism that is devised to implement it, and secondly, from the other elements in society. It has been called justifiably, a "calculated risk."[6]

2. The question of the conditions of Democracy, i.e., what must exist for Democracy to exist, is one of the great problems of the age. Unfortunately, a great deal of contemporary discussion of it is bedevilled by an essential ambiguity in the nature of the question. It is often unclear whether the question is *logical,* i.e., what conditions must be satisfied for us to say correctly that Democracy exists, or *empirical,* i.e., what conditions must exist elsewhere in society for Democracy to come into existence and to survive.[7] Such ambiguity is common in theoretical arguments, but in this context there are two additional factors to account for its persistence. One is the absence of any developed sociology of politics; and the other is the extreme prestige attached to the word "Democracy," so that writers tend to take over any concomitant of Democracy that they like and write about it as if it were part of Democracy.

In contemporary discussions of the conditions of Democracy, three issues have been singled out for particular attention:

a. The connection between Democracy and Socialism. Those who assert that there is a real connection between the two may be divided into three groups:

First, there are the Marxists. These are sometimes taken to assert that Democracy is incomplete without socialism. This, however, is a misunderstanding of their true position. For what they wish to do is not so much to extend the concept of Democracy as to transpose it completely. Believing in what has been called the "impotence of politics,"[8] they are indifferent to constitutional and political organization, but at the same time want to secure the full prestige of this concept for their own preference in what they consider to be the truly important field—that of economic organization. It is significant that the use of the word "Democracy" as a word of praise in Marxist thought dates from the time when it became a universally honorific word.

Secondly, there are the Democratic Socialists. Of these the Guild Socialists used to argue that a society could not truly be called "democratic" unless all the institutions in it were themselves democratic. Amongst these institutions were to be numbered factories and other industrial plants, and the democratization of such institutions necessarily involves workers' control, i.e., Socialism.[9] Nowadays, most Socialists would prefer to use less *a priori* arguments. Some would use a pragmatic argument, namely that political Democracy cannot be truly safe without economic reorganization: and again others would prefer a moral argument to the effect that there is an inconsistency in applying the principle of equality in the field of politics and denying it in the field of economics.

Thirdly, there are the conservatives who argue that Democracy is in its nature incompatible with Socialism. There are a number of arguments raised in current discussion to this effect: they are differentiated according to the feature of Democracy that they hold to be the ground of this incompatibility. Some have held this to be competition, others tolerance, others the existence of property. A recent argument that has attracted attention is that which maintains that Democracy requires freedom, freedom requires the Rule of Law, and Socialism in its advocacy of bureaucratic planning has to dispense with the Rule of Law.[10] Against this it has been urged in the first place, that the Rule of Law guarantees security, not freedom; and secondly, that even if economic planning does contract freedom in some directions, it extends it in others and the overall effect may well be an increase rather than a diminution.[11]

b. The connection between Democracy and the belief in Democracy. Since John Stuart Mill who claimed (ironically enough) that Democracy was not suitable for "Malays and Bedouins," it has been generally conceded by even the most fervent democrats that there are some conditions that a population must satisfy for it to be fit for Democracy. However, despite the practical urgency of this problem with the break-up of the old colonial empires, our knowledge of what these conditions are has not increased. On one condition—which to some appears to have a certain intuitive obviousness—controversy has been bitter: viz., the belief in, or acceptance of, Democracy. Now if this condition is taken as applying to society as a whole it is obviously true, perhaps logically so. But it does not follow from this that it is therefore true of every single member of a society. Society to be democratic must believe in Democracy; but how many members it can successfully contain who do not themselves believe in Democracy, is a question incapable of any *a priori* answer. It depends on the restraints that these dissidents are prepared to put upon their own behavior, on the moral or spiritual authority that they wield over others, and on the extent to which their behavior can be neutralized by other factors in society (free speech, the press, education, etc.).

c. The connection between Democracy and Constitutionalism. It would be common ground to nearly all supporters of Democracy that there are certain laws or regulations that ought not to be passed even if the greater part or indeed the whole of the people favor them. To some it has seemed desirable to inscribe these "moral limitations" of Democracy in a charter or Constitution. Some English thinkers have gloried in the fact that liberties enjoyed in Great Britain are to be found not in any Constitution but in the accumulated precedents of common law.[12] It would seem, however, that though this may well be something to be grateful for, it is not a matter for pride, and it is perfectly natural that other, and in particular younger, Democracies should prefer to express their ideals in a more systematic if necessarily more "artificial" fashion.

However, the issue somewhat changes when the Constitution is regarded not merely as a systematic statement of the liberties recognized in society but as a method of guaranteeing them. In such cases the Constitution is accompanied by some mechanism for enforcing provisions like that of judicial review. To certain thinkers this has seemed the obvious requirement of Democracy; by others it has been regarded as inequitable, incompetent, and unnecessary. It is inequitable because it tries to limit the power of the living majority by means of the "the dead hand" of the past: it is incompetent because the only cases where it is likely to arise are just those where the Constitution itself will require "interpretation"; and it is unnecessary because a society that is likely to accept the findings of such a mechanism is unlikely seriously to offend against the spirit of its Constitution. These strictures are sometimes supported by a historical examination of the record of actual mechanisms, e.g., the history of "judicial review" in the U.S. as an instrument of Democracy.[13]

3. There are in circulation in Anglo-Saxon thought a number of arguments, all purporting to justify Democracy. These arguments vary greatly in acceptability according to the number and validity of the principles they invoke, the truth of the factual assumptions they make use of, and the relevance of the kind of Democracy for which they argue to the kind that we experience.

a. To exercise rule or to enjoy any form of political authority is a kind of moral education. On egalitarian grounds the opportunity for such self-improvement should be extended to as many as possible. In Democracy it is extended to all: therefore Democracy is the best of all forms of government. This argument, which is originally to be found in Aristotle (*Pol.* III. 1277b), may have had some application within the confines of the Polis, but applied to the conditions of the modern world it seems hopelessly unrealistic. Significantly enough, it is the characteristic argument of a kind of Liberalism which is or was peculiarly associated with a classical education.

b. The second argument is that true opinion on political and moral matters is the privilege of the common man. Accordingly, power in a community should reside with him: and this it does only in a Democracy. Hence the superiority of Democracy. As we have seen, this argument is central to the Greek conception of Democracy. In modern thought it has received reinforcement from a certain sentimental theory of the goodness of human nature uncorrupted by wealth, luxury and education. In contrast to this, Democracy has come in for much criticism based on the so-called discovery of man's "irrationality" by modern psychology. Much of this criticism is confused, and, if it proves anything, proves not so much the weakness of Democracy as the weakness of this particular argument for it.

c. A more materialistic version of the preceding argument makes the ordinary man the best judge not of what is right for the community but of his own interests. In consequence, if the people are allowed to control the government, then the interests of the people will be dominant. Democracy is identified with popular control, and therefore vindicated. This argument is the argument of the Utilitarians, supported in their case by a thoroughgoing psychological egoism. It also has been subjected to a great deal of empirical criticism. Recent sociology has, for instance, cast doubt on the classical notions of class by bringing out what has been called (perhaps misleadingly) the "subjective" element in class determination. Nevertheless the argument has considerable weight.

d. A further retreat from the positions maintained in the two previous arguments leads to the completely sceptical argument for Democracy. According to this argument, it is impossible for anyone to discover what is the right course of action for the community, or where the true interests of its inhabitants reside. From this it follows that everyone in the community should be allowed to do what he wants to do as far as is socially possible. The only society in which this can happen is the one in which everyone has some control in the government: therefore Democracy is favored. As a variant of this argument, it may be maintained that even if one can discover what is ideally the right course of action to pursue, it would be wrong to insist on it unless everyone in the community recognized its rightness. Accordingly in practice one must adopt a sceptical attitude towards government and allow people to have the laws, institutions, etc., that they want: hence Democracy.

It seems to be certainly the case that scepticism does involve Democracy—even if the link is not as rigorous or as formal as some would believe. It does not follow from this, though—as certain critics of Democracy would have us believe—that Democracy involves scepticism.

e. At the opposite end of the scale it is maintained that everyone has a natural right to control government and that this right is recognized only in Democracy: therefore Democracy is the best form of government. This argument has been subjected to two lines of criticism, both of which are misguided. The first is that the conception of "a natural right" is metaphysical. Now natural rights are capable of, and often receive, a metaphysical interpretation, but this is not necessary. To say that something is a natural right may merely be a way of saying that it is an ultimate value. Secondly, it has been urged that it is absurd to allow that everyone has a natural right to exercise control over government when in fact not everyone can do so. But this argument assumes that the right in question is, in the terminology of jurisprudence, "a right proper" (i.e., correlative to duty) whereas it seems more natural to assume that it is a liberty or privilege.[14]

f. Finally, it may be maintained that it is irrelevant whether Democracy does in fact maximize welfare, safeguard rights, accord with natural law, etc., for the fact is that under modern conditions it is the only working possibility. No member of an emancipated industrial society will put up with political tutelage. He insists on having a fair chance of influencing the government in accordance with his own desires and ideas; and by a "fair" chance he means a chance "as good as the next man's." This argument was succinctly summarized in the nineteenth century by the conservative James Fitz-James Stephen who said that in Democracy we count heads to avoid breaking them; and it remains to-day one of the best arguments in favor of Democracy on account of its extreme economy.

4. The relation of the concept of Democracy to other notions such as Equality, Liberty, etc., falls outside the scope of this article.

NOTES

1. G. A. Paul, "Democracy," *Chambers Encyclopaedia,* 4 (1944), 430-1.
2. Bernard Bosanquet, *The Philosophical Theory of the State* (London, 1899).
3. J. L. Talmon, *The Origins of Totalitarian Democracy* (London, 1952).
4. E. J. Nanson, "Methods of Election," *Transactions and Proceedings of the Royal Society of Victoria,* 19 (1883), 197-240; Kenneth Arrow, *Social Choices and Individual Values* (New York, 1951).
5. Robert A. Dahl, *A Preface to Democratic Theory* (Chicago, 1956).
6. Robert A. Dahl and Charles Lindblom, *Politics, Economics and Welfare* (New York, 1953).
7. Joseph A. Schumpeter, *Capitalism, Socialism and Democracy* (New York, 1947).
8. Karl R. Popper, *The Open Society and Its Enemies* (London, 1945).
9. G. D. H. Cole, *Guild Socialism Re-Stated* (London, 1920).
10. F. A. von Hayek, *The Road to Serfdom* (London, 1944).
11. Hans Kelsen, "Democracy and Socialism," *Conference on Jurisprudence and Politics* (Chicago, 1954), 63-87.
12. A. V. Dicey, *Introduction to the Study of the Law of the Constitution* (London, 1885).
13. Henry S. Commager, *Majority Rule and Minority Rights* (New York-London, 1943).
14. Richard Wollheim and Isaiah Berlin, "Equality," *Proceedings of the Aristotelian Society,* 30 (1956), 281-326.

ADDITIONAL REFERENCES ADDED BY R. WOLLHEIM

LORD LINDSAY OF BIRKER, *The Modern Democratic State,* Vol. 1 (London, 1943); G. H. SABINE, "The Two Democratic Traditions," *Philosophical Review,* 61 (1952); S. I. BENN AND R. PETERS, *Social Principles and the Democratic State* (London, 1959); H. B. MAYO, *An Introduction to Democratic Theory* (New York, 1960); C. L. BECKER, *Modern Democracy* (New Haven, 1941); A. P. GRIFFITHS AND R. WOLLHEIM, "How can one person represent another?" *Proceedings of the Aristotelian Society,* Supplementary Volume XXXIV (1960); W. J. MACKENZIE, *Free Elections* (London, 1958); UNESCO, *Democracy in a World of Tensions* (Paris, 1951).

PART THREE

MARXISM AND COMMUNISM

INTRODUCTORY NOTE

In this Part, the study of revisionism will provide the most significant clues. The many and complex facets of revisionism are demonstrated by Z. A. Jordan in his article, "The Philosophical Background of Revisionism in Poland." One type, "orthodox" revisionism comes from the Party leaders and other politicians who find it necessary to change their policies and to modify official doctrines according to the needs of the day. Orthodox revisionists are being influenced by the ideas of lower-echelon theoreticians who have no share in power but who do adhere to the Marxist methodological dogmatism. L. G. Churchward, for example, points out, in his paper "Contemporary Soviet Theory of the Soviet State," that "re-thinking of the theory of the Soviet State has been chiefly done at a lower level."

Another impetus to ideological debate within the communist camp has come from the "philosophical" revisionists—philosophers and theoreticians who reject the dogmatic attitude of the former group and persist in probing the validity of doctrinal foundations. Their impact on the orthodox group cannot be denied. Indeed, the two groups frequently overlap. The two types of revisionism—orthodox and philosophical—constantly interact. With reference to Polish revisionism, Jordan says that "the line of division between orthodoxy and revisionism is constantly shifting, for even the most rigid orthodoxy is not immune from change." Occasionally—in accordance with the classical tradition —this may even lead to a fusion of philosophy and action at the leadership level. In his paper "Marxism Today," Bertram D. Wolfe does not hesitate to say that "today all *orthodox* Marxists in *partibus infidelium* are at the same time revisionists—albeit reluctant ones."

Revisionism is an inseparable part of the communist system—a system based on a Marxist orthodoxy with strong chiliastic elements. Heresy is always a potential threat to Marxism for several reasons. Marx and Engels were the first revisionists, as Wolfe points out, and several of Marx's predictions and theories proved false (including the theory of historical materialism, which has been refuted by the success of Soviet Communism), and his legacy has proved ambiguous. Any evolutionary path followed by Marxism is necessarily "revisionist."

Leopold Labedz emphasizes in "Ideology: The Fourth Stage" that revisionist conflict has always presented a serious danger to Marxism; these disputes have shown that strict adherence to an ideology makes adjustments precarious, compromise uncertain, and the conflict more dangerous. If accepted as guiding rules of behavior, political ideologies become decisive factors. For this reason, the study of revisionism, which helps us to unveil the role and purpose of ideologies, is important. The precise content of ideologies seems of little consequence. They seem to operate in the same manner as Georges Sorel's myths—as an inducement to action. The masses may thereby be prompted to violence in the form of uprisings and revolutions, as well as to acceptance of physical danger and other hardships. To the leaders and theoreticians an ideology is a point of reference, a stabilizer, a peg on which the argument can be hung, an arsenal of weapons with which to fight opponents, a body of tactical rules with which to outmaneuver the "comrades" who are challenging one's position and authority. To the faithful, it serves as a beacon illuminating both the desired goal and the prescribed way.

In his article "Historical Determinism and Political Fiat in Soviet Communism," Sidney Hook stresses that "important political corollaries follow from a recognition of what [the communists'] true ideology is." As a rule, communists consolidate political power, acting in the name of Marxist doctrine. Marxism plays the role of a false consciousness "which masks from the protagonists themselves the causes, grounds and motives of action." Hook surveys the unchanging ideological factors in Soviet Communism and asks what considerations determine the fundamental line of Bolshevik policy.

Yet, Labedz observes, ideology is an operative factor despite the ideological inconsistencies, which are an accepted part of the Soviet system as well as is the increasing "discrepancy between the maturing Soviet social structure and fundamentalist ideological prescriptions." The tension between the rationality of means and the irrationality of ideological ends can lead in time to the fading away of Marxism. Labedz concludes that "resistance to Communist expansion is the best way to direct Soviet ideology towards internal euthanasia."

Is there any inner logic in revisionism, any recurrent theme or permanent feature? Has Khrushchev's reaction against Stalinism anything in common with those of Tito and Mao? Insofar as "external" revisionism is concerned, one thing is clear: "What makes Tito a 'revisionist' and Mao a 'dogmatist' is not so much any specific article of belief to which they are committed but whether or not they accept the hegemony of the Soviet Union," says Hook in a recent article.[1]

Certain recurrent issues reveal the logic of revisionism. It is a relative concept (thus to the Russians the Chinese are revisionists—they are also referred to as "dogmatists"—and vice versa), but it revolves around the same issues: a separate road to communism, a revolutionary time-table, the attitude toward the socialist movements of the world (either sympathetic or competitive), and the approach to capitalist countries (either "positive" or "negative" coexistence).

Revisionism is a rejection of the official line of the dominant communist authority in the name of Marxist dogma, ostensibly to preserve the purity of the orthodox doctrines, but in practice for the sake of "one-upmanship" in the struggle for power, or to preserve one's own dominion and status, or at least to gain a certain measure of autonomy. From the point of view of the results achieved and roads followed, a tentative classification of various revisionisms might take the following form.

In extreme cases revisionism takes the form of *power-revisionism*, best illustrated by Sino-Soviet relations, in which ideology has been deliberately invoked to antagonize the opponent, and in which, as Donald S. Zagoria points out in "Russia and China: Two Roads to Communism," "the conflict over revolutionary strategy abroad is acute." Mao not only rejects the Soviet line of policy but tries to impose his own. As Arthur A. Cohen demonstrates in his paper "How Original is 'Maoism'?" ideological differences (behind power-revisionism) between Maoism, Marxism-Leninism, and Soviet Communism are not important. The differences are those of method and form.[2]

Another type is *thaw-revisionism*, an essentially intellectual movement with a certain impact on politics, demanding a greater amount of national autonomy and a greater degree of personal freedom, as in Poland. It has a moral orientation. It is permeated by the sense of moral responsibility and moral autonomy—a characteristic feature of philosophic revisionism, whose leading representative is Leszek Kolakowski.

The third type is the *opportunist-revisionism* of the Yugoslav brand, inspired by the political conditions caused by that country's relative isolation from the communist camp and Tito's excommunication by Stalin. Revisionism was used in that case to rationalize the situation. In his "Yugoslav Communist Theory," Fred Warner Neal discusses the framework which the Yugoslav communists have erected to explain and justify their position and bulwark their views.

It appears, then, that revisionism can serve as a justification for what has happened and as a guide for future action. It is a symptom of political struggle and its limits are defined by the ideological framework within which the communist system operates. It does not lead to the diffusion of political power within any state of the communist bloc, but is a "schism among the faithful"—directed against the monolithic nature of the bloc itself and leading to a polycentric structure.

The other topical theme, apart from revisionism in the study of Marxism, is alienation, an idea rediscovered by revisionists. The main credit is given to Georg Lukacs. The concept is concerned with a neurotic personality torn by opposing tendencies to mastery and subjection, and at war with itself and the world. Daniel Bell's paper, "In Search of Marxist Humanism," is concerned with the debate on alienation.

Discredited in many fields, Marx appears to the modern man as a false prophet responsible for a fictitious abstract model. While neo-Marxism is receding into a dream world, some neo-Marxists, as Wolfe pointed out, are involved in a rescue operation, trying to salvage, among other things, Marx's humanism from his unpublished early writings. Robert Tucker's recent book *Philosophy and Myth in Karl*

Marx (1961), which deals with the alienated world of the juvenile Marx, is symptomatic of the current interest in Marxist problems shown by Anglo-Saxon countries—an echo of a debate in which Continental Marxicologists have been engaged for some time and one which Sidney Hook now sees as a mere *tour de force* (cf. his article in *Encounter* quoted above). In his article on historical determinism, included in this symposium, Hook says that certain aspects of Marxist humanism have been vindicated by the Soviet experience "that one cannot build a socialist economy in a backward country except at a morally prohibitive cost."

NOTES

1. "Revisionism at Bay," *Encounter*, September, 1962.
2. Cohen's treatment of Mao's body of thought has been referred to as "de-Maotization." Cf. *Studies in Soviet Thought,* Vol. II, No. 3, September 1962, p. 238.

MARXISM TODAY

Bertram D. Wolfe

The 110 years since the *Communist Manifesto* pronounced the "downfall of the bourgeoisie and the victory of the proletariat equally inevitable" have not dealt kindly with Marx's predictions. At wholesale and at retail they have failed to materialize. The very approach which claimed to make of sociology a "science" and lay bare "the law of motion" of industrial society has proved irrelevant.

Yet the other nineteenth century social thinkers and social critics remain buried in the textbooks, while the name of Marx has become a household word. Some reject him without knowing his work; others accept him in equal ignorance. There are lands where no intellectual dares approach his specialty except under a protective umbrella of quotations from Marx and from those calling themselves Marxists. The rulers of one third of mankind have raised him to Founder of the Faith by which they claim to chart their course. In the new nations of Asia many invoke his name though they know little of his doctrine. In the West—and these are the ones who will chiefly concern us in this article—a number of intellectuals continue to call themselves Marxists. And non-Marxists in the free world, if they do but study his writings dispassionately—as dispassionately as men can read things so charged with passion—are likely to recognize in him a great moralist and stylist, and a seminal thinker whose insights can still fructify the social disciplines (let us not fall into Marx's error of calling them sciences): history, sociology, economics, and political philosophy.

The practitioners of these disciplines are today a little shamefaced about the fact that man's values must form a constitutive part of his examination of his own activities. Were it not for this false shame, political philosophy would not now be so nearly in eclipse. And it, too,

Reprinted from the *Antioch Review,* vol. XVIII, no. 4 (Winter, 1958), 471-487. By permission of the author and the publisher.

would be acknowledging a substantial debt to Marx and his fellow utopians for insights in that branch of political philosophy which may be called social criticism, and which concerns itself with the imperfections of any society-in-being as measured against its own potentialities and against man's flickering yet undying vision of the good life.

II

More than a century ago, when Marx undertook to analyze industrial society and lay bare its "law of motion" and its destiny, he saw it heading towards immediate and total catastrophe. The cataclysm was mere days or weeks away. First it was to come with the next street skirmish. Then it was to come out of a war to be begun before the year was up. A little later, it was to come out of the next downswing of the business cycle ("the revolution remains as inevitable as the next crisis itself").

With a zeal, a fanfare, and an explicitness that no fortune-teller would risk, Marx was forever climbing out on a limb of prophecy, and forever falling from the dead branch. No other serious thinker of the nineteenth century was so frequently, egregiously, and totally wrong in his predictions.

Worse than the fate of his prophecies concerning wars, the fall of ministries, sovereigns, dynasties, and regimes, was the fate of his general law. Industrial society, he held, was destined to transform itself with great speed, indeed was even then completing its transformation, into a society completely polarized and torn in two as though by mitosis, a tiny handful of huge exploiters at one pole and an overwhelming mass of miserable, dehumanized, and outraged proletarians at the other. Proletarian misery and dehumanization were to become absolute. All other classes would be ruined and disappear into the proletariat. The outraged and the injured, having lost their last stake in society and their last semblance of humanity, were to rise in their wrath, expropriate the handful of expropriators, burst the integument of existing society, and humanize all mankind. Today excluded from any stake in the nation, tomorrow the proletariat would "constitute itself the nation." That tomorrow was *tomorrow*, not some years or decades hence. (Even when Engels died in 1895 he still gave the old order "until the end of the century.")

The Communist Manifesto, which proclaimed the end of nationalism, was intended to serve as the program for the revolutions of 1848. But those revolutions proved to be the greatest explosion of national feeling that the world had known. Though the *Manifesto* had failed to touch the problems of German national unification, within a few weeks of its issuing, Marx and Engels, being Germans, made that problem a central concern. Indeed, it was to remain a central concern for most of the rest of their lives, until "the old boy, Bismarck, did our work for us." [1]

The proletariat, which in 1848 already "had no country to defend," would still be found in 1914, and once more in 1939, defending their respective countries. Indeed, nationalism was to prove the one cause for which the millions were ready to fight and die; and in the course of the twentieth century, it would spread from Europe, which was its home, to Asia and Africa, where the nation had hitherto been unknown.

When barricades and street fighting did not end "the system" in 1848, Marx began to call for war. *Die Neue Rheinische Zeitung*, which he was then editing, became the most warlike paper in Europe, indeed the most warlike in the whole history of European journalism. He called for war of the German people on Prussia, for war on all the German principalities, for war on Denmark, for war on Russia, for war simultaneously on Russia, Prussia, England, and Denmark at once.[2]

Until three years before Marx's death in 1883, he and Engels continued to take sides zealously in every "capitalist" war, while Marx urged unceasingly on Germany and England and France that they declare war on Russia. But in the final decade of his life, he began to catch a glimpse of the fearful outlines of the holocaust that was to come in 1914. For his native land he felt that this would be "a 'defensive' war, not one of those newfangled 'localized' wars but a race war against the allied races of Slavs and Latins." He realized that its outcome would be uncertain; that the European civilization which he ambivalently loved and hated would be in ruins; that the nations would fight for their very lives and all the peoples would defend their countries. He lost his taste for war as an engine of progress. Three years before he died, he wrote soberly to the Russian Narodnik, Danielson: "A European war I would consider a terrible misfortune."

Engels had time to develop this feeling further. The twelve years remaining to him after Marx's death he spent largely in activities that can only be described in Lenin's language as "social pacifism"—an earnest effort to use the international socialist movement to avert the calamity. At the same time, he drew up plans for universal military service in a "popular militia" with "professional officers' cadres," to make Germany better able to defend herself if her existence were thus threatened. And he solemnly warned the French people that if they entered into an alliance with Russia for war on Germany, they would find the German socialists and workingmen rallying to the defense of their country. In 1891 he even urged on Bebel that the Socialists in the Reichstag should vote for the military appropriations that year since it looked as if war might be coming "next spring." So the last twelve years of his life were seriously dedicated to that "pacifism" and "defencism" which Lenin was to denounce in 1914 as "treason to Marxism."

Thus, by recognizing the error of some few of their positions and predictions, Marx and Engels became "the first revisionists." The Orthodox take unction from this as a sign that the founders were "scientific" and "no dogmatists," although they are loathe to touch whatever Marx and Engels left untouched, or to allow, with Marx and Engels dead, that there are any authorized revisionists among the living.

This revision was not limited to war and nationalism and changes in the timetable of revolution. Thus in 1850 Marx had assured the proletariat that it was a senseless "utopia" to expect "the slightest improvement in its position *within* the bourgeois republic." But in the sixties Marx began to hail the legal shortening of the working day as "a consequence of the pressure of society" and as "the victory of a principle, in which the political economy of the bourgeoisie has capitulated to the political economy of the working class . . . as the result of a half century of civil war." If this makes us wonder what Marx can here mean by "civil war," our wonder is increased by his coming to recognize that in America, England, and Holland (Engels later added France), "the social revolution" (which of course had to be a *revolution*) might be achieved by peaceful democratic process, "barricades being unnecessary because there, if they but want to, the proletariat can win victory at the polls."

And after Marx's death, Engels, whose writings on philosophy had always been more extensive, more systematic, more explicit, and more "philosophical" as well as intellectually weaker than the aphorisms of Marx in that field, took it upon himself to admit in letters to disciples that Marx's and his economic reductivism had been one-sided and neglectful of the complexity and autonomy of institutions and the realms of the spirit—but then he took refuge in the evasive device that "in the long run" the economic or the material factor was "decisive." [3]

III

Whatever their reluctant revisions in the light of their experience with a recalcitrant and bewilderingly changing world, at the core of Marx's thinking and emotions there remained to the end an irreducible holistic and apocalyptic element.

Still he continued to think of industrial society in mythic Hegelian totalist terms as "the system." Still he persisted in believing that whatever defects he perceived were integral to the system and could not be removed defect by defect but only by scrapping the system and replacing it with another system. Still he was sure that he knew the framework of rigidities beyond which the most rapidly changing world in the history of man could not further change without a shattering of the hypothetically rigid framework. Still he assigned to a particular class the "mission" of shattering the framework. Still he was sure that he could descry, and at no great distance, a day of wrath and doom. Still he was insistent that continuous alteration (reform) changed "essentially" nothing—except that it prepared the chosen class by giving it more leisure for comprehending its "mission," which was not the elimination of recognizable evils (reform) but sudden and total transformation (revolution).

Volume I of *Capital*, the only volume that Marx completed, is possessed by this contradiction. The book contains rich treasures of empirical materials: historical sketches, studies of technology, analyses of the development of modern industry, statistical material, keen sociological observations. But great sections which derive from British Parliamentary Bluebooks testify eloquently to the awakening conscience of British society. A paean to the victory of the Ten Hours Bill and other social legislation tells the reader that the lot of the working class is improving, its power and organization growing stronger, its needs winning the support of all disinterested sections of society. "Capital is under compulsion from society." "The factory magnates have resigned themselves to the inevitable." "The power of resistance of capital has gradually weakened . . . the power of attack of the working class has grown with the number of its allies. . . . Hence the comparatively rapid advance since 1860."

This seems clear enough, and comforting. Then suddenly we run up against, at the volume's very end, the "conclusion" to all the empirical material: the general law or general line of the volume—"The Historical Tendency of Capitalist Accumulation." Capital, we learn, came into the world conceived in original sin, "a congenital bloodstain on its cheek, dripping with blood and dirt from head to foot, from every pore." And it is destined now, by the workings of "the immanent laws of capitalist production itself," to leave the world in a cataclysm. One capitalist kills many. The other classes are being proletarianized too.

Along with the constantly diminishing number of magnates of capital . . . grows the mass of misery, oppression, slavery, degradation, exploitation; but with this grows too the revolt of the working class. . . . The monopoly of capital becomes a fetter upon the mode of production. Centralization of the means of production, and socialization of labor, at last reach a point where they become incompatible with their capitalist integument. This integument is burst asunder. The knell of capitalist private property sounds. The expropriators are expropriated.

But was it for this that all the vast researches were undertaken and all the empirical material accumulated? This "conclusion" Marx had reached when he was but cracking the bindings on the first books on economics, back in 1844. The "general law" was up his sleeve before his concrete "investigations" began. Perhaps it is intended to seem more impressive now, surrounded by all this concrete material. But the material, far from bolstering, refutes the "general law"! The grand conclusion is but our old friend, the pre-economics prophecy of 1844: the prophecy of the imminent Apocalypse.

IV

In a sober moment, Marx had written: "No social order ever perishes before all the productive forces for which there is room in it have developed." This, alas, on examination, proves no more explicit than any other of Marx's sweeping generalizations. Nor any truer, as the Russian and Chinese Revolutions were to demonstrate. With singular perversity, history was to vouchsafe social revolutions in underdeveloped countries on the eve of industrialization, or only part way along the road, and was to deny them in the advanced industrial societies which Marx's law specifically dedicated to revolution.

Moreover, not only had the industrial society Marx knew not reached the end of its development in 1844—or in 1848 when he delivered the doom so stirringly, or in 1867 when he tacked it on to the empirical material that so largely contradicted it. Actually, the industrial society Marx knew was scarcely at the beginning of the development of its "productive forces."

That industrial revolution which Marx had studied—the change from manpower, animal, wind, and waterpower, to steampower, and from cottage handicraft to machinofacture—was but the first industrial revolution. It was to be followed by a second—the age of electricity. And by a third, a fourth, and a fifth—conveyor belt, combustion engine, synthetic chemistry, electronics, automation, atomic fission atom fusion. True, this latest revolution does seem to make a cataclysm unpleasantly possible, but it is not Marx's cataclysm.

In place of the polarization Marx had predicted, the very opposite has occurred. The intermediate classes that were to have been proletarianized have greatly changed their character and vastly multiplied. The industrial proletariat has lost in numerical weight in the total population but has gained greatly in status and in organized economic and political power. The service trades, which Marx contemptuously treated as sheer economic waste and as "parastic servitors to the parasites," have increased steadily in number and variety, and in the advanced countries have become servitors to the working population.

The state, too, has proved refractory. Supposed to be the "executive committee" of a numerically dwindling bourgeoisie, its democratization has made it ever more subject to the labor vote, farm vote, and vote of the intermediate classes. Out of labor's influence on government, and out of the general, quite classless, pressure of society as a whole, have come state regulation of economic life, legal limitation of hours, minimum wage, protection of health and conditions of labor, legalization of the right to organize, institutionalization of collective bargaining, and the whole sweep of security legislation. The French socialist, Paul Deat, has summed up this process as a "socialization of power." And the German socialist Paul Lensch, having in mind that the working man has not only defended his country but has come to recognize that it is his primary field of activity, has written: "The state has undergone a process of socialization, while socialism has undergone a process of nationalization."

More startling is the series of economic novelties which have made the abstractions of the nineteenth century economists, Marx's as well as let us say Bastiat's, totally obsolete as modes of generalization and understanding. These include protectionism, currency manipulation, deficit spending, price floors and price ceilings, state fostered cartellization in one land and anti-trust prosecution in another, and, in vast areas of the world, autarky. Whether these features are to be welcomed or feared, they have produced a world which makes the projections of Marx and his opponents alike irrelevant.

Unkindest cut of all, the worker himself has not consented to being increasingly proletarianized. He has displayed stubbornness, tirelessness, courage, skill, incapacity to recognize when he is licked, and the power to enlist the sympathy of the bulk of society, in fighting off this "prophetic assignment."

"It isn't a question," Marx had written, "of what this or that proletarian, or even the entire proletariat, may for a time *imagine* to be its goal. It is a question of *what the proletariat is,* and what that *being* will historically force it to do."

But unlike the declassed intellectuals who offered them leadership, the workers themselves have never been attracted to this "mission." They have had no stomach for being reduced to nought the better to prepare themselves for being all. It is *against this* that *their* "class struggle" is directed. Against this they have used their numbers, their solidarity, their influence on other parts of society, even their competition with each other. To win the suffrage, to exert influence and control over governments, to legalize and contractualize improvements in their "being" in the many hours of their lives that they spend in labor, to secure equal status and citizenship with the rest of society, to win some security and dignity within the "system," to become "something" in the world in which they have their "being," not "everything" in a world which exists only in the fantasy of the utopians of which Marx was perhaps the greatest—it is to these aims that they rallied. And to these aims modern society as a whole has rallied also.

As Hendrik Brugmans. Rector of the Collège d'Europe, himself a dedicated Socialist, has put it: "Those who 'being nought were to want to become all' become something, and the whole scheme loses its tidy outlines." [4]

V

The secret of Marxism's power to survive the shipwreck of all his prophecies lies in its inherently dual character.

On the one hand it claims to be a science. It claims to have made sciences out of history, sociology, economics, politics; to do for them what Darwin has done for the biological sciences; indeed, to do even more—to explain the past, make clear the present, foresee and control the future. But so badly has a century of actual history dealt with these claims that in the Western World where one is free to question, no Marxist intellectual now ventures to mediate between Marxism and the non-believer without a large measure of what the lawyers call "confession and avoidance." Indeed, when they are pressed, they are apt to discard one by one all the *results* arrived at by Marx's "method" and to insist only on the validity of the method. Thus we are confronted with a spectacle which would have astonished Bernstein and Kautsky alike: today all *orthodox* Marxists *in partibus infidelium* are at the same time revisionists—albeit reluctant ones.

If as a "science" Marxism has been stripped down to a "method" which has produced only invalid results, on the other hand, Marxism's staying powers lie in the fact that it is also an *ism*. There is no Lockeism, no Smithism, no Millism, no Weberism, no Durkheimism, no Micheletism, Rankeism, or Gibbonism, but there *is* a Marxism. It is an ideology in the precise sense in which Marx himself used the term. It is a creed, which can be clung to by faith where the intellect questions and rebels. It is charged with emotion, cannot be shaken by the mere refutation of any number of detailed matters; it is maintained by rationalizations, gives ground yet resists; it is filled with the thunder of denunciation and sustained by a sense of righteousness and the assurance of prophecy.

In an age prepared for by nearly two thousand years of Christianity but in which the faith of millions had grown dim and the altar seemed to them vacant of its image, Marxism arose to offer a fresh vision of the Last Things, a new hope of Apocalypse: a day of wrath when the mighty should be humbled and the lowly exalted; a new thousand-year kingdom of justice and freedom and happiness on earth; a world where life would lose its uncertainties and cease to play unexpected tricks on men. History was to be given a new meaning, a new goal, and a new end in Time (the "end of pre-history" Marx called it). A new integral faith and providential certitude were to guide man's uncertain steps and faltering thoughts. The initiate were to be the new Elect, armed with both understanding and vision. And the "proletarian," the most lowly and humbled, becoming ever more abased and outraged and injured, was to be crucified, crowned first with thorns then armed with the vengeful lightning, to become, not only for his own class but for all mankind, the new Redeemer. Then at last man would become as God, master of his own destiny, maker of his own future, conscious architect of his world. Moreover, he would become, if not omnipotent, at least omnicompetent: the very division of labor which had made possible the modern world society was to be ended and man become whole.[5]

Thus Marxism attracts, as Henri de Man wrote of its attraction for him, because it seems "as certain as science, as integral as religion." Hebraic prophecy and Hebrew-Christian chiliastic expectations are syncretised with the worship of that Faustian demon of an earlier age which became the fashionable deity of nineteenth century worship: Science. The two powerful cults reinforce each other; according to the audience addressed, the Marxists of our day lean more heavily on the one or the other.

Yet it is hard to see what there is left of "science" in a method all of the prophecies of which have proved false and irrelevant. Surely it cannot be the three quotations, endlessly repeated, two from Engels and one from Marx, to the effect that their creed is no dogma but a guide to action, or that "I myself am no Marxist." A few reluctant revisions in the face of history's refutation can hardly be elevated into a simulacrum of the humble and tentative way in which real scientists advance and test hypotheses.

If there is anything "scientific" about Marxism beyond the invocation of the word, it lies in its critical and empirical observation of the society of Marx's day. But in this critique, Marx is in nowise superior to the other utopians who were his masters. Even the invocation of the magic word was common coin when Marx, not yet a Socialist, came to Paris to study their works. All of the utopians had the idea that they could make of their generous and value-charged criticism of the defects of the existing, and their speculative dreams of the perfect society, a "science."

Saint-Simon called his critique and vision "the science of universal gravitation." He wrote when Newton was still lord of scientific thought and gravitation its archetype. By the time Engels got around to making the same claim for Marx, Newton had just been dispossessed from the zenith by Darwin and gravitation by evolution.

Fourier called his critique and vision "the certain science." Proudhon called his plans for the construction of the future perfect society and his critique of the existing order "scientific socialism." And Marx and Engels, before they quarrelled with Proudhon and expropriated the term, were proud of this workingman autodidact and pleased to recognize in him "the founder of the science of national economy."

What distinguished Marx from the other utopians was a canny refusal to be detailed and specific about his utopia. But this was only true of his later writings. Now that history has made mincemeat of Marx's specific predictions and general "law of motion," the neo-Marxists of our day tend to take refuge in the more generous vision of some of his earliest work, much of it only recently published. However, in these early works Marx is as visionary as any other utopian.

VI

Today all neo-Marxists who must speak to those who are intellectually free are engaged in an enormous rescue operation. One branch seeks to rescue Marx's abstract model of the economy from the ravages of time; the other flees from the shipwrecked galleon of economic prophecy to the blessed isle of Marx's earlier utopian visions. The watchword of the one school is "Marx's method"; of the other, "Marx's humanism."

In Marx's writings there is a Marx for any circle one approaches, for every changing fashion and mood. One has but to pick and choose.

Since Marx was an aphoristic writer, orphic, sporadic, and frequently self-contradictory rather than systematic, and since at his best he is a great stylist and deals with matters of deep human concern, his utterances have a resonance, reverberate in such fashion that a few of them may be made to go a great way. It is fatally easy to find one's self a minuscule body of quotations and enlarge them by repetition, contemplation, and exegesis. Chipping thus a fragment from a huge and roughhewn figure, the neo-Marxist proclaims: "Behold my Marx!" or "Behold the real Marx!"

The word "humanist" is tricky. Marx was more horrendous in 1844 to 1850 and became more humane and less in love with "terror" and "popular excesses" as he grew older. But there are more quotes for the "humanist" in the earlier writings. The trouble with those who would make of him a "humanist" or an "existentialist" in line with fashions of our day is that the tiny splinters they take are almost all from his earliest writings, things he set down before he was fully formed and had become the "economist" and "scientist" which was his pride and major claim. Always the same handful of quotations, striking aphorisms culled from an enormous amount of nonsense and scorn and spite. Always the same handful of quotations about *Entfremdung* ("alienation"), a term he derived from Hegel and sometimes used ironically "to make myself intelligible to the philosophers." To this is added a single, important concept from *Capital*, the concept of "fetishism." The whole "humanist" Marx can be printed in a single magazine article, but—with the exception of the truly important concept of fetishism—most of Marx's strengths and his weaknesses would alike be missing.

An honorable exception must be made of Maximilien Rubel, author of *Karl Marx: Essai de Biographie Intellectuelle* (Paris, 1957). He is the most attractive and the most learned of the neo-Marxist "humanists." He at least does not work with a handful of quotations out of context, but is a Marxicologist in the great tradition of Mehring and Ryazanov. He has pored over everything Marx has written—more than the two aforementioned Marxicologists, for some new manuscripts of the early period have only recently come to light. With the exception of the horrendous worshipper of terror, excesses, and war, and the unpleasant side of Marx revealed in his letters and in the mockery and unjust polemics against some of those closest to him, Rubel has taken all his writings into the account. But he rescues Marx from himself by the simple device of refusing to believe Marx meant his arrogant, cocksure prophecies, his claims to foreknow the "inevitable" future, his pretensions to have made of the social disciplines exact sciences on the order of natural sciences.

Rubel's Marx is simply a great moralist (*éthicien*) and a great social critic, who has pondered deeply the defects of existing society, and the *possibilities*, not inevitabilities, of a better one. His Marx modestly tells the proletariat and mankind as a whole what they "inevitably" must do *if* they want, as he has faith that they "inevitably" must want, that "better society" which is his vision. Thus Marx is put back among the utopians which his pretensions to "science" taught him and Engels to patronize and scorn. The only trouble with this Marx is that it is the attractive and engaging Maximilien Rubel written large, and supplied with a great bush of beard, and not at all the Marx of the dogmas, quarrels, hatreds, envies, pretensions, and prophecies.

VII

For the other branch of neo-Marxists who would cling to Marx the economist and scientist, the rescue operation consists of efforts to explain, or explain away, the treacherous behavior of actual economic developments by treating each novelty of history as a "deviation" from the "essential" and the "lawful" and the "predestined in the long run." An effort is made to show that though there may be shoals, or even dry land or great mountain peaks, where there was supposed to be deep water, still the course the great pilot set was "essentially" right. "Sly history's" novelties do not make the old road map useless, they merely represent long and "explainable," if unexpected, detours.

When a theory shows itself incapable of explaining or even describing reality [writes Herbert Luthy], its believers set themselves to writing books where they explain why the theory remains sound at bottom all the same, and wherein reality has erred. Thus it is that pre-Keplerian astronomy hardened into an impenetrable thicket of auxiliary hypotheses minutely elaborated, tables of deviations, squarings of the circle, with the sole purpose of making room for the re-entry of the incompatible results of new observations into the established system of geocentric astronomy or into the circular orbits of Copernicus.[6]

The theoretical economists of the nineteenth century, and Marx who was their disciple and their critic, worked with an abstract model of the economy which, in part deliberately and in part unconsciously, abstracted from such "aberrations" as state intervention and regulation, state fostering and restraining, nationalization, protectionism, currency manipulation, the influence of organized groups, legislated cartellization and legislated competition, enforcement by public or quasi-public bodies of quantities, qualities, price levels, import quotas and prohibitions, and the embryonic germs of the welfare state and autarky. Theirs was a world of autonomous economic forces, with free movement of men, money, goods, and ideas. The intervention of all these extra-economic forces they treated as negligible or as having entered into a permanent decline with the end of mercantilism.

This abstract model was still a useful conceptual instrument for approaching the world of the first half of the nineteenth century. But with the manifest decline of *laissez faire,* theoretical economics itself went into eclipse, since reality departed farther and farther from the models based on the "free" working of economic forces. Then came the age of the epigones, exegetes, and fragmentalists—men who worked on some fragmentary aspect such as statistical series, currency and budgetary manipulation, or the like. It was not only Marxism that was painfully lacking in original thinkers after the death of Marx.

Even when he was writing his *Capital* it was already becoming manifest that the public powers and organized groups were intervening in the "raw" or "autonomous" economic processes with ever greater scope and rigor, to regulate their consequences and alter their direction. Even when these efforts at regulation had, as they often did, consequences that were unintended, the "autonomy" of the economic process was nevertheless at an end. Whether *laissez faire* is regarded as a blessing insuring "eternal harmonies," or a curse on industrial society leading it straight to the jungle of civil war, the abstract model, which was a useful and not too far-fetched conceptual fiction when his masters were writing, had already become useless and increasingly misleading when Marx began his *Capital*.

In justice to Marx perhaps it may be noted that the first volume of *Capital*, the only one he himself completed, is but a fragment of his intended work. As he originally outlined his work it was to consist of six parts: (1) Capital; (2) Landed Property; (3) Wage Labor; (4) The State; (5) Foreign Trade; (6) The World Market. Though Engels threw some portions of manuscript intended for the later parts into Volume III, actually all three volumes are but an expansion of the first section of the projected study. Particularly section 4, on "The State," was never reached by Marx at all.[7]

Thus it is possible to imagine that if Marx had gotten around to his volume on "The State," an empirical study of its functioning might have made him recognize its growing role not only as a regulator of the conditions of labor but of the economy as a whole. However, with the exception of his remarks on English labor laws, there is little in his occasional *obiter dicta* and aphorisms on the state which would lead us to believe that he might so drastically have revised his outlook and his method.[8]

Hence "orthodox" neo-Marxism has gotten farther and farther from reality, and has limited itself to expounding his doctrine as he left it, or, to cite Luthy once more, "to making an exegesis of the history of the world in so far as it is a history of the deviations from the Marxist schema."

As Hayek and Roepke have sought to keep alive the vanished dream of the eternal harmonies of Bastiat, so Hilferding, Luxemburg, Lenin, Bukharin, and Sternberg have sought to keep alive the eternal disharmonies of the (in essence) identical dream world of Marx. The epigones of the one school and the other still continue to feel at home in this world of abstract schemata, for only there can they theorize freely and pleasantly abstract from both historical survivals and historical novelties, from all the extra-economic and noneconomic factors that make the real world so complex, so unmanageable, so resistant and unpredictable. Actually, both schools live in a lost world, for what the later nineteenth century witnessed and the twentieth century has enormously accelerated, is the total breakdown of the usefulness of the concept of autonomous economic laws, and the total shipwreck of all the predictions that Marx derived from the assumption of their autonomy.

NOTES

1. I have treated this question in detail in an article on "Nationalism and Internationalism in Marx and Engels," . . . in the December 1958 issue of *The American Slavic and East European Review.*

2. Such calls for war are to be found in the *Marx/Engels Gesamtausgabe* (hereafter called MEGA for short), I/7, pp. 24, 30, 92, 181, 204, 354-5, 376.

3. It is noteworthy that Marx used the terms "materialist conception of history" and "dialectical" but never spoke of "historical materialism" or "dialectical materialism." These were of Engels' coinage, and it was Engels who expounded them. Marx never espoused a positive ontology or epistemology, either. Moreover, when Engels wrote to him that he was intending to read the dialectic into nature, Marx answered cautiously and a bit ironically that he "did not want to venture any judgment until he had had time to reflect on the matter and to consult 'the authorities,'" (Letter of May 31, 1873). Though Marx died ten years later, the "judgment" never came.

4. From his suggestive introduction to the brilliant critique of Marx by Milorad M. Drachkovitch, *De Karl Marx à Léon Blum*, Geneva, 1954, p. 10.

5. "In the Communist society," Marx wrote, "where every one has no exclusive circle of activity but can train himself in any branch he wants to, society regulates general production, and just by that makes it possible for me to do one thing today and another tomorrow: to hunt mornings, fish afternoons, raise cattle evenings, criticize after dinner, in whatever way I please, without ever having to become a fisherman, a herdsman, or a critic." MEGA, I/5, p. 22.

It remained for a philosophical disciple of Hegel, Heidegger, and Marx, Herbert Marcuse, to add the final "existentialist" touch to the wonders of this utopia by suggesting that the change in the forms of ownership and regulation of industry would lead to "living without anxiety." (Introduction by Herbert Marcuse to Raya Dunayevskaya, *Marxism and Freedom,* New York, 1958, p. 10.)

6. Herbert Luthy, "L'Histoire du Monde: Une Deviation?", *Preuves,* Paris, May 1958, pp. 68-78.

7. For an analysis of this point see Maximilien Rubel, *Karl Marx*, p. 333. For Marx's own statement of his plan see *Grundrisse der Kritik der politischen Oekonomie,* Berlin, 1953, pp. 29, 139 and 175; *Zur Kritik der politischen Oekonomie,* Berlin, 8th Edition, 1921, pp. XLVI and LIII; Marx's letter to LaSalle, Feb. 22, 1858 and his letter to Engels, April 2, 1858. When Marx was old and ill and had but two more years to live, Kautsky asked him about arrangements for the publication of his *Complete Works,* to which he responded sadly: "Those works—they will have to be written first."

8. I have in mind not so much his childishly simple conception of the modern state as "the executive committee of the capitalist class," as his "philosophical" insurance against stumbling on the truth. He not only treated the economy as "autonomous," he held that it was determinative. It was the state that was not and could not be autonomous, but was determined as to form and function by the economy. From his first admonition to the Young Hegelians that "the state does not have primacy over private property but private property has power over the state" (*MEGA, I/1*, p. 498) to Engels' last protective retreat to the imprecise and evasive "in the long run," neither Marx nor Engels ever abandoned the view that the economy determines the nature and functions of the state.

IN SEARCH OF MARXIST HUMANISM:
THE DEBATE ON ALIENATION *

Daniel Bell

There is today, in England and in France, a renewed interest in Marx. One sees this in the pages of the English *Universities and Left Review*, and the French *Arguments*, the magazines of the post-Stalinist left-wing generation in these countries. One hears this in detailed discussion of the writings of the Polish and East German "revisionists," and par- ticularly of the "subterranean" ideas of Georg Lukacs, the Hungarian Marxist philosopher, one of the sources of revisionism. One reads this in the literary journals, such as Lucien Goldmann's long essay "La Réification," in the February-March 1959 issue of *Les Temps Modernes.*

This new interest revolves around the theme of alienation. Marx is read not as an economist or political theorist—not for the labour theory of value or the falling rate of profit, not for the theory of the State or even of social classes, and certainly not as the founder of dialectical materialism—but as a philosopher who first laid bare the estrangement of man from an oppressive society. Alienation is taken to be the critical tool of the Marxist method, and the new canon is derived from the early, and in his lifetime unpublished, philosophical manuscripts of Marx. Even non-Marxists accept this new emphasis. Thus in Père Jean-Yves Calvez's comprehensive *La Pensée de Karl Marx,* published in 1956, four hundred and forty of a total of six hundred and forty pages are devoted to the concept of alienation and its use in social and political analysis.

All of this is rather novel. Rarely in the thirties, for example, when the first burst of Marxist scholarship occurred, did one find in the exeget- ical and expository writings on Marx a discussion of alienation. In Sidney Hook's pioneer account of Marx's intellectual development, *From Hegel to Marx,* published in 1936, the word "alienation" does not occur *once* in the text. It was not, of course, that Hook was unaware of the

Reprinted from the *Soviet Survey,* no. 32 (April-June, 1960), 21-31. By per- mission of the author and the publisher.

idea of alienation and the role it played in Hegelian thought. (His book, based on these early manuscripts, had traced in patient detail Marx's thought to his immediate forebears: to Feuerbach, who, in his discussion of religion, had developed the concept of alienation; to Bruno Bauer, who had emphasized the "critical method" in philosophy; to Moses Hess, who first sketched the picture of humanistic communism; and to the other young Hegelians for whom the relationship of freedom to necessity was the paramount concern.) But the intellectual problem for Hook, as it was for *all* "classical" Marxists, was, first, a defence of the idea of materialism as a viable modern philosophy—and this Hook sought to do by reading Marx uniquely as a naturalist—and, second, to resolve the "contradiction" between Marx's social determinism (i.e., that one's consciousness and knowledge are shaped by one's existence and class position), and Marx's, and Lenin's, class teleology (or the fact that socialist purpose and goal are instilled into the worker from the "outside") [1]—and this Hook sought to do by reading Marx as a pragmatist. The intellectual issue for Marxists in the thirties was the validity of historical materialism.

Different times, different *Zeitgeist*. The reason for this change is clear. In Europe today, a school of neo-Marxists, having rejected Stalinism (and, implicity, historical materialism, which, in its projection of "higher" stages of society, had been used to justify the Bolshevik use of terror), has gone back to Marx's early writings to find a new humanist foundation for Socialism. The revisionist philosophers in Eastern Europe do so to find doctrinal support against the official party theologues. The French post-Stalinists, such as Lucien Goldmann or Edgar Morin, see in the idea of alienation a more sophisticated, radical critique of contemporary society than the simplified and stilted Marxist analysis of class. And the young English socialists, such as Charles Taylor of All Souls College, see in the concept of alienation a means of reformulating the idea of community.

While all this is a fresh, and even fruitful, way of making a criticism of contemporary society, it is *not* the "historical Marx." For, as the following analysis argues, Marx had repudiated the idea of alienation divorced from his specific economic analysis of property relations under capitalism, and, in so doing, had closed off a road which would have given us a broader and more useful analysis of society and personality than the Marxian dogmatics which did prevail. While one may be sympathetic to the idea of alienation, it is only further myth-making to read this concept back as the central theme of Marx. As a political effort by the revisionists, bound within the Marxist camp, it may have some polemical value. As a stage of the pilgrim's progress of those coming out of the Marxist forest, it is understandable. As an intellectual effort, it is false. If the concept of alienation is to have any meaning, it must stand on its own feet, without the crutch of Marx. This, then, is the burden of this paper.

For the "left-Hegelians," the teachers and colleagues of Marx, the chief task of philosophy was to specify the conditions under which "Man" could achieve his freedom. They accepted the question which Hegel had opened up; they were dissatisfied with his formulation of the problem.

The goal of Man, Hegel had said, was freedom, a condition, he defined, in which man would be self-willed and where his "essence" would become his own possession—in which he would regain his "self." But man was "separated" from his essence and bound by two conditions which seemed inherent in the world: necessity and alienation. Necessity meant a dependence on nature and the acceptance of the limitations which nature imposed on men, both in the sense of the limitation of natural resources and the limitations of physical strength. Alienation, in its original connotation, was the radical dissociation of the "self" into both actor and thing, into a *subject* that strives to control its own fate, and an *object* which is manipulated by others.[2] In the development of science, man could, perhaps, overcome necessity and master nature. But how was one to overcome the Orphic separateness of subject and object? Alienation was an ontological fact, in the structure of grammar as well as of life; for the self was not just an "I" seeking to shape the world according to its intentions, but also a "me," an object whose identity is built up by the pictures that others have of "me." Thus the condition of complete freedom, in which the self seeks only to be an "I," a shaper of events in accordance with its own will, rather than being shaped by others, is a seeming impossibility. In the face of this irreducible dualism of subject-object, of "I" and "me," how does one achieve the goal of being "self-willed"?

Bruno Bauer, one of the first teachers and friends of Marx, felt that the solution lay in developing a "critical" philosophy which exposed the "mystery" of human relationships (i.e., the *real* motives behind social acts). Most human beings born into the world, said Bauer, simply accept it and are oblivious to the sources of their morals and beliefs, of their rationality and irrationality; they are "determined" by the world. By subjecting all beliefs to criticism, however, men would become self-conscious, reason would be restored to them, and therewith their self-possession. The overcoming of the dualism, therefore, was to be through the achievement of self-consciousness.

Feuerbach, to whom Marx gave credit for making the first real breach in the system of Hegelian abstractions, sought to locate the source of alienation in religious superstition and fetishism. The most radical of all the left-Hegelians, Feuerbach called himself Luther II. Where Luther had sought to demolish an institution that mediated between Man and God, the second Luther sought to destroy God himself. Man would be free, he said, if he could demythologize religion. Man was bound because he took the best of himself, his sensibility, and projected it onto some external object, or spirit, which he called divine.[3] But the history of all thought was a history of progressive disenchantment, and if, finally, in Christianity, the image of God had been transformed from a parochial river deity into a universal abstraction, the function of criticism—using the radical tool of alienation or self-estrangement—was to replace theology by anthropology, to dethrone God and enthrone Man. The way to overcome alienation was to bring the divine back into man, to reintegrate himself through a religion of humanity, through a religion of self-love. Men's relation to each other, said Feuerbach, in first employing terms that, ironically, were adopted later by Martin Buber for religious purposes, had to be on an I-Thou basis.[4] Philosophy was to be directed to life, man was to be liberated from the "spectre of abstractions" and released from the thongs of the supernatural. Religion was only capable of creating "false consciousness." Philosophy would reveal "true consciousness." And, by placing Man rather than God at the centre of consciousness, Feuerbach sought to bring the "infinite into the finite."

This uncompromising attack on religion was equally a sharp attack on all established institutions. But beyond that, the spreading use of the concept of alienation had a more radical consequence in the minds of the left-Hegelians, because it initiated a direct break in the history of philosophy by ushering in the period of modernity. In classical philosophy, the ideal man was the contemplative one. Neither the middle ages nor the transitional period to contemporary times (the 17th to the mid-19th century) was ever wholly able to detach itself from the ideal of the Stoa. Even Goethe, who gave us in Faust the first modern man, the man of ambition unchained, reverted, in his ethical image of the human ideal, to the Greek. In discussing freedom, however, Hegel had introduced a new principle, the principle of *action;* for man, in order to realize his self, had to strive actively to overcome the subject-object dualism that bound him. In action a man finds himself; by his choices he defines his character. For Hegel, however, the principle of action had remained abstract. In Feuerbach, while the principle of alienation is sharply defined and the source of alienation is located in religion, an abstraction remains because Feuerbach was talking of Man in general. In Marx, action was given specificity in a radical new emphasis on *work.* Man becomes man, becomes alive through work, for through work man loses his isolation and becomes a social or co-operative being, and thus learns of himself; and through work he is able to transform nature as well.[5]

In locating man's alienation in work, Marx had taken the revolutionary step of grounding philosophy in concrete human activity. The road by which he "freed" himself from the Hegelian tyranny of abstraction was a long and difficult one.[6] As a Hegelian, Marx thought first of the alienation of work in terms of idealistic dualities. Man, in working, reifies himself in objective things (i.e., in products which embody his work). This is *labour (Arbeit)* and is part of the "alien and hostile world standing over against him." In labour, man is "under the domination, compulsion and yoke of another man." Against this is the state of freedom where man would transform nature, and himself, by free, conscious, spontaneous, creative work. Two things stood in the way of achieving this freedom: the fact that in the alienation of work man lost control over the *process* of work, and lost control, too, of the *product* of his labour.[7] For Marx, therefore, the answer to Hegel was clear: the alienation of man lay not in some philosophical abstraction of Mind, but in the property system. In the organization of work—in labour becoming a commodity—man became an object used by others, and unable, therefore, to obtain satisfaction in his own activity. By becoming himself a commodity, he lost his sense of identity; he lost the sense of "himself."

The extraordinary thing was that Marx had taken a concept which German philosophy had seen as an ontological fact, and had given it a social content. As ontology, as an ultimate, man could only accept alienation. As a social fact, rooted in a specific system of historical relations, alienation could be overcome by changing the social system. But in narrowing the concept, Marx ran two risks: of falsely identifying the source of alienation only in the private property system; and of introducing a note of utopianism in the idea that once the private property system was abolished man would immediately be free.

The question of why men were propertyless turned Marx to economics. For a man whose name is so inextricably linked with the "dismal science," Marx was never really interested in economics. His correspondence with Engels in later years is studded with contemptuous references to the subject and he resented the fact that his detailed explorations prevented him from carrying on other studies. But he continued because, for him, economics was the practical side of philosophy —it would unveil the mystery of alienation—and because he had found in the categories of political economy the material expression of that alienation: the process of economic exploitation.

This development is seen most clearly in the *Economic-Philosophical Manuscripts*, which Marx had written in 1844 at the age of twenty-six. The *Manuscripts*, in the history of Marxist thought, is the bridge from the left-Hegelianism of the early Marx to the Marxism we have come to know. The title itself is both literal and symbolic. Beginning as an anthropology it ends as a political economy. In it one finds the first conceptualization of alienation as rooted in work (rather than in abstract spirit, or religion), and the beginnings of the analysis of property. And in the analysis of property, one finds the direct transmutation, which is so crucial in the development of Marx's thought, of philosophical into economic categories.

In search for an answer to Hegel's question, Marx had sought to pin down concretely the ways in which the human being was "robbed" of his potential possibilities of realizing his "self." For Feuerbach, religion was the means whereby man was alienated from himself; for in religion man externalized his real "self." For Marx, now, the idea of the "self" had become too abstract. The key to the problem was the nature of work—the process whereby man became a social being —but the question remained as to what barred man from realizing his full nature in work. The answer, he thought, lay in the operation of the property system. But how? In the capitalist system, in the bargain made between worker and employer, the individual was formally free. What, then, was the means whereby a man, unbeknownst even to himself, was alienated and enslaved? Marx found the answer in money. Money is the most impersonal form of value. It is seemingly neutral. A man who has a direct obligation to another, as a serf does to a master, knows directly the source of power over him. But one who sells his labour power for money may feel himself to be free. The product of the labourer can thus be easily "abstracted" into money and, through the exchange system, be "abstracted" from him.[8]

Money, thus, is the concrete embodiment of the philosophical abstraction which Hegel had described airily as "spirit," and the commodity process the means whereby the labourer, by exchanging his labour power for money, is robbed of his freedom unawares. Political economy became for Marx what religion was for Feuerbach, a means whereby human values are "projected" outside of man and achieve an existence independent of him and over him. And so alienation, conceived initially by Marx as a process whereby an individual lost his capacity to express himself in work, now became seen as exploitation, or the appropriation of a labourer's surplus product by the capitalist. Thus a philosophical expression which embodies, actually, a socio-psychological insight became transformed into an economic category.

The irony, however, was that in moving from "philosophy" to "reality," from Hegelian phenomenology to political economy, Marx moved from one kind of abstraction to another. In his system, self-alienation became transformed: man as "generic man" (i.e., Man writ large) becomes divided into classes of men.[9] For Marx now, the only social reality is not Man, nor the individual, but economic classes. Individuals and their motives count for naught.[10] The only form of consciousness which can be translated into action—and which can explain history, past, present, and future—is class consciousness.

In *The German Ideology*, written in 1846, the idea of the "self" has disappeared from Marx's writings. Marx now mocks the left-Hegelians for talking of "human nature, of Man in general who belongs to no class, has no reality and subsists only in the realm of philosophical fantasy." In attacking the "true Socialist," Marx writes: "It is characteristic of all these high-sounding phrases about liberation, etc., that it is always 'man' who is liberated . . . it would appear from [their] claims that 'wealth' and 'money' have ceased to exist. . . ." [11]

In *The Communist Manifesto*, the attack is widened, and made cruelly sardonic. The German *literati*, says Marx, "wrote their philosophical nonsense beneath the French original. For instance, beneath the French criticism of the economic functions of money, they wrote 'alienation of humanity'. . . ." And mocking his erstwhile philosophical comrades, Marx speaks scornfully of "this transcendental robe in which the German Socialists wrapped their sorry 'eternal truths' . . . the robe of speculative cobwebs, embroidered with the flowers of rhetoric, steeped in the dew of sickly sentiment." [12]

In saying that there is no human nature "inherent in each separate individual," as Marx does in his sixth thesis on Feuerbach, but only social man, and then only classes, one introduces a new *persona*. Marx makes this explicit in his preface to *Capital*, written in 1867: "Here individuals are dealt with only insofar as they are the personifications of economic categories, embodiments of particular class-relations and class interests. My standpoint, from which the evolution of the economic formation of society is viewed as a process of natural history, can, less than any other, make the individual responsible for relations whose creature he socially remains, however he may subjectively raise himself above them."

Thus, individual responsibility is turned into class morality, and the variability of individual action subsumed under impersonal mechanisms. And the ground is laid for the loss of freedom in a new tyranny that finds its justifications in the narrowed view of exploitation which Marx had fashioned.

To sum up the argument thus far: In his early philosophical writings, Marx had seen, against Hegel, that alienation or the failure to realize one's potential as a self, was rooted primarily in work, rather than in the abstract development of consciousness. In the organization of work, men become "means" for the aggrandisement of others, rather than "ends" in themselves. As alienated labour, there was a twofold loss: men lost control over the *conditions* of work, and men lost the *product* of their labour. This dual conception is present, in a different form, in the later Marx: the loss of control of work is seen as *dehumanization,* occasioned by the division of labour and intensified by technology; the loss of product, as *exploitation,* because a portion of man's labour (surplus value) was appropriated by the employer.

But except for literary and illustrative references in *Capital* to the dehumanization of labour and the fragmentation of work, this first aspect, as problem, was glossed over by Marx. In common with some later (bourgeois?) sociologists, Marx felt that there was no solution to the loss of "self" in work inherent in technology. Under communism—in the "final" society—the division of labour, the cause of dehumanization, would be eliminated so that by variety in work man would be able to develop his varied aptitudes. But these fragmentary discussions take on a utopian hue.[13] In actuality one had to accept not only the division of labour, but hierarchical organization as well. In a polemic against some Italian anarchists who had argued that technology had imposed on man a "veritable despotism," Engels argued that it was utopian to question the nature of authority in a factory: "At least with regard to the hours of work one may write upon the portals of these factories: *Lasciate ogni autonomia, voi che entrate!* [leave, ye that enter in, all autonomy behind!]. If man by dint of his knowledge and inventive genius, has subdued the forces of nature, the latter avenge themselves upon him by subjecting him, insofar as he employs them, to a veritable despotism, independent of all social organization. Wanting to abolish authority in large-scale industry is tantamount to wanting to abolish industry itself, to destroy the power loom in order to return to the spinning wheel.[14]

What became central to *Capital* was the concrete social relationships created by private property, those of employer-and-employee, rather than the processes generated by manufacture. Dehumanization was a creature of technology; exploitation that of capitalism. The solution was simple, if one-sided: abolish private property, and the system of exploitation would disappear. "In contemporary capitalist society men are dominated by economic relations created by themselves, by means of production which they have produced, as if by an alien power," said Engels. "When society, by taking possession of all means of production and managing them on a planned basis, has freed itself and all of its members from the bondage in which they are at present held by means of production which they themselves have produced but which now confront them as irresistible, alien power; when consequently man no longer proposes, but also disposes—only then will the last alien power which is now reflected in religion vanish. And with it will also vanish the religious reflection itself, for the simple reason that there will be nothing left to reflect." [15]

When critics argued that technological organization might still "deform and debilitate" the worker, the Marxist called this utopian. When sceptics asserted that socialism itself might become an exploitative society, the Marxist had a ready answer: the source of exploitation, and of power, was economic, and political office was only an administrative extension of economic power; once economic power was socialized, there could no longer be classes, or a basis whereby man could exploit man. By this extension it became "clear" that the Soviet Union was a "workers' state," and no basis for exploitation existed. Thus the concept of alienation came, down one road, to a twisted end.

Having found the answer to the "mysteries" of Hegel in political economy, Marx promptly forgot all about philosophy. ("The philosophers have only *interpreted* the world differently; the point, however, is to change it," he had scrawled in his *Theses on Feuerbach*.) In 1846, Marx and Engels had completed a long criticism of post-Hegelian philosophy in two large octavo volumes and (except for some gnomic references in the *Critique of the Gotha Programme* in 1875) neither of them returned to the subject until forty years later when Engels, after the death of Marx, was, to his surprise, asked by the *Neue Zeit*, the

German Socialist theoretical magazine, to review a book on Feuerbach by C. N. Starcke, a then well-known anthropologist. Engels reluctantly consented and wrote a long review which, slightly expanded, was published two years later in 1888 as a small brochure entitled *Ludwig Feuerbach and the Outcome of Classical German Philosophy*. In writing the review Engels went back to some mouldering manuscripts of Marx and found among his papers the hastily scribbled eleven theses on Feuerbach, totalling in all a few pages, which he appended to the brochure. In the Foreword, Engels alludes to the large manuscript (without mentioning even its title, *The German Ideology*), and says merely that because of the reluctance of the publishers it was not printed. "We abandoned the manuscript to the gnawings of the mice all the more willingly," wrote Engels, "as we had achieved our main purpose—to clear our own minds." [16] (The gnawing was literal, since many pages, in fact, had been completely chewed up!)

But it is also clear that while, as young philosophy students, the debates with the other young Hegelians were necessary for the purposes of "self clarification," the absorption of both into concrete economic study and political activity had made the earlier philosophical problems increasingly unreal to them. In a letter to his American translator, Florence Kelley Wischnewetzky, in February 1886, Engels writes, apropos of his *Anti-Dühring*, "the semi-Hegelian language of a good many passages of my old book is not only untranslatable but has lost the greater part of its meaning even in German." [17] And in 1893 a Russian visitor to Engels, Alexis Voden, found Engels incredulous when the question of publishing the early philosophical manuscripts was raised. In a memoir, Voden recalled: "Our next conversation was on the early works of Marx and Engels. At first Engels was embarrassed when I expressed interest in these works. He mentioned that Marx had also written poetry in his student years, but it could hardly interest anybody. . . . Was not the fragment on Feuerbach which Engels considered the most meaty of the 'old works' sufficient?" Which was more important, Engels asked, "for him to spend the rest of his life publishing old manuscripts from the publicistic works of the 1840's or to set to work, when Book III of *Capital* came out, on the publication of Marx's manuscripts on the history of the theories of surplus value?" And for Engels the answer was obvious. Besides, said Engels, "in order to penetrate into that 'old story' one needed to have an interest in Hegel himself, which was not the case with anybody then, or to be exact, 'neither with Kautsky nor with Bernstein.'" [18]

In fact, except for *The Holy Family*,[19] a crazy-quilt bag of essays deriding Bruno Bauer and his two brothers, who with their friends constituted the "holy family," none of the early philosophical writings of Marx was published either in his lifetime or that of Engels. Nor is it clear whether the major exegetes, Kautsky, Plekhanov, and Lenin, were ever aware of their content. None of the questions of alienation appears in their writing. The chief concern of the post-Marxist writers, when they dealt with philosophy, was simply to defend a materialist viewpoint against idealism.

The contemporary "rediscovery" of the idea of alienation in Marxist thought is due to Georg Lukacs, the Hungarian philosopher who did have an interest in Hegel. The idea of alienation, because of its natural affinity to romanticism, had already played an important role in German sociology, particularly in the thought of Georg Simmel, who had been a teacher of Lukacs. Simmel, writing about the "anonymity" of modern man, first located the source of alienation in industrial society, which destroyed man's self-identity by "dispersing" him into a cluster of separate roles. Later Simmel widened the concept to see alienation as an ineluctable outcome between man's creativity and the pressure of social institutions (not unlike Freud's later image of the inescapable tension between instinct and civilization).

Lukacs, coming to Marx after World War I, was able, without knowing of the early *Manuscripts,* to "read back" from Marx into Hegel the alienation of labour as the self-alienation of Man from the Absolute Idea. The Kautsky-Lenin generation had construed Marxism as a scientific, non-moral, analysis of society. But in Lukacs' interpretation, Marx's economic analysis of society was turned inside out and became the work, as Morris Watnick put it, "of a moral philosopher articulating the future of man's existence in the accents of a secular eschatology." Lukacs' interpretation, which was included in a collection of essays entitled *Geschichte und Klassenbewusstsein* (History and Class Consciousness), published in 1923, smacked of idealism to the orthodox Marxists, and Lukacs quickly came under fire in Moscow. Among the Communists the book was proscribed, although the work continued to enjoy a *sub rosa* reputation among the Communist intelligentsia, less for its discussion of alienation, however, than for another essay which, in covert form, rationalized the elite position of, and the need for outward submission of, the Communist intellectual to the party. When Lukacs fled Germany in the early thirties and took refuge in the Soviet Union, he was forced, eleven years after the publication of the essays, again to repudiate his book, and this time in an abject act of self-abasement.[20]

When the early philosophical works of Marx were unearthed and published, Lukacs had the satisfaction of seeing how accurately he had been able to reconstruct the thought of the young Marx.[21] But this did not spare him from attack. The dogma, drawn from Lenin, had become fixed.

The early philosophical writings were published in 1932 in Germany. But in the floodtide of Hitlerism, of the destruction of the Social-Democratic and Communist parties, and the dispersal of the German scholarly community, there was little time or incentive to read these inchoate and fragmentary works. In the disillusionments with Stalinism in the late thirties, particularly following the Moscow trials, in some small intellectual radical circles in New York, in the increasing sense of rootlessness felt by a young generation, in the resumption of scholarly activity by a group of German scholars in New York, notably the Frankfurt Institute of Social Research of Max Horkheimer, and the publication of its *Zeitschrift*, first in German and then in English, there arose some small interest in the early writings of Marx, and particularly the idea of alienation. But the application of the idea was psychological and literary and soon found a louder resonance from surprisingly other sources.

The interest in the idea of alienation that unfolded rapidly in the late forties and early fifties came largely from the rediscovery of Kierkegaard and Kafka, and from the sense of despair that both epitomized.

Kierkegaard represented the other great, neglected trunk which had emerged from the deep Hegelian roots. Where the "left-Hegelians" had sought a rational answer to the question of alienation, Kierkegaard argued that none existed. No rational act could overcome the subject-object dualism; any attempt to set rational limits to comprehension ends in the "absurd." Only by a "leap of faith" could man establish a relationship with ultimate powers beyond himself. Thus, from ontology, Kierkegaard took the concept of alienation and gave it a religious content; and where Marx had sought to narrow the description of alienation into the exploitative social relationships created by the economic system, Kierkegaard universalized it as an ineluctable, pervasive condition of man.

There were deep reasons for this attraction to the idea of despair —and faith. The sadism of the Nazis, the ruthlessness of war, the existence of concentration camps, the use of terror, had called into question the deepest beliefs of the generation. One could argue, as did Sidney Hook, for example, that the Stalinist terror grew out of the specific historical circumstances which shaped the Russian dictatorship, and that its existence was no indictment of rationalism. But a more compelling reason—at least, psychologically speaking—seemed to come from the neo-orthodox arguments of Reinhold Niebuhr that such corruption of power was inevitable when men, in their pride, identified their own egos with the demiurge of History, and that rationalism, by encouraging utopian beliefs in man's perfectibility, had left men unarmed against the corruption which lurked in socialism.

From a second source, the "tragic vein" of German sociology, came new, intellectual support for the idea of alienation. In the influence of Karl Mannheim, and later of Max Weber, the idea of alienation merged with the idea of "bureaucratization." The two had absorbed Marx's ideas and gone beyond him. The drift of all society, said Weber, was towards the creation of large-scale organization, hierarchically organized and centrally directed, in which the individual counted for naught. Marx's emphasis on the wage worker as being "separated" from the means of production became, in Weber's perspective, as Gerth and Mills succinctly put it, "merely one special case of a universal trend. The modern soldier is equally 'separated' from the means of violence, the scientist from the means of enquiry and the civil servant from the means of administration." And the irony, said Weber, is that, from one perspective, capitalism and socialism were simply two different faces of the same, inexorable trend.

Out of all this came the impact of the idea of alienation. The intellectual saw men becoming depersonalized, used as a "thing" in the operation of society as a machine; the intellectual himself felt increasingly estranged from the society. The idea of alienation, thus, was a judgment *on* society. It also reflected the self-conscious position of the intellectual *in* the society.

The themes of alienation, anomie, bureaucratization, depersonalization, privatization have been common coin in sociological literature for more than a decade and a half. In the light of all this, the recent attempts to proclaim the theme of alienation in the early Marx as a great new theoretical advance in the understanding of contemporary society is indeed strange. The reasons for this—which lie in the sociology of knowledge—are fairly simple. There is today a new political generation in England and France—and in the Communist countries of eastern Europe—whose only political perspective had been Marxism. Following the Khrushchev disclosures at the 20th Party congress and the events in Hungary, this generation became disillusioned about Stalinism. It wants to find its own footing, and, like any generation, has to find it in its own way and in its own language. The post-Stalinist radical generation in England and France still wants to think in political terms (and the dissidents and revisionists in eastern Germany and Poland, by the nature of their situation are forced to argue in philosophical categories) —hence the umbilical cords to Marx.[22]

But the difficulty is that there are no apocalyptic ideas or fresh ideological causes. There may be immediate issues such as nuclear tests or educational policy, but no comprehensive political vision which can fire young imaginations and fill the emotional void that obviously exists. The idea of alienation has gained a new edge because of the disorientation of the radical intellectual in the mass society where tradition, avant-garde and middle-brow culture all jostle each other uneasily— but that is already a far different topic.

Having started out with the idea that in the young Marx there was a double vision of the nature of alienation, I would like to conclude with some brief remarks about the road that Marxism did not take. Marxist thought developed along one narrow road of economic conceptions of property and exploitation, while the other road, which might have led to new, humanistic concepts of work and labour, was left unexplored.

In the transmutation of the concept of alienation, a root insight was lost—that alienation is a consequence of the *organization* of work as well, and that in the effort to give a man a sense of meaning in his daily life, one must examine the work process itself. In manufacture, said Marx, the worker is "deformed into a detail worker," he becomes an appendage to the machine. All this was laid at the door of capitalist society. Yet there is little evidence that the Communist countries have sought to reverse the process, to explore new combinations of work, to re-examine the engineering process, or to question the concept of efficiency that underlies the contemporary organization of work. If anything, in the intense pressure for production, the lack of free trade union movements and independent agencies, which can act as a control or check on the managers and the State, has meant that the workers in the Communist countries are even more exploited than those in western lands. Technology stands as a "given."

One need not accept the fatalism of the machine process [23]—or wait for new utopias in automation—to see that changes are possible. These range from such large-scale changes as genuine decentralization, which brings work to the workers rather than transporting large masses of workers to the work place, to the relatively minute but important changes in the pace of work, such as extending job cycles, job enlargement, allowing natural rhythms in work, etc. The "flow of demand," to use the sociological jargon, must come from the worker rather than from the constraints imposed upon him. If one believes, for example, that the worker is not a commodity, then one should take the step of abolishing wage payment by the piece, or eliminating the distinction whereby one man gets paid a salary and another an hourly wage. If one accepts the heritage of the humanist tradition, then the work place itself, and not the market, must be the centre of determination of the organization of work. The fulness of life can and must be found in the nature of work itself.

NOTES

* Presented in a symposium on "The Nature and Value of Marxism Today," at the meeting of the American Philosophical Association, at Columbia University, 29 December 1959.

The idea of alienation as *derived* from Marx, and employed by intellectuals today, has a double meaning which can best be distinguished as *estrangement* and *reification*. The first is essentially a socio-psychological condition in which the individual experiences a sense of distance, or a divorce from his society or his community; he cannot belong, he is deracinated. The second, a philosophical category with psychological overtones, implies that an individual is treated as an object and turned into a *thing* and loses his identity in the process; in contemporary parlance, he is depersonalized. The two shades of meaning, of estrangement and depersonalization, are sociologically quite distinct.

As Marx used the term, alienation equally had a double, yet obliquely different set of meanings from current usage. The first, of *Entäusserung*, implies the "externalization" of aspects of one's self, with the overtone that such externalization comes through the sale (in a legal-commercial sense) of one's labour. The product that one sells remains as an object, independent of one's self, but one with which there is the twofold sense of identification and loss. The second term, of *Entfremdung*, implies simple estrangement, or the detaching of one's self from another, of divorce. (Feuerbach's usage, while emphasizing the fact that in religion one externalizes part of one's self, tended to emphasize the sense of estrangement.)

These double usages by Marx are found in the early manuscripts and the unpublished philosophical works. In his later writings, the psychological nuances of the term "alienation" have disappeared, and in the form in which the idea of alienation appears in *Capital*, as the "fetishism of commodities," it is clearly in the idea of *reification*. People buy commodities, things, not realizing that each commodity has "embedded" within it labour power, nor are they aware of the social organization required to produce and distribute products. A serf has a direct obligation to a lord and the relationship is naked and direct. The exchange of products in a market "hides" the social relationships because the personal ties have become impersonal, and labour, both in the creation of commodities and in the sale of its own labour power, is now an object.

The contemporary use of alienation, as estrangement, is a far cry from the transmuted ideas of alienation as used by Marx in *Capital*. And to a considerable extent, the current usage "reads back" into Marx overtones of contemporary society that were only dimly heard at the time.

In tracing the idea of alienation, in the present essay, I am concerned largely with the meanings which are present, I think, in the early writings. The larger ambiguous term of alienation is retained because the contemporary political debate begins with that concept.

For a discussion of the terminology, see translator's note to the *Economic-Philosophical Manuscripts* (English-language edition, pp. 10-13), and the citations in Note 6 below.

1. A troublesome issue that still remains unresolved in Marxist theory, for if the intellectuals create the social ideology, while the workers, left to themselves, achieve only trade union consciousness, as Lenin maintained, what, then, is the meaning of Marx's statement that existence determines consciousness, and that class fashions ideology?

2. "For freedom," says Hegel in his *Logic*, "it is necessary that we should feel no presence of something, which is not ourselves." Finitude is bondage, the consciousness of an object is a limitation: freedom is "that voyage into the open where nothing is below us or above us, and we stand in solitude with ourselves alone" (Wallace edition, pp. 49, 66, cited by Robert Tucker; see footnote 6 below).

3. See Ludwig Feuerbach, *The Essence of Christianity* (Harper Torchbook edition, 1957), p. 30.

4. For a discussion of Feuerbach's use of the I-Thou concept, see the introduction by Karl Barth to *The Essence of Christianity, ibid.*, p. xiii.

5. The key statement of this idea in Marx is to be found, first, in the *Economic-Philosophic Manuscripts of 1844*. An English edition was published in Moscow in 1959. See pp. 67-84, and esp. pp. 73-77. A more condensed version of this idea is to be found in Part One of *The German Ideology* (International Publishers, 1939), esp. pp. 7-8.

6. A comprehensive exposition of the early views of Marx can be found in Robert C. Tucker, *The Self and Revolution: A Moral Critique of Marx*, unpublished Ph.D. dissertation (Harvard, 1957). This study, revised and expanded, will be published by the Cambridge University Press under the title, *The Alienated World of Karl Marx*. I am indebted to Mr. Tucker for many insights. A lucid discussion of the nature of Marx's early writings can be found in Jean Hippolyte's *Etudes sur Marx et Hegel* (Librairie Marcel Rivière et Cie, 1955), esp. pp. 147-155. An overly simple exposition can be found in H. P. Adams, *Karl Marx in his Early Writings* (London, 1940); a provocative discussion in Hannah Arendt's *The Human Condition* (Chicago, 1958).

7. For a further discussion, see Herbert Marcuse, *Reason and Revolution: Hegel and the Rise of Social Theory* (New York, 1941), pp. 276-277.

8. "Money is the alienated *ability of mankind.* That which I am unable to do

as a *man*, and of which, therefore all my individual powers are incapable, I am able to do by means of *money*. Money thus turns each of these powers into something which in itself it is not—turns it, that is, into its *contrary.*" *Economic-Philosophical Manuscripts, op. cit.*, p. 139 (italics in the original).

It is this conception of money as the hidden mechanism whereby people became exploited (money "the common whore . . . [which] confounds all human and natural qualities") that lay behind Marx's withering analysis of the Jew, as the dealer in money, in economic society. It is this conception, too, that underlay the extraordinarily naive act of the Bolshevik regime in the first days after the October Revolution of abolishing all money in an effort to make the relationship of man to man "direct." The novel implications of this development in Marx's thought, of the *shift* in the early manuscripts from philosophy to political economy, have been explored in great detail by Professor Tucker (*op. cit.*).

9. For a neglected discussion of the idea of "generic man" and "historical man" in Marx, see Solomon F. Bloom, *The World of Nations: A Study of the National Implications in the Work of Karl Marx* (New York, 1941), Chap. I, pp. 1-10.

10. In *The German Ideology* Marx poses the question of how individual self-interest becomes transformed into ideology. "How does it come about," he asks, "that personal interests grow, despite the persons, into class-interests, into common interests which win an independent existence over against individual persons, in this independence take on the shape of general interests, enter as such into opposition with the real individuals, and in this opposition, according to which they are defined as general interests, can be conceived by the consciousness as ideal, even as religious, sacred interests?"

Having posed the question so concisely, Marx, exasperatingly, never goes on to answer it. Sidney Hook, in his article on "Materialism" in the *Encyclopedia of the Social Sciences*, sought to rephrase the problem in these terms: "What are the specific mechanisms by which the economic conditions influence the habits and motives of classes, granted that individuals are actuated by motives that are not always a function of individual self-interest? Since classes are composed of individuals, how are class interests furthered by the non-economic motives of individuals?" Having rephrased the question even more sharply, Hook, too, left it unanswered. So far no Marxist theoretician has detailed the crucial psychological and institutional nexuses which transform the personifications, or masks of class-role, into the self-identity of the individual.

See, *The German Ideology, op. cit.*, p. 203; *E.S.S.*, Vol. X, p. 219; and the discussions by Robert Tucker.

11. *Ibid.*, p. 96.

12. *The Communist Manifesto*, p. 233, in Karl Marx, *Selected Works* (Moscow, 1935), Volume I.

13. In *Capital*, Marx writes powerfully of the crippling effects of the detailed division of labour, and then, in a footnote, quotes approvingly the image of work provided by a French workman who had returned from San Francisco: "I never could have believed, that I was capable of working at various occupations I was employed on in California. I was firmly convinced that I was fit for nothing but letterpress printing. . . . Once in the midst of this world of adventurers, who change their occupation as often as they do their shirt, egad, I did as the others. As mining did not turn out remunerative enough, I left it for the town, where in succession I became typographer, slater, plumber, &c. In consequence of thus finding out that I am fit for any sort of work, I feel less of a mollusc and more of a man." (Marx, *Capital*, Chicago 1906, Vol. I, Part IV, Section 9, esp. pp. 532-535. The footnote is from p. 534.)

14. F. Engels, "On Authority," in *Marx & Engels: Basic Writings on Politics & Philosophy*, edited by Lewis S. Feuer (Anchor Books, 1959), p. 483.

15. Frederick Engels, *Anti-Dühring* (Chicago, 1935), pp. 332-333.

16. Frederick Engels, *Ludwig Feuerbach and the Outcome of German Classical Philosophy*, in Karl Marx, *Selected Works, op. cit.*, Vol. I, p. 147.

17. Engels to Florence Kelley Wischnewetzky, February 25, 1886, in Karl Marx and Frederick Engels, *Letters to Americans* (New York, 1953), p. 151.

18. A. Voden, "Talks with Engels," in *Reminiscences of Marx and Engels* (Moscow, undated), pp. 330-331.

19. The first part of *The Holy Family*, subtitled the "Critique of Critical Critique," is devoted to an alleged misreading by Edgar Bauer of Proudhon's work on property. The book then jumps to a detailed analysis of Eugene Sue's *The Mysteries of Paris* and to the alleged misreading of this volume—which is about the sick and wretched of Paris—by a supporter of Bauer who had used the volume to demonstrate the "critical method." The last sections deal with the French Revolution and the rise of French materialism. In his heavy-handed way, Marx was fond of pinning religious tags on his opponents. Not only are the Bauers called the "holy family" but in *The German Ideology* Max Stirner is called "Saint Max." Although Marx drew most of his ideas from his peers—self-consciousness from Bauer, alienation from Feuerbach, communism from Moses Hess, the stages of property from Proudhon—he was not content simply to synthesize these ideas, but he had to attack, and usually viciously, all these individuals in the determined effort to appear wholly original.

20. This statement is quoted by Morris Watnick in his study, "Georg Lukacs: An Intellectual Biography," *Soviet Survey*, No. 24, p. 54. Mr. Watnick's extended discussion of Lukacs' ideas can be found in *Soviet Survey*, Nos. 23, 24, 25, 27 (1958-59).

Lukacs' book is generally unobtainable here. A chapter from it under the title "What is Orthodox Marxism," appeared in *The New International*, Summer, 1957. Sections of the book have been translated into French, in the review *Arguments* published by Les Editions de Minuit. There are some brief, but penetrating remarks on Lukacs—and the problem of the intellectual accepting the soldierly discipline of Communism—in Franz Borkenau's *World Communism* (New York, 1939), pp. 172-175.

21. The early philosophical writings, principally the incomplete *Economic-Philosophical Manuscripts*, and *The German Ideology* were first published (with small sections missing) in 1932 by S. Landshut and J. P. Mayer under the title of *Der historiche Materialismus*, in two volumes. (Some small fragments of the third part of *The German Ideology*, on Max Stirner, had been published by Edward Bernstein in *Dokumente des Sozialismus*, in 1902-03.) A detailed description of the early manuscripts, particularly of *The German Ideology*, was published by D. Riazanov in Vol. I of the *Marx-Engels Archiv* in 1927. The complete texts are available in the *Marx-Engels Gesamtausgabe* under the direction of V. Adoratski (Berlin, 1932). A new edition of the early papers was published by S. Landshut in 1953, under the title of *Die Frühschriften von Karl Marx*. A complete guide to the works of Marx can be found in Maximilien Rubel, *Bibliographie des Oeuvres de Karl Marx* (Paris, 1956).

22. So eager are the young neo-Marxists to maintain a tie to Marxism or to provide some notion of fresh thinking and discovery that such a bright young Scottish philosopher as Alasdair MacIntyre is led to write such a farrago as appeared in *The Listener* of 8 January 1959, entitled "Dr. Marx and Dr. Zhivago": "Humanity and the one true bearer of the human essence in our time, the industrial proletariat, has to break through and make new forms. So alienated man remakes and regains himself. This is the picture which the young Marx elaborated, the picture out of which the mature Marxist theory grew. In this picture there is a place for those members of bourgeois society who, humane and sensitive as they are, cling to the ideals and culture they know and therefore cannot make the transition to the new society. Such surely is Zhivago."

23. For an elaboration of this argument, see my essay "Work and Its Discontents: The Cult of Efficiency in America" (Beacon Press, 1956).

SOVIET IDEOLOGY

HISTORICAL DETERMINISM AND POLITICAL FIAT IN SOVIET COMMUNISM

Sidney Hook

Despite their concern about the Soviet Union, the statesmen and generals of the Western world have shown very little interest in its ideology. They have been inclined to regard it as having about as much relevance to Soviet practice as Christian theology to the practices of the West. Few students of Soviet policy, however, would deny that some understanding of Communist (Bolshevik) ideology is relevant to charting, and possibly predicting, the course of conduct followed by the Kremlin. But there is no agreement on how significant that influence is in relation to other considerations, material and ideal.

Some observers seek to explain Soviet practice in terms of the psychology of its leaders or as an expression of the psychology of the Russian Slavic people, naturally or mystically interpreted. Others see it as little different from the traditional policy of national expansion followed by earlier Russian regimes from Peter the Great to Nicholas II. Still others view Soviet policy as a jockeying for a strategic global position in a balance of power the laws of whose equilibrium are invariant for all social systems. Another influential school sees in Communism a kind of Christian heresy embodied in the institutional vestiges of Byzantinism but perverted to a form in which the secular power *openly* declares itself to be the source of all spiritual and temporal authority.

All of these conceptions would be contemptuously dismissed by the Russian Communists themselves as an "ideological" reading of the Russian historical experience since 1917. Strictly speaking the term "ideological" in the vocabulary of the Russian Communists connotes a "false

Reprinted from the *Proceedings of the American Philosophical Society*, vol. 99, no. 1 (January, 1955), 1-10. By permission of the author and the publisher.

consciousness" which distorts objective historical truth. The truths of history, according to their own account, are specific applications on the level of human affairs of certain fundamental truths embodied in the alleged laws of materialistic dialectics.

These laws, simply summarized, state that all change, including historical change, takes place in virtue of the operation of *internal* and *necessary* causes. The tempo according to which they manifest themselves may be retarded or accelerated by causes *external* to the system under consideration but in no case can they be permanently arrested in their development. Thus in considering the history of any given society, factors like climate, geography, the presence or absence of raw materials, the influence of great men, are assigned at most the role of peripheral factors. They are unable to supply the key to the main movement which always lies in the mode of economic production. The proximity of cultures, the diffusion of cultural forms and practices are relegated to the rank of stimuli which are of themselves never sufficient causes of significant social change. An encounter between civilizations gives rise to a fundamental change only when the internal state of one or both has reached a point of internal readiness or preparedness such that it can confidently be predicted that even without the specific stimulus of contact, the change would have taken place anyhow at a subsequent date. Ideas and ideologies, although not denied some causal influence, are strictly subordinate to the basic immanent economic "contradictions" which constitute the dynamic force in all social evolution.

This conception of an overriding objective historical necessity, triggered by subjective factors and contingent events, is canonic doctrine for all Communists in all countries. It is of course the cardinal tenet of the orthodox Marxism professed by Communists everywhere, especially Lenin,[1] and has remained so down to today. Anyone who has read Mao Tse-Tung will find in his writings the same ideas down to the very illustrations which Stalin took from Lenin who copied them out of Engels.[2]

The uses to which the doctrine of historical determinism has been put are many and profound. Every major policy including the conquest of political power in October, 1917, has been justified in its terms. The Bolsheviks have prided themselves upon being activists, unflinching in resolution and prepared for any personal sacrifice. But the more they set themselves to storm the gates of heaven, or achieve the "classless society," the more they felt themselves absolved from ordinary principles of ethical responsibility in virtue of the operation of the economic necessities which they insisted they were helping to fulfill. The establishment of the dictatorship, the programs of industrialization and collectivization, the ironclad control of culture, the major turns in foreign policy—all were defended as, in the last analysis, compelled either by the economic decline of capitalism or by the necessity of building and defending the socialist economy.

This attitude with some variations has been often adopted by

Western admirers of the Russian Revolution who have bravely accepted all the hardships and deprivations of the Russian masses on the ground that the Bolsheviks had no real alternatives open to them. Hard and ruthless as Bolshevik actions were, they were not the result of arbitrary decisions, for in a certain sense they were not free decisions at all. The hands of the Kremlin were forced by economic events. They could not have acted differently and succeeded in building socialism. Thus, Harold J. Laski, who towards the end of his life believed that Soviet civilization held up to the Western world an image of its own future, contended that the reduction in the living standards of the Russian people, the liquidation of all democratic institutions including free workers' soviets, the terror and concentration camp regime was the only way in which the socialist economy could have been set up. A democratic course would never have permitted the sacrifice of basic consumption needs for massive investments in capital goods industries. This would have meant inability to stand up against Hitler's war machine.[3] Believing then that capitalist countries must expand or face ruin, and that their expansion could be achieved only by war, the Communists were compelled to follow the logic of the historical situation. Had they pursued instead the gradualist path of democratic socialism or moved towards something like the welfare economies of England and the United States, Hitler would have triumphed. So runs the argument.

I

The question I propose to discuss in this paper is whether in actual fact Communist practice has been guided by its doctrinal justifications, whether Bolshevik historical behavior can be squared with its professed Marxist theory, and, if not, what set of considerations actually determines the fundamental line of Bolshevik policy.

The first observation which suggests itself to an unbiased inquiry is that the Communists have inflated the elements of voluntarism in the Marxist system of thought to a point where they have burst out of its framework. From a Communist point of view this is a most heretical and impious charge. To imply that a Communist is not a Marxist is tantamount in the eyes of believers to asserting that one can be Catholic without being Christian. None the less a sober assessment of Communist practice seems to lead to this conclusion—and this independently of whether one regards Marx's thought as sound or unsound.

One of Marx's central contributions to the study of culture is his theory of historical materialism. It is plagued by all sorts of ambiguities, loose formulations, and difficulties. But its intent is clear. It asserts that politics is a reflex of economics, that the human will does not possess all degrees of historical freedom. Human action is either the mode by which social inevitabilities come to pass or, in a freer and more charitable reading, it is responsible for choices between narrowly limited alternatives in conditions of historical crisis. No Marxist of any persuasion would admit that political action can create a new social order unless the necessary antecedent economic conditions for its successful functioning were already present. Marx, Engels, Kautsky, Plechanov, and the entire Sanhedrin of Social-Democratic expositors of Marx, including Lenin before the First World War,[4] described these economic conditions, and their social and cultural corollaries. A matured capitalist economy with an industrial proletariat schooled by modern processes of production and inspired by an enlightened world view was considered a necessary if not sufficient condition for the great social transformation that would forever end economic class society and the exploitation of man by man. The socialist revolution was expected in advanced industrial countries like England and the United States, not in one of the most economically backward countries of Europe. The Communists, than whom there are none more vehement in their protestations of Marxist orthodoxy, none the less seized political power in Russia, destroyed the regime which at one time Lenin declared "the freest" in the world, characterized "by the absence of oppression of the masses," [5] and built a collectivist economy. Marx had proclaimed in his *Introduction to the Critique of Political Economy* that "no social order ever perishes before all the productive forces for which there is room in it have developed." [6] There was plenty of room for the development of productive forces in the Russia of 1917, certainly not less than in the United States of 1917, which was decades ahead of Russia, and yet more than doubled its productive capacity since then.

At first, Lenin and Trotsky rationalized the Communist conquest of power by considering the world economy as a whole and claiming that on a world scale there was no room for further expansion—again in the teeth of the facts, since world capitalism, measured by increase in productivity, has developed on a tremendous scale. Lenin asserted that capitalism breaks down "at its weakest link" which Russia was supposed to be; Trotsky discovered a "law of combined development" which enables backward countries to telescope their social development so that they can skip a phase of industrial development.[7] These *ad hoc* doctrines could just as well explain a socialist revolution at the time in Spain or Turkey which were still weaker links in the capitalist chain. If valid they would have held even for the time of Marx and Engels, making nonsense of their earlier predictions.

But all this was preliminary to a more far-reaching abandonment of Marxism. The assumption of Lenin and Trotsky was that the world socialist revolution would begin after power was taken in Russia, and that the more highly industrialized countries would lead the march to socialism with Russia once more making up the rear. When this did not happen, the Communists set themselves to do what Marxist theory declared economically impossible, i.e., to build a collectivist economy even though the necessary presuppositions were absent. Their very success refuted the theory which presumably guided them. If socialism

be defined as collective ownership of the instruments of mass production, then we must regard it as one of history's greatest ironies that
Marx has been decisively proved wrong by his most vehement disciples.

To be sure socialism can be defined not merely as a collectivist
economy but as one functioning under democratic political controls in
which case there can be no talk of socialism under a totalitarian dictatorship. But orthodox Marxism cannot consistently define a culture save
on the basis of its economy. After all, it is quite explicit that democracy
and dictatorship both are merely superstructural addenda. Just as capitalism still remains capitalism whether it functions under democratic
or dictatorial forms so, in accordance with this line of thinking, socialism
remains socialism irrespective of whether it is administered under a
democracy or dictatorship. At any rate in most contexts socialism is a
category of economic, not political, classification.

We are not interested here in the exegetical conflicts between doctrinaire Marxists but in readily verified historical facts which cannot be
explained away. A year to the day after the Communists seized power
in Russia, Lenin unveiled a memorial to Marx and Engels. In his speech
he acclaimed as their great historical merit their "scientific analysis of
the inevitability of the collapse of capitalism and its transition to communism." [8] At that very time against great odds, Lenin and his party
were trying to make the inevitable come to pass. It was their will to
power, together with the ineptitude and disunity of their opponents,
which was shaping day-by-day events, and nothing remotely resembling
any social or economic necessity.

II

In no aspect of Communist domestic policy is this clearer than in
the transformation of the Marxist concept of "the dictatorship of the
proletariat" (a phrase infrequently used by Marx as synonymous with
a workers' democracy) into a dictatorship of the Communist Party—
and its leaders—over the proletariat.

Marx never made any clear distinction between his party and the
proletariat and seems to have accepted a kind of "theory of spontaneity"
according to which the workers, following the pattern set by the Paris
Commune, would democratically control their political and industrial
life. He assumed that the socialist revolution when it occurred would
have a clear majority of the population in its support. After the February
Revolution the Soviets became the special organ of workers, soldiers, and
peasants as distinct from the Provisional Government which looked
towards the Constituent Assembly for an authoritative democratic mandate. There is no evidence that at any definite time the actual will of
the majority of the Russian population was reflected in the Soviets.
Representation was uneven, the city Soviets exercised disproportionate
influence and there were no direct elections to the Provincial and all

Union Soviets. But they did provide a more or less free area of discussion and debate of representatives of the Russian working population and soldiery.

When Lenin returned to Russia from abroad in April, 1917, he called for the transfer of all political power to the Soviets despite the fact that "we [the Bolsheviks] are in the minority." [9] The Soviets were the political form through which the dictatorship of the proletariat was to be exercised. He made effective capital of the call "All Power to the Soviets" until it appears that the Soviets, repelled by the premature attempts at the seizure of power by the Bolsheviks in July, showed clearly that they were prepared to defend the Provisional government against further insurrectionary attempts. Then in a revealing and much neglected essay, *On Slogans,* Lenin frankly acknowledged that the appeal for all power to the Soviets, hitherto defended as a democratic principle, was nothing but a slogan. He called for its abandonment, despite the fact that the Soviets still represented the largest group of workers and peasants, and for the preparation of an insurrectionary program. "The slogan of the power passing to the Soviets would at present sound quixotic and mocking," he wrote.[10]

The Sixth Congress of the Bolshevik Party formally approved Lenin's new proposal which was a clear declaration that the Bolsheviks would attempt to seize power behind the backs of the Soviet democracy. After the Kornilov affair, Lenin again proposed the slogan "All Power to the Soviets," suspended it when rebuffed by other working class and peasant parties, and returned to it only when the Bolsheviks got a majority in the Petersburg and Moscow Soviets. Trotsky candidly admits that the slogans under which the Bolsheviks carried out their insurrection meant merely "All Power to the *Bolshevik* Soviets." [11]

Although Lenin, and Stalin after him, speak of "the dictatorship of the proletariat" as an "historic necessity," [12] no attempt is ever made to show how the actual nature of such a dictatorship determines any specific *political* institutional form, except that representation shifts from a geographical to an occupational basis. The "dictatorship of the bourgeoisie" is presumed to be present under parliamentary institutions, no matter how democratic, as well as under the rule of a dictator. Yet at no time have the Bolsheviks held that such political dictatorship, or even Fascism as a political system, is *inevitably* bound up with capitalist development. It is always pictured as a consequence of political weakness or betrayal. Why, then, must "the dictatorship of the proletariat" take a *politically* dictatorial form? Neither Lenin nor any other Bolshevik theoretician offers any plausible explanation in terms of their own Marxist doctrines.

The truth seems to be that, confronted with an opportunity to seize power, the Communists abandoned the entire democratic heritage of the Marxist tradition. Despite an elaborate semantic by-play with the terms "democratic" and "leadership," it is clear that neither Lenin nor Stalin regarded majority rule as a necessary element in their conception of democracy. Their idea was first to seize power and then count the votes to determine who won the confidence of the majority. Stalin quotes Lenin with full approval: "If the proletariat is to win over the majority of the population, it *must first of all overthrow the bourgeoisie and seize the powers of the state.*" [13]

The term "proletariat" is a very elastic one and the Communists stretch it to suit their convenience. Strickly speaking it is the class of industrial workers who not only constitute a minority of the population in most countries but a *minority of workers* in industrially backward countries such as Russia was in 1917. In order, therefore, to win over even a majority of the workers, "the victorious proletariat" must seize power. Only *then* will it be in a position "to gain the sympathy and win the support of the majority of the working (though non-proletarian) masses whose wants will be satisfied at the cost of the exploiters." [14]

It remains to ask only, to lift the curtain on the last corner of obscurity: who is the "revolutionary proletariat" which seizes power, overthrows the bourgeoisie, lays down the new rules of suffrage, counts the votes, and determines when the confidence of a majority of workers and, ultimately of the majority of the population, has been won? The actions as well as the writings of the Bolshevik leaders leave no doubt that the answer is the Communist Party.

The relation between the Party and class has always been a very embarrassing one to Communist theoreticians especially since they are well aware that Marx never spoke of the dictatorship of the Party and condemned analogous notions in Bakunin and Blanqui as conspiratorial perversions. Lenin is impatient and scornful of those who counterpose "the dictatorship of the Party" to the "dictatorship of the class." He seeks to conceal the mechanics of political control in which every element is cunningly prearranged in a conceptual maze in which, because the party allegedly knows the interests of the workers better than they do themselves, there is no need for the flummery of freely given consent. When all ambiguities are resolved, the so-called dictatorship of the proletariat in the Soviet Union and elsewhere is an open dictatorship of a minority Communist Party, or of the leaders of that Party, *over* the proletariat and the population at large. For all of his refusal to face the issues clearly, and his introduction of the dialectic to swallow contradictions, Lenin admits, and Stalin after him, that the dictatorship of the proletariat is *substantially* the "dictatorship of the Party." Long before the Stalin constitution declared it to be the law of the land, Lenin admitted: "In the Soviet Union the land where the dictatorship of the proletariat is in force, no important political or organizational problem is ever decided by our Soviets and other mass organizations without directives from the Party." [15] The theory and practice of democratic centralism guarantees that the dictatorship of the party sooner or later leads to the outlawry of party factions and to the dictatorship of the Politbureau.

I am not laboring these points to establish what is obvious to anyone who has the slightest acquaintance with the Soviet Union. I cite them to indicate that the theory and practice of Communism, and this is true not only in the Soviet Union but in every country in which Communists have come to power, cannot in essential respects be identified with some of the central doctrines, right, wrong, or confused, of Marxism. The Communists are not the midwives of a social revolution waiting to be born. They are the engineers or professional technicians of revolution at any time and at any place.

Important political corollaries follow from a recognition of what their true ideology is. The Communists are very jealous of their claim to be Marxists; they preen themselves upon their realism, and scornfully distinguish themselves from all varieties of Utopian socialism. But their realism is an entirely different sort of thing from what we should expect from historical materialists. They are not at all realistic about the objective economic presuppositions of socialism, about the problem of finding substitutes for capitalist accumulation, and calculating the costs of enforced technical development. They are realistic only about the problems of conquering political power.[16] Once they have conquered power and can hold on to it by any means, then *by definition* that country is ripe for socialism. The achievement of socialism through the dictatorship of the party is on the agenda of history at any time in any country. Only the prospects of success must be carefully assessed. The Communist Party is, therefore, not only a revolutionary party in virtue of its program but a revolution-making party.

III

Logically the attempt to build socialism irrespective of the material economic presuppositions can be carried out at a rapid or slow tempo, by partial and piecemeal collectivization or by one fell decree, by the use of pilot plants and force of example or by physical coercion. Similarly, the existence of a political dictatorship does not necessitate a dictatorship in *all* fields of culture as the history of most dictatorships up to the twentieth century shows. The party regime set up by Lenin did not inescapably lead to the cultural totalitarianism of Stalin despite the beginnings already clearly discernible under the former. Decisions were made at each point—decisions which were not merely technical but moral since their consequences had profound bearings on the welfare of others. The evidence is clear that every major decision taken, with the exception of the period immediately following War Communism, turned the screws of totalitarian control on Soviet society and culture more tightly. Here, too, the Communists acted *in the name* of the doctrines of Marxism, comforting themselves with the belief that they were recognizing and yielding to the iron necessities of history. In reality they were substituting their own driving wills to consolidate their political power for the driving forces of social development. There is no convincing evidence that the initial decision to seize power in a backward country compelled them to wield that power as they did.

It may be illuminating to discuss from this point of view phenomena as disparate as the enforced total collectivization of agriculture and the straitjacketing of art and science by the state philosophy of dialectical materialism.

Marx predicted that the laws of capitalist production would hold for agriculture as well as for industry. His predictions were so far from becoming true that it led to modifications of the agrarian program of Social-Democrats everywhere. Although according to Marx nationalization of the land was not strictly a socialist measure and could be carried out even under capitalism, most Social Democratic parties soft pedaled this note in rural countries where a strong independent peasantry existed with no feudal background. In Russia nationalization of the land was decreed immediately after the October Revolution but in practice this meant only the expropriation of the landlords without compensation, distribution of their land, and the multiplication and strengthening of millions of independent peasant holdings. In effect the Communists had carried out the agrarian program of the non-Marxist Social Revolutionary Party. The number of collective or government farms established up to 1927 was insignificant. Marxist theory has assumed that the peasants would be put off their lands and proletarianized by the growth of agricultural capitalism. Since this did not happen even in capitalist countries, it could hardly happen in a country in which capitalism had been abolished. The only thing the Bolsheviks could rely on was the force of example, i.e., the greater productivity of the state farms and cooperatives, and the power to supply the technical means to make agriculture viable. Measured by achievement, the force of example turned out to be quite unimpressive. It made no inroads on the peasant's psychology. The state of industry made it impossible to bring economic pressure on the peasants. Wheat, not steel, was king in a socialist economy of scarcity. There was no economic necessity to collectivize the farms in order to guarantee grain deliveries since by relaxing the pace of industrialization the basic technological needs of the peasants could have been gradually met. *A fortiori* there was no economic necessity to collectivize agriculture in a span of four years and in such a fashion that in some respects Soviet agriculture is worse off today than when the program was introduced—aside from the millions of lives destroyed and the ghastly suffering produced in the process. The ruthlessness of the drive defeated the anticipated economic advantages. In a sense, the agricultural revolution undertaken ten years after power had been won had a much more profound effect upon Russian life than the social revolution of the decade which preceded it. Official sources make no secret of the fact that this revolution was commanded and initiated from above. Its effect was to make the Soviet peasant once more a serf—with two differences. He was a serf exclusively of the state and his contributions and rewards were computed by modern book-keeping methods.

Lenin had placed his hope on the Russian peasants growing into socialism through their village cooperatives aided by Soviet power and electrification. This was a viable procedure. Stalin destroyed the peasant cooperatives, drove the peasants into collective farms which at the time lacked electrification, and launched a program of hypertrophic capital goods construction while the masses lacked adequate food, clothing, and shelter. The "permanent revolution" of Lenin and Trotsky resulted in a permanent shortage of consumption goods and a permanent state of political insecurity. There was nothing inevitable about this development. Once decisions were taken, of course, they limited possible alternatives. But there were always alternatives open which permitted the use of methods more or less democratic, more or less humane.

Some Marxist critics of the Communists who share their professed determinism see in the grim features of Soviet life the unavoidable consequences of the first fall from the state of Marxist virtue and orthodoxy. It is true of course that some decisions and actions entail others. The consequence of taking the first step over the precipice is a further and faster fall. Such criticism if valid would absolve the Communists of any moral responsibility for actions subsequent to their conquest of power. But there is no evidence that the historical concatenation of events in Russia or elsewhere hangs only from one fateful action or that its justification can be derived from one poisoned premise. This may be best seen from an analysis of Soviet controls on culture.

IV

The totalitarianization of Soviet culture has gone so far that it emerges as a culturally unique trait of modern times. Can it be derived from any of the Marxist premises of Bolshevik ideology? Was it required, did it in any way help, the programs of industrialization and collectivization?

Marxist doctrine views the cultural superstructure as a natural outgrowth of the development of the mode of production, not as a hothouse plant that can be made to flourish by forced feeding. Law and political action can have reciprocal effects on the economy but they cannot legislate for literature, art, music, or philosophy. To the extent that they are authentic they are largely "unconscious" expressions of the acceptances and rejections, the moods, the hopes, dreams, and frustrations of the world in which men find themselves. Even science on this oversimplified, monistic view is a derivative response to the needs of production which indirectly influence the basic problems of research. The planned society envisaged by Marx and Engels did not include a planned spiritual life for man but a liberation of the creative spirit from economic and political restraints, and enjoyment of a complete cultural autonomy. The picture is as naive as the prediction of the disappearance of the state but it indicates a perspective of liberation for culture, not one of its coordination by the police power.

Nor, to answer our second question above, has anyone ever presented a particle of evidence that the styles of socialist realism or formalism or any other aesthetic matter on which the Central Executive Committee of the Russian Communist Party has taken a stand possess the slightest practical bearing on productivity in Soviet industry or agriculture. The same is true for moot questions in theoretical science from the Einstein theory of relativity in its cosmic implication to the principle of indeterminancy in atomic physics.

The most that can be argued is that since the philosophy of dialectical materialism asserts that all things are interrelated, different theoretical positions in any field, ranging from art to zoology, must ultimately lead in practice to different political positions. Since by definition the Communist Party has the only true political position, it therefore has the most reliable, if not infallible, criterion on what is sound or unsound in any field whatsoever.

The premise of the argument is false: not all things are interrelated. But even if true, the reasoning is faulty. It would justify scientists claiming a right to a veto on the wisdom of the Politbureau on the presumed ground that its political decisions have scientific implications on which they are the authorities. The patent fact is, however, that the character of any art form or of any specific scientific theory is irrelevant to questions of politics. The attitude towards modern art or to classical and folk music on the part of Truman, Stalin, Churchill, and Hitler was pretty much the same despite their different political faiths. Zhdanov's fulminations against modernism in poetry, music, and literature sound very much like the tirades of philistines everywhere,[17] with the immense difference that the latter would never dream of erecting their private prejudices into public law. The secret of the party line in music is neither the economy of socialist society nor the philosophy of dialectical materialism but simply and solely Stalin's ear—or the ear of whatever tyrants succeed him. This entire episode of cultural degradation was made *possible* by a form of party dictatorship which in turn meant the dictatorship of the leader or leading group. Under other leadership it might not have happened and still have left unaffected the iron clad control of the Party on the political life of Soviet society.

V

There remains to consider the claim that the foreign policy of the Soviet Union was the key to its domestic policy, particularly its prevision of military intervention by its enemies. It is true that the forced pace of Soviet industrialization permitted the Soviet Union to meet

Hitler's invasion with weapons and the auxiliary material of war essential to its victory. Without discounting the immense aid received from its allies, the great bulk of the arms and equipment of the Red Army was manufactured in the Soviet Union. Was there not, therefore, an objective logic in the domestic policies and decisions of the Soviet leaders especially in their programs of industrialization and collectivization which provided an arms and grain reserve? If their policies were based upon an analysis of the development of European economy and politics must we not recognize that Marxist doctrine played a role—an intelligent and important one—in the pattern of Soviet events? Can we not say of the Soviet leaders that without being as Talmudic as their Marxist critics in other camps they were not less principled but vastly more creative? Have they not been vindicated by the judgment of history, by their victory over Hitler?

Before an affirmative answer to these questions can be given, we would first have to inquire into the extent to which in foreign affairs the Bolsheviks were the architects of their own isolation and Russia's trial by ordeal; and second, what the likelihood is that they would have been able to withstand the full weight of Nazi ferocity if they had been compelled to face Hitler alone—from which they were saved, by no plan or merit of their own.

The first point that requires examination is the responsibility of the Bolshevik leaders for the victory of Fascism in Germany and Italy. A united working-class movement in either one of those countries would have created a political situation in which neither Hitler nor Mussolini might have come to power. But with greater zeal than they attacked capitalism, the Communists set themselves the task of smashing Social Democracy. The organization of the Communist International, the sabotage of the Weimar Republic, including insurrectionary attempts, the promulgation of the doctrine of social-fascism were all parts of an unremitting crusade aimed first at the liquidation of democratic socialism. Even Harold Laski, who inconsistently hailed the Soviet system as the hope of the world, admits it probable "that had Lenin not precipitated the fatal split in the working classes implied in the foundation of the Communist International, certainly not Hitler, and perhaps not Mussolini, would have attained to power." [18]

What Lenin began, Stalin carried to grotesque lengths in his theory of social-fascism, promulgated as early as 1924, faithfully followed by the entire Communist world movement until the Seventh Congress of the Communist International in 1935, never officially abrogated, and periodically revived since then. According to this theory the Social Democrats were "the moderate wing of fascism. These organizations [Fascist and Social-Democratic] do not negate but supplement each other. They are not antipodes, they are twins." [19] This meant it was absurd to expect genuine united action with Social Democrats to combat Fascism since it would be uniting with one group of Fascists to combat another.

The truth is that the rise of Fascism as a social and political movement was never anticipated by the Communists either on the basis of their professed Marxist faith or of any other. When it appeared on the scene the Communists completely mistook and underestimated its significance. They assumed it would collapse of its own weight shortly after it came to power. They were confident if it did not collapse that they would liquidate it but "only over the corpse of Social Democracy." As late as the May Day pronouncements of the Communist International in 1933, five months after Hitler had been in power, the Kremlin declared that the chief enemy of the German working class was not Hitler but German Social Democracy. On May 2, 1933, Hitler destroyed the Social-Democratic and Communist trade-unions alike.

Having encouraged Fascism to come to power in hopes that the Soviet Union could stand by while the "imperialist Western powers" destroyed each other, the Communist leaders became frightened at the prospects of their isolation and of a concerted world crusade against Bolshevism; they sought to overcome this dangerous isolation by pursuing two radically different approaches—a "popular front" tactic in which Communists dressed themselves in liberal wool and bleated democratic slogans, and by secret overtures to Hitler. The second won out after Munich. By signing a pact with Hitler and guaranteeing him against a second front, Stalin helped precipitate the Second World War. When Hitler turned on Stalin both of them expected an immediate peace among all the capitalist countries, democratic and nondemocratic. Although Lenin and Stalin never ceased pointing to "contradictions" among capitalist powers, both had been predicting a world capitalist crusade against the Soviet Union with different countries slated in the lead at different times. And indeed nothing in the Marxist doctrine, which sees in war not only the continuation of politics but a reflex of the clash of economic interests, prepared the Soviet leaders for their grand alliance with one set of capitalist powers *against* another capitalist power which posed as "a savior" of Europe and Christianity from Bolshevism.

It is extremely problematical whether the Soviet Union could have survived, alone and unaided, the full brunt of a German invasion without allies in the West, especially in view of the millions of defections to Hitler's armies by Russian soldiers and peasants at the outset of the war.

In view of all this one is entitled to considerable skepticism concerning the claim that the programs of industrialization and collectivization and total terror were a necessary consequence of a foreign policy of defence against intervention. The threat of intervention worked in two ways. Before, during, and after the Civil War, the Bolsheviks never concealed their own program of intervention by revolutionary subversion into the affairs of other countries. This intervention included the possibility of direct military engagement by Soviet military forces beyond their own borders. This is made manifest in many passages. In an edition of Stalin's *Problems of Leninism* published as recently as 1953 in Moscow, the Soviet regime includes Stalin's discussion, fortified by citations from Lenin, of the way in which the first socialist country can render assistance to revolutionary Communist movements in other countries.

In what should this assistance be expressed?

It should be expressed, first, in the victorious country achieving "the utmost possible in one country *for* the development, support and awakening of the revolution *in all* countries." (See Lenin, 23: 385.)

Second, it should be expressed in that the "victorious proletariat" of one country, "having expropriated the capitalists and organized socialist production, would stand up *against* the rest of the world, the capitalist world, attracting to its cause the oppressed classes of other countries, raising revolts in those countries against the capitalists, and in the event of necessity coming out even with armed force against the exploiting classes and their states." (See Lenin, 18: 232-233.) [20]

In the eyes of the Bolsheviks, all this is dialectically interrelated with "peaceful coexistence." This passage should be pondered together with another important text of Stalin's in which he explains how before the seizure of power every act of planned aggression was represented as a measure of defence.[21]

VI

I close with some considerations by way of summary:

1. The orthodox Marxist theory of social development has received its definitive refutation at the hands of those who flaunt their Marxism to the world.

2. The so-called scientific socialism of Marx and Engels does not guide the Communists in their actions. They are neither historical nor economic determinists. Marxism in the Soviet Union functions strictly in the way Marx defined an ideology, i.e., as a "false consciousness" which masks from the protagonists themselves the causes, grounds, and motives of action.

3. There is no reason to doubt the Communists' belief in their proclaimed goal which is the establishment of a world wide economy planned from above and functioning under the tightest totalitarian controls which force, ingenuity, and terror can establish. Meanwhile the prediction that the state will some day wither away serves as a consoling myth. Soviet internationalism, unless conflicts develop between the Chinese and Russian Communists of which at present there are no indications whatsoever, except journalistic suspicion, is Russian nationalism whose actual content has little in common with Russian nationalism of the past.

4. The actual guiding doctrine of the Communist regime, as distinct from its official ideology of Marxism, is a kind of latter-day Utopianism, a social engineering whose goals recognize no limits except physical or

biological impossibility and whose means are of indefinite flexibility. The goals are fixed, pursued with fanaticism, and never tested by the consequences of the means employed to achieve them. If we wish to predict and cope with Communist behavior, much more important than Communist social philosophy is the Communist theory, strategy, and tactics of world revolution.

5. It is paradoxical but of great significance that the propaganda appeals used by the Communists are more often "ideal" than "material" or "economic." Peace, independence, justice, equality, nationalism, and other psychologically powerful themes are central. When its own existence hung precariously in the balance, the Kremlin rallied support to itself under the slogan of "defence of Mother Russia," not "defence of socialism." Psychological factors are realistically surveyed not from the point of view of what can be achieved but of what human beings can be made to believe.

6. Although the existence of the Soviet Union refutes the Marxian theory of historical materialism, it may be argued that in a not recondite sense the humanistic aspect of Marxism has been vindicated by the character of Soviet culture. In declaring it impossible to build a socialist economy where the objective preconditions were absent Marx was mistaken. But he assumed that there were certain human needs and moral values which would guide political action and which would limit what human beings are prepared to do to other human beings. That one cannot build a socialist economy in a backward country except at a morally prohibitive cost is the sense of his socialist humanism. If we are completely indifferent to questions of human cost and suffering, only physical and biological necessities limit action. We can make even a desert bloom if we are prepared to fertilize it with human corpses and water it with rivers of blood and tears. Allowing for comparable starting points, the costs in suffering exacted from the peoples of the Soviet Union as a price for industrialization exceeded by far those endured by the Japanese in the thirty years, by the Germans in the forty years, and the English in the fifty years required to build their large scale industry. Marxists have sometimes implicitly recognized the fact that a moral judgment is involved in every effort to change the course of events. This was realized even by Lenin himself before the Revolution of 1917. He once declared with explicit reference to Russia that: "Whoever wants to approach socialism by another path, other than by political democracy, will inevitably arrive at absurd and reactionary conclusions in the economic and in the political sense." [22]

This judgment has been confirmed. Lenin and his followers have helped destroy the traditional historical determinisms which set too narrow limits on what human will and action can achieve. But thereby they have brought home to sensitive and reflective men everywhere the centrality of the problem of moral choice and responsibility in historical affairs.

NOTES

1. See especially Lenin's comments on historical materialism in the collection of his writings from 1895 to 1923 on Marx and Marxism, issued by the Marx-Engels-Lenin Institute, entitled *Marx-Engels-Marxism,* New York and Moscow, Cooperative Publishing Society of Foreign Workers in the U.S.S.R., 1935.

2. Mao Tse-Tung, *On contradictions,* English translation, New York, International Publishers, 1953.

3. Laski, H. J., Reflections on the revolution of our times, 55 ff., New York, Viking Press, 1943.

4. At the time of the Revolution of 1905, Lenin wrote, "Finally we wish to say that by making it the task of the provisional revolutionary government to achieve the minimum program, the resolution therefore eliminates the absurd, semi-anarchist idea that the maximum program, the conquest of power for a socialist revolution, can be immediately achieved. The present degree of economic development of Russia (an objective condition) and the degree of class consciousness and organization of the broad masses of the proletariat (a subjective condition indissolubly connected with the objective condition), make the immediate, complete emancipation of the working class impossible." Lenin, V. I., *Selected works,* 3:52, Moscow and New York, International Publishers, 1938.

5. Lenin, V. I., *Collected works,* 20:107, New York, International Publishers, 1929.

6. Marx-Engels, *Selected works,* 1:329, Moscow, 1950.

7. For a discussion of Lenin's and Trotsky's views, *cf.* Trotsky, L., *History of Russian Revolution,* 3, Appendix 2, New York, Simon and Schuster, 1932.

8. Lenin, V. I., *Collected works,* 23:291, New York, International Publishers, 1945.

9. Lenin, V. I., *Collected works,* 20:107, New York, International Publishers, 1929.

10. Lenin, V. I., *Collected works,* 21:45, New York, International Publishers, 1932.

11. Trotsky, L., *History of Russian Revolution,* 2:320, New York, Simon and Schuster, 1932.

12. Stalin, J., *Leninism,* 1:29, New York, International Publishers, 1928.

13. *Ibid.,* 1:123, my italics.

14. *Ibid.*

15. Lenin, V. I., *Selected works,* 10:88, Moscow and New York, 1938.

16. *Cf.* Plamenatz, J., *German Marxism and Russian Communism,* 294, New York, Longman's, 1954.

17. Zhdanov, A., *Essays in literature, philosophy and music,* Eng. trans., 76, New York, International Publishers, 1950. The essay on music is the translation of the text of a speech delivered to a conference of leading Soviet musicians called by the Central Executive Committee of the Russian Communist Party.

18. Laski, H. J., *Reflections on the revolution of our time,* 84, New York, Viking Press, 1943.

19. Stalin, J., *Collected works,* 6:294, Moscow, Foreign Languages Publishing House, 1953.

20. *Op. cit.,* 147.

21. Stalin, J., *Collected works,* 6:357, Moscow, 1953.

22. Lenin, V., *Selected works,* 3:52, Moscow and New York, 1938.

IDEOLOGY: THE FOURTH STAGE

Leopold Labedz

Marxism in Russia has gone through three stages and now seems to be entering its fourth. The first stage was that of transplantation. Marxism was a doctrine born in the West, and the members of the Russian intelligentsia who adopted it had been for decades subject to Western cultural and political influences. The doctrine emerged in the wake of the German romantic movement, the disenchantment of the intelligentsia with the results of the French revolution, the abortive revolutions of 1848, and the revulsion from the social effects of early industrialization. It contained two essential ingredients that strengthened its appeal to the intelligentsia of a backward country: revolutionary fervor and a chiliastic hope. It called for modernization, and not, like *Narodnichestvo* (populism), for a revival of moribund peasant institutions. But although its millenarianism suited the Russian messianic tradition, the premises of its class-analysis were not in line with Russian revolutionary attitudes, which had little patience with an evolutionary process, even a Marxist one.

Intellectually, however, the early Marxists under Plekhanov emerged victorious from the debate with the *Narodniks*, about what would now be called the "Russian road to socialism." They demonstrated "conclusively" that the hopes of Russian socialism were naive, that the stage of capitalism could not be skipped, that the peasant commune (*obshchina*) was in process of disintegration under the impact of market relationships, that the Russian peasant was not "a communist by nature," and that capitalism had already established itself in Russia and was rapidly developing.

This, the Plekhanov phase of the Marxist movement, came to an end soon; with Lenin's *What is to be Done?* bolshevism—or Leninism—was born. It created the premises for the triumph of the very heresy which

Reprinted from *Problems of Communism,* vol. VIII, no. 6 (November-December, 1959), 1-10. By permission of the author and the publisher.

AUTHOR'S NOTE: At the time this article was written, I could only predict the emergence of the Khrushchevian ideological formulas and point to the probability of their development. The revision of Stalin's interpretation of Marxist tenets and their replacement by the Khrushchevian ones came only later.—L. L.

Russian Marxism had begun by opposing, the concept of jumping the economic stages Marx himself had postulated. The organizational principle of the party "of the new type"—closely knit, revolutionary and highly centralized—was, of course, the most important among these premises, but not the only one.

MARXISM IN PRACTICE

The second stage in the destinies of Marxism in Russia was that of adaptation. Bolshevism has often been described as a blend of Marxism and populism. This is true but incomplete. Other Marxist trends were also affected by the historical background and environmental pressures in Russia: Mensheviks were often no less "impatient," and it was Trotsky's idea of permanent revolution—the notion that the two classic Marxist revolutions, the "bourgeois" and the "proletarian," could be "telescoped" into one—that was practically implemented by Lenin in October 1917 after his abandonment (in the April Theses) of his previous views on the character and perspectives of the revolution. But there is little doubt that it was in bolshevism that some of the most characteristic ideas of the Populist theoreticians of the 19th century found their safest anchor: Pisarev's utilitarian ethics, Tkachev's attribution of a special role to the revolutionary elite, Nechaev's acceptance of the use of force and fraud as "normal," Lavrov's emphasis on the role of the party, and the general fascination with the idea of the dictatorship of the revolutionary minority. Despite the obvious continuity between bolshevism and its predecessors, however, there is also an element of genuine novelty in Leninism: in the principle of "democratic centralism" it contained the nucleus of a totalitarian chain-reaction.

The third stage, that of implementation, came with the victory of the revolution. The Marxists had "solved" the problem of how to win power in the un-Marxist conditions presented by a proletarian island in a peasant sea; now they were confronted with the problem of exercising that power in a backward country lacking, according to their own Marxist premises, the industrial prerequisites of socialism. The hope, based on these premises, of a "proletarian revolution" in the more advanced countries soon vanished, and the next step beyond the original orthodoxy became inevitable: Stalinism replaced Leninism. Lenin had replaced the Marxist theory of revolution with his own, more practicable theory in the given circumstances. Stalin abandoned other tenets of the original Marxist creed as well.

The process has been referred to as a transition from theory to ideology. But it was both more and less than that. Having suffered a theoretical defeat through its own victory after the revolution in Russia, Marxism was caught up in a vicious circle of theoretical contradictions. It was not the unity but the disunity of theory and practice that began to be embodied in Soviet institutions. The theory therefore could not simply be thrown overboard, while the ideology was retained; both had to undergo a complex transformation. The theory was elevated to the status of a state doctrine; orthodoxy crystallized into a ritual, and policies were justified by invoking first principles that had no relation to the circumstances. It was not that the theory was "betrayed"; it simply became more irrelevant. The facts that did not fit it had to be explained away.

The reason why the theory could not be abandoned and replaced by another was, of course, because the legitimacy of the system itself was based upon it. Therefore subordinate propositions had to be introduced with each new twist of policy; such propositions often logically nullified the original theory, but helped to preserve it by shifting the emphasis from its heuristic aspect (purporting to explain past and current experience) to the future it envisaged. The theory thus acquired an autonomous sphere of existence largely impervious to the facts of the present and therefore invulnerable to logical argument.

Even earlier Marxism, in becoming an ideology of mass movements and acquiring the characteristic features of systems of mass-belief, had come to assume the inadmissibility of doubts lest the faith of the believers be endangered. Despite the fact that *de omnibus dubitandum* was one of Marx's favorite maxims, his followers soon became accustomed to settling their arguments by an appeal to the scriptures, and quotation-mongering became an obligatory game. When the doctrine became the basis of a state, the believers could no longer appeal to the scriptures on their own; interpretations were prescribed by those who controlled the state.

AN IDEOLOGY, NOT A THEORY

As a total *Weltanschauung* Marxism was a theory which aspired both to explain the facts of nature and society and at the same time to evaluate those facts. The statements of fact and value were thus intrinsically mixed, and despite its protestations to the contrary, Marxism was from the first an "ideology" in its own sense of the term—that is, a "false consciousness" and not, as it claimed to be, a "scientific theory of socialism." Unlike a scientific theory, it was not ready to revise its assumptions in the light of experience, so that revisionism always presented a mortal danger. Previously Marxism had merely been "an illusion of an epoch"; after becoming a ruling ideology it was transformed into a falsified consciousness, with all the instruments of the state devoted to this falsification. Indoctrination was geared to fill the gap between experience and theory, not merely to expound a certain system of values. The new scholastic species, the ideological functionaries, performed the task of doctrinal exposition according to the requirements of the moment. Like other casuists before them, they could always find a suitable quotation.

It is this last aspect which led many Western commentators to conclude that under Stalin ideology had become a mere appendage of Machiavellian *Realpolitik*—a cynical camouflage playing no role whatever in political decisions, which were dictated by hard-headed considerations of the interests of the party or the state.

The reality was more complex. It is true that when the "Stalinist school of falsification" replaced the Leninist school of rationalization, ideology seemed to be reduced to a secondary role. But this was partly a matter of degree and partly an optical illusion. Lenin had a strong element of *Realpolitik* in him, without ceasing to be an *ideologue;* Stalin, the "realist politician," aspired all his life to be the supreme ideologist. The question here is not one of personalities. The party could not exist without the ideology providing its doctrinal legitimacy. Ideology may be manipulated to suit policy, but it is still there, not merely reflecting the needs of the rulers but shaping their mentalities as well. Doctrinal rationalization has not ended with Lenin, nor has falsification ended with Stalin.

THE STALINIST LEGACY

The vicissitudes of "destalinization" and "restalinization" tended to obscure the simple fact that the post-Stalin regime emerged as a continuation of the one he left; all the leaders struggling for the succession were members of the victorious Stalinist faction in the 1920's and 1930's, and the repudiation of its role would have amounted to their repudiating themselves. Khrushchev went furthest in his "secret speech" of 1956 but limited his denunciation to Stalin personally. This stand has since been modified, or at least clarified, in the newly published version of party history, which explicitly approves Stalin's actions in the 1920's and 1930's—with the exception of the Great Purge. Thus the need to legitimize the post-Stalinist regime set the limit to doctrinal change.

Such changes as have been made are presented only as a continuation of Leninist orthodoxy, straightening the path where Stalin strayed from it. This is, of course, quite deceptive. "Khrushchevism," despite historical continuity, is no more a return to Leninism than Stalinism was a straight continuation of it.[1] The new adaptation takes those elements from Lenin's ambiguous legacy that suit its present purposes, as Stalin did in his time, and as Lenin himself did with Marx.

The history of Soviet thought can be regarded as a struggle of doctrine with reality, or as a process of adjustment to intractable reality. When the latter is finally accepted, the doctrinal formula of acceptance is referred to as "the creative development of Marxism." Before such a formula emerges, a period of groping precedes it in which various formulations are thrashed out in esoteric discussions until finally one of them is consecrated in the official orthodoxy. The evolution of such formulas can be traced as precisely as that of a species in a museum of natural history. The Stalinist contributions to the "creative development of Marxism"— "socialism in one country," the theory of the reinforced state, class structure in the socialist society, and the new twists given to the problems of egalitarianism, "the law of value," and the relationship between the economic basis and the ideological superstructure—all of these have a long history of gradual reformulation until they acquired their ultimate shape in the Stalinist dogma. It is possible to trace their emergence to political or economic needs, and to see how in their final form they were related to such needs—with the least apparent damage done to the doctrine.

Yet ideological inconsistencies became routine in the Soviet system and they continue under Khrushchev. There have been obvious signs in recent years of groping for new theoretical adjustments, and now that Khrushchev's writ is law it is probable that some of the new experimental formulas which have been put forward will be proclaimed as his contributions to the "creative development of Marxism." Indeed, the expression is already being used in respect to some such formulations, and if they serve the ideological requirements of the new situation they may become a part of the new theodicy.

THE FOURTH STAGE OF MARXISM

The Stalinist phase in Soviet ideology was doctrinally characterized as "the building of socialism." Khrushchev has announced that the process is completed and has promised the achievement of communism in the near future. Indeed, according to his pronouncements, the Soviet Union has already entered the "higher stage" and is engaged in attaining the final doctrinal aim, the Communist society.

This may well be the most difficult period for the doctrine. In the past its dynamic appeal was preserved as a result of its teleological view of history and its retention of certain ideas derived from nineteenth-century utopian socialism. However, these elements could not stand up to a confrontation with reality, and therefore the doctrine had to operate "beyond the reality principle" by projecting ultimate aims into the future. Obviously the moment of reckoning would come, should the aims be considered to have been achieved, the historical mission of the proletariat fulfilled, and the *terminus ad quem* of pre-history attained.

Achievement of communism can, of course, be repeatedly postponed, but ultimately there are only limited ways out of the doctrinal dilemma. One is for the ideology to become a set of dead formulas, not only to the population at large but to the party as well. It is perfectly obvious, however, that the *apparatchiki* have a vital vested interest in the perpetuation of the ideology. It is this feature that makes Soviet communism historically *sui generis*. In the case of the French Revolution, long before forty years had passed, the revolutionary dynamic had been exhausted, the Jacobin formulas and even Thermidor were forgotten, and "liberté, égalité, fraternité" was becoming a motto for the façades of public buildings (including prisons). Should ideology cease to be an operative factor in the Soviet Union, the party could not hold out for long against divisive social forces and sectional interests. It would be the end of the unity of the political elite and of the permanent revolution from above.

But nothing at the moment warrants such a forecast. The chiliastic element in the ideology cannot be reconciled with "the achievement of communism," but it can be projected beyond the geographic frontiers of the Communist bloc to perpetuate the "ideological" dynamic. Herein lies one alternative to abandonment of the doctrine. Needless to say, it is incomparably more dangerous to free societies and to the prospects of "peaceful coexistence."

EFFECTS OF RITUALIZATION

The outcome is, of course, not predetermined and will depend not only on internal Soviet developments but on outside factors—the courses pursued in the non-Communist world, the direction taken by Chinese revolutionary fervor, etc. Internally, the ideological future will depend on the rate of *embourgeoisement* and the degree to which this affects the party. Both the content and the role of ideology are bound to be affected by general social change as the Soviet Union acquires a more mature industrial economy. The party, which is not the ruling social class but the ruling political elite, is aware of these antithetical elements and tries to perpetuate its position at the top of society by new injections of social mobility. Khrushchev's educational reform and the recent wage and salary changes are two instances of the Bonapartist technique of playing lower strata of the population against the higher to preserve the party's equilibrating position. But such attempts cannot be effective indefinitely. The Soviet social structure is crystallizing, and no amount of permanent revolution from above (especially without terror) can arrest the process in the long run.

With *embourgeoisement* the doctrinaire fanaticism of the *apparat-chiki* may subside or they may be corrupted by cynicism. It is clear that as the doctrine to which they adhere has become more ritualistic it has lost its positive content. But if ritual diminishes the meaning of a religion to the believer, it helps on the other hand to preserve the church. Since there are different degrees of initiation according to rank, the ritual sterilization of ideology has varying impacts at different levels of the hierarchy. Eventually the "historical purpose" of Marxist eschatology may cease to be convincing at any level. Even those initiated into the tactical motivation of changes in the party line may cease to regard them as simple teleological detours, necessary to reach the ultimate goal. It has happened before that those charged with the administration of the faith end by losing it.

Soviet *apparatchiki* of today, however, are still far from the sophistication of the Renaissance cardinals. And at their apex is a ruler for whom simplified Marxism is a part of folklore, a vital element which shaped his mentality in the *rabfak* (workers' school), as the popular wisdom of Russian proverbs did before he received his formal education. Here is a very different figure from those of the past.

The Leninist generation of Bolshevik leaders, recruited from the intelligentsia, consisted of ideologues. Stalin, a member of the semi-intelligentsia, resented their intellectual superiority, but aspired himself to provide ideological guidance, entering personally into doctrinal disputes. While it is true that his main venture into philosophy (the celebrated section on dialectical and historical materialism in the fourth chapter of the *Short Course* of the party history) was written with the help of Yudin, until recently Soviet ambassador in Peking, Stalin never left his doctrinal pronouncements entirely to ghost-writers.

Khrushchev on the other hand relies on his *vydvizhentsy* (those promoted from the bench or the plough) who are even cruder intellectually than their Stalinist predecessors. He leaves doctrinal formulations to these ideological functionaries, and it is only when a formula is ready for *oformleniie* (final formulation) that he puts his stamp on it. While the appearance is maintained that ideology has acquired a new Supreme Interpreter without whom the system could not properly function, the new interpretation is no longer made by him personally, but rather by the party ideologists. The era of philosopher-kings in the Soviet Union is ended. It is therefore more likely that social factors and forces will become a greater influence in shaping doctrinal change.

DOCTRINAL INNOVATIONS

What specific changes can already be discerned in the content and the role of ideology in this early period of the post-Stalin era, and what is likely to be the physiognomy of the fourth stage of Marxism in Russia?

First—and perhaps inevitably—with the announcement that the ultimate goal of communism was in sight, the ambivalence so characteristic of Marxism and Leninism seems to have become even more marked.

The economic and administrative reforms of Khrushchev have again raised the perennial problems of the theory of state and the law of value. In general Stalin's doctrinal legacy in this area is approved, but with certain important exceptions and modifications. Those of his ideas which have been repudiated are neatly summarized in the *Political Dictionary*:

The Economic Problems of Socialism in the USSR [Stalin's last *opus* of 1952] had a great influence on the elaboration of some theses of the political economy of socialism. At the same time the work contains a series of erroneous and questionable theses, such as for instance the statement that commodity circulation begins to hinder the development of the productive forces of the country and that a gradual transition to natural exchange is necessary; the underestimation of the role of the law of value in the sphere of productivity, in particular in relation to the means of production; the assertion about the inevitability of the contraction of capitalist production after World War II and about the inevitability in contemporary conditions of wars between the capitalist countries.[2]

In simple language this means that under Khrushchev monetary economy is taken for granted, at least for the time being, and that direct distribution through rationing is not yet contemplated; that the problem of pricing capital goods has been recognized as a problem; that the prospects for capitalism set out in the postwar "Varga controversy" have finally been recognized as fallacious,[3] and that Stalin's hope of wars between the western countries is taken for what it was, a nonsensical fantasy of a paranoidal dictator.

With the greater importance attached to "the law of value," Soviet economic theory has begun to show signs of stirring out of the long slumber into which it had fallen during Stalin's lifetime. Although the Polish and Yugoslav economic revisionists are attacked, and the more heretical Soviet economists (like Kronrod) scorned, there are indications that the pragmatic needs of the Soviet economy in its more mature phase force the acceptance of the economic facts of life, including the problem of the price-mechanism and market relationships.

THE CASE FOR A STRONG STATE

In contrast to the critical assessment of Stalin's doctrinal positions in the economic sphere, his contributions to the "creative development of Marxism" in the political sphere are now accepted almost in toto.

After initial waverings in 1956 the Soviet theoreticians reached a new doctrinal equilibrium on the theory of state.

Khrushchev in his "secret speech" condemned as erroneous the doctrinal premise of Stalin's terrorism, his thesis that class struggle grows more intense with the advance of socialism. This thesis had served as a basis for the Stalinist theory of state under socialism; since the internal class struggle was becoming more acute, the state—far from "withering away"—had to grow stronger. (His other ingenuous justification of the strong state was, of course, the concept of "capitalist encirclement.")

During 1956-57 the condemned thesis was referred to in Soviet publications as one of Stalin's mistaken notions, although it was not linked with its logical Marxist corollary concerning the diminishing role of the state. On the contrary, Soviet dialecticians indulged in an involved argument which pointed to the old conclusion that the state must remain strong even under communism.

Though Stalin was "rehabilitated" in 1957, his thesis on the intensification of the class struggle under socialism has not returned to favor. But neither is it treated any more as one of his doctrinal sins. It has been quietly forgotten, as witnessed by the fact that it got no critical mention at all in the two most recent authoritative publications on theory, *The Political Dictionary* (1958) and the new party history (1959).

On the other hand, Stalin's theory of state is now accepted in principle and full credit is given to him:

Generalizing the historical experience accumulated by the party after the death of V. I. Lenin, a new contribution to the Marxist-Leninist teaching on the state was made by J. V. Stalin. In particular he showed the necessity of strengthening the Soviet state in every respect in conditions of capitalist encirclement, boldly posed the question of the insufficiency of the well-known formula of F. Engels about the withering away of the state, and gave a new formulation to the question of the possibility of preserving the state even under communism, if the danger of an attack from outside still exists.[4]

The sanctioned view of the state's role—at least for the present—seemed clear enough as expressed by Khrushchev himself, in an interview with a United Press correspondent in 1957: "It would be a serious error, a leftist deviation, if we were now to weaken our state organs of rule, to abolish the organs of coercion." [5] This line has been elaborated by the ideologists, e.g.:

The Communist Party takes constant care at the present time to strengthen the Soviet state and to make it more efficient in every respect. The theses "On the Fortieth Anniversary of the Great Socialist October Revolution" proclaim: "In present conditions Soviet society still needs a strong popular state for the defense of its socialist achievements and for taking charge of the building of communism." [6]

CHANGING STATE FUNCTIONS

In rather startling contradiction to such statements, however, certain modifications have been made concerning the role of the state in the future. The theory inherited by today's ideological functionaries from the Stalin epoch divided the basic phases of societal development into two: first, the revolutionary transition from capitalism to socialism, and second, the gradual transition to communism. In each of these phases the state has certain functions to fulfill. Among the functions listed in the first phase were: suppression of the overthrown exploiting classes, defense of the country, and performance of administrative-organizational and cultural-educational work by state organs. In the second phase the first of these functions is abolished, but the other two are retained and another is added: the task of safeguarding socialist property from thieves and embezzlers of the national wealth.[7]

While the basic stages of development have remained the same, in present theory there has been a subtle twist in scholastic argumentation to emphasize the Khrushchevian shift from methods of direct coercion to those of persuasive pressure. The argument centers on a semantic nuance. Stalin was declared wrong in regarding "the administrative-organizational and cultural-educational work of the state organs as one function of the Soviet state." [8] His view was incorrect because, "as a result of joining these two functions, an impression is involuntarily created of the subordinate significance of cultural-educational work in relation to administrative-organizational activity." It is expedient to delimit the two because "the methods and forms of performing these two functions, [as well as] the organization and activity of the ad- ministrative organs of the economy and [those of] culture have their own peculiarities." [9] The Soviet intelligentsia supposedly can now rest assured that the peculiarities of the administrative function will not be applied in the intellectual sphere.

The functions of the Soviet state in the period of transition to com- munism remain the same as those enumerated in the Stalinist theory of state, but their content and relationship to the society are now presented differently. By a new dialectical turn Soviet scholastic experts have again tried to deal with that thorn in their flesh, the "withering away of the state." In a word, the abatement of terror and Khrushchev's ad- ministrative and judicial reforms have been heralded as steps in the direction of a diminution of state power:

The socialist state remains during the whole period of the construction of communism, but the content of its functions and the forms of its activity change. Gradually, the role of the administrative functions, connected with state coercion, is diminished. Thus the premises are being created for the withering away of the state which will take place at the higher stage of communism provided there is no danger of attack by the imperialist powers. At the higher stage of communism the importance of the planned direction of production and distribution . . . and [of] cultural values will increase even more. The state organs performing these functions under socialism will be replaced at the higher phase of communism by social organs of economic- cultural self-government.[10]

At the 21st Congress Khrushchev gave as an example of such "self- government" the action of the extrajudicial bodies set up under the so-called "anti-parasite" laws. The formation of the workers' militia (which existed previously as *Brigadmils*—Brigades for Cooperation with the Militia) is also hailed as "a step in the handing over of state func- tions to social organizations," [11] and therefore as part of the process of the withering away of the state. Various ossified institutions, including trade unions and the soviets (workers' councils), are now claimed to contribute to the same end.

A skeptical observer may have some difficulty in visualizing how much more "withered away" the Soviet state under communism will be in comparison to the capitalist states, with which it will presumably "coexist." The Soviet theoreticians have shown no such doubts, boldly proclaiming that "the 21st Congress of the CPSU has elaborated the problem of the concrete forms of the withering away of the state." They do confirm, however, that progress toward the goal will be a "protracted process." According to the theoretical organ of the party, *Kommunist:*

[The organs of state coercion] are still necessary in present conditions, but the social content of their activity has already changed essentially. At the 21st Congress it was noted that drastic coercion is at present directed against thieves, crooks, embezzlers of socialist property, parasites, malicious hooligans, murderers, and other criminal elements. Together with the creation of the conditions of the transition to communism, with the increase of the consciousness of the masses, coercion inside the country will diminish more and more. . . . in the Soviet Union the sprouts of Communist social self-government have already appeared, and they represent the forms which will secure the further development of socialist democracy.[12]

One may wonder what "further development" these "sprouts" can accomplish—if, as is claimed in the new party history, social democracy already "secures to all Soviet citizens genuine freedom of speech, of the press, of assembly, meetings and demonstrations. . . ." [13] But then, the dialectical process is unending.

In elaborating his aforementioned theories of class struggle and state power during the building of socialism, Stalin argued "dialectically" that "any dialectical thinker understands that, in order to wither away, the state must first grow stronger" (speech before the 16th Party Congress). According to Khrushchev, the new phase of building communism has initiated the process of the withering away of the state. But he has made use of Stalin's argument for other purposes—and in the first instance, for the defense of the strong party.

Although at the higher stage of communism both the party and the state are destined to disappear, only the state seems to be involved in the process for the indefinite future:

To be sure, the party will not exist forever. Marxism-Leninism teaches that when the party has accomplished the construction of the higher stage of communism, which then ceases to be an object of struggle, only then will there be no more necessity for the party as a political organization. This means that class differences will then finally disappear, as well as the essential differences between physical and mental labor, between town and country, and that the consciousness of all the toilers will be raised to the level of their Communist vanguard. But this is a question of the distant future. All the present practice of the construction of communism points to one necessity: the steadfast strengthening of the guiding role of the party in all spheres of life in Soviet society.[14]

In short, as with the state, in order to wither away the party must first grow stronger. Although Engels' third dialectical law, the negation of negation, which fell into disfavor in Stalin's time, is now readmitted, it is still the second dialectical law, the interpenetration of opposites, which reigns supreme.

COMMODITY CIRCULATION

When Stalin proclaimed the achievement of socialism he justified it theoretically on the ground that with collectivization and the liquidation of NEP, the institution of private ownership of the means of production had ceased to exist in the USSR. Henceforth, there existed two sectors in the Soviet socialist economy: the state sector, consisting of nationalized industry and *sovkhozes* (state farms), and the cooperative sector, consisting of *kolkhozes* (collective farms) and *artels* (cooperatives). The transition to communism was said to involve "the raising of the private, cooperative sector to the level of the public, state sector"— in other words, total nationalization, not only of industry but also of agriculture.

Khrushchev's dissolution of the MTS (machine-tractor stations) and pronouncements on the "withering away of the state" have introduced new difficulties in doctrinal formulations and explanations touching upon the above concept.

Previously, the MTS were regarded as the nuclei of communism in the countryside. Stalin wrote in his *Economic Problems of Socialism* that selling the MTS to the collective farms would extend commodity circulation and would thereby hinder the transition to communism, which was incompatible with commodity circulation. But as this "retrograde step, turning back the wheel of history" (Stalin's words) has in fact been taken by his successor, Soviet theories have had to be revamped.

The theoretician Ostrovityanov produced the new rationale by applying the familiar dialectical argument, this time not to the withering away of the state or of the party, but to commodity circulation:

The dialectics of the development of socialist economy consists in the fact that we will reach the withering away of commodity production and money circulation at the highest phase of communism, as a result of the all-round development of commodity and money relationships at the socialist stage of development.[15]

The innovations on the withering away of the state create an even greater doctrinal quandary. How can the higher phase of communism be defined as a transition to the stage when the state takes over all productive property, if at the same time this transition is characterized by the gradual withering away of the state itself?

But as Stalin himself has said, "there are no fortresses which the

Bolsheviks cannot conquer"—especially semantic fortresses besieged by theoreticians. P. Fedoseev, the head of the Institute of Philosophy—who ranks with Pospelov, Ponomarev, and Ostrovityanov as a leading ideologist of the Khrushchev regime—provided a somewhat involved answer:

As long as the state exists, the public (*obshchenarodnaia*) form of property remains the nationalized means of production, *i.e.*, state property. When the state withers away the public means of production will cease to be state property. However, until then, the state socialist sector of production, based on public property, will play a leading role in the advancement of society to communism. There is no basic, qualitative difference between state socialist property and the future communist non-state form of property; the difference here is only in the degree of development at different stages of one and the same social-economic formation.[16]

Stalin might well admire this display of dialectical dexterity.

The social effect of the transition to communism should be the classless society—the economic effect, the change to the distribution principle, "to each according to his needs."

Today, as in Stalin's time, it is asserted that class distinctions in the USSR are being obliterated: but now the additional claim is made that the difference between mental and physical labor has already begun to disappear. The reduction in the number of unskilled workers and Khrushchev's educational reform are mentioned in substantiation of this thesis.[17]

The distribution of products "according to needs," which in the orthodox theory was incompatible with commodity circulation and monetary exchange, now gets another doctrinal twist. At the 21st Congress Khrushchev declared that "an individual's needs are not unlimited," but cautiously added: "Of course, when we speak about satisfying the needs of the people we do not mean capricious demands and pretentions to luxury, but the healthy needs of a civilized man." [18]

Who decides what these "healthy needs" are is not made explicit. Presumably not the individual, but the state—in the time it has to spare from withering away. Nor are the criteria of distribution "according to needs" under communism made explicit, though Ostrovityanov has explained that they will not be too egalitarian:

The tendency to decrease differentiation in the remuneration of labor during the period of the transition to communism by no means signifies a tendency towards a leveling off in consumption. . . . The Communist principle of distribution does not signify equalitarianism and leveling of consumption, but a full satisfaction of the variegated and rising needs and tastes of the members of society.[19]

THE EVOLUTION OF KHRUSHCHEVISM

Any analysis attributing purely ideological motivation to Soviet political behavior is bound to result in confusion. So must the other extreme, that of reducing ideology to pure rationalization and denying its role altogether. Clearly in the first case, if true, there would be little doctrinal change; in the second, there would be no such pressing need as is evident for doctrinal justification, nor for the whole elaborate edifice of sophistry built whenever intractable reality forces "a creative development of Marxism."

Doctrinal adjustments reflect both internal Soviet social change and the international situation. That much goes without saying. But can one discern any long-term principles governing the relation between these factors? Such principles would help us to understand not only the role of "dialectical pragmatism" and doctrinal rationalization, but how they relate to each other: not only the evolution of the content of the ideology but perhaps also its changing function. For it is clear that doctrinal change under Khrushchev, as under Lenin and Stalin, is accompanied by a subtle change in the role of the ideology itself. The complexity of the evolution cannot be reduced to a single causative factor, but it can be related to a series of significant historical elements.

Each stage in the development of Marxism in Russia is obviously connected with the concomitant stage of economic development: transplantation occurred in the pre-industrial phase; adaptation took place in the period of early industrialization; and the present phase will be affected by the fact that the Soviet Union has become a mature economy.

Marxism in Russia, in its early phase, was a product of the revolutionary intelligentsia; under Stalin it was put in the hands of the semi-intelligentsia; and Khrushchev represents the *vydvizhentsy* who have arrived to take it in charge. Only in the next phase, when the new Soviet intelligentsia will acquire greater sophistication and the sons will again replace the fathers, is there a chance that it will lose some of its primitive flavor.

However, though economic and social change are bound to affect the content and role of ideology, constituting an ever-greater threat to the concept of party supremacy, it would be rash to infer that the party's position and political role will soon be automatically or basically changed. The party tries to forestall such effects by its technique of what might be termed "permanent revolution" from above. At the same time technocratic advance, as a result of the pressure for higher skills and greater specialization, is not without some advantages to the "theocrats": greater specialization makes it more, not less, difficult for the individual to relate his specialized knowledge to general developments. In the present set-up it is only the ideological "experts" who have the knowledge and position to deal with general political issues, and the party is the only institution providing the link between various bureaucracies in the society.

The evolution of Khrushchevism has not, of course, depended on domestic developments alone, nor will it in the future. More attention is being paid to the international aspect of communism. According to the present doctrine socialism has become a world system. One of the new functions of the Soviet state is "the strengthening of the inviolable friendship, brotherly cooperation and mutual help of the countries of the world system of socialism." [20] The new party history, unlike the old *Short Course*, offers tribute to foreign Communist leaders. The opposition between the "socialist" and "capitalist" systems is stressed in Soviet publications as much as ever, although the present emphasis is on proving the superiority of the Communist system through "peaceful competition."

The basic ambivalence of Russian Marxism remains. Communism in one bloc is an even greater anomaly in doctrinal terms than socialism in one country. The two "souls" of Bolshevism, the Marxist and the Jacobin, have as their historical roots orthodox universality on the one hand, the populist nationalist appeal on the other. These two aspects of Bolshevism have so far been reinforcing each other, thus increasing the danger of expansionism against the outside world. While there has always been a potential conflict between nationalist and universalist messianism in the motivation of Soviet policy, the contradiction is still not antinomical, although conceivably it might become so.

More important at present as a cause of ambivalence is the growing discrepancy between the maturing Soviet social structure and fundamentalist ideological prescriptions. The gap is steadily widening, and the legitimacy of the system is therefore under constant threat. Industrial development has introduced the necessity of rationalism in the organization of the economy, an element which the Soviet rulers can neglect only at their own peril and at the risk of undermining the international position of the USSR. The formal rationality of organization, the rationality of means, can of course coexist with the substantive irrationality of ideological ends. But the divorce between the two in Soviet society contributes further to the atrophy of faith. The *apparatchiki* have long ceased to believe that the average man will rise to the stature of Aristotle or Goethe, an idea expressed by Trotsky but shared by others in the romantic period of the revolution. The Soviet "organization man" is probably disinclined to believe that the "new Soviet man" will ever rise "above these heights to the new peaks," and must find it increasingly difficult to swallow the rest of the ideological nonsense with which he is bombarded—on the state withering away, on the disappearance of the differences between mental and manual occupations, on the imminence of distribution "according to needs," etc. Whereas Lenin suggested that the establishment of a Communist society might require a century or two, Khrushchev is promising it here and now, or in the not too distant future—thereby bringing nearer the day of reckoning, the confrontation of utopia with reality. Surely he must realize the utter incongruity of reducing the problem of achieving the Realm of Freedom to a question of *per capita* production of meat and milk.

The alternative possibilities of the evolution of Khrushchevism remain open. The tension between ideology and rationality is becoming more—not less—acute. As suggested earlier, one way out of this dilemma is a withering away not of the state, or the party, or commodity circulation, but of the Marxist faith itself. The other is a renewed cycle of ideological "restructuring of reality," either through new attempts to make Soviet reality conform to Marxist blueprints, or through the application of fundamentalism to the global community of non-believers, resulting in increased pressure on the "bourgeois world."

The history of Bolshevism offers many examples of such alternating cyclical phases. NEP was hailed as a return to normalcy, the end of revolutionary romanticism and the beginning of a new stability. Khrushchev's reforms, the easing of the position of the masses, the greater degree of security for the Soviet elite, and the higher role given to rationality in the productive process, do not do away with the basic cause of tension created by the issue of the legitimacy of the system. The flying pyramids, the sputniks and luniks, may perhaps divert attention from the chasm between theory and practice, but they hardly can bridge it. The present reformist phase of internal adjustment may well give way to another attempt to change this world, before conquering other worlds.

Those who hope that Khrushchevism will evolve harmlessly in and by itself, who ignore the expansionist element within it, do not understand the nature of the Communist system. Doctrines have a way of resisting social change, and doctrinaires change their views with utmost reluctance. Only when repeated attempts to violate reality are to no avail do they adjust themselves to it and proceed to produce another "creative contribution to Marxism." Resistance to Communist expansion is the best way to direct Soviet ideology towards internal euthanasia. Only in this way can the process of *embourgeoisement* come to fruition, and ideology and utopia be replaced by a domesticated ideological ritual and subtopia. When and if this happens, it will be legitimate for Soviet citizens to say along with Oscar Wilde: "The map of the world which does not contain an island of utopia is not even worth looking at."

NOTES

1. See "Lenin and 'Peaceful Coexistence'" [*Problems of Communism*, vol. VIII, no. 6 (November-December, 1959), p. 53].

2. B. N. Ponomarev, *Politicheskii Slovar*, Second Edition, Moscow, 1958, p. 556. One concept mentioned perhaps requires a word. According to the "law of value"

the commodity exchange is correlated with the amount of abstract, socially necessary labor used in the production of commodities. In Soviet usage the "law of value" refers euphemistically also to the market relationships permitted in the Soviet economy.

3. Cf. M. E. Varga, "The Problems of the Postwar Industrial Cycles and the New Crisis of Overproduction," *Kommunist*, No. 8, June 1958.

4. M. V. Kharlamov, *The Activity of the CPSU for Further Strengthening of the Soviet Socialist State*, Moscow, 1958, p. 9.

5. *Pravda*, November 19, 1957.

6. Kharlamov, *op. cit.*, p. 11.

7. M. P. Kareva *et al.*, *Teoria Gosudarstva i Prava* (The Theory of State and Law), Moscow, 1955, pp. 210-240.

8. V. V. Nikolaev, "On the Stages of Development of the Soviet Socialist State," *Voprosy Filosofii*, No. 4, 1957, p. 10.

9. P. S. Romashkin, "The Development of the Functions of the Soviet state in the Process of Transition to Communism," in *Voprosy Stroitelstva Kommunizma v SSSR*, Soviet Academy of Science, Moscow, 1959, p. 113. This book and the new party history are the two basic texts on Soviet ideology under Khrushchev.

10. K. V. Ostrovityanov, "Some Problems of the Construction of Communism in the USSR and the Tasks of the Social Sciences," *ibid.*, p. 21.

11. *Trud*, November 23, 1958.

12. A. Davletkeldnev, "The Development by the 21st CPSU Congress of Teaching on the Socialist State," *Kommunist*, No. 11, July 1959, pp. 9-20.

13. *The History of the Communist Party of the Soviet Union*, Moscow, 1959, p. 662. For discussion of the theory of the state under Khrushchev, see also, *inter alia:* M. P. Kareva, "The Theoretical Significance of the Experience of the Soviet Socialist State," in *Voprosy Sovetskovo Gosudarstva i Prava*, Moscow, 1957; and D. A. Kerimov *et al.*, "Marxist-Leninist Teaching on the Socialist State and Law," in *Sorok Let Sovetskovo Prava*, Leningrad, 1957.

14. G. Shitarev, "The Elevation of the Leading Role of the Party in the Building of Communism," *Kommunist*, No. 12, August 1958, pp. 12-13.

15. Ostrovityanov, *op. cit.*, p. 25; cf. also D. Chesnokov, "The Development of the Forces and Relations of Production in the Period of the Intensified Construction of Communism," *Kommunist*, No. 10, July 1959.

16. P. Fedoseev, "The Development of the Relations of Production in the Transition from Socialism to Communism," in *Voprosy Stroitelstva Kommunizma v SSSR*, Moscow, 1959, pp. 71-72.

17. Cf. the present writer's article on "The New Soviet Intelligentsia," *Soviet Survey*, July-September 1959, pp. 103-11.

18. *Izvestiia*, January 29, 1959.

19. Ostrovityanov, *op. cit.*, pp. 35-36.

20. Romashkin, *op. cit.*, p. 116.

CONTEMPORARY SOVIET THEORY
OF THE SOVIET STATE

L. G. Churchward

In the eight years that have passed since the death of Stalin various aspects of his theory have been subjected to re-examination and re-appraisal by Soviet writers. While some aspects of this theory—such as those relating to imperialism, war, and the nature of relations between capitalism and socialism—have been re-interpreted at the highest level, the re-thinking of the theory of the Soviet State has been chiefly done at a lower level, by academics and journalists rather than by the top politicians of the party. A study of this revision is important not only for its own sake but because of the light it throws on the nature and extent of ideological change in the Soviet Union since 1953.

Stalin's theory of the Soviet State (mainly formulated between 1933 and 1939) had a dual origin. In the first place it incorporated the Marxist theory of the state. In the second place it took account, at least to a certain extent, of the facts of political power in the USSR itself and this caused a certain re-formulation of the original Marxist theory. The original Marxist theory of the state contained three essential propositions. In the first place the state was regarded as an agency for the mediation of class conflicts in the name of society but not necessarily in the interests of society as a whole. Thus Engels wrote in 1884 that "the state arose from the need to keep class antagonisms in check." [1] Secondly, the state was regarded as an agency or machine for the oppression of one class by another. Engels stated that "the state arose in the thick of the fight between classes," and that it was "normally the state of the most powerful, economically ruling class." [2] The relationship between these two propositions was not always stated with consistency. Engels, in "The Origin of the Family, Private Property and the State" (1884) wrote that in "exceptional periods," when the warring classes are nearly equal in forces, the state power may act as an

Reprinted from *Soviet Studies*, vol. XII, no. 4 (April, 1961), 404-419. By permission of the author and the publishers.

"apparent mediator" and acquire "for a moment a certain independence in relation to both." This, he said, applied to the absolute monarchy of the seventeenth and eighteenth centuries which balanced the nobility against the bourgeoisie and to the Bonapartist Empires which balanced the bourgeoisie against the proletariat. More often the state served as the instrument of the ruling class. Thus Engels wrote in 1892: "The State was the official representative of society as a whole: the gathering of it together into a visible embodiment. But it was this only in so far as it was the state of that class which itself represented, for the time being, society as a whole; in ancient times the state of the slave-owning citizens; in the middle ages, the feudal lords; in our time, the bourgeoisie." [3] Lenin in "The State and Revolution" (completed in August 1917) ignored this qualification in the Marxist theory of the state and regarded the state as purely "an organ of class rule, an organ for the oppression of one class by another." [4] On this point both Stalin and his heirs have followed Lenin. Thus the 1958 edition of the Soviet Political Dictionary defines the state as "the political organization of society, the organ of the dictatorship of the economically dominant class." [5]

The third of the essential Marxist propositions about the state is that it is a temporary phenomenon. It arose with the emergence of class divisions in society and it will die with the final abolition of classes. The state, as an agency of oppression, will eventually "wither away," although various non-coercive social organizations will remain. When does the withering away process begin? Lenin, in "The State and Revolution," considered that it would be "a rather lengthy process" of "a protracted nature," and that it would not be completed until the higher stage of socialist society, communism, had been achieved. Here he followed Marx and Engels. At the same time Lenin in August 1917 clearly underestimated the complexity of the proletarian state structure. Thus he wrote that:

The exploiters are naturally unable to suppress the people without a very complex machine for performing this task but *the people* can suppress the exploiters even with a very simple "machine," almost without a "machine," without a special apparatus, by the simple *organisation* of the armed masses. . . .[6]

This view was rapidly modified by Lenin when confronted with the necessity of organizing a complex proletarian state to defend and extend the revolution. This positive role of the proletarian state during the transition from capitalism to communism was to be given even greater stress by Stalin.

The fullest statement of Stalin's theory of the Soviet state is contained in his report to the XVIII Congress of the CPSU(B) in March 1939.[7] The statement was undoubtedly provoked not merely by speculation within the party on the question of the withering away of the state since the 1936 announcement that socialism had been achieved, but by a recognition of the need to provide some rationalization for the obvious increase in the coercive role of the Soviet state during the period of the purges.

Stalin accepted Engels' forecast that the state would wither away under socialism, when there was no longer any class to be held in subjection, but he held that they had not considered the possibility of socialism being established in one country ahead of others. Since the Soviet socialist state existed within a circle of capitalist states the Soviet state could not be expected to wither away. The prime reason for the continuation of the state under socialism was the need to defend the conquests of socialism from foreign attack. The state would remain even under communism "unless the danger of foreign military attack has disappeared."

However, while the state remained under socialism and would perhaps remain under communism, the form of the state was changing and would continue to change in line with the development of Soviet society and with changes in the international situation. Stalin considered that the Soviet state had passed through two main phases in its development since 1917. The first phase he defined as "the period from the October Revolution to the elimination of the exploiting classes," i.e. apparently to 1931. The second phase he defined as "the period from the elimination of the capitalist elements in town and country to the complete victory of the socialist economic system and the adoption of the new Constitution," [8] i.e. from 1931 to 1936. The main functions of the Soviet state in the first phase were stated to be three, the suppression of the overthrown classes within the country, the defence of the country from foreign attack, and the beginning of the work of economic organization and cultural education. However, the third function was poorly developed in this period. The principal tasks of the Soviet state in the second phase were said to be four. First, the establishment of the socialist economic system all over the country and the elimination of the last remnants of the capitalist system. Second, the function of class suppression was largely replaced by that of protecting socialist property. Third, the function of defending the country from external attack was fully maintained. Fourth, the function of economic organization and cultural education remained and became fully developed:

Now the main task of the state inside the country is the work of peaceful economic organization and cultural education. As for our army, punitive organs, and intelligence service, their edge is no longer turned to the inside of the country but to the outside against external enemies.[9]

Stalin's theory of the Soviet state, as expounded in the years 1933-39 was not seriously challenged inside the Soviet Union in his lifetime. The inflexibility of Stalin's thinking in his closing years is reflected in his re-affirmation in 1950 of his 1939 explanation of the survival of the Soviet state being conditioned by the capitalist encirclement of the

USSR.[10] The concepts of "socialism in one country" and "capitalist encirclement" which were clearly inexact descriptions of post-war international relations were never explicitly revised by Stalin, although in a sense the Zhdanov report on the International Situation (September 1947)[11] and Stalin's "Economic Problems of Socialism in the USSR" (1952) provided the basis for the fuller revaluation of situation and theory which was carried out at the XX Congress in 1956. It was an appreciation of such facts as that the "socialist sixth" had become the "socialist third," that socialism had expanded beyond a single country into an alliance of socialist states, that imperialism was on the retreat in the Colonial World, that enabled the leadership at the XX Congress to introduce certain modifications into Stalinist ideology. Perhaps because of this the revisions which were made at this Congress were in the fields of international relations and revolutionary strategy [12] rather than directly on the theory of the state. Criticism of Stalin's theory of the state was not initiated by the XX Congress although it was undoubtedly stimulated by it. The criticism has also gained something from the limited revival of empirical studies in the sphere of government as such studies have served to bring out some of the deficiencies of Stalin's over-schematic picture of the Soviet state. The theory is being currently re-examined at three points, the nature of the contradictions in Soviet society (a question which involves the class basis of the state), the periodization of the Soviet state and its functions in the various stages of its development, and the role of the socialist state in the transition to communism. The limits of this revision will become clear as we summarize the main arguments of recent years on each of these questions.

The question of the contradictions within Soviet society has been raised several times since 1953, especially amongst writers and philosophers. The publication of V. Kozlovski's book *Antagonistic and Non-antagonistic Contradictions* [13] in 1954 provoked quite an extended discussion in the journal *Voprosy filosofi* during 1955 and 1956. The controversy was conducted in highly philosophical, almost metaphysical terms, but some at least of the writers [14] argued, in contrast to Stalin, that there were elements of antagonistic contradiction (i.e. of class struggle) still operating in Soviet society. Yet at this time no one conceded the possibility of contradictions operating between government and people. This was first raised in Communist circles by Mao Tse-tung in February 1957.[15] At first Soviet spokesmen denied its applicability to the USSR but before the end of 1958 Soviet philosophers had begun to take up Mao's argument and apply it in part to the Soviet Union.[16]

It would make it easier for Soviet writers to explain the tensions in contemporary Soviet society if they were prepared to concede that socialism had not been fully established. Molotov, in his speech to the Supreme Soviet, 8 February 1955, made such a revision when he stated that, "Side by side with the Soviet Union, where the foundations [*osnovy*] of socialist society have already been built, there are also the people's democracies, which have taken only the first, but highly important steps, in the direction of socialism." However, this "revision" was quickly repudiated.[17]

Discussions about the nature of the contradictions in Soviet society are concerned with the theoretical basis for explaining the Soviet state rather than with the nature of the Soviet state itself. However the early discussion referred to above was followed in 1958-59 by a more direct discussion on the development and functions of the Soviet state. One of the first writers to grapple with this problem was M. I. Piskotin whose article "Concerning the Question of the Functions of the Soviet State in the Present Period" appeared in the journal *Sovetskoye gosudarstvo i pravo* in January 1958. Piskotin argues that Stalin's 1939 statement on the basic functions of the Soviet state requires a more detailed formulation based not merely on the nature of the Soviet state but on the existing functions of the state at various levels. He re-formulates the functions of the present Soviet state as four:

1. the maintenance of the socialist system and the socialist order in society;
2. economic-organizational, including the main work of organizing production and regulating the distribution of the basic products and socal services;
3. cultural-educational; and,
4. external, including the defence of the country and the maintenance of economic, political and cultural links with friendly countries.[18]

Piskotin's minor amendments to Stalin were extended in a later article in the same journal by A. M. Davidovich.[19] Davidovich argues that the recognition of periods in the development of the Soviet state and law should be based on changes in the superstructure as well as changes in the social structure. On the basis of the social structure alone only two phases in the development of the Soviet state can be recognized, the first lasting until the early 1930s, the second phase covering the entire period since 1933. He divides the first phase into four periods:

1. The period of the Great October Sociaist Revolution and the establishment of the Soviet State and Law (November 1917-July 1918).
2. The period of Foreign Intervention and Civil War (1918-20).
3. The period of Economic Recovery and the introduction of the first USSR Constitution (1921-25).
4. The period of Reconstruction of the national economy and strengthening the USSR (from the XIV Congress in December 1925 to the end of the first five-year plan in 1932).

The second phase in the development of the Soviet state is also divided into four periods:

1. The period of Reconstruction of the USSR Economy and the Victory of Socialism in the USSR and the preparation and adoption of a new Constitution (1932-1937).

2. The period of the Introduction of the New Constitution and the establishment of the New State Structure (1937-41).
3. The period of the Great Patriotic War (June 1941-1945).
4. The period of the Further Development of the USSR in the direction of rapid transition towards Communism (1945 to the present day).

While admitting certain changes in recent years Davidovich argues that basically the same conditions have operated over the whole period since 1945.

The September 1958 issue of *Sovetskoye gosudarstvo i pravo* contained a criticism of Davidovich's article by A. S. Fedoseyev.[20] Fedoseyev agrees with Davidovich on the two basic phases in the development of the Soviet state but he suggests 1936 rather than 1933 as the dividing line between the two phases. He argues that while the economic basis was clearly socialist by 1933 the adjustment of the superstructure of state and law to this basis was not completed until 1936.[21] Periodization of Soviet state and law must be based on a combination of changes both in the basis and in the superstructure. Using this approach he arrives at the following periodization:

Phase I. Soviet State and Law during the period of the transition from capitalism to socialism 1917-1936.

1. Period of the Great October Socialist Revolution and the foundation of the Soviet State and Law (November 1917-July 1918).
2. Soviet State and Law during the Period of the Wars of Intervention and the Civil War (1918-1920).
3. Soviet State and Law during the period of the New Economic Policy (1921-29).
4. Soviet State and Law during the period of developing socialist advance on all fronts and the victory of socialism (1929-36).

Phase 2. Soviet State and Law in the period of the Completion of the Building of Socialism and the gradual transition to Communism. December 1936 to the present.

1. Soviet State and Law in the period of the further democratization of Soviet society and the state system (1936-41).
2. Soviet State and Law in the period of the Great Patriotic War (June 1941-1945).
3. Soviet State and Law in the period of transition to peaceful economic construction (1945-53).
4. Soviet State and Law in the period of further development of the USSR on the road of imminent transition to Communism and the development of Soviet socialist democracy (September 1953 to the present day).

Not the least interesting thing about the above scheme is that it recognizes 1953 as a dividing line, although it begins the present period from the September 1953 plenum of the Central Committee of the CPSU rather than from the death of Stalin in March 1953. Perhaps this is more logical than the earlier date since the September plenum marked the first clear emergence of Khrushchev's policies and leadership.

A. I. Lepeshkin, writing in 1958,[22] solves the problem of the dividing line between the two phases in the development of the Soviet state by suggesting that the years 1933-37 should be regarded as a period of overlapping between the two phases. He agrees with other recent writers who have criticized Stalin's formulation—the defence of the USSR— as inadequate for the period since 1945 because Soviet foreign policy now extends beyond the defence of the USSR to the defence and strengthening of the world socialist system.

The problem of the functions and development of the Soviet state was one of the subjects reported on at the Conference of the Social Sciences Section of the USSR Academy of Sciences in Moscow, 23-26 June 1958.[23] The main report on the subject was given by P. S. Romashkin,[24] Director of the Law Institute of the Academy of Sciences. Romashkin's concern was with the basic functions of the Soviet state in the two main phases of its development rather than with periodization within these phases, and with the functions of the Soviet state during the transition to communism. He criticized Stalin for understating the importance of the economic-organizational and cultural-educational functions of the Soviet state during the first phase and for his omission of the function of the defence of socialist legality and individual rights of Soviet citizens during both phases. He also considered that Stalin's formulation on the foreign policy function of the Soviet state in both phases was incomplete, since in the first phase it was concerned with maintaining the peaceful coexistence of socialism and capitalism as well as with the defence of the USSR, while in the second phase it was concerned with strengthening friendship and fraternal cooperation between countries of the socialist camp as well as with improving relations with capitalist states.

In the discussion that followed the various reports to this Conference several writers commented on the problems of the role of the Soviet state. Thus V. V. Nikolayev [25] criticized Romashkin for his failure to tie the question of the functions of the Soviet state to the tasks of the state in the fulfillment of its historic role. Stalin did this when he formulated the basic task of the Soviet state in each main stage of its development. Thus in the second phase of its development the primary task of the Soviet state was the development and perfecting of socialist production relations. M. S. Strogovich,[26] on the other hand, argued that the functions exercised by the Soviet state in its various phases were objective functions and not the fabrication of scholars. In the main he agreed with Romashkin rather than with Nikolayev and argued that the function of the defence of the rights and legal interests of Soviet citizens began in the first phase but that it achieved its full development only during the second phase. The fact that this was not recognized until recently he blamed on the influence of the personality cult which had kept Stalin's formulations uncriticized for so many years. The defence of socialist legality would be an essential function of the Soviet state so long as it was concerned with the building of communism.

The role of the state in the transition to communism was merely a matter of speculation in 1936. The problem has become more urgent over the past two years with the official pronouncements prior to and, at the XXI Congress of the CPSU, that the Soviet Union was on the eve of the transition to communism. Unlike the debate on the question of the functions of the Soviet state this discussion has been initiated and wholly inspired by official Communist Party statements. A further factor has been the criticism of the Soviet state and of the Soviet bureaucracy by Yugoslav socialists.[27]

The main reports at the XXI Congress in January-February 1959, especially those by Khrushchev and Suslov,[28] emphasized the view that there was no clear-cut division between socialism and communism, that there was no "impenetrable barrier," "no wall separating these two stages of social development," and that the transition to communism in the future would proceed at an accelerated tempo.

On the question of the "withering away of the state" it was argued that this implied "the development of the socialist state into communist self-administration (*samoupravleniye*). For under communism too, there will remain certain public functions similar to those now performed by the state, but their nature and the methods by which they will be exercised will differ from those obtaining in the present stage." [29] Khrushchev argued that this transfer of functions from state to social organizations was already happening and he gave as examples the handling of many health services and other social services in the cities by trade unions and the transfer of the control of physical culture and sports from a State Committee to a Voluntary Sports Organization, a proposal which was carried into effect in April 1959. Other indications of the growth of social organizations were the Comradeship Courts and the Volunteer Militia. However such developments did not imply a weakening of the role of the socialist state in the building of communism but rather its strengthening since it would broaden popular participation. The state will continue to be necessary because of its defence role and because of its economic role. Even under communism some form of social organizations would be necessary although it was impossible to say in advance precisely what these would be.

Soviet journalists, propagandists and academics have merely detailed these official utterances. Thus K. Sevrikov and Yu. Filonovich, writing in *Izvestiya* 12 February 1959, stated that:

With the full victory of Communism, the State, it is true, will disappear. But that does not mean that social life will not be regulated in any way. Without this society cannot function normally, cannot direct the necessary development of its internal resources. Without it society would be changed into a formless and unorganized mass of people. Communist society will be a highly organized and harmonious cooperation of free and equal workers. It will regulate its relations through some kind of organizations and with the help of established norms. It is impossible right now to say what these organizations will be, but undoubtedly they will be organizations acting by the authorization of society. It follows that right now we must prepare for that, must cultivate and develop corresponding social habits, must implant in people the skill to live in communist society and to direct its affairs.

All this is speculation about the distant future and is generally consistent with Marx and Engels' formula about "the rule over persons giving place to the administration over things." Stalin's modification of the theory, namely that the state might survive under communism if imperialism survived, is still retained. Thus P. S. Romashkin states:

> The state must be retained under communism if the imperialist camp survives until then; it will be necessary for the military defence of communist society against imperialism. But the main functions of the state under communism would be external ones.[30]

This is not held to contradict the Marxist conception of the state as merely a class agency because the existence of a communist state under such conditions would be based on the continuation of class contradictions in the international arena.[31]

In the period of transition from socialism to communism the state will change its role but it will not immediately wither away. The transition from socialism to communism requires in fact the further strengthening of the socialist state, the further development of Soviet socialist democracy, the broadening of the spheres of activity of all mass organizations and the increased role of the Communist Party.

> There is no other way to bring about the withering away of the state. This will be so not only in the period of transition from capitalism to socialism, but in the period of socialism when the state has some functions withering away and others being transformed but it continues to exist.[32]

The Soviet state is thus held to be developing in a contradictory fashion, simultaneously reducing some functions and enlarging others.[33] Functions which are alleged to be currently declining are those of police control and certain administrative functions such as control of public health, sport and physical culture. Developing functions—apart from defence— are those defined by Stalin as economic-organizational and cultural-educational. The former is expanding because the transition to communism is held to be not a cautious, gradual progress but one of accelerated development in industry and agriculture, requiring strong state direction. The latter function is increasing not merely because of the need to struggle more strongly against capitalist survivals in the communal psychology [34] but because of the need for educating people to the requirements of communist society.[35]

The following statement from a recent Soviet pamphlet is a good example of this dialectical view of the present and future role of the Soviet state:

> The State of socialist society, with the greater and greater development of socialist democracy gradually transfers functions of administration to different democratic institutions and social organizations. It follows that the withering away of the socialist State should be understood as the transfer of separate state functions to different social organizations and the transformation of the State as a social political organ into social communist self-administration. This of necessity is a prolonged process and cannot be completed as the result of the victory of communism in one country or even in a group of countries. However the tendency is such that the very strengthening and development of the functions of the socialist State leads to the transformation step by step of different state functions into functions of social self-administration.[36]

Two special points which have come up in the discussion of the eventual withering away of the socialist state are the fate of the Party and of local Soviets. The transfer of additional functions from central to local Soviets was mentioned by Khrushchev in January 1959 as part of the process of transforming state agencies into social organizations. The apparent contradiction between this claim and the fact that local Soviets are obviously a part of the state structure is resolved only when it is remembered that local Soviets are not merely state agencies but are simultaneously agencies of mass participation and social control.[37] As such they are expected to survive the establishment of communism and the withering away of the state. But the Soviets which survive under communism will eventually cease to be agencies of state power and will serve merely as social agencies.

As with the Soviet state it is considered necessary for the role of the Communist Party to be strengthened rather than diminished during the transition to communism. The need for Party leadership will increase as various administrative functions are progressively transferred from state to social organizations. It is sometimes freely admitted that continued Party control is necessary to prevent the development of anti-social tendencies such as "localism" or "departmentalism."[38] The Party will survive the establishment of communist society but its methods and forms of work and its internal structure will change. Thus we find that recent prescriptions on the process of the withering away of the socialist state frequently omit any mention of the ultimate fate of the Party. The recent Academy of Sciences textbook on the "Foundations of Marxist Philosophy" covers the problem in these terms:

> The withering away of the state involves: (1) the disappearance of the need for coercion by the state and its agencies; (2) the transformation of the economic-organizational and cultural-educational functions from state to social functions; (3) the involvement of all citizens in social administrative matters and the necessary transformation in the organs of political power. When all

traces of class divisions in society have been transformed, when communism has become victorious throughout the entire world, the need for the state will no longer arise. Society will no longer need special detachments of armed people in order to maintain order and discipline. And then, as Engels expressed it, it will be possible to relegate the state machine to the museum of history along with the spinning wheel and the bronze axe.[39]

If any mention is made of the eventual withering away of the Party it is as something which can happen only in the remote future, under conditions of mature communism. Thus D. I. Chesnokov has recently stated that:

The Party will occupy the leading position during a long time in communist society.
Even in the early stages of the victory of communism on a world scale the Party as the embodiment of all that is most progressive and original will need to exist. The people will need many years, decades of life under communism while all the new mechanism of social organization is sorted out and coordinated, till at length the conditions will be created for the withering away of the Party. This process will be long and protracted. It will be realized as all members of society will reach the level of consciousness and organizational experience of party members. Gradually the difference between Communists and non-Party persons will disappear. The Party will turn into a universal organization coinciding with the organizations of self-administration.[40]

Thus the Party will wither away only when communism is victorious all over the world. Eventually, when communism has become universally victorious neither State nor Party will remain although there will be a complex of social organizations which will be formed by the merging and absorption of now separate organizations like Soviets, trade unions, cooperatives and the Party.

It is not my intention to discuss here the general truth or untruth of the Marxist theory of the state. My concern is solely with the extent to which this theory has been revised in recent years and the extent to which it facilitates or prevents an intellectual analysis of changes in the actual state structure. The first conclusion I would draw is that the rethinking of the Soviet theory of the state has been done entirely within the general framework of Stalinist formulae. Criticism has been at a secondary level such as the date at which the Soviet state may be said to have entered the second or socialist phase of its development, or the precise functions of the Soviet state in the two main phases of its development. General propositions such as the class basis of the state, the fundamental differences between socialist states and capitalist states,[41] the survival of the state and party even under communism, have been retained. Revision of these general propositions has consisted essentially of a restatement with additional detail. This revision may be said to reflect changes in the objective situation in which the Soviet Union has operated—for example, the contrast between the capitalist encirclement of the Soviet Union in 1933-9 and the socialist camp of the post-1949 world—and the subjective evaluation of these changes in the Soviet Union itself.[42]

Secondly, Soviet Marxism does provide a general theory against which many if not all of the changes in the Soviet state system in recent years may be examined and assessed. Thus the reduction in the size and complexity of the Soviet administrative apparatus[43] or the increase in the powers and actual performance of local Soviets[44] since 1954 do indicate a modification and, at certain levels, a reduction of state functions, although not necessarily a withering away of the state. I have already referred to the claims which Soviet authors make about the significance of social organizations replacing state organizations. This is not a new development (trade union control of social insurance goes back to 1933) but it has been enormously extended since 1957. The decision to extend trade union powers taken by the December 1957 plenum of the Central Committee of the CPSU was quickly implemented and the new legislation extending the functions of factory, works and local trade union committees and establishing Permanent Production Conferences in medium and large factories was completed by July 1958.[45] The general effect of this legislation has been to extend considerably the role of both trade union committees and trade unionists in the supervision of industrial production, plan fulfillment, technical development, workers' safety, social insurance and welfare. Most Western critics would regard this as merely additional evidence that Soviet trade unions are state agencies. But does the performance of functions which are generally regarded in capitalist democracies as "government functions" necessarily transform Soviet trade unions into state agencies? This sort of development is perhaps more easily understood within the context of Soviet theory. The same might be said for the increasing role of trade unions in judicial matters. Besides serving as appeal tribunals for labour disputes trade union committees supervise the Comradeship Courts established within the factories and industrial plants.[46]

If we turn to rural government we find somewhat similar developments. The effectiveness of Village and District Soviets has long been challenged by the size of the economic units in the areas which they have supervised. Between 1953 and 1958 the Machine Tractor Stations —agencies of the central state—largely replaced the District Soviets as the immediate supervisory agencies over the sowing and harvesting plans of both collective and state farms. Although the abolition of the Machine Tractor Stations in 1958 seemed to lead immediately to a revival of the agricultural control functions of the raiispolkom[47] this development has been more than matched by the development of inter-kolkhoz organizations. Construction of capital works, housing and social buildings (such as schools, kindergartens, hospitals, clubs, bath houses, etc.) and even machinery maintenance is now more often handled by inter-kolkhoz agencies whose activities sometimes extend to a dozen or more neighbouring kolkhozy.[48] Despite recent attempts to increase the powers of Village Soviets it would appear that in certain regions much of the work of these Soviets is in fact initiated by the village meeting (*skhod*), i.e. by a social rather than a state agency.[49] Developments such as these obviously involve considerable modification in the structure of local government although it would be rash to predict for the Soviet Union an early absorption of the local political-administrative apparatus into the economic apparatus as has happened in China. In the Soviet Union development of social organizations is only partly competitive with the local Soviets. More often it is complementary. This is explained in contemporary Soviet theory as the simultaneous transfer of state functions to social agencies and the slow transformation of state agencies such as local Soviets into purely social organizations.

Soviet theory also provides a basis for the partial explanation of recent modifications in Soviet foreign policy. It is obvious that there has been a qualitative change in the nature of Soviet foreign policy, a change which might be categorized as the extension of a policy aimed at national defence into one aimed at the defence and mutual development of a system of socialist states. It is the recognition of this change that has produced the modification of Stalin's formulation of the external function of the Soviet state as being exclusively that of national defence.

It should also be noted that Soviet scholars are quite ready to recognize the existence of evidence which seems to contradict the official view that the size and complexity of the administrative structure is being steadily reduced. Many writers have pointed to such inconsistencies or contradictions as the increase in the size of Gosplan staffs since 1957 and the increase in the size of regional bureaucracy occasioned by the establishment of the sovnarkhozy.[50]

Occasionally a writer will challenge the official conclusions about the relevancy of a particular change to the objective of establishing communism. Thus A. V. Mitskevich has recently challenged the official interpretation of the use of social agencies (such as Comradeship Courts and Volunteer Militia) to handle petty crime and disorder as indicative of the gradual transformation of the coercive apparatus of the state into control by social organizations:

Such a practice leads only to unnecessary parallelism in the work of the social and state organs of order. It doesn't lead to the promotion of habits of self-administration, but only leads to the replacement of one coercive apparatus by another.[51]

It is not unlikely that some Soviet writer may soon discover that recent trends towards decentralization, reduction of the administrative apparatus, extension of the powers of local government and greater use of social organizations not only have earlier parallels but that the earlier parallels were sometimes connected in theoretical discussion with the question of the transformation of the state.[52] If and when such an opinion is reached the critic will have arrived at the point where the conclusion that current administrative changes do not necessarily indicate a trend towards the elimination of the state would seem to be inescapable. These changes undoubtedly represent a conscious attempt to adjust the superstructure to the changed material and cultural basis of Soviet society [53] but it is an open question as to whether or not they indicate any basic transformation in the state as such.

While I have argued that current Soviet theory of the state does serve some useful purpose in the evaluation of empirical changes in the Soviet state it is clear that many problems of the Soviet state in its historical development are not adequately explained by this theory. Such problems as the position of Stalin,[54] Soviet bureaucracy,[55] the internal function of the police and the coercive powers of the state over the entire period of its existence are not easily understood within the context of the Marxist theory of the state, at least as it is currently handled in the USSR.

NOTES

1. F. Engels, *The Origins of the Family, Private Property and the State* (Sydney, Current Book Distributors, 1942) p. 124.

2. *Ibid.* p. 124.

3. F. Engels, *Socialism: Utopian and Scientific* (London, Allen & Unwin, 1932) pp. 75-76.

4. V. I. Lenin, *The State and Revolution*, in *Selected Works* (London, Lawrence & Wishart, 1946) vol. 7 p. 9.

5. *Politicheski slovar* (2nd edition, ed. B. N. Ponomarev, M., 1958) p. 136.

6. V. I. Lenin *op. cit.*, 82-83.

7. J. Stalin, *Problems of Leninism* (Moscow, FLPH, 1945) pp. 631-8. This can be compared with earlier and later formulations, e.g., Report to the Joint Plenum of the CC and the CCC, CPSU(B), January 1933 (*Works*, M., 1955, vol. 13 pp. 211 ff.); "On the Draft Constitution of the USSR," 25 Nov. 1936 (*Problems of Leninism* pp. 540-68); *Concerning Marxism and Linguistics*, 1950, Soviet News Booklet (London, 1950) pp. 36-37.

8. J. Stalin, *Problems of Leninism* pp. 636-7.

9. *Ibid.* p. 637. Contrast Stalin's statement in January 1933: "The abolition of classes is not achieved by the extinction of the class struggle, but by its intensification. The state will wither away, not as a result of the weakening of the state power, but as a result of strengthening it to the utmost, which is necessary for finally crushing the remnants of the dying classes and for organising defence against the capitalist encirclement, which is far from having been done away with as yet, and will not soon be done away with." (Report to the Joint Plenum of the CC and the CCC, CPSU[B], 7-12 Jan. in *Works* vol. 13 p. 215.)

10. "Soviet Marxists, on the basis of studying the present-day world situation, came to the conclusion that in the conditions of capitalist encirclement, when the Socialist revolution has been victorious only in one country, and capitalism reigns in all other countries, the land of victorious revolution should not weaken, but in every way strengthen its state, State organs, intelligence organs, and army, if that land does not want to be crushed by the capitalist encirclement." (Reply to Cde. A. Kholopov, in *Concerning Marxism and Linguistics* p. 36.)

11. A. Zhdanov, *The International Situation* (M., FLPH, 1947) (speech delivered at the Conference of Communist Parties held in Poland, September 1947).

12. Cf. N. S. Khrushchev, *Report of the Central Committee of the CPSU to the XX Party Congress, 14 February 1956* (M., FLPH, 1956) pp. 38-46. The questions dealt with by Khrushchev in this section of his report were peaceful coexistence of capitalism and socialism, the possibility of preventing war in the

present period, and forms of transition to socialism in different countries. The latter question, which might perhaps have invited a review of Stalin's theory of the state in fact avoided it as working-class control (the dictatorship of the proletariat) was made a condition for any peaceful transition to socialism.

13. V. Kozlovski, *Antagonisticheskiye i neantagonisticheskiye protivorechiya* (M. 1954).

14. Cf. the article by L. N. Kogan and I. D. Glazunov in *Voprosy filosofii* 1955 no. 6.

15. "On the Correct Handling of Contradictions among the People" (speech to the 11th Session of the Supreme State Conference, 27 February 1957; English text in Supplement to *People's China* no. 13, I.vii.57).

16. I. S. Serikov, *Voprosy filosofii* 1958 no. 10 pp. 131-6.

17. See *Kommunist* 1955 no. 14.

18. *Sovetskoye gosudarstvo i pravo (SGP)* 1958 no. 1 p. 100.

19. *SGP* 1958 no. 3 pp. 112-19.

20. *SGP* 1958 no. 9 pp. 33-42.

21. D. I. Chesnokov, in *Voprosy filosofii* 1958 no. 7 pp. 30-47, had also argued for 1936 as the dividing line between the two phases in the development of the Soviet state.

22. A. I. Lepeshkin, *Fazy razvitiya i funktsii Sovetskovo gosudarstva* (M., 1958).

23. *Voprosy stroitelstva kommunizma v SSSR* (M., 1959).

24. *Ibid.* pp. 105-28 (also printed in *SGP* 1958 no. 10 pp. 3-18).

25. *Ibid.* pp. 274-9.

26. *Ibid.* pp. 294-302.

27. Cf. N. S. Khrushchev, "Control Figures for the Economic Development of the USSR for 1959-1965," *Izvestiya* 28.i.59; D. I. Chesnokov, *Voprosy filosofii* 1958 no. 7 pp. 30-47; A. I. Lepeshkin *op. cit.*; P. S. Romashkin *SGP* 1958 no. 10 pp. 3-18, *et al.*

28. N. S. Khrushchev, "Control Figures . . . ," *Izvestiya* 28.i.59; Suslov's speech in *Izvestiya* 31.i.59.

29. N. S. Khrushchev, "Control Figures . . . ," *Izvestiya* 28.i.59.

30. *SGP* 1958 no. 10. p. 17.

31. Cf. I. G. Aleksandrov, *SGP* 1958 no. 12 pp. 3-15.

32. *Voprosy filosofii* 1958 no. 7 p. 47.

33. "Clearly the withering away of the state is a complex and contradictory process. Its dialectic is such that one function of the state is completely transformed or disappears while another is retained or even strengthened." (*Osnovy Marksizma-Leninizma*, M., 1959 p. 722.)
"... it is impossible to contrapose the task of strengthening the socialist state with the perspective of its withering away; they are two sides of the one medal." (*Osnovy marksistkoi filosofii*, M., 1959 p. 535.)

34. Cf. P. S. Romashkin *loc. cit.*, "It is impossible to build communism without further intense struggle against capitalist survivals in the consciousness of the people."

35. V. Nikolayev, *Rol Sovetskovo gosudarstva v period razvernutovo stroitelstva kommunizma* (M., 1959). Cf. P. S. Romashkin *SGP* 1960 no. 2 pp. 17-30.

36. I. A. Khylabich, *V chem opasnost sovremennovo revizionizma?* (M., 1960) p. 30.

37. Cf. D. I. Chesnokov, *Ot gosudarstvennosti k obshchestvennomu samoupravleniyu* (M., 1960) p. 39; and F. Kalinychev and V. Vasilev in *Sovety deputatov trudyashchikhsya* 1960 no. 9 pp. 32-41.

38. *Osnovy Marksizma-Leninizma* p. 724.

39. *Osnovy marksistskoi filosofii* pp. 535-6. The same vagueness about the eventual fate of the Party is present in Khrushchev's speech at the XXI Congress, 27 Jan. 1959.

40. D. I. Chesnokov *op. cit.*, pp. 25-26.

41. Cf. the statement by A. L. Lepeshkin in *Fazy razvitiya . . .* p. 22: "J. V. Stalin was absolutely correct in formularizing that the functions of economic-organizational and cultural-educational work were inherent only in socialist states.

No exploiting states possess these functions." This is not only a dubious and narrow interpretation of the Marxist theory of the state but it makes it difficult if not impossible to explain the positive role of the capitalist state in recent decades.

42. N. S. Khrushchev's admission in his report to the XXI Congress of the CPSU, 27 January 1959, that "the socialist countries will enter the higher phase of communist society more or less simultaneously . . . ," represents a tacit but inexplicit revision of Stalin's 1939 claim that communism in one country was possible. Cf. R. J. Medalie, "The Communist Theory of the State," *The American Slavic and East European Review* vol. 18 Dec. 1959 pp. 510-25.

43. Soviet statistics are far from adequate on this point. Perhaps the clearest guide to the general trend is provided by the fact that budget expenditure on administration has been falling absolutely each year since 1954, and that it has fallen on a percentage basis from 3.9% in 1940 to 1.6% in 1959. Cf. *Finansy SSSR* 1960 no. 3 p. 80.

44. Over the three years 1957-9 more than 40 regulations extending the powers and scope of local Soviets were issued by the Supreme Soviets of the Union Republics (Yu. A. Tikhomirov, SGP 1960 no. 1 pp. 76-88).

45. *Izvestiya* 16.vii.58. Cf. *Soviet Studies* vol. X pp. 176-83.

46. Comradeship Courts functioning in localities are supervised by the Executive Committee of the relevant local Soviet. Decisions of Comradeship Courts may be appealed to People's Courts (Draft Regulations on Comradeship Courts, *Izvestiya* 24.x.59); cf. *Yuridicheski spravochnik deputata mestnovo Soveta* (ed. D. S. Karev, Moscow University Press, 1960) pp. 110-12; and R. Schlesinger, "Social Law—I," *Soviet Studies* vol. XII pp. 56-82.

47. Cf. L. G. Churchward, "The Agricultural Reorganization and the Rural Districts Soviet," *Soviet Studies* vol. X pp. 94-97.

48. Cf. G. Abakumov, *Soviet deputatov trudyashchikhsya* 1959 no. 2 pp. 47-50. L. Vandenko in *ibid.* 1959 no. 8 pp. 38-43 reported that interkolkhoz construction agencies in the Chernigov oblast in 1958 handled construction-maintenance work valued at 63 million rubles, constructed over 260 animal husbandry and agricultural buildings and 29 cultural welfare buildings. In one raion up to 90% of all construction work was being handled by the interkolkhoz construction organization. In 1958 the Chernigov kolkhozy established an Oblast Interkolkhoz Construction Agency for coordinating the work of the raion agencies.

49. Although the existing Regulations governing the General Meeting in Villages and Settlements date from March 1927 (in the RSFSR) there has been a considerable revival and extension of their activities in recent years. For example, a Village Meeting in the Kuibyshev oblast, recently singled out by *Izvestiya* for special praise, decided such questions as the establishment of a Voluntary Militia Squad, a Construction Brigade, and a 2-3 year Construction Plan (*Izvestiya* 19.x.60).

50. E.g. A. Kozlov in *Izvestiya* 9.iv.59 claimed that the Ukrainian Gosplan apparatus was now six times as large as it was in 1955, and M. Savalev in *Sovety deputatov trudyashchikhsya* 1960 no. 1 p. 15 claimed that there were 85,000 employed directly in the apparatus of the sovnarkhozy and in the administration of subsidiary organizations.

51. SGP 1959 no. 9 pp. 24-33.

52. Cf. E. H. Carr, *A History of Soviet Russia* vol. 6 (Socialism in One Country 1924-1926 Part Two) (London, Macmillan, 1959) pp. 294, 303, 365-72.

53. Cf. L. G. Churchward, "Continuity and Change in Soviet Local Government 1947-1957," *Soviet Studies* vol. IX pp. 256-85.

54. Cf. "Why is the Personality Cult alien to the spirit of Marxism-Leninism?" (*Pravda* 28.iii.56) and the Statement of the CPSU Central Committee "On Overcoming the Personality Cult and its Consequences," 30 June 1956 (*Pravda* 2.vii.56).

55. Present bureaucracy is explained in terms of individual shortcomings, survivals of earlier bureaucratic practices and the influence of the personality cult. It is nowhere analysed in social (class) and historical terms as both Lenin and Trotsky attempted in 1923 (cf. V. I. Lenin, *Luchshe menshe, da luchshe*, and L. D. Trotsky, "The New Course").

REVISIONISM AND POLYCENTRISM

YUGOSLAV COMMUNIST THEORY

Fred Warner Neal

One does not have to accept the Marxist claim to a unity of theory and practice to see that, as far as modern Communism is concerned, there is a striking degree of correlation. This does not mean that Communist politics invariably follow Communist theory in all its aspects. Nor does it mean that many Communist theories have not obtained primarily as rationalizations of situations occurring outside, or even contrary to, any theoretical framework. It does mean, however, that generally speaking ideology provides a binding orientation for the direction of society, a view of both tactical and strategic goals and a guide to the thinking of at least the leadership.

This is neither more nor less true of the Yugoslav Communists than of others. But the ideological peregrinations of the Yugoslavs merit especial attention, not only because they underpin the most striking nationalist manifestation of an international movement but also because they constitute what is perhaps the most interesting and significant development in Marxist theory since the Bolshevik Revolution. A short review of Yugoslav theory is particularly interesting at this time. Most of the various bits and pieces comprising it were brought together in the Program adopted at the Seventh Congress of the Yugoslav League of Communists in April, 1958. Although Soviet-Yugoslav relations today are, perhaps, worse than at any period since 1953-54, at the time of the Congress they appeared to many in the West to be dangerously cordial and likely to be even more intimate. As if to lend support to this view, the Yugoslavs made certain revisions in their Draft Program to meet Soviet criticisms.[1] Thus the state of Yugoslav theoretical formulations at the time of the Seventh Congress gives some indication of the extent to which Yugoslavs' basic doctrines

Reprinted from the *American Slavic & East European Review*, vol. XIX, no. 1 (February, 1960), 42-62. By permission of the author and the publishers.

were affected by the ups and downs of relations between Moscow and Belgrade.

In discussing Yugoslav theory as a cohesive ideology and in distinguishing it from Soviet theory, it is necessary to begin with two important qualifications. The first is that the essential bases of Yugoslav theory, no less than Soviet theory and all other modern-day socialist theory, has its roots deep in Marxism. This is true both of historical analysis and ultimate goals, to say nothing of methods of reasoning. Thus there is an essential core of theory which is the same in both the Soviet and Yugoslav cases. This involves primarily the concepts of dialectical materialism, and the class struggle, the nature of the contradictions in capitalism and the inevitable triumph of socialism and Communism. The following quotation from Edvard Kardelj's address to the Seventh Congress of the Yugoslav League of Communists illustrates the point:

As far as the final goal of the League of Communists is concerned, the Draft Program . . . proceeds from the scientific premise that the final disappearance of capitalism and its vestiges from history is inevitable; that it is just as inevitable for society to undergo a revolutionary transfer to socialist relationships, to gradual and continual development of the latter toward higher forms until the achievement of communism, as a form of relationship among people where, on the basis of highly developed productive forces, everyone works according to his ability and receives according to his needs. This historical evolution of society simultaneously is the final aim of the ideological, political and economic activity of Communsts.[2]

Similarly, both Soviet and Yugoslav Communist ideologies have their roots in the theories advanced by Lenin. But whereas in the Soviet case the roots have become enmeshed with the tree itself to form the single doctrine of Marxism-Leninism, in the Yugoslav case the Leninist roots remain roots, with some of Lenin's theories incorporated into Titoist theory and others not.

This fact has relevance in the second qualification, which is that it is useful to differentiate between tactical-operational theories and basic, strategic doctrine. Marx is detailed enough when it comes to historical analysis and bold enough—if somewhat fuzzy—when speaking of end goals. But where he is not clear at all is about the present and how to reach the future. Much of Lenin's addenda to Marxist doctrine concerns interpretations of developments since the time of Marx and ways and means of establishing socialism in Russia. This tactical side of Communist doctrine to an even greater extent characterizes those theoretical contributions which come under the head of that unpopular term Stalinism.

It is primarily in the realms of interpretations of the original Marxist gospel, and of operational theory, that Yugoslav ideology differs so sharply from its Soviet model. However, Yugoslav theoretical innovations are not confined to methodology and in certain instances take original positions on basic strategic issues also. In Belgrade, Stalinism is openly repudiated. Leninism is not quite repudiated as such, although important parts of it have been abandoned or recast. All this is done in the name of Marxism.

The specific facets of Yugoslav Communist theory are better understood if considered in the context in which they arose. Even before Yugoslavia was expelled from the Cominform in June, 1948, there were differences between the Yugoslav and Soviet Communist leaders. These differences were not primarily of an ideological nature, however. They grew out of the peculiar national background of the Yugoslavs and, more importantly, out of the peculiar political conditions in which the Tito Communists found themselves. What distinguished the Yugoslav Communists after the war was that, unlike their comrades elsewhere in Eastern Europe, they were not dependent on the Soviet Union for either coming to power or staying in power. What is more, as a result of the wartime coalition on which it rode to victory, the Tito regime, minority dictatorship though it was, had a wider popular following than did the regimes in the satellites-proper, and this, in itself, was a factor in Tito's power position. To comply with all Soviet wishes in the realm of either political and economic policies would have adversely affected that position. Thus the Yugoslavs demurred at certain Soviet demands, gently but nonetheless firmly. To the aging and arbitrary autocrat in the Kremlin, this in itself amounted to a theoretical deviation, a departure from the idea, which Stalin had elevated to a theory, that other Communist parties must subordinate themselves to Soviet leadership. This is not to say that there may not have been genuine Soviet concern of a theoretical nature regarding such things as Yugoslav agricultural policies or the role of the Yugoslav Party. But it was certainly the refusal—or, better said, inability—of the Yugoslavs to follow Soviet dictates generally that lead to their excommunication.[3]

In this connection, it is also useful to recall that the Yugoslavs did not "withdraw" from the Soviet community or "escape" from Soviet domination. They were pushed out, protestingly and against their will. Indeed, they were horrified at the idea, and, at first, met their excommunication by repeating humble oaths of allegiance to Stalin and the Soviet Union. They were, in fact, for some time simply unable to believe that an anathema had been pronounced on them by the Soviet Union and its great *vozhd*, the country and the leader which they worshipped in near-religious fashion. Their reaction can only be compared to that which one might expect in American Roman Catholics if suddenly the whole American hierarchy found itself excommunicated by the Vatican. The Yugoslav leaders actually suffered psychosomatic illnesses as a result of the Cominform expulsion, and the rank-and-file suffered confusion which can only be termed extreme.[4]

It was inevitable that once the Yugoslav leaders were able to comprehend their situation they would come up with a new theoretical framework. First of all, it was necessary to explain what had happened to them, and why. Second, there was needed a justification for their position as a Communist state not only outside but in opposition to the Communist community. And, thirdly, their rude expulsion from the Cominform freed them from their blinders of Soviet ideology and permitted them—or forced them—to see themselves and their nation, the Soviet Union and the world, capitalism and socialism, man and the society, if not as they actually were, at least in a way different from how they looked through Soviet glasses. Their view was perhaps still distorted, like that of Plato's men coming out of the cave, but it now had a perspective that was not exclusively Soviet. The Yugoslav leaders were still Marxists, still Communists, but, in a real and basic sense, different Marxists and different Communists—and different persons—than they were before.

The new theories emerged slowly, beginning with a critical view of Soviet theory and practice. It was easier for the Yugoslavs to express what they were against than what they were for. Out of these early theories grew new practices, and out of these in turn emerged new theories. The Yugoslavs were concentrating on building a system rather than an ideology. They were charting unexplored territory. Inevitably they experimented. And inevitably their theoretical framework came to have a pragmatic character about it that itself constituted a big departure from what might be termed Soviet theoretical practice.

It is not unnatural, therefore, that in their basic Marxism the Yugoslavs emphasize those pragmatic aspects of it as an evolving theory. Thus the Program of the League of Communists adopted at the 1958 Congress declares:

Marxism is not a doctrine established forever or a system of dogmas. Marxism is a theory of the social process which develops through successive historic phases. Marxism, therefore, implies a creative application of the theory and its further development, primarily by drawing general conclusions from the practice of socialist development and through attainments of scientific thinking of mankind.[5]

The Program goes on to quote Lenin approvingly as follows:

"We do not at all look on Marx's theory as something finished and inviolable. . . . We do not pretend that Marx or Marxists know the road to socialism in all its concrete aspects. This is nonsense. We know the direction of that road and we know which class forces lead the way, but concretely, practically, only the experience of millions will tell, when they get down to work."[6]

The major theoretical positions which distinguish the Yugoslav Communists may be divided into the following groups: (1) national forms of socialism, the nature of transition from capitalism and proletarian internationalism; (2) the roles of the state and party under socialism and the nature of the dictatorship of the proletariat; (3) owner-

ship, surplus value and the nature of state capitalism; (4) socialism in
the villages; and (5) the relationship of democracy to socialism.

Yugoslavia is the prime exemplar of what has come to be called
national communism because of the Titoists' insistence on "independent
paths to socialism." The Yugoslav dislike of the term national communism arises not only because it suggests bourgeois nationalism, which
they, as other Communists, deplore, but also because it tends to
further their isolation from the world Communist community. Further,
of course, it is technically a misnomer, since Yugoslav theory foresees
communism ultimately as a world system, with national differences
obliterated. What the Yugoslavs have is really "national socialism,"
although this term is obviously ruled out because of its associations
with Nazi Germany.[7]

The theoretical basis for the insistence on independent paths to
socialism and different forms of socialism lies in Lenin's theory of
the uneven development of capitalism. Since capitalism develops unevenly, with some states ripe for transition to the next stage ahead of
others, so, the Yugoslavs reason, does socialism develop unevenly. Since
socialism is seen as a reflection of reality and reality differs from country
to country, therefore each nation must develop its own approach to
and its own forms of socialism. Failure to adhere to this principle means
unnecessary difficulties in developing socialism and possibly even failure,
with resulting harm to the whole socialist movement.[8]

For these reasons, the Yugoslavs say, Lenin espoused the equality
of socialist states, and for these reasons also one form of socialism is
held to be as good as another. Although the experiences of one socialist state affect the forms in others, these experiences belong to the
whole working class movement, and no one socialist state can occupy
a leading position. The Yugoslavs distinguish between the situation
today, when several socialist states exist, and the situation between
the wars, when the USSR was the sole socialist state. During the earlier
period it may have been the duty of all Communists to work for
the USSR and even follow Soviet orders. But Stalin's efforts to carry
this situation over into the period of several socialist states is considered
a deviation from Leninism and retarded socialist development generally.[9]

The contradictions inherent in capitalism have weakened it, say
the Yugoslavs, but not necessarily in the manner Marx foresaw. The
trend has been for capitalism to cope with its contradictions through
greater state intervention in the economy. These are seen as socialist
tendencies, even though not so intended. This means that the nature
of capitalism has changed. "Pure capitalism" no longer exists, because
all contemporary capitalism has within it not only socialist tendencies
but some socialist forms.[10]

Nor is there "pure socialism," because "vestiges of old systems in-
termingle and laws of commodity production operate. . . . Certain
contradictions and antagonisms of the last phase of capitalism are

carried over into the first phase of construction of socialist society." [11] Thus, it follows, there are obviously contradictions in socialism as well as in capitalism. These center around conflicts "between the collective and individual interests of producers, between the state and labor, between the state and social self-government, between communal and central administrations, between coercion and freedom and between general policies and personal self-determination of man." [12]

From these views, the Yugoslavs derive a number of important and interesting theoretical positions concerning the transition from capitalism to socialism and the relations of socialist and capitalist states.

First of all, they assert, in contemporary conditions the forces of socialism in the world are much stronger than they were during the periods on which Marx and then Lenin based their observations. Secondly, the socialist forces are diverse. "The conception that Communist parties have a monopoly on every aspect of the movement toward socialism and that socialism is expressed only in them and through them is theoretically incorrect and very harmful in practice." [13] Therefore, Belgrade believes that Communist parties, rather than opposing, must cooperate with social democratic parties, the labor movement as a whole and even, in certain cases, those capitalist forces which, consciously or unconsciously, are held to be furthering socialist tendencies.

Thirdly, the prospects of a peaceful transition from capitalism to socialism are not only present but greater than in previous periods. There is, in fact, posited a unity of revolution and evolution, which are two aspects of a single process. Evolution, to the Yugoslavs, represents a quantitative piling up of factors in social development which at a certain stage "cause an indispensable leap from quantity to higher quality." While a sharp revolutionary conflict may be necessary to achieve the "leap," in Yugoslav eyes it is preferable, to the extent it is possible, to achieve the transition by evolution because in this way socialism will better be able to develop once it takes hold. "Socialist thinking no longer concentrates on the mere overthrow of the old capitalist system." [14]

On the other hand, however, the Yugoslavs reject the theory of automatism, according to which capitalism, because of its internal contradictions, will inevitably be transformed into socialism and Communism. The tendency is there, but the very adaptations of socialist forms by the capitalist state tend to bolster the capitalist system. As Lenin said, there is no absolutely hopeless situation which would drive capitalism to automatic transition to socialism. Results depend "not only on objective conditions but also on the conscious action of socialist forces." [15]

Does this mean that a dictatorship of the proletariat is necessary to effect the transition from capitalism to socialism? Yes, probably, but, to the Yugoslavs, dictatorship of the proletariat means no special "form of state or method or organization of the political system" but rather a situation in which the working class will have the strength to determine the direction of society. In the past this has in practice meant the Leninist form, but in contemporary conditions it can and inevitably will take other forms, among which parliamentary government is included as a possibility.[16]

The fourth conclusion the Yugoslavs draw from their view that neither pure capitalism nor pure socialism exist is that the conflict between the two systems, at the level of states, is not fundamental. Prior to the Twentieth Congress of the Soviet Communist party, this was the principal basis of the Yugoslav rejection of the Marxist theory that capitalism inevitably breeds war. Now, however, the Yugoslavs bulwark this rejection with Khrushchev's reasoning that war is not inevitable because of the strength of socialist forces in the world. Further, they are influenced explicitly, as Khrushchev certainly was implicitly, by the hard facts of nuclear weaponry.[17]

Thus coexistence is not only considered possible but necessary, because socialism, as the inevitable development in the world, is now inextricably tied to peace, without which it, as all else, is likely to be destroyed. Whereas for Lenin, Kardelj says, coexistence was primarily a defensive tactic, today it must be a continuing policy. This is so not only because socialism is no longer on the defensive, but also because the alternative is, to put it mildly, against the interests of socialism.[18]

From this position stems the well-known and controversial Yugoslav opposition to "division of the world into military blocs." In the first place, the real division of the forces of capitalism and socialism, as the Yugoslavs see it, is not geographic but is present inside both capitalist areas and socialist areas. Thus blocs based on geographic distribution cannot affect either the progress of socialism or the defense of capitalism against it. But blocs, regardless of whether they comprise capitalist or socialist states, are held to jeopardize coexistence and thus increase the risks of war, which is in the interest of neither side.

For these reasons, argue the Yugoslav theorists, there is little to choose between either the capitalist bloc or socialist bloc. They see NATO as arising from "Stalinist aggression." But because it is anti-Communist in character, they say, it gave rise to the Warsaw Pact bloc. They insist that it is in the interest of socialist forces to work for elimination of both.[19]

It was on this point, more than any other, that the Soviet leaders denounced the Draft Program of the Yugoslav League at its Seventh Congress. As a result of this criticism, the Yugoslavs revised the Program to spell out more in detail the differences between the blocs. Thus the Warsaw Pact was seen as now more defensive than NATO, and as comprising states which are striving more actively than the NATO states for relaxation of international tensions. Nonetheless, according to the Yugoslav view, the continued existence of the blocs is a manifestation of "reactionary forces" in both camps, in that of the socialists as well as that of the capitalists.[20]

This brings up the Yugoslav view of proletarian internationalism. As is well known—to borrow a familiar phrase—Proletarian Internationalism to the Kremlin and its *po-putchiki* means primarily recognizing the Soviet Union as the center of the Communist movement and the leading socialist nation and following the Soviet position in international affairs. Practically, this means active affiliation with the Soviet bloc. Conversely, it means abstaining from criticism of the Soviet Union or Soviet policies. It is perfectly obvious that the Yugoslav Communist theories do not fit this concept. Tito is of the opinion that this—as manifested by the Yugoslav refusal to sign the Declaration of the twelve Communist parties in Moscow in 1957—is the essence of the present Soviet campaign against Yugoslavia, although he minimizes its theoretical significance.[21]

Nevertheless, the Yugoslavs do espouse a theory of proletarian internationalism of their own. In fact, the Program adopted at the Seventh Congress says: "In all its contacts with other Communists, Socialist, Progressive and anti-imperialist movements and in all its international relations in general, the League of Communists of Yugoslavia has upheld and will continue to uphold the great idea of proletarian socialist internationalism as its guiding principle." [22]

It is easier to say what proletarian internationalism does not mean to the Yugoslavs than what it does mean. Apparently the Yugoslav concept means little more than a feeling of ideological solidarity among the "socialist forces" including but by no means limited to Communist parties. There should also be cooperation but only on a basis of equality and without formal organization. When stressing such principles, Kardelj admits, the Yugoslavs "are guided primarily by experience from the past." Although recognizing that conditions have changed since Cominform days, Kardelj warns that "contradictions of the transitional period and the powerful influences of the present international situation on relationships between socialist countries can still be a source of diverse mistakes and negative tendencies." [23]

One final position derives from these Yugoslav views. This is the rejection of the Leninist theory of just and unjust wars. "Socialism cannot be exported or imposed by force on other peoples," declared Kardelj, and "no one can prescribe the socialist forms any one country shall apply." It follows, he said, that "we consider as aggressive every attempt at interference in the internal life of a socialist country for the purpose of restoring the old order or of encouraging the vestiges of reactionary forces." [24]

This is an interesting, although not altogether successful, attempt to harmonize the Yugoslav stand on just and unjust wars, first formulated as early as 1951, with Belgrade's ambivalent stand on the Soviet intervention in Hungary in 1956. Although the intervention was both criticized and deplored by Tito at the time; he also admitted that if it was necessary to "save socialism" in Hungary it was justified. In 1951 Kardelj had specifically excluded from the category of just wars attempts of "the Soviet Union . . . to bring happiness to other peoples by forcing its political system and hegemony on them." [25] In 1958, although obliquely maintaining this position by reference to "encouraging the vestiges of reactionary forces,"—which to the Yugoslavs means Cominform or Stalinist influence—Kardelj now implies that a greater danger is intervention "aimed at restoration of the capitalist order."

The second major area of special Yugoslav theoretical development concerns the role of the state. The state is seen as an indispensable force in the beginning of the transition period. But once the "initial transition period" has been accomplished—as manifested by nationalization of the means of production and isolation of "exploiting elements" —then, in order for progress toward socialism, the state must begin to wither away. Although the withering away does not have to be accomplished in any concrete time period, it must begin. Indeed, a state is not really a socialist state unless it is in the process of withering away, and the withering away "arises as the fundamental and decisive question of the socialist system." [26]

Soviet theory, of course, also embraces the concept of the withering away of the state. The basic difference here in Yugoslav ideology is the insistence that the process must get underway in order for a society to be launched truly on the road to socialism.

The withering away begins in practice, according to Kardelj, first in the fields of state economic functions, education, cultural activities and social services, e.g., in those areas where the Yugoslav state has in fact divested itself of direct control and management. However, Kardelj warns, the role of the state as "an instrument of power . . . against anti-socialist forces and activities or as regards protection of the country's independence"—e.g., police and army—will diminish more slowly. The process, he explains, will depend on how long "in international relations the influence of antagonistic social contradictions dominates and reactionary social forces are still to be reckoned with as a factor capable of jeopardizing the existence of the free development of socialism.[27] (Since the Yugoslavs interpret these words to refer to safeguards against not only anti-Communist activity but "Cominform-type" activity as well, the comparison suggested with ideas advanced by Stalin to justify his maintenance of state power is inexact.)

The tendency of the state, once reconstituted as the dictatorship of the proletariat, not to wither away is seen as a major contradiction in the socialist process. This tendency is held to be nurtured by remnants of capitalist elements, and unless it is promptly overcome, the dictatorship of the proletariat, instead of moving toward socialism, degenerates into state capitalism.

The 1958 Program repeats the earlier analysis of the Soviet system as it existed prior to the Twentieth Party Congress that it demonstrated state capitalist tendencies and attempted to bulwark them with "a pragmatic revision of . . . Marxism-Leninism." But it also adds that following the Twentieth Congress "various deformities in the USSR born under the influence of the above-mentioned tendencies gradually began to be removed." This apparently gave the Yugoslav Communists hope that conditions now exist in the Soviet Union to "make possible the further successful development in this process, furnishing a new incentive in the advance of socialism." [28]

Yet even this bringing up to date of the Yugoslav analysis of Soviet developments falls short of an appraisal which fits the Yugoslav requirement of the beginning of the withering away of the state as a prerequisite for socialism. The contradiction is all the greater since the Soviet Union claims not only to have socialism but now to be advanced on the road to Communism itself.

The main danger in state capitalist tendencies, as seen by the Yugoslavs, is that "state bureaucratism" may develop into an independent system of its own.[29] This is particularly true in the case of state management and control of industry. In Yugoslav theory, state ownership of the means of production is a vital beginning for socialism, but what counts is not only ownership but control. Thus nationalization is seen as only the first, and the lowest, step in the transition. As long as it does not progress beyond this, worker ownership is only fictional. The workers actually have no control, because control is lodged in the state bureaucracy which tends to administer the means of production in a way to perpetuate its own control. In such cases, the state bureaucracy is a form of state capitalism in which surplus value is appropriated by the state bureaucracy much as under capitalism surplus value is appropriated by the private owners. Indeed, under capitalism an independent labor movement is, at least theoretically, better able to protect the interest of workers than under a dictatorship of the proletariat turned state capitalism. Under the latter, surplus value acts as a contradiction in the same way as it does under capitalism.

Although this formula was first enunciated by the now disgraced Milovan Djilas, who incorporated some of it in his book *The New Class,* the essence of the theory is retained in the 1958 Program.[30]

The manifestations of such "statist deformations" are not confined to the economic system, but permeate social relationships and foreign policy as well. Nor are they caused by the "cult of the individual." Rather the "cult of the individual is caused by the political and economic system, of which it is a characteristic." [31]

It is in connection with their interpretation of the concept of the withering away of the state that the Yugoslavs are, perhaps, best known. Since mere nationalization was only the first step, and since its concomitant, state control, constituted a grave danger, the Yugoslavs had to devise "a higher form of socialism in which the state would begin to wither away." First they invoked the concept of "social property." This was national ownership but not state ownership, "social but not state control." [32] The mechanism for its implementation was found in worker-management. Under this arrangement, councils elected by workers in each factory organize production and dispose of proceeds of their work by and large according to their own wishes.

This process was accompanied by a sweeping decentralization which amounted to elimination of virtually all state agencies concerned with directing the economy. The Yugoslav equivalent of the Gosplan was not completely eliminated, but its functions were drastically changed. The social plan became little more then estimates of production, not legally binding on individual producing units, which themselves planned and carried out their output, prices and wages. The state was to influence and indirectly channel the economy by use of state investment funds and control of taxes and credit and, to some extent, foreign trade. Later indirect controls came to include associations of producing units. Although certain controls were lodged in local governments, still, within these limits, the Yugoslav economy became virtually a free, but not a private, enterprise economy. This meant, according to the Yugoslavs, that socialism would be promoted not only by more direct participation of citizens in running the economy but also by "freeing the initiative of the producers to develop according to basic economic laws." [33] The initiative of individual producers thus freed is certain, the Yugoslavs feel, to represent "a greater economic power than capitalist initiative" and guarantees that "socialism must come out a victor in economic competition with capitalism." [34]

While the state is withering away, what becomes of the Communist Party? It was Tito's declaration in 1952 that the Party, too, would wither away along with the state that set in motion a chain of ideas culminating with Djilas' proposal that it do so forthwith. Therefore, Tito abruptly pulled back, declaring that "there can be no withering away or winding up of the League of Communists until the last class enemy has been immobilized, until the broadest body of our citizens are socialist in outlook." Rather, said Tito, at the Central Committee "trial" of Djilas, the Party must become stronger, while its withering away would be a "lengthy process," developing only "through trials and difficulties." [35]

Nevertheless, the 1958 Program promises that the League of Communists "will gradually disappear . . . as the forms of direct socialist democracy become stronger, develop and expand. This disappearance will proceed parallel to the objective process of the withering away of social antagonisms and all forms of coercion which historically grew out of these antagonisms." [36]

Interpreting this, Kardelj explained that the method of the withering away of the party would be a gradual merger of its power "into the direct power of the working masses themselves." [37]

Although the latest ideological pronouncements do not deal extensively with the concept of withering away of the party as such, they do reiterate earlier admonitions that state and party functions must be clearly separated. They warn that bureaucracy is a danger not only in the state but in the party as well and emphasize that the danger of "bureaucratic statism" is greatest where government decision-making is concentrated in Party hands. Further, the Communist Party, it is repeated, cannot have *the* leading role in a socialist society but only *a* leading role, in cooperation with other organizations. Above all, it is insisted, the task of the Communists is not to order and direct but to lead by education and propaganda.[38]

Practical application of these innovations in the theory of the party has led to a prohibition of party functionaries being heads of local government units and to extension of considerable autonomy, comparatively, to local and basic units.[39] Furthermore, there was a considerable reduction in size in the party apparatus, and many Party functions were eliminated. In most cases, however, these have been taken over by the Socialist Alliance, a mass organization embracing virtually everybody but thoroughly, if indirectly, controlled by the Party.[40] Of course, it goes without saying that, despite all theorizing, the Party still maintains the dominant place in Yugoslav society. As Kardelj put it to the Seventh Congress, "we would be guilty of hypocrisy if we did not admit that at present the Communists in our country do exert, as they should, a direct influence on the key positions of power. . . ."[41]

Meanwhile, the Yugoslavs had run aground, theoretically as well as practically, on that old stumbling block of Communism, agriculture. Having abandoned the collective farms and accepted the private peasant as a long-run feature of Yugoslav life, they still were committed to collectivization of agriculture as a goal and still regarded the private peasant as a negative, if not hostile, force.

To cope with this situation theoretically, they made their first open and specific repudiation of Leninism as such. They rejected the Leninist doctrine that socialism in the villages was necessary for socialism in the country. Instead, Kardelj devised the concept of what might be called "socialism by osmosis." That is, instead of proceeding with socialism in the villages, the Yugoslavs would let the peasants alone—limiting capitalist influences by imposing a limit on land holdings—and proceed with developing socialism elsewhere through industrialization. The theory was that as this process proceeded, a generally socialist *Zeitgeist* would be created which would ultimately alter the individualist outlook of the peasants. When it did, they would be in a mood for the acceptance of cooperatives "of some sort, although not the Soviet kolkhozi." This would take a long time, "maybe 25 or 50 years," according to Kardelj. In the meantime, through development of voluntary cooperatives of other types, especially in the areas of storage and processing, the "softening" of the peasants' individualism would be accelerated.[42]

Repeating implicitly and explicitly these views, the 1958 formulations on agriculture constitute both an admission of past mistakes, a pledge not to repeat them, a doctrinal assertion of the necessity for some kind of collectivization ultimately and a hope that somehow it will be accomplished. Although such theorizing leaves the Yugoslavs in some difficult dilemmas as far as practice is concerned, it nevertheless does provide an ideological justification for their abandonment of collectivization.[43]

The final area in which Yugoslav theory has made new departures concerns the meaning of democracy in a socialist system. The Yugoslavs are more careful to point out what their kind of democracy does not mean. It does not mean a multi-party system. It does not mean freedom of anti-socialist criticism that would endanger the system. It does not mean establishment of all the forms of "bourgeois democracy," even if socialist forces "should obtain complete mastery" of them, because such forms contain the seeds of capitalism; but adaptation of certain forms of bourgeois democracy is possible.[44]

Socialist democracy, to the Yugoslavs, means particularly "direct and mass democracy, in contrast with bourgeois democracy which, both in theory and practice, is indirect democracy through intermediaries. . . ." Such direct democracy comes about when, as a result of the withering away of state functions, masses of citizens themselves make political decisions affecting their lives.

Although the first step in this process was seen as establishment of workers' councils, it was further manifested in a variety of political instrumentalities—ranging from voters' meetings to citizen-action committees in local government and direct citizen management of such institutions as schools and hospitals. Furthermore, there has been an extension of citizen participation in certain utilities, of which the publishing is considered one, with the discussion of extending the principle to workers' councils generally.[45]

That much of this citizen participation in government is controlled and directed by the Socialist Alliance, which is something of a broad mass organization for the Party, affects the practical application of the theory but not the theory itself.

The emphasis in Yugoslav socialist democracy is on local government, particularly on the new form of the Commune. The Commune is seen as, next to Communism itself, the end product of Yugoslav socialist decentralization. Communal organizations—generally at the level of a district or county—have supervision over economic enterprises, big and little, in their area, and control over most investment in both industry and agriculture. They are not the same as local government, but in most areas have taken over many of the functions, especially the economic functions, of local government. The Commune thus "represents the outstanding institution of direct socialist democracy. . . . The Commune is not only primarily a school of democracy, but democracy itself—the basic cell of self-management of citizens in common affairs."[46] Further development of communal activities in the fields of child care, food supply, laundry services and the like is seen as "the way to socialization of the technological basis of housekeeping."[47]

Not all aspects of Yugoslav socialist democracy are direct, however. One in particular involves worker representation in parliamentary bodies at all levels in the form of the council of producers. All law-making bodies in Yugoslavia are bicameral, and the council of producers is one of two chambers. Its members are elected directly by workers, on a basis of the contributions to national income made by their particular branch of production. The theory is that as workers' councils give workers control of factories, so producers' councils give them a direct voice in government, especially in economic affairs.[48]

In its non-institutional aspects, Yugoslav Communism insists that Socialist democracy must be concerned with individual freedom and human rights. This is referred to as "socialist humanism." It involves the necessity of free expression. "Conditions are being created," boasts the 1958 Program, "for considerate hearing of everybody's opinion." [49]

"Socialist humanism," however, operates only within the framework of a socialist society, that is, only as long as it does not endanger the system. "Only those forms of democracy can be a suitable instrument of social advance," according to Kardelj, "which allow . . . socialist economic and social relationships to 'rest' comfortably." [50] Among the democratic forms specifically excluded by Tito is freedom of the press.[51]

Out of these concepts grows the Yugoslav variety of socialist legality, which, it is held, must govern society in a period of peaceful socialist development. To the Yugoslavs, "socialist legality means necessarily the rule of law with equality and possession of certain unlimited subjective rights by individuals." Especially is it the right of citizens to secure protection from state action through the courts. "The working class and socialist society," Kardelj asserts, should "feel safe not only from remnants of the bourgeoisie, but also, as Marx says, from their own officials." At the same time, the courts must safeguard socialism. Thus while technically they are independent of the state they are not independent of the system.[52] This distinction is more clearly stated in theory than it is maintained in practice.

From their theory of socialist democracy, the Yugoslavs delimit the right of either state or party to interfere with development of art or science. Although the Yugoslav Communists believe "in the social conditioning of science and art and their great role in society," they also reject "all pragmatic distortion of Marxist views on the role of science and art in society and all transformations of science and art into instruments of daily political affairs. They take "a position against the 'theory' which, in the name of abstract concepts of freedom, actually abolishes true freedom of scientific and artistic creation and subordinates it to reactionary political tendencies. . . . The ideological role of the League of Communists must not be that of a dogmatic judge of trends, schools and styles in science and art." [53]

Amplifying this, the poet Oskar Davičo explained that the stand of the League of Communists on art does not violate Marxist precepts or mean "depolitization." Rejecting socialist realism completely, he says that real art "speaks to everyone" and inevitably expresses the realities of its period better than they can be expressed by politicians.[54]

Stepping out of the strange world of Marxist reasoning and language, what conclusions can one draw from this half-original, half-fundamentalist framework which the Yugoslav Communists have erected to explain and justify their position and bulwark their views?

First of all, here is a fresh approach to contemporary Marxism that maintains most of what is appealing to those interested in the theory and omits or alters much of what is distasteful to those who, although attracted to Marxism, are repelled by Soviet dogmatism and brutality. In one sense, it offers a bridge between the positions of the Second and Third Internationals, although it is certainly closer to the latter. There are, as Soviet spokesmen have charged, some elements of both "right and left deviation" in Yugoslav theory, some elements of both Trotsky and Bukharin. But whereas the practical effect of this position may be to foster "Bernsteinism," in their ideology structure-proper the Yugoslavs have skirted but avoided this cardinal sin.[55]

Practically, the new Yugoslav theories indicate directions non-Soviet Communist thinking might take if freed from the fetters imposed by the Kremlin. Certainly there is provided an ample theoretical base—if one is really needed—for a socialist state outside Soviet hegemony, for socialism in one country (other than the Soviet Union) based on national interest. It does not necessarily follow that the Yugoslav path is open to other countries. The Yugoslavs themselves did not set upon it willingly, and their theories and practice derive in no small degree from conditions peculiar to Yugoslavia. Yet the Yugoslav development, theoretical and otherwise, obviously has had a great impact on the whole Communist movement, including the USSR as well as the satellites. One need not feel that the Yugoslav example was a primary factor in the 1956 events in Hungary, or even in the so-called "October Revolution" in Poland, to realize that there was nevertheless a connection.

Furthermore, if the world holds together, it is not improbable that national differences among the satellite countries will grow, with more independence from Soviet tutelage. If so, Yugoslav theory offers an ideological basis, well within the confines of Marxism and even Marxism-Leninism, for a more democratic development, in which more attention can be paid to human values and individual rights. Since, to the extent that the satellites have it within their power to accelerate this course, it is almost certain that the Communists, rather than the non-Communists, will do it, the existence of Yugoslav Marxist flags marking the way may be of significance.[56]

Along the same lines, Yugoslav theory is important for other countries which may well, unfortunately, take the Communist path in the future. Such countries are likely, both because of geography and time, to be less under the influence of a dominant Communist power, and the value of having other directions pointed out to them in a way theoretical minds can understand may be of great importance.[57]

At least as important is the devastating criticism to which Yugoslav theoretical analysis subjects Soviet development and policies and Soviet theories. The criticism is all the more meaningful because of the wide area of agreement between the Yugoslav and Soviet Communists.

Yet, at the same time, Yugoslav theory has had less impact than the Yugoslavs themselves would like to believe. Certainly recent Soviet and Chinese developments, to the small extent they indicate appreciation of the Yugoslav position, resulted more from the realities of their own arms, foreign and domestic, than from Yugoslav influence. That the Yugoslav impact on Western Communist parties has been so small testifies to the extent of their allegiance to Moscow. In non-Communist underdeveloped countries, Titoism thus far seems to have more attraction for the Second than for the Third International socialists.

One could draw other conclusions also. One of them is that the areas of similarity in Yugoslav and Soviet theoretical approaches are as important as the difference, that Communists, no matter what variety, are Communists and as such should never be confused with Western-type democrats.

And, finally, certainly not the least significant aspect of Yugoslav theory is its importance to the Yugoslav Communists themselves. "Theory," observed Stalin, ". . . gives practical people strength and orientation, a clarity of perspective, confidence at work, faith. . . ." [58] Even during the period of their closest rapprochement with the Soviet Union, the Yugoslav Communists remained faithful to their basic tenets. The existence of a cohesive body of theory bulwarking the unique Yugoslav approach to Communism and nationalism does not prove that they will not ever abandon their new directions for the mirage of Socialist Unity under Soviet tutelage, but it does make that eventuality far less likely than might otherwise be the case. This theoretical framework is perhaps the most important factor setting off Yugoslav developments from those in Poland. In Poland, the new reforms have far more of an "NEP" tactical quality about them just because of the virtually complete absence of a new theoretical orientation. [59] The Polish Communists have already begun withdrawing from the positions of October, 1956. The extent of freedom and relaxation in Poland thus [is] fundamentally less substantial than . . . in Yugoslavia, even where, on the surface, [it] may seem more so.

NOTES

1. Cf. *Nacrt Programa Saveza Kommunista Jugoslavije* (Belgrade: Kultura, 1958). The Draft Program was distributed in March both in Yugoslavia and to leaders of foreign Communist parties. The final program is included in *Sedmi Kongres SKJ* (Belgrade: Kultura, 1958). For an English text, see Stoyan Pribechevich's translation, *Yugoslavia's Way, The Program of the League of the Communists of Yugoslavia* (New York: All Nations Press, 1958).

2. Edvard Kardelj, "Povodom Nacrta Programa Saveza Komunista Jugoslavije," *Sedmi Kongres SKJ*, p. 147.

3. Cf. Fred Warner Neal, *Titoism in Action: The Reforms in Yugoslavia after 1948* (Berkeley: University of California Press, 1958), pp. 2-3, and Robert Lee Wolff, *The Balkans in Our Time* (Cambridge: Harvard University Press, 1956), p. 321 and p. 355.

4. Neal, pp. 3-5.

5. *Yugoslavia's Way*, p. 133.

6. *Ibid.*

7. See *Yugoslavia's Way*, p. 65, p. 73, and Neal, p. 18.

8. See Josip Broz Tito, "Zadaci Saveza Komunista," *Sedmi Kongres*, pp. 35-36, and Kardelj, p. 173.

9. *Ibid.* See also *Yugoslavia's Way*, pp. 39-40. The 1958 view repeats earlier analyses of the Soviet experience, although now blame is to some extent more directly on Stalin personally. However, see discussion of the "cult of the individual," below.

10. *Yugoslavia's Way*, p. 14, p. 24. See also Neal, p. 17.

11. *Yugoslavia's Way*, p. 74.

12. *Ibid.*, pp. 148-49.

13. *Ibid.* See discussion on Party, below, and also Resolution of the Seventh Congress, *Sedmi Kongres*, pp. 443-57.

14. *Yugoslavia's Way*, p. 23.

15. Kardelj, pp. 156-58.

16. *Yugoslavia's Way*, p. 106, pp. 111-14.

17. Cf. *ibid.*, pp. 74-75, and Kardelj, pp. 166-67.

18. Kardelj, pp. 164-65.

19. *Ibid.*, p. 166, and Tito, *Sedmi Kongres*, p. 13.

20. *Yugoslavia's Way*, pp. 70-77, and Kardelj, p. 166 and pp. 180-81. Except for such alterations, the difference between the Draft Program and that finally adopted was more one of tone than of substance, which, of course, was what annoyed the Russians. Cf. *Borba*, November 14, 1958, p. 1.

21. Cf. Tito's remarks at Labin, in Istria, *Borba*, June 15, 1958, p. 1.

22. *Yugoslavia's Way*, p. 67.

23. Kardelj, pp. 159-60.

24. *Ibid.*, p. 126.

25. Cf. Kardelj, *Medjunarodna Scena i Jugoslovenski Polozaj* (Belgrade, 1951), pp. 6-8.

26. *Yugoslavia's Way*, p. 30, p. 116. For a similar view, expressed earlier, see Jovan Djordjević, "Some Principles of Socialist Democracy in Yugoslavia," *New Yugoslav Law*, Nos. 3-4 (July-December, 1952), p. 16.

27. Kardelj, p. 176.

28. *Yugoslavia's Way*, p. 15, pp. 44-45 and p. 118. Whereas earlier pronouncements, especially those made by Milovan Djilas, stated flatly that the Soviet Union is an example of state capitalism rather than socialism, the present view avoids this judgment about the present, implying, without quite saying so, that it is no longer valid.

29. *Ibid.*, pp. 118-19.

30. *Yugoslavia's Way*, pp. 124-25, p. 129, p. 140. For the earlier and more concrete formulation, see Neal, pp. 20-21. Djilas' analysis was specifically aimed at Stalin's theory that the concept of surplus value is applicable only under capitalism. Although ignored in the 1958 Program itself, Djilas was sharply condemned by various speakers at the Seventh Congress.

31. Kardelj, p. 161. See also answer to questions on this point in *Mladost*, Belgrade, March 6, 1957.

32. For Yugoslav views spelling out these concepts, see Neal, pp. 20-21. These are embraced in the 1958 Program. *Yugoslavia's Way*, pp. 128-29 and pp. 133-34.

33. Cf. Neal, pp. 120-59. See also Charles P. McVicker, *Titoism, Pattern for International Communism* (New York: St. Martin's Press, 1957), pp. 61-106.

34. *Yugoslavia's Way*, p. 155.

35. See Neal, pp. 67-73.

36. *Yugoslavia's Way*, p. 235. The present theory omits Tito's earlier linking of the withering away of the Party to the withering away of the state.

37. Kardelj, p. 178.

38. *Yugoslavia's Way*, p. 120, p. 165, p. 239. See also Kardelj, p. 178, and Neal, Ch. III.

39. However, democratic centralism explicitly remains the guiding principle of the League of Communists. See "Statut Saveza Komunista Jugoslavije," *Sedmi Kongres*, p. 428.

40. Cf. Neal, Ch. III.

41. Kardelj, p. 178.

42. Cf. Neal, pp. 208-10.

43. *Yugoslavia's Way*, pp. 130-31 and pp. 141-42.

44. *Ibid.*, pp. 162-64, and Kardelj, pp. 171-72. For earlier rejections of "bourgeois democracy," see Neal, p. 23.

45. *Yugoslavia's Way*, pp. 165-75.

46. *Ibid.*, p. 176.

47. *Ibid.*, p. 177. The agency for these activities is the so-called *Stanbena Zajednica*, or housing neighborhood, the development of which is currently a favor theme with Yugoslav Communists. See, for example, *Borba*, July 10, 1958.

48. *Yugoslavia's Way*, pp. 178-79. See also reference to council of producers in the Resolution of the Seventh Congress, *Sedmi Kongres*, p. 448. For description of the council of producers, see Neal, pp. 96-98. Sharp discrimination against peasants results from the method of electing members of councils of producers. Cf. Neal, pp. 112-14.

49. *Yugoslavia's Way*, p. 238. McVicker, especially, is impressed with this "humane variety of Marxism" in Yugoslavia. McVicker, p. xii.

50. Kardelj, p. 172.

51. Tito, *Sedmi Kongres*, pp. 87-88.

52. *Yugoslavia's Way*, p. 183. See also Radomir Lukić, "Legality in Socialist Countries," *Review of International Affairs*, October 1, 1958, pp. 8-11, and Kardelj, p. 172. For a more extensive exposition of this theme, see Neal, pp. 214-19, and McVicker, Ch. IX.

53. *Yugoslavia's Way*, pp. 254-55.

54. Oskar Davičo, "Two Kinds of Prejudices in Aesthetics and a Subjective Factor," *Review of International Affairs*, November 16, 1958, pp. 12-15.

55. For Yugoslav views on Bernsteinism, see *Komunist*, Nos. 1-2 (January-February, 1954), pp. 32-41, and Neal, p. 18 and p. 71.

56. It should be remembered that in Poland and even in Hungary initially agitation for reform was begun not by anti-Communists but by "nationalists" among the Communists.

57. For instance, Prof. Marshall Windmiller of the University of California at Berkeley is of the opinion that in India there has been extensive Yugoslav influence not only on the Congress Party but also on the Communists.

58. J. S. Stalin, *Voprosy Leninizma* (Moscow: Gosizdat, 1934), pp. 299-300.

59. During his visit to Poland in the fall of 1958, the writer was told repeatedly by Party and government officials that their reforms had no formal ideological connotations but were adopted simply because they would work better. Events of the fall and winter months of 1959 appear to bear out the less substantial nature of some Polish reforms.

HOW ORIGINAL IS "MAOISM"?

Arthur A. Cohen

Liu Shao-Ch'i, heir apparent to Mao Tse-tung as head of the Chinese Communist Party, claimed in 1945 that Mao had formulated a "theory" of the Chinese revolution which constituted a new "development" of Communist doctrine on the revolutionary conquest of power. Liu's tribute heralded the beginning of what has since proven to be an ambitious and persistent effort not only to exalt "the ideology of Mao" as the sole guide for the Chinese Communist Party and people, but also to propagate an image of the Chinese party leader as the foremost living theorist of the world Communist movement.[1] At least one Chinese party spokesman has credited Mao with more than fourteen major contributions to Communist doctrine.

The Chinese pretensions to Mao's ideological primacy have figured as a highly important and thorny issue in the still continuing conflict of views between Moscow and Peking. If only for that reason, a fresh attempt to evaluate those pretensions seems worthwhile—especially since the Chinese claims presumably will remain a factor in the Sino-Soviet relationship even after Mao's death, just as divergent Chinese and Soviet assessments of Stalin's contribution have played a part in that relationship since the death of the former Soviet dictator.

MAO AS A MARXIST PHILOSOPHER

The first area in which the Chinese Communists claim that Mao has made a major creative contribution is that of Marxist philosophy, in particular his elaboration of Marxian dialectical materialism. This claim has been based principally on two essays attributed to Mao—"On Practice" and "On Contradiction"—both alleged to have been originally written by him in 1937, but actually published in their present form only in 1950 and 1952, respectively.

Reprinted from *Problems of Communism*, vol. X, no. 6 (November-December, 1961), 34-42. By permission of the author and the publisher.

Chinese Communist writers on theory credit Mao's "On Practice" with novel theoretical formulations in two specific respects. Li Ta terms the essay "a development of the Marxist-Leninist theory of practice," [2] while others such as Ai Ssu-ch'i claim that it "clarifies and develops Engels' and Lenin's famous principle of absolute and relative truth." [3]

It is difficult to grant validity to either of these contentions. Li's claim appears without basis inasmuch as "On Practice" contains little more than paraphrased passages of Lenin's discussion of the theory of knowledge in his *Philosophical Notebooks* and *Materialism and Empirio-Criticism*. As for Ai Ssu-ch'i's thesis of a Maoist contribution to the Marxist theory of truth, a close reading of the relevant portions of Mao's essay similarly reveals the discussion to be merely a reiteration, rather than a creative development, of ideas already set forth in Lenin's *Materialism and Empirio-Criticism* and Engels' *Anti-Dühring*. Nor does "On Practice" have anything to add to the ideas of Engels and Lenin on appearance and essence, or to Marx's critical reformulation of "the primary of practice in knowledge" as elaborated in the writings of Engels, Lenin, and Stalin.

Thus, nowhere in "On Practice" does Mao introduce a genuinely novel idea or make a constructive contribution to dialectical materialist doctrine on practice. Indeed, in a rather unusual commentary on Mao's treatise, published in a Chinese Communist journal, Professor Feng Yu-lan, perhaps the greatest living historian of Chinese philosophical thought, acknowledges in effect that even pre-modern Chinese philosophers— particularly Mo Ti, Wang Ch'ung, and Wang Chuan-shan—had anticipated all of Mao's ideas on the role of practice in the knowing process.[4]

The Chinese case with respect to the second of Mao's philosophical essays, "On Contradiction," is similarly exaggerated, but perhaps a shade stronger. Ai Ssu-ch'i claims that in this work Mao "further developed Lenin's brilliant idea that 'the dialectic, briefly defined, is the theory of the unity of opposites'" and also "further defined the correct relationship between internal contradiction and external causation in the development of things." [5] Actually, the essay says nothing new on the unity of opposites or the "particularity" of contradiction, nor does it "further define" the laws of causation beyond the concept of the "necessary self-movement" of things as expounded in Hegel's *Logic* and subsequently in the writings of Engels and Lenin. Mao does indeed seem to have come up with one novel formulation, namely the contention that any contradiction has a "principal aspect" which is the determinant of qualitative change; but this rather suspect idea is the extent of his originality as a dialectical materialist and Marxist philosopher.

Quite apart from the question of the substantive value of "On Practice" and "On Contradiction" as a contribution to Marxist philosophy, there is also the question of whether the two essays were, in fact, written by Mao in substantially their present form in 1937, as the Chinese Communists claim. According to the Chinese Communist version, "On Practice" was written in July and "On Contradiction" in August of that year.[6] Introductory editors' notes accompanying the essays in Volumes I and II of Mao's *Selected Works* (published in October 1951 and April 1952, respectively) state that both were originally presented by Mao as lectures at Yenan in 1937, and only the note to "On Contradiction" indicates a revision of the original text prior to its inclusion in Volume II.

Actually, there is considerable evidence casting doubt on this Chinese Communist version, and it may therefore be worthwhile to summarize the available facts. To begin with, as far as can be determined, "On Practice" was published in China for the first time in the central party organ *Jen-min jih-pao* on December 29, 1950 (it was also published in the Soviet journal *Bolshevik*, No. 23, December 1950, and commented on in *Pravda*, December 18, 1950); and "On Contradiction" first appeared in print in China, also in *Jen-min jih-pao*, on April 1, 1952. Although earlier collections of Mao's major writings to date had been published in the mid-1940's, they did not include either of these essays. Moreover, in a philosophical article published in May 1941, the Communist writer Hsiao Chou specifically discussed the theory of practice without making any reference to Mao's purported essay on the same subject.[7]

It is also curious that Volume I of Mao's *Selected Works*, as published in October 1951, included "On Practice" but not "On Contradiction," and that the latter appeared out of proper chronological sequence in Volume II, published in April 1952 just after the essay had come out for the first time in *Jen-min jih-pao*. A statement by the Committee on Publication of Mao's Works, appearing on the flyleaf of Volume II, offered no explanation of this curious fact, merely noting that " 'On Contradiction' . . . should have been in Volume I to accord with the author's chronology" and would be transferred there in a later reprinting of the volume. This would strongly suggest that "On Contradiction" had not been ready for publication even as late as October 1951 when Volume I appeared.

Still further reason for doubting the Chinese version is furnished by the sharp contrast in caliber of Marxist thinking between "On Practice" and "On Contradiction," as published in 1950 and 1952, and another example of philosophical writing by Mao dating back, in actual fact, to 1940. The latter—part of an essay on dialectical materialism printed in a Shanghai magazine in March 1940 [8]—appears to be the only sample of Mao's writing on Marxist philosophy to have been actually published prior to 1950, and it sheds revealing light on the primitiveness of his philosophical ideas as of that period. In it Mao makes many mistakes— for example, his attribution to "idealists" of views which in fact were held by well-versed Marxists—and the entire fragment is a jumble of statements that are questionable as philosophy, Marxist or otherwise. Even Mao's lieutenants apparently regarded the essay as a catastrophe. According to General Sheng Shih-ts'ai, the onetime warlord of Sinkiang

Province, the Yenan Communist Fang Lin refused to show him the essay in 1940 with the remark, "You had better not read it. From the theoretical point of view, Chairman Mao's 'Dialectics' is full of errors." [9]

If this was the caliber of Mao's philosophical thinking in 1940, it is difficult to believe that any lectures he may have prepared and given at Yenan in 1937 on the Marxist theories of practice and contradiction could have been anything but equally primitive and unsophisticated. By contrast, however, "On Practice" and "On Contradiction" in the form in which they were first published in 1950 and 1952 clearly show the hand of a theorist who, if not original in his thinking, at least develops his arguments along well-schooled and correct Marxist-Leninist lines. It therefore seems reasonable to conclude that the published versions either were written at a much later date than the Chinese claim, or represent such drastic revisions of Mao's purported 1937 lectures as to be altogether different from them.

THE MAOIST "THEORY" OF REVOLUTION

So much for Mao's pretensions to eminence as a "developer" of Marxist dialectical materialism. Is there any stronger foundation for the claim that he made an original and unique contribution to Communist doctrine concerning the fundamentals of the revolutionary process?

Chinese Communist writers, it is true, have conceded that Mao's general analysis of the problems of the Chinese revolution conformed essentially to the concepts of Lenin and Stalin. Chang Ju-hsin, for example, wrote in 1953 that during the period of the First Revolutionary Civil War (1924-27) "Comrade Mao Tse-tung, . . . the faithful student and comrade-in-arms of Stalin, upheld the viewpoints of Lenin and Stalin in regard to the problems of the revolution in China." [10]

But the Chinese nevertheless insist that Mao's conclusions had an independent value of their own. That is to say, they derived from Mao's own analysis of Chinese conditions and were not just a direct appropriation of Leninist-Stalinist ideas. In the same article quoted above (which was, in fact, a tribute to Stalin published shortly after his death), Chang Ju-hsin went on to say that Mao arrived at "identical conclusions with those of Stalin regarding the fundamental problems of the Chinese revolution."

Another Chinese Communist writer, Shen Chih-yuan, takes a similar line in an article published early in 1952. Although acknowledging Mao's general debt to Lenin and Stalin, he qualifies this by saying that in the period 1924-27 the writings of Lenin and Stalin "had been disseminated in China only to a very small extent." "Yet," he adds, "Chairman Mao, already in this very period or even somewhat earlier, had finished his analysis of classes in Chinese society and his report on the peasant movement in Hunan . . . exercising independent powers of reflection." [11] But both Chang and Shen fail to mention an important historical fact, namely, that the policies actually followed by the Chinese Communists in the middle and latter 1920's, as well as the theoretical justifications for them, were laid down and sent to China in numerous Comintern directives initiated and approved by Stalin.

This has not deterred the Chinese from being quite specific in their claims on behalf of Mao. Ch'en Po-ta, Mao's chief eulogist, wrote in 1951 that Mao "consistently adhered to . . . the Lenin-Stalin theory on the leadership of the proletariat *and developed this theory in a concrete manner* (Italics added)." [12] Ch'en was referring to the concept of proletarian rather than bourgeois leadership of the first stage of revolution directed at the overthrow of "feudalism and monarchy." But it is difficult to see in what way Mao "developed" or elaborated upon Lenin's thesis, set forth as early as 1905 in his "Two Tactics of Social Democracy in the Democratic Revolution," that the proletariat must be the "leader," and not a subsidiary of the bourgeoisie, in carrying out the bourgeois-democratic revolution.

Again, Chang Ju-hsin maintains that Mao was the first to propound the twofold thesis that revolutions in backward countries, such as China, are primarily peasant revolutions, and that the poor peasants constitute the most important force and the most reliable ally of the workers in these revolutions.[13] This claim, however, ignores the evidence in one of Lenin's early writings—"The Agrarian Program of Social Democracy" (1907)—attesting to his recognition, long before Mao, of the important role of the peasantry, and particularly the poor peasantry, in the early stage of the revolutionary process. Lenin wrote:

We must have a clear idea of the character and significance of precisely the peasant agrarian revolution as one of the varieties of bourgeois revolution. . . . A section of the Marxists, the Right Wing, persistently made shift with an abstract, stereotyped conception of the bourgeois revolution and failed to perceive the peculiar features of the present bourgeois revolution, which is precisely a peasant revolution.

In the same work Lenin spoke of the "rural proletariat" as the primary revolutionary force in the countryside, using this term in the same sense as Engels had given it in "The Peasant Question in France and Germany" (1894)—that is, to designate poor farm workers as distinct from big and small rural landowners.

There is further evidence on this point in statements by Lenin's contemporaries. Speaking critically of Lenin's program for revolution, the Menshevik leader G. V. Plekhanov wrote (in his "The Working Class and the Social Democratic Intelligentsia"): "It is not Marxism that we find in Lenin's views, but—to use a term of ill repute—peasant insurrectionism, a new version of the theory of heroes leading the rabble." Again, in 1924, Zinoviev saw the very key to Leninism in the importance it attached to the agrarian question. "Leninism," he wrote, "is Marxism in the epoch of imperialist war and of the world revolution *which began directly in a country where the peasantry predominates.*" [14]

Thus, there was no departure from Leninism when P'eng P'ai, a member of the newborn Chinese Communist Party, went into the countryside of Kwangtung Province in 1921 to organize the peasants, or when Mao himself in 1927 went to inquire into the revolutionary peasant uprisings in Hunan Province. The product of Mao's inquiry was his March 1927 "Report of an Investigation into the Peasant Movement in Hunan," perhaps the most striking thing he ever wrote. In it Mao gave an estimate of the total strength and revolutionary potential of the Hunan peasant movement, crediting the peasant associations with 70 percent of the revolutionary work in the province, and the urban population and military units with only 30 percent. There is every indication that Mao's findings were viewed at the time by his fellow Communists—and by the Comintern—simply as a useful and accurate estimate of the revolutionary potentialities of the Hunan peasantry, and not at all as the formulation of a heretical new "theory" of revolution. That this was the case is evidenced by the fact that the report was published in the Chinese party's official journal, as well as in Moscow. (So, also, were P'eng P'ai's reports of the same year on his experiences in organizing the first peasant soviet in China.)

It was only after 1950, when the Chinese Communists began laboring in earnest to build up Mao's prestige as an eminent "theorist," that his 1927 report was invested with a new aura of doctrinal orginality. What had formerly been looked upon merely as a competent on-the-spot account of the Hunan peasant uprisings was now exalted as a brilliant Marxist-Leninist "theoretical" analysis of the Chinese revolution in general. (In keeping with this new treatment, Mao's original reference to the inconspicuous role of the urban population in the Hunan revolts was expunged from the report when it was republished in Volume I of his *Selected Works* in October 1951.) But, as pointed out above, even if the report could be construed as outlining a Maoist "theory" of revolution, its recognition of the peasantry as an important revolutionary force can hardly be regarded as any advance over the ideas formulated earlier by Lenin.

MAOIST STRATEGY AND TACTICS

Mao's early writings, then, contain nothing to substantiate the claim of a creative development of Communist revolutionary doctrine. But the Chinese case for Mao does not stop there. It is a familiar Communist thesis that the leader who directs a Communist party in revolution contributes, by his formulations of actual strategy and tactics, to the "theory" of revolution itself. If the scope of "theory" is thus broadened, Mao can indeed be credited with two distinctive contributions—

i.e., the strategy of waging revolution from self-sustaining rural bases and the tactics of guerrilla warfare.

According to Ch'en Po-ta, Mao "worked out a series of complete conclusions . . . that it was possible for the revolution to achieve victory first in the countryside, and that it was possible to establish long-term revolutionary bases there." [15] These conclusions were set forth by Mao in a report written in November 1928—"Struggle in the Chingkang Mountains"—in which he enumerated the prerequisites for establishing such bases and formulated a specific plan of organization. It can reasonably be argued that this Maoist strategy for waging the revolutionary struggle in China constituted a *practical* advance over Lenin's general idea of establishing peasant soviets in backward countries.

Ch'en also points to guerrilla warfare as another distinctive feature of the Maoist strategy of revolution. This likewise seems justified, although it is difficult to determine to what extent Mao's espousal of guerrilla tactics was actually inspired by Chu Te—described by a prewar American military observer of the Chinese Red Army as "pre-eminent" in this field [16]—and other Chinese Communist military leaders. The fact that Chinese Communist publications in recent years have made no mention of Chu's numerous writings on guerrilla warfare, the tactics of protracted war, and "quick-decision attack" suggests that Chu's light may well have been concealed in order that Mao's might shine more brightly.

What is most important, however, is that Mao's whole scheme of waging a prolonged revolutionary struggle from self-sustaining Communist bases in the countryside, utilizing tactics of guerrilla warfare, was conceived not as a general "theory" of revolution, but as a concrete, practical strategy for the conquest of power in the specific conditions that prevailed in China. It was, in fact, dictated by those conditions and represented perhaps the only strategy which could enable the Chinese Communists to carry on the revolutionary struggle. Mao's approach to the problem of gaining ruling power was consistently pragmatic, not theoretical; it was based on the key premise that it was necessary to win by whatever means offered themselves at the moment. Consequently, his writings contain sanction for a wide variety of actions appropriate to almost any set of circumstances.

Mao's eulogists have even attempted to give his pragmatic, common-sense approach the status of a new precept of Communist strategy. In a review hailing the appearance of Volume IV of Mao's *Selected Works* in November 1960, two Chinese Communist writers called Mao's "paper tiger" concept—defined as "slighting the enemy strategically and taking full account of him tactically"—"a new development of enormous significance in the theory of Marxist-Leninist strategy and tactics." [17] It is nothing of the sort, it is just a platitude. Virtually every revolutionary leader, including many a non-Communist nationalist, has exercised caution in the face of superior enemy strength. Stalin himself was a past

master in showing contempt for the enemy "strategically" while exercising caution "tactically." After all, only a lunatic would fail to act
cautiously if what he considered a "paper tiger" appeared for the
moment to have the capacities of a real one.

A further point should be mentioned in connection with the Maoist
strategy of revolution. Mao's writings of 1928, in which he formulated
the idea of establishing rural revolutionary bases, carried the implication
that this was a strategy specifically applicable to the peculiar political
and geographical environment of China. After 1949, however, the
Chinese Communists began taking the line that Mao's formula for
revolution—now designated "the road of Mao Tse-tung"—furnished a
model strategy for all backward countries. Thus, when one of Mao's
original writings—"Why Can China's Red Political Power Exist?"
(October 1928)—was republished in the first volume of his *Selected
Works* in 1951, a footnote was appended to it emphasizing the applicability of the Chinese revolutionary experience to other countries "of
the East." The key passage in the footnote reads:

Thus, just as the Chinese people have done, all or at least some of the colonial
peoples of the East can hold big or small base areas and maintain revolutionary
regimes for an extended period, carry on a protracted revolutionary war to
encircle the cities from the countryside and proceed gradually to take over
the cities and win nationwide victory in their respective countries.[18]

This Chinese Communist line has been a thorn in Moscow's side
ever since it was enunciated—and it is even more irritating now that
the Peking regime is actively competing with the Russians for influence
not only in the underdeveloped countries of Asia but also in Africa
and Latin America. Peking can claim, if only by implication, that every
leader of a rural-based nationalist revolutionary movement in the colonial
and underdeveloped areas of the world is following "the road of Mao
Tse-tung," whether he ever heard of Mao or not. Here, Moscow is at
a disadvantage, for it cannot cite Lenin and Stalin as architects of this
special kind of revolutionary strategy.

PEOPLE'S DEMOCRATIC DICTATORSHIP

Besides his contribution to the practical strategy, if not the "theory,"
of revolution, Mao is claimed to have formulated a distinctly new
concept of the type of transitional state to be instituted following the
Communist acquisition of power. This Maoist concept goes under the
name of "people's democratic dictatorship."

According to Marx, the overthrow of the bourgeois state by proletarian revolution was to be followed by the establishment of an interim
state structure defined as a "dictatorship of the proletariat," which
would rule during the period of transition toward the ultimate stateless

and classless society of full communism. Engels, Lenin, Trotsky, and Stalin all elaborated upon the concept of proletarian dictatorship in their writings.

What Marx originally envisioned was a state under the dictatorship of a single class, the workers. In his "Two Tactics," however, Lenin—over the objections of Trotsky—broadened Marx's concept of a one-class dictatorship, envisaging instead a "democratic dictatorship of the proletariat and peasantry" as the provisional form to be assumed by a revolutionary government. Similarly, in 1926, Stalin predicted the establishment, specifically in China, of a revolutionary government which "will in general resemble in character the government we used to talk about in our country in 1905, that is, something in the nature of a democratic dictatorship of the proletariat and peasantry." [19] Although the new international Communist line decreed by the Comintern in 1935, which directed Communist collaboration with other leftist parties in forming "popular front" governments, could perhaps be regarded as containing the germ of a broader concept of the post-revolutionary state, there was no actual redefinition of ideological theory on this point, in terms of class structure, until Mao enunciated his concept of "people's democratic dictatorship."

The essential difference between the established Leninist-Stalinist concept of proletarian dictatorship and Mao's new concept of people's democratic dictatorship lay in the fact that the latter envisaged, instead of a two-class dictatorship, a "joint dictatorship of several revolutionary classes." Mao first enunciated this idea of multiclass rulership in his *Chinese Revolution and the CCP*, written in 1939, and he further elaborated it in *On New Democracy* (1940) and *On the People's Democratic Dictatorship* (1949). The most notable feature of the Maoist concept, as developed in these writings, was its inclusion of the "revolutionary segment of the national bourgeoisie"—meaning, actually, the most cooperative elements of the capitalist class—among those who would share ruling power in the post-revolutionary state pending the transition to socialism, and thence to eventual communism.

The Chinese Communists naturally have lost no opportunity to play up Mao's concept of people's democratic dictatorship—with some justification—as a "creative development of the Marxist-Leninist doctrine of the dictatorship of the proletariat." [20] Moreover, much as in the case of the Maoist strategy of revolution, Peking spokesmen not merely insisted— at least, until 1954—that Chinese-style people's dictatorship differed distinctly from Soviet-type proletarian dictatorship, but also suggested that it was an especially appropriate model for Communist movements in the colonial and underdeveloped areas to adopt in the event of revolutionary success.

This too, of course, was galling to the Soviet leadership, and Soviet writers, in discussing Mao's concept of people's democratic dictatorship, generally glossed over its originality by equating it with Lenin's formula of two-class dictatorship. Then, in 1954, there were signs of a Chinese retreat. An article in the Chinese Communist theoretical review *Hsueh-hsi* (*Study*) acknowledged that there was no "essential" difference between "proletarian" and "people's democratic" dictatorship, and that the only difference was one of "form." [21] This Chinese compromise evidently satisfied Moscow and was formalized in 1956 at the Eighth Congress of the Chinese Communist Party.

If there *were* any actual differences between the Chinese Communist "people's democratic dictatorship" in its formative years and the Soviet totalitarian state, these have long since ceased to exist in fact, if not in theory. Despite the continued existence of so-called "democratic" (non-Communist) parties in China, power is monopolized as exclusively by the CPC as by the CPSU, and the Chinese Communist dictatorship has imposed its will on capitalists and non-capitalists alike, with a ruthlessness that has even been offensive to some other members of the Communist bloc.

CONTRADICTIONS IN SOCIALIST SOCIETY

One of the more recent contributions to Communist theory that have been claimed for Mao concerns the ideas he formulated in 1957 on the subject of contradictions within socialist society. These ideas were enunciated by Mao in an address delivered at a meeting of the Supreme State Conference in February 1957—the speech that paved the way for the spectacular developments of the "hundred flowers" campaign. The text of the address was not made public at the time but eventually appeared in the Chinese Communist press—apparently in drastically revised form—under the title, "On the Correct Handling of Contradictions Among the People." [22]

In an article published in June 1960, a Chinese Communist writer on Marxist philosophy claimed that Mao's 1957 speech had "for the first time distinguished between two kinds of contradiction in society . . . antagonistic and non-antagonistic." [23] This is false, as such a distinction had been made as far back as 1939 by Soviet theoreticians M. Rozental and P. Yudin, and had subsequently been elaborated upon by Andrei Zhdanov in 1947, Yudin in 1948, and B. Kedrov in 1951. Even some Chinese Communist theorists had already written along the same line in 1956.

The fact of the matter is that the significance of Mao's discourse did not reside in the elaboration of any new theoretical concept, but lay rather—typically enough—in the realm of practical policy. In effect, the speech took the Marxist idea of "contradictions" (i.e., conflicts) out of the context of philosophical theory and made it the basis—indeed, almost a slogan—for a nationwide campaign aimed at "rectifying" bureaucratic tendencies among party officials and regaining the support of disaffected intellectuals.

From the policy standpoint, however, Mao's February 1957 pro-

nouncement did contain some significant departures from Soviet precedent. Whereas Stalin, in his *Problems of Leninism* (1926), had conceded
merely the *possibility* of conflict between the Communist Party and
the working class, Mao went beyond this to state that "a contradiction
between leaders and led . . . *does exist* . . . under socialism." Again,
whereas Soviet practice sanctioned criticism only when it was directed
at derelictions on the part of individual party functionaries, Mao's
pronouncement invited non-Communists to join in criticizing not only
individual officials but the whole Communist Party. Mao further deviated
from Soviet precedent in transferring certain contradictions between
the working class and the bourgeoisie, defined as "antagonistic" in the
USSR, to the "non-antagonistic" category in Communist China; and he
also made the startling announcement that strikes—forbidden by the
Soviet regime—would be tolerated by the Peking government provided
they were "small in scale." Conflicts involving criticisms of official conduct, declared Mao, ought properly to be resolved in one of two ways:
either those who voiced the criticisms should be satisfactorily shown
that they were mistaken; or, if the criticisms were found justified, the
offending officials should "rectify" their errors.

Some, if not most, of these Maoist innovations were looked upon by
Moscow with strong distaste. In China itself, moreover, the outpouring
of anti-party criticism during the climactic phase of the "hundred flowers"
campaign brought a sharp shift away from the policies of liberalization
which Mao's speech of February 1957 had seemed to foreshadow. Today,
virtually the only aspect of this pronouncement which still seems to be
an acceptable topic of discussion in Chinese Communist theoretical
journals is the matter of "non-antagonistic" contradiction between the
working class and the bourgeoisie.

THE TRANSITION TO COMMUNISM

Originality has also been claimed for a number of Mao's ideas on
the subject of China's transition to socialism and eventual communism.
For the most part these claims have related to Maoist policies strictly in
the realm of economics, an area outside this writer's competence, and
will therefore not be discussed here. However, one claim of a more
general nature which deserves attention concerns Mao's ideas regarding
the transformation of the capitalist class. In a June 1955 article, a Chinese
Communist theorist credited Mao with formulating the unprecedented
principle that capitalists can be peacefully "reconstructed" or "reformed"
(*kai-tsao*) into reliable members of socialist society, rather than being
forcibly liquidated as a class. The article stated:

In a state where the proletariat has seized power under definite social and
historical conditions, the establishment of the principle that capitalist elements
can be basically reformed under socialist guidance is another brilliant con-

tribution of Comrade Mao Tse-tung to the treasure house of Marxism-Leninism. This theory never before appeared in the classical works of Marxism-Leninism, and no country in the world [before China] has ever gone through this kind of experience.[24]

Actually, both Marx and Lenin had envisaged peaceful alternatives to the physical extermination of capitalists, although Mao certainly carried their ideas much farther. Lenin, in his "Unavoidable Catastrophe and Boundless Promises" (May 1917), stated that individual capitalists or "even the majority of capitalists" would not be deprived of everything, and that "the proletariat . . . intends to place them at useful, honorable tasks, subject to the control of the workers themselves." Again, in May 1918, Lenin cited Marx's own conjecture that capitalists might "come over to socialism peacefully." It remained for Mao, however, to formulate the idea that the capitalists, as a class, could be transformed *mentally* into workers in a socialist society. This was a novel concept indeed, and its implementation was aided by the development of the the equally new Maoist technique of mass "thought remolding," or "brainwashing."

But it is above all the "people's communes" which Chinese Communist writers cite as blazing a new Maoist path towards the goal of full communism. They concede that Marx, Engels, Lenin, and Stalin developed almost all of the general principles that will underlie the fully Communist society of the future, and they also admit that Stalin already had something to say about communes before Mao elaborated and actually implemented the idea in developing the Chinese commune system. However, Mao's great and decisive contribution, the Chinese claim, lay precisely in his fashioning of the people's communes—spontaneously "created by the Chinese masses"—so that they might serve as a concrete organizational instrumentality for effecting the transition from socialist "collective ownership" to communist "ownership by the whole people." Thus, one Chinese Communist theorist wrote in 1959:

Comrade Mao Tse-tung's major contribution was his ability to see the significance of the people's communes in long-range historical perspective. Guided by Marxist-Leninist theories, he combined the lessons of the great classics and improved the communes so that they became the best form to be used in completing the building of socialism as well as the best organizational form for China's transition to a communist society.[25]

Chinese Communist claims regarding the communes were most exaggerated in the early period of their existence in 1958, when they were exuberantly hailed as marking the start of China's transition from socialism to communism. This boast, signifying in effect that Communist China not only had progressed as far in one decade as the Soviet Union had in four, but also had discovered a short cut from socialism to communism which did not require a high degree of industrialization and technological development, aroused both anger and apprehension in

Moscow. Soviet pressure was evidently brought to bear on Peking, with the result that Chinese Communist spokesmen began backtracking from the earlier line that China had already embarked on the building of full communism.[26] Moreover, despite continued lip service to the commune concept on the part of the Peking regime, the actual role and importance of the communes have gradually declined since 1959, with the production brigades and teams tending to become the real basic units of rural economic activity in China.

"MAOISM" IN PERSPECTIVE

What conclusion, then, can be drawn regarding the validity of the Chinese Communist claims of a distinctive "ideology of Mao Tse-tung" or, as it has even been called, "Mao Tse-tung-ism"? [27] Can Mao justifiably be credited with having developed—as these designations are so obviously intended to suggest—a new and unique strain of Marxism-Leninism?

In the light of preceding analysis of the allegedly "original" elements in Mao's thought, there appears to be slight justification for attributing to him any really significant, new contribution to the basic philosophy and theory of communism. Mao, in fact, has been much less a philosopher and theorist than a talented and resourceful political leader. While he has indeed introduced a number of innovations in the course of his career, these have been primarily innovations of method inspired and shaped by practical considerations, rather than substantive modifications of theory or principle.

One of the Chinese Communists' most cherished slogans says that "politics takes command"—and if the words "over theory" are added, it fits Mao perfectly. For, in Mao's book, theory is primarily a tool to be manipulated for the purpose of rationalizing and legitimizing a policy deemed necessary on pragmatic grounds. Thus, his pronouncements are characteristically couched in a style keyed to the reasoning of the simplest Chinese peasant in order to assure that the policy he is expounding will be immediately comprehended and obeyed without question.

Mao can, in fact, be extraordinarily nimble in his use of dialectics for political ends. In his original, unpublished speech of February 1957 on contradictions, he was reliably reported to have said that the "antagonistic" contradiction between the Chinese Communist regime and Chiang Kai-shek would automatically become "non-antagonistic" if Chiang returned Taiwan to People's China! (This was one of the passages excised from the text as finally published in June 1957.) It may be said that Mao, in manipulating theory to fit political objectives, has acted as an apt disciple of Lenin and Stalin, but it would be hard to imagine Lenin and Stalin stretching theory quite so flagrantly as Mao sometimes has. And though he now attacks Khrushchev's departures from Marxist-Leninist orthodoxy, Mao must labor to conceal his own practical deviations.

In sum, if one can speak at all of "an ideology of Mao" or "Maoism," and of a distinctive "Chinese" communism, they differ from Marxist-Leninism and from Soviet communism primarily in matters of method and form, and not of essential substance. The differences are no greater than those which distinguish the African elephant from his cousin in India. Yet, the Chinese Communists must go on asserting the individuality of "Maoism" and of the Chinese brand of communism, not only because Mao's personal ambition to be recognized as the world's foremost Communist thinker is every bit as intense as Stalin's was, but also because Communist China as a nation aspires to a position of world prestige and power no less imposing than that held by the Soviet Union.

NOTES

1. E.g., an article in the *Honan Jih-pao* (Chengchow), January 14, 1960, declared: "Comrade Mao Tse-tung is the most outstanding representative of the proletariat in our country, and the greatest and most outstanding revolutionary leader, statesman, and theorist of Marxism-Leninism in the modern era."

2. Li Ta, " 'On Practice'—The Philosophical Foundation of Mao Tse-tung's Ideology," in *Selected Essays for the Study of "On Practice"* (2nd ed.), Chung-nan Jen-min Ch'u-pan-she, Hankow, December 1951, p. 72.

3. Ai Ssu-ch'i, "Comrade Mao Tse-tung Develops the Theory of Truth," *ibid.*, p. 56.

4. Feng Yu-lan. "Mao Tse-tung's 'On Practice' and Chinese Philosophy," *People's China* (Peking), November 16, 1951. Feng, however, felt constrained to conclude his article by saying that Mao had "successfully solved a problem which has claimed the attention of so many brilliant minds through the centuries."

5. Ai Ssu-ch'i, "Comprehend the Dialectic from the Aspect of 'On Contradiction,' " in *Study "On Contradiction"* (1st ed.) Hsin-chien-she Ch'u-pan-she, Peking, September 25, 1952, pp. 5, 7.

6. See editors' note accompanying the English translation of Mao's "On Contradiction," published in *People's China*, July 1, 1952.

7. Hsiao Chou, "Study Theory and Practice," *Ch'un-chung* (The Masses), Vol. IV, No. 14, May 20, 1941, pp. 397-400.

8. Mao Tse-tung, "Dialectical Materialism, Part II," *Min-chu* (Democracy), Vol. 1, No. 2, March 1940.

9. Allen S. Whiting and General Sheng Shih-ts'ai, *Sinkiang—Pawn or Pivot?*, Michigan State University Press, 1958, pp. 229-31.

10. Chang Ju-hsin, "Stalin's Great Theoretical Contributions to the Chinese Revolution," *Jen-min jih-pao* (Peking), April 3, 1953.

11. Shen Chih-yuan, "*Study the Selected Works of Mao Tse-tung, Volume I,* Hsin-chien-she Chu-pan-she, Peking, January 20, 1952, pp. 25-26.

12. Ch'en Po-ta "Mao Tse-tung's Theory of the Chinese Revolution is the Integration of Marxism-Leninism with the Practice of the Chinese Revolution," *Hsueh-hsi* (Peking), July 1, 1951.

13. Chang Ju-hsin, *On Two Works of Comrade Mao Tse-tung during the First Revolutionary Civil War,* (pamphlet), Jen-min Chu-pan-she, Peking, September 1953, p. 6.

14. "Bolshevism or Trotskyism," *Pravda*, November 20, 1924.

15. Ch'en, *op. cit.*

16. Major Evans F. Carlson, "The Chinese Army: Its Organization and Military Efficiency," in *Institute of Pacific Relations*, Vol. VII, Sec. 3, October 6, 1939, p. 20.

17. Teng Li-ch'un and Wu Chiang, "Dialectics is the Algebra of Revolution: Read the *Selected Works* of Mao Tse-tung, Volume IV," *Hung Ch'i* (Red Flag), Nos. 20-21 (combined), November 1, 1960, p. 25.

18. See English edition of Mao's *Selected Works*, Vol. I, International Publishers, New York, 1954, footnote 7 on p. 304.

19. J. V. Stalin, "Prospects of the Revolution in China," *Works*, Vol. VIII, Foreign Languages Publishing House, Moscow, 1954, pp. 38-39.

20. E.g., Liu P'ing-lin, "Seriously Study Comrade Mao Tse-tung's Doctrine of the Dictatorship of the Proletariat," *Ta-chung Jih-pao* (Tsinan), May 12, 1960.

21. Ti Chao-pai, "State Capitalism in Our Transition Period," *Hsueh-hsi*, February 2, 1954.

22. Text published by New China News Agency, June 18, 1957.

23. Wu Chiang, "The Victory of the Dialectical Law of History," *Che-hsueh Yen-chiu* (Philosophical Research), No. 6, June 10, 1960.

24. Shu Wei-kuang, "The Gradual Leap in China's Transition Period," *ibid.*, No. 1, June 1955.

25. Fan Hung, *Study Marx, Engels, Lenin, and Stalin on the Theory of Communism* (pamphlet), Peking, April 1959, pp. 42-51.

26. Sripati Chandra-sekhar, an Indian visitor to Communist China in 1959, quoted officials in Peking as boasting to him that the Chiliyin Commune, near Chengchow, was "the latest development, where we have gone one step ahead of the Soviet Union." See Chandra-sekhar's article, "Mao's War with the Chinese Family," *New York Times Magazine*, May 17, 1959, p. 73.

27. The latter term was used in an Editors' Introductory Note prefacing an earlier collection of Mao's writings, *Mao Tse-tung Hsuan Chi*, published in Dairen in November 1947.

RUSSIA AND CHINA: TWO ROADS TO COMMUNISM

Donald S. Zagoria

The present Sino-Soviet conflict began, broadly speaking, in the fall of 1957, when the two basic complexes of issues arose around which the controversy has since been waged. The first and most persistent element in the conflict concerns communism's global strategy. Peking rejected the Khrushchev version of "peaceful coexistence" as unworkable. The second revolved about domestic revolutionary strategy, how to build socialism and communism in a country already ruled by a communist party.

Although the conflict over revolutionary strategy abroad is more

Reprinted from *Survey*, no. 38 (October, 1961), 137-145. By permission of the author and the publisher.

acute than the conflict over how to build communism, the two issues cannot really be separated. For its part Peking not only rejects the "general line" of Soviet policy; in many areas of the world, particularly in the underdeveloped countries, it seeks to impose its own line. It seeks to change the strategy of many of the communist parties in the underdeveloped countries in a left-wing direction, and in those underdeveloped countries ruled by communist parties, it seeks to export some of its own experience in building communism at a headlong pace with limited resources and a rapidly growing population. The Russians, for their part, although aware that they cannot impose their will on the Chinese, will not allow the Chinese to set themselves up as leaders of communism's Eastern empire. The result is competition in many areas, which has already produced profound changes in the relations between Moscow and Peking, in the relations within the communist world, and, not least important, in the relations between the communist bloc and the Western world.

THE PRINCIPAL DIFFERENCES

The differences between Moscow and Peking on the "transition to communism" turn first of all on the question of timing. The Chinese conception of how to build communism is shaped by the desire to go faster than the Russians believe desirable or feasible. While the Chinese suggest that the Russians, by taking the slow road to communism, are putting into jeopardy the social revolution in the bloc itself, the Russians accuse the Chinese of trying to move faster than "objective conditions" allow. The newly published Soviet party programme gives warning, as the Russians have done persistently since late 1958, against trying to jump over stages in the advance toward communism.[1]

Secondly, there is the specific question of the communes. For a variety of reasons, the Russians have been cool towards the Chinese commune experiment, which they believe is premature and potentially disruptive for China's economy; it is, in any case, an ideological challenge to them. This is so because the Chinese claim that the commune, however modified since it was first introduced, and however much it will change in the future, is the final unit of communist society, a unit for which the Russians are still groping. Moreover, the Chinese have introduced in the commune a part-supply system which they claim represents a "sprout" of the final communist form of distribution according to need, a form of distribution which the Russians say must await the distant future.[2]

Third, the Chinese conception is characterised by a radicalism or fundamentalism which contrasts sharply with the more pragmatic Soviet attitude. It was symptomatic of this Chinese fundamentalism that in September and October 1958, various Chinese spokesmen went not to contemporary Soviet writing but to the works of Marx, Engels, and Lenin to justify their path to communism.[3] In so doing, they implied that the Russians had abandoned the classical ideological goals and were interested merely in building a modern and powerful economy. This approach has forced the Russians to counter it by putting more emphasis in their propaganda on the spiritual and ideological goals of communist society.

A fourth difference between Soviet and Chinese views is the Chinese insistence on unceasing experimentation with social institutions whenever they seem to hold up revolutionary advance, as opposed to the Soviet stress on continuity and consolidation. The Maoist insistence on ceaseless experimentation is more than a rationale for the erratic commune experiment. It has deep roots in Mao's philosophy, as shown particularly in his writings on contradictions. These indicate that "contradictions" can never be fully eliminated from human society, even after the full triumph of communism. The same emphasis on ceaseless struggle and experimentation is manifest in his "creative development" of the Marxist-Leninist theory of uninterrupted revolution.[4] First officially noted by Liu Shao-ch'i when he set out the "general line" at the 8th Party Congress in May 1958, Mao's theory of uninterrupted revolution has been the subject of much discussion since. In one of the most revealing of such discussions, the Chinese journal *Study* wrote in October 1958:

There are some who ask in alarm: when you advocate uninterrupted revolution in a socialist society, what is the object of the revolution? *Actually, viewed from the standpoint of Marxists, the objects of revolution always are the production relations and the superstructure, which at the time are lagging behind the development of the productive forces and therefore interfering with the development of the productive forces.* . . . Marxists must not conceal contradictions and also must not shun revolution. . . . Whoever understands these general truths will not think it strange that it is still necessary to advocate uninterrupted revolution in a socialist society (my italics, D. Z.).

The theory was both a rejection of Soviet gradualism in the advance toward communism and a complete reversal of the Soviet and Marxist view of the domestic revolutionary process. For what it clearly indicated was that the "superstructure" may lag behind and interfere with the development of "productive forces." The transition to communism—like the world revolution—is marked by continuing struggle, by leaps forward, by periods of rapid advance and periods of consolidation, and, above all, by continuing experimentation.

The Chinese evidently consider that Khrushchev, by making of the "construction of communism" a rather sluggish process whose primary purpose is to increase the material production base rather than to explore new social forms, puts into jeopardy the achievement of the final revolutionary goal. They apparently fear that Khrushchev, who follows the gradualist Soviet tradition, will make of the "transition to communism" a meaningless slogan. Thus in 1958, one Chinese writer said, clearly with the Russians in mind:

According to some, the victory of the proletariat and the advent of a socialist society mean the end of the social revolution, after which there will be all sorts of phenomena of crystallisation, ranging from economic matters to the superstructure and tendencies toward absoluteness, all resulting in interference with the development, by leaps forward of the forces of production.[5]

And in 1960, Lu Ting-i, member of the CCP Politburo, criticised "the kind of theory" which holds that

. . . there is no need to develop the socialist system, but only to consolidate it, and even if it is to be developed, to go forward to communism, still there is no need to undergo a struggle and to pass through a qualitative leap; and thus the process of the uninterrupted revolution of human society goes up to this point and no farther.[6]

WHOSE MODEL ?

The Russians and the Chinese not only differ between themselves on how to make the "transition to communism" but—perhaps more important—they differ on the applicability of the Soviet model to other countries. In his draft theses for the 21st Congress, Khrushchev said:

V. I. Lenin foresaw that the Soviet Union would exert chief influence on the entire course of world development by its economic construction. Lenin said: "If Russia becomes covered with a dense network of electricity stations and powerful technical equipment, our communist economic construction will become a model for the future socialist Europe and Asia." [7]

In sharp contrast to this, the Chinese contended in effect that Mao has solved the problem of socialist and communist construction for all under-developed areas as well as for China. In one of the first discussions of the Chinese communes ever to appear, as early as July 1958, Ch'en Po-ta, in an article significantly titled "Under the Banner of Chairman Mao," contended that Mao had followed Lenin's injunction to the countries of the East to develop Marxist theory creatively "in the light of special conditions unknown to European countries." [8]

If Mao had indeed solved the problems of socialist and communist construction for the under-developed countries, did it not also follow that Peking should be accorded leadership of the revolutionary movement in those areas? There is, of course, one omission in this chain of reasoning. In effect, the Chinese communists were claiming in 1958 that Mao had discovered a special path for building communism in backward countries once the communists had taken power. They had not then renewed their earlier claims of 1949-51 that the Chinese road to power was also relevant in those countries. In 1959 they were to fill this gap, and to carry their claims to their logical conclusion. Mao knew best how to make the revolution, how to consolidate it, and how to proceed toward communism. In the countries of the East, the CCP was in effect once again claiming leadership of the revolutionary movement. Having pointed to some of the basic differences between Soviet and Chinese views on the transition to communism, we may now try to find some of the explanations for them.

DIFFERING NATIONAL CIRCUMSTANCES

The Chinese communists' primitive agriculture barely manages to keep ahead of population growth; enormous industrial strains are generated by their headlong efforts to outstrip some advanced capitalist countries in the space of a few decades. China is, in the words of Mao, "poor and blank." The Russians, on the other hand, have a developed economy long past the point of take-off, an economy which does not produce the tensions and strains inevitable in any country, and particularly a communist one, in the midst of vast social and economic change.

Communist China's "general line," introduced in 1958, including the commune programme and the "leap forward," represented a direct institutional response to the chronic economic problems that had always plagued the Chinese communists and had, by the summer of 1957, become acute.

It is apparent that some time between the summer and early fall of 1957, there was a struggle between two factions within the Chinese Communist Party, one advocating a radical turn to the "left" and the other advocating a massive retreat on the lines of the Soviet NEP.[9] The left wing of the party won the day. It had concluded that China's acute problems could not be solved by continuing to copy Soviet experience, as had been done in China's first Five-Year Plan from 1953 to 1957. A radical solution to these problems was required, and this solution was the distinctive path to communism evolved in 1958—a path whose most notable feature was the communes. The principal aims of the communes were to develop cottage industries, to centralise control over all means of production in the countryside, to increase control over peasant consumption, and to mobilise China's one abundant resource, its manpower, for huge peasant labour armies on a scale unprecedented in modern history. A closely related aim was to substitute ideological for material incentives by holding out the prospect of an early passage to the final communist paradise via communes.

Looked at in this perspective, much of the Chinese communist conception of the process of building communism, with its emphasis on continuing struggle, on the strength of the masses once aroused, on the power of ideology, can be attributed to the desperate need to find a solution to acute economic problems.

This does not of course entirely explain the Chinese insistence on exporting their ideology. Differing ideological perspectives induced by different national circumstances would not have produced so great a strain on Sino-Soviet relations if the Chinese had not suggested, as they did, that their new path to communism was valid for all under-developed countries. If we probe this question of what might be called Chinese evangelism a bit further, it soon becomes evident that deeply-rooted in Chinese communist history and ideology is the conviction that its revolution is the model for Asia and other colonial and semi-colonial areas. As early as the spring of 1946, in an interview of extraordinary importance which has never received adequate attention in the West, Liu Shao Ch'i told Anna Louise Strong that Mao had discovered an Asiatic form of Marxism, that Marx and Lenin were Europeans and therefore, by implication, not very interested in or capable of solving Asian problems, that Mao was the first to have succeeded in adapting Marxism to China, and that Mao's revolutionary theories charted a path to power not only for the Chinese people "but for the billion folk that live in the colonial countries of South-east Asia." The passage deserves reproduction in full:

Mao Tse-tung's great accomplishment has been to change Marxism from a European to an Asiatic form. Marx and Lenin were Europeans; they wrote in European languages about European histories and problems, seldom dis-cussing Asia or China. The basic principles of Marxism are undoubtedly adaptable to all countries, but to apply their general truth to concrete revolu-tionary practices in China is a difficult task. Mao Tse-tung is Chinese; he analyses Chinese problems and guides the Chinese people in their struggle to victory. He uses Marxist-Leninist principles to explain Chinese history and the practical problems of China. He is the first that has succeeded in doing so. Not only has he applied Marxist methods to solve the problems of 450 million people, but he has thus popularised Marxism among the Chinese people as a weapon for them to use. On every kind of problem— the nation, the peasants, strategy, the construction of the party, literature and culture, military affairs, finance and economy, methods of work, philosophy —Mao has not only applied Marxism to new conditions but has given it a new development. He has created a Chinese or Asiatic form of Marxism. . . . There are similar conditions in other lands of South-east Asia. The courses chosen by China will influence them all.[10]

From 1949 to 1951, the two years following the Chinese communist seizure of power, Mao's claims to ideological autonomy and his insistence that he had discovered a model to be followed in other colonial and semi-colonial countries was probably the cause of considerable friction with Stalin. A well-documented survey of the period shows:

1. Chinese propagandists explicitly claimed that Mao's political theories on revolution were independently arrived at, while the Russians consistently endeavoured to show Mao's complete theoretical de-pendence on Stalin.

2. The Chinese asserted that Mao's writing on the Chinese revolution embodies an ideology—the "ideology of Mao Tse-tung"; there was no recognition of such an ideology in Soviet writings.
3. Between 1949 and 1951 the Chinese viewed their revolution as the model to be followed in other undeveloped countries and they referred to this model revolutionary path as "Mao's road." Such themes were absent from Soviet writings, which conceded only that the Chinese revolution had "inspired" the people of backward countries in their own revolutionary movements.[11]

The political significance of such claims is difficult to exaggerate. First of all, they suggest that Mao has always put himself on a level not with Stalin, let alone Khrushchev, but with Marx and Lenin, the founding fathers of communism. In the light of this image, Mao's attitude to the hearty peasant who now sits on top of the world communist movement is easy to imagine. Second, the claims imply that Mao has never accepted a position subordinate to Moscow with regard to Chinese domestic or foreign policies. Third, they suggest that Mao has always considered himself to be leader of the revolution in all under-developed areas, including Asia, Africa, and Latin America.

In 1951 the claims for "Mao's ideology" ceased to be made, probably because Mao's economic and military dependence on Stalin forced him to greater caution and modesty. But in 1958, as the Chinese communists were becoming more powerful and the balance of forces in the international communist world was changing, similar claims again appeared. Mao was now described as a "great prophet" and "one of the most outstanding Marxist-Leninist revolutionaries, statesmen, and theoreticians of our age." [12] By the end of 1959, Mao's ideology was being increasingly equated with Marxism-Leninism and sometimes given priority over it. There were also invidious remarks about "so-called Western Marxists" who did not understand the problems of the "East."

For Sino-Soviet relations, one of the implications of the growing cult of Mao was obvious. Mao was once again, as in the period from 1949-51, being portrayed as an independent source of authority and strategy, who had adapted Marxism to China and whose theories were relevant for all colonial and former colonial peoples.

DIFFERING REVOLUTIONARY HISTORIES

Still another factor behind the differences on the transition is the differing revolutionary histories of the two parties. The Russians had experimented with agrarian communes in the early years of their revolution and had found that such a drastic form of socialisation was not feasible. In Stalin's report to the 17th Party Congress in 1934, his only major pronouncement on the communes, he ascribed their failure to three factors: under-developed technology, a shortage of products, and a premature practising of egalitarianism. The future commune, he wrote, could arise only on the basis of abundance of products and a developed technology. It is of course true that the Chinese communes of 1958 were a far cry from the Bolshevik agrarian communes of the 1920s. But the common denominator of both was the attempt to introduce egalitarian distribution, to socialise all means of production, and to introduce a system in which each individual would work selflessly for the good of the state. The Russian failure had been marked enough to convince them that such drastic forms of socialisation required a production base which would allow the sharing of plenty rather than the rationing of scarcity. It left a deeply engrained belief, repeatedly expressed by Stalin and his successors, that the transition to communism would have to be gradual; the vestiges of capitalism could not be eliminated overnight. It was this firm belief, rooted in Soviet history, that led the Soviet leaders to view with grave reserve the Chinese attempt to introduce communes at a relatively early stage of revolutionary development.

By 1960 the conflict over the communes and the transition to communism had receded into the background, to be replaced by the more acute conflict over global strategy. As a continuing potential source of discord, however, the issue remains. In their vigorous attacks on Soviet policy in April 1960, the Chinese continued to take issue with Soviet views on the transition to communism and continued to reassert the Chinese path and its relevance to under-developed countries. The CCP contended that revolutions in Oriental countries would "undoubtedly display even greater peculiarities than the Russian revolution"; they protested against "*foreign* and Chinese philistines" who had "their heads stuffed with metaphysics" and did not understand the revolutionary dialectics of the general line, the leap forward, and the communes.[13] The claims implying doctrinal innovation were soft-pedalled when the structure of the communes had to be modified, and some "leftist" mistakes were admitted. The Soviet view is made explicit in the new programme, which claims universal validity for the Soviet path to communism and studiously avoids any reference to the Chinese experiments.

IMPLICATIONS FOR WORLD COMMUNISM

An analysis of the issues dividing Moscow and Peking ultimately leads to the most basic of all—the question of authority within the communist world. The Chinese communists are not attempting to supplant Russian leadership of the communist world now; it is a position which, they are well aware, they are not yet sufficiently strong to occupy. Nor are the Russians, for their part, seeking to enforce unquestioning obedience, which they know to be no longer possible. They are arguing, instead, over the extent to which authority can be divided between two autonomous communist states with divergent interests and needs and differing ideological perspectives.

If Russia and China offer different models to other communist states, which one should the other communist states follow? The Russians remain convinced that their model is by and large universally valid both for Europe and Asia. The Chinese seem to be equally convinced that the problems of building socialism and communism in under-developed areas, predominantly agricultural, with large peasant populations, relatively little arable land in comparison to total population, are quite different from the problems of building socialism and communism in relatively more advanced countries. A "division of labour" on this question between Moscow and Peking thus seems out of the question. For the Russians to concede that the Chinese model is valid in all under-developed areas would be tantamount to surrendering to Peking the hegemony of the revolutionary movement in Asia, Africa, and Latin America. For the Chinese to concede that the Russian model is universally valid would be tantamount to accepting Soviet hegemony in the communist world as it exists today and in the future communist empire that both parties envisage for tomorrow.

If the smaller communist parties throughout the world choose, as seems increasingly likely, not to follow either the Soviet or Chinese model, but to pick and choose from both and to adapt the experience of both to their own peculiar national environments, this in turn threatens in the long run to undermine the ideological and therefore political unity of the communist world.

To the extent that each communist party adapts general Marxist-Leninist principles to its own national setting, "nationalist deviations" are bound to occur. What may at first appear as ideological relativism opens the door to ideological erosion. And without ideological sanction the Communist Party loses its very claim to existence.

This is the basic dilemma that has arisen and will continue to plague the communist world. The most likely result is that there will begin to appear other variants of socialism and particular brands of communism. Just as the smaller communist states have already taken advantage of the Sino-Soviet conflict over global strategy to advance their own foreign policy interests as they perceive them, so they will take advantage of the conflict over the "transition to communism" to adapt general principles to their own peculiar national environments. While this is by no means an insurmountable problem for the communist bloc, and certainly does not diminish the very real challenge which communism presents to the Western world, it will have important consequences. Ideological ties will become looser and authority in the communist world will become increasingly more diffused. The Russians will have to govern the bloc within the limits of an international communist consensus. As several writers have already pointed out, the spectre of polycentrism is here to stay.

NOTES

1. Much of the section on the "transition to communism" in the new programme must be viewed against the background of Mao's challenge of Soviet doctrine.

2. For a perceptive comment on the communes as a divisive force in Sino-Soviet relations, see Richard Lowenthal, "Shifts and Rifts in the Russo-Chinese Alliance," *Problems of Communism*, Jan.-Feb. 1959. Lowenthal makes the important point that the Chinese ideological challenge to the Russians was deliberate.

3. In articles about the proper form of distribution in both socialist and communist societies, *People's Daily* throughout October and November 1958 appealed almost exclusively to the authority of Marx and Engels. In seeking to justify the "emancipation" of women, writers cited Engels' *Origin of the Family, Private Property and the State*. In articles on education under communism, authority was again sought from Engels. In not one case did the Chinese press refer to recent Soviet experience or doctrine on building communism.

4. The theory of uninterrupted revolution is of course accepted in its Leninist form in the Soviet Union, but is given greater emphasis in Mao's writings in reference to the post-revolutionary period.

5. Wu Chiang, "A partisan of the uninterrupted revolution theory must be a consistent dialectic materialist," *Che-Hsüeh Yen-chiu (Philosophical Study)*, No. 8, 1959, cited by Stuart R. Schram, "La 'revolution permanente' en Chine," *Revue française de science politique*, September 1960, a good discussion of the evolution of the concept of uninterrupted revolution. Later Wu Chiang wrote that "there is a theory which maintains that development need not pass through struggle and qualitative leap." Although "well-intentioned," this theory in fact impeded the development of socialism because it would lead to a "lifeless society." See *Selections from the China Mainland Magazines*, No. 225, 6 September 1960, pp. 10-11.

6. "Unite Under Lenin's Revolutionary Banner," in *Long Live Leninism*, Peking Foreign Languages Press, 1960, pp. 94-95.

7. *Pravda*, 14 November 1958: cited by John Bradbury in *The China Quarterly*, April-June 1961, p. 20.

8. "Under the Banner of Comrade Mao Tse-tung," *Red Flag*, 16 July 1958; *Extracts From the China Mainland Magazines*, No. 138, 11 August 1958, p. 13.

9. Reflections of the Right's thinking were to appear in November, after the Left wing of the Party had gained the ascendancy. Thus, on 3 November, the journal *Study* railed against "certain people" who wanted to "learn from all" (presumably including the West), and believed that there should be "free competition and fluctuation of prices." The journal denounced such views as "preposterous" and said they would "obliterate the basic differences between socialist and capitalist economy." "Study the Experience of the Soviet Union in its Construction," Hsüeh Hsi, No. 21, 3 November 1957, in *Extracts*, No. 120, 24 February 1958, pp. 5-6.

10. Anna Louise Strong, "The Thought of Mao Tse-tung," *Amerasia*; June 1947, p. 161.

11. Unpublished manuscript by Arthur Cohen, Phillip Bridgham, and Herb Jaffe, "Chinese and Soviet Views on Mao as a Marxist Theorist and on the Significance of the Chinese Revolution for the Asian Revolutionary Movement."

12. Liu Lan-tao, *People's Daily*, 28 September 1959, in *Ten Glorious Years*, Peking Foreign Languages Press, 1960, p. 296.

13. "Forward Along the Path of the Great Lenin," *People's Daily* editorial, 22 April 1960, and Lu Ting-yi, "Unite Under Lenin's Revolutionary Banner," both in *Long Live Leninism*, pp. 60-63 and 94-96.

THE PHILOSOPHICAL BACKGROUND OF
REVISIONISM IN POLAND

Z. A. Jordan

A serious difficulty confronts anyone who attempts to give an account of the contemporary dispute over revisionism within the Marxist-Leninist movement. This difficulty is inherent in the subject matter of the controversy. The problems at issue cover a vast area which has no sharp boundaries, and the problems themselves are often related to one another by a thin or illusory link of fact and logic.

The dispute over revisionism deals with problems belonging to philosophy and to the historical and social sciences. But the fierce controversies which revisionism has provoked in the past and in our own time are neither purely academic nor abstract. They are concerned with those aspects of our thinking and knowledge that touch upon and affect our conduct in life. They try to penetrate into the no man's land where thought is transformed into action or action finds expression in thought, where knowledge is considered from the point of view of its bearing upon and relation to the social and existential conditions of human life. The protagonists in the dispute not only try to persuade each other of the justness of their views, but also to influence or change their respective attitudes to certain basic problems of individual and social existence. Perhaps this accounts for the fact that the dispute over revisionism combines the characteristics of an academic debate, of a political controversy, and of an Existentialist tournament. The latter is a joust in which lances are replaced by soul-searching examinations of such questions as the meaning of life and history, man's lived participation in the world and his experience of extreme situations, the liberty of conscious action and the moral responsibility of the individual, and the true sense of happiness and humanity.

It should be observed that the term "revisionism" originated with and is used almost exclusively by the supporters of the orthodox Marxist-Leninist doctrine to describe the views of those who undertake a critical

Reprinted from *East Europe*, vol. 11, no. 6 (June, 1962), 11-17, 26-29; and *loc. cit.*, no. 7 (July, 1962), 14-23. By permission of the author and the publisher.

analysis of orthodoxy from the Marxian viewpoint, examine its logical consistency and test its conformity with historical or social reality. When "revisionism" is mentioned by party politicians in their speeches, when it appears in the polemical exchanges of journalists, in the pronouncements of ideologists or in the arguments of political and philosophical writers, it is likely to have a different meaning each time. An expression as equivocal as "revisionism" loses its cognitive meaning. Instead of referring to the object which it is supposed to designate, it acquires a purely emotive sense, that is, it expresses solely the emotions of the speaker. A term that becomes an emotive sign can no longer be used as a vehicle for communicating thought and exchanging views.

To justify this assertion let us briefly examine the various meanings of "revisionism" to be found in some recent speeches and publications of the Polish supporters of Marxist-Leninist orthodoxy.

THE ORTHODOX VIEWS ON REVISIONISM

According to Gomulka, revisionism is a negation of or deviation from the principles common to the entire international communist movement, or, as he put it, "from the universal truths of Marxism-Leninism, verified by the practice of the class struggle." [1] Gomulka specified that the common principles which he had in mind were those formulated in the Declaration of the Conference of Twelve Communist Parties, held in Moscow in November 1957. Gomulka's definition of revisionism was intended to serve a political and pragmatic purpose, namely, the re-establishment of ideological unity and discipline within his party.

Since the common principles of the Moscow Declaration are not unambiguous and may be variously understood, Gomulka's definition calls for amplification. Revisionism involves a rejection of or deviation from the universal truths of Marxism-Leninism in their interpretation given by the party leadership. Consequently, a revisionist is a member of the party who questions the infallibility of the party leaders in matters of ideology and policy.

Adam Schaff, the leading philosopher and ideologist of the party, has taken a different approach. In his view, revisionism is a spiritual progeny of the "marriage between Existentialism and the Kantian doctrine." It is an intellectual attitude that has nothing to do with politics or ideology intended to initiate a course of political action. The revisionists have defined their own position best by wishing to be known as *clercs*, that is, as intellectuals divorced from life and devoted to the search for abstract truth. According to Schaff, they live in the thin air of the Existentialist nonsense, indulge in intellectual snobbery and delight in mutual admiration. As a school of thought they have, however, nothing original to say. What they divulge in their esoteric writings has been said before them by the revisionist Eduard Bernstein, by the bourgeois philosophers Hermann Cohen, Paul Natorp and Karl Vorlaender, by the political writers Henri de Man and Léon Blum, and, finally, by Jean-Paul Sartre. The intellectual originality of the revisionists is a myth, invented by their clamorous, conceited and befuddled admirers.

Revisionism in Poland, continues Schaff, is detached from life and politics and is an expression of a sterile and futile philosophy engrossed in moralizing. On this account the revisionists find gratification in imitating Existentialism, in going back to Kant and in reconstructing "Marxism" on the basis of Kantian ethics, which provides a "classical formulation of subjectivism in morals." Thus they testify to their ideological bankruptcy and philosophical ignorance, for their reconstruction of "Marxism" amounts to the renunciation of the social revolution in favor of moral transformation of the individual and society, and thus implies the liquidation of "Marxism" as a distinct political movement and philosophical school.[2]

Stefan Zolkiewski, a historian of literature, a versatile writer and, like Schaff, a member of the party's Central Committee, combined Gomulka's and Schaff's evaluations of revisionism and supplemented them with his own ideas, many of them familiar to the reader of *Pravda*, *Izvestia* and *Kommunist*. He described revisionism as an intellectual attitude of readiness to give up the theoretical coherence of Marxism-Leninism and to look for new conceptions in non-Marxist systems of thought. He was inclined to call "revisionism" any attempt to criticize "hastily and unjustifiably the correct Marxist views." He linked revisionism with social-democratic reformism and the admiration for bourgeois social and political institutions. He spoke of revisionism as the rejection of the "Marxist" standpoint in political and social theories, in economics, historiography and philosophy, paving the way for bourgeois schools of thought. In Zolkiewski's opinion, revisionism is inspired not only by Neo-Kantian philosophy and Existentialism, but also by neo-positivism, and in addition by the old socialist humanism and by contemporary militant anti-communism. Since it abandons historicism, by which Zolkiewski meant a historical and relativistic approach to morals, revisionism returns to pre-Hegelian positions in philosophy and to Kant's categorical imperative. The latter is an attribute of human nature, which is subject to no change in its social and historical development.[3]

This odd assortment of incoherent opinions and mutually exclusive evaluations reveals the variety of meanings given to "revisionism" by the supporters of orthodoxy. Freud spoke of condensations in the dream-work, by which he meant the composite, blurred and indistinct pictures appearing in the manifest dream and blending into a single object fragments of several persons or places or events. Stanislaw Ossowski, the sociologist, coined an analogous term, "conceptual condensations," to refer to concepts amalgamating characteristics abstracted from various segments of reality. The way in which the term "revisionism" is used by the Marxist-Leninists justifies its classification as a "conceptual condensation." It is hardly more than a repository and a collective label for all those views which the Marxist-Leninists abhor and with which they disagree. It is an emotionally charged term used, as was "idealism" in the past, not in a descriptive or classificatory sense, but rather to convey angry condemnation or contemptuous disapproval. As Tadeusz Kotarbinski once put it, such labels are "dynamic name-callings." [4] Being a "conceptual condensation," emotionally charged, the term "revisionism" is a weapon in the political struggle, one by means of which the opponent is to be discredited and degraded. Thus, it tells more about those who use it than about those to whom it ostensibly applies.

But the use of the term "revisionism" implies the existence of something that must not be revised. Gomulka, Schaff and Zolkiewski are in complete agreement that revisionism is a deviation, a negation or a distortion of the incontrovertible truths codified in the doctrine of Marxism-Leninism. Gomulka enumerated the universal principles which make up the absolute truth of Marxism-Leninism. Neither Schaff nor Zolkiewski followed in Gomulka's footsteps, but they assured us that Marxism-Leninism is based on unalterable truths discovered by its founders. Zolkiewski emphasized that revisionism questions and abandons the "correct Marxist views" and Schaff wrote: "Revisionism is a nullification of the Marxist theory and implies its liquidation through the rejection, against the evidence of facts, of the basic Marxist presuppositions." [5]

When a Marxist-Leninist dismisses revisionist views as errors of thinking and evidence of ignorance, he assumes explicitly or implicitly that Marxism-Leninism includes some presuppositions which can neither be altered nor falsified by experience. In the sense accepted in the methodology of science, a Marxist-Leninist is, therefore, a methodological dogmatist. Scientific method, based on a critical rationalist approach, recognizes no dogmas, no incontrovertible and irrevocable truths beyond the reach of questioning and revision. If the presuppositions could neither be changed nor refuted, they would have to be the necessary assumptions of all thought, like Kant's categories—a view conclusively shown to be untenable—or else they would have to be revealed knowledge that is irrefutable because it does not refer to the world of experience.

"Erroneous" and "Creative" Revisionism Schaff took note of this implication and tried to invalidate it. He rightly observed that revisionism is a historical concept that was applied for the first time to the activities of Eduard Bernstein in German Social Democracy at the turn of the century. This erroneous anti-revolutionary revisionism, he said, has provided the model for all subsequent similar attempts to revise "Marxism." In line with Gomulka's pronouncement,[6] Schaff suggested that an anti-revolutionary revision of Marxism-Leninism should be called "liquidationist revisionism," for it transforms a revolutionary ideology into harmless reformism, depriving Marxism-Leninism of its distinctive characteristics and reducing it, as it were, to a state of liquidation.

On the other hand, said Schaff, there is a creative revision of the Marxist-Leninist doctrine which also warrants the name of revisionism.

Since creative revision is an essential characteristic of Marxism-Leninism, the latter is not a set of dogmas but a system of continuously developing thought, *quod erat demonstrandum*. He dismisses the objection that Marxism-Leninism is dogmatic as "semantic confusion," resulting from an ambiguous use of language and unjustifiable in the light of facts. "Marxism" is an essentially revisionist doctrine, but its revisionism is creative and not "liquidationist" or erroneous.[7]

Schaff supported his arguments by a critical examination of dogmatism, in which the methodological meaning of this term merges with its political connotation known from the internal party disputes in the pre-October period. "Dogmatism" in this latter sense means "Stalinism." "Marxism," Schaff wrote, contains no view which must be retained if it disagrees with facts, or which cannot be questioned and abandoned if unknown facts and new arguments emerge. Facts satisfactorily established should be recognized, whatever authority may be claimed against them. One should think for oneself and make no compromise in the search for truth. An opposite view regarding each of these rules results in or involves dogmatism.[8]

These observations, directed against the dogmatists in the party, that is, against the Stalinists, make of Schaff an orthodox revisionist (the meaning of this term will be given later), but do not exempt him from the objection of being a dogmatist in the methodological sense. Who is to decide, we can ask Schaff, whether a given revision is creative or erroneous? Does he accept without qualification and restriction the view that only experience and logical inference, irrespective of where they may lead, should settle the issue? If he does accept this view, why does he speak of a "nullification of the Marxist theory," a "rejection of the basic Marxist assumptions" and a "liquidationist revisionism"? We may go on to ask whether it is really true that the question [of] which revisionism is creative and which erroneous is resolved by an appeal to facts and not to authority, by factual and logical considerations and not by ideology. Is it really true that every statement falsified by the development of events, new observations and investigations must be rejected? Is no basic "Marxist" assumption exempt from the discussion? Can everybody think for himself and make no compromise in the search for truth?

All these questions have been answered by Schaff himself. While defending the right of the Marxist-Leninists to differ in their opinions and to produce differing solutions of the same problem, he concluded his spirited criticism of Stalinism with the following proviso:

But granted all the tolerance and the taking of a broad view of these matters, it should be stated that there are definite limits which no one can transgress if he does not wish to sever his connections with Marxism.[9]

Schaff's assertion that Marxism-Leninism is free from dogmatism clearly involves an elementary error. To show this, we have first to explain what a nominal and a projecting definition are. We say that a definition is nominal (or verbal) if it is a statement regarding the actual use of a term (word) in a given language. A nominal definition which is a declaration of intention as to how one wishes to use a certain term may be called a projecting definition of this term. If a nominal definition is a statement about how a certain expression is used, a nominal definition is either a true or a false statement. But a projecting definition has no claim to truth, not even as a statement about language, for it is not a proposition at all. Moreover, in neither case can a nominal definition function as a premise in inference about matters of fact.

Now, it is clear that Schaff's definition of "Marxism" is a verbal and projecting definition. What he says in the argument under discussion amounts to a declaration that he intends to use the expression "system of continuously developing thought" as a substitute for the term "Marxism." Nothing can be inferred from such a declaration, irrespective of whether we accept or reject it in our own language. In particular, from the verbal definition: "Marxism" means "system of continuously developing thought," we cannot derive the conclusion that Marxism *is* a system of continuously developing thought. Similarly, the nominal definition: "Marxist policies" means the same as "policies which do not restrict the search for truth," does not allow us to draw the conclusion that Marxist policies support the search for truth.[10] A proposal of policy cannot be derived from facts and still less from a projecting definition. If we give the Earth the name Heaven and call Heaven the Earth, by ascribing to our arbitrary verbal definition the claim to truth we could easily persuade ourselves that we all live in Heaven. Words have no power to create or change or affect in any way their referents. To cherish this expectation is to indulge in the belief in magic. Magical rites may give confidence to their performer, but empirical ends cannot be obtained by the mere utterance of some prescribed words.

A few years ago Polish Marxist-Leninists announced their determination to make up for neglect of formal logic and of the logical analysis of language, which they recognized to be among the most important tools of the philosopher. They failed, however, to follow their celebrated rule that theory is a guide to action. This is clear from the example just considered, as well as from the argument intended to establish the conclusion that "Marxism" is not a set of dogmas but an ever-creative thought. Having once discarded logic in order to replace it by dialectics, Marxist-Leninists now accept the universal validity of logic, and, in particular, of the principle of non-contradiction. That is, they adhere to the view that a conjunction of contradictory statements is always a falsehood. Yet they also believe that one such conjunction is true; for on the one hand they say that "Marxism" is a creative revision of all views including their own, while on the other they assert that a revision of the "Marxist" assumptions is not permissible. To put it differently, Marxist-Leninists state that their doctrine is both unalterable and not unalterable, according to what the situation requires in a particular case.

Schaff's creative revisionism is but a protective coating to conceal the hard core of dogmatism resulting from the acceptance of truths based on authority. To resolve the question whether a revision is "creative" or "erroneous," we do not need—according to him—to consider what is to be revised and how the revision is justified. The decisive thing is the person by whom the revision is accomplished or approved. This also applies to the following statement that appears to be perfectly sound and unquestionable: a revision is creative if and only if the revision is true, that is, is in agreement with reality. For only the appropriate authority has ultimately the right to decide what is in conformity with reality and what does not correspond to the facts of social life and historical development. When this right is claimed by an individual or a minority deprived of political power, they must be wrong and their revision erroneous. Although all men are equal, some of them are more equal than others. To ignore this principle is an infringement upon the foundation of power, order and authority, which is included in what Zolkiewski calls *the requirements of the Marxist methodology.*

The methodological dogmatism inherent in Schaff's creative revisionism is an attitude characteristic of people who are politically committed. He who strives for the realization of his ideals is usually inclined to regard his beliefs as incontrovertible truths, that is, as dogmas. His faith protects his beliefs from doubt, and his ideology conditions his way of thinking and of perceiving the world. This is all too human and nothing to wonder about provided that a committed man is free from fanaticism and intolerance. But it is a fatal error if these attitudes of mind and modes of thought characteristic for a politician and ideologist are presumed to be scholarly or scientific, and identified with the rules accepted in scientific procedure. The sociology of science, to which Schaff often refers for support, provides evidence that neither scholars nor scientists are exempt from ideological preconceptions. But the sociology of science does not and cannot prove that on this account the line of division between science and ideology becomes blurred or disappears altogether. The rules of scientific procedure by means of which a scientific statement is validated enable us to eliminate the distorting influence of ideological and other preconceptions.

The distinction between a "creative" and an "erroneous" revisionism cannot be maintained without the support of the so-called institutional Marxism, that is, without conceiving Marxism as a closed doctrine,[11] the content of which is determined by a privileged group of followers. A closed, institutionalized doctrine cannot be a science or a scientific view of the world. To think otherwise is either the result of a misunderstanding about what science is, or an attempt, to use C. L. Stevenson's expression, to offer a persuasive definition. While purporting to be a descriptive statement, a persuasive definition expresses an attitude of approval or disapproval and guides, evokes, or prescribes similar attitudes to other people with respect to what it ostensibly tries only to describe.

The Concept of Orthodoxy The line of division between orthodoxy and revisionism is constantly shifting, for even the most rigid orthodoxy is not immune from change. The dispute over the question [of] which views are orthodox and which revisionist has raged without interruption since the deaths of Marx and Engels. The dispute most often deals with issues which never concerned Marx and Engels. One of the disputed solutions will be designated "the only correct Marxist standpoint," and the others labelled "anti-Marxist" or "revisionist." We may conclude that not only the concept of revisionism but also that of orthodoxy is relative and changing in its content. There is no such thing as a changeless orthodoxy. Each orthodoxy is a result of the revision of the preceding one, and upon each the honorific title of "authentic Marxism" is conferred *ex post*. While novel pronouncements of the orthodoxy may be disguised in familiar terms, a new use and meaning is given to these terms and a new content is thereby expressed by equiform statements.

Karl Mannheim and other sociologists have analyzed this phenomenon and explained its social functions. The functional conception of ideology, initiated by Durkheim and developed by Mannheim,[12] considers an ideology as an instrument by means of which the patterns of interaction in and between particular social groups are maintained or changed without the social foundation of power relationships being thereby modified. An ideology that not only is altered, as it must be under the pressure of new practical requirements, but also expressly recognizes the effected changes, could not achieve both of those objectives at once. The social function of an ideology is essentially conservative; it serves the purpose of maintaining the *status quo*, the existing political institutions, the economy and the class structure. This is one of the many uses of "ideology" which can be found in the writings of Marx. Ideology considered from this viewpoint is for Marx the whole system of legal, moral and religious ideas which provide the ruling class with the justification and legitimation of the social system that serves its interests. But Marx believed that the working class, having achieved power, would have no use for this kind of ideology. Either Marx was wrong or his expectations still await their fulfillment.

A description of orthodoxy which fails to take note of the changes in its content would also be a persuasive definition. The orthodoxy of Marxism-Leninism should not be identified with some definite "principles," "correct views" or "basic Marxist assumptions"; this would suggest that orthodoxy is never altered, which is simply untrue. Orthodoxy is better described as a temper, an intellectual attitude of readiness to accept some truths as incontrovertible and obligatory for all concerned at a given stage of development, as the communist leaders have often emphasized.[13] This intellectual attitude is the psychological counterpart of methodological dogmatism in which the common formal factor of every orthodoxy should be seen. Thus, while the alleged incontrovertible truths are not in fact immutable, but change their meaning and content in time, the permanent elements of orthodoxy are the intellectual dispositions and attitudes of its supporters who regard the authoritatively pronounced truths as incontrovertible and immutable.

The orthodox temper of mind is also characterized by the caution with which truths are altered to suit the requirements of changing circumstances, "lest revolutionary socialism be turned into opportunism." A Marxist-Leninist cannot admit that he alters his ideology, for the function of an ideology is to provide its followers with a common cognitive orientation, which frequent changes would destroy. The ideology of a ruling group must never lose the aura of universal and ultimate truth, beneficial to all mankind, which only a selfish, ignorant and servile simpleton could fail to understand, for otherwise, as mentioned earlier, it would cease to be a means of retaining power in the hands of the rulers. To paraphrase Durkheim's views, whatever changes are made should not appear to the individual as "learned machinations destined to conceal from men the traps in which they have caught themselves" but as necessary products of given causes and of a force "which is superior to him and before which he bows." [14]

THE GERMAN ANTECEDENTS

We shall leave a more detailed description of orthodox revisionism until later and take up now some preliminary issues concerning the characteristics of proper revisionism, which also will be conceived as a set of intellectual attitudes and methodological rules of procedure. Some of these characteristics are universal, others are specific with respect to place and time.

It has been mentioned above that Schaff considers revisionism in Poland as an offspring of the marriage between Existentialism and the Kantian doctrine. In the course of time the Existentialist ancestor assumed for him the more important role. To put it in terms of genetics, Existentialism has become the dominant and the Kantian doctrine the recessive characteristic in the inheritance mass of revisionism.[15] This was due to the evolution of the views of Schaff himself. Schaff, who had once felt an utter contempt for Existentialism, that is, the Existentialism of Sartre (he ignores all the other Existentialist thinkers and invariably identifies Sartre's doctrine with Existentialism *tout court*) has recently reached the conclusion that the problems raised by Sartre are of considerable significance. Although the solutions produced by Sartre and his Polish revisionist imitators are unacceptable, he feels that the problems themselves should not be ignored. Moreover, they can be fully accommodated within "Marxism," which also provides the best basis for Existentialist investigations.

Schaff's proposal may sound novel, but it is not an entirely new development. The so-called philosophic anthropology was an integral part of Marx's early interest in philosophy, for which, apart from other less important contributions, *The Economic and Philosophic Manuscripts of 1844* provide the main evidence. The manuscripts were published for the first time in 1932 and then ignored by Marxian scholars, including the representatives of orthodoxy. Nothing was heard about them until Henri Lefèbvre tried to use them in the 'forties to interpret the teaching of the "later Marx"; then Heinrich Popitz published his influential study *Der entfremdete Mensch* (1953), followed by a comprehensive re-interpretation of Marx's thought in the light of *The Economic and Philosophic Manuscripts of 1844* by the French Jesuit Jean-Yves Calvez in his *La Pensée de Karl Marx* (1956). The influence of the "early Marx" was reflected in the writings of Ernst Bloch, Sartre and Leszek Kolakowski, who was the first Polish Marxian scholar to undertake a philosophical elucidation of *The Economic and Philosophic Manuscripts of 1844*, a task extremely hard to perform in view of the esoteric Hegelian style of Marx's work.[16] English readers were given in Robert C. Tucker's study *Philosophy and Myth in Karl Marx* [17] a clear and incisive exposition of what the author calls *original Marxism*. In Poland, Czeslaw Nowinski tried to use the Marxian anthropological approach in his interpretation of Leninism.[18] Finally, Schaff announced that it was desirable and imperative to take up studies concerned with a materialistically conceived Existentialism.

Since Existentialism was in disgrace among Marxist-Leninists everywhere, this was an important development, particularly with respect to the Soviet-bloc countries outside Poland. In Poland it was a sign, implicitly conceded by Schaff in his *Marxism and Existentialism*, that, after the disclosures about Stalin's rule, problems of moral conflict, sense of guilt and self-esteem could no longer be managed by means of ideology alone. Schaff recognized that some more effective means was necessary to release the tension arising from the reckoning with the past and from conflicts of personality exposed to discrepant or irreconcilable demands. As will be seen, his attitude clearly resulted from or was decisively influenced by the activities of the denounced revisionists. It also testified to his awareness of the increasing intellectual isolation in which the Marxist-Leninists found themselves. Existentialism, wrote William Barrett, is a philosophy "that was able to cross the frontier from the Academy into the world at large." Marxist-Leninists were anxious to leave perhaps not so much the Academy as their party offices and to mingle with the crowd outside.

Having clarified this intellectual development in Poland, about which there has been some misunderstanding in the past, let us return to the Kantian origin of Polish revisionism. While the supporters of Marxist-Leninist orthodoxy have often mentioned the Kantian and Bernsteinian ancestry of Polish revisionism, they have never explained exactly what its link with Kant or Bernstein was. It is worth our while to consider briefly the more than 60-year-old dispute over revisionism within German Social Democracy, for its analysis is enlightening in many respects.

At first sight, the two things seem to have nothing in common. German revisionism was, above all, a political movement, concerned with the program and tactics to be adopted by the Social Democratic Party. It was, therefore, a pragmatic dispute, and not a theoretical one. This does not imply that questions of economics and philosophy did not enter into the dispute, but that practical problems of securing power were the primary issue while the theoretical problems were brought in to support arguments advocating different policies. This was clear to the chief protagonists in the dispute, which, according to Kautsky, was "about a question of tactics and not about matters of principle." A similar observation came from Bernstein, who defined revisionism as a "conception of practical action" (*Theorie einer Praxis*).[19]

The main difference of opinion between Bernstein and Kautsky, from which all the others derive, can be stated in either political or historiosophic terms. Bernstein believed that a steady trend of change and reform—the extension of the franchise, labor legislation, trade-unionism, the widening of educational facilities, a controlled economic expansion which was bound to increase the size of the working class and to strengthen its class consciousness—would secure the transition to socialism. There was no question that this trend was at work in Germany at that time (though about its significance there could and did exist a difference of opinion) and that it had made the Social Democracy the most powerful socialist party in the world.[20]

Bernstein's belief that socialism could be attained by evolution reflected a conception of the historical process which deviated from the view then widely accepted as truly Marxian. According to Bernstein, historical inevitability no longer held sway over the life of men. The determination of their acts by historical forces was being replaced by man's free choice, conscious effort, and control over his natural and social environment. Consequently, as Bernstein put it, socialism was no longer inevitable, but "what ought to be" (*etwas was sein soll*), a conception of a definite social order permeated with ideals. Socialism should be identified either with these ideals or with the movement toward them, for people were becoming free to strive for the realization of their aspirations and to act in accordance with moral demands (*sittliche Forderungen*) transcending what they actually experienced.[21]

Kautsky rejected Bernstein's analysis and evaluation of the development of events, and accepted a view of history closer to Marx's classical formulation. Socialism is not what ought to be but what has to be. "Socialism is inevitable since the class struggle and the victory of the proletariat are inevitable," reads the closing sentence of the *Ethik und materialistische Geschichtsauffassung*. The historical process is subject to laws, these laws determine the course of events and the ultimate establishment of socialism that is not a condition of society which "we merely wish for and desire, but which has to come about because it is necessary." [22] The transition to socialism cannot be accomplished by evolution; a gradual change only paves the way for a socialist revolution, without which the autocracy cannot be abolished and democracy firmly established.

As far as political principles, distinct from historiosophic assumptions, were concerned, the differences between Kautsky and Bernstein were less considerable than might be imagined. The reasons for this were numerous and complicated, but are of no interest in this context. Kautsky and Bernstein shared the same ideal of socialism, they both believed in democracy as the founding stone of socialism. Bernstein lived for many years in England and he kept in close contact not only with Engels but also with the Fabians, who deeply influenced him. But Kautsky was no less a sincere democrat than Bernstein. It should be remembered that Kautsky rendered great services to the socialist movement by his staunch defense of democracy against Lenin's doctrine and practice of minority dictatorship, for which Lenin branded him a renegade. Kautsky and Bernstein were in agreement on matters of basic importance and on the goals to be achieved by the socialist movement. They disagreed on the subject of the most suitable and effective means by which the goals were to be reached. The disagreement made of Bernstein a revisionist, while the agreement prevented him from becoming a founder of a distinct political party or a school of political thought. In the course of time the issues were cleared and the verdict was passed. Neither Kautsky nor Bernstein was entirely right or entirely wrong, but the socialist movement in Western Europe has in its majority followed Bernstein rather than Kautsky.

Polish revisionism differs from its German predecessor in both of the respects so far considered. In Polish revisionism theoretical questions have predominated over pragmatic issues. Moreover, there is no agreement on fundamentals between the supporters of Marxist-Leninist orthodoxy and their revisionist opponents. As there is no such agreement, the opponents of orthodoxy should not really be called revisionists at all.

The fact that theoretical problems predominate over matters of practice in Polish revisionism is due to two main circumstances. The leading Polish revisionists are not politicians, although some of them have a deep and abiding interest in political issues. They come from the ranks of philosophers, sociologists, economists, historians, literary critics, writers and even poets. They have been supported in their intellectual activities by skilled logicians, methodologists, social scientists, linguistic scholars, and also scientists (above all, the theoretical physicist Leopold Infeld). This accounts for the theoretical orientation of Polish revisionism and also for its strength. For while some of the revisionists combine literary talent, intellectual ability and professional competence, which make of them formidable opponents of the orthodox doctrine, they can also count on and actually receive assistance from scholars and scientists who are not at all involved in the dispute over revisionism. Neither science nor scholarship produces dogmas, and every dogma hampers their advance. He who fights dogmatism is an ally of all unprejudiced minds.

The fact that Polish revisionism is concerned mainly, if not exclusively, with problems of philosophy, sociology, history and economics is due, above all, to circumstances of time and place. Until recently Poland was a totalitarian country and it is still an authoritarian state. All political issues remain the exclusive preserve of the communist party or rather of its leadership. This means that no open discussion concerning political principles is possible in public unless the disputants fully accept the premises endorsed by the party leadership. If it is to survive at all, revisionism must keep within the bounds of high abstraction and very general theorizing. Since access to free political activity is blocked, effort must be concentrated on theoretical issues and on exercising influence on the minds of others.

It was noted above that, unlike their German predecessors, Polish revisionists and the supporters of the orthodox doctrine do not agree on fundamentals. This does not imply that as far as the ultimate goals of socialism are concerned, Gomulka on the one hand and Kolakowski, for instance, on the other, could not agree. Both, each in his own way, are sincere socialists probably in full agreement about the distant goals. But the supporters of orthodoxy and the revisionists differ deeply and basically in their views on how to get there and still more on where to start from. What for the former is a prerequisite of the transition to socialism, is for the latter a sure way of destroying the chances of ever achieving socialism.

However tolerant an orthodox Polish Marxist-Leninist of today may be in accepting the right of dissent in matters of theory and ideology, he firmly adheres to what we may call two meta-dogmata.[23] He believes that the founders of Marxism-Leninism discovered certain absolute truths, and this act of faith involves for him the unquestioning acceptance of the principles of Marxist-Leninist philosophy. He also believes in the meta-dogma that in any set of given historical and social conditions there is one and only one road leading to socialism, that which is known to the leaders of the communist party and outside which there is no salvation for mankind (Blakeley calls it the *meta-dogma of the communist destiny of humanity*). These two acts of faith provide the guarantee of the truth of two dogmas. First, Marxist-Leninist philosophy comprises true knowledge about the world, society, history, man and his involvement in society and history; whoever fails to accept this body of knowledge must necessarily be in error. Second, only the party, that is, the leadership of the party, can and should determine what is the best policy on any matter of major importance. The leadership is an infallible authority in all ideological questions, for ideology provides definitions of the situation and makes collective action possible. Whoever defies this authority, no matter what his reasons, must necessarily be wrong.

A revisionist rejects the meta-dogmata and their consequences. Like so many before him, he doubts that faith is the fulfillment of reason. He believes that all men are fallible and that it is absurd to assume that a single group has a monopoly on knowledge and truth, whether in matters of theory or of practical significance. A revisionist is convinced that theories protected from rationalistic criticism by administrative methods are not theories at all but objects of "devotional worship," as one of them put it, concealing "the absence of intelligence and courage." Unrestricted freedom of thought is the only guarantee in our possession that knowledge may advance and errors be discovered. The practice of democracy is a necessary condition for the realization of democracy, and it is inseparable from a genuine transition to socialism. In this respect the supporters of the orthodox doctrine and the revisionists are separated by an impassable chasm, and there is no possibility of constructing a bridge over the dividing gulf unless one or the other radically changes his initial position. The fundamental character of this disagreement accounts for the fact that it is of great significance for the whole society, irrespective of other differences that might divide particular sections of the community from the revisionists.

When we ask how this disagreement arose and where to look for its ultimate source, we have to go back to the philosophical issues involved in the dispute over revisionism at the turn of the century. For in this respect there seems to be a real similarity between the old German revisionism and the new revisionism in Poland.

THE INEVITABILITY OF REVISIONISM

The philosophical issues involved in the dispute concern the relation between value judgments and statements of fact. They are a permanent source of revisionism within the Marxian doctrine and within every subsequent interpretation which claims exclusive rights as an authentic continuation of the teaching of the founder.

It was Hume who, in a famous passage of the *Treatise on Human Nature,* made philosophers aware of the logical impossibility of deducing normative propositions from declarative propositions.

In every system of morality which I have hitherto met with, I have always remarked that the author proceeds for some time in the ordinary way of reasoning, and establishes the being of a God, or makes observations concerning human affairs; when of a sudden I am surprised to find, that instead of the usual copulation of propositions, *is* or *is not*, I meet with no proposition that is not connected with an *ought* or *ought not*. The change is imperceptible, but it is, however, of the last consequence. For as this *ought* or *ought not* expresses some new relation or affirmation, it is necessary that it should be observed and explained, and at the same time, that a reason should be given, for what seems altogether inconceivable, how this new relation can be a deduction from others which are entirely different from it.[24]

This argument has been taken up by other modern thinkers who have restated it in various forms. Facts are discovered, norms and rules of conduct are man-made, and the logical gap between them cannot be bridged. When a man adopts or follows a norm, what he does is as much a fact as any other fact. But what he adopts is not a fact related to other facts or to be inferred from them, but a normative proposition either to be deduced from other normative statements or to be accepted axiomatically. We can reject an adopted norm in favor of another which we regard as superior to the rejected norm. Even the standards, however, by which this preference is made, are, to quote Karl Popper, "of our making in the sense that our decision in favor of them is our own decision and that we alone carry the responsibility for adopting them. The standards are not to be found in nature. Nature consists of facts and of regularities and is in itself neither moral nor immoral." [25]

This does not imply, as the supporters of the "naive monism of facts and norms" often contend, that values are something fictitious and arbitrary or that they do not play an important part in individual and social life. Values are a social product, the result of experiences of many past generations, and the man who appeals to them takes advantage of the inheritance of the society to which he belongs. What is important is to realize the distinctive nature of value judgments and normative propositions on the one hand, of statements of fact on the other, and to apply the appropriate rules of procedure to each of these classes of statements. When Zolkiewski says that "empiricism in the social sciences" leads to the rejection and neglect of the world of values, we fail to follow his astonishing train of thought. It is impossible to find the implicated view in Popper's *The Poverty of Historicism* (and still less in *The Open Society and Its Enemies*) to which Zolkiewski refers for supporting evidence.[26] There is a kind of criticism of which we should not fail to take notice, and another kind which we can afford to ignore. We shall proceed, therefore, to the analysis of so-called scientific socialism in the light of the established distinction between normative and declarative statements.

It appears that Marx never saw the need for this distinction or appreciated its importance, a fact in which we can see the influence of Hegelian dialectics and *Weltorientierung* toward justifying any arbitrary deduction. The same applies to Engels to an even greater extent. One can say of Marx that he clearly saw the errors of others when they inferred statements of fact from normative propositions or from propositions which implicitly contained or implied a value judgment. One of the many uses of the Marxian concept of ideology is to show up any procedure that regards normative assumptions as a legitimate logical basis for positive knowledge about reality. But Marx was unaware of his own error in the opposite direction inherent in the deduction of value statements from statements of fact. He believed (and was confirmed in his belief by Engels) that he had managed to overcome the irreducibility of the two classes of statements in his theory of scientific socialism. This is not, however, the case. The continuous rediscovery of Marx's error by successive generations is an ever-present source of revisionism. As nobody has succeeded thus far in removing Marx's error and since there is, in fact, no chance of its ever being removed, for the problem involved is logically insoluble, we are forced to the conclusion that the Marxian doctrine logically involves the inevitability of revisionism.

It was during the dispute over revisionism within German Social Democracy that Marx's error was duly noted and formulated for the first time. The social and historical sciences might possibly justify the conclusion that socialism is inevitable, that is, that the transition to socialism can be predicted on the basis of the natural laws which determine social change and historical development (to simplify the argument, we do not wish to examine the question as to whether the Marxian doctrine provides a sufficient logical basis for making such a valid prediction, although we do not believe that it does). But sociological and historical knowledge cannot logically establish the normative statement that socialism is morally desirable or that men ought to strive and exert themselves to bring socialism about. Therefore, either socialism is inevitable in the sense defined above, but then it cannot be shown to be morally desirable, or we accept socialism as something worth striving for, but then it cannot be inevitable. For normative and value statements cannot be deduced from declarative propositions, and no proposition expressing what people ought to do can validate a statement of fact.[27]

Having established this point, the German revisionists reach a further conclusion, namely that if the Marxian doctrine is a positive, or, as we would say today, a correlational or theoretical science, it must be amplified by a moral philosophy. This moral philosophy was found in Kant's ethical theory or rather in his critical philosophy, by means of which Kant tried to establish universally valid foundations for a system of ethics. Kant's procedure consists essentially in an analysis of moral experience intended to reveal the presuppositions which make it possible, and the principles which justify other moral norms and their application in any particular case.

Now it is not difficult to understand why the solution was and continues to be unacceptable to a faithful supporter of the Marxian doctrine. Some of the reasons were stated by Kautsky in his *Ethik und materialistische Geschichtsauffassung*, first published in 1906 in reply to Hermann Cohen's *Ethik des reinen Willens* (1905): Kant eliminated all empirical elements from ethics, implied that social progress depends on the moral improvement of the individual, and thus provided bourgeois thinkers with an intellectual instrument by means of which they could try to reconcile class antagonism and prevent the revolution.[28] Moreover, according to Marx and Engels, morality is always class morality; that is, it is essentially the expression of class interests. Socialist morality cannot, therefore, be derived from universal ethics, binding upon the whole of mankind. To amplify the teaching of Marx with the Kantian ethics is an absurd undertaking, as absurd as nourishing fire by adding water. In this way, however, the supporters of scientific socialism have made revisionism logically inevitable by opposing any revision in its original formulation.

The essential philosophical issue involved in the dispute over revisionism within German Social Democracy has provided the premises on which an important trend in Polish revisionism is also based, and has determined its further development. The premises have been stated over and over again in Poland in recent years, but nowhere better than in the writings of Leszek Kolakowski, who has examined them with a rare combination of intellectual vigor and moral fervor. We shall draw upon his contributions to describe the views of Polish revisionism on the relation between moral and cognitive components in the socialist ideology.

The perception of the moral world of obligation, Kolakowski wrote, is irreducible to the knowledge of facts, events, and natural laws:

> The practical choice must be made in a world defined by "obligation" and not by "existence." These two categories, *Sollen* and *Sein*, characterize two attitudes and two visions of reality between which we fruitlessly but constantly try to establish contact.[29]

Since these two attitudes to the world are irreducible to each other, we are always faced by the necessity of making a choice which can be described only by the extreme characteristics of the recurring alternatives: we have to choose between utopianism and opportunism, between a romantic arbitrariness and a submissive compliance to the perceived reality. Although historical necessity is not a figment of the imagination, we can never define its limits with sufficient precision to establish in each particular case that part which is and that which is not determined by the historical process, independent of the will of the individual. The past is irrevocable, it cannot be made different from what in fact it was; the irrevocability of what is only to happen is always doubtful, further located possibilities are undecided and leave room for choice and a realistically conceived decision. While our present actions cannot affect the past, they can have an effect upon the future. Therefore, no doctrine and no faith can release us from the moral choice and moral responsibility each individual has to face.

It is not true that historiosophy defines our main choices in life. Our moral sensibility does. We are not communists because we have considered communism a historical necessity. We are communists because we are on the side of the oppressed against the oppressors, on the side of the poor against their masters and on the side of the persecuted against their persecutors. Although we know that the theoretically correct division of society is not a division into the rich and the poor nor into the persecuted and the persecutors, yet, when apart from the theoretical approach we are to make a practical choice, that is to make a wager, we are then motivated morally, and not by theoretical consciousness. It cannot be otherwise because even the most convincing theory is not in a position to make us move a finger. A practical choice is a choice of values, *i.e.* a moral act, and that means something for which everybody is personally responsible.[30]

The assumption of the autonomy and the responsibility of the individual in the act of moral choice does not involve the acceptance of Sartre's Existentialist anthropology with its conception of man who is abandoned, lonely and tragic, and who struggles against the absurdity of the natural world or against the anguish of nothingness pressing upon him at the margin of his existence. Rather, it goes back to Socrates who never ceased to question all authority in matters of morals, who constantly searched for universally valid moral norms, and who elevated the conscience of the individual to the position of the supreme judge of the court of moral appeal. The above-mentioned assumption does not imply either, as Schaff interpreted Kolakowski's views, that "man as much spins moral ideas out of the innermost of his mind as does the spider its cobweb."[31] Kolakowski stated in a quite unambiguous manner that the moral convictions of the individual are subject to various determinations, some resulting from the universal conditions of social life, others from specific conditions of class society or membership in a definite class, profession or other social group.[32] He wished to emphasize an entirely different aspect of the problem, namely, what he calls the "barracks-like and monastic interpretation of the Hegelian concept of freedom," in which—from the assumption that freedom is the understanding of necessity—the conclusion is inferred that in a socialist society the individual should acquire the awareness of the inevitability of everything that happens in his life provided that it happens for the sake of society. He also voiced his opposition to the view that in a socialist society the conflict between the freedom of the individual and freedom in the larger society is bound to disappear. Moreover, he contended (and explained in greater detail in his essay *Essence and Existence in the Concept of Freedom*, to which the reader is referred) that "an individual existence never realizes the class essence in a pure and unpolluted form, nor can it be exhaustively described in terms of its class membership; the course of an individual existence is no more determinable by the general laws of the class struggle than are the movements of particular gaseous particles determined by the laws of statistical mechanics although the latter, irrespective of their inapplicability to particular molecules, remain valid with respect to their aggregate."[33] Finally, Kolakowski made use of Moritz Schlick's famous argument produced in *Fragen der Ethik* to establish the point that determinism and moral responsibility are not mutually exclusive but complementary. If there are determinants of human behavior, this fact does not imply that the individual acts under compulsion, that is, that he cannot act otherwise than he in fact does. The determination of the behavior of an individual by social conditions and his own past is not to be identified with an external compulsion, and only an external compulsion deprives the individual of his freedom of choice and releases him from moral responsibility. For all these reasons the view should be adopted that

ultimately the decision and the act remain in the power of the individual. Kolakowski quoted Whitman:

> Not I, not anyone else can travel that road for you,
> You must travel it for yourself,

and concluded that we follow the main road of our life on our own
responsibility.[34]

We do not wish to suggest that Kolakowski formulated his views
under the influence of the revisionist discussion within German Social
Democracy which, in the first decade of our century, had produced a
voluminous flood of publications. We only wish to draw attention to
the similarity of approach and the line of argument followed by two
revisionist trends separated from each other by more than half a
century. Kolakowski's views originated in his analysis of the Stalinist
doctrine and of the individual and collective experiences suffered during
the period of "errors and distortions." Stalinism provided the model of
a doctrine which tries to deduce moral obligation from historical necessity. Kolakowski used this doctrine to show the logical errors involved
in such a deduction and the horrors resulting from its application. These
horrors are bound to be inflicted upon mankind whenever a doctrine
claims a complete and infallible knowledge of the future. It then asserts
that the moral problem of the individual lies not in measuring the
historical events by the standards of one's own sense of justice but only
in adapting one's own sense of justice to historical necessity. This leads
to a submissive compliance to the commands and wishes of those in
power and to the belief in the immorality of history. For the sense of
moral duty is associated with the conviction that a certain type of
human behavior is an end in itself, and not merely a means to an end.
But if the moral judgment is subject to decrees of historical necessity,
there is no single thing which can be considered as an end in itself. In
other words, moral values cease to exist altogether and there is no room
left in man's life for moral obligation *sensu stricto*, since this becomes
indistinguishable from obedience to the will of the mighty and the
powerful.

It should be easy to understand why Kolakowski was branded by
the supporters of the orthodox doctrine as the chief revisionist in Poland.
He richly earned this distinction by restating with force and conviction
the irreducibility of value judgments to statements of fact, by the reassertion of the independence of morality from speculative theories about
society and history, by endowing the moral law with the Kantian
reverence and by his insistence on the moral autonomy and responsibility of the individual. He also deserves the reputation of the chief
revisionist since he did not hesitate to draw practical conclusions from
his analysis. The memory of the cruelties, inhumanity and bondage
experienced in the Stalinist period endowed his discovery of a logical
error with the intensity of a protest against the "attempts to give to

historiosophy a normative interpretation," that is, against regarding the standards of moral evaluation as logical conclusions inferred from the knowledge of "historical laws." The moral autonomy and responsibility of the individual, within the framework of the determination of his moral beliefs by the historical and social conditions of his life, constitute the cornerstone of all sound social and political endeavors. They not only are his inalienable right, supported by the demands of his conscience, but also his duty.

No one is exempted from the moral duty to fight against a system of government, a doctrine or a social condition which he considers to be vile and inhuman, by resorting to the argument that he finds them to be historically necessary. We protest against this form of moral relativism, in which it is assumed that the criteria of the moral evaluation of human conduct can be deduced from the knowledge of the mysteries of the *Weltgeist*.[35]

It is not a futile and helpless indulgence in moralizing, as the supporters of the orthodox doctrine maintain, but the reassertion of the moral attitude to life, that is a characteristic feature of Polish revisionism. Owing to this attitude it is not divorced either from politics or from life. Politics in the current meaning of this term consists in the threat or actual use of power which enforces conformity and submission. But politics also refers to various forms of persuasion by means of which the social attitudes and behavior of one's fellow men are influenced and molded. In this latter sense the activities of the revisionists carry political implications. They make people aware that the facts of social life are alterable; that they cannot shift the responsibility for changing these facts to anybody else; and that thus the responsibility is entirely theirs.

ORTHODOX REVISIONISM

Revisionism in Poland not only has a moral orientation, but also a distinctive philosophical content. To describe it, we first have to distinguish the two sorts of revisionism existing in Poland, orthodox and philosophic revisionism. We shall begin our exposition with the former.

There are three main trends of thought which, together, make up orthodox revisionism. The first consists in changing the interpretation of some Marxist-Leninist presuppositions, in conferring a new meaning upon them, while leaving their verbal formulation unaltered. The second trend of orthodox revisionism is revealed in a shift of emphasis to one of the component parts of the doctrine at the expense of another. Finally, the third tendency is expressed in its readiness to take up new problems which were previously ignored because of their alleged idealistic significance and bourgeois origin.

The appearance of orthodox revisionism is to be accounted for by the specific circumstances which Marxism-Leninism met in Poland. Between the two wars Poland had a large and thriving school of philosophy, known in the world of learning as the Warsaw School or simply as the Polish school. It excelled in formal logic, philosophy of language and philosophy of science. It set up high standards of precision in speech and thought, and demanded familiarity with and competence in the procedures of deductive and empirical sciences. It was positivistically and scientifically oriented; it avoided and combatted the traditional trend in philosophy given to speculations unrelated to scientific knowledge and unchecked by logical analysis. In addition to having a thriving school of philosophy, Poland enjoyed a world-wide reputation for its school of mathematical logic. This reputation has persisted after World War II. Next to the United States, Poland is the most important center of logical investigations in the world.

Marxism-Leninism was confronted in Poland with a strong tradition of philosophic achievement, a large group of philosophers highly skilled in logical and scientific procedure, and a strong native attachment to the importance of matters of the mind. In these circumstances Marxism-Leninism could not prevail by the simple claim that everybody was wrong and only the followers of Marxism-Leninism were right. It was no more successful in the Stalinist period when this claim was upheld by a complete suppression of freedom of speech and thought. For even in the silence enforced by censorship, the question "What is the evidence for what you declare to be the absolute truth?" sounded loud, impressed the followers of Marxism-Leninism themselves, and put them under constant intellectual pressure. Not the philosophers, but the Marxist-Leninists began retreating. At first the retreat took the form of certain minor deviations or shifts of emphasis. These persisted and tended to increase the original distance from orthodoxy, and in the course of time they produced a Marxist-Leninist philosophy markedly different from that existing in the Soviet Union.

The native philosophical tradition explains the appearance of the first two new orientations in the orthodox revisionism which have just been mentioned. An example of the first of these trends is the revision of the thesis, originated by Engels, that an "objective contradiction" is inherent in all objects and phenomena of nature. Until recently Marxist-Leninists staunchly adhered to the opinion that this "objective contradiction" is a logical contradiction, a view which, for reasons we do not need to enter into, has far-reaching and disastrous consequences. Orthodox revisionism, mainly owing to Schaff's persuasive powers, effected an interpretative change and adopted the view now prevailing among the Marxist-Leninists in Poland and increasingly gaining ground in the Soviet Union, that the "objective contradiction" is of a dialectical nature, or more plainly, is no contradiction *sensu stricto* at all. This was an important revision, for it released a chain reaction of successive reinterpretations. The recognition of the universal validity of the principles of logic involved further revisions and this process is not yet by any means completed.[36]

Another example of the first tendency in orthodox revisionism is a new interpretation of the principle of partisanship. The principle is both a prescriptive and a proscriptive norm. As a proscription the principle of partisanship commands the rejection of any view incompatible with the position of the communist party, since such views are erroneous by definition. As a positive norm the principle of partisanship requires a rigorous, consistent, partisan and active commitment to the defense of views recognized by the communist party, the abandonment of "academic objectivism" and the treatment of any dissenting opinion as pure nonsense, significant only as an expression of the interests of the bourgeoisie and its hostility to Soviet socialism. On the other hand a necessary condition of acquiring true knowledge, "an objective, undistorted reflection of reality," is the adoption of the standpoint of the proletariat and its interests. It is the right and the privilege of the leaders of the communist party to decide what these interests are in each particular case, for truth is an illusion if it is not seen in accordance with what the party leaders consider it to be.[37]

The principle of partisanship in a new interpretation, produced by Oskar Lange, is reduced to the distinction between the conservative and the progressive type of ideology. The conservative ideology tends to mystify, and the progressive to illuminate, social reality. Since between the two extremes, which are never realized in a pure form, there are other intermediate attitudes, the conservative and the progressive ideology seem to be ideal types in Max Weber's sense. Moreover, Lange emphasizes the fact that the conservative attitude may also stimulate a limited but real scientific advance, just as the progressive attitude may produce mystifications. Utopian pre-Marxian socialism, revisionist deviations from scientific socialism, the period of dogmatism and the "cult of personality" in recent years, provide examples of distorted knowledge and biased conceptions in the international workers' movement. Therefore, the proletarian and the progressive attitude does not automatically guarantee an adequate reflection of social reality.

The principle of partisanship, as now understood, can be reduced to the following statement: there are two types of ideological attitudes, the progressive and the conservative; the latter is motivated by the desire to maintain the established order and acts as a stimulus to the inquisitiveness of the mind only in so far as new facts are thereby discovered that aid in the perpetuation of the existing institutions; the former, being connected with the workers' movement and the construction of socialism, is, in principle, free from inhibitions, stimulates the discovery of the whole truth about social reality and thus is bound to favor scientific progress.[38]

The second tendency characteristic for orthodox revisionism can be exemplified by its anti-Hegelian orientation, with which is associated the return to the positivistic elements in Marx's philosophy (it is a well established fact that in the Marxian doctrine naturalism and positivism are curiously blended with some remnants of Hegel's speculative philosophy). This implies a retreat from bewildering speculations to the standpoint of common sense, an increasing respect for facts, genuine knowledge, scientific method and its achievements. These consequences of the anti-Hegelian orientation, also originated by Schaff, are particularly apparent among the younger philosophers, former supporters of the Marxist-Leninist orthodoxy, interested in the problems of dialectical materialism. Dialectical materialism has always been conceived both as an ontological and as a methodological doctrine. The revision of dialectical materialism differentiates between its ontological and methodological aspects, giving preference to the latter and modernizing its content by taking advantage of the contemporary philosophy of science. This trend has many supporters, among whom Helena Eilstein should be mentioned in particular.

Before Lange published his intellectually refreshing *Political Economy*, the demand for the rejection of the principle of partisanship had been voiced by the philosophical revisionists or the "liquidators," as they are called by the supporters of orthodoxy. The reader should be referred in this context to Kolakowski's essay *The World View and Criticism* [39] and to a series of articles published by Jozef Chalasinski, one of Poland's leading sociologists, in *Nauka Polska* and *Przeglad Kulturalny* in the years 1954-1955; they were the first swallows of the "spring" to come in October 1956.[40] But the final rejection of the principle of partisanship, with all its consequences in philosophy and the social sciences, required Lange's authoritative support in order to be accepted by other orthodox revisionists, at least in theory, for in practice there still remains much to be desired.[41]

So far the most favorable outcome of this rejection has been the abandonment of the so-called nihilistic criticism or lazy-minded Marxism, *marxisme paresseux*, as it was called by Sartre in an article published in the monthly *Tworczosc* in 1957.[42] The nihilistic criticism was based on the assumption that Marxism-Leninism had an exclusive monopoly on perceiving, formulating and solving new and "genuine" philosophical problems. This assumption entailed the conclusion that its opponents never were and never could have been right. Only a Marxist-Leninist knew or was able to discover anything worth knowing, indulging in a somewhat immodest belief that he did not expect to learn anything worthwhile from other people.

The criticism based on the above assumption was extremely simple. It was enough to show that the opponent expressed a view incompatible with the Marxist-Leninist doctrine to classify him as an idealist, irrespective of whether he was or was not aware of what his views implied "objectively." Idealism was not only an erroneous philosophy but also a political crime; for idealism was identified with bourgeois and imperialistic ideology. As Kolakowski put it, by reducing the opponent's viewpoint to absurdities and hostile political declarations this method became part of a ritualistic ceremonial which could successfully combine ignorance of the subject with an utter contempt for the writer under criticism.

At present this practice of the past has been repudiated. Schaff recognized that philosophical opponents should not be ignored nor should they be accused of merely indulging in the utterances of hostile absurdities. "It is not the case that some trends in philosophy have a monopoly on truth and others on falsehood. . . . In reality, the position is much more complicated. Even important truths might occur in systems which are otherwise false and downright anti-scientific. . . . Falsehoods, even important ones, might occur in systems otherwise entirely true." The method of "Marxist criticism" was abandoned, for according to Schaff it had nothing in common with scientific procedure. Furthermore, since it failed to carry conviction, it was ineffective. Finally, it impoverished the cognitive content and atrophied the intellectual function of "Marxist philosophy." [43]

A Western reader might regard this discovery as the forcing of an open door and as a truth both trivial and naive. This view was also voiced in Poland. It was said that truisms known for centuries could not be regarded as landmarks of scientific advance. Kolakowski wrote: "Deeply degrading are the statements that historical evidence should not be falsified, that science and scholarship demand that their assertions should be validated, that criticism of an opponent should be objective, and so forth." [44] But an opposing view also had its supporters. The revisions introduced by Schaff to the ruling orthodoxy, wrote a prominent Polish philosopher, "should be warmly welcomed by everybody who has a high level of philosophical thinking in Poland at heart." [45] This may be the advice of wisdom with which one should agree. For the doubtful discoveries had to be announced before some real progress could be made. Moreover, they mark some advance in tolerance, which, although still precarious and conditional, should be welcomed and respected wherever it appears.

A few years ago Kolakowski emphasized that the founders of "Marxism" did not solve all the problems which were facing materialistic philosophy, and that its professional supporters seem to have been little aware of this fact. He saw the greatest weakness of "Marxist philosophy" in its inability to ask new questions, its insensitivity to the rise of new issues, its intellectual blindness with respect to new facts and its indifference to every problem that could not be formulated in terms of orthodoxy. He concluded that "Marxism" would not cure itself from ossification and atrophy unless it began asking questions which its opponents failed to ask or managed to solve, and, in general, unless it modernized its conceptual framework the revision of which was overdue.[46]

Orthodox revisionism now accepts Kolakowski's suggestion, for it tacitly recognizes that Marxism-Leninism could not otherwise extricate itself from the intellectual doldrums. Moreover, the abandonment of the nihilistic criticism required that the traditional scope of problems considered in Marxist-Leninist philosophy be extended and include questions so far neglected because of their origin in bourgeois philosophical thought. These problems, Schaff argued, should be taken up and developed on the ground of "Marxist philosophy" before it is too late, that is, before Marxism-Leninism fails entirely to satisfy the intellectual needs of contemporary man.[47]

While the orthodox revisionism of Schaff is mainly due to the pressure exercised by the native philosophical tradition, it is philosophical revisionism which has pushed him to an innovating extension of the traditional Marxist-Leninist philosophical interests. Having first demanded that this expansion should include the philosophy of language, which he calls "semantics"—Schaff published his *Introduction to Semantics* in 1960—he has now moved on in a different direction. He has suggested that Marxism-Leninism should take up a debate with Existentialism and personalism and develop its own philosophical anthropology—which he prefers to call "philosophy of man." This philosophy of man is given a clearly Existentialist orientation and is to take up the themes that belong to the original Existentialist preoccupations. It is to deal with questions concerning the meaning of human existence, what attitude we should take to the irreducible reality of time, in what sense we can say that man molds his life, controls his destiny and is responsible for his acts. It is to face the ultimate situation of existence: the uncertainty of the world, suffering, anxiety, struggle, failure, guilt and death, and to illuminate them all by showing the way that life is to be lived. "Marxist" Existentialism must be materialistic, however, and it cannot endorse Sartre's concept of liberty. Consequently, the encyclopedic philosophy of man, as envisaged by Schaff, having absorbed the problems with which theologians and sages, poets and imaginative writers, Existentialists and moralists, speculative social philosophers and philosophers of history all deal, is to be firmly based on and accommodated within historical materialism.[48]

If we now try to take a general view of the recent developments and trends characteristic for orthodox revisionism, the first thing to be emphasized is the absence of an immanent evolution of thought. Unlike the development of other contemporary philosophical schools, such as analytic or linguistic philosophy, logical empiricism or phenomenology, orthodox revisionism has evolved in response to external stimuli, to the social and intellectual pressures of its environment. We have pointed out, in passing, its heavy debt in ideas to the native tradition of scientific philosophy and to philosophical revisionism. These observations could be multiplied and expanded. Moreover, there is some evidence that it is not a philosopher's search for truth that inspires the endeavors of orthodox revisionists. They do not make any secret of the fact that they are trying to contain and to countervail the "weakening of the influence of Marxism-Leninism," and to use their expected gains in the class struggle for the allegiance of men, that is, that their motive is political and their purpose pragmatic.[49]

This statement must not be understood to imply that orthodox revisionism should be dismissed and ignored, as a political trend without theoretical significance and implications. This conclusion would be wrong and unjustifiable, for orthodox revisionism did bring about some definite improvements, introduced some measure of tolerance and provided some scope for a free discussion. Moreover, every human act has several consequences, both intended and unintended, and orthodox revisionism is no exception to this rule. But we should not go to the other extreme and assume that orthodox revisionism is an expression of intensive and inventive thinking. The instrumental character of Marxism-Leninism, that is, the subordination of the theoretical and cognitive purpose to the requirements of effective social and political action, has not been altered. Instrumentalism characterized Marxism-Leninism at its inception and has been its *idée maîtresse* ever since; orthodox revisionism has not emancipated itself from this inheritance.

Neither has it freed itself from methodological dogmatism. While it rightly asserts that science knows no irrevocable truths, it recognizes them within its own doctrine: "There are definite limits which no one can transgress if he does not wish to sever his connections with Marxism." We can take comfort in the fact that the number of dogmas decreases and their content slowly evaporates into thin air. But as long as this dogmatic attitude prevails, freedom of thought is not secure and Marxism-Leninism continues to be a threat to the advancement of knowledge.

PHILOSOPHIC REVISIONISM

The fundamental factor which differentiates the philosophic revisionist from the orthodox, and which entails all the other differences, is the rejection by the philosophic revisionist of methodological dogmatism in every form. He adheres without any restriction to the rule that Marx recommended to his followers: *de omnibus dubitandum.* In his view, the establishment of incontrovertible truth is incompatible with the nature of science and holds back the advancement of knowledge. The scientific attitude means criticizing everything.

Every kind of restriction on the rule of methodical rationalistic doubt, he believes, leads to dogmatism and, ultimately, to an overt or concealed oppression of thought. If a list of incontrovertible truths, the validity of which cannot be critically examined, is accepted, philosophic thinking degenerates into apologetics and exposition of views fixed in advance, based neither on observation nor on inference. Furthermore, if there is a repository of incontrovertible truths, there emerges in its wake one form or another of extra-scientific control over science and scholarship. Truths do not come from nowhere. They have to be formulated and there must, therefore, be a group of individuals who decide authoritatively which truths are to be included in the list. These individuals must be powerful enough to protect them from the destructive impact of rational criticism. No dogmatism is able to survive on its own; it needs the support of legitimized violence which by means of various restrictions and controls over thinking minds makes dogma-

tism secure. But under the protection of authority and administrative
prohibitions the difference between truth and falsehood, myth and
reality disappears. To define in advance the limits of permissible discussion is always wrong and ineffective; ultimately it only exposes the
theoretical weakness of the views protected by administrative privileges.

The communist party does not need intellectuals in order that they admire
the wisdom of its decisions but only in order that its decisions be wise. Thus,
they are needed by communism as men free in their thinking; as opportunists
they are expendable. . . . . Communist intellectuals defending independent thinking from the pressure of politics are acting not only in the name of an abstractly
conceived freedom of science, but also for the sake of the interests of
communism.[50]

Kolakowski maintains that an unrestricted freedom of investigation,
of the choice of methods, of thought and expression is a necessary condition before thought, being free, may search for truth and be useful to
a revolutionary movement. It is imperative that a movement that aspires
to effect a complete reconstruction of social life in every respect should
be able to make use of a theory constantly revised and modernized.
Only on this condition can a revolutionary movement retain its position
in promoting social changes in the world, only then can it react quickly
to new situations and effectively conduct the struggle for the right of
secular thought.

It is harmful to restrict scientific inquiry in any way for political
reasons and to announce in advance that a definite result of such
inquiry is true and politically correct. The imposition of definite results
on scientific research implies the demand to provide justification for
views which might be the object of faith but are no concern of science.
To define some beliefs as incontrovertible is dangerous and reckless in
its theoretical and practical consequences, and abolishes the distinction
between science and theology.

Communist intellectuals have the duty but also the right, to bear responsibility
for the ideological development of the revolutionary movement. They have,
however, neither the duty nor the right to adopt for this purpose any assumption recognized in advanced as being exempt from rational control and
discussion.[51]

Adherence to these principles calls for a revision of the whole
Marxian tradition, distorted by the codifiers and lost in the discussions
on "authentic Marxism," with which orthodoxy has nothing but its
name in common. The attitude of philosophic revisionism to the Marxian
tradition has been formulated by Kolakowski in his essay *Permanent
and Transitory Aspects of Marxism*.[52] Its main findings have determined
the direction in which philosophic revisionism has continued to develop.

The main problem facing a Marxian scholar today can be reduced
to the question: Are there any objective criteria for an unambiguous

decision as to what is and what is not "authentic Marxism"? Before approaching this problem another issue must first be clarified: the term "Marxism" must be defined. The ambiguity of meaning makes "Marxism" an ideological label and a war-call rather than a term designating certain intellectual attitudes or a set of philosophical propositions.

"Marxism" might be considered to mean "institutional Marxism" in the sense given to this term by Stanislaw Ossowski.[53] Ossowski examined institutional Marxism as a social and political phenomenon and gave a sociological analysis of it in terms of Durkheim's sociology of religion. While accepting Ossowski's sociological analysis, Kolakowski was interested in a definition of institutional Marxism which would ascribe its philosophical content, rather than its social function.

This is not feasible, however, for the content of institutional Marxism cannot be described by enumerating its accepted views. The views known at a particular time to be eternal verities are in fact alterable according to the requirements of time and place. The supposed incontrovertible truths turn out to be the necessities and beliefs of the hour imposed as political orthodoxies. For instance, until February 1956 only an anti-Marxist, a reformist, a metaphysician—in brief, an idealist could believe that socialism might be achieved without a revolution. Since February 1956 the former idealist has become a genuine Marxist and the former genuine Marxist has assumed the role of an anti-party idealist. The content of institutional Marxism can be defined precisely only in one way, namely, by indicating an Office or an Authority with which the content obligatory at a given moment is deposited. A supporter of institutional Marxism is not a man with definite views but one ready to recognize institutionally approved beliefs.

Orthodox revisionism has some characteristics in common with institutional Marxism. The distinction between a creative and an erroneous revision presupposes the recognition of an Office or an Authority, which acts as an umpire and pronounces its verdict on the controversial issues. Moreover, an orthodox revisionist knows for certain that there are limits that cannot be transgressed by a true believer, but he is reluctant to say where these limits should be drawn, for this is the privilege of the Office.

The term "Marxism" also refers to various attempts to apply Marx's conceptual apparatus in the analysis of events and developments not considered by Marx himself. Bernstein, Kautsky, Plekhanov, Lenin, Trotsky, Bukharin, Lukacs, Bloch and many others are called Marxist in just this sense. It is with respect to this group of writers and thinkers that there is a constant controversy as to whether they deserve the name of Marxists. The controversy over "authentic Marxism" is closely associated with another, namely whether all thinking men can be divided into Marxists and non-Marxists or whether such a division should be abandoned as irrelevant.

According to Kolakowski these controversies are purely verbal. Let us take as an example a sociologist or an economist who, by applying the Marxian theory of classes in the analysis of contemporary societies, reaches the conclusion that the predictions, based on the Marxian theory, concerning the polarization of the proletariat and the bourgeoisie or the progressive pauperization of the working class have not been confirmed. One could say that this conclusion deviates from the teaching of Marx in one respect and follows it in another. For the findings are not compatible with the theories of Marx, but the conclusion, the rejection of a hypothesis disconfirmed by facts, is fully compatible with the methodological rule that was recognized by Marx.

Since Marx's death, economics, sociology and historiography have made a great advance. Whole new areas of facts have been opened to research, new theories and concepts have been formulated, and new methods have been tried out and applied. Is Max Weber's theory of ideal types idealistic, that is, non-Marxist, as Schaff asserts, or is it only an unsuccessful attempt to construct models in the historical and social sciences, not without some methodological merits, as Lange believes? Should one reject Lenin's philosophic definition of matter in the light of new discoveries in physics, as Helena Eilstein suggests, or guard it as the apple of one's eyes, as Nowinski recommends? Such questions could be multiplied at will. Is there any rational justification for qualifying as "Marxist" or "non-Marxist" such theories as functionalism in sociology and social anthropology, such research methods as questionnaire technique and the input-output analysis in sociology and economics, such new disciplines as psychoanalysis or philosophy of language?

In the natural course of events, according to Kolakowski, the division of scholars and scientists into "Marxist" and "non-Marxist" has lost significance and become meaningless. One can rightly say that there are a number of views which are typically Marxian. This can be said about the views that the division of society into classes is of basic importance in the analysis of social and historical phenomena; that the thinking of the scholar is exposed to limitations and distortions determined by the specific social conditions of his life; that the moralizing approach in the evaluation of historical events should be abandoned; that the nature of man is not immutable but that it is the product of his social history; that the social sciences have both a cognitive and a practical purpose, that they should be applied to further the abolition of class divisions, the realization of egalitarianism, the emancipation of men from toil and exploitation. It is enough, however, to formulate these Marxian beliefs to realize that they have been accepted by all, including those who for other reasons could be classified as "non-Marxists," and that these ideas have entered the blood stream of science and scholarship, thus losing their former typically Marxian character. As far as more specific Marxian hypotheses are concerned, not all of them have withstood the test of time and confirmation, others have been reformulated or more precisely stated and included in the common stock of knowledge. These developments only testify to the advancement of knowledge. There is no reason to mourn over the fact that Marxism as a distinct school of thought, as a sum total of views originated by Marx, is losing its importance in the social and historical sciences and is gradually bound to disappear altogether. The names of Newton, Linnaeus, Harvey or Gauss suffer no depreciation although there exists no "Newtonism," "Linnaeism," "Harveyism" or "Gaussism" today.

The greatest triumph of an eminent scholar comes precisely when his achievements cease to be a separate school of thought; when they melt into the very tissue of scientific life and become a component part of it, losing in the process their separate existence. This process is, of course, different and much slower in the social sciences and humanities, but even there it is an essential part of progress.[54]

The position of Marx in philosophy is different. Friedrich Waismann said that what is deeply exciting about philosophy is not the clarifying of thought or the correct use of language or any other of the things ascribed to philosophy today. If he were to express it in a single word he would say without hesitation that it is a matter of vision.

What is decisive is a new way of seeing and, what goes with it, the will to transform the whole intellectual scene. This is the real thing and everything else is subservient to it.[55]

Kolakowski shares a similar view of philosophy. The value and greatness of a philosophic system lie not in its specific content but in its breaking through inherited preconceptions and conventions, in its new way of perceiving the world. The Marxian system as a vision of the world retains its original significance just as Platonism or Cartesianism does.

"Marxism" in this meaning of the term does not refer to a doctrine which can be either accepted as a whole or rejected as a whole. It does not mean a universal system but a vibrant philosophical inspiration, affecting our whole way of looking at the world; a stimulus forever active in the social intelligence and social memory of mankind. Its permanent validity is a consequence of the new and ever-important perspectives which it opened to us: enabling us to look at human affairs through the prism of universal history; to see, on the one hand, how man in society is formed in the struggle against nature, and, on the other hand, the simultaneous process of humanizing nature by man's work; to consider thinking as a product of practical activity; to unmask myths of consciousness as being the result of ever-recurring alienations in social existence and to trace them back to their proper sources. These perspectives enable us, furthermore, to analyze social existence with its incessant conflicts and struggles. These conflicts and struggles, these countless multitudes of individual goals and desires, individual sufferings and disappointments, individual defeats and victories, present nonetheless a picture of a general evolution which—we have every right to believe—means, in the grand scale of history, not retrogression but progress.[56]

The Two Revisionisms Compared A confrontation of orthodox and philosophic revisionism was necessary in order to reveal their deep and essential differences. Orthodox revisionism originates in political interests. Sensitive to opinion, exposed to the pressure of scholars and scientists, and aware of its own precarious situation, orthodox revisionism has undertaken a reconstruction of orthodoxy to make of it a more effective instrument of social action.

Philosophic revisionism, on the other hand, is a philosophic trend. This is shown by its rationalistic and critical attitude as well as by its readiness to re-examine and test every view, whenever there are reasons to do so. The analysis of philosophical issues is a logical procedure. Its results are not subject to sanctions or evaluations made from a practical point of view, to be judged by politically favorable or unfavorable (alleged or real) consequences which they might involve. Philosophic revisionism rejects the division of views into those which are and those which are not methodologically irrevocable, for neither observation nor reasoning justify such a principle of division. No view is incontrovertible, for no view can claim conclusive evidence. We can hope to attain scientific objectivity if and only if every view and presupposition can be freely criticized. The test of the rationality of our beliefs consists in their being permanently subject to discussion, to further investigation and logical control. Neither the belief in the truth of our views nor a subjectively felt need for such belief constitutes an objective criterion of truth. Durkheim pointed out that "sentiments," whether they pertain to physical or social things, "enjoy no privilege not possessed by other sentiments, for their origin is the same. . . . Sentiment is a subject for scientific study, not the criterion of scientific truth." [57]

Orthodox revisionism is dogmatic, instrumentalist and irrationalistic; philosophical revisionism is anti-dogmatic, critical and anti-irrationalistic. For these reasons the latter, rather than the former, manifests orientations closely akin to the scientific attitude, according to which every truth is regarded as transitory and superior to others only if it is better confirmed and thus more probable in the light of the knowledge available at the time. As Bertrand Russell has said:

The triumphs of science are due to the substitution of observation and inference for authority. Every attempt to revive authority in intellectual matters is a retrograde step. And it is part of the scientific attitude that the pronouncements of science do not claim to be certain, but only the most probable on the basis of present evidence. One of the great benefits that science confers upon those who understand its spirit is that it enables them to live without the delusive support of subjective authority.[58]

The clash of the orthodox and the philosophic revisionists is a conflict between those who are anxious to act effectively and those who wish to think correctly. Our personal and social experience seems to justify the opinion that effective action depends on knowledge, and not conversely, for he who subordinates his thinking to the requirements of action does not, as a rule, act effectively or think rightly. The orthodox revisionists appear now to recognize the truth of this, for they blame their instrumentalist approach, "a too narrowly conceived practicism," for their errors in the past. Still, the orthodox revisionists are unable to shake themselves free from their inveterate habits. Because ideology holds the highest rank in their hierarchy of values, they continue to support theories justifying views accepted in advance. Moreover, making use of these theories in support of a great variety of beliefs and practical proposals, they are bound the more to value these theories, the more vague and ambiguous they are. Finally, while the orthodox revisionists have reduced the number of incontrovertible truths and "correct views," they have never abandoned them entirely and unconditionally. They are in full agreement with the so-called highest authority in the state, that is, with the leaders of the communist party, that "there can be no creative Marxism against the ideological principles of the party policy."[59]

THE LAST STAGE IN THE DEVELOPMENT OF PHILOSOPHIC REVISIONISM

It was mentioned earlier that the moral orientation is one of the characteristic features of philosophic revisionism. For those of the philosophic revisionists who are natural scientists, sociologists, economists, historians and philosophers interested in the theory and methodology of science, the re-discovery of the principle of the individual's moral autonomy and responsibility constituted the end of their revisionist activities. Before Descartes set out on his intellectual journey he provided himself with some moral maxims which allowed him to remain resolute in his action while his reason compelled him to suspend his judgment. Having acquired in the principle of moral autonomy and responsibility the Cartesian code of morals, this group of philosophic revisionists were able to resume their scientific studies without further delay. Their revisionism consisted in the emancipation of their minds from the political pressure which was undermining the integrity and independence of thought. Once this task was accomplished there remained nothing that differentiated them from their fellow scholars methodologically.

The case is different with those revisionists who suddenly halted between philosophic and orthodox revisionism and gradually returned under the protective wings of the orthodoxy. Their revisionist past makes of them ambivalent personalities and minds, split between the attraction of intellectual work emancipated from ideological determination and the orthodox position demanding from them the defense of certain definite views and the rejection of others for the sake of "the internal consistency of the Marxist system." The problem of the philosophic revisionists who converted back to orthodoxy might interest the psychologist and sociologist, but there is nothing to be said about them from a philosophic point of view. People may be inclined to accept a system of beliefs be-

cause it justifies their behavior. Practical considerations, wrote L. J.
Russell, tend to "sanction types of action previously condemned or to
condemn types of action previously sanctioned." [60] If this happens,
views once approved have to be replaced by beliefs more in harmony
with the type of life which people lead.

Finally, there remains a group of philosophic revisionists whose main
object of interest is neither natural science nor any discipline of the
humanities and of the social sciences, nor scientific philosophy, but a
humanistically oriented philosophy. Leszek Kolakowski is the most
prominent representative of this trend. In what direction does the
evolution of their views now move? In what relation do these
views stand to their position in moral philosophy and philosophical
anthropology?

By humanistic philosophy should be understood that trend of
philosophical thought which emphasizes the specificity of the problems
examined in the humanities and which is opposed to the application of
the scientific method to philosophy. Thinkers who are most representative for humanistic philosophy excel, as a rule, in the history of
philosophical thought and make their knowledge in this particular
domain the subject matter of their meta-theoretical investigations. They
examine different types of *Weltanschauungen*, of attitudes toward the
world and life; they try to discover their structural and typological
traits as well as their social and historical functions. They believe that
in this way they can reach a vantage point from which they are able to
view the whole course of the philosophical history of man, the various
attempts to answer the questions concerning the meaning of life, man's
place in nature and the relation of the individual to society. The final
aim of all these endeavors is both to gain understanding and to illuminate the way life is to be lived. On this account humanistic philosophy is also called *the philosophy of life*.

Kolakowski represents this trend in philosophy. He ascribes to it a
particular importance at the present time in view of the widespread
influence of technocratic ideologies which expect to solve specifically
social problems by purely technical means. At present, one of the main
tasks of humanistic philosophy is to formulate ideas likely to foster
social bonds and coherence among men that would countervail atomiz-
ing tendencies in modern societies. These tendencies grow in strength
owing to the increasing power of technocratic ideas over the human
mind.[61]

According to Kolakowski, philosophy is a humanistic discipline:

The component elements of the world, perceived in philosophical reflection,
are not singled out by the thinker because knowledge of them is essential for
human skill in controlling nature. They are chosen for attention in view of the
fact that knowledge of them influences and molds the relations among men as
social beings. . . . A specific feature of a cognitive philosophical attitude is the
humanization of every object of knowledge. The proper meaning of any knowledge about the world is only then discovered in philosophy when its practical
and human meaning is revealed.[62]

The meaning to which Kolakowski refers is the significance and importance of a fact, a theory or a *Weltanschauung* for the transformation of the social and moral attitudes of men. This makes of philosophy a humanistic, that is, an evaluating discipline; it gives it an "anthropocentric" orientation and includes it in Hume's "science of man"; it attributes to it a practical function reflected in its significance for man's moral life.[63]

Being committed to this conception of philosophy, Kolakowski never hesitates to answer questions with no verifiable solution which, however, call for an immediate answer in view of a wide and deep interest in them and of their significance for social behavior. For this reason also, Kolakowski rejects the "positivistic rationalism" accepted by a great majority of his contemporaries and fellow thinkers. The concepts of verifiability and meaningfulness used in logical empiricism do not coincide with the sense of these terms as applied in everyday life and the practical activity of men. Humanistic philosophy rejects the "absolute in every form," and consequently must also reject the "absolute" of logical empiricism that restricts philosophy to the investigation of the foundations of science and to the logical systematization of scientific knowledge as a whole.[64]

Kolakowski starts from an assumption, to be found in the philosophy of Marx, that man holds a unique position in the world of natural science, for he is able not only to adapt himself to the environment but also to create. This creative power is responsible for the fact that man, a component part of the natural world, emancipates himself from and opposes himself to nature. As man severs his direct dependence upon nature, he gradually gains the awareness that "whatever he might be and whatever he might become, he owes only to himself," above all to his reason, which is his main instrument for finding his bearings in the world. This awareness is acquired by man only at the age of historical maturity. It gives rise to the ideology of rationalism, to an intellectual reflection of the situation in which man realizes his exclusive responsibility for himself with all the consequences implied by it.

The basic assumptions of the ideology of rationalism are clearly derived from the "young Marx." They underlie Marx's speculations in his youthful work *The Economic and Philosophic Manuscripts of 1844* and Kolakowski's own interpretation of it given in the already-mentioned contribution, *Karl Marx and the Classical Definition of Truth*. But probably neither the young Marx nor Kolakowski was aware of the fact that he was following in Kant's footsteps and exploring Kant's conception of Enlightenment. To quote Kant himself:

Enlightenment is the emergence of man from his self-incurred minority. Minority is incapacity to use one's reason without the guidance of another. This minority is self-incurred if its cause is not due to the lack of reason but of determination and courage to exercise reason without the guidance of another. *Sapere aude!* Have the courage to take advantage of your own reason is thus the motto of the Enlightenment.[65]

Man attains historical maturity by his involvement in social life, by the advancement of arts and knowledge, which express his strivings for self-fulfillment. Although he emerged from nature, he can attain the goals of his aspirations only in opposition to nature. The laws which man wants to follow and realize in social life are not those discovered by natural science. "Social progress means a checking of the cosmic process at every step," said T. H. Huxley in the celebrated address *Evolution and Ethics.* Kolakowski moves in the same direction. The creative power of man allows him to discover that he depends only on himself—this is not, as we shall see, another variation on the Existentialist theme of "living in a world without God"—and this knowledge about the world and himself gives rise to his sense of moral responsibility and of responsibility for himself. The history of man's efforts to achieve moral and intellectual maturity is expressed in his successive views of the world and life.

The principle of moral autonomy and responsibility of the individual and the principle of intellectual autonomy and responsibility are complementary. They are only different aspects of the individual acting in a world of natural necessity, social determination and moral obligation. The situations by which the individual is faced and which he creates by his defiance of nature require a total mobilization of his intellectual and moral resources. This should be clear if one realizes that most of the views of the world and life are a "collection of instruments by means of which man gives up his own responsibility and tries to extend his childhood indefinitely."[66] They are the means of silencing the mature consciousness by surrendering personal responsibility and obligation to some cosmic principle or human agency, by subordinating one's own decisions to providence or revelation, to historical necessity or inevitable progress, to ideology or to authority, to biological predestination or to natural fate. Each of these cosmic or human agencies reflected in various views of the world might be transformed into a dogma "inhibiting intellectually and coercing morally." Each of them carries a temptation to find in it a permanent refuge from our responsibility for ourselves and with respect to ourselves. The ideology of rationalism is an attitude that makes us ready to withstand and reject such temptations that render the mind insensible to the unknown possibilities in the world and unwilling to accept self-reliance in all matters.

Rationalism demands that every point of view be regarded as a tentative approach. It demands tolerance for the possibilities that are still unexplored and an awareness of the fact that it is humiliating to act as if something, whatever it might be—God, the doctrine or fate—might take over our own toil, for it can never reveal to us that it is capable of it.[67]

Every absolute truth is a relic of the human consciousness at the stage of historical childhood and an attempt to repudiate our self-reliance. In contradistinction to this inertial inclination, rationalism sharpens the mind's awareness to what is not yet accomplished, what remains still unknown and concealed in the future. It accepts the risk of error associated with it but rejects the hazard incurred in venturing upon the risk of a dogma. Rationalism is not a confession of despair and loneliness, but an attitude expressing hope, the philosophy of an "unfulfilled world" and of a "permanently unfulfilled man." The impossibility of accounting for the presence and action of man in the world by appealing to some transcendent reasons or causes outside him may allow us to view the future as contingent, unknown and undetermined. The ideology of rationalism is the "gay science" of a fully emancipated mind.

Having described Kolakowski's path from philosophic revisionism to his own sort of humanistic philosophy we can take leave of him and wish him farewell. We take leave of him with a feeling of affection, which his indomitable spirit inspires, and with a feeling of respect for all his achievement. People inclined to identify political power with authority, and realism with an exclusive concern with political power, have announced that revisionism in Poland and elsewhere has collapsed. They unwittingly follow in the footsteps of past and present authoritarian rulers who think of intellectual issues as pure epiphenomena and as matters to be administratively managed. We do not share this viewpoint nor this verdict, which in the light of the evidence submitted in the preceding pages would seem to be premature and unjustifiable.

Philosophic revisionism, which has been a primary cause of recent social upheaval, has not been extinguished. One of its stages has been completed, only to open the way for a new one. Taking leave of Kolakowski, the philosophical revisionist, we welcome at the same time a young thinker who considers the emancipation of the mind from all dogmatism and restrictions, self- or otherwise imposed, as the aim and calling of the philosopher. The scope of Kolakowski's activities has been extended. The revisionist of a certain form of orthodoxy obstructing progress toward the historical maturity of the mind has become an iconoclast of all absolute doctrines that block the field of intellectual vision and conceal the "plurality of reality" from men's perception of the world.

NOTES

1. *Nowe Drogi*, 1959, 4/118, p. 80.
2. A. Schaff, *Spor o zagadnienia moralnosci*, Warszawa, Ksiazka i Wiedza, 1958, pp. 56-70.
3. S. Zolkiewski, *Kultura i polityka*, Warszawa, PIW, 1958, pp. 205-211; *Perspektywy literatury XX wieku*, Warszawa, PIW 1960, pp. 121-123; *Nauka Polska* IX, 1961, 1/33, p. 27.
4. T. Kotarbinski, *Wybor pism*, T. 2, Warszawa, PWN, 1958, p. 192.
5. A. Schaff, *op. cit.*, p. 31; S. Zolkiewski, *Nowe Drogi* 1959, 7/121, p. 68.
6. W. Gomulka, *Przemowienia*, T. 2, Warszawa, Ksiazka i Wiedza, 1959, p. 19.
7. A. Schaff, *op. cit.* pp. 30-34.
8. A. Schaff, *op. cit.* pp. 29-30.

9. A. Schaff, *Nowe Drogi* 1961, 3/142, p. 81.

10. This inference comes from another publication of Schaff; see A. Schaff, *Marksizm a egzystencjalizm*, Warszawa, Ksiazka i Wiedza, 1961, p. 126.

11. The qualification "closed" is used here in the same sense in which Karl Popper applied it in *The Open Society and Its Enemies*. A doctrine is closed if it is a system of beliefs buttressed by magical taboos; a doctrine is open if it is accepted on the authority of one's own intelligence and thus liable to revision at any time.

12. The functional conception of ideology was recently discussed by J. Hochfeld in *Studia Filozoficzne* 1960, 6/21.

13. See D. Joravsky, *Soviet Marxism and Natural Science*, London, Routledge and Kegan Paul, 1961, p. 14.

14. E. Durkheim, *The Rules of Sociological Method*, Chicago, The University of Chicago Press, 1938, p. 123.

15. See A. Schaff, *Nowe Drogi* 1959, 13/127, p. 17; *Marksizm a egzystencjalizm*, pp. 9-10.

16. L. Kolakowski, *Studia Filozoficzne* 1959, 2/11. Kolakowski was sharply criticized by Schaff in *Nowe Drogi* 1959, 13/127.

17. Cambridge University Press, 1961.

18. Cz. Nowinski, "Filozofia zaangazowania," *Kultura i Spoleczenstwo* IV, 1960, No. 1-2.

19. K. Kautsky, *Der Weg zur Macht*, 3. Aufl. Berlin 1920, p. 15; E. Bernstein in *Sozialistische Auslandspolitik*, No. 7, 1915, quoted in E. Matthias, "Kautsky und der Kautskyanismus," *Marxismusstudien* (Tuebingen), 2. Folge, 1957, p. 165, 168.

20. Bernstein could have referred to the fact that Engels shared some of his views toward the end of his life. See Ch. Gneuss, "Um den Einklang von Theorie und Praxis, Eduard Bernstein und der Revisionismus," *Marxismusstudien* (Tuebingen), 2. Folge, 1957, pp. 198-226.

21. E. Bernstein, *Wie ist wissenschaftlicher Sozialismus moeglich?*, Berlin, Verlag der Sozialistischen Monatshefte, 1901, pp. 18-19.

22. K. Kautsky, *Ethik und materialistische Geschichtsauffassung*, Stuttgart, 1910, p. 144, cf. pp. 141-142.

23. As far as the concept of meta-dogmata is concerned, see T. Blakeley, "Method in Soviet Philosophy," in J. M. Bochenski and T. J. Blakeley (Eds.), *Studies in Soviet Thought*, Dordrecht, D. Reidel Publishing Company, 1961, pp. 17-27. Probably every comprehensive view of the world has its own meta-dogmata. For instance, as Popper observed, the rationalist attitude presupposes faith in reason which could be described as its meta-dogma. See *The Open Society and Its Enemies*, Chapter 24, II. This dose not mean that there are no differences in universality between various meta-dogmata, by which they can be evaluated.

24. D. Hume, *The Treatise on Human Nature*, III, Pt. I, 1.

25. K. Popper, *The Open Society and Its Enemies*, Princeton, University Press, 1950, p. 62.

26. S. Zolkiewski, *Kultura i polityka*, pp. 277-286. On the other hand, Schaff made exactly the opposite objection and accused Popper of adopting the "Kantian axiology"; see A. Schaff, *Obiektywny charakter praw historii*, Warszawa, PWN, 1955, pp. 115-116, 133-138. Popper's contributions to the philosophy and methodology of science aroused an unconcealed and intransigent hostility among political scholars in the Soviet-bloc countries, the reasons of which one can guess without being able to forget the lack of courtesy to a philosopher clearly greatly superior to his opponents.

27. One of the clearest, though not entirely satisfactory expositions of this view, held by the German revisionists, can be found in E. Bernstein, *Wie ist wissenschaftlicher Sozialismus moeglich*, pp. 18-22, 32-38. That so-called scientific socialism involves contradiction is an opinion widely held and often explained in detail. One of the best analyses was provided by H. B. Acton, *The Illusion of the*

Epoch, London, Cohen and West, 1955. So far, however, nobody seems to have drawn the conclusion therefrom that the Marxian doctrine involves the inevitability of revisionism.

28. Notwithstanding the respect due to Kautsky for his integrity and a long life devoted to a single noble purpose, it should be frankly stated that *Ethik und materialistische Geschichtsauffassung* is a work of almost childlike philosophical naiveté. Although Marxist-Leninists everywhere took serious exception to this little book, they nevertheless used its arguments against the Kantian ethics and have done so until quite recently. It is worthwhile emphasizing that Kautsky is criticized today not only for his social Darwinism, but also for his endorsement of strict determinism. See Marek Fritzhand's Introduction to the Polish translation of *Ethik und materialistische Geschichtsauffassung,* republished in 1959 (Warszawa, Ksiazka i Wiedza).

29. L. Kolakowski, "History and Responsibility," *Nowa Kultura* VIII, 1957, 38/391, p. 4. Although Kolakowski was classified as a "liquidator" on account of this view and others derived from it, the view itself is now accepted by the orthodox revisionists. See A. Schaff, *Marksizm a egzystencjalizm,* pp. 83-84.

30. L. Kolakowski, *op. cit. Nowa Kultura* VIII, 1957, 37/390, p. 4.

31. A. Schaff, *Spor o zagadnienia moralnosci,* p. 66. Kolakowski replied to this objection in "Zakresowe i funkcjonalne rozumienie filozofii," *Kultura i Spoleczenstwo* VI, 1962, No. 1, p. 11.

32. L. Kolakowski, "History and Responsibility," *Nowa Kultura* VIII, 1957, 37/390, p. 4.

33. L. Kolakowski, *Swiatopoglad i zycie codzienne,* Warszawa, PIW, 1957, p. 117. This essay is an expanded version of the paper read at the conference of the Philosophical Section of the German Academy of Science in East Berlin, held March 8-10, 1956, devoted to "The Problem of Freedom in the Light of Scientific Socialism." Among other speakers at this conference were E. Bloch and W. Harich. The addresses delivered at the conference and the discussions were published in a separate volume by *Akademie Verlag* (Berlin, 1956) but it was soon withdrawn from circulation. It is now a bibliographical rarity.

34. L. Kolakowski, "History and Responsibility," *Nowa Kultura* VIII, 1957, 37/390, p. 5. Some of these views were later incorporated into the orthodox doctrine. See A. Schaff, *Spor o zagadnienia moralnosci,* pp. 94-95, *Marksizm a egzystencjalizm,* pp. 83-84, 105-110.

35. L. Kolakowski, *op. cit. Nowa Kultura* VIII, 1957, 36/389, p. 4.

36. For some further details see Z. Jordan, "The Development of Philosophy and Marxism-Leninism in Poland since the War" in J. M. Bochenski and T. Blakeley (Eds.), *Studies in Soviet Thought,* Dordrecht, D. Reidel Publishing Company, 1961, pp. 92-93.

37. See A. Schaff, *Obiektywny charakter praw historii,* p. 29.

38. O. Lange, *Ekonomia polityczna,* T. 1, Warszawa, PWN, 1959, pp. 276-294. While teaching in the United States, Lange published the article "The Scope and Method of Economics" (*Review of Economic Studies,* 13, 1945/46), which was reprinted in H. Feigl and M. Brodbeck (Eds.), *Readings in the Philosophy of Science,* New York, Appleton-Century-Crofts, 1953, pp. 744-754. In this paper Lange produced a similar argument, but in a more scholarly way than he did in *Ekonomia Polityczna,* and thus also more persuasive.

39. Reprinted in *Swiatopoglad i zycie codzienne.*

40. The most important of these articles are to be found in *Nauka Polska* II, 1954, 1/5, 3/7, 4/8; III, 1955, 2/10, *Przeglad Kulturalny* IV, 1955, 39/159, 41/161.

41. See e.g. Tadeusz Kotarbinski's forceful plea published in *Przeglad Kulturalny* (X, 1961, 43/478), followed by statements of Leopold Infeld, Roman Ingarden, Julian Krzyzanowski, Wladyslaw Wolter, Stanislaw Ehrlich, Wlodzimierz Zonn, to which Henryk Jablonski replied with a blunt "no," Stefan Zolkiewski and Adam

Schaff with a more gentle but no less firm refusal, put in evasive and ambiguous terms. See *Przeglad Kulturalny* X, 1961, 47/482, 48/483, 49/484, 50/485, XI, 1962, 2/489, 3/490, 8/495, 9/496, *Zycie Warszawy*, December 9, 1961.

42. J. Paul Sartre, "Marksizm i egzystencjalizm," *Tworczosc*, 1957, No. 4, pp. 33-79. This article has been incorporated with some changes into Sartre's latest work *Critique de la raison dialectique* and makes up its first two chapters.

43. A. Schaff, *Wstep do semantyki*, Warszawa, PWN, 1960, pp. 90-93, 350-351.

44. L. Kolakowski, *Nowe Drogi* 1956, 9/87, p. 27.

45. M. Kokoszynska, *Studia Filozoficzne* 1961, 1/22, p. 147.

46. L. Kolakowski, *Swiatopoglad i zycie codzienne*, pp. 61-66.

47. A. Schaff, *Marksizm a egzystencjalizm*, pp. 44-46, *Nowe Drogi* 1961, 3/142, p. 80.

48. A. Schaff, *Marksizm a egzystencjalizm*, pp. 130-133.

49. A. Schaff, *op. cit.* p. 47.

50. L. Kolakowski, *Nowe Drogi* 1956, 9/87, p. 31.

51. L. Kolakowski, *op. cit.* p. 29.

52. This essay, originally published in *Nowa Kultura* VIII, 1957, 4/357, was translated into English and published in P. Mayewski (Ed.), *The Broken Mirror, A Collection of Writings from Contemporary Poland*, New York, Random House, 1958, pp. 157-174. Direct quotations from Kolakowski's essay make use of this translation.

53. S. Ossowski, "Doktryna marksistowska na tle dzisiejszej epoki," *Mysl Wspolczesna* 1947, 12/19.

54. L. Kolakowski, *Permanent and Transitory Aspects of Marxism*, p. 173 (translation of George Krzywicki).

55. F. Waismann, "How I see Philosophy," in H. D. Lewis (Ed.), *Contemporary British Philosophy, Personal Statements*, London, Allen and Unwin, 1956, p. 483.

56. L. Kolakowski, *op. cit.* p. 174.

57. E. Durkheim, *The Rules of Sociological Method*, pp. 33-34.

58. Bertrand Russell, *The Impact of Science on Society*, London, Allen and Unwin, 1952, pp. 110-111.

59. *Polityka* II, 1958, 50/94, p. 3.

60. L. J. Russell, "Belief and Action" in H. D. Lewis (Ed.), *Contemporary British Philosophy, Personal Statements*, p. 405.

61. L. Kolakowski, *Kultura i Spoleczenstwo* IV, 1960, No. 1-2, pp. 77-78.

62. L. Kolakowski, *Swiatopoglad i zycie codzienne*, pp. 23-24.

63. L. Kolakowski, *op. cit.* p. 23, 25. Cf. L. Kolakowski, *Kultura i Spoleczenstwo*, VI, 1962, No. 1, pp. 3-19.

64. L. Kolakowski, *Argumenty* III, 1959, 19/48.

65. I. Kant, "Was ist Aufklaerung," *Ausgewaehlte kleine Schriften*, Leipzig, Verlag von Felix Meiner, n.d., p. 1. Bertrand Russell's famous essay "A Free Man's Worship" (published in the collection *Mysticism and Logic*), expresses a similar point of view. See also its most recent restatement in K. R. Popper's *The Open Society and Its Enemies*, Chapter 5, II-V.

66. L. Kolakowski, *op. cit.* p. 8.

67. L. Kolakowski, *ibid.* p. 8.

PART FOUR

VARIETIES OF
DEMOCRATIC IDEOLOGIES

INTRODUCTORY NOTE

Are the main democratic ideologies being reformulated with reference to basic democratic tenets or to their own historical foundations? How do democratic influences fare in a world torn by violent ideological conflict? What is new in the contemporary democratic "isms"?

Gordon K. Lewis' opening paragraph in "Twentieth-Century Capitalism and Socialism" sets forth many of the problems involved. Pointing to the American resurgence of conservatism, the British dissatisfaction with the "less attractive aspects" of a welfare-society, plus the suspicion that classical liberalism has "by-passed too easily the moral issues of power and authority," he notes that both American liberals and British Socialists are beginning to re-examine their major assumptions and are now searching for "new doctrinal outlines." Lewis shows the vast sociological and cultural background of the doctrinal dispute over democratic ideologies, and discounts the pseudo-objective, non-committed, tentative, and academic attitudes in the current ideological debate. Referring to the role of the intellectuals, he says: "Not to take a stand on issues is to commit the real *trahison des clercs.* . . ."

There are curious ideational and ideological relationships between various democratic ideologies and the idea of democracy itself. If these ideas—particularly socialism and liberalism—are ideologies, democracy in a sense is not. It does not provide a comprehensive theory of the state, which would include the purpose of government and the place of the individual, expressed in doctrinal terms. Democracy has ideological strains only insofar as it is a "liberal" or "socialistic" democracy; in other respects, it is only a system of government. It is in the latter sense that Francis W. Coker refers to the term "democracy" in his paper, "Some Present-Day Critics of Liberalism."

Conservatism is also in a peculiar position. In his "Conservatism as an Ideology," Samuel P. Huntington argues that "conservatism differs from all other ideologies except radicalism: it lacks what might be termed a substantive ideal. . . . In any society, there may be institutions to be conserved, but there are never conservative institutions. The lack of conservative ideal necessarily vitiates the autonomous definition of conservatism."

Conservatism has been given a number of attributes by the authors represented in this symposium: it is institutional (immanent) as opposed

[290]

to ideational (transcendent); it is positional (static) as opposed to inherent; thus, in Huntington's opinion, it needs no revision or elaboration. In his paper, "The Anatomy of Conservatives," Francis Wilson agrees that there is a situational element in conservatism.

There are divergent views on conservatism's content. "The philosophical content of American conservatism . . . is nebulous," says Lewis. Ludwig Freund, another student of conservatism (not participating in this symposium), speaks of "a whole series of ideologies differentiated by their national environments." Francis Wilson grapples with the intricate problem of defining conservative philosophy: "Any design of ideology must rest on some primary idea of the cosmos," he says. But, he points out, conservatism is a political position, not something stemming from primary philosophical ideas. What most writers on conservatism do, he says, is compose a model "or the design of the ideology [which] . . . constitutes a summary at the surface." In other words, the model is made up of the views held by various articulate intellectuals. However, he says, ". . . it must be conceded that the statement of the ideological paradigm is not a probing philosophical experience." According to Wilson, conservative philosophy rests on a model of the universe, history, and a view of truth. On the other hand, Lewis' tone is skeptical: he speaks of a conservative *mood* rather than of a conservative *philosophy*.

There is some agreement that no dichotomy exists between conservatism and liberalism. Such is Huntington's view. Francis Wilson asserts that any political and intellectual life might be considered either liberal or conservative. He speaks primarily in terms of the American experience: "In America the European Tory system did not take root, and the liberalism of the Europeans became the conservatism of Americans." This is why he feels American conservatism must be "steeped in aspects of the liberal tradition."

The split personality or "self-contradictory" nature of American conservatism arises from the fact that although it is forced to defend liberal values, it shows signs of reaction against the illogicalities of both classical liberalism and modern American liberal thought. Totalitarian ideologies, by entrenching themselves in the world, have increased the conservatives' awareness of the dangers in the liberal ideology, which condones the activities of those seeking to destroy liberal democracy.

Conservatives find in the liberal ideology many values worth preserving. In fact, Peter Viereck, a leading neoconservative writer, claims that "in certain American situations the only thing conservatives find at hand to conserve is—liberalism." What the liberals must realize is the need for espousing certain conservative and static attitudes toward the existing institutions. Huntington argues that "only by surrendering their liberal ideas for the present can liberals successfully defend their liberal institutions for the future. . . . To continue to expound the philosophy of liberalism simply gives the enemy a weapon with which to attack the society of liberalism. The defense of American institu-

tions requires a conscious articulate conservatism which can spring
only from liberals deeply concerned with the preservation of those
institutions."

The problem of liberalism is that its ideals—concrete freedoms in
various aspects of life—have been largely taken over by socialist and
conservative programs. Socialism has now become "democratic socialism."
In his article on "Modern Liberalism," Ernst Bieri asserts that "socialism discovered the fundamental importance of liberal thought for
the protection of freedom and of democracy." Socialism is bound to
adopt liberal goals because many of its own aspirations have been
fulfilled and because it has started to focus its attention on the ends
of reform rather than its means. In his article, "A New Ism for
Socialism," Sidney Hook describes the socialist position as follows:
"Socialists began to realize that large-scale industrialization and mass
culture, whether under capitalism or socialism, often imperil the individual's sense of independence, of integrity, of counting for something. They returned to their original insight that the organization of
production was only a means to an end—to a free, secure, and significant life."

Socialism is detaching itself from its Marxist foundations and is becoming, in Hook's phrase, "a broad movement of social reform." Bieri
speaks of the new socialism as a "proved bulwark against the Communists" and as an expansion and fulfillment of democracy. "The fulfillment is to consist in supplementing the 'merely political' by economic
and social democracy." As David J. Saposs has shown in "The Split
between Asian and Western Socialism," the socialist New Look does
not apply to Asia. The socialist movement in Asia is trying to cut itself
off from Western democratic socialism and is "an obstacle to the
strengthening of democratic forces."

The success of democratic socialism—with its rejection of Marxist
dogmatic philosophy and its swing away from doctrine toward reform
—is an indirect tribute to liberalism. Having displaced the old liberals,
British socialists became not only their heirs in the technical, parliamentary sense, but also preserved their traditional role as advocates of
social equality. The extension of equality in the international sphere,
to the developing nations in particular, is in tune with both that
tradition and the socialist doctrine itself. In this matter British socialism
is not necessarily flexible or fully liberal. But the significance of the
present neoliberal "disguise" is that it helps to reassert the crucial value
of liberal democratic ideals.

Liberalism provides the ideas on which society can thrive, as well as
those very basic assumptions and valuable goals without which democracy
would be but an empty institutional shell. Francis Coker's paper, which
deals with several contemporary critics of liberalism, is also a reassertion of his belief in inviolable freedoms and inalienable rights, in
order, and in consensus—those liberal values which make democracy
strong.

The lack of consensus on the nature of current ideologies of a strictly democratic variety shows the need not merely for reinterpretation of basic postulates, but even more for their formulation. There is no urgent need to preserve historical tradition or continuity of dogma. It seems that there has not been much agreement regarding the nature of foundations. Too much has always been taken for granted. Although the democratic system offers far greater possibilities in the realm of interpretation than does totalitarianism (which is confined to rather definite limits), it offers far fewer incentives in this respect. Despite democracy's doctrinal freedom of interpretation, until now, opportunities have not been pursued with great vigor, except for a few brilliant exceptions, and insuperable difficulties have as a rule been emphasized. As a result, pluralistic tendencies have not been fully investigated, nor have the ideological relationships of various currents been fully explored.

Section I

DEMOCRATIC SOCIALISM

TWENTIETH-CENTURY CAPITALISM AND SOCIALISM: THE PRESENT STATE OF THE ANGLO-AMERICAN DEBATE

Gordon K. Lewis

I

Liberalism, wrote Herzen in a famous sentence, is not the doctor, it is the disease. Within our own generation that doubt has entered the liberal citadel itself and both of its major champions, the American liberal and the British socialist, have been driven into a re-examination of their major assumptions of thought. On the American side, the resurgence of Conservatism as a respectable philosophy, on the British side a growing dissatisfaction with the less attractive aspects of a welfare-society founded upon administrative Fabianism—both of them reinforced by a deep suspicion (as Orwell's popularity is symptomatic) that classical Liberalism by-passed too easily the moral issues of power and authority —has given rise to a search for new doctrinal outlines. There is a new emphasis upon the theme of social order and consensus, in itself a natural outcome of war: in that sense, the spirit of the age is to be compared with that of Augustan England, which was prepared to pay any price to prevent the repetition of the religious wars of the previous century. In England, the emphasis has become an intellectual preoccupation with the secular Establishment as a whole; in the United States it has become an effort to confer intellectual validity upon the dominant institutions—the churches, the business corporation, the entertainment industries—of the society, and an effort, beyond that, of the American

Reprinted from *Western Political Quarterly,* vol. XII, no. 1, Part I (March, 1959), 78-110. By permission of the author and the publisher.

[294]

intellectual to forego the tradition of his willing isolationism classically embodied in *The Education of Henry Adams*. If, indeed, America refused to listen to Adams in the Gilded Age, it listens almost religiously to his successors, so that the social scientist enjoys a contemporary prestige that almost amounts to a Chinese bureaucratization of his function. The outcome of all this is an Anglo-American literature of social and political science that throws interesting light upon the condition of the Western intelligentsia at mid-century.

The literature, of course, must be seen within the framework of the social revolution of the times. Both Conservative and Republican have maintained intact the essential changes, respectively, of the Labour and the New Deal regimes, so that in the American case the radical sentiment has had to go to the edges of the American society—the Puerto Rican problem, the issue of the American Mexican, the Negro case— to satisfy its drive, while in the English case a book like Professor Cole's *Post-war Condition of Britain* catalogues a welfare state so extensive that it has to be compared with the same author's *Condition of Britain* of 1937 for the full scope of the transformation to be recognized. The seminal themes of progressivism—mass destitution, large-scale unemployment, wide disparities of wealth and poverty—have been more or less satisfied, and so far they have not been replaced by preoccupations as compellingly urgent. The result, in politics, has been a return to a period of dull government, for "Butskellism" and Eisenhower Republicanism are nothing much more than rationalizations for electoral tempers which merely desire to consolidate the economic and social gains of the earlier period. It is symptomatic of that temper, to take only one example, that Lord Altrincham's astringent comments in the *National Review* on the British Monarchy should have captured public attention so dramatically, while his intrinsically more important articles in the *Sunday Observer* on a new Toryism should have passed by relatively unnoticed.[1] In social relations, all this has meant the *embourgeoisement* of social classes to such an extent that the suburbanite has become almost a symbol of a new social respectability, while new types—the soldier and the scientist, for example—have entered the power elite as a tribute to the new importance of technology in the modern administrative society. Conversely, there has been a decline in the prestige of older figures, the diplomat, the intellectual, the gentleman-politician, all of whom, as types, have depended less on the sciences than upon the arts for their eminence. It is suggestive, as illustration, that an analysis of the new governing personnel of the British nationalized industries should show that they are predominantly managers, senior technicians, and directors, to the comparative neglect of the types that have traditionally serviced British public bodies —the conventional company man, the retired army officer, the orthodox civil servant.[2]

The figure of the businessman, likewise, has become metamorphosed from the Robber Baron into the dedicated public servant fulfilling a new doctrine of social trusteeship, although there is evidence to suggest, from

the recent studies of *Fortune* magazine, for example, that he is not altogether happy with the façade of half-conscious hypocrisy involved in the
change.[3] The hero-figure of Mr. Cameron Hawley's *Cash McCall* is, in
this sense, an unsatisfactory combination of the old-style business adventurer running roughshod over defeated rivals and the new image
of the business-statesman acting out the role of the cultured gentleman.
All this has meant, too, a rehabilitation of the status of government itself.
Public administration and planning, once Fabian heresies, have become
almost new professions, although that has meant an accompanying
tendency to sacrifice their social purpose to a narrow concern with
method and technique, so that Pope's famous couplet has almost become
the slogan of their practitioners. State, society, business—all in their
turn have become socialized. The old distinctions of the academic textbooks based on Mill and Green—state versus society, the legitimate
province of government, the distinction between self-regarding and other-
regarding actions—have been replaced by the more complex topics of
a more complex social order, although many Oxford textbooks still
manage to ignore the change. Altogether, it is now possible to see that
World War II precipitated to full fruition changes so massive that they
demand a revolution in the basic assumptions of analysis. For wars, as
Marx said of revolutions, are the locomotives of history. Yet contemporary political science has produced nothing like the kind of work—
Calvin's *Institutes*, Rousseau's *Social Contract*, Darwin's *Origin of Species*
—which sums up the new temper of a new age, and gives it form,
rationale, direction; nor has it given birth to the sort of thinker, significantly outside of the academic profession—Veblen, Shaw, the Webbs
—who provocatively states the terms of a new intellectual orientation.
The orientation is there, nonetheless, and the observer can at least sketch
the boundaries of its nature.

II

The decline of intellectual communism, to begin with, has given rise
to a moral rehabilitation of capitalism. In America, it is true, there has
been little of the dramatic apostacy of the European intellectual driven
to deny the infallibility of the Red Pope, odd cases like that of Chambers
excepted. For American liberalism, in fact, never did go much beyond
the basic premises of the American ethic; its individualism, its reliance
upon the individual leader like Roosevelt or Wilson—what Lewis Mum-
ford has termed its "pragmatic acquiescence" in the ideology of wealth
and success. The New Deal increased the power of the state against
economic forces; but it was a power less concerned with investment in
central business enterprise than with government undertakings in
public relief, public works, and subsidies to private enterprise. As H.
G. Wells pointed out early in the century in *The Future in America*,
the progressives were merely the Whigs of a political balance of which

the Republicans were the Tories; and neither possessed in any real strength what Wells termed a "sense of the state." That is why the greatest liberal candidate for the Presidency since Wilson, Adlai Stevenson, was not so much a radical intellectual as a well-educated and sensitive lay gentleman, in the Victorian manner, profoundly conservative, by any European standards, in his social philosophy. As a consequence, the American liberal has had little difficulty in adjusting himself to the new conservative mood, to a society of luxuriant prodigality of material wealth in which perhaps his deepest unhappiness stems from the ability of that society to convert his most angry criticism into a saleable commodity. Even his search for a distinctively American culture can be seen as that return to native grounds which is not new but at least as old as Emerson's address on the American Scholar.

Nothing could better illustrate this than the ease with which the liberal writers have accepted the thesis of the Capitalist Revolution. Professor Berle uses his earlier analysis of the relationship between the modern corporation and private property to present now a view of corporate enterprise and power as a study in politics and institutional economics, out of which a planning may emerge that assumes the readiness of business to regulate itself by its own professional ethic.[4] Professor Galbraith's book converts the very size of the modern corporation into its own first principle of defense, although his concept of "countervailing power" is not much more than an elaboration of an important element in pluralist theory.[5] Mr. Lilienthal's book, finally, is an almost passionate panegyric of corporate bigness, although its argument assumes without proof that there is a logical connection between big technology and big business.[6] In one sense, of course, the thesis common to all of these books—that the antiquarian portrait of a Jeffersonian America must yield to the conditions of modern institutions—is legitimately argued, for it gets away from the confusions attendant on the philosophy of economic individualism implicit in the technique of anti-trust legislation. It finally establishes the point that one main stream of American social thought, embodied in the Brandeis viewpoint, was a romantic anachronism because it assumed the power of the state to enforce a return to a genuinely free competitive condition; that is implicit, ironically enough, in Brandeis' own warning to the Commercial Club of Boston in 1905 that the chief makers of socialism were the great captains of industry who perverted legislatures in order to build up monopoly power.[7] Modern society is institutionalized, professionalized, bureaucratized to a degree where even in the United States the term "bureaucrat" has largely ceased to be a term of abuse. The American debate has to get away from the Jeffersonian illusions implicit in Woodrow Wilson's remark that America is the prize amateur nation of the world.

To say that, however, is not to deny that the new theories present as many difficulties as they resolve. The Schumpeterian thesis of a dynamic capitalism, to which they all owe something, has been no less successful

in creating its own folklore than the theoretical economics it has as-
sailed. There is sufficient literature to establish doubt, for example,
whether competition between the corporate few means a high productive
level and a low costs system. A president of the world's largest steel
company could tell a revealing story in 1950 of its productive inefficiency
and managerial ineptitude before World War II; [8] while the evidence of
a former executive of the General Electric Company forcibly suggests that
the real reason for that company's phenomenal success has been less its
record as a technical innovator than its monopolization of new patents
in order that they may be quietly suppressed.[9] Nor does the history of
recent scientific invention support the defense of the great corporations
as pioneers in the field; the whole tenor of corporate research, rather,
is toward the discouragement of original research in first principles and
the growth of applied technology on the vulgar assumption that there is
nothing fundamental left to discover,[10] and it is reinforced by the growing dependence of the university scientist upon government departments
that emphasize applied research to the detriment of original work, with
disastrous consequences for scientific freedom.[11] What has been defended, in turn, as the "new competition" of product rivalry and innovation turns out, on examination, to be not the survival of the fittest (it
is worth noting that Mr. Lilienthal's lyrical paean to "competition" comes
perilously close to a restatement of the confusions of social Darwinism),[12]
nor a mechanism for the freer entry of new firms into an area, but
rather an extremely limited form of competition between a variety of
products many of which are produced by the same corporation. There is
no perfect monopoly. At the same time, competition between large-scale
giants is different, in degree and kind, from competition between a large
number of small units. "The rude fact appears to be," concedes Mr.
Berle, "that when 45 per cent of American industry is dominated by 135
corporations which necessarily must administer their prices, no one else
is going to risk the logical results of wholly free competition." [13] What
Professor Fellner has somewhat euphemistically styled "spontaneous co-
ordination" between the units of corporate business disguises, in effect,
a vast system of power, half-economic, half-administrative, concerned
more with institutional stability than with the sort of bold adventure
which would justify the *conquistador*-like tone of the apologetic literature.

It is interesting to note the new rationale of the system. Professor
Galbraith's book, in the first place, along with the revival of Bentley's
well-known work, has popularized an economic variant of the federalist
theory of group balance. Yet it is worth emphasizing that an economic
federalism is applauded at a time when much of political science has
underlined the grave defects of political federalism. For if it be true
that federalism prevents the omnipotence of any one unit in the whole,
it is equally true that it frequently stands in the way of the good of the
whole. Thus, to take only two examples, a national policy for the development of the great Western lands has been frustrated by the growth
of "private federations" which have used the state legislatures as a

defense mechanism against federal regulation, while the rigidity of state boundaries has made practicaly impossible the rational resolution of the problem of river control in the Missouri and Colorado basins, with the device of the interstate compact further encouraging the subordination of regional goals to local and state particularism.[14] Federalism freezes an existing complex of power-arrangements; rearrangement of power to respond to social and technological change is made more difficult than usual. The national interest is lost in the name of local democracy. There is nothing in the doctrine of "countervailing power" to prevent a similar outcome in the industrial field. In many ways, of course, it is a persuasive doctrine, for it quite eliminates the need for further extension of state jurisdiction save as that jurisdiction becomes, in Green's phrase, a remover of obstacles to group co-ordination; and it is interesting to note that the attack upon nationalization in recent English social theory, as in Mr. Crosland's book, *The Future of Socialism*, is based upon a similar plea for a system of checks and balances. Yet its assumptions are fragile to a degree. It assumes an effective equality of power in the participating groups; yet the disparity of informal representation of interest-groups in Washington, as revealed in a document like the Buchanan Committee Report, shows how much the ability of a group to be heard rests upon the ability to hire professional influence. It assumes a natural harmony of interests, which in effect translates the Utilitarian myth of competing equal selves in the economic market to a new level of group personality; yet there is little reason to expect that the competition of groups will produce a pre-established social harmony any more than the competing individuals of the Utilitarian calculus. In both cases, the public good is left to fend for itself.

The argument assumes a mythical equality of groups. It reflects the characteristic preoccupation of contemporary social science with the assiduous cataloging of the merely quantitative problems of power, as distinct from the qualitative problems. It places a premium upon consensus about ultimate ends; which really means the ends of the most powerful groups of the society. And in American society, for all of the elaborate description of group variety, those groups are those of the power elite. Despite the New Deal reforms, which were basically the outcome of the distrust of the American gentleman-class for a vulgar business-society, the basic decisions of the economy are still controlled by the corporate managerial class. The determination of operations, the location of plants, the markets to be supplied, the commodities to be produced, the rate of capital expansion, the patterns of research—all of these still remain the province of management. "For practical purposes," Mr. Berle frankly admits, "the judgment of the market place in relation to application of capital has little application in the greatest and most dynamic areas of American industry."[15] So vital, in turn, are those decisions for the national economic health that government itself is inescapably driven to adjust its own monetary and fiscal policies to the final consideration that no large corporation in any strategic field must be allowed to fail. Its own planning, consequently, as in the case of the Full Employment Act of 1946, becomes subordinated to the private decisions of a small number of business executives, so that, as one eminent business leader has commented, the major assumption of such an important congressional statute is that "mass unemployment is a cancer that is inherent in our private enterprise economy. The bill, therefore, proposes that the President of the United States shall conduct an annual physical examination on our body economic, and that if he sees this cancer spreading he shall recommend adequate medical treatment which Congress may then prescribe according to its own best judgment. To the extent that it can, the Congress is expected actually to eliminate the cancerous growth. If that is not possible, however, it is instructed to provide a hypodermic, in the form of deficit spending by government, which will keep the sufferer from realizing that the cancer is still there." [16]

The role of government is thus reduced to the undignified and limited one of spurious arbiter between power-blocs that compete as mercilessly but less publicly than the Robber Barons. The assumption of that role is that one great interest will cancel out the other, an assumption endemic in American political thought since Madison wrote the *Federalist Paper No. 10*. Unfortunately, Madison's prophecy has never matured. Rather, the pressures on the political process have become cumulative. "While this process seems neat and automatic," a Congressional Committee has concluded, "it simply does not operate as it is supposed to. Even if it did, it would represent a degrading conception of democratic politics in which the highest function of government would be to yield to the strongest pressure. Absolute responsiveness to group interests is one thing, but truly representative government is quite another." [17] The legitimate right of the pressure group to be heard has become an illegitimate claim to a right to govern. When stripped of its romantic verbiage, the theory of balance turns out to be a rationalization of a power-struggle between groups that have power without much responsibility. Its protagonists should remember Lord Acton's dictum that there is no example in history of a balanced constitution having lasted a century.

This is not to say that the American business class is devoid of its own fair share of *civisme*. For the principle of the New Capitalism is a frank appeal to that *civisme*. It has received expression, indubitably sincere, in books like Clarence Randall's *A Creed for Free Enterprise* and Howard Bowen's *Social Responsibilities of the Businessman*. But neither book possesses a real doctrine. The appeal that both make to the social sense of the business leader reflects little more than an assumption that the American *esprit de corps* runs so deeply in the national character that no one group of men will violate in any serious measure the unwritten rules that serve the general interest. Mr. Berle, who is fond of bold historical analogies, has attempted to discover a more original thesis, almost a principle of legitimacy. He anticipates a business aristocracy actuated by "certain great philosophical premises," which will do for capitalism what, in different ways, the doctrine that the king could do no wrong did for the medieval kingship and what Augustine Christianity did for the medieval church.[18] The historian is tempted to reply that in both of those cases the beauty of the theory was counterbalanced by the failure of either of those great medieval institutions to practice its injunctions; for in the first case it took parliamentary revolt and a civil war to prevent the degradation of Stuart kingship into the "right divine to govern wrong," while in the second the splendid dream of the *Civitas Dei* produced those great Princes of the Church who, by 1500, had built a vast ecclesiasticism the corruptions of which were satirized by every great writer of the period from Chaucer to Erasmus. The very essence of the American tradition, indeed, has been that no single class can ever be trusted with power on the basis of utter faith in its goodwill, for every such class, historically, has been able without conscious perjury to identify its own private interest with the public good. Nor is it enough to point to the patent civic temper of contemporary business leadership, for it is a temper that has been less self-induced out of a genuine mood of conversion than evolved by forces—the New Deal, trade-unionism, progressive public opinion—which the world of business originally fought against as threats to its way of life. "The fact is," wrote Lord Acton to Mary Gladstone in a passage appropriate to this point, "that education, intelligence, wealth, are a security against certain faults of conduct, not against errors of policy. . . . The danger is not that a particular class is unfit to govern. Every class is unfit to govern." [19] All that the last thirty years have done is really to insulate American corporate business against certain faults of conduct, not against continued errors of policy.

Even more. It is not perhaps unfair to enquire whether, even now, American business has been so completely converted to social trusteeship as is assumed by the contemporary eulogistic literature. In a society where the slogan frequently hides the reality, the social analyst has to penetrate behind the hidden persuaders of mass-opinion to the basic sentiment underneath. "A society," concludes Professor Mills in his mordant study, "that is in its higher circles and on its middle levels widely believed to be a network of smart rackets does not produce men with an inner moral sense; a society that is merely expedient does not produce men of conscience. A society that narrows the meaning of 'success' to the big money and in its terms condemns failure as the chief vice, raising money to the plane of absolute value, will produce the sharp operator and the shady deal." [20] It is possible that the sentence is spoiled by an excessive readiness to attribute motive (a quite un-Marxist procedure) to the new amalgam of big executive, big political militarist and powerful government official that compose the power elite, for, as Mill insisted, it is the man that makes the motive and not the motive the man. There is, as it were, a touch of venom about the analysis which robs its author of the capacity to see the men he describes, not merely as an arrogant power-group, but also as individuals convinced of the rightness of their perspective. At the same time, the indictment is a formidable one. And it is even reinforced, in a way, by the interesting studies of the "new men" made by magazines such as *Fortune,* and brought together in a book like Mr. Whyte's *The Organization Man.* Mr. Whyte aptly demonstrates how many of the public poses of the business leader— group dynamics, "democratic" leadership, the gospel of service, the overtones of "culture"—are concessions he makes to the fantasy-world of the publicity men. "Rightly or wrongly," Mr. Whyte observes, "the executive considers civic work a diffusion of energy, and only those who see a clear relationship between civic work and their careers perform it with any real enthusiasm." [21] He lives in a world strangely unreal to his instincts. He must act "according to the role that he is cast for— the calm eye that never strays from the other's face, the easy, controlled laughter, the whole demeanour that tells onlookers that here certainly is a man without neurosis and inner rumblings. Yet again the drive, the fierce desire to control one's own destiny, cannot help but produce the inner conflicts that the demeanour would deny." [22] Social consciousness has thus not altered the inborn nature of the business world; instead, it has served merely to add an unnatural burden of guilt to the corporate struggle. The Organization Man is thus but the Robber Baron writ small. Because the New Deal operated, at best, on merely an empirical level, it could not provide the liberal businessman with the positive philosophy he would have needed to offset that fate, and whatever item of philosophy it possessed has consequently become merged into the economic paternalism of corporate business.

III

Out of all this the twin ideals of Liberalism, the democratic People and the socially conscious State, have been subjected to a new sophisticated criticism by the new orthodoxies of social science. The first has suffered from its connection with mass-culture, the second from a growing preoccupation with totalitarianism and authoritarianism as elements in the clinical pathology of Power. In one sense, the trend is hardly surprising. Every age of disillusion likes to emphasize the beast in human nature; it is not for nothing that the cynical maxims of Hobbes and La Rochefoucauld seem more plausible today than the sentiments of Locke or Jefferson. Every age of anxiety, likewise, becomes fascinated with the private experience; that is why men can reveal without shame their private agonies of spirit in much the same way as the religious controversialists of the seventeenth century wrote their autobiographies of salvation in the conviction that their citations from Scripture were incontestable proof of the creeds they had embraced. Nor is antistatism (the revival of Anarchism as a philosophy, as in Camus, is symptomatic) likely to be lightly dismissed by anyone who appreciates the growth of the police-state since 1914. A political science that underestimates all this is in danger of becoming a pathetic anachronism.

The end-result, however, has been a sociological literature employed in the service of an antidemocratic pessimism. The concept of "totalitarianism" has been used to establish not merely, as did Hobbes, a study of politics from the viewpoint of administration and social psychology, but going even beyond Hobbes, to maintain that power can rarely be used for any real public good. The consequent tendency to slur over the vital yet subtle line that divides authority from authoritarianism can be seen, to take a seminal book of the movements, in Dr. Arendt's identification of forces like Lord Cromer's imperialism and General Smuts's white racialism as precursors of totalitarian bureaucracy, or in Dr. Talmon's effort to trace a causal relationship in a chain of historical guilt between the Robespierrean revolutionary fanaticism and modern "totalitarian democracy"; and it is worth observing that even a mind as scholarly as Collingwood's could commit a similar confusion in his angry indictment of the Germans in his *New Leviathan*. All these, in turn, are part of a sociological passion for exact definition, for an architectonic generalization which can be fatal to the variety of experience; and one of its outcomes is a tendency to see the contemporary totalitarian state as a monolithic and ferocious efficiency, when in fact the findings of historians like Trevor Roper and Edward Crankshaw on the German Gestapo machine conclusively indicate the need for a somewhat less apocalyptic note in that field of study. The concept, again, of the "authoritarian personality" has tended to identify traits such as dogmatic exaggeration or excessive enthusiasm or even at times the mere possession of a political faith as elements of the "antidemocratic" person; the historian is reminded of the eighteenth-century distrust of "enthusiasm" as the certain proof that its owners were prepared to commence a religious war. The outcome of all this is a curious logic in which the exercise of legitimate authority is confused with the habit of authoritarian intolerance and in which the widespread fear of totalitarianism is allowed to become a belief that any extension of public authority must mean a further step on the road that leads to the nightmare of 1984.

For the pessimism has gone far beyond writers like von Mises or Professor Hayek. It is there in more liberal outlooks like that of Professor Boulding in his *The Organizational Revolution*.[23] It is there in Mr. Lippmann's attempt to curb representative institutions by the invocation of Natural Law, an attempt that ignores how much of the history of that famous concept has been its usage as a weapon in the cause of revolutionary popular sovereignty against Royalist political doctrine. It is there in the argument of Dr. Niebuhr's *Irony of American History*, although the author does not go so far as to present the idea of Reason itself— as in the writings of Whittaker Chambers—as the great Gnostic heresy of Western civilization and thus make it utterly alien to the very nature of American experience. The historical foundations, themselves of the modern welfare state, are called into question by a sort of historical revisionism. It is instructive thus, to note the difference between an earlier work such as Professor Nevins' *Ordeal of the Union* and Mr. Bruce Catton's *This Hallowed Ground*, for whereas the one sees the Civil War as the breakdown of the democratic process, the other reconstructs it as a kind of mystic collective experience that contributes, through a mysterious paradox never really explained, to the growth of American nationalism. In much the same way Professor Hayek's edited volume, *Capitalism and the Historians*, misconstrues the argument of historians such as the Hammonds to mean that the living-standards of the English working class failed to rise under capitalism, while his own thesis—that the new capitalism unilaterally improves those standards— is not supported by the evidence of all of his contributors, notably the contribution of Professor Ashton.[24] The New Deal period in America, finally, has likewise been revised to appear as a Garden of Eden in which the American liberal lost his innocence, so that not only an acceptance of communism but even a social indignation at the plight of the migratory agricultural worker is converted into a betrayal of the American tradition.[25] Altogether, what is conveyed is the lesson that the political state has now reached the terminus of its growth, either because there is nothing left to reform or because further enlargement of its power would usher in the absolutist society.

On all this, certain observations are in order. First, the presumption that liberal capitalism has finally resolved the problem of organizing plenty in peace is at least arguable. There has been, of course, an enormous spread of the national wealth, as studies like those of Professor Miller demonstrate. Yet that has been the outcome of a massive war and postwar rearmament program rather than of domestic polity. The study of Kuznets and Jenks shows how the New Deal failed to effect any significant redistribution of income-shares between the different groups of the economy.[26] The postwar period, likewise, owes its impressive prosperity in increasing measure to a sort of built-in defense cycle characterized by, first, the emergence of the federal government as the major patron of the great corporations, especially in th aircraft, oil, steel, and rubber industries, and second, a merger between the coroporation economy and the military bureaucracy and a corresponding elevation in the status of the military in the realm not only of business but also of foreign policy and the diplomatic service. And it is suggestive, for that last point, that a recent study of the history of military-civilian relationships, Professor Huntington's *The Soldier and the State*, should end with a plea for the establishment of a highly professional American officers corps sustained in the national estimation by a shift in basic American values from liberalism to conservatism.[27]

The economic-military alliance has in fact spawned a vast quasi-military public works program in the capital-goods industries of the nation. The implications of that fact both for the American civilian-soldier relationship and for the future of research-patterns in science have been widely canvassed. What has not been so widely noted is that it begins to set up a nexus between business and war which could leave the classic Marxist interpretation dangerously unanswered; although even a critic as radical as Mr. Strachey has remarked that this does not as yet prove that capitalism cannot sustain itself by a domestic consumer demand-pattern.[28] The second point is that, as the state-power has thus increased, it has encouraged the growth of a type of state-capitalism wherein the interests of government and business have become inextricably interwoven. That is evident in the manner in which the federal regulation of business have become a vehicle for the federal protection of business. Professor Bernstein's careful analysis of the regulatory commissions serves to reinforce the earlier conclusion of Professor Cushman's study that the insulation from political and partisan influence embodied in the idea of the independent agency has merely made their members more responsive to the pressures of the regulated groups.[29] Studies like those of Professor Wilcox and of Adams and Gray likewise reveal how the application of the antitrust legislation has been undertaken on the premise that the established rights of corporate property must not be modified, with the curious consequence that the giant corporate enterprises have gained many of the privileges accorded to the regulated utilities without at the same time having to accept the restraints imposed upon the latter.[30] The charges entered by the book of Adams and Gray are ironically underwritten by the assumption of its authors that the processes they have catalogued can be seen as a betrayal of a valid doctrine of absolute divorce between political and economic forces somehow rooted in the famous funeral speech of the Athenian Pericles.[31] What is sufficiently clear is that the liberal fear of the state as the necessary enemy of business enterprise (the fear is the assumption of Mr. Lilienthal's plea for a Basic Economic Act which would repeal the antitrust legislation) [32] belongs emphatically to the historical lumber-room of exhausted ideas.

Thirdly, and finally, it ought to be noted that the conservatism of the period is related to a sociology of mass-society and mass-culture. The sociology has been born of a marriage between Ortega y Gasset's famous book and the insights of modern psychoanalytical theory, fashioned in its most recent manifestations by the West Coast school of political sociologists (it is curious how American social science, like American jazz, has engendered its regional schools). Its main consequence, in its terms of public policy, has been to argue for an outlook so completely deterministic as to make the seminal tenet of liberalism—that Reason can help reshape Society—seem utterly untenable. Social science, as it were, does not merely supplement social action—it supersedes it. The final irony is that, anti-Communist as that social science is, it is in some ways even more deterministic than classical Marxism, for the latter does possess nominative elements in its theoretical structure, which make room for the deployment of free will in the social process. Few, of course, would deny that the contemporary state of popular culture has deceived some of the more ardent hopes of the

democratic ideologists after the French Revolution. But it is at least arguable that the facts are susceptible to alternative interpretations. For if the
lonely crowd prefers jazz to Beethoven or the novels of Mickey Spillane
to those of Jane Austen, or Elvis Presley to Maria Callas, there is evidence enough to suggest that that is not because people, in the mass,
are made that way but because their tastes have been shaped in large
measure by, first, the omnipresent search for profit and power and second, by a vulgar underestimation of potential taste on the part of those
who control the great entertainment industries. Mr. Seldes's book, *The
Public Arts*, thus insists that because the great "public" has been viewed
as an undifferentiated "audience" and because, in his own apt phrase,
the radio and television and movies have devoted themselves to the
business of exploiting personality rather than of developing character,[33]
the result is a vast audience whose conformity and intellectual passivity
are cited as their own cause instead of being recognized as results that
flow from the terrible abuse of the mass media by the advertising sponsor and the network executive. We are told, in defense, that the public
gets what it wants; it would be more correct to say that it wants what
it gets. The abdication of leadership in public taste is thus justified in
terms of a "democratic" acquiescence in "popular" demand which quite
evades the question as to whether the "demand" itself has not been
shaped in large part by the forces that invoke it as an alibi. Nor is this
necessarily to pretend, Rousseau-like, that a "good" populace is corrupted by a "bad" power group, for those who actively resist the conventional and the orthodox and the popular in any society are probably
always a minority group. It is not so much that the amusement "huck-
sters set out deliberately to debase the public taste as that they have lost
any desire to improve that taste.[34] The indictment is all the more interesting because it comes from an author who, on the whole, accepts the principle of private ownership and corporate competitiveness in the entertainment media as the essentially American foundation of their role.

There are two footnotes to be added on this particular issue in the
social sciences. The first is that the American discussion on "mass culture" tends frequently to a quite unhistorical view of the problem. It
tends to overdramatize the contemporary dilemma by assumptions about
the arts and literature in the preindustrial societies, assumptions that
betray the weak status of history in the social sciences. Critics such as
Mr. Dwight McDonald have thus posited the thesis of an earlier "popular culture" when, in grim reality, if such a culture ever existed at all
it existed as a reflection, in its themes, of aristocratic society and was
probably no less dull than its modern counterpart. It would be difficult
to argue, at least, that the brutal force of the more popular Restoration
comedies was better than modern burlesque, and it would be impossible
to believe that the popular amusements of the English proletariat of the
eighteenth century, as seen in Hogarth's prints or in Defoe's novels,
were morally or aesthetically superior to their twentieth-century counter-
parts. Nor should the life of the privileged classes in the earlier societies

be idealized as a contrast to the degradation of contemporary tastes (the basis of much of the New Conservatism as well as of the new sociological liberalism). Burke's "natural gentleman," in real life, was the type that peoples the diaries of contemporary observers like Croker and Greville; Plato's intellectual aristocrats were the men who crowd the dark pages of Thucydides. It is even more doubtful if the artists and writers of the earlier periods were more free, in terms of their dependence upon their respective audiences, than their modern successors who must rely upon the patronage of the large philanthropic foundations or, in England, upon the institutions of the Establishment. The story of Cellini's relations with the Duke of Florence is not a happy one, and the lives of thinkers like Bayle and Spinoza and Descartes are not exactly reassuring examples of generous patronage. The famous letter of Dr. Johnson to Lord Chesterfield is, indeed, the beginning of a new freedom for the writer in the bourgeois age. Nor does this mean, of course, that men must embrace the reverse snobbishness of a cultural nationalism that equates Gershwin with Mozart, a trend perceptible in the new "affirmation" of American culture. What it does mean, perhaps is that America no longer needs a new sociological version of the "genteel tradition" any more than it needs a sterile denial of an European tradition that it no longer has any real reason to fear.

The second footnote is to draw attention to the fact that in making a sharp distinction between the "mass" and the "elite" political sociology commits a double mistake. It commits an ideological mistake, for it confuses the democratic claim for equality with a perverted claim for identity, and the mistake reinforces the temptation of its advocates to insulate themselves from the majority. And it commits a descriptive mistake, because the evidence indicates that the groups that have been selected for the role of the American "elite" are perhaps as "massified" as the faces in the crowd themselves. The American middle class, to begin with, inhabits a world of "white-collar" conformity and status-preoccupation. The higher education concerns itself either with "civic studies" that identify citizenship with social adjustment or, as the bitter pen-portraits of Mary McCarthy and Randall Jarrell show, with an elaborate ballet of professional jealousies and snobberies divorced from the world of the average American, and even ready at times to hand over that world, in the name of "research," to other less amiable forces. The technicians belie the romantic hopes of Veblen and Burnham by a preoccupation with their special skills rather than with the *summum bonum*. Most significant of all, the higher reaches of the corporate world live an existence in which great ambition soars little higher than a vague collective attachment to the total firm. Mr. Whyte's book has exhibited its characteristic features: the bogus religion of "community" which stifles individual initiative; the sacrifice of content to technique, of eccentricity to "wellroundedness," of any dynamic philosophy to the comfortable stability of the "acceptance world"; the insistent reiteration that all is for the best in the best of possible worlds; a new orthodoxy which sees tension between individual and society as an index of private sickness rather than as the necessary condition of creativity. The externals of that existence, moreover—the group dynamics, the gospel of "service," the social entertainment—in reality disguise an acquisitive society as ruthless in its own way to the failure or the half-successful in the physical and psychological ravage it exacts as the old-fashioned Calvinist capitalism; and quite as morally empty. The massive price that a society has to pay when it sets up as the sole criterion of "success" the final appointment to the desk of the top executive has been nicely analyzed in *The Executive Life;* and even when the summit has been reached it is for many an empty victory. Its final portrait is "an image of intense loneliness in high places, of strain that always increases with each step up the ladder, of the impoverishment of life itself in the single-minded drive for success, and finally, when age imposes retirement from work, a picture of stagnation, futility, purposelessness." [35] An American people invited to ape such an elite may well suspect that, in the famous charge of Melanchthon against Luther, they have been brought out of the bondage of Egypt only to perish in the wilderness of the desert.

What is astonishing about all this is not the enthusiasm of the Organization Man for his world, an enthusiasm frequently engagingly real, but the failure of the intellectual elite to perform its classic role of the Socratic gadfly. Nor is this a failure of nerve or, as some socialist critics have argued, the failure of men who have "sold out" to the society. Rather, it is, in part, the failure of pragmatism as a philosophy of liberal politics, for a theory of consequences makes it difficult to resist conclusive argument—no more conclusive than in American life—of flamboyant success in material productivity. In part, too, it is the logical impossibility of making any sort of moral criticism of phenomena once it is accepted that they are the concomitants of "mass society." Thus, Mr. Whyte's own analysis ends in a morally compromising advice to the individual to "cheat" the organization by deceiving his corporate superiors in the "personality tests," [36] as if, by such an act, he can hope to change the world that he inhabits. Mr. Riesman's plea, again, for "utopian" and "autonomous" thinking sounds pathetically inconsequential in the light of his description of the power of conformism in the national life.[37] Mr. Mills' denunciation of the power elite, once more, is an essay in brilliant sterility, since against the co-operating mood of the liberals he can only offer an imprecise resentment; the classic escape of socialist thought—the invocation of working-class energy against the "system"—is denied him because he accepts the pessimism of the "mass" thesis.[38] In part, finally, the presumption that all the great problems are solved has been encouraged by a narrow concentration upon the prosperity and leisure of the upper middle class to the neglect of other elements; yet Mr. Miller's analysis demonstrates that there its still a bottom fifth of the nation that has not benefited from income redistribution. A book like Mr. Lynes's *A Surfeit of Honey* is misleading for that very reason.

All of these factors, in turn, have been supplemented by a social science that has not as yet worked out any satisfactory relationships between ends and means in its theoretical presuppositions. Its architects have attempted the logically impossible task of constructing a positivist foundation for a naturalistic ethic, so that they have been caught between a scientific politics in which only scientifically verifiable propositions are "true" and the American belief in "natural" rights. The consequent insistence that all facts are born free and equal has led to a fatal disability to identify the really paramount issues, so that vast effort gets wasted in the analysis of the life-habits of the corporation executive or, as in England, in the speech habits of the upper classes, with very little awareness of the truth that knowledge, to be meaningful, has to be related to some great ends themselves founded upon what Newman styled a grammar of assent. Professor Sorokin's book has catalogued the shortcomings of the discipline: the humorless platitudes, the tautologies, the confusing of obscurity with profundity, the false air of precision based upon a limited understanding of the scientific method, the ponderous Germanic style, the reliance upon dubious psychological assumptions; the analysis is only marred by the shrill note of the heretic whose earlier work has been responsible at one time for the growth of the sociological movement.[39] The "scientism" encourages a belief in a spurious disengagement from political action on the ground, equally spurious, that objectivity about method must involve neutrality about ultimate issues. Once that is done, there can be no answer to the totalitarian nihilist since, having denied the validity of values generally, the social scientist cannot consistently uphold his own. Nor can he challenge the morality of any phenomenon, McCarthyism for example, since it presents itself as another "fact" to be absorbed in a valueless compendium of data.

It would be easy to fashion out of all this an obscurantist attack upon the central principle of social science—the application of rational intelligence to the study of society. The temper of the *Times Literary Supplement* review of the Sorokin book indicates an English tendency so to do.[40] Yet sociology, as such, has a reputable English genealogy. The influence of Marx upon the Fabians was deep, despite the effort of Edward Pease in his book of 1916 to discount it. The investigations of Booth and, before him, of Mayhew, Hobhouse's analysis of irrationality in society, the comparative study of social institutions going back to Maine, the sociological history of religions in Robertson Smith, the social thinkers of the Scots Enlightenment—all exemplify a British source of sociological discipline often unacknowledged by American schools. These men and their work have been resisted by the older English universities, whose curricula have been adjusted to the ideological indoctrination of the British governing elite. Yet they recall a vital Victorian source of social studies; even more, they knew that "research" is merely the prelude to the great debate on public policy where decisions are fashioned by subjective factors. They did not claim to be a new elite, and the last chapter of the Webb's *Methods of Social Study* of 1932 is an eloquent warning against the folly of such a claim. But they did see that not to take a stand on issues is to commit the real *trahison des clercs*. That is why a book like Professor Deane's dissertation on the figure of Laski goes wrong when it assumes that to have proven "bias" on the part of its subject is to have indicated some sort of imperfection above which more responsible men rise, and that intellectual gifts would be better devoted to "scholarship" than to "propaganda." The thesis ignores the fact, first, that the most valuable of our political literature has been composed by men who knew their subject, like Machiavelli and Burke and Lenin, from a firsthand experience of its workings and, second, that a thinker might feel so urgently the exacting demands of his period's problems that it would seem in his view not to be so much a question of a nice balance between "scholarship" and "propaganda" as a question of the very survival of those conditions without which intellectual life in any real form could not survive. Pascal's *Lettres Provinciales* and Milton's Salmasian tracts were both thus written, and to say the authors were wrong would be to have required of them a prophetic insight of unnatural proportions. There is a temptation to rewrite the intellectual history of the nineteen-thirties in that strain, to portray its enthusiasms as either a conscious betrayal of liberalism or as the delusions of, in Mr. Fiedler's phrase, a paranoid world. The whole argument of psychological motivation proves too much, for, granted its premises, it must concede that all attitudes, not simply radical ones, have their roots in personal neurosis. Not to concede is to give way to the fatuous distortions of a book like Professor von Mises' *The Anti-Capitalistic Mentality,* in which an entire corpus of social and economic literature is dismissed as the outcome of personal frustrations; the argument degrades thought to the status of an *annexe* of emotional anxiety.[41] The example is an extreme one. Yet much of the literature of psychopathology and politics accepts a similarly dangerous identification of intellectual radicalism with emotional abnormality without sufficiently appreciating that concepts such as mental "health" and social "normality" rest upon disciplines that do not share a common exactitude in their respective definitions or knowledge. To embrace that sort of identification is to yield up the proper function of the social scientist, which is to unite rational enquiry with moral passion. Ideally, he should combine the virtues of the Enlightenment, its endless curiosity, its faith in nature, its confidence in the power of reason to shape conduct, with a readiness, once the "facts" are garnered, to take sides, to adopt (which is the real appeal of Orwell) a fiercely moral foundation of politics. It is a classical tradition in political thought; Mr. Parkin's recent essay on Burke has reminded us that Burke must be seen, not merely as an exponent of practical statecraft or leader of a revolt against the eighteenth century, but above all as a moral theorist.[42] In this way, the problem of value is not evaded. It is incorporated into a system that reconciles research and value, humanism and science, that seeks to fulfill the great dream of the philosopher-scientists of the seventeenth century. Only in that way can the social scientist avoid the charge that the discipline he practices is the instrument of an authoritarian social engineering.

IV

If there has been a "decline of Liberalism," the debate has at least been taken up by both the British Left and the American Right. For neither the British Right nor the American Left has had much to contribute. The latter has never been intellectually prepossessing; it has been isolated as an urban expression; and it has been frequently romantically American, as a book like Gustavus Myers's *America Strikes Back* of 1935 shows. The former has already given up its postwar effort to construct a "new Conservatism" and with exceptions such as lively minds like Christopher Hollis or Quintin Hogg, its doctrinal foundations, if any, remain, as Mr. Churchill's new *History of the English-Speaking Peoples* bears witness, those of an idea of political liberty set within the grand Whiggery of Augustan England. Theory, in the one case, has been sterilized by the pervasive influence of Pragmatism, in the other case by the splendid prejudice of the English conservative that ideas are not necessary to a governing class that has ruled without interruption for some three hundred years.

That postwar America is conservative is not in doubt. Nor is it difficult to trace the sources of that mood: a luxuriant material prodigality, the disappearance of the worst features of prewar poverty, the solid comfort of the new suburbanites, the search for status of the rising minority-groups as they have climbed the economic ladder and, in reaction to the latter, the invocation of an "old American" tradition on the part of the older ethnic strains of the American aristocracy. But a conservative mood is not a conservative philosophy and, so far, what has passed for the latter has been little more than a reaction against some of the more naïve or illogical assumptions of classical Liberalism; and even that is not new, for the fallacies of rationalism were noted by Mill's conservative critics as soon as his mid-Victorian essay was published.[43] Beyond that, it is difficult to see anything solid in the American "new Conservatism." The genealogy it invokes has been an assortment of names from Adams to Babbitt that have little in common save a dislike for the business spirit. Unlike its English counterpart, it has been unable to release its feelings in an unashamed passion for the restoration of a social order long dissolved. It has failed, finally, to identify any strategically located social class in the American structure which could conceivably become the vehicle of a conservative program.

As a consequence, the movement is involved in paradox. It attempts to transplant English Tory Democracy to the American scene. But there is a vast chasm between the great American fortunes and the great houses of the English political tradition described in diaries like those of Croker and Greville, for while the latter have regarded politics as the highest function of a governing class and as the trust the gentleman owes to classes less fortunately placed than his own, the former have been so preoccupied with wealth-making that they have rarely come to see politics in the grand manner. While the English gentleman has embraced a Burkean-Disraelian paternalism based upon an alliance of aristocrat and worker, the American businessman has been, as a class, hostile to the growth of the welfare state. Professor Rossiter is thus obliged to confess that the class has altogether failed to support the conservative philosophy and that its history can be summed up, indeed, as the "alienation" of the "conservative" from conservatism.[44] Similarly, Mr. Viereck, after a lively plea for a return to patrician values, notes with honest frankness that there is nothing to justify any hope of such a return and that, in any case, if conservatism has anything to do with historical tradition, the Truman Democrats have a more august tradition than the Taft Republicans since the latter's origins go back no further than the Gilded Age.[45] The public-spirited patrician is, of course, not unknown in America. But he is rarely in an openly conservative camp. From Jefferson to Stevenson, he has been in the liberal camp. The socially conscious business leader—who must be the head and center of an American conservatism if it is to be real— is rare indeed, and even as energetic a champion as Mr. Viereck is driven to acknowledge that much of the contemporary language about "business responsibility" is hypocritical and therefore much less pleasing than the honest arrogance of the Robber Barons.[46] Mr. Lippmann's conception, once more, of the political executive who will be the dis- interested guardian of the public interest assumes that democracy can safely discard its institutional safeguards against abuse of power and surrender itself to the self-restraining wisdom of his executive elite. Yet history offers no example of a ruling class that has not abused such a threat, and, indeed, it is of the essence of American political thought that it has been belligerently sceptical of the doctrine of trusteeship.

The philosophical content of American conservatism, as a result, is nebulous. A representative book such as Professor Rossiter's *Conserva- tism in America* invokes both the Burkean *mystique* and laissez-faire individualism so much that it is difficult to say whether its author is liberal or conservative. The logical dilemma here, indeed, is that if the conservatism is to be something more than simply a romantic nostalgia for traditions that have no American foundation it is driven back into the pervasive liberal rhetoric of the American debate and thus becomes merely a reiteration that there must be a conservation of liberal values. The only way to avoid the dilemma is to espouse openly an antiliberal ethic. It is in that sense that the real conservatives are writers like Whittaker Chambers, whose *Witness* is a neo-Catholic essay in religious obscurantism; [47] or writers like Professor Kirk, whose nostalgia for the

Augustan territorial aristocracy leads him, in his *Program for Conservatives*, into a thoroughgoing attack upon the mild social liberalism that Shaftesbury or Disraeli might have espoused. This portion of the "radicals of the right" has at least the merit of being "radical" in the sense that it rejects the status quo and the politics of liberal compromise.[48] Its supreme irony is that its noble regret, as in Professor Kirk, for the Churchillian dream of Augustan nobility, becomes transmuted, once it comes down to practical policies, into a support of a Bourbon Republican party of which there is a famous passage of sardonic criticism in one of Mr. Churchill's own early speeches. For those conservatives, again, who see little hope in any social class there is only a retreat into a conservatism of private taste and individual manners; Mr. Viereck thus turns his back on politics and argues for a purely academic conservative ethic.[49] All in all, the American conservatives have sought to impose an English gentlemanly code upon an American democratic experience and have thereby violated the chief impulse of conservative thought pregnant in Burke's dictum that it is urgent to attend to the nature rather than to the reasonings of men. "To write about conservative politics in America," a recent writer has recorded, "is to chronicle the political performance of American business." [50] No American philosophy, of any brand, can ignore that truth.

Even more. The conditioned reflex of conservatism is to resist change, even to insist that change does not take place. It lacks, in Mannheim's sentence, all those reflections and illuminations of the historical process which come from a progressive impulse. As it states its theory it is tempted to rewrite history as a footnote to the theory. It is instructive to record how the American conservative thus reconstructs American history in such a way as to demote the ineluctably basic factor of the national experience. Professor Rossiter's thesis that the American Revolution was in no real sense a revolution at all [51] thus mistakes the fact that they were therefore not innovators, for there clearly was that revolutionary break with tradition all conservatism resists. Professor Boorstin's thesis, likewise, of a constitutional conservatism as the major issue of the Civil War [52] is only valid so long as Calhoun, and not Madison, for example, is cited as the correct commentator upon the original intent of the Constitution; yet not only was Madison the chief framer of the Constitution, but he also vigorously contested in his own day Calhoun's denial that the constitutional intent was to erect a government founded upon the revolutionary dogma of popular sovereignty.[53] In a similar fashion, Professor McCloskey manages to transform an Anglophobe Yankee entrepreneur like Andrew Carnegie into a "conservative," and Professor Kirk claims Cardinal Newman for the same portrait gallery; yet the one penned a well-known popular defense of capitalist individualism, while the other advanced a theory of doctrinal development which, as his Anglican critics perceived, was calculated to destroy the very foundations of the Church of England. The entire historiographical procedure is weak because it applauds as "conservative" processes of change denounced in their own day by contemporary conservatives as presumptuous irreverence. It is curious that the American followers of Burke do not see that what Burke himself was doing in his *Appeal from the New to the Old Whigs* was to canonize the Revolution of 1688 into a conservative act when in reality the Whiggism of its leaders was a revolutionary act against prescriptive authority properly perceived by contemporary conservatives like the Non-Jurors. It is a fallacy of antecedent that afflicts all social philosophies; Marx committed a similar distortion of history in acclaiming the Ten Hours Bill of 1847 as a proof of the growing revolutionary maturity of the Victorian working class. Conservatism shares with radicalism the dangers of such utopianism. It theorizes as much as the system-making philosophies it attacks. Professor Pares has pointed out, in this respect, how much of Burke's ideas were impossibly idealist in eighteenth-century England and that subsequent generations have wrongly assumed he had the best of the argument on matters such as party and political representation only because of the success of the two-party system in the later period of Victorian England.[54] The contemporary American conservatives no more offer means of having their ideas accepted by the business class or the politicians than did Burke suggest how his own ideas could be accepted by the great territorial magnates of his time. Nor—to take another example—do they show how their argument for a revival of religious belief has any real meaning in a society where religion has become just a therapeutic mechanism for the invocation of "peace of mind" in people whose sense of purpose in life has been eroded by a luxuriant materialism.[55] The same is true of British conservatism. Young conservatives such as Mr. Quintin Hogg have urged the same return to religion as a social tie.[56] But all the most recent evidence indicates that traditional religious sanctions mean little to the average Englishman; the working-class man who said of his mates, "They'd sooner go to a pub than a church and so would I," [57] was expressing a hostile attitude so widespread as almost to justify the conclusion that a French sort of anticlericalism is present in the popular English attitudes to the churches.[58] The conservative, clearly enough, is isolated from the crowd. And if he seeks to rationalize that fact through a theory of "elites" and "masses" he does so only by abdicating the traditional conservative ideal of an alliance of scholar-gentleman and populace against the business ethic.

V

The contribution of the British Left starts, of course, from an acceptance of the welfare state. Its Fabian strain has throughout emphasized the paramountcy of the community welfare as the prime goal of policy. It has thus avoided the liberal emphasis upon freedom as consisting primarily in the protection of individual self against social restraint. Much of the contemporary liberal discussion still upholds the emphasis and some of its elements, as in logical positivism and analytical philosophy, have consequently moved further and further away from the basic interrelationship of man, nature, and society as the foundation of worthwhile enquiry into the problems. The Lockean influence, in this respect, has been a narrowing one; for even if Locke's doctrine affords a guarantee of personal liberty it ignores the problem of social growth and is insufficient as a basis for the formation and maintenance of organized society; and if Hobbes's system resulted in a justification of the absolutism of the state, Locke's system involved the assertion of the absolutism of the individual citizen.[59] Much of what passes for criticism of the welfare society has been reiteration of that solipsist individualism.

The welfare state, of course, is not the socialist commonwealth. England is still at bottom a class-ridden society, a Dickensian mixture of aristocratic remnants, plutocratic influence and middle-class sentiment. Professions such as the law and medicine, although not closed castes, still carry the marks of hereditary occupations.[60] Institutions such as the Anglican Church continue to be bastions of social privilege and bishops, as a class, come overwhelmingly from a single social stratum trained in select schools like Marlborough and Merchant Taylors.[61] The Diplomatic Service, despite the Eden reforms of 1943 and despite the proof, in the figure of Mr. Bevin, that a trade-union leader can become an outstanding Foreign Secretary, still resists effective democratization, and since 1945 only the occasional ambassador, Lord Halifax or Sir Oliver Franks, has been drawn from outside the ranks of the traditional career men.[62] The sociology of the peerage shows that, in its present state, approximately three-quarters of its members come from the "public schools" and that, the creation of some one hundred new peers by Labour Cabinets since 1945 notwithstanding, an ennobled individual very rapidly acquires the conservative instincts of *noblesse oblige* and, in addition, sends his sons to Eton or Harrow and himself will seek out a business position rarely below the board-room level. It is also of interest to note that two of the major occupational sources of the class are ex-Army regular officers (39 per cent of all peers) and lawyers (25 per cent of new peers).[63] Behind all this there lies the common source of a privileged educational system that has been substantially untouched by reform. For apart from the grotesque exclusiveness of the "public school," recent investigations of educational opportunity at both the grammar-school and university level suggest that, in the first place, a boy coming from a middle-class home has a greater chance of entering a grammar school than a boy from a working-class home and, secondly, the growing democratization of "Oxbridge" has meant, in terms of social attitudes, an assimilation of the working-class student into the value-system of the traditional upper-class influence.[64] The consequence, as Professor Pear has displayed in his fascinating study, is that English life is still pretty well dominated by

a set of social prejudices and class differentiations based not so much
upon gradations of income as upon the more subtle differences of speech,
manners, dress, leisure pursuits, even modes of eating and drinking;
and all of them defended in terms of a vague ideology of "character"
calculated to sustain the national habits of class separatism. Nor has
this been seriously changed by the advent of new elites that, in themselves, are doing much to break down the more comic aspects of that
separatism and to challenge the conservative spirit of the older professions, for although they are more hospitable to talent and ability
they have not seriously challenged the basic societal values, and, indeed
themselves constitute covert elites profoundly disturbing to the principle of national community.[65] The group-novel of C. P. Snow is a vast
fictional footnote to that truth.

If it be true that the democratic spirit is modifying all this, at least
three comments need to be added. The first is that much of the change
stems from quite nonsocialist causes. For just as much of the Liberal
social legislation of 1906-14 was the outcome of a militant trade-
unionism which the Webbs distrusted, so much of the Labour welfare
legislation since 1940 has been the outcome of a mental revolution born
itself of that process of war which the Webbs again, unlike Marx,
neglected to appreciate as a major precipitant of social change. The
second point is that Great Britain is still far from being either an
economic or a social democracy. Essential industries like food processing, engineering, chemicals, shipbuilding, armaments, automobile
manufacture, have been left relatively untouched by any principle of
economic democracy, and it is doubtful whether the American method
of "trust busting," implicit in the Monopolies and Restrictive Practices
Act of 1948, will be any more successful in Britain than it has been in
the United States. The British welfare-capitalism, like the American, has
of course disproved the Marxian prophecy of increasing pauperization.
But compared to the living-standards of the American labor-aristocracy
or to those of his own upper middle class, the British worker still lives
a narrow and cramped life. He travels a little more, but only a little
more, than his father; his housing is still frequently bleak and ugly;
he still does not regard things like the telephone or the automobile as his
natural right; it is even possible to argue, as Mr. Hoggart has done in
his controversial book, *The Abuse of Literacy*, that his cultural standards have declined in the last generation. Nor should the income-
redistribution of the welfare state be exaggerated, for it would probably
be true to say, as Mr. Strachey has urged, that it has done little more
than to enable the working classes to hold their own and thereby to
keep just about in step with the general rise in wealth.[66] It follows from
this, as the third point, that the welfare state has not so much radically
revised British social relationships as permitted the rise of a relatively
larger minority of talented lower-class individuals into the strata above
them. Public taxation has done little to eliminate the unearned income
of the functionless shareholders of public companies, on the one hand,

or the capital gains that have generated a new style of conspicuous consumption in the English rich, on the other; nor, even more important as a source of inegalitarianism, has it done much to reform a social value system wherein long and arduous work is often meanly rewarded and easy and satisfying work is generally well-paid. There is still a dual educational system, with the new modern school catering mainly for the lower-class pupil and the "public school" for the more prosperous elements of the middle classes, the latter being patronized, ironically, by many Labour parents. Altogether, English society remains still pretty much the prisoner of a deep and intractable social snobbishness. The snobbishness is frequently most ardently supported by those who have most recently benefited from it; it is not for nothing that the symbolic hero-figure of the society has become the type of Lucky Jim, half graspingly selfish, half belligerently class-conscious, just as after 1832 the symbol of the new middle class was the figure of Becky Sharp. The religion of inequality remains; only more devotees have been permitted into the temple. The truth is an old truth in English social development. "The lowest plebeian by birth," observed Bulwer-Lytton caustically in his brilliant yet neglected book, *England and the English*, on the transition after 1832 from aristocracy to middle-class rule, "has only to be of importance to become the bitterest aristocrat in policy. The road to honours is apparently popular; but each man rising from the herd has endeavored to restrain the very principle of popularity by which he has risen. So that, while the power of attaining eminent station has been open to all ranks, yet in proportion as that power bore any individual aloft, you might see it purifying itself of all democratic properties, and beautifully melting into that aristocratic atmosphere which it was permitted to attain."[67]

Two recent books have attempted a restatement of socialist theory in the light of all this, Mr. Crosland's *The Future of Socialism* and Mr. Strachey's *Contemporary Capitalism*. Mr. Crosland's book is a frank attempt at revisionism based on the supposition that postwar welfare policies have solved in effect the great question of the ownership of production-means within the economy. It is its thesis that because of new factors—the growing supersession of the shareholder by the managerial personnel, the enlarged power of the trade-union, more economic equality—the issue of ownership is increasingly irrelevant, so that nationalization becomes an obsolete item of social theory. The argument reflects the assumption that the national economy is now safely launched upon a smooth passage into a sort of Swedo-American community. Yet the assumption is not incontrovertible. To begin with, it accepts the managerialist thesis when it is recognized that, even in the leading American capitalism, the reality of economic power is still held by an alliance of the traditional rich and the chief corporation executives wherein the managers play a secondary role.[68] And even if the thesis were true, it is quite alien to socialist thought to assume that such a grave responsibility to society should rest on the uncertain foundations

of correct behavior on the part of a managerial elite. It is true, as Mr.
Crosland argues, that the technique of the public corporation is not
utterly satisfactory. But that is not sufficient reason for abandoning the
technique. It could be seen, indeed, as reason for improving it by various
methods—a modernization of parliamentary control; a new concept of
the role of the political minister; the widening of opportunity in promotion on the boards, at present blocked both by trade-union conservatism and a managerial suspicion of the university man; the role of the
trade-unions themselves in public ownership, especially, on this last
point, the growth of new administrative bodies such as Development
Councils that might break the still powerful separation between management and labour.[69] Mr. Crosland's attack upon nationalization is all
the more remarkable in the light of his own rather drastic suggestions
for forced income redistribution by way of gift taxes, capital gains
taxation, and transfer of unearned income to the community, for if the
question of the ownership of production-means is as insignificant as
asserted then it is difficult to appreciate the reasons for such fiscal
radicalism. The present conspicuous consumption of English wealth
that offends Mr. Crosland flows in large part from the private ownership of corporate power in the private sector of the economy. The
educational privileges Mr. Crosland rightly resents are again in themselves the outcome of uncontrolled private means. What emerges from
all this is a welfare society characterized by a permanent continuation
of capitalist enterprise of substantial proportions, the effects of which
shall be counterbalanced by a type of public strategic participation, as
outlined in a document like *Twentieth Century Socialism*. Such a
society would be divided, not only by entrepreneurial forms, but by
two sets of social values, one of profit-making, the other of public
service. Nor is there much evidence to support the assumption that in
the long run the leaders of the private sector will be converted to the
ethics of socialist organization. It seems far more likely that the public
sector will be placed on the defensive; indeed, the "new thinking" of
the Labour party threatens to relegate the state-power, in its *Industry
and Society* statement of policy, to the role of an accessory preoccupied with the comparatively functionless status of a partner in private
firms by the acquisition of industrial shares. Undoubtedly, the rule
of the public servant has its own dangers and Mr. Crossman has noted
them in his Fabian pamphlet, *Socialism and the New Despotism*. But
to permit an awareness of the dangers to become an attack upon the
principle of public control itself . . . would be to embrace the entire
catalogue of logical fallacies about "bureaucracy" characteristic of the
von Hayek school of economic thought.[70]

It is the eminent defect of books like Mr. Crosland's that they
abjure a general theory and thereby offer an unsatisfactory empiricism.
It is the merit of books like Mr. Strachey's that they recognize the need
for theory, since the "practical" assumptions upon which all men act
are, at bottom, based upon a theory of the universe. It is Mr. Strachey's

argument that the theory the Left needs is still Marxism, but a Marxism stripped of the Stalinist orthodoxy and of its errors of historical prophecy. The vast diagram of capitalism that Marx mapped out is to be seen as the work of a pioneer sociologist in a developing rationalist tradition rather than as that of a sort of Hebraic prophet prophesying doom. Its theoretical elements must be seen, as Marx said of the labor theory of value in his letter to Schmidt, as operative concepts that stand or fall by their utility in describing the realities of industrial society. Where Marx went wrong was to assume that tendencies like the level of subsistence-wages and growing institutional concentration would lead to the increasing pauperization of the mass, without appreciating that in later capitalism those tendencies would be overruled by essentially noneconomic forces such as the growth of democratic working-class institutions. Where he was right was to diagnose the innate tendency of capitalism, in its laws of capital accumualtion, to ever-growing inequalities; and if these have been mitigated in the century since he wrote it is not because of the inherent benevolence of the system but because of the economic consequences of democracy. Marx himself would have taken account of these new developments had he lived; for his massive structure was no eighteenth-century mechanico-materialism but an attempt to apply rational enquiry to the changing processes of society. His great mistake was to assume the permanency of the conditions of the brutalized mid-Victorian capitalism of his own day; but it is a mistake that is unpardonable in the modern Marxist.

What emerges from all this? In the first place, the improvement in the workers' lot since Marx wrote must be seen, not as an intrinsic trait of capitalism nor, Fabian-wise, as the conversion of its governing class to social liberalism, but as the result of organized action by worker and farmer to counteract the tendencies of the system. Secondly, political democracy thus acts upon economic forces in a mode of mutual influence, and to fail to see that is to embrace the misleading Stalinist picture of modern capitalism. The task before the Labour parties is to see the struggle in terms of the effort of democracy to preserve and extend the democratic forces that thus impinge on capitalism. And, third, it is urgent to recognize the essential fragility of the democratic character even of British society. Its institutions, in that society, have only been completed within the last thirty-five years. Its classic inventions, such as freedom of the press, have failed to fulfill the dreams of their early democratic champions. There is still far too little real participation of the average citizen in the processes of government. Democratic control over the main national institutions, however real in the political field, is still very imperfect in the economic and industrial field. The snobbishness which gives unequal rewards to the "wage-earner" and the "salary-earner" remains powerful and widespread. Above all, there are ominous signs indicating that the climate of political opinion in upper-class English society is becoming increasingly illiberal and antidemocratic. For as the possibility has grown, in however small a way, that the apparatus of the state-power may be employed in the interests of the majority there has grown up in response a rediscovery of the early nineteenth-century doctrine that "the State" is the most hideous engine of oppression conceived of by the mind of man. It is symptomatic that a conservative political mystic like Lord Percy of Newcastle can be acclaimed as a sort of new Burke, and that Mill's fears of majority rule are enthusiastically restated by Mr. Beloff and Professor Oakeshott.[71]

Despite its weaknesses—the social scientist will note the absence of any real sociology in the argument—the book has the supreme merit of disproving the popular American belief that the Labour party has exhausted its promise. The achievement after 1945 was wholly exceptional in that it was able to inherit the *élan* of a wartime social revolution and, even then, it was far more an extension of the social services of the 1906 variety and far less the use of the tax weapon for a radical transformation of national wealth and income. It has been more distributist than productionist; the Labour party has hardly begun to seize hold of the vast possibilities of science and technology; it is suggestive that Great Britain still retains a national road system that is hopelessly obsolete in terms of modern needs. To recognize all this might be the medicine Labour needs in order to shake off its present mood of cautious apology.

VI

Yet political programs do not survive without faith. And the most distinct impression that analysis of the Anglo-American debate leaves is the feeling that both American liberalism and British socialism have lost much of their faith in the democratic dogma. The one has sought to innoculate itself against erratic beliefs by asserting that it has no beliefs at all, and the subsequent corrosion of morale and intellectual courage in the American college liberal professor is grimly catalogued in the Lazarsfeld Report for the Fund for the Republic. The other has allowed itself to become too much absorbed by the aristocratic spirit of the English Establishment—against which Dickens waged a ceaseless war for a whole lifetime—so that, with all the rest, it has become the target of the frustrations of a younger generation for whom all politics have become flat, stale, and unprofitable. The personal outcome, on the American side, is the characteristic figure of the middle-class professional man, such as Hamilton Basso's hero of Anson Page in *The View from Pompey's Head*, who has finally gained in middle age all the rewards that professional success can offer but is still haunted by a pervasive sense of failure, of promise unfulfilled; while on the English side it is the characteristic figure of the Fabian public man, such as Bernard Sands in Angus Wilson's *Hemlock and After*, whose sophisticated humanism has faded into a pursuit of socially marginal private pleasures because, at bottom, it has never been much more than an expression of upper-class social sensibility. The retreat from social obligation has in turn been encouraged by a nice neo-Tractarian pre-occupation with the private mood and the personal experience, with all of its concomitant features—a mania for self-accusation, the anarchy of self-revelation, a distrust in the power of reason to solve the problems of life, an alliance, at its worst, of intellectual charm and moral bankruptcy in the ideal person-types that it worships. As all this becomes the mood of the educated classes of Western European-American society the historian is forcibly reminded of the mood of educated Romans on the eve of the victory of a popular Christianity they could neither understand nor appreciate. He sees men once again on the threshold of a new era in which their old faiths must either reform themselves to fill the spiritual vacuum of a tired age or be supplanted by new faiths more meaningful for the experience of the world-masses who have lived their silent lives beyond the privileged orbit of the Western-Christian tradition.

For in the long run men yield their allegiance less to the logic that illuminates than to the faith that sets the heart on fire. The heart of man, as Newman emphasized in a great passage, "is commonly reached not through the reason, but through the imagination by means of direct impressions, by the testimony of facts and events, by history and by description. Persons influence us, voices melt us, looks subdue us, deeds inflame us. Many a man will live and die upon a dogma; no man will be a martyr for a conclusion." That great truth of human nature is perhaps the secret to the renovation of liberalism in an illiberal age. It was a truth Beatrice Webb glimpsed as she sought to assess the meaning of the collapse of British socialism after 1931. "Have we the material," she asked, "in the British Labour Movement from which can be evolved something of the nature of a religious order—a congregation of the faithful who will also be skilful technicians in social reconstruction? What undid the two Labour Governments was not merely their lack of knowledge and the will to apply what knowledge they had, but also their acceptance, as individuals, of the way of life of men of property and men of rank. It is a hard saying and one that condemns ourselves as well as others of the Labour Government: You cannot engineer an equalitarian state if you yourself are enjoying the pomp and circumstance of the city of the rich surrounded by the city of the poor." [72] That sentiment was to produce later the fantastic misunderstandings in the Webbs' famous book on Soviet Russia wherein the Communist party was seen as such a religious order but the grim implications of that fact for democracy and individual freedom were quite disregarded, and disregarded largely because the Webbs failed to see that the Messianic fervor of the Bolshevik, his apocalyptic dogmatism, his ruthless selflessness, were things to be understood adequately only within the large perspective of the fact that Soviet Russia owes as much to its origins in Byzantium as it does to its revolt against Western Christianity.

Yet the truth remains a vital truth for any Western movement that seeks to meet the challenge of the new modern political religions. It must know what it is for as well as what it is against. It must have moral passion. Above all, it must consciously seek real understanding between intellectual and people. So long as the intellectual cultivates a nice contempt for an undifferentiated "mass" or so long as he merely feels a helpless shame at losing his own working-class roots—much of the nature of the "angry young men" in Britain flows from that source—he will utterly sterilize the possibility of such an understanding.

The understanding will need to effect itself, indubitably, at two levels. To begin with, it must rise above its neo-Churchillian tendency to assume that the world is restricted in effect to the contemporary Atlantic world. For fifty years of Europe are no longer equal to a cycle of Cathay. There exist other great world religions, such as Islam and Hinduism, that surpass in their massive following the historic Christian churches of the West, and it is doubtful if world leadership can now so blandly assume the "Christian" answer to the present discontents. Anglo-American thought has hardly begun to appreciate the meaning of the observation of the Indian delegate to the General Assembly of the United Nations in its 1954 session that it is in Europe that the great wars of the modern period have all begun and that it is from Europe that they have been carried to other parts of the world. What flows from all this, secondly, is that just as in the nineteenth century the central challenge to liberalism lay in the answer it provided to domestic inequality in the industrializing societies, in the twentieth century it lies in the answer that must be provided to the growing international inequality between the technologically advanced and the underdeveloped nations. Both American liberalism and British socialism have been handicapped in this endeavor, the one because of the deep and pervasive strength of American isolationism, the other because of the fact that the Fabians assumed the continuing existence of the British international hegemony based upon the massive power of the London financial market in the world economic system. They have misunderstood the character of the new colonial nationalisms, again, because there is a temptation of American liberalism to see all anti-imperial effort through the historically distorting perspective of 1776, and a temptation, likewise, in British socialism to imagine its own British middle-class culture-pattern as the natural model for the colonial peoples as they move towards national self-government. Both of them have yet fully to sense that men are passing through one of those seminal moments in history, such as the breakdown of the Roman Empire or the Reformation or the French Revolution, when a whole civilization must undertake fundamental readjustment to new and strange forces or else, like a score of civilizations before it, perish because it has failed to act as flexibly as the age inescapably demands.

NOTES

1. Lord Altrincham, "A New Toryism," *Observer* (London), June 9 and 16, 1957.
2. *The Men on the Boards* (London: Acton Society Trust, 1957).
3. Fortune Editors, *The Executive Life* (Garden City: Doubleday, 1956), pp. 62-63, 71-72.
4. A. A. Berle, *The 20th Century Capitalist Revolution* (New York: Harcourt, Brace, 1954), pp. 46-52.
5. J. K. Galbraith, *American Capitalism. The Concept of Countervailing Power* (Boston: Houghton Mifflin, 1952.)
6. David E. Lilienthal, *Big Business; A New Era* (New York: Harper, 1956).
7. Samuel J. Konefsky, *The Legacy of Holmes and Brandeis* (New York: Macmillan, 1956), p. 78.
8. *Study of Monopoly,* Hearing before Subcommittee on the Judiciary on H.R. 14, Pt. 4A, "Steel," 81st Cong., 2d Sess., 627 *et seq.* (1950).
9. T. K. Quinn, *Giant Business: Threat to Democracy* (New York: Exposition Press, 1952), chap. 6.
10. William H. Whyte, *The Organization Man* (New York: Simon & Schuster, 1956), Part V, "The Organization Scientist," especially pp. 205-17.
11. *Federal Funds for Scientific Research and Development at Non-Profit Institutions, 1950-51 and 1951-52* (Washington: Government Printing Office, 1953).
12. Lilienthal, *op. cit.,* p. 54.
13. Berle, *op. cit.,* pp. 50-51.
14. Arthur MacMahon (ed.), *Federalism Mature and Emergent* (Garden City: Doubleday, 1955), pp. 322-23, 345-46.
15. Berle, *op. cit.,* p. 40.
16. Ira Mosher, remarks quoted in *Hearings before a Subcommittee of the Committee on Banking and Currency* on S. 380, 79th Cong., 1st Sess., 124 (1945).
17. *General Interim Report of House Select Committee on Lobbying Activities,* H.R., 81st Cong., 2d Sess. 63 (1950).
18. Berle, *op. cit.,* chaps. iii and v.
19. Herbert Paul (ed.), *Letters of Lord Acton to Mary Gladstone* (London: George Allen, 1904), p. 93.
20. C. Wright Mills, *The Power Elite* (New York: Oxford University Press, 1956), p. 347.
21. Whyte, *op. cit.,* pp. 148-49.
22. *Ibid.,* pp. 155-56.
23. Kenneth Boulding, *The Organizational Revolution* (New York: Harper, 1953), chaps. viii and x.
24. F. A. von Hayek (ed.), *Capitalism and the Historians; Essays by T. S. Ashton and Others* (Chicago: University of Chicago Press, 1954), pp. 40-41.
25. Leslie A. Fiedler, *An End to Innocence; Essays on Culture and Politics* (Boston: Beacon Press, 1955), p. 10.
26. Simon Kuznets and Elizabeth Jenks, *Shares of Upper Income Groups in Income and Savings* (New York: National Bureau of Economic Research, 1953), pp. xxxv-xxxix and 37-43.
27. Mills, *op. cit.,* chaps. 8 and 9; Matthew Josephson, *The Big Guns,* reprint from the *Nation* (New York, 1957); Burton M. Sapin and Richard C. Snyder, *The Role of the Military in American Foreign Policy* (New York: Doubleday, 1954); and *Military in American Foreign Policy* (New York: Doubleday, 1954) and Samuel P. Huntington, *The Soldier and the State* (Cambridge: Harvard University Press, 1957), pp. 463-64.
28. John Strachey, *Contemporary Capitalism* (New York: Random House, 1956), pp. 295-303.

29. Marver H. Bernstein, *Regulating Business by Independent Commission* (Princeton: Princeton University Press, 1955), pp. 294-96. See the earlier remarks of Cushman in *The Independent Regulatory Commissions* (New York: Oxford University Press, 1941), pp. 730-31.

30. C. Wilcox, *Public Policies toward Business* (Homewood, Ill.: Irwin, 1955); Walter Adams and Horace M. Gray, *Monopoly in America: The Government as Promoter* (New York: Macmillan, 1955).

31. Adams and Gray, *op. cit.*, pp. 172-78.

32. Lilienthal, *op. cit.*, pp. 181-88.

33. Gilbert Seldes, *The Public Arts* (New York: Simon & Schuster, 1956), p. 84.

34. *Ibid.*, p. 294.

35. *Fortune* Editors, *op. cit.*, p. 82.

36. Whyte, *op. cit.*, chap. 14.

37. David Riesman, Nathan Glazer, Reuel Denny, *The Lonely Crowd* (New York: Doubleday Anchor Book Edition, 1953), pp. 346-49.

38. Mills, *op. cit.*, chap. 13.

39. Pitirim Sorokin, *Fads and Foibles in Modern Sociology and Related Sciences* (Chicago: Henry Regnery, 1956), *passim*.

40. "The Language of Sociology," *Times Literary Supplement* (London), November 2, 1956, p. 651.

41. Ludwig von Mises, *The Anti-Capitalistic Mentality* (Princeton: Van Nostrand, 1956), pp. 11-33.

42. Charles Parkin, *The Moral Basis of Burke's Political Thought* (Cambridge: Cambridge University Press, 1956), pp. 4-5.

43. J. C. Rees, *Mill and his Early Critics* (Leicester: University College, 1956), *passim*.

44. Clinton L. Rossiter, *Conservatism in American* (New York: Knopf, 1955), pp. 231-34.

45. Peter Viereck, *The Shame and Glory of the Intellectuals* (Boston: Beacon Press, 1953), p. 254.

46. *Ibid.*, pp. 261-62.

47. Whittaker Chambers, *Witness* (New York: Random House, 1952), pp. 82-83.

48. Daniel Bell (ed.), *The New American Right* (New York: Criterion Books, 1955), pp. 189-92.

49. Viereck, *op. cit.*, p. 248.

50. Gordon A. Harrison, *Road to the Right; the Tradition and Hope of American Conservatism* (New York: Morrow, 1954), p. vii.

51. Clinton Rossiter, *Seedtime of the Republic; The Origin of the American Tradition of Political Liberty* (New York: Harcourt, Brace, 1953), pp. 312 ff.

52. Daniel Boorstin, *The Genius of American Politics* (Chicago: University of Chicago Press, 1953), pp. 99 ff.

53. Stuart Gerry Brown, *The First Republicans; Political Philosophy and Public Policy in the Party of Jefferson and Madison* (Syracuse: Syracuse University Press, 1954), pp. 44-46.

54. Richard Pares, *King George III and the Politicians* (New York: Oxford University Press, 1954), p. 117.

55. Will Herberg, *Protestant, Catholic, Jew. An Essay in American Religious Sociology* (Garden City: Doubleday, 1955), pp. 283-85.

56. Quintin Hogg, *The Case for Conservatism* (London: Penguin Books, 1948), p. 18.

57. B. Seebohm Rowntree, and G. R. Lavers, *English Life and Leisure. A Social Study* (London: Longmans, Green, 1951), p. 347.

58. *Ibid.*, pp. 345-46.

59. Wm. Cunningham, *The Common Weal. Six Lectures on Political Philosophy* (Cambridge: Cambridge University Press, 1917), pp. 34-35.

60. *University Education and Business* (Cambridge: Cambridge University Press, 1945), *passim.; Donald Dewey, "Professor Schumpeter on Socialism; The

Case of Britain," *Journal of Political Economy*, LVIII (June, 1950), pp. 208-9.
61. *Economist* (London), October 20, 1956, pp. 214-15.
62. *Tribune* (London), March 21, 1947. For a study of the class structure of the Higher Civil Service see R. K. Kelsall, *Higher Civil Servants* in Britain. (London: Routledge & Kegan Paul, 1955), especially chapter 7.
63. *Economist* (London), July 21, 1956, pp. 199-201; July 28, 1956, pp. 297-98.
64. T. H. Pear, *English Social Differences* (London: Allen & Unwin, 1955), chap. 10.
65. *Ibid.*, p. 291.
66. Strachey, *op. cit.*, pp. 128-29.
67. Edward Bulwer-Lytton, *England and the English* (London: Richard Bentley, 1833), I, 18.
68. Mills, *op. cit.*, chap. 7; Quinn, *op. cit.*, chaps. 15 and 16.
69. The Acton Society Trust, *Studies in Nationalized Industry. Problems of Promotion Policy; The Future of the Unions; The Framework of Joint Consultation* (London: 1951-52). See also *Special Report from Select Committee on Nationalized Industries* (London: HMSO, 120, November, 1955); and National Coal Board, *Report of the Advisory Committee on Organization* (London, February, 1955).
70. C. A. R. Crosland, *The Future of Socialism* (London: Jonathan Cape, 1956); Socialist Union, *Twentieth Century Socialism* (London: Penguin Books, 1956).
71. Strachey, *op. cit.*, pp. 331-35.
72. Margaret Cole (ed.), *Beatrice Webb's Diaries 1924-1932* (London: Longmans, Green, 1956), II, 295.

A NEW ISM FOR SOCIALISM

Sidney Hook

Socialist parties in Europe and in some countries of Asia are undergoing important transformations under the whiplash of recent electoral defeats. More and more they are surrendering their traditional ideology and becoming broad movements of social reform.

Their familiar programs and slogans have proved unable to win them public support in the face of the relatively high levels of prosperity and employment achieved under conservative governments. Despite increased industrialization and urbanization (processes which, according to Socialist theory, were expected to prepare the way for Socialist

Reprinted from the *New York Times Magazine*, April 10, 1960. By permission of the author and the publisher.

triumph) the appeal of their message—even to the workers whose
interests they were organized to further—has declined. This appears to
be as true in the Scandinavian countries as in Israel, in England as in
central Europe. The rise of a new Social Democratic party in Japan
under Nishio Suchero is also in line with this tendency.

The momentous change in the orientation of socialism has been
dramatized by these three events: the abandonment of the traditional
Marxist program by the West German Social Democratic party; the
post-election discussion of the British Labor party at Blackpool and in
the English Labor press, and last summer's meeting of the Sixth
Congress of the Socialist International at Hamburg.

The German Social Democratic party, launched with the blessings
of Marx and Engels, has always been a classic example of Socialist
orthodoxy. Last fall the party adopted a new "program of principles."
Not only did that program avoid the usual Marxist clichés—even terms
like "class" and "class struggle" were replaced by euphemisms—but it
openly acknowledged the value of private enterprise in major sectors
of the economy. For "common or public ownership" it substituted the
more flexible notion of "public control." The adoption of such a program
(summed up in the pronouncement "as much competition as possible,
as much planning as necessary") can be compared to the abandonment
of basic doctrines by a religion.

In England the Labor party, under the leadership of Hugh Gaitskell,
faces the possibility of a similar turn. British Labor has always placed
its greatest emphasis upon the nationalization of industry. But at the
Blackpool conference following the general elections, Gaitskell cautiously suggested that the emphasis be shifted from nationalization to
social welfare aspects of the program.

Aroused by the Gaitskell proposal, the war horses of Socialist
orthodoxy are calling for a return to "Socialist first principles," which
to them means more nationalization. Since they still muster the support
of an old and eloquent rank and file, who distrust the dulcet tones and
uncalloused hands of the younger intellectual leaders, it will probably
take some time before any change is officially adopted.

The deliberations last summer of the Sixth Congress of the Socialist
International emphasized the view that Socialists must now speak not
only for a class but for the public welfare. Hardly anyone at the congress identified public welfare with nationalization. The dominant mood
was expressed in a remark of the Dutch Socialist Voogd: "The most
important question for Socialists is no longer who owns the means of
production in society but how people live in society."

The ideological revolution signaled by these three events can be
summarized as a recognition by Socialists that today, when democracy
is threatened by totalitarianism and war, the political rather than the
economic structure of a country is more important in achieving Socialist
goals.

The importance of this change from doctrinaire to liberal socialism

can be understood only against the background of the traditional Socialist credo and the four chief reasons offered for its acceptance.

First among the cardinal articles of Socialist belief was public
ownership or nationalization of the means of production. This was
justified on two main grounds: economic, and ethical or political.
Nationalization, it was felt, merely continued a process of economic
expansion and monopoly already observable in capitalist society. But
there was this important difference: since industry would be operated
for public service rather than for private profit, its wheels could always
be kept turning and the evils of the business cycle avoided.

Nationalization would also put an end to unemployment, for there
would be no curb on production so long as there was a social need
for what was produced. Just as important was the ethical or political
justification. Since property is a form of power, those who own the means
of production exert a very great control over those who must live by
them. Socialists hoped that nationalization would free workers from the
arbitrary exercise of power by those who owned industry.

The second main feature of socialism was planning. It was regarded
as the only means by which waste of natural and human resources
could be avoided. Viewing the economic plant of society as a whole,
Socialists argued that planning would eliminate duplication and the
unnecessary costs of competition. It would also strengthen those public
services, from conservation of natural resources to education, with which
government must be increasingly concerned.

Third was socialism's emphasis upon human welfare and social
justice. Socialists believed that, just as all who consumed the wealth
produced by society owed it some service, so society was obligated
to provide adequate vocational opportunities for all who were able and
willing to work. Private industry could do this only fitfully, depending
upon market conditions. In its drive toward efficiency and profitable
labor-saving machinery, it could not concern itself with human and
social costs of technological innovation.

Further, Socialists believed society—in order to provide equality of
opportunity—must reward according to need as well as capacity. Depending upon the level of the the productive forces, it must provide
a constantly rising floor of compensation for all who do useful work,
and a steadily declining ceiling of income for those who live on
inherited wealth.

The fourth element in socialism was humanistic—the desire to bring
about a society in which every individual would mature into an independent harmonious personality, developing as far as his abilities permitted. He would be either a creator or, more likely, someone capable of
making creative and meaningful use of leisure. Socialists were always
fond of saying, "Nothing of genuine value or culture is too good for
the workers."

It was hoped that under socialism there would be a revulsion against
monetary values, that human beings would learn that life's real wealth

can be found only where one finds its joys—in human beings and ideas, in art, religion and science.

What happened to all these brave aspirations? To the surprise of Socialists, some of them were realized through gradual changes in the existing economic system. The capitalism of "the robber barons" gave way to a mixed economy, which was no longer a strictly free-enterprise system either in law or in fact.

Even more striking was the discovery that public ownership was not a cure-all, that human beings could be exploited and feel themselves exploited just as much by publicly owned industries as by private ones. Of this, the Communist countries furnished frightening proof. It was clear that in the absence of democratic processes, bureaucrats have far greater power over human beings—including the power of life and death—than do private owners, subject as they are to law and the countervailing force of strong and free labor unions.

Furthermore, the principles of social welfare and responsibility for the unemployed, the aged, the sick and disabled—traditional staples of the Socialist program—were adopted by those who were not Socialists. This was a universal phenomenon. The Democratic party platform of 1932 reads very much like the Republican party platform; but the record of New Deal achievements reads like the Socialist party platform of 1932—nationalization excepted.

Similarly, when the Tory party came to power in England, although it opposed further nationalization, it did not scrap the social services introduced by the Labor party. Indeed, at one time it even boasted that it had constructed more public housing than had Labor.

Rising standards of living after the war, coupled with almost full employment and the allure of modern gadgetry, took some of the fighting spirit out of the Socialist rank and file—just as the previous period of tight wartime controls had left many of them with mixed feelings about the desirability of socialism. Socialism became a movement associated with middle age, respectability and moral earnestness. It seemed to bore the young, who were looking for a good time rather than a good cause.

Finally and most important, one must list the revitalization of the ethical and democratic aspects of socialism. Socialists began to realize that large-scale industrialization and mass culture, whether under capitalism or socialism, often imperil the individual's sense of independence, of integrity, of counting for something. They returned to their original insight that the organization of production was only a means to an end—to a free, secure and significant life.

To a cog in a vast machine it matters little who sits at the levers of power—individual owner, government bureaucrat or corporate manager. What does matter, to a human being who seeks to find some meaning in his work and life, is whether he can share or influence power, whatever the legal forms of ownership. (The German Socialists have concluded that one of the ways they can best further the interest of working people is by a policy of "codetermination" which would give workers the right to elect representatives to the managerial boards of industry.)

All this represents, if not a complete abandonment of Marxism, at least a profound retreat from or revision of Marxism. Socialists are still pledged to continue the class struggle, despite their new vocabulary. But it is obvious to European Socialists that they have much more in common with their democratic non-Socialist brethren than with the Communists, whose shadow lies athwart the Continent. When threatened, the freedoms to speak and agitate, to organize and strike become better understood and more precious than before.

Does all this mean that Socialists consider their great battles have been won? It is difficult to answer unequivocally yes or no. Considerable pockets of poverty still exist. The legal forms of ownership are in the main unaltered. Nonetheless, in the area of social welfare—especially recognition of both state and industry responsibility for raising the living standards and humanizing the lives of the working population—some of the major battles have been substantially won. The opponents of socialism have accepted the welfare state in practice if not in theory—though they have sometimes done this to prevent Socialists from carrying out a more extreme program.

If this is so, does socialism have a future as a separate movement and as a separate political party? That it will have some role is indisputable. Whether it will be successful, in terms of winning elections is less certain. Let us consider the two points independently.

Once the monolithic, chock-a-block conception of socialism is discarded, Socialist parties can no longer speak in prophetic or apocalyptic tones. They can no longer offer total solutions, only piecemeal proposals to improve this or that. They once believed that a basic economic change was sufficient for the solution of all capitalist society's major problems.

Today they know better. The evils of society, in their present view, do not all flow from free enterprise as such. Therefore Socialist party platforms of the future will not call for across-the-board nationalization, but will admit the desirability of combining competition and free enterprise in some sectors of the economy with public service corporations of various kinds in others.

With this new orientation, Socialist parties will become the parties of continuous social reform, spokesmen for all forgotten or oppressed groups, the tribunes for more social welfare. They not only will fight for measures that will increase production and insure maximum employment, but will seek to equalize opportunities, to raise the standards of health, housing, education and culture.

The reforms they advocate may be similar to those drawn up by conservative parties, but Socialists will demand more public funds for social welfare and more guarantees that the rise in standards of living will not be accompanied by erosion of personal freedoms. Socialist parties will therefore present themselves not as class parties but as the protagonists of all worthy causes that further the democratic way of life.

Will this role win elections? The answer is much more uncertain, even though the emphasis on reform rather than doctrinaire socialism recently enabled the German Socialists to win their first election over Adenauer's Christian Democratic Union in predominantly Catholic Bavaria.

Except when a country is aroused by grave political abuses, elections are won by the patient and continuous work of political organization. There is reason to believe that what Socialists may gain in popular appeal they may lose in organizational cohesiveness, once the fervor of Messianism is lost. The transformation of the Socialist parties into opposition reform parties may cost them the devotion and day-in-day-out support of the "Jimmy Higginses," the humble rank and file whose faith rests on a shining vision rather than on the slow, unexciting evidence of progress. And it may well become more difficult to attract young men and women out to transform the world.

At any rate, political life in England, Germany and other countries in which the Socialist parties complete this evolution will not be as dramatic in the near future as in the past. It will be more responsible, less sloganized, more literate. (The Russian and Chinese Communists and the repercussions of their foreign policy on the domestic scene can be counted on to keep it from becoming boring.)

Outside the arena of party politics, socialism will become an ethical movement, applying the methods of scientific intelligence to the problems of national and international life. The stronger such a movement grows, the closer we in the free world will come to a society without ideologies or permanent political factions in which men will temporarily divide over specific issues independently of their overarching religious or philosophical commitments.

The rise of Fascist and Communist totalitarianism in the twentieth century should be the most powerful argument in persuading the genuinely democratic parties of the free world that what they have in common is more important than what divides them. Differences there will always be; but however grave, they need not be divisive to a point of violent conflict if common needs and aspirations and a faith in intelligence are taken as a basis for settling them.

THE SPLIT BETWEEN ASIAN AND
WESTERN SOCIALISM

David J. Saposs

The dominating ideology in the international labor movement in the West is still Socialist, but a Socialism with a new look. Marxism has been discarded, although more by force of circumstances than conscious design, and the movement is still influenced by some Marxian reasoning; but, in general, Western Socialism has ceased to be class conscious and become reformist. It seeks the welfare state, but not revolution. The growing Christian (predominantly Catholic) labor movement in Western Europe has also arrived at maturity, and its social philosophy is likewise oriented toward the welfare state.

The old controversy over the interpretation of Marx was not revived in the labor movements in continental Europe after this war, as it was after World War I. This tacit abandonment of Marxism became fully apparent when the Socialist International was revived as a permanent organization in Frankfurt during the summer of 1951. The program and pronouncements of the convention used none of the Marxian terminology so characteristic of prewar Socialist literature, and this momentous omission was not challenged in the discussions there. The 1952 Milan Conference of the Socialist International followed the precedent established at Frankfurt, and at the 1953 Stockholm Conference it was repeated. Such clichés as the materialistic or economic conception of history, exploitation of the workers, expropriating the expropriators, the class struggle, are no longer mentioned. The former sacred tenet that the workers are the class chosen to fulfill the holy mission of bringing about the inevitable capitulation of capitalism has fallen into limbo. The central theme of the new official pronouncements revolves about problems of social justice, economic planning, full employment, democracy and human rights. Emphasis is placed on the need to avoid deflation with its consequent depression and unemployment, and, of

Reprinted from *Foreign Affairs*, vol. 32, no. 4 (July, 1954), 588-594. By permission of the author and the Council on Foreign Relations, Inc., New York.

course, on the rôle of the trade union movement in promoting social justice.

To be sure, differences exist on policy, with the British Socialists still clinging to nationalization, the Germans featuring "codetermination" in industry and the Scandinavians empirically emphasizing efficiency and production, with better distribution of the proceeds. But the Communists are the only group within the Western democracies still consistently quoting Marx—albeit hyphenated to Lenin and Stalin—and talking revolution, often obfuscated by their need to adapt their pronouncements and activities to the changing tactics of Soviet foreign policy.

In Asia and other underdeveloped areas, however, the situation is different. A deep schism seems to be developing in the world Socialist movement, led by the Asian Socialist parties. The separatist group revealed itself at the 1951 congress of the Socialist International in Frankfurt; and at the succeeding Milan Congress this group announced the intention of organizing an independent Asian Socialist movement. Its Congress convened in Rangoon in January 1953. European Socialist notables, including Clement R. Attlee, attended as fraternal delegates and urged the conference to remain an organic part of the Socialist International, arguing strongly against the formation of a separate Asian Socialist Conference. Notwithstanding the prominence of these fraternal delegates from the Socialist Parties of the Western democracies and the eloquence of their appeal, their advice was not heeded. A separate and independent Asian Socialist Conference was formed. The only concession made to the Socialist International was the proviso that the affiliates with the Asian Socialist Conference could retain affiliation with the Socialist International if they desired. It was further announced that the Asian organization would undertake to maintain close contact with the Socialist International, but it was emphatically stipulated that the Asian Conference would have no organic connection with the International.

The new Asian organization differs basically from the Western-oriented Socialists, although its thinking has not yet been clarified. Many of its adherents, like the left-wing Socialist Party of Japan, feature revolutionary radicalism and hail Marx as their true prophet. With mild reservations they regard Russia as the Socialist fatherland, uncritically accepting its claims of accomplishments and looking to it for inspiration. Such left-wing elements point to the United States and the capitalist world as the enemy; Soviet interpretations of events and accusations against the Western democracies are unquestioningly supported. Similarly, this faction supports all proposals made by the Communists for ostensibly improving relations between the East and the West.

However, such left-wing Socialists have resisted the Communist efforts to take over their parties, and, so far, have maintained their independence. They have no open relations with the Cominform and its affiliates, differing in this respect from the Nenni Socialists in Italy, for example. On the other hand, they are devout champions of revolutionary radicalism, seeking the overthrow of the present social order and its replacement by a Socialist society. In Japan, the right-wing Socialist Party reflects the prevailing national sentiment which believes in a strong domestic police force, but it opposed Japanese rearmament and does not want the government to lean toward the United States and the other Western democracies.

In some Asian countries—Burma and India, for example—Socialists tend to blend their doctrine with the prevailing religious or social philosophies, most of them steering clear of Marxism and revolutionary radicalism and advocating an advanced program of social reform, stimulated by the existing feudalism. Thus they emphasize land reform, anti-imperialism and national independence, to be attained through moderate means. Like the more extreme faction, however, they too are friendly toward Russia. Even the more moderate elements, influenced by Communist anti-imperialist and anti-capitalist propaganda, which is reinforced by their own suspicion of the motives of the West (particularly the United States) and by their fear of offending their Communist neighbor, China, are inclined to equate Russia with the United States. Neutralism in international affairs is their watchword. The Asian Conference disapproved of Communist totalitarian policies, such as the use of force, denial of freedom and negation of human rights, but the tendency is to regard these features as transitory and incidental. Even the moderates tend to accept the professions of accomplishment by the Communist countries at face value, hoping that they themselves can achieve their objectives without resort to brutality.

Thus both wings of the Socialist movement in Asia are neutralist. Some, as in Burma, are primarily influenced by their juxtaposition to Communist countries; others in India are still operating under the spell of Gandhi. Their conceptions of neutrality sometimes transcend normal understanding. Recently the Socialist Government of Burma refused economic aid from the United States so that its neutrality would not be compromised. However, it proposes to negotiate an economic treaty with Soviet Russia. This same Government has deported deserting Chinese Communist army personnel that claimed political asylum in Burma, justifying this inhuman action by the contention that its neutral policy forced it to deny political asylum to offenders against "a friendly nation," notwithstanding that these soldiers were returned to certain death. But such neutralists were horrified at the execution of the Rosenberg atom spies in the United States.

Such states of mind can be only temporary, although it is clear that the Asian Socialist Parties of both right and left are determined to separate themselves from the movement dominated by the Western democratic Socialists. The left wing, which clings to the doctrine of the overthrow of capitalism, by revolutionary means if need be, predicates its doctrine on Marxist reasoning and tempers its neutralism by being "neutral against" the United States in favor of Russia. The right wing sponsors moderate procedures and immediate social reform with emphasis on particular Asian problems. It is not critical of Russia and is more readily attracted by Soviet claims than is its Western Socialist counterpart. However, it favors accepting Western economic and technological assistance, with no military or diplomatic alliances. It considers itself a firm adherent of democracy.

The Communists are using the Asian neutralist Socialists to their advantage, but whether they will capture them is questionable. They seem to be making headway in Japan, both with the left-wing Socialists and the principal trade union organizations; the Sohyo trade-union group shifted from "neutralism" to "world-wide collaboration of peace forces," the line now advocated by the Communists, and some of its leaders even declared that Soviet Russia and China were the forces making for peace. However, when leaders of the left-wing Socialist Party criticized this attitude as contrary to neutralism, the Sohyo spokesman retreated. On the whole, it does not seem likely that the Communists will capture the Asian Socialist Conference.

The determination to maintain a separate organization is rationalized by the Asian Socialists on the ground that Asia is confronted with problems which differ from those of the rest of the world. They point out that Asia is primarily agricultural and underdeveloped, that it still suffers from imperialism and colonialism, and that these are problems which the Western World does not understand: only by separate organization, the Asians say, can they cope with the particular problems of the Far East.

This rationale, as well as many of the current demands of the Asian Socialist Conference, highlight the contrast with the conditions that generated the Western Socialist movement in its earlier stages. Socialism in the Western countries was founded on an emerging industrialism, and it adapted its principles, policies and tactics to the expansion and growing stability of capitalism. On the other hand, most of Asia and the other underdeveloped countries of the world still operate under feudalistic customs and régimes. Insofar as there is an emerging industralism, it is based primarily on plantation and extractive industries closely allied to agriculture. Nevertheless, the thinking of Socialists in these countries is complicated by their desire to seek salvation through industrialism. Some of these countries have enacted most advanced social legislation, as recommended in I.L.O. conventions, but little effort is made to enforce these laws.

Politically, the Asian Socialists, in common with the rest of the population in Asia, are still thinking in colonial and semi-colonial terms; their reactions are chiefly based on past experience, influenced by resentment at the fact that they are either still linked to Western countries, or obligated to them. They know that they are economically dependent on Western capital, equipment, technological know-how and supervisory skill, but psychologically they are disturbed at having to accept such assistance. Hence, in emphasizing immediate demands for social improvements, the Asian Socialist Parties have nationalistic, racial, economic and political issues uppermost in their minds. Their pragmatic demands are limited primarily to the solution of agrarian problems and those related to agriculture, such as stimulation and regulation of cottage industries, use of small machines in manufacturing as well as in agriculture, cheap power development. Even the few that look to industrialism for ultimate salvation find it necessary to fall in line with those who stress these immediate demands in order to alleviate pressing social evils.

In contrast, the Socialist parties of the Western democracies, with a rationale stimulated by an emerging industrialism, called for social and labor legislation that would promote the interests of the new wage-earning class—demands for sanitary working conditions, proper light in the factories, accident prevention, workmen's compensation, maximum hours of labor and minimum wages, abolition of child labor, special protection for women workers and social insurance. They also sought to promote better living conditions through housing programs, price controls and food subsidies, and consumer cooperative movements. In time the Asian Socialists will probably adjust their program accordingly.

There is little or no prospect for the old-fashioned revolutionary radicalism in countries and areas with a highly stabilized social structure and a mature industrialization, where workers enjoy "status" and a feeling of belonging. In the viable Western democracies, the small residue of Socialists still attracted by the siren-call of revolution will gravitate, if they have not already done so, toward the Communist movement. It should be noted that the Communist movement has been rapidly losing ground in the countries enjoying a relatively stable social structure—Western Europe (except France and Italy), Australasia, North America. In Italy and France, the Communists seem to be gaining in the political field, and, judging from elections of representatives to works councils, are either retaining their strength or gaining in the industrial field. Outside of these exceptions there are few regions where the Communists have succeeded in maintaining their position. In general their strength has so receded that they are a minor element in the labor movement.

Even in Japan in the recent election the Communists polled only 700,-000 votes and elected only one member to the Lower House of Parliament; but there they are growing stronger in the unions. They made a more formidable showing in the first election in India and are a considerable threat to the Congress Party in many areas—a development that has alerted the dominant political organization to the necessity of seeking alliances with other non-Communist elements. On the whole, open Communist strength is receding in effectiveness in the democratic world. It is naturally more difficult to gauge its conspiratorial and surreptitious activities. Since the Catholic trade-union movement, in common with the Canadian and American labor movements, is clearly committed to an advanced program of social reform and some form of the welfare state, the labor movements of the Western democracies are drawing closer together ideologically.

Thus three political internationals operating in the labor movement are likely to emerge as a result of the new developments—the Western group, the Communists and the Asian neutralists. The last-named, in a sense a "third-force" group, will probably have a strong appeal to the people in other underdeveloped countries, such as Africa and Latin America. It should prove to be a rival of the Communists, in that it will appeal to the outspoken anti-capitalist, anti-imperialist, race-conscious elements, who shy away from aligning themselves with either the Western-oriented movements or the totalitarian forces behind the Iron Curtain. Though there seems little danger that it will be captured by the Communists, it might be tempted to collaborate with them, and it may experience defections. It will, however, be playing the Communist game indirectly, and will thereby render a serious disservice to the democratic world. It will no doubt prosper in underdeveloped areas, particularly among peoples who are still laboring under the shell-shock of colonialism and imperialism, and who have suffered from discrimination because of color. The ultra-radical element which used to be temperamentally attracted to syndicalism in the West, and which thrived in the countries with the most unstable social structures, might also gravitate toward this group.

Eventually, the relations of the Communists to this neutralist group are certain to become strained. At present, Asian Socialism is an obstacle to the strengthening of democratic forces; but it is also a barrier between the Communists and the masses. If the Communists come to believe that the neutralism of the Asian Socialists is hindering them more than it is helping them, they are bound to turn on it, as they have on other movements which they have failed to direct or control.

THE ANATOMY OF CONSERVATIVES

Francis G. Wilson

I

The critics of conservatives seem to center on the proposition that the "new conservatism" is not really a properly intelligible position. There is a tendency, often implicit, to say that conservatism has no status as a program, ideology, or political philosophy. The gravamen of the charge is either that conservatives are irrational; that they have lost their sense of reality; or that they represent a form of inverted or reversed utopianism, or doctrinairism, that cannot be taken seriously. However, the denial of status as a political position takes a variety of forms and some of these must be noted before we enter into the positive argument of this paper.

1. In the extreme, critics have insisted that conservatism is a kind of political tropism. The conservative exhibits a kind of inborn inclination, or fixed personality drift, or trait, that is purely and simply negative. The contemporary emphasis on the study of personality, and the view that personality traits are extremely difficult or impossible to modify, have lent support to the contention that conservatives by their tropism are excluded from any connection with rationality. On the assumption that the conservative represents a clinical case of "the authoritarian personality" it has been said that we have only a "pseudo-conservatism" in the United States.[1]

2. Again, the differences between conservatives and others—especially the liberals—is one of mood and bias, rather than discernible stands on public questions. Exponents of this view deny that conserva-

Reprinted from *Ethics*, vol. LXX, no. 4 (July, 1960), 265-281. By permission of the author and the publisher.

tives have a position or that there can be any serious distinction between liberals and conservatives. Still, Rossiter has insisted on the irresponsibility of the "ultra" conservatives, who are presumably those who reject the "revolutions" of the last generation in both domestic and foreign policy. Pushed to an extreme the "mood and bias" argument would deny also the historical foundations of conservative argument, as well as national variants in conservative thought and program. But it is quite clear that the legitimacy and quality of the conservative's position are minimized to invisibility if the position taken is short of being "ultra." [2]

3. Another denial of the existential quality of conservatism would reduce it simply to a reaction against change. That there is a "situational" element in conservatism can hardly be denied, for the prudential judgments of conservatives differ in different countries, in different times, and there are sharp differences in social philosophy. The conservative, it is said, expresses his nature in opposition, mostly futile, to change, whatever may be its social or political character. Nor is it merely a matter of definition that is involved here, for one is concerned with the existential quality of the conservative mind. Moreover, the struggle to prevent change can be either limited and immediate, or it can be discovered in critical historical situations such as the attempts to turn back the Reformation, to limit the impact of the French Revolution and its revolutions by filiation, to retard the march of democratic parliamentary institutions, and the effort to check the technological revolutions of modern society. Thus, conservatism is situational and positional. The critics have said that on the positive side the "new conservative" is so vague in his immediate political stands and in his interpretation of traditional personalities that conservatism has little or no rational relevance to the modern world. [3]

4. In a view of more savage criticism, it is said that conservatives then and now, old or new, are simply reactionary, unprogressive, and feudalistic characters attempting to steal the social show. Such has been the condemnation voiced by the left-wing revolutionary and more positively by the long sequence of the disciples of Karl Marx. Reaction has been defined in the most elusive manner, and "unprogressive" is surely an epithet of the ideological wars. "Feudal" as used by Marxians has, of course, no relation to any historical or existential meaning. For in Marxism it is an abstract idea, a definitional symbol, used to castigate the enemy. In more specific terms, the conservative as a reactionary has been described as the European "economic liberal," defender of the free-market economy, the defender of capitalism, and the opponent of democracy, popular sovereignty, and liberty. In other situations, the conservative has been identified with the totalitarian minds defending the totalitarian regime, and, indeed, simply as a fascist. Obviously, in such a war of Giant Ideology, as Russell Kirk expresses it, the most extreme example is often chosen as the most typical. In recent times, as well, the conservative has been identified in communist propaganda with the thrust of imperialism, particularly the alleged effort of the

United States to dominate the world. Lenin's *Imperialism* is certainly one of the most important of the ideological textbooks against conservatism in our time.[4]

5. At a higher level of dialectic the conservative is charged with being reactionary in his commitment to a philosophy, which is again a denial of rationality and the right to claim honorable status among political positions. The conservative is usually theistic rather than deistic or agnostic; he believes in sin rather than atrophied personal moral responsibility; he asserts the imperfect qualities in the composite of human nature, and he denies that central hypothesis of progressivism, the perfectibility of man. The conservative is likely to be a traditional Christian or believer in a religious faith, while the enemy has emancipated himself from the superstitions and priestcraft of other and more primitive eras. But there have been impressive changes in both the defense of theistic philosophy and of Christian-inspired conservatism. Kuehnelt-Leddihn has written, "There are close ties between the New Conservatism and the notions of Burke, von Stein, Görres, A. v. Müller, Chateaubriand, E. L. v. Gerlach, Lacordaire, Montalembert, and even of Peguy, but very few links with the ideology of De Maistre and almost none at all with that of De Bonald or Maurras." In other words, the new conservatism is profoundly hostile to nationalism, while it was not in a previous time.[5]

II

1. The attempt to explain the anatomy of conservatives begins here with the proposition that conservatism must be accepted as a legitimate political position. As a "position" it must be studied both in a general sense and in particular situations. It is a dialectical force that arises when there are political oppositions, such as between liberals or revolutionaries and conservatives. Such conflict and contradiction are found, naturally, where political and social consensus has been in process of breaking down, for where there is deep consensus there is hardly a conscious position at all, and there is no conservatism in a practical sense. When there is conflict about ideals and solutions of human uncertainties in the typically "human situation," there can be a classification of conservatives, for the conservative is aware of his commitment or engagement to a position in a changing situation. In any given struggle a pattern of argument emerges, and ideas from the past are incorporated in the present. But a point to be emphasized is this: classification is most effective and meaningful to the student of conservatives when value systems are the groundwork of classification. Surely the great ideas or the great conflicts in ideas must matter most: the struggle between religious affirmation and indifference or hostility; realism in a factual or naturalistic sense, and realism as the attainment of truth and value, or a belief that in the end it is the truth that will work; the struggle between methods of inquiry, between naturalism,

even with a theistic interpretation, and intuition or the self-evident statement. No doubt, one of the deepest of all the conflicts is the materialistic
insistence on what life is against the spiritual interpretation of man's
nature.

To the conscious conservative his commitment is an adherence to
order and to the symbols of order that both justify and sustain it. A
conservative is more likely to view history as Eric Voegelin has in his
magnificent *Order and History,* one of the most profoundly conservative studies of history in our time. He has presented a central theme
concerning the attitude of those who would create and conserve institutions: the historical process is to be understood as the movement of
decisive civilizations and societies either toward or away from union
with God. Every important order has interpreted itself in relation to
its conception of an order that is both in nature and is ultramundane,
and there is always a search for symbols that can represent this order
in the life of a society. In Volume I Voegelin speaks of Israel, and for
Israel order was discovered primarily in revelation, as for the Hellenes
it was primarily in philosophy. With Israel for the first time mankind
learned what it means to have a history and move in time toward the
consummation of both man's will and God's intention. This movement
and this process of history is symbolized in scripture, in the liturgy
of the religion of Yahweh, in sacred poems and secular history, as well
as in drama and philosophy.[6] If one proposes to say that a conservative
is a situational thinker, then one must inquire deeply into "situations,"
for the transmundane interpretation of situation cannot in the more
recent views of history be excluded; "situation" cannot be limited to a
few details of pragmatic history without the infusion of meaning
through value; formal history is not enough in itself to sustain a thesis
about the situation in which the mind of the conservative works.

2. Let us consider the problematic of position and situation for the
conservative.

a. First of all, there is a level of discussion to be noted. While it is
true that the inarticulate man may live either with a common acceptance
of tradition or with an uneasy sense of hostility toward those who oppose
him, at a more formal level discussion is carried on either by intellectuals, by the writer or teacher, or by the political leader. Intellectuals
have been said to sense their remoteness from the masses; hence their
willingness to become members of the Marxist movement, which promises them an end to their alienation. The conservative intellectual is, no
doubt, more successful than the revolutionary in integrating his personality with non-intellectual people. Still, it is especially part of the work
of the politician to insist that he has contact with common men and to
discuss the politics of issues that are understood at least to a limited
extent by just anyone who may happen to hear.

The eloquence of intellectual conservatives must in logic begin
with some sort of philosophy of conservatism. In turn, this philosophy
rests remotely on a model of the universe and more immediately on
history; it is a paradigm of causation, motivation, and sequence, and it

involves of necessity some position on ordinary or perennial philosophical issues. In contrast, the political leader is the purveyor of prudential judgments on policy and proposals for political reform. There is surely a conservative theory of reform, such as that of the French Catholic intellectuals who criticized industrialism during the nineteenth century. Benjamin Disraeli and Richard Oastler in England may be cited as conservatives who had a theory of reform having little in common with the reforms urged either by the triumphant liberals or by the emergent socialists. In the contemporary situation the conservative is seeking to develop new positions in the ideological void that covers much of Europe. The restoration of symbols of order, including a Christian social policy and the restoration of the institution of monarchy, has been foremost in the minds of many European conservatives.[7]

b. In the second place, a statement of the common maxims and policies of the conservative should be offered. We deal here with the models, or designs, of a generalized conservative system that any of its adherents might advocate. The model or design is frequently like a Kantian conception which is defined formally to begin with while admitting that no single instance of what is defined may be strictly in accordance with the definition. The paradigm or the stylization is a kind of historical average; it is protographic and logical rather than existential. However, such a summary of maxim and policy is a construction of an idea resting on a considerable body of Western experience. Any design of ideology must rest on some primary idea of the cosmos. But since conservatism is a political position (as viewed in this discussion), the propositions that make up the "creed" are not usually primary ideas in speculative philosophy. Most writers on conservatives have attempted to state a series of propositions that are commonly associated with conservative positions, and these statements constitute the model or the design of the ideology. The model, then, constitutes a summary at the surface; it consists of views held by intellectuals and those who in any case are articulate, but it must be conceded that the statement of the ideological paradigm is not a probing philosophical experience.

First, conservatives have variant but similar attitudes toward the continuity of experience. Most conservatives would say there are patterns in behavior to be observed in history, and these patterns give rise to clues of what is possible or probable in politics. Obviously not all history by any means is a proper subject of admiration, but "pattern," if it exists, is objective. Undoubtedly, the Irish look on their historical experience somewhat differently from the conservatives and Unionists in Great Britain.

Second, where history has been kind, as Englishmen have generally seen it, the attitude of Edmund Burke is appropriate. His antagonism to "sophisters and calculators" becomes understandable. History and statesmanship, as Burke urged, involve more than the metaphysics of an undergraduate and the arithmetic of an excise man. There is faith in prescription, and the love and enjoyment of tradition, as Walter Bagehot noted. Social time has its mysteries.[8]

Third, T. S. Eliot once said there must be an orthodoxy by which the tradition of practice, policy, and institution may be judged. The orthodoxy by which tradition is judged is the conservative acceptance of a moral order, or perhaps one should say it is the tradition itself as a deposit of truth, something that is handed on without basic change. Russell Kirk has spoken of the belief that a divine intent rules society. In Catholic terms this means natural law and rights, and in ordinary Protestant expression it is moral law. In any terms, it means a new Aristotelianism rather than pragmatism.[9]

Fourth, conservatives in their majority view have held that it is appropriate to have some distrust of human nature. The conservative "realist" may have the psychological distortions of judgment in mind, but the Christian conservative will probably consider the effect of sin, and, indeed, the effect of original sin. Such a view of practical, behavioral human nature suggests limits to humanitarian reform. In application reform and change are surely not the same; change can, in some instances, make reform impossible. In 1896, in a speech on Princeton University during the American Revolution, Woodrow Wilson said he believed, "There is nothing so conservative of life as growth. . . . But not all change is progress, not all growth is the manifestation of life. Let one part of the body be in haste to outgrow the rest and you have malignant disease, the threat of death." Or, as John Stuart Mill said in *Representative Government*, the people must be able and willing to do the things necessary to support a higher form of government than the one they may have.

Fifth, there is a further conservative view related to the distrust of human nature which is the rejection of the principle of equality. In the extreme in European society it has meant the distinctions of orders and classes. However, in commercial society it means almost simply the justification of the unequal distribution of wealth and the correlation of unequal function with unequal reward as a principle of distributive or social justice. Equality, however, seems to be the great passion of the twentieth century. Viscount Kilmuir said in June, 1953, reflecting a British conservative view, "Equality is intellectual and biological nonsense. Even in the French Revolution it took only five years for the concept of equality to change into that of equality of opportunity." [10]

Sixth, the conservative view holds that government must be limited in its power. Internal restrictions may be used, a careful arrangement of the preconditions of majority rule, and the attempt may be made to assure a pluralistic society. The revolutionist demands a high level of consensus, while the conservative will settle for a low one. It is at this point that the conservative suspicion of the planned society appears, and this suspicion is found both among those who favor an effective free-market economy and those who might accept much of the modification of individualism found in the old program of Disraeli's Tory democracy.

Seventh, conservatives are defenders of property, private property, before they are defenders of capitalism or a particular system of the manufacture and distribution of goods. Capitalism is a late comer, while property in many forms is an ancient institution.[11]

c. An additional problem of position and situation for conservatives concerns the "prudential judgment" of politics and programs. Here the political leader becomes primarily the advocate of policies which he believes will bring nearer the realization of the ideals in national tradition. Policy is always emergent in the history and symbolism of a given time. Since prudential judgment is exercised in the atmosphere of national tradition—that is, the deposit of unchanging value—and within a given nation, it must vary from situation to situation. Policy naturally involves the controversies which whirl around the interpretation of tradition. Against the political leader and his allies among the intellectuals there is often a struggle by segments of public opinion to secure different interpretations of the meaning of national experience. Here one deals with the existential rather than with the potential. The interpretation of tradition is often an argument about what has actually happened in national history. One may say there is in conservatism a national character which is reflected both in values and in established institutions. The application of tradition signifies commitment to policy, and policy may be generally regarded as an explicit statement of prudential judgment. If the intellectual conservative may be classified according to his theories of the truth or validity of ideas, the political leader who is a conservative may be classified according to the national character of the policies he urges for the common good.

The American is fully aware of the controversy concerning the meaning of his tradition. Among the intellectuals there is usually a struggle over the right to say what tradition means. One large school insists that the only American tradition is the liberal attitude as there has never been anything else either in the colonies or in the United States. The contention is focused on this point: there has been no feudalism in America to overthrow. But others have said there is here a practical and pragmatic attitude toward life; hence philosophical views, often metaphysical in import, have had no meaning for Americans. The American tradition is the tradition of having no philosophy; it is a philosophy of no-philosophy. On the other hand, mere practicality is not pragmatism since pragmatism is an epistemology; it is a philosophy; and it might as well be obvious that the principle of natural rights, so deeply embedded in our historic system (including the civil libertarianism of our mid-century times), constitutes a philosophical system. While the liberal has been saying that the only tradition of America is liberalism, the conservative case has been centered on the hypothesis that conservative views have been creatively important in American history. There is, therefore, a formative conservative view in American experience. Must not the "political theology" of *The Federalist* be considered a conservative statement of first rank? Are not most political leaders and writings ambivalent to a degree in their positions? Jefferson was surely not all "liberal and democratic," and John Adams should not be considered all conservative.

Any political and intellectual life might be considered either liberal or conservative, with moments of the other interspersed within a general drift of attitude. But the problem is to discover as much as possible about the attitudes, motivations, and specific beliefs of an individual as he looks out at the social world. It is the individual, not a group, who makes his commitment to society and not to some form of social abstraction. Each individual, as well as each intellectual and political leader, must agree within himself what he will either support or reject and that he will feel harmonious with or alienated from the social world around him. The problem is one of attitude and judgment in a given situation. Conservatives say that certain ideas in America are valid and that they constitute the core of the tradition. The constitution—interpreted in a given manner—is the central symbol of order and the representation of the political cosmos. Private property, the free market, the protection of agriculture, the maintenance of national defense and the system of government, the idea that the United States is a Christian nation, and the maintenance of local autonomy and popular control over schools—all form, to many, the essence of our tradition. Conservatives, likewise, have generally favored stable money, the payment of debts, and the recognition of the moral responsibility of each individual. Curiously, too, when the modern existentialist stresses individual responsibility and the freedom of the will, he speaks like the traditional mind which stressed the moral code and the freedom of the will.

III

We have now reached a point where it should be asked: What is the central theme that creates some kind of taxonomic satisfaction in the study of conservatism? Gerhart Niemeyer has offered a forceful concept in these words:

In essence, conservative theorizing has consisted in attempts to restate the understandings on which a given country actually was based. . . . Conservatives, in thus formulating political truth, have not necessarily desired to return to the past. Nor have they forsworn change and a better future. Essentially what they have done is to point out the laws of spontaneity in the order of a community, lest impatient change seek channels of alienating force. These men were not always called conservatives, just as their opponents were not always named liberals. But the conservative concern, always the same, has been consistently with the "planners," the thinkers of abstract schemes, the know-better innovators, the politically unresponsive intellectuals.[12]

The theory of the community or the country involves the creation of an order to which the individual citizen can give his commitment, or his allegiance, and one which he can regard as legitimate. Most articulate and intellectual conservatives are driven in the end to ask also: What kind of a philosophy is necessary as the underpinning of such a community? And they will say, I think, with Niemeyer that behind the thought of men like Coke, Burke, Donoso Cortés, Richard Hooker, or the French critics of the Great Revolution, like Maistre or Bonald, is some kind of Aristotelian-Christian theory of the social nature of man and the society in which he may live. These conservatives, like Woodrow Wilson in the foundation of his thought, would say that just as folly may be observed in history, so wisdom can be gained. The revolutionary mind, and the liberal mind, I think, are more likely to be Kantian than Aristotelian; such minds are surely materialistic if one considers the whole impact of skepticism and dialectical materialism on modern man. The revolutionist may be existential in the atheistic sense, or pragmatic, and an adherent of radical empiricism; but the neo-Aristotelian believes that we can know real things and essential structures; that there is a free spiritual principle in man; that God exists and is providential; and that there is a universal moral law. It is the function of the conservative to state such a position, and it is the function of the conservative leader to formulate prudential judgments that will assist in the realization of the proper symbols of order. It is thus that one may seek to meet a crisis in the existence of the community.

Such a theory of the community is different in a profound sense from what has been called a modern "liberal" theory of society. The community has been emphasized at times to such a degree that there is support for an absolute majority rule, which in itself would be the definition of the truth of the community. There would be no recognition of a weightier or wiser part in making political decisions, for all decisions would flow from the easy spirit of democratic groupings. Freedom is to be attained through "belongingness" and "togetherness," and through the development of the personality under the guidance of psychologists rather than moral teachers; the objective of education and of life in the community would be "life normality and group conformity" and the process of learning might be regarded as a phase of group dynamics. It is a little like the *Zusammengehörighkeitsgefühl* of the *Hitlerjugend*. Indeed, some philosophers have sensed in the pragmatic or instrumentalist group life an approach to the idealist theory of the community, which would be always morally superior to the individual.

The conservative's view of the community seeks to reject extremes. He rejects the utopia of the individual who lives in isolation like a god, as Aristotle noted, and also the utopia in which all members have a full expression of the ego. In the utopia of the isolated individual, the person must renounce the community and mean it; this very renunciation must be his condition of human happiness. A probing issue is raised: What are the ideal types of men? Even the most dedicated in the more strict of monastic orders of life find the process of self-realization in union with God a slow and painful process. The saint, the wise man, the hero, the farmer, the artist, the servant of the city or the church,

the person with beauty and talent, and those who practice the arts—
have all been praised as ideal types, and all of them experience the
necessity of "withdrawal" to solitude for a time. But nearly all of whom
we have any record have returned from the transforming experience of
self-communion to the activity of life in the community. The utopia of
solitude is the preparation for life in society.[13]

Likewise, the conservative is unimpressed with the utopia of the
submerged ego, the life in the group in which the personality realizes
its own perfect importance, its unmeasured prestige, and the complete
absence of any problem of security. In such a group there would be no
need for any catharsis by violence against others, and frustration or
pressure would be just words in other people's tracts for the times. In
such a society the individual would never withdraw since withdrawal
would be unsocial and dangerous to the individual who draws away from
contented life with his fellowship.

Conservatives seek the balanced community, however difficult in
practice it may be to attain it. Balance itself would be difficult both to
define and to attain in policy under whatever system of society it might
be sought. If the conservative attains his end he secures to the creative
individual the proper conditions of life in the community so that there
would be no alienation of those who might search for the utopia of the
sublime life. Neither the intellectual nor the worker must be devalued
and alienated from his social world. The burning ego of those who
exploit must be restrained in so far as the politics of the possible says
it can be done.

IV

Let us shift the discussion now to a more difficult level. It has been
seen that to the conservative the primary object of inquiry is the community. The conservative life is a search for an authentic community
which the individual feels to be legitimate and in which he shares in a
commonly recognized consensus. It is a consensus, indeed, which is
shared by the intellectual and the common man, or by any and all
classes. The conservative community is always one in which there is
some alleviation of class struggle and in which, it is said, *stasis* may be
avoided altogether.

But this means that conservative inquiry into the community is far
more than an inquiry conducted by observing political behavior. It is
an inquiry that gives valid propositions; that is, the inquiry into community must result in truth. Now, the critics of conservatives in the
past century believed they could reach truth, but in more recent days
they have contented themselves with historical relativism, pragmatic
workability, behavioral or operative consensus, and scientific analogy in
social statement. If all conservatives have engaged in the quest for the
truth of a community, and if this has meant some form of philosophy,

one may surely classify the conservatives in accordance with their modes of discovering meaning in symbols of order. What conservatives would recognize, it seems, is that there must be a basis for truth that is more than pragmatic history; history has its uses, but the conservative would say, I think, that the philosophical inquiry is valid, for the philosopher can state the paradigmatic meaning that may be woven into the pragmatic event. Even the reason of the political leader concerned with prudential judgment and the enactment of policy can probe into the issue of meaning.

1. On the one hand, meaning is sought in the sense of the transcendent, and in the opening toward God. To live in history is to live with God and the destiny He will allow or provide for those who, like the children of Israel, formulated the principle for the first time.[14] At the other extreme, one might cite Latin naturalism, including the views of Ortega y Gasset, Santayana, and Unamuno. At times philosophy erupts into the discussion of general policy, and policy is chosen because it seems to stand in agreement with primary philosophical views. Behind any such conception of policy, which is held to be the expression of truth, there is a model or a design of the universe; and the state, the government, and the system of politics are regarded as harmonious with a larger conception of the existential. The larger events of the revolution of heavenly bodies are said to have suggested by analogy the whole notion of "revolution." Thomas Hobbes was surely one of the first to use "revolution" in the modern sense of the word.[15] In modern times secular philosophers have looked at the world as a machine, as a kind of organism, and as historical process, while the religious thinker has included the providential within his design or law of the universe.[16] The theistic view may, of course, be found with many shadings. Isaac Newton, who provided modern man with a mechanical system, was deeply theistic and providential in his thought. Or even law in history may be seen in the state as power or force, realism in the empirical sense. So the German historian Heinrich von Treitschke idolized Machiavelli, and Treitschke exercised a greater spiritual influence on succeeding generations of academic youth in Germany than any other conservative before him.[17] Still, Treitschke was an earnest Christian; the laws of God and the laws of realistic or factual politics did not conflict though moral attainment was surely the higher and ultimate objective of political life. The state as power was the creation of the will of God himself.

The formulation of a theory of law or design in the world is a search for a basis of valid conclusions. Conservatives seek ideas to justify a social order, indeed, but the justification occurs because the ideas are true, and being true they are embodied in institutions that must be defended.[18] The conservative ideology rests on a view of truth, and public policy as prudential judgment is considered to be an expression of deeper strata of thinking about justice, right, and law in the universe. For the conservative as an intellectual, the model of proof of value rests upon a twofold foundation: "history" as a method of inquiry, and "philosophy" as a method of inquiry. Fact and value in either case are united, and empiricism is a "method" by which the facts of history and philosophy are joined into the satisfactory demonstration of judgment.

a. In the demonstration of the validity of ideas history had been, in truth, one of the great weapons of the conservative. From history one may derive a behavioral criticism of both revolution and reform. In some views history and evolution have blended together into a single tool of social inquiry. As a tool for the attainment of truth, history is used in three significant ways: as the criticism of institutions, as the buttress of empirical realism, and as the embodiment of an ideal, a paradigm, or an orthodoxy that may stand in judgment on a social and political tradition. The uses of history separate conservative traditions with a great width, for human experience with history is diverse, and ultimately history is a tool that is judged for its utility in each situation.

History as a criticism of institutions is most lucid in the statement and defense of tradition. One starts with what is considered excellent, and those traditional and habitual forms of life which are in accordance are approved and proved through historical study. As a criticism of institutions history seems to say "the truth will work" even though some stretch of pragmatic history may have shown the failure of the symbols of order that are being defended. Institutions are criticized for their deviation from the standard of truth, or the word, or the law. But history as a criticism of situations and institutions is an agency for use in the application of an idea. It is a means to judge a situation by the standard which stands intellectually and traditionally outside of the whole of the historical moment. Judgment arises less from history and more from the energy of judgment that is injected into the historical.

In contrast, the historical realist attempts to see the facts separated from value; he asks whether something works, and in the spirit of pragmatism he says that it is true if it works. The judgment found in tradition is subjective, conventional, limited in time; and because values beyond the empirical are subjective, the fact judges the value. Now most conservatives would, I believe, be found in the camp which says that fact and value are organic and may not be separated effectively in Humean fashion. But this organicity works in two ways; for just as facts speak to values, values speak to facts, and the judgment is one of conscience and intellect on the part of the person who is doing the judging. Still, there is a class of conservatives who are in effect radical in their empiricism and who assume that a knowledge of facts will generate a proper judgment of values. Scientific realists in international relations are among the most common proponents of this view. Such realists, who persuade interests and facts to speak for themselves, find in history the confirmation of their judgment of contemporary affairs.[19]

History as value or as ideal seeks, in a sort of Kantian manner, to use history to create the ideal. The conservative's history looks toward the future though it is a future that is generally in no hurry to arrive. History as value becomes a standard by which tradition is judged.[20]

b. Against the conservative whose concern is some use of history as a tool for gaining social truth we must observe the conservative whose deepest effort is to attain an engagement or commitment on philosophical issues. Conservatives have commonly been attached to certain of the great philosophical positions, primarily the Aristotelian, the Christian, the Thomist, and the Hegelian. The conservative intellectual is, of course, a philosopher—of necessity so—and he is driven to ask an ontological question, or the existential question, What is man? Through philosophy one acquires a basis for judging experience and an insight into the justice of a social system. When one speaks of the unity of the "Great Tradition" of the West there is behind it a sense of community in philosophical method which has its ultimate roots in the Greek, Roman, and Jewish heritage. From the Greeks one might learn the face of reason, from the Romans the symbols of order in a legal system, and from the Jewish-Christian tradition the realization that history is lived or judged under God. There is a paradigm or order that transcends the pragmatic events of the "kingdom" or of the "war." From the groundwork in philosophy one can discern agreement in social purpose in the creation of a society, and a sense that there is communication about order throughout the civilized West. To the conservative, the great symbols grounded on ontological inquiry have been order, law, the social inequality of man, the ownership of property, and the family. With all of the variation in the system there is some unity; but there is also imperfect realization, and there is evolution or change.

Some have said this is the tradition of every intellectual grounded in the West, not only Aristotle, Adam Smith and Burke, and not only the Tory and the Whig, but the liberals. Actually, the whole idea of a self-conscious conservatism did not originate until there had been an attack on tradition through an attack on religion and the theistic order of life. The conservative was born in the eighteenth century in the defense of religion, of the Church, and of the social order that had lived in symbiosis with the Church from time immemorial. While the critic might like to make the conservative reaction a tropism, the conscious conservative will assert he is essentially in the Aristotelian tradition, and he will not permit the denial of the importance of the truth of the community. But the conservative must often assert, against the liberal, that he is an intellectual.

2. It has been suggested that the conservative may be dissected in accordance with his method of searching for the meaning and the nature of the community. In a more specific sense he may be called either one who uses history as a tool for his course of discovery or one who uses philosophy more directly. But conservatives may be classified

in accordance with their programs of the prudential judgment. We face
an immense variety of programs, for the national tradition will dictate
the possibilities of practical policy and politics. Yet, there are issues
that transcend a national situation, such as international communism, the
energy of capitalism, or pressures at the point of contact between the
great religious systems. Theology, like philosophy, is in conservatism, a
basis for a program; it demands by its logic to be translated into action.

It is in this area that most of the criticism of the conservative occurs.
It is said that he has no program, that he is an exponent of do-nothing
politics, or that what he does is reactionary, unprogressive, or dangerous.
Here the conservative is charged with sponsoring outmoded political
doctrine, of being a standpatter, and, indeed, simply as an opponent to
change. On the other hand, he may be charged with a subversive attachment to change, resulting in a rejection of legal process and the
espousal of revolution.[21] Still, the main charge in the anti-conservative
barrage is that of doing little or nothing save resisting salutary change.
F. M. Cornford in his whimsical classic on academic politics has defined
conservative liberals and liberal conservatives as follows:

A Conservative Liberal is a broad-minded man, who thinks that something
ought to be done, only not anything that anyone now desires, but something
which was not done in 1881-82. A Liberal Conservative is a broad-minded
man, who thinks that something ought to be done, only not anything that anyone now desires; and that most things which were done in 1881-82 ought
to be undone.[22]

The range of conservative prudential judgments about policy have
varied enormously from country to country, from time to time, and
from one culture to another. Often, at this point, the conservative is
charged with an unperceptive traditionalism, such as a Burkean unwillingness to reform Parliament, or a Metternichian unwillingness to accept
the liberalism of the French Revolution and its daughter revolutions
in Europe. But to the conservatives, aside from those who attempt to be
"realistic" or scientific Machiavellians, their assumptions reach back
into the ethical groundwork of their society and their history. The issue
is expressed in the immediate and the human, but it is grounded in the
national past. In a democracy such as ours one may praise both rights
and majority rule, but in Spain a conservative like Calvo Serer may
become the leading advocate of reforms that will bring about a Christian
society and the restoration of monarchy.[23] In France, Raymond Aron
has identified three kinds of conservatism: opposition to the Third
Republic; the right wing in Parliament, including opposition to the Latin
Liberal conception of the separation of church and state, the defense of
laissez-faire and the free market economy; and the Boulangist-Gaul-
list position, which has been charged with showing vaguely fascist
tendencies.[24]

For the American, one of the most difficult of all the problems of conservative symbolism has been the divergence between historic Toryism and the liberal, laissez-faire theory in Europe. In America the European Tory system did not take root, and the liberalism of the Europeans became the conservatism of Americans. The Tories in England launched one of the most effective early attacks on free trade in factory society, and the liberals in England (until after the middle of the century) opposed factory legislation. Adam Smith, as an exponent of capitalism, was in general a believer in free trade though there were many limitations which in his mind were compatible with free competition. We find Burke, the founder of conservatism, a liberal in this instance, since he supported the ideas of Adam Smith. Might not one say that the idea of free competition has been ambivalent, appealing to all liberals and to some conservatives? Might we not also say, in consequence, that the acceptance of free trade by the conservatives in America was a slow business? Did not the democratic tide of Jacksonianism defend free trade while conservatives remained Hamiltonians? After the middle of the century the liberals in both England and America began to be more sympathetic toward collectivism, and the conservatives slowly but certainly moved toward a more forceful presentation of free competition as an aspect of capitalism.

What the contemporary, collectivist opponent of American conservatives can hardly realize is that there has been a conservative theory of reform in Europe, exemplified in Disraeli and the continental aristocratic critics of industrialism. Though a particular reform may be accepted by both English Conservatives and Laborites, for example, the principle and the tradition behind the reform can readily be different. Industrial reform is the largest of the areas of political change involved in modern society, but it is not the only one by any means.

Much of the prudential judgment of conservatives has been an effort to maintain some of the traditional orders of society against the impact of revolutions. The French Revolution, the revolution of 1848, World War I and World War II, the Russian revolution, the Fascist revolutions, the incredible spread of communist ideology throughout Asia, and the threat of further revolutions under communist inspiration in the Near East and in Africa, not to mention the Americas—have destroyed much of the relevance of many institutions and ideas that only a short time ago seemed lasting. Can the United States or any Western power succeed in convincing the Asian and the African that the Western states are not imperialistic? Can it be shown that they are only trying to serve well the international community of which we are all a part? Clearly the Romantic and antirevolutionary thinking of Adam Müller cannot be restored to favor nor can the details of the institutional arguments of Edmund Burke. However, both Müller and Burke must be numbered among the heroes of the conservative movement.

The conservative prudential judgment has sought to restrain the communist revolution; and, by so doing, it has hoped to maintain the spirit and structure of nineteenth-century economic, religious, cultural, and political institutions. In the end the conservative hopes for a victory over both fascists and communists and a resolution of the various "colonial" issues. But the victory over fascism in World War II strengthened the communists, while at the same time only a limited vitality was restored to parliaments, to capitalists, and to the influence of religious leaders.

V

Not all conservatives have been alike in this large enterprise. Many systems of policy may obviously be listed under conservatism. But it is clarifying to make some statement of the differences between conservatism in Europe and America. Both similarity and difference may be observed, and one of the most similar aspects of ideological thinking in both places has been "schools" of thought in Western politics. In his study of the history of political ideas Gaetano Mosca noted, first, that from the end of the eighteenth and through the nineteenth century there have been those who, following Montesquieu, have formed the liberal current; second, along with these there have been those who were democrats, aiming primarily at political equality through universal suffrage; third, one may observe the socialists who would complete political equality with an economic revolution; and, fourth, those who have formulated the principle of national union and independence, and sought to attain it in Germany, Italy, Poland, and in other countries.[25] The "schools" of political thought have spread throughout the West, and much of Montesquieu has been used by conservative thinkers. The nationalistic theory of the last century was upheld both by those who sought a revolution for the new and by those who wanted to restore through nationalism the ancient use and wont of political life.

Since movements of ideas and ideologies are now more widespread than in the past, one can well expect similarities between Europe and America that are greater than in the days when Thomas Paine and Joel Barlow were American missionaries of the "republican creed" to European society. The conservative wherever he is in the West is an enemy of the march of militant communism. One may say, indeed, that one of the deeper causes of the crisis in Europe since August, 1914, has been extreme nationalism and the philosophies and ideologies that have gone with it in each country where the infection became acute. While there has been no effective, extreme nationalism in the United States, the conservatives of Europe have been increasingly hostile to the ravages of nationalistic passion. One thing seems to be clear: many conservatives in Europe have been weaned away from a liberalistic, free-market capitalism, and they have turned much of their loyalty to a functional or corporative organization of the economic process. In other words, social gains should be preserved, and there should be an effective functional organization of workers and management or owners. Thus, the young conservative imagines a world beyond both socialism and communism on the one hand, and beyond liberal and capitalistic society on the other. Conservatism can, thus, become a third vision of how man may earn his daily bread.

In Catholic Europe the conservative turns to the defense of the church, while conservatives in America are bound to be defenders of a pluralistic society which includes Protestants, Catholics, and Jews. In Lutheran Europe the conservative can defend a state-supported church and the confessional school which receives money from the state, while the Lutheran in America may be the defender of a different public-law setting for his religious life. In England the Anglican and monarchist tradition yet stands as the symbol of stability to the continental conservative where there has been a resurgence of monarchism. But in America our conservatism must be republican and thus must reject an Anglicanism that is tied to the monarchy though our modern republican creed can hardly be influenced by the utopianism of the vision of progress of the years immediately after the American Revolution.

In our time, of course, the secular mind turns to the ingredients of "liberalism" in the American political psyche. Ludwig Freund has said "there is no place in this country for a conservative movement in the European sense" because, first, liberal ideas of the Enlightenment deeply influenced the formation of the American tradition, and it was in opposition to many of these ideas that European conservatism was formulated. American conservatism must, thus, be steeped in aspects of the liberal tradition. The main difference between political parties within the American consensus is one of degree and emphasis. "Do they believe more in the humanistic tradition of liberalism as symbolized by Locke, Montesquieu, and Thomas Paine or in the *economic* aspects of liberalism as embodied in the teachings of the Manchester school of thought?" [26] But times change, and the position of the liberal element is not the same as it once was. Liberalism in America has grown collectivistic, and the conservative may now affirm the principle of the free-market against the liberal. But, as Gerhart Niemeyer has argued, conservatives fear that the "innocent ideologists" in the fight against communism are insufficiently firm.

Hence it is no accident that over the issue of communism conservatives have attacked not only liberal actions and policies, but the very pattern of modern liberal thought. The sight of totalitarian actuality has sharpened the conservatives' sense of dangerous potentialities inherent in liberal ideology.[27]

There has been more than a faint suggestion that American and European conservatives in the new age are sensing that they have much in common because of the weakness of European liberalism and the successes of communism. But European liberals in the same situation may sense they have something in common with conservatives. As Kuehnelt-Leddihn has said:

A hundred years ago the Liberals worshipped Adam Smith, Spencer, J. S. Mill, and Bentham, while the nineteenth-century Conservatives devoured De Maistre, Bonald, Carlyle, Cortés, and C. L. von Haller. Today the New Liberals as well as the New Conservatives are living on a *common* diet of Alexis de Tocqueville, Acton, Burckhardt, Vinet, Röpke, Hayek, Dawson, Jouvenal, Martini, and Somary.[28]

NOTES

1. Consult Richard Hofstadter, "The Pseudo-Conservative Revolt," *American Scholar,* XXIV (Winter, 1954-55), 9 ff.; Herbert L. McCloskey, "Conservatism and Personality," *American Political Science Review,* LII (March, 1958), 27-45. For excellent criticisms of this method see David L. Spitz, "Power and Personality: The Appeal to the 'Right Man' in Democratic States," *ibid.,* pp. 84-107; Willmoore Kendall, "Comment on McCloskey's Conservatism and Personality," *ibid.,* pp. 506-10.

2. Clinton Rossiter, *Conservatism in America* (1955). See the significant review of this work by Gerhart Niemeyer, *Journal of Public Law* (Emory University), IV (Fall, 1955), 441 ff.

3. See Samuel P. Huntington, "Conservatism as an Ideology," *American Political Science Review,* LI (June, 1957), 454-73, for a development of such a point of view.

4. Bernard L. Kronick has said: "Natural conservatism is both the result of habit and the product of fear. Thus it is the psychological basis of all other conservatism. Many kinds of fear are present in conservatism" (see "Conservatism: A Definition," *Southwestern Social Science Quarterly,* XXVIII [September, 1947], 171-79, 173).

5. Erik von Kuehnelt-Leddihn, "The New Conservatism in Europe," *Southwest Review,* Winter, 1955, p. 2. M. M. Auerbach, *The Conservative Illusion* (1959), may be consulted on the philosophical issue in the criticism of conservatism.

6. See Edward Gargan, "The Ultimate Service of History," *Critic,* XVI (June-July, 1958), 7-8.

7. See *Modern Age,* Vol. II (Summer, 1958), for a discussion of the social theory of Otto von Habsburg who illustrates some of the current theories of the reform of the social order.

8. From the Greek criticisms of democracy to the present, some conservatives have had distrust of the extreme forms of populistic politics: democratic mass movements can easily become despotic. See Amaury de Riencourt, *The Coming Caesars* (1957); R. H. Luthin, *American Demagogues* (1954); Donald R. Richberg, *Labor Union Monopoly: A Clear and Present Danger* (1957).

9. On tradition see Josef Pieper, "The Concept of Tradition," *Review of Politics,* XX (October, 1958), 465-91. On p. 490 he notes tradition is both resistance and incentive at the same time.

10. R. A. Butler (ed.), *The New Conservatism: An Anthology of Post-war Thought* (1955), p. 85.

11. A great range of literature might be cited but the following may suffice: Russell Kirk, *The Conservative Mind* (1953); *A Program for Conservatives* (1954); *Beyond the Dreams of Avarice* (1956); Peter Viereck, *Conservatism Revisited* (1949); *Conservatism from John Adams to Churchill* (1956); F. G. Wilson, *The Case for Conservatism* (1951); "A Theory of Conservatism," *American Political Science Review,* XXXV (1941), 29 ff.; Daniel Bell (ed.), *The New American Right* (1955); Walter Lippmann, *Essays in the Public Philosophy* (1955); Daniel Boorstin, *The Genius of American Politics* (1953); Ludwig Freund, "The New American Conservatism and European Conservatism," *Ethics,* LXVI (October, 1955), 10 ff.;

W. M. McGovern and D. S. Collier, *Radicals and Conservatives* (1957); W. M. Chamberlin, *The Evolution of a Conservative* (1959).

12. See Niemeyer's review of Rossiter, *Conservatism in America*, in *Journal of Public Law* (Emory University Law School), IV (Fall, 1955), 443.

13. Consult Arnold J. Toynbee, *A Study of History* (Abridgment, 1947), pp. 217 ff., for his discussion of the "withdrawal and return" of the creative personality. Cf. E. V. Walter, "The Political Sense of Ford Maddox Ford," *New Republic*, March 26, 1956, pp. 17-19: "In the aristocratic imagination, there are four royal roads to the sublime life: the saintly, the wise, the heroic and the bucolic."

14. See Eric Voegelin, *Israel and Revelation* (1956), *passim*. The theistic conservatism of John H. Hallowell, *Main Currents in Modern Political Thought* (1950) and *The Moral Foundations of Democracy* (1954) is a significant contribution to American conservative thinking.

15. This analogy is present at the end of the "Review and Conclusion" of the *Leviathan*.

16. Karl W. Deutsch, "On Communication Models in the Social Sciences," *Public Opinion Quarterly*, XVI (Fall, 1952), 356 ff.

17. Freund, *op. cit.*, p. 15.

18. Huntington, *op. cit.*, p. 454.

19. Voegelin has said: "In Protagoras appears, for the first time, the type of thinker who is a skeptic, or agnostic, with regard to transcendent reality and, at the same time, a conservative with regard to historical order." For further illustrations he mentions Pyrrho toward the end of the fourth century and Montaigne, Bayle, and Hume in post-Reformation times. Voegelin regards the position unstable, to be maintained only if "the theoretical question of validity and its source will not be raised" (Eric Voegelin, *Order and History*, Vol. II: *The World of the Polis* [1957], p. 308).

20. See T. S. Eliot, *After Strange Gods: A Primer of Modern Heresy* (1934).

21. See Robert J. Harris, *Journal of Politics*, XX (February, 1958), 232, in a review of Jackson Kilpatrick, *The Sovereign States* (1957).

22. *Microcosmographia Academica, Being a Guide for the Young Academic Politician* (5th ed., 1953), p. 4.

23. See Rafael Calvo Serer, *Política de integración* (1955); *Teoría de la restauración* (2d ed., 1955).

24. (1) Raymond Aron, "Espoir et peur du siècle," *Western World*, No. 7 (November, 1957); René Rémond, *La Droite en France de 1815 à nos jours* (1954). Rémond shows that the right itself is a microcosm in which diverse traditions and diverse ideologies cross and enter into combat. Thomas Molnar, "French Conservative Thought Today," *Modern Age*, III (Summer, 1959), 283-98, has made an excellent statement of the positions to be found among French conservatives.

25. See Ferruccio Pergolessi, "Notas sobre la 'ciencia politica' de Gaetano Mosca," *Revista de estudios políticos*, LXXXIX (September-October, 1956), 83-84, summarizing Mosca's *Storia delle dottrine politiche* (1st ed., 1933), Pergolessi's long article is a remarkably complete study of Mosca, both in idea and in bibliography.

26. Freund, *op. cit.*, p. 16. Since World War II the Christian Democrats in France have believed in the neo-Thomist theory of man and society. They have had a "long-range desire to reconcile the church and the Enlightenment" and to cure the division that has prevailed since 1789. In addition the "reconciliation" would be based on a peaceful replacement of the capitalist economy "with a system based on the private ownership and the public management of property." Also some form of pluralism should be attained in which there would be a decentralized social order and a recognition of group rights. Each person should be free to associate himself with groups having a philosophy acceptable to his view of life. See Willard Ross Yates, "Power, Principle, and the Doctrine of the *Mouvement Républicain Populaire*," *The American Political Science Review*, LII (June, 1958), 421.

27. Niemeyer, *op. cit.*, p. 444.

28. Kuehnelt-Leddihn, *op. cit.*, p. 9.

CONSERVATISM AS AN IDEOLOGY

Samuel P. Huntington

Does conservative political thought have a place in America today? The answer to this question depends upon the general nature of conservatism as an ideology: its distinguishing characteristics, its substance, and the conditions under which it arises. By ideology I mean a system of ideas concerned with the distribution of political and social values and acquiesced in by a significant social group.[1] Interpretations of the role and relevance of conservative thought on the contemporary scene vary greatly. Underlying the debate, however, are three broad and conflicting conceptions of the nature of conservatism as an ideology. This essay deals with the relative merits of these concepts.

I. THEORIES OF CONSERVATISM

First, the *aristocratic* theory defines conservatism as the ideology of a single specific and unique historical movement: the reaction of the feudal-aristocratic-agrarian classes to the French Revolution, liberalism, and the rise of the bourgeoisie at the end of the eighteenth century and during the first half of the nineteenth century. In Mannheim's words, modern conservatism is "a function of *one particular* historical and sociological situation."[2] Liberalism is the ideology of the bourgeoisie, socialism and Marxism the ideologies of the proletariat, and conservatism the ideology of the aristocracy. Conservatism thus becomes indissolubly associated with feudalism, status, the *ancien régime,* landed interests, medievalism, and nobility; it becomes irreconcilably opposed to the middle class, labor, commercialism, industrialism, democracy, liberalism, and individualism. This concept of conservatism is popular among critics of the "New Conservatism." For, as Louis Hartz has brilliantly demonstrated, the United States lacks a feudal tradition. Hence, the efforts of intellectuals and publicists to propagate conservative ideas in middle-class America must be doomed to failure.

Reprinted from *The American Political Science Review,* vol. LI, no. 2 (June, 1957), 454-473. By permission of the author and the publisher.

Second, the *autonomous* definition of conservatism holds that conservatism is not necessarily connected with the interests of any particular group, nor, indeed, is its appearance dependent upon any specific historical configuration of social forces. Conservatism is an autonomous system of ideas which are generally valid. It is defined in terms of universal values such as justice, order, balance, moderation. Whether or not a particular individual holds these values high depends not on his social affiliations but upon his personal capacity to see their inherent truth and desirability. Conservatism, in this sense, is, as Russell Kirk says, simply a matter of "will and intelligence"; the principles of conservatism "are not confined to the interests of a single class"; conservatives may be drawn from "all classes and occupations. . . ." [3] This theory of conservatism is obviously popular among the "New Conservatives." It implies not only that conservatism is relevant and desirable in contemporary America, but that it is the preferable political philosophy under any historical circumstances.

Third, the *situational* definition views conservatism as the ideology arising out of a distinct but recurring type of historical situation in which a fundamental challenge is directed at established institutions and in which the supporters of those institutions employ the conservative ideology in their defense.[4] Thus, conservatism is that system of ideas employed to justify any established social order, no matter where or when it exists, against any fundamental challenge to its nature or being, no matter from what quarter. The essence of conservatism is the passionate affirmation of the value of existing institutions. This does not mean that conservatism opposes all change. Indeed, in order to preserve the fundamental elements of society, it may be necessary to acquiesce in change on secondary issues. No person can espouse the conservative ideology, however, unless he is fundamentally happy with the established order and committed to its defense against any serious challenge. Conservatism in this sense is possible in the United States today only if there is a basic challenge to existing American institutions which impels their defenders to articulate conservative values.

Now, the question may be legitimately raised: What is gained by arguing over definitions? Are not all definitions essentially arbitrary? How is it possible to demonstrate the superiority of one to another? This argument is valid if no common assumptions exist among the conflicting theories. Such, however, is not the case with the three definitions of conservatism. They differ only with respect to the relation of conservative ideology to the historical process. The aristocratic definition limits conservatism to a particular social class in a particular society. The autonomous definition permits the appearance of conservatism at any stage in history. The situational definition holds that conservatism appears when challenging and defending social groups stand in a particular relation to each other. Yet all three approaches agree fundamentally as to the content of conservatism as an ideology: the substance of the values and ideas in which conservatives believe. Russell Kirk, for instance, criticizes Arthur Schlesinger, Jr., for identifying conservatism with feudalism, but he agrees substantially with Schlesinger's statement of the essentials of the conservative ideology.[5]

All the analysts of conservatism, moreover, unite in identifying Edmund Burke as the conservative archetype and in assuming that the basic elements of his thought are the basic elements of conservatism. These areas of consensus permit a rational evaluation of the three definitions. The historical function of conservatism must be derived from its substance. That theory of conservatism is to be preferred which most adequately and completely explains the manifestations in history of the Burkeian ideology. The thesis of this article is that the situational theory most closely meets these criteria.

II. IDEATIONAL AND INSTITUTIONAL IDEOLOGIES: THE ABSENCE OF A CONSERVATIVE IDEAL

Among writers espousing all three definitions of conservatism substantial agreement exists that at least the following are major components of the conservative creed—the essential elements of Burke's theory.

1. Man is basically a religious animal, and religion is the foundation of civil society. A divine sanction infuses the legitimate, existing, social order.
2. Society is the natural, organic product of slow historical growth. Existing institutions embody the wisdom of previous generations. Right is a function of time. "Prescription," in the words of Burke, "is the most solid of all titles. . . ."
3. Man is a creature of instinct and emotion as well as reason. Prudence, prejudice, experience, and habit are better guides than reason, logic, abstractions, and metaphysics. Truth exists not in universal propositions but in concrete experiences.
4. The community is superior to the individual. The rights of men derive from their duties. Evil is rooted in human nature, not in any particular social institutions.
5. Except in an ultimate moral sense, men are unequal. Social organization is complex and always includes a variety of classes, orders, and groups. Differentiation, hierarchy, and leadership are the inevitable characteristics of any civil society.
6. A presumption exists "in favour of any settled scheme of government against any untried project. . . ." Man's hopes are high, but his vision is short. Efforts to remedy existing evils usually result in even greater ones.

Assuming these propositions to be a fair summary of representative conservative ideas, what do they suggest as to the relative merit of the aristocratic, autonomous, and situational theories? Nothing in these conservative principles limits them exclusively to the feudal-aristocratic reaction. To be sure, the ideology stresses the inevitability of classes and leadership in society, but it does not particularize any specific form of social organization or source of leadership. Nor is there anything in the ideology which presumes a partiality towards an agrarian society, the feudal system of land tenure, monarchy, or a titled aristocracy. Similarly, the autonomous theory is inadequate because the conservative ideology lacks the broad sweep and catholic appeal of an ideology of universal and permanent relevance. Indeed, conservatism itself stresses the particular nature of truth and warns of the danger of overarching principles. Manifestly, the ideology has little appeal to anyone discontented with the status quo. In short, the aristocratic definition fails because no necessary connection exists between aristocracy or feudalism, on the one hand and conservatism on the other: nonaristocrats can expound conservative ideology; aristocrats can expound nonconservative ideologies.

The autonomous definition fails because the appearance of conservatism in history is not a matter of random chance. The aristocratic definition restricts conservatism to too small a segment of the social process. The autonomous definition frees it too completely from any connection with the social process. The characteristic elements of conservative thought—the "divine tactic" in history; prescription and tradition; the dislike of abstraction and metaphysics; the distrust of individual human reason; the organic conception of society; the stress on the evil in man; the acceptance of social differentiation—all serve the overriding purpose of justifying the established order. The essence of conservatism is the rationalization of existing institutions in terms of history, God, nature, and man.

The usefulness of the conservative ideology in justifying any existing order is manifest from the above summary of Burkeian principles. Nowhere in that summary is there any indication of the character of the institutions which these ideas might be used to defend. In this respect conservatism differs from all other ideologies except radicalism: it lacks what might be termed a substantive ideal. Most ideologies posit some vision as to how political society should be organized. The words "liberalism," "democracy," "communism," "fascism," all convey an intimation as to what should be the distribution of power and other values in society, the relative importance of the state and other social institutions, the relations among economic, political, and military structures, the general system of government and representation, the forms of executive and legislative institutions. But what is the political vision of conservatism? Is it possible to describe a conservative society? On the contrary, the essence of conservatism is that it is literally, in Mühlenfeld's phrase, *"Politik ohne Wunschbilder."*

It may be argued, for instance, that the Portuguese political system is closer to the authoritarian ideal than the British and American systems, that the British system is closer to the socialist ideal than the Portuguese and American systems, that the American system is closer to the democratic ideal than the British and Portuguese systems, and that all three systems are far from the communist ideal. But which of the three is closest to the conservative ideal? Portugal? Great Britain? The United States? It is impossible to say because no conservative ideal exists to serve as the standard of judgment. No political philosopher has ever described a conservative utopia. In any society, there may be institutions to be conserved, but there are never conservative institutions. The lack of a conservative ideal necessarily vitiates the autonomous definition of conservatism.

The ideals of nonconservative ideologies change from thinker to thinker and generation to generation, but their fundamental characteristic remains the same: the ascription of value to theoretically-defined formulations and the appraisal of existing reality in terms of those formulations. Nonconservative ideologies are thus *ideational* or transcendent in nature, while conservatism is *institutional* or immanent. All the common ideational ideologies of modern western society approach existing institutions with an "ought demand" that the institutions be reshaped to embody the values of the ideology. In this sense all ideational theories involve some degree of radicalism, i.e., criticism of existing institutions. The greater the gap between existing institutional reality and the ideal of the nonconservative ideology, the more radical is the ideology with respect to that reality. Radicalism is thus the opposite of conservatism, and, like conservatism, it denotes an attitude toward institutions rather than a belief in any particular ideals. Conservatism and radicalism derive from orientations toward the process of change rather than toward the purpose and direction of change.

The conservative ideology is the product of intense ideological and social conflict. It appears only when the challengers to the established institutions reject the fundamentals of the ideational theory in terms of which those institutions have been molded and created. If the challengers do not question the basic values of the prevailing philosophy, the controversy between those for and against institutional change is carried on with reference to the commonly accepted ideational philosophy. Each group attempts to show that its policies are more in accord with the common ideals than those of the other group. After the Civil War in America, for instance, the conflict between American Whig and American Democrat was fought, as Hartz has pointed out, within a shared framework of Lockean values. Consensus precluded conservatism.

When the challenges fundamentally disagree with the ideology of the existing society, however, and affirm a basically different set of values, the common framework of discussion is destroyed. The rejection of the prevailing ideology by the challengers compels it to be abandoned by the defenders also. No ideational theory can be used to defend established institutions satisfactorily, even when those institutions in general reflect the values of that ideology. The perfect nature of the ideology's ideal and the imperfect nature and inevitable mutation of the institutions create a gap between the two. The ideal becomes a standard by which to criticize the institutions, much to the embarrassment of those who believe in the ideal and yet still wish to defend the institutions.[6] Eventually the defenders are faced with an unavoidable choice: either they must abandon their ideology in order to defend their institutions and substitute a conservative philosophy for their old ideational theory, or they must adhere to their ideational theory at the risk of further contributing to the downfall of those institutions which largely embody their ideals. The defense of any set of institutions against a fundamental challenge, consequently, must be phrased in terms of the conservative logic, sanctity, and necessity of the institutions *qua* institutions irrespective of the degree to which they correspond to the prescriptions of this or that ideational philosophy.[7]

The challenging social force must present a clear and present danger to the institutions. The mere articulation of a dissident ideology does not produce conservatism until that ideology is embraced by significant social groups. The *philosophes* of the mid-eighteenth century generated no conservative ideology; the events of 1789 and the subsequent years did. Conservatism, in Mannheim's words, "first becomes conscious and reflective when other ways of life and thought appear on the scene, against which it is compelled to take up arms in the ideological struggle." [8] If the defenders of the established order are successful, in due course they gradually cease to articulate their conservative ideology and substitute for it a new version of their old ideational theory. If their defense is unsuccessful, they abandon either their old ideational premises or their new conservative ideology. If they are inclined to be congenital conservatives, they will accept the new order as the inevitable work of destiny. Burke, Bonald, and de Maistre, for instance, all in part believed that the triumph of the French Revolution might be decreed by Providence and that once this became obvious, it would "not be resolute and firm, but perverse and obstinate" to oppose it.[9]

On the other hand, the unsuccessful conservative who remains attached to the ideals of his old ideational philosophy becomes a reactionary, i.e., a critic of existing society who wishes to recreate in the future an ideal which he assumes to have existed in the past. He is a radical. No valid distinction exists between "change backward" and "change forward." Change is change; history neither retreats nor repeats; and all change is away from the status quo. As time passes, the ideal of the reactionary becomes less and less related to any actual society of the past. The past is romanticized, and, in the end, the reactionary comes to support a return to an idealized "Golden Age" which never in fact existed. He becomes indistinguishable from other radicals, and he normally displays all the distinctive characteristics of the radical psychology.

The nature of conservatism as an institutional ideology precludes any permanent and inherent affiliation or opposition between it and any particular ideational ideology. No necessary dichotomy exists, therefore, between conservatism and liberalism. The assumption that such an

opposition does exist derives, of course, from the aristocratic theory of
conservatism and reflects an overconcern with a single phase of western
history at the end of the 18th and the beginning of the 19th centuries.
The effort to erect this ephemeral relationship into a continuing phenomenon of political history only serves to obscure the fact that in the
proper historical circumstances conservatism may well be necessary for
the defense of liberal institutions. The true enemy of the conservative
is not the liberal but the extreme radical no matter what ideational theory
he may espouse. Different radicals advance different panaceas, but they
all have the same psychology which conservative thinkers have not been
slow to identify. Hooker's sixteenth-century Puritan, Metternich's "presumptuous man," Burke's "metaphysical scribbler," Hawthorne's Hol-
lingsworth, Cortés' "self-worshipping man," Hoffer's twentieth century
"true believer," are all one and the same.

The distinction between conservatism and the ideational ideologies
has led some nonconservatives to deny any intellectual content to conservatism and has led some conservatives to attack all ideologies. Both
the critics and the defenders of conservatism are wrong, however, when
they minimize its intellectual significance. Conservatism is the intellectual rationale of the permanent institutional prerequisites of human
existence. It has a high and necessary function. It is the rational defense of being against mind, of order against chaos. When the foundations of society are threatened, the conservative ideology reminds men of
the necessity of some institutions and the desirability of the existing ones.
All ideologies need not be ideational ideologies. The theory of conservatism is of a different order and purpose than other common political
theories, but it is still theory. Conservatism is not just the absence of
change. It is the articulate, systematic, theoretical resistance to change.

III. INHERENT AND POSITIONAL IDEOLOGIES:
THE ABSENCE OF A CONSERVATIVE TRADITION

Most writers agree, and it is assumed here, that Burke is properly
called a conservative. The question, consequently, is: Can Burke best
be understood as the spokesman for the feudal aristocratic order, the
expounder of values and ideals universally valid, or as the defender of
established institutions? The aristocratic definition fails to explain Burke
because: (1) the English society Burke defended was neither primarily
feudal nor exclusively aristocratic; (2) Burke was concerned with the
defense of other established societies, notably in India and America;
and (3) insofar as Burke had views on the desirable organization of
society, he was a liberal, a Whig, and a free trader. The autonomous
concept similarly does not offer a complete explanation of Burke because: (1) Burke's political writings and speeches were all directed to
immediate problems and needs; (2) he rejected the desirability and the
possibility of a moral or political philosophy of universal applicability;

and (3) the principal elements of his political thought are relevant chiefly to the limited purpose of justifying established institutions.

On the Continent at the beginning of the nineteenth century Burke's ideas were used to defend aristocracy and feudalism against the rising middle class. The English society and constitution with which Burke was concerned, however, were quite different from those existing across the Channel. The fact that his ideas could be used to justify the established order in both places demonstrates not the similarity of the two orders but the transferability of his philosophy. In a penetrating epigram, Louis Hartz has declared that "In America Burke equalled Locke." This is true enough, but it was equally true in England. Burke defended the English constitution of his day first against the efforts of George III to reassert the influence of the Crown over Parliament and then against the efforts of the democrats to broaden the control of the people over Parliament. He was a conservative because one hundred years after Locke he was still attempting to preserve the institutions of 1689. A devotee of mixed government, he was resolved, he said, "to keep an established church, an established monarchy, an established aristocracy, and an established democracy, each in the degree it exists, and in no greater." [10] Burke recognized that the people had an important, although limited, role to play in the English system.[11] Accepting aristocracy as an inherent and necessary element of the British constitution, he showed, however, little partiality towards it. A commoner himself, he suffered on more than one occasion from the aristocratic disdain of the great lords who tended to view him as an "Irish adventurer." Like Jefferson and Adams, Burke was a supporter of a natural aristocracy, not an artificial aristocracy.[12]

The social order which Burke defended was to a large extent commercial, and it was becoming increasingly industrial. The eighteenth century had seen the rise of the Bank of England, the South Sea Bubble, joint stock companies, expanding shipping and trade, the accumulation of commercial fortunes and industrial capital, a rash of industrial inventions, and the steady growth of manufacturing. Commerce was "the dominant factor" in eighteenth-century England.[13] Voltaire's astonishment that the great gentlemen of England were not ashamed of trade was but one indication of the difference between English and continental society. For thirty years before Burke arrived in London in 1750 the promotion of industry had been a primary objective of the English government. By 1790, when according to the aristocratic theory of conservatism Burke was defending the feudal corporate order, the Industrial Revolution in England was already a generation old. Was Burke repelled by the growth of commerce and industry? Did he seek to return to the feudal agrarian order of a previous age? Far from it. For Burke, as Namier declares, "trade was the soul of empire." As early as 1770 Burke stated his position in no uncertain terms: "There is no such thing as the landed interest separate from the trading interest. . . . *Turn your land into trade.*" [14] Is this the advice of a feudal apologist? Six years later Burke praised to the skies "for sagacity and penetration of mind, extent of views, accurate distinction, just and natural connexion and dependence of parts" a book which accurately reflected his own views on economics: *The Wealth of Nations*.[15] In Parliament Burke was consistently for laisser faire; the state should stay out of economic matters; the laws of commerce were the laws of nature; labor itself was an "article of trade." Is it any wonder that Adam Smith, after discussing political economy with Burke, should declare that Burke "was the only man, who, without communication, thought on these topics exactly as he did"?[16] If Burke is an apologist for the feudal corporate order, what becomes of Adam Smith? The plain fact of the matter is that, insofar as he had views on the desirable organization of society, in politics Burke was a liberal and a Whig, the defender of the Lockean constitution; in economics, he was a liberal free trader, his ideas at one with those of Adam Smith. There was little or nothing that was corporate, or feudal, or aristocratic about him at all.

While Burke preferred a balanced constitution and a commercial economy, his preference derived not so much from their peculiar virtues as from the fact of their existence. Montesquieu and Adam Smith developed the ideational rationale for the institutions which Burke accepted. Burke's contribution was different. He was concerned not with the substance of institutions but with their preservation. Impartially he defended Whig institutions in England, democratic institutions in America, autocratic institutions in France, and Hindu institutions in India. Indian institutions, he warned, for example, must be based "upon their own principles not upon ours," denouncing those Britishers in India who subverted "the most established rights and the most ancient and most revered institutions of ages and nations."[17] "He changed his front," as Morley remarked in a classic phrase, "but he never changed his ground." Since Morley, scholars have united in clearing Burke of charges of inconsistency. But if Burke was consistent, how can he have been an aristocrat? If his primary concern had been the preservation of the feudal corporate order in Europe, why would he have any concern for America or India? Most conservatives adopt conservative ideas in order to defend one particular established order. In this respect their conservatism is instrumental rather than primary. Burke, however, was the conservative archetype because his impulse was to defend all existing institutions wherever located and however challenged.

Supporters of the aristocratic theory of conservatism argue that modern conservatism originated with the reaction to the French Revolution. They are mistaken. It is possible to identify at least four major manifestations of conservatism in western political history. The first was the response in the sixteenth and seventeenth centuries to the challenge of centralized national authority to medieval political institutions and the challenge of the Reformation to established church-state relationships. On the Continent, for instance, Francis Hotman in his *Franco-Gallia* and Juan de Mariana in his *De Rege et Regis Institutione* attempted a conservative defense of the medieval pluralistic order against the growing power of the national monarchs. That Hotman was a Frenchman and a Protestant and Mariana a Spaniard and a Jesuit made little difference. They had similar purposes and similar arguments. Unfortunately for both, however, the historical facts did not entirely support the uses which they made of them, and the trend toward royal power had already undermined most of the significant institutions of the old order. As a result, the argument of the monarchomachs was shifted from a conservative base to an ideational one. It was restated in terms of principle rather than precedent. *Franco-Gallia* was eclipsed by the *Vindiciae,* and Mariana was overshadowed by Suarez.[18]

In England, on the other hand, the existence of a strong national monarchy and of a national church permitted a conservative defense of both. The ideas which on the Continent had been used to defend the estates against royal authority were used in England to defend royal authority against political dissidents and theological radicals. The political thinking of the Tudor apologists—Tyndale, Gardiner, Hooker, and numerous others—was suffused with conservative appeals to order and obedience.[19] Rebellion and anarchy were held out as the worst of evils; disobedience was an effort to break a divinely ordained chain of being. Restated again and again in Tudor literature was Shakespeare's warning: "Take but degree away, untune that string, And, Hark! what discord follows. . . ."

Toward the end of the sixteenth century as the Puritan attack gathered strength and became more extreme—the episcopacy came under sustained criticism in 1570—the need arose for a more thorough conservative defense of the national civil and religious establishment. This need was met by Richard Hooker in his *Laws of Ecclesiastical Polity* published in 1594. This multivolume work stands as a towering and eloquent statement of the conservative ideology. Here, two hundred years before Burke, was delineated every significant strand of Burkean thought.[20] The substance of their conservatism is virtually identical. Yet the institutions they were defending and the challenges to which they were reacting were dissimilar. The Tudor constitution of 1590 differed from the Whig constitution of 1790. The threat to Hooker's institutions came from Puritan sects advocating the complete separation of Church and State, the supremacy of faith over reason, and the authority of scripture against the authority of the church. The Puritans viewed man as depraved and evil; they were spiritualistic, deterministic, anti-intellectual, fundamentalist, and pessimistic. The challenge to Burke's institutions, on the other hand, came from democratic groups assured of the efficacy of reason and possessed of an unbounded confidence in human nature and man's capacity for progress. They were everything which the Puritans were not: materialistic, rationalistic, anti-religious, optimistic, and libertarian. Yet despite the differences, the similar situations in which Hooker and Burke found themselves led them to expound similar political ideas.

The second great manifestation of conservatism was the response to the French Revolution. That social upheaval, the ideologies it advanced, and the classes it propelled towards power were undoubtedly the greatest threat to existing institutions in the history of western civilization up to that time. Consequently, they produced the greatest outpouring of conservative thought in western history. The conservative response to the Revolution was largely but not exclusively a defense of the feudal, agrarian, aristocratic order against a rising, urban, enlightened middle class. Nonetheless, the Revolution endangered not only feudal aristocratic institutions but all established institutions. In England Burke made a conservative defense of a commercial society and a moderate, liberal constitution. In America, the Federalists—from John Adams through Hamilton to Fisher Ames—expounded conservative ideas to defend a liberal constitution against what they thought to be the threat of a democratic revolution. On the Continent, too, the initial conservative reaction came not from the feudal aristocrats but from thinkers associated with more liberal, commercial, and bureaucratic elements. In Germany, for instance, Brandes, Rehberg, and Möser, representatives of the north German cities where the middle class was strongest, made the first attacks on the Revolution.[21] A few of the continental conservatives, such as Gentz, were liberal in their economics. Even among the spokesmen for the aristocracy, differences existed in the societies which they defended: the France of Bonald and de Maistre, the Prussia of von der Marwitz and Haller, and the Austria of Gentz, Metternich, and Müller did not have identical social structures. Nevertheless, the common strands of conservatism ran through the political ideas of the Reaction thinkers irrespective of the immediate social order which they desired to preserve.

The conservatism of the feudal-aristocratic thinkers of the Reaction was the product of their temporary defensive position rather than of the permanent and inherent nature of their class interests. The fundamental character of those interests did not change in 1789. Yet prior to that year the aristocracy produced no significant conservative thinking. They had no need for it. On the other hand, after the aristocrats were driven from power, they ceased to be conservative without surrendering their aristocratic ideals. In France, in particular, aristocratic thought, once conservative, rapidly became reactionary and eventually became radical. De Maistre had exalted order and stability. In the bourgeois democracy of the Third Republic *L'Action Française* preached violence and the "coup de force." The revolutionaries were on the Right.[22]

The third manifestation of conservatism was the response of the governing classes to the popular lower class demands for a share in the direction of society in the middle years of the nineteenth century. The single most important symbol of this challenge was the cry for the extension of the suffrage. It was a challenge, however, that involved only a partial divergence from accepted values and, consequently, occasioned a weak conservative response. In France, in particular, where the middle classes had to face in two directions, the typical exponents of their viewpoint—Royer-Collard and Guizot, for instance—expounded liberal ideas against the aristocrats and conservative ideas against the masses. In Germany, where a major upheaval had not destroyed the structure of society, Stahl, Ranke, Savigny, and Ludwig von Gerlach articulated a more broadly conceived conservatism emphasizing the organic growth of society. In England, Coleridge and, subsequently, Newman, Maine, and Lecky warned of the dangers of substituting popular rule for class rule. In the United States, the neo-Federalists, Story, Choate, Kent, made a brief conservative defense of a restricted governing class before they were overwhelmed by the Jacksonian tidal wave.

A fourth manifestation of conservatism was the outpouring of political thought produced in the southern United States by the challenge of industrialism, free labor, and abolition in the middle of the nineteenth century. Prior to 1830 southern political thought was shaped largely in the Jeffersonian image. After 1830 southern thinking became increasingly conservative as a result of the increasingly articulate theories of abolition and the rise of northern industry and population. William Lloyd Garrison—the epitome of the radical reformer—founded *The Liberator* in 1831 and in the same year Nat Turner led his slave insurrection. The combination of forces which these events symbolized forced the South on the defensive and led it to abandon its Jeffersonian heritage and develop a conservative apologia in the language of Burke. It was possible to be at once a Jeffersonian and a slaveowner only so long as no one set the Declaration of Independence against slavery. When this happened, the slaveowner had to abandon either his liberalism or his livelihood. Inevitably the ideational philosophy was sacrificed and replaced by a far-reaching conservatism.[23] Just as the rising tide of Puritan radicalism against the Tudor establishment eventually produced Hooker, the rising tide of abolitionist reform eventually produced Calhoun and Fitzhugh. In their writings and in those of the others of the "reactionary enlightenment"—Holmes, Hammond, Hughes, and Harper, in particular—there was "duplicated in every essential aspect the argument of Europe's feudal reaction."[24] All the basic ideas of Burke were reproduced in the treatises and pamphlets with which they came to the defense of their established social order against a threat which was concrete, potent, and eventually successful.

Louis Hartz has suggested that southern conservatism was a "fraud."[25] Starting from the aristocratic conception of conservatism, Hartz argues that there was an inherent conflict in the effort of the southerners to use Burke to defend slavery, on the one hand, and a political tradition containing many elements of liberalism, on the other. Notwithstanding definite inconsistencies in the southern system, however, there was no inconsistency in the South's use of Burke to defend that system. The conservative philosophy was appropriate to the defense of the institutions of Jefferson, the "peculiar institution" of slavery, or any combination of the two. It was no more of a fraud for Calhoun to combine Burke and slavery than it was for Burke himself to combine Burke and laisser faire. Nor does the fact that southern conservative political thought ended with the Civil War prove that the southerners were "false Burkes, halfway Burkes." When the southern social-political system was destroyed, the theory elaborated in its defense necessarily had to die with it. Hartz himself describes southern conservatism as "one of the great and creative episodes in the history of American thought." Could it be this, however, if it were simply a "fraud," an artificial importation without roots in the American situation? Is it not possible to avoid this problem by a more simple explanation of southern conservatism? The southern experience was a clear example of a society shifting from a liberal ideational theory to an uncompromising conservatism as the result of the rise of a fundamental challenge to its existence. Given the change in the southern position, the change in the southern thought was both necessary and natural.

The basic inadequacy of the aristocratic theory of conservatism is that it conceives conservatism to be an *inherent* ideology rather than a *positional* ideology. An inherent ideology is the theoretical expression of the interests of a continuing social group. It is derived from the fundamental common characteristics which make the group a group. Consequently, an inherent ideology evolves and changes as the interests and needs of the group change, but, at the same time, it maintains certain essential characteristics reflecting the continuing and inherent identity of the group. True to its essential nature as the ideology of the bourgeois middle class, the liberalism of one generation has differed from and yet grown out of the liberalism of a previous generation. An inherent philosophy may also be differently interpreted and expressed by conflicting subschools existing at the same time. American liberalism has been split between a Whig, "property rights," version, on the one hand, and a popular, "human rights," version, on the other. None the less, American Whig and American democrat both share the essentials of Locke. Marxism, too, has existed in a variety of forms and evolved through a number of phases, all of which, however, have retained the same underlying fundamentals which distinguish Marxism as a theory. It is thus possible to relate the various expressions of an inherent theory to each other, to trace patterns of development and influence, and to identify schisms and subvarieties within the common intellectual tradition. In brief: the substance of an inherent theory evolves and proliferates, and the expressions of the theory are interrelated and interdependent. The theory and its exponents all constitute a *school of thought.*

Positional ideologies are quite different. They do not reflect the continuing interests and needs of a particular social group. Rather they depend upon the relations existing among groups. A group may espouse one positional ideology when its relations with other groups assume one form and another positional ideology when those relations assume a different form. Positional ideologies reflect the changing external environment of a group rather than its permanent internal characteristics.

Inherent ideologies are functions of groups no matter what their positions; positional ideologies are functions of situations no matter what groups occupy those situations.[26] With positional ideologies, it is a question not of "who" but of "where." Thus, the theory of "states' rights" in the United States has been primarily a positional ideology espoused by a succession of different groups whenever their power in the central government vis-à-vis their opponent groups has been less than their power in the states.

If the situational definition of conservatism is correct, conservatism is a positional ideology. Conservatism develops to meet a specific historical need. When the need disappears, the conservative philosophy subsides. In each case, the articulation of conservatism is a response to a specific social situation. The manifestation of conservatism at any one time and place has little connection with its manifestation at any other time and place. Conservatism thus reflects no permanent group interest. Depending upon the existence of a particular relation among groups rather than upon the existence of the groups themselves, it lasts only so long as the relation lasts, not so long as the groups last. And the relation is necessarily ephemeral, seldom continuing more than one generation. Consequently, the conservative ideology is not developed and transmitted with alterations, elaboration, and revision from one age to the next. Nor does it have a set of basic writings to be annotated, interpreted, and argued over by contending sets of disciples. The manifestations of conservatism are simply parallel ideological reactions to similar social situations. The substance of conservatism is essentially static. Conservative thought is repetitive, not evolutionary. Its manifestations are historically isolated and discrete. Thus, paradoxical though it may seem, conservatism, the defender of tradition, is itself without tradition; conservatism, the appeal to history, is without history.

The static and repetitious character of conservative thought is reflected in the extent to which conservatism lends itself to itemization. More so than any other political ideology, conservatism can be condensed into a brief catalog of principles or concepts which constitute the conservative catechism common to all conservative thinkers. Both the proponents and critics of conservatism agree that the essence of conservatism can be summed up in a small number of basic ideas. The number of these ideas may vary in the different formulations, but their content is universally the same. Hearnshaw, for instance, lists "twelve principles of conservatism," Kirk "six canons of conservative thought," and Rossiter "'twenty-one points' of the Conservative tradition." [27]

In part, these brief and similar catalogs of conservative ideas simply reflect the general consensus on the substance of conservatism as an ideology. But, in addition, they reflect the static and limited nature of that ideology. Other ideologies have basic ideas which recur in various manifestations. But these ideas are the starting point, not the sum and substance of the ideology. Individualism is basic to liberalism but the individualism of Locke is quite different from that of Bentham. Class conflict is basic to Marxism, but the class struggle in Kautsky is different from the class struggle in Lenin. Conservatives, however, do not subdivide into schools, nor do they, like liberals and Marxists, engage in fiery arguments over the meaning of their faith. Individual conservative thinkers, of course, may phrase their ideas in slightly different ways and may modify them in the light of their particular ideational leanings. But in general they simply repeat their catechism, and once they have said their catechism, they have said all there is to be said of the substance of conservative thought. A history of liberal or Marxist thought reveals the transmutation of the ideology through different times and circumstances. A history of conservative thinkers, such as Kirk's *Conservative Mind*, necessarily involves the repetition over and over again of the same ideas.

This peculiar character of conservative thought explains one frequently commented upon aspect of conservatism cited by Mannheim: "The careers of most conservatives and reactionaries show revolutionary periods in their youth." [28] Many of the early nineteenth century conservatives—Görres, Gentz, Müller in Germany; Coleridge, Wordsworth, Southey in England—were initially enthusiasts for the French Revolution. The Federalists began as successful revolutionaries, and America's premier conservative, John C. Calhoun, started his career as a fire-eating Jeffersonian nationalist. Why does this pattern exist? Is it not simply because conservatism is not the permanent ideological expression of the needs of any social group? No one is born to conservatism in the way in which a Mill is born to utilitarianism. The impulse to conservatism comes from the social challenge before the theorist, not the intellectual tradition behind him. Men are driven to conservatism by the shock of events, by the horrible feeling that a society or institution which they have approved or taken for granted and with which they have been intimately connected may suddenly cease to exist. The conservative thinkers of one age, consequently, have little influence on those of the next. There are few second generation conservatives. Hooker, for instance, anticipated Burke in all the essentials of conservative philosophy; but Burke's conservatism was derived not from a study of Hooker but from the impact of events about him. Similarly, in France, "Maistre never had a school, so to speak." In the United States, Fitzhugh, the apologist for the South, gained little inspiration from earlier conservative thinkers.[29] Each individual statement of the conservative position, in itself, moreover, tends to be generated by some immediate intellectual challenge. Christopher Morris describes the *Laws of Ecclesiastical Polity* as a "livre de circonstance." The same phrase could apply equally well to the *Elemente der Staatskunst*, the *Reflections on the Revolution in France*, and *A Disquisition on Government*.[30]

IV. THE RELEVANCE OF CONSERVATISM

In the light of the above analysis, what role has the conservative ideology in America today? Is the "New Conservatism" really conservative? Does room exist for a more profound and far-reaching exposition of conservative ideas?

Much of the New Conservatism is characterized by at least three deficiencies as a conservative movement. First, many New Conservatives appear uncertain as to what they wish to defend. Some simply continue the old identification of conservatism with business liberalism. Others are radical aristocrats, ill at ease in and disgusted with American society as it exists today. Desiring to import European aristocracy to bourgeois America, they dream of an age of less democracy, less equality, less industrialism, an age in which the elite ruled and the mass knew their place. Their rejection of the existing American political and social system makes it impossible for them to be truly conservative. Russell Kirk's view of contemporary America, for instance, could hardly be more unflattering: "near to suicide," "cheap," "materialistic," "sterile," "standardized." [31] Is this the language of a conservative? Or is it the language of a maligner of existing society? Instead of a vigorous defense of American constitutional democracy, Kirk's books are filled with a strained, sentimental, nostalgic, antiquarian longing for a society which is past. He and his associates are out of tune and out of step in modern America.

Secondly, many New Conservatives are astonishingly vague as to the nature and source of the threat to what they wish to conserve. Historically, conservatism has always been the response to a direct and immediate challenge. Conservatives have not usually been in doubt as to the identity of their opponents. Among the New Conservatives, however, the enemy is seldom brought clearly into focus. To some, the foe is Liberalism, although little agreement exists as to the meaning of this term. To others, it is modernism, totalitarianism, popularism, secularism, or materialism. For some New Conservatives the enemy is irrationalism and to others it is rationalism. This confusion, of course, merely reflects the fact that the economic prosperity and political consensus of American society make any conservatism oriented towards domestic enemies absurdly superfluous. Hooker, Burke, and Calhoun fought real political battles against real political enemies. Lacking any flesh and blood social-political challenge, however, the New Conservatives fashion imaginary threats out of abstract "isms."

A third deficiency of the New Conservatism is the effort to uncover a conservative intellectual tradition in America. Apparently desiring the security of identification with an intellectual movement, the New Conservatives scurry through America's past, resurrecting political and intellectual figures long since forgotten. Few enterprises could be more futile or irrelevant. In *The Conservative Mind,* for instance, Russell Kirk defines a conservative as one who stands by established institutions. Yet in his efforts to find a conservative tradition in America, Kirk classifies as conservative: James Russell Lowell, who was "frightened" by what he saw about him; Brooks Adams, who was "disgusted with American society"; Henry Adams, who has become the classic symbol of frustrated alienation; [32] Irving Babbitt, who fled from America to Buddhism; and Santayana, who fled from America to his Roman cloister. All these men were malcontents, and in many respects they were much more fundamentally malcontent than Debs, Henry George, de Leon, and Lafollette, whom presumably Kirk would never dream of classifying as conservatives. The New Conservatives' search for forebears merely reflects their own uncertainty of purpose, role, and identity. They seek to conserve an intellectual tradition which does not exist rather than institutions which do exist. Were they true conservatives, immediately engaged in the defense of an institution or society against a real and imminent threat, they would have little interest in establishing a conservative pedigree.

The dubious side of the New Conservatism, however, does not exhaust the possibilities of conservatism in America today. Some New Conservatives recognize the essentially situational character of conservative ideology. They realize the sterility of a conservative defense of one segment of American society against another segment. The only threat extensive and deep enough to elicit a conservative response today is the challenge of communism and the Soviet Union to American society as a whole. In this respect, as Max Beloff has pointed out, a marked parallel exists between the position of the South in the 1850s and the position of the United States in the 1950s: both societies challenged by an expanding external order. [33] Just as the South produced a conservative defense in Fitzhugh and Calhoun, it is not unreasonable to expect that America too will have its conservative apologists. The more profound recent writings in a conservative vein, such as those of Niebuhr, were in many respects a direct response to the challenge of foreign totalitarianism. As an island of plenty and freedom in a straitened world, America has much to defend.

American institutions, however, are liberal, popular, and democratic. They can best be defended by those who believe in liberalism, popular control, and democratic government. Just as aristocrats were the conservatives in Prussia in 1820 and slaveowners were the conservatives in the South in 1850, so the liberals must be the conservatives in America today. Historically, American liberals have been idealists, pressing forward the goals of greater freedom, social equality, and more meaningful democracy. The articulate exposition of a liberal ideology was necessary to convert others to liberal ideas and to reform existing institutions continuously along liberal lines. Today, however, the greatest need is not so much the creation of more liberal institutions as the successful defense of those which already exist. This defense requires American liberals to lay aside their liberal ideology and to accept the values of conservatism for the duration of the threat. Only by surrendering their liberal ideas for the present can liberals successfully defend their liberal institutions for the future. Liberals should not fear this change. Is a liberal any less liberal because he adjusts his thinking so as to defend most effectively the most liberal institutions in the world? To continue to expound the philosophy of liberalism simply gives the enemy a weapon with which to attack the society of liberalism.[34] The defense of American institutions requires a conscious articulate conservatism which can spring only from liberals deeply concerned with the preservation of those institutions. As Boorstin, Niebuhr, and others have pointed out, the American political genius is manifest not in our ideas but in our institutions. The stimulus to conservatism comes not from the outworn creeds of third-rate thinkers but from the successful performance of first-rate institutions. Current conflict rather than ancient dogma will yield a "New Conservatism" which is truly conservative.

Conservatism is not, as the aristocratic interpretation argues, the monopoly of one particular class in history. Nor is it, as the autonomous school contends, appropriate in every age and place. It is, instead, relevant in a particular type of historical situation. That is the situation in which American liberalism finds itself today. Until the challenge of communism and the Soviet Union is eliminated or neutralized, a major aim of American liberals must be to preserve what they have created. This is a limited goal but a necessary one. Conservatism does not ask ultimate questions and hence does not give final answers. But it does remind men of the institutional prerequisites of social order. And when these prerequisites are threatened, conservatism is not only appropriate, it is essential. In preserving the achievements of American liberalism, American liberals have no recourse but to turn to conservatism. For them especially, conservative ideology has a place in America today.

NOTES

1. This essay deals only with conservative theory. It is not concerned with conservative instincts, attitudes, political parties, or governmental policies. For contrasting views on the meaning of ideology, see Karl Mannheim, *Ideology and Utopia* (New York, 1949), pp. 49 ff. and Carl J. Friedrich and Zbigniew K. Brzezinski, *Totalitarian Dictatorship and Autocracy* (Cambridge, 1956), pp. 71 ff.

2. Karl Mannheim, "Conservative Thought," *Essays on Sociology and Social Psychology*, ed. Paul Kecskemeti (New York, 1953), pp. 98-99. For contemporary use of the aristocratic definition with respect to the "New Conservatism," see Arthur M. Schlesinger, Jr., "The New Conservatism in America: A Liberal Comment," *Confluence*, Vol. 2, pp. 61-71 (December, 1953), and "The New Conservatism: Politics of Nostalgia," *Reporter*, Vol. 12, pp. 9-12 (June 16, 1955); Bernard Crick, "The Strange Quest for an American Conservatism," *Review of Politics*, Vol. 17, pp. 361-63 (July, 1955); Gordon K. Lewis, "The Metaphysics of Conservatism," *Western Political Quarterly*, Vol. 6, pp. 731-32 (December, 1953).

3. Russell Kirk, *A Program for Conservatives* (Chicago, 1954), pp. 22, 38-39; Peter Viereck, *Conservatism Revisited* (New York, 1949), p. 9.

4. See Clinton Rossiter, *Conservatism in America* (New York, 1955), p. 9; Francis G. Wilson, "A Theory of Conservatism" [*The American Political Science Review*],

Vol. 35, pp. 39-40 (February, 1941); Raymond English, "Conservatism: The Forbidden Faith," *American Scholar*, Vol. 21, pp. 399-401 (October, 1952); Arthur M. Schlesinger, Jr., "Conservative vs. Liberal—A Debate," *New York Times Magazine*, March 4, 1956, pp. 11 ff.

5. See Kirk, *op. cit.*, p. 37, and compare Schlesinger's summary of conservative concepts, *Confluence*, Vol. 2, pp. 64-65, with Kirk's summary, *The Conservative Mind* (Chicago, 1953), pp. 3-10. See also below, note 27.

6. Hence any theory of natural law as a set of transcendent and universal moral principles is inherently nonconservative. Mannheim, consequently, is quite right in identifying opposition to natural law as a distinguishing characteristic of conservatism, *op. cit.*, pp. 116-19. On Burke's denial of natural law, see Alfred Cobban, *Edmund Burke and the Revolt against the Eighteenth Century* (London, 1929), pp. 40 ff., 75, and Leo Strauss, *Natural Right and History* (Chicago, 1953), pp. 13-14 and 318-19, who makes the point that Burke differed from previous thinkers precisely in that he did not judge the British constitution by a standard transcending it. The efforts of contemporary publicists such as Russell Kirk to appear conservative and yet at the same time to espouse a universal natural law are manifestly inconsistent.

7. Since conservatism is the ideological justification of established social and political institutions, a conservative defense of sheer chaos or of a society in a continuing state of rapid revolutionary change would be impossible except for an individual so nimble, so cunning, so strong as to be confident of his talent for flourishing as an outlaw. This raises the question as to the chances of conservatism in a modern totalitarian state. If totalitarian society is, as Franz Neumann described Nazi Germany, "a non-state, a chaos, a rule of lawlessness and anarchy," a conservative defense of such a society is impossible. On the other hand, if a totalitarian regime under attack did articulate a theory characterized by a number of conservative elements, this in itself would be supporting evidence that it had "settled down" and was no longer in a state of permanent revolution. The answer to this general question obviously depends upon the nature of totalitarianism rather than on the nature of conservatism. See Carl J. Friedrich (ed.), *Totalitarianism* (Cambridge, 1954); Hannah Arendt, "Ideology and Terror: A Novel Form of Government," *Review of Politics*, Vol. 15, pp. 303-27 (July, 1953); Franz Neumann, *Behemoth: The Structure and Practice of National Socialism* (New York, 1942); Zbigniew K. Brzezinski, "Totalitarianism and Rationality" *[The American Political Science Review]*, Vol. 50, p. 751 (Sept., 1956).

8. *Op. cit.*, p. 115.

9. See Bonald's famous comment: "Quand Dieu a voulu punir la France, il a fait retirer les Bourbons." "Pensées sur Divers Sujets," *Oeuvres* (Paris, 1817), Vol. 6, 172. Also: Joseph de Maistre, "Considerations sur la France," *Oeuvres* (Bruxelles, 1838), Vol. 7, Ch. 1, 2; and Strauss's discussion of Burke, *op. cit.*, pp. 317-19.

10. "Reflections on the Revolution in France," *Works* (Boston, 1865), Vol. 3, p. 352 (hereafter cited as *Works*).

11. See *e.g.*, "Thoughts on the Cause of the Present Discontents," *Works*, Vol. 1, pp. 436, 440-41, 469, 472-74, 491-93, 508.

12. For Burke's views on aristocracy, see *ibid.*, Vol. 1, p. 458; "An Appeal from the New to the Old Whigs," *ibid.*, Vol. 4, pp. 174-75; "Reflections on the Revolution in France," *ibid.*, Vol. 3, p. 297; "Speech on the Second Reading of a Bill for the Repeal of the Marriage Act," *The Works of Edmund Burke* (London, World's Classics), Vol. 3, p. 385; John MacCunn, *The Political Philosophy of Burke* (London, 1913), pp. 157-60, 173 ff., 258-68. On Burke's difficulties with the aristocracy, see John Viscount Morley, *Burke* (London, 1923), pp. 198-208. ·

13. L. B. Namier, *England in the Age of the American Revolution* (London, 1930), pp. 15, 38, 40: "Trade was not despised in eighteenth-century England— it was acknowledged to be the great concern of the nation. . . ." See also W. E. H. Lecky, *A History of England in the Eighteenth Century* (New York, 1878), Vol. 1, p. 433: "In very few periods in English political history was the commercial element more conspicuous in administration. . . . The questions which excited most interest

were chiefly financial and commercial ones." And J. L. and Barbara Hammond, *The Rise of Modern Industry* (New York, 1926), pp. 64-65: "In eighteenth-century England, industry seemed the most important thing in the world. All classes put industrial expansion high among the objects of public policy. . . ." On the beginning of the Industrial Revolution in England and the prestige of commerce and industry, see also: W. Cunningham, *The Industrial Revolution* (Cambridge, 1908), p. 494; W. T. Selley, *England in the Eighteenth Century* (London, 1934), pp. 218-19; Witt Bowden, *The Rise of the Great Manufacturers in England, 1760-1790* (Allentown, 1919), *passim*.

14. *Cavendish Debates,* Vol. 1, p. 476, quoted in Robert H. Murray, *Edmund Burke: A Biography* (Oxford, 1931), p. 192 (italics added).

15. *Annual Register,* 1776, Vol. 19, p. 241.

16. Robert Bisset, *The Life of Edmund Burke,* 2 vols. 2d ed. (London, 1800), Vol. 2, p. 429.

17. Quoted in Morley, *Burke,* pp. 190-91, 245, and George H. Sabine, *A History of Political Theory* (New York, 1950, rev. ed.), p. 616.

18. Some conservative elements persisted in the *Vindiciae,* but they were obscured by the appeal to the social contract and natural law. *Cf.* J. N. Figgis, *From Gerson to Grotius* (Cambridge, 1916), pp. 174-79 and Sabine, *A History of Political Theory,* pp. 375-77.

19. See Charles Nevinson (ed.), *Latter Writings of Bishop Hopper* (Cambridge, 1852), esp. "Annotations on Romans XIII," pp. 93-116; Pierre Janelle (ed.), *Obedience in Church and State: Three Political Tracts by Stephen Gardiner* (Cambridge, 1930); Henry Walter (ed.), *Doctrinal Treatises by William Tyndale* (Cambridge, 1848), esp. pp. 173 ff., 195-97, 240 ff.; Christopher Morris, *Political Thought in England, Tyndale to Hooker* (London, 1953), pp. 15, 17, 57, 68-77. One hundred years later Bramhall duplicated those arguments in his controversies with Hobbes. See John Bramhall, *Works* (Oxford, 1844), Vol. 3, "A Fair Warning to take Heed of the Scotch Discipline," and "The Serpent-Salve, or, the Observator's Grounds Discussed," esp. pp. 236, 241, 272, 298, 309, 318; John Bowle, *Hobbes and His Critics* (New York, 1952), pp. 114 ff.; T. S. Eliot, *For Lancelot Andrewes* (Garden City, 1929), pp. 27-46.

20. For typical conservative expressions in the *Laws of Ecclesiastical Polity,* see: Pref., i, 2, iii, 7, iv, 4, vi, 5-6; I, v, 1, x, 4; IV, i, e, iv, 2, xxi, 2, xiv, 1-2; V, vii, 3, lxxi, 4; VII, i, 1-2; VIII, ii, 2, 17. On Hooker's conservatism generally, see Sheldon Wolin, "Richard Hooker and English Conservatism," *Western Political Quarterly,* Vol. VI, pp. 28-47 (March, 1953). On the nature of the Puritan challenge and the origins of Hooker's work, see C. J. Sisson, *The Judicious Marriage of Mr. Hooker and the Birth of the Laws of Ecclesiastical Polity* (Cambridge, 1940), *passim,* and E. T. Davies, *The Political Ideas of Richard Hooker* (London, 1946), Ch. 1, 2.

21. See Reinhold Aris, *History of Political Thought in Germany* (London, 1936), pp. 54-58, 256. Brandes and Rehberg wrote their conservative works before reading Burke. Möser was closer to feudalism, but even he, as Mannheim points out, "Conservative Thought," pp. 144-45, had little use for the nobility, and was primarily concerned with the preservation of the medieval social system as a whole.

22. Joseph C. Murray, "The Political Thought of Joseph de Maistre," *Review of Politics,* Vol. 11, p. 86 (January, 1949); Charles A. Micaud, *The French Right and Nazi Germany, 1933-1939* (Durham, 1943), pp. 1-15.

23. For the change in southern thinking about 1830, see William E. Dodd, *The Cotton Kingdom* (New Haven, 1921), pp. 48 ff., and Arthur Y. Lloyd, *The Slavery Controversy* (Chapel Hill, 1939), pp. 119 ff.

24. Louis Hartz, *The Liberal Tradition in America* (New York, 1955), p. 146.

25. *Ibid.,* pp. 147. ff.

26. The significance of positional ideologies has been obscured by the assumption, deriving from Mannheim's sociology of knowledge, that every ideology has a "carrier" in the form of a specific social group or class. The argument here is

that ideologies may also have "carriers" in the form of recurring patterns of relations among groups.

27. F. J. C. Hearnshaw, *Conservatism in England* (London, 1933), pp. 22 ff.; Kirk, *Conservative Mind*, pp. 7-8; Rossiter, *Conservatism in America*, pp. 61-62; Mannheim, "Conservative Thought," p. 114; Lord Hugh Cecil, *Conservatism* (London, 1937), p. 48; William O. Shanahan, "The Social Outlook of Prussian Conservatism," *Review of Politics*, Vol. 15, pp. 222-25 (April, 1953); R. J. White (ed.), *The Conservative Tradition* (London, 1950), pp. 1-10.

28. "Conservative Thought," p. 120.

29. Murray, *Review of Politics*, Vol. 11, p. 86; Arnaud B. Leavelle and Thomas I. Cook, "George Fitzhugh and the Theory of American Conservatism," *Journal of Politics*, Vol. 7, pp. 146-47 (May, 1945).

30. Its lack of both an intellectual tradition and a substantive ideal account for another peculiar aspect of conservatism: the extent to which it has been ignored by political scientists writing on political theory. In the political theory textbooks conservatism rarely, if ever, appears, and when it does it is treated, on the whole, in a very skimpy manner. Similarly, there are no decent histories of conservative thought. The reason for this lies partly in the nature of conservatism and partly in the training of political scientists. The latter learn to analyze historical schools of thought, to trace the development of ideas, to identify the influence of one man or another, and to search out the ideological schisms and doctrinal divergencies in a school of thought. They are also taught to dissect the substantive ideals of ideologies in terms of their inherent logic and consistency, the theories of man and nature which they reflect, and the group interests which they rationalize and project. Lacking an intellectual tradition and a substantive ideal, conservatism does not lend itself to fruitful analysis along these lines. Not knowing what questions to ask about conservatism or how to evaluate its significance, political scientists have tended to ignore it.

31. *Conservative Mind*, pp. 10, 428, and *Program for Conservatives*, *passim*. It is essential to distinguish between those such as Kirk who criticize the institutions *and* the theory of modern liberal democracy and those such as Reinhold Niebuhr who limit their critique to the theory of liberalism while praising the inherent wisdom of its institutions.

32. But see Henry S. Kariel's reinterpretation of him, "The Limits of Social Science: Henry Adams' Quest for Order" in *[The American Political Science Review]*, Vol. 50, p. 1074 (December, 1956).

33. *Foreign Policy and the Democratic Process* (Baltimore, 1955), pp. 5-7.

34. A good example is the common experience of the American in Europe who extols the United States as the land of freedom, equality, and democracy, and then is asked: "What about the Negro in the South?" In reply, the American inevitably stresses the magnitude of the social problems involved, the inevitability of gradualness, the impossibility of altering habits overnight by legislative fiat, and the tensions caused by too rapid social change. In short, he drops the liberal language of equality and freedom and turns to primarily conservative concepts and arguments.

SOME PRESENT-DAY CRITICS
OF LIBERALISM

Francis W. Coker

I. INTRODUCTION

"Liberalism" is a late modern word, appearing first (along with "conservatism," "socialism," and "communism") in the early nineteenth century. Its basic ideas are old. The particular freedoms called for have changed as the denials of freedom have changed. The demands have been for liberation from oppressive political rule or intolerant ecclesiastical authority; or from a status of slavery or serfdom; from restraints embodied in laws and customs that hamper the rise of new productive forces, or from limitations on equal opportunity resulting from narrow concentrations of private economic power; from limitations on voting rights and from interferences with freedom of religion, speech, and association. The constant concern has been with pleas for deliverance from restraints which, although perhaps widely regarded at a given time as a normal part of life, have come to be regarded, by some in the community, as unnatural and intolerable.

The founding of such pleas on ideas about man's natural traits also follows a long tradition. It is "the rational principle within us," said Aristotle, that distinguishes man from "the animals," who "do not apprehend reason, but simply obey their instincts." "Language," Aristotle continued, is the sign of this special human faculty; for the distinctive function of language is to express, not "feelings of pain and pleasure"—animals have that faculty—but "perceptions of good and evil, the just and the unjust, and other similar qualities." Again (accord-

---

Reprinted from *The American Political Science Review*, vol. XLVII, no. 1 (March, 1953), 1-27. By permission of the author and the publisher.

ing to Aristotle): although man is the least self-sufficient being—meant by his nature to live in close association with other men in an organized political community—he is, in the rightly organized community, subject only to the commands of persons who rule under "the laws," which are "sovereign over personal rule, whether it be exercised by a single person or a body of persons."[1] It is in this ancient Greek idea of "freedom under the law" that some historians of ideas have located the origin of "western liberalism," and it is chiefly in this sense that liberalism has been called "the tradition of the West."[2]

Later examples of such ideas about freedom and reason are familiar, in both religious and secular literature: St. Paul exhorting his readers to heed "the inner law," in man's "mind," "written in the hearts of men"; early Christian jurists maintaining that it is man's nature to be free, so that restraints should be regarded as temporary expedients to correct deviations from normal human behavior; officials of a powerful medieval church intervening to protect citizens from arbitrary political rulers; various secular and ecclesiastical writers, from Cicero on, holding that rulers and people are equally bound by the dictates of right reason; writers of the Renaissance (a rebirth of early Christian as well as of ancient pagan ideas) and the Enlightenment, holding that men can achieve significant values on earth if they set their minds and hearts on releasing themselves from the handicaps of outmoded institutions and an adverse environment; and the later modern phrasing of these beliefs —holding that man, by virtue of his nature, has inalienable rights and that we can best discover truth about man and society through free inquiry and the dialectic of free discussion, or (more concretely) that the "civil liberties" (such as are set forth in modern "bills of rights") must be maintained as essential means for realizing man's highest intellectual, moral, and spiritual values and for reaching viable decisions in a democracy. Such ideas, it has been widely held, have provided approaches towards solving the never fully solvable problem considered in ancient, medieval, and modern political discussions: how to maintain a united community directed by strong and efficient government, without producing incompetent, incomplete citizens.

Such ideas do not, of course, make up the whole of the tradition of the West. There have always been advocates of the opposite, or complementary, values of order, stability, and consensus. These values also have been associated with ideas about the nature and destiny of man: with conceptions, that is, of man as a being who attains fulfillment of his nature chiefly by playing his assigned, directed part in maintaining the existence and well-being of some group (e.g., a nation, class, or "community") in which alone he can find his own existence maintained and explained. Man's chief right or duty, in the extremer forms of such a doctrine, is to "conform," accepting as his own the common or general opinion or will of his group.

When the modern liberal has challenged the reasonableness or justice of particular orders made by official spokesmen for a ruling group, he has sometimes been rebuked as an advocate of disorder or disunity; or if he has appealed for the restoration of earlier freedoms, he has been rebuffed as one vainly trying to revive outmoded ideas. When, in a community with a democratic form of government, he challenges the justice or practicality of a particular decision of the official political majority, he is represented as rejecting the principle of majority rule; and when his reasoning in behalf of freedom runs counter to the reasoning of spokesmen for a particular religion, he is sometimes charged with exalting reason above faith.

The present-day criticisms of liberalism are varied (often mutually contradictory) and they issue from various sources. Some identical criticisms are made by groups that are frequently regarded as sharply opposed to one another in their ideas about man and society and the ways of governing a community. Thus fascists and communists are alike in describing liberals as deluded idealists or incompetent intellectuals. Spokesmen for these groups are emphatic and sweeping in their rejections. Both reject the idea that private citizens can have rights against political rulers. Both disparage free, "objective," inquiry as a means for discovering truth about either the physical world or about man and society; and both regard freedom of discussion as useless for arriving at any viable consensus in the political community. Said Oswald Spengler: the liberal's concern for individual or minority rights and freedoms leads only to "blindness," "cowardice," and "spiritual indiscipline"; he described the modern liberal as either "bourgeois" or "plebeian" and said he meant both of those words to be understood as "terms of abuse." Lenin said that freedom of criticism usually amounts to "freedom from every thought-out theory," and he called the liberal an "arm-chair fool." [3]

There are a wide variety of criticisms offered by writers who are somewhat more moderate in their disparagement and who operate more clearly within the general limits of our western tradition. Some of these criticisms appear as items in general appraisals of the modern western mind; others appear in a systematic consideration of liberalism as the most characteristic feature of the modern mind. Some of these writers are friendly critics, offering warnings against what they regard as the liberal's exaggerated statement and application of his liberal negations and affirmations. Others regard the present-day political liberal as essentially wrong: wrong in advocating the wrong policies, because he concerns himself with matters that have no essential relation to the major problems of political life; or wrong in resting his policies on insecure moral and spiritual foundations, with wrong ideas about man's natural needs, motivations, and capacities, and about man's ultimate spiritual dimensions. In each of these groups, a wide variety of attitudes is displayed towards modern liberalism and the modern liberal, as indicated by the variety of descriptive terms they employ. Liberalism, they say, has become an essentially "negative," "neutral," "middle-of-the-road," "stereotyped," "mechanical," doctrine; or it is a "dogmatic," "pretentious," "aggressive," positively "dangerous" doctrine. The liberal, they say, is "a-moral," "secular," "religiously indifferent," "anti-religious"; or he is too much the "perfectionist"—"self-righteous" and "priggish" in his appraisal of political policies. Thus also the liberal is variously identified by these critics as distinctively "sentimental," "idealistic," "romantic," "utopian," "intellectual," "academic," and "nineteenth-century." Some of the critics—conceding that there were once virtues in the characteristic liberal doctrines (suitable for the period in which they appeared), yet regarding those doctrines as no longer useful or safe—offer the consolation that liberalism, having done its essential negative, destructive work, is now destined to "disappear."

This paper will deal with two groups of critics of liberalism, considered as a set of ideas about the rights of man in a political community.[4] The two groups have sharply opposed ideas as to just how the liberal is wrong in such matters, and also as to the intellectual and moral levels upon which a discussion of such matters can be profitably conducted. Professors Willmoore Kendall and J. Austin Ranney believe that the liberal wrongly interjects moral considerations into a political discussion; and that he is thereby specifically wrong in regarding individuals and minorities as having inviolable rights in a democracy. Reinhold Niebuhr, T. S. Eliot, and Professors John H. Hallowell and Sebastian De Grazia regard the liberal as wrong in leaving moral (and theological) considerations out of his political discussions; or that he is wrong specifically in trusting to an assumed natural reasonableness and ingenuity and spontaneous goodness in man as the adequate foundation upon which to construct a policy for making human rights secure in the political community.

II. THE "MAJORITY-RULE DEMOCRATS"

Professor Kendall objects to the liberal's advocacy of "rights" in a political community—of freedoms, that is, which are natural to man, and which, accordingly, citizens ought to demand and rulers ought to acknowledge and protect.[5] Such a discussion, he contends, irrationally mixes moral with political ideas, violating "the frontier that divides political theory from ethics." Political theory, as Mr. Kendall defines it, is "value free." Advocating the values of free speech, religious freedom, and fair law enforcement belongs only to other disciplines, such as "ethics and theology." Political theory deals with the efficiency of means for the realization of political ends, not with the consistency of such ends or means with man's more basic values or preferences. It is concerned with "the method by which political decisions are to be made," not with the reasonableness, justice, or morality of the decisions.

Mr. Kendall objects particularly to the liberal's attempt to combine a discussion of the rights of individuals or minorities (other than the right to take part in making political decisions) with a discussion of democracy. "Democracy," properly understood, is the name for a form of government. It means government by "the people"; and this means, in practice, government by a "majority of the electorate," since unanimity among voters is never attainable. Thus, Mr. Kendall continues, a democrat may properly be called a "majoritarian." "The majoritarian is the man who finds the majority principle more congenial to his values than any other, but the finding on this is, or should be, value free. . . . The problem a democratic community faces is, as it seems to us, merely that of deciding in what persons amongst us our democratic values require us to lodge its power." Discussing "the merits of the majority's (i.e., the community's) setting aside the traditional civil liberties has no more place in a discussion of the majority principle than a thesis regarding the merits of an economy's producing dum-dum bullets would have in a discussion of the pricing system."

Thus "democracy," in this majoritarian political theory, means "absolute," "unlimited," majority rule. If there are limits on a majority's rule, some other group, "outside" the majority, has to define the limits and the methods of applying them, and you then have rule by a minority. "In a democracy the last word must be with the majority." The American people, declares Professor Ranney, have in vain wanted both "majority rule and inviolable rights." We can't have both: we have to decide "whether democracy to us means majority rule *or* minority rights"; minority rights "means" minority rule. In a democracy, Professors Ranney and Kendall jointly declare, "no political decisions should be made by any body smaller than fifty per cent plus one of all its members. . . . The only restraint upon popular majorities consonant with democracy is such a sense of self-restraint as those majorities happen to possess."

To make the government of the United States the sort of democracy described by Professors Kendall and Ranney would require radical changes in our constitutional system. Professor Ranney lists the following necessary changes: Abolishing staggered national elections, the equal representation of the states in the Senate, and Senate filibusters. Further changes would have to be made, it would seem, if the majority is never to be restrained by a minority. Thus to make Congress—and the presidency also, if we are to have more than one agency representing the majority—more nearly the representative of a bare majority, we would have to do away with all special majorities, change the present apportionment of the vote for President, and provide for a nationally defined suffrage and a national policing of the elections; and then, in order to give unlimited governing power to these bare-majority representatives, we would have to abolish, or let majorities in Congress or in popular referenda abolish or ignore, all the constitutional guarantees against governmental interferences with the traditional civil liberties.

This argument for unlimited majority rule is aimed particularly at the "judicial veto" as it operates in the enforcement of the constitutional guarantees. You don't have democracy, Kendall says, if you have a supreme court "armed with a bill of rights that forbids the majority to do certain things." "No form of government," Ranney and Kendall jointly declare, "in which the popular majority is checked by some other agency (such, for example, as a court exercising the power of judicial veto of legislative acts), external and not responsible to the majority, has any legitimate title whatever to the label of 'democratic.'" Although in a given democratic community there may be certain traditional, commonly assumed and accepted, standards generally followed in appraisals of the rightness of majority decisions, it is still, in a genuine democracy, only a bare majority that decides what the standards mean, in their political applications, and when and how they are to be applied, or when and how they are to be changed or abandoned.[6]

The foregoing indicates the reasoning of the majoritarian in excluding from political theory all discussion of rights in a democratic community, except the right of "political" equality—i.e., the right of every voter to participate equally in the community's decision-making process. Yet Kendall admits into his theory most of the specific freedoms which the liberal treats as rights. He agrees that certain freedoms are necessary as means for obtaining majority decisions. A majority-rule system must have the proper "institutions" for forming majority decisions, with "guarantees" that use of the institutions will be available to all who are to be counted in the process of arriving at a majority decision. "Since the majority-rule democrats do not believe that the people can be counted upon to produce a majority will except where certain conditions are satisfied, they insist upon institutions calculated to facilitate the emergence of such a will (popular education, ventilation of public issues before the widest possible audience and with fullest guarantees that all points of view will find expression, such freedom of organization for political parties as will assure a maximum of competition between them for majority support, etc.)."[7] A majority puts an end to majority rule if it prevents existing minorities from growing into new majorities.

Here the majority-rule democrat may appear to be adopting liberal political ideas. But this is only an appearance. Admitting the right or necessity, in a democracy, for a free exchange of views and for freedom of assembly and organization, is not injecting moral or liberal ideas or "values" into political theory. For such freedoms, in the majoritarian's theory, are only means, not ends; you can't have democracy without them, but they are not essential rights; and an existing majority can, through the proper democratic procedures, decide to destroy them, thus exercising its unlimited power by deciding to end majority rule; or it may unwittingly make decisions that bring about that result. Democracy, in Mr. Kendall's words, can "commit suicide." It is in this way that the majority-rule democrat keeps himself "intellectually" safe on the political side of the barrier he has erected between his politics and his ethics, holds on to his dogma that democracy means unlimited majority rule, and sticks to his judgment that liberals talk non-sense when they talk about inalienable rights of individuals or minorities under a democratic form of government.

Comment on the Majoritarians. It seems proper to insist that in a political discussion the word "democracy" should be used to identify a form of government—a location of "highest" decision-making authority—and not as the name for some humane governmental policy. The former has been the prevailing meaning of the word since the Greeks started, in the fifth century, B.C., talking about the desirable results that might be achieved by placing political decisions in the hands of "the people." A government in which a few rule in the interest of the many may be called a good government, but not, in a proper political vocabulary, a democracy. It also seems proper to say that democracy means "majority rule" since that is as near as we ever get to rule by all the people. It may be agreed also that democracy means "unlimited" majority rule, in one sense of the word "unlimited" as it is used in political discussions. The most ardent advocate of "inviolable" and "inalienable" rights of individuals and minorities understands that a ruling group can violate these rights; and he knows that in any government there is some formally designated person or group of persons possessing an authoritative "last word." Even in states in which the ordinary governing bodies rule legally only within limits set forth in a written constitution, there are other constitutionally designated bodies that can legally abolish those limits. In this familiar meaning of unlimited ruling power Professor Ranney is correct in saying that if the American people want democracy they can not have inviolable rights—i.e., rights that the finally deciding "majority" may not legally violate. That majority can legally deprive any individual or group of life, liberty, and property by any means it chooses, and make the deprivations effective to the full extent of whatever coercive or persuasive powers it possesses.

It may be agreed, finally, that political theory is not altogether theory about "values." As a special technical discipline, political theory can be said to consist of objective, "value-free," descriptions and explanations of observed regularities in the relations among political events; or of deductions from postulated premises about political behavior, or of generalizations based on a rational weighing of the best available evidences in this field. That sort of political theory (or political science) can be useful in appraising governmental forms and activities in terms of their efficiency in realizing stated preferences concerning the location and scope of governmental power. These preferences may be derived from various sorts of basic values and modified by various experiences in the pursuit of the values. A political theorist of this sort is not obligated to look into the meaning of the values. If he offers only to give advice to a community whose values (whatever they may be) lead it to want a government organized and operated in conformity with the wishes (whatever they may be) of a relatively large number of the members of the community, he may properly confine his efforts to pointing out the ways whereby such a people—given their particular capacities and habits and the limitations of their particular environment—are most likely to get that sort of government. It thus seems proper to say that political theory of this sort or to this extent is (or ought to be) "value-free."

To agree to the foregoing definitions—of democracy as "majority rule," of a majority's "power" as, in an important aspect, "absolute," and of political theory as, in some aspects, "value-free,"—is not, however, to agree that this excludes from a rational political discussion all consideration of the values that appear to determine a preference for a democratic form of government, or all consideration of the desirability of establishing judicially applicable limitations upon the powers of the ordinary policy-declaring bodies in a democracy. The meaning of a preference for a democratic form of government is rarely fully indicated by a specification of the number or qualifications of the people who are to take part in making the final decisions. There are different kinds of majority rule, and a desire for one kind does not commit anybody to a desire for another kind. Plato and Aristotle (discussing democracy as a form of government) set forth what they regarded as the essential differences between a "pure" democracy, in which the majority rules in the interest of all the people and in accord with traditional customs or unwritten laws of the community, and a "corrupt" democracy, in which the majority rules in its own interest and without regard for those higher obligations.[8] Similar evaluations appear in many of the later classical statements of political theory. Thus ideas on majority rule are combined with ideas on inalienable rights in the theoretical systems of both Locke and Jefferson.[9]

James Bryce and Ernest Barker also (both cited by Ranney and Kendall as writers who properly treat democracy as a form of government) have these "mixed" ideas about democracy. Each specifies the ends that majority rule must serve if it is to fit his conception of a rational preference for a democratic form of government. Bryce explained that by "democracy" he meant rule by a majority that safeguards "independence of thought," and a "free play of the intellect," permits the expression of "unpopular opinions," and bears with opposition "because it has faith in the victory of truth." "Not less than any other form of government," said Bryce, "does democracy need to cherish Individual Liberty." [10] Said Barker: A democracy that "rests merely on the will of numbers rests merely on force. If we keep the name and the idea of democracy, we must find some other basis. . . . It is not the majority, as a majority, that matters. It is each human being, as such." The "essence" of democracy, Barker continued, "what matters," is a majority that seeks "full development of personality and individuality," tolerates "differences in doctrine," encourages "discussion of competing ideas," and intervenes in the life of the individual "with a restrained and cautious hand." [11]

Most systematic discussions of democracy (as a form of government) consider the desirable limitations on majority rule. Most of the present-day democracies have written constitutions containing provisions designed to restrain the powers of bare, temporary, majorities: orders and prohibitions intended (in Bryce's words) to operate as "mitigations of the faults to which democracy is liable." "The annals of democratic governments consist largely of an account of the various expedients resorted to for this purpose," said Bryce. He discussed, in this connection, the familiar expedients of indirect election, upper legislative chambers, over-lapping terms, and "checks and balances" (including judicial review) in the distribution of governing powers.[12]

Why should a community, having a general preference for majority rule, be debarred from choosing the means it considers most useful in making majority decisions more generally acceptable and effective? The American Congress seems traditionally committed to the belief that a "judicial veto" is a useful means to this end. At various times, Congress has been urged to enact or initiate measures designed to destroy or limit the judicial veto. In rejecting or ignoring such proposals, Congress may be reflecting some sort of a persistent popular opinion that legislative decisions will be more willingly and intelligently observed if we retain this safeguard; a belief that with the veto—as it operates in retarding, warning, yet not finally frustrating, a popular will—we are more likely to have the sort of community best fitted for long-run majority rule. Bryce (describing our judiciary as "in fact and in name an independent branch of the government side by side with the Executive and the Legislature") said that he regarded our use of judicial review, in placing certain matters "out of reach of legislative or executive action," as one of our most significant contributions to the "practical art" of democratic government. The American people, he said, had "resolved to put certain rules out of the reach of temporary impulses springing from passion or caprice, and to make these rules the permanent expression of their calm thought and deliberate purpose. It is a recognition of the truth that majorities are not always right, and need to be protected against themselves by being obliged to recur, at moments of haste or excitement, to maxims they had adopted at times of cool reflection." [13] Other commentators, here and abroad, have described this feature of our system as a successful experiment in the limitation of governmental power in a democracy.

In insisting on rights the liberal does not mean that rulers cannot violate rights; he means, frankly, that rulers ought not to violate rights. The liberal recognizes the necessity of having somewhere in the governmental structure a "last-saying" authority. As a democrat he recognizes the necessity of placing that authority in the hands of a relatively large number of the sane adult citizens. He acknowledges the citizen's moral and rational obligation to obey governmental commands which his conscience and reason may condemn as violations of rights. The liberal is not a philosophical anarchist; he does not advocate either active or passive resistance to law enforcement. He understands that majorities as well as minorities have rights. None of this, however, commits him to the conclusion that if you want majority rule you can reasonably attach importance to the protection of rights only insofar as the exercise of such rights operates as a means for the formation of majority decisions. And none of this commits the liberal democrat to Professor Kendall's apparent belief that if you criticize any political opinion held by the majority you are presuming to substitute your own "values and lights for those of the people" (or "the majority of the people"), and thereby renouncing any consistent belief in democracy as a form of government.

Discussion of the proper scope of governmental action—of matters to be controlled and matters to be left free from control—has usually been regarded as a proper part of political theory, no less important than the question as to who should rule. Ideas about powers to be exercised and freedoms to be respected by a ruling majority have rarely been sharply separated from ideas about the ethical status of majority rule. Ancient, medieval, and modern political theorists have attempted to explain the values implicit in the political preferences of a people and to show how far and in what ways they can be reconciled with one another. Values may lead to a desire for both majority rule and inviolable rights, with guarantees that majority rule will not be used to destroy other freedoms we value. We give up the full achievement of some preferences, in part, in order not to thwart the achievement of other preferences. Thus a "value-free" political theory is likely to be of limited utility for a people strongly influenced by values. Rule by a majority that undertakes to rule without understanding the values that influence the attitudes of substantial minorities is likely to become impotent majority rule. Minorities as well as majorities exercise power in a democracy. Thus, said Bryce (still discussing democracy as a form of government): "Every people that has tried to govern itself has recognized the necessity for precautions against the errors it may commit, be they injurious to the interests of the State as a whole or in the disregard of those natural or primordial rights which belong to individual citizens." [14]

The liberal insists that these rights should not be disregarded. He believes that rights to religious freedom, freedom of speech, and fair trials should be acknowledged and protected by his government, even at the cost of accepting what the Greeks called "counter-devices" in a governmental system. It seems to him strange to say that people who want majority rule cannot regard as inviolable the freedoms that make majority rule possible and durable; and strange to say that people cannot reasonably desire both democracy and the conditions that make democracy desirable.

III. THE RELIGIOUS CRITICS

With the critics now to be considered, disparagement of liberalism forms part of a general lamentation over the moral and spiritual degeneration of modern society. In their specific criticisms, some of these critics approve main items in the liberal program for political action, while rejecting liberalism as a political philosophy; others reject both the philosophy and the program. The common idea in these criticisms is that liberals are wrong or ineffective in their political policy because they have not understood the nature of the evils with which political action deals. Conceiving man as by nature reasonable, magnanimous, and cooperative, the liberals have believed that existing injustices, discomforts, and insecurities in the political community can be corrected by benevolently motivated, rationally devised, institutional reforms. They fail to realize that our misdeeds and mistakes, in public as in private life, are natural and persistent manifestations of man's innate sinfulness and irrationality.

Perhaps the lengthiest and most emphatic criticism of liberalism, on religious grounds, is to be found in the works of a theologian most sympathetic with liberal aims. Reinhold Niebuhr—a progressive, humanitarian, internationally-minded theologian—has set forth, in several books, his ideas as to why the liberal's schemes for bringing freedom, justice, comfort, and peace into the world have achieved so little. Organize and plan, the liberal says, in his pleas to good and reasonable men: redistribute wealth; educate the masses; use our vast material resources and technical knowledge in eliminating disease and raising the standard of living for everyone; abolish tyrannies and set up democratic governments everywhere; reduce armaments and establish world tribunals for the peaceful and impartial settlement of international disputes. Such hopes, Niebuhr says, are vain. Good plans are futile unless they are undertaken by men wise enough to understand the depth of man's unwisdom and with a moral enlightenment that enables them to realize the strength and pervasiveness of human sinfulness. These views are best summarized in the following quotations from two of Niebuhr's books:

The utopian illusions and sentimental aberrations of modern liberal culture are really all derived from the basic error of negating the fact of original sin. This error . . . continually betrays modern man to equate the goodness of men with the virtue of their various schemes for social justice and international peace. . . . Obviously there are vary degrees of sin and guilt and some men and nations are more guilty than others of disobedience to the heavenly vision. Also there are specific evils in history, arising from the specific maladjustments in social and political organization. But these evils can be dealt with most adequately if men do not give themselves to the illusion that some particular organization of society might be found in which men would no longer stand in contradiction to the law of their being.[15]

The assumption of rationalists in the past centuries has been that either education or the equalization of economic interests would finally fashion the mind into a perfect instrument of universal and absolute knowledge, and would ultimately destroy social friction by eliminating the partial perspectives which prompt men to assess social issues in conflicting terms. But this assumption fails to recognize that the most intelligent and disinterested person can never escape his fate as a child of nature and finitude. . . . Thus even the most refined spiritual achievements of humans can never result in an unqualified synthesis of human hopes and aspirations. At some point they will always accentuate social conflict by making men more stubborn in the defense of their interests, under the illusion that their interests represent universal values.[16]

Niebuhr has recently illustrated these views, about man and his history, in a special study of the ironies of our American experience. We have demonstrated in a special way, he believes, an irrational faith in reason and a moral blindness to man's inherent immorality. The Puritan and Calvinist settlers believed they were creating "a new heaven and a new earth." The Constitutional Fathers, and we, their heirs, have continued to trust in our superior virtues and talents in making new beginnings in a corrupt world. Here then are some of the ironies in our actual achievement: a nation of greatest productive efficiency, we are involved in a global controversy threatening wholesale destruction; disparaging materialism, we have been its most expert practitioners; having achieved a high state of economic security at home, we are involved in unprecedented global insecurity; having made ourselves the world's most powerful nation, we are yet forced to accommodate our most fateful decisions to the demands or needs of other nations. "A nation with an inordinate degree of political power is doubly tempted to exceed the bounds of historical possibilities, if it is informed by an idealism which does not understand the limits of man's wisdom and volition in history." [17]

Niebuhr repeats these views in several of his books. Man, he says, "cannot rise to a simple triumph over historical fate." Our natural will to survive becomes a constant search for security, which in turn is transmuted into a competition for power and superiority. Sin, ignominy, and misery are our lot on earth. Yet this fervent pessimism by no means leads Niebuhr into any advocacy of negativism or passivism in his attitudes towards political action. For man, Niebuhr explains, is a complex being: a part of "nature" and involved in its limitations, yet also outside nature, and able to understand and appraise and in some measure transcend those limitations. Goodness and dignity are, in some measure, our lot. Sinful in his "original" nature, man can yet seek to become righteous; he faces the never realizable yet never escapable command to "be perfect." To qualify himself for making a better among the imperfect choices, he must first put himself in the proper moral and spiritual state. He must recover the traditional Christian virtues of acknowledging and repenting of one's sins. And he must try to understand the complexities of human history—"the limits of all human striving, the fragmentariness of all human wisdom, the precariousness of all historical configurations of power, and the mixture of good and evil in all virtue."

Thus repentance, rebirth, and a search for understanding are key words in Niebuhr's moral commandments. But so also is realism. The Christian must be practical; ready to choose the less over the more imperfect choices available to him at any given time. Indeed Niebuhr's criticisms do not actually separate him from liberals in the efforts to achieve justice and peace and make human rights secure. He agrees that citizens have fateful decisions to make, political reforms to be striven for actively and courageously. Thus the fault of liberals appears to be (in Niebuhr's diagnosis) not that they have rejected moral criteria, but that they have failed to qualify themselves, spiritually and intellectually, for a genuine application of moral criteria. The liberal's illusions about the possible scope of moral achievement at any given time often result in net losses for morality.

T. S. Eliot's criticisms of liberalism appear in several of his essays and short books. Like Niebuhr he believes that the typical defects of modern society are to be found in an exaggerated faith in human "reason" and "perfectibility" and in the lack of a religion or of any other sort of basic belief.[18] Our ordinary political distinctions today, between the democratic and the totalitarian countries, rest, Eliot believes, on nothing very significant. Indeed the totalitarian countries might be said to be more democratic than the democracies, since their policies may reflect a clearer popular will. The democracies and the dictatorships are alike, however, in their essential secularism. In a few of the western countries (Spain, Portugal, and Ireland) religion retains a slight hold. For the rest, the real division is between the pagan countries (communist and fascist) and the neutral countries (e.g., the United States, France, the British dominions, and possibly England). The pagan peoples have at least the virtues of not pretending to be religious and yet of having some sort of positive beliefs, however shallow and inconsistent. The neutral countries have no philosophy of any sort; to call them "Christian" is "an abuse of terms"; for they are Christian only in the sense that "no one is penalized for the formal profession of Christianity."

Both democracy and liberalism are, Eliot believes, typical manifestations of the degeneration of the modern West. He has little that is specific to say about democracy, and regards the word as now devoid of concrete definition; it means too many things to mean anything. "If anybody ever attacked democracy, I might discover what the word meant." Liberalism, Eliot agrees, once meant something concrete and valuable. In early modern times the beliefs we associate with that term supplied a useful negative element in the prevailing ideology and policy, counteracting old abuses by actively opposing an active, coercive intolerance at a time when the disputants were in essential agreement in their general religious and moral ideals. Present-day liberalism, Eliot believes, serves no present-day needs. It has, like democracy, become a spineless creed, lacking any beliefs strong enough to stand up against the diabolic faith of racism, class war, and the selfish imperialisms of capitalism and revolutionary socialism. Or if either democracy or liberalism can be said to have a religion, it is the religion of materialism, "the worship of profit. . . . Democratic liberal society, assembled around nothing more permanent than a congeries of banks, insurance companies, and industries," has no belief in anything more essential than "compound interest and the maintenance of dividends." The cure for this modern disease of the West cannot be found in good intentions and secular institutional changes. There must be a change in beliefs, or a change from non-belief to belief. "If you will not have God you should pay your respects to Hitler or Stalin."

The western world, then, Eliot believes, can be saved only by religion;

and only by the right religion, which is (for the West) Christianity.[19] And, like any other religion, Christianity must be authoritatively set forth and actively propagated under political auspices. The liberal idea that religion is "a matter of mere private belief and that Christians should be able to accommodate themselves to any world that treats them good-naturedly, is becoming less and less tenable": the Christian God is "a jealous God." The restoration of Christianity requires the restoration of Christian institutions. A Christian society must be founded on a Christian political philosophy; and it must be organized in such a way as to promote a wide understanding and acceptance of the Christian hierarchy of values. This does not require the adoption of any one of the traditional "forms of government." The form of the government of a Christian society may be a monarchy, aristocracy, or democracy, or a "corporative state" of the sort described in encyclicals of Pope Pius XI. "To identify any particular form of government with Christianity" is to confound "the permanent with the transitory, the absolute with the contingent."

Eliot's scheme for a Christian organization of society consists of "The Christian State," "The Community of Christians," and "The Christian Community," and an established Christian Church. By a "Christian State," Eliot means "the government" (in the ordinary sense of the word): the "rulers" (directors of policy) and the whole personnel engaged in the work of legislation, administration, and law enforcement. The rulers do not have to be believing Christians: they may be infidels in their private beliefs, but they must govern as Christians, conforming to "the temper and traditions" of a Christian people; they may "frequently perform un-Christian acts," but must "never attempt to defend their actions on Christian principles." By a "Community of Christians" Eliot means an elite gathered from among clerics, teachers, and intellectually and morally superior laymen; the function of this group will be to help bring Christian principles into education, public policy, and the private economy. The "Christian Community" is the general body of citizens in whom the Christian faith has been ingrained; for this group—"the masses"—Christianity will be essentially a matter of unconscious habit, with ordinary people conforming as a matter of course to established religious observances and traditional patterns of Christian behavior. The form of an established Christian Church, and its relation to the state, might vary in different Christian countries; but everywhere its function would be to speak with "final authority" in the interpreting matters of faith and morals.

Eliot recognizes the difficulties in the way of establishing his Christian society anywhere. Actual tendencies in social behavior—exaggeration of the profit motive, exploitation of labor, and an unfair distribution of wealth—are, he believes, carrying society in the opposite direction. Few will dispute that "a great deal of the machinery of modern life is merely a sanction for un-Christian aims." Although Eliot in such passages indicates a humane interpretation of Christian economic principles, he by no means identifies this with any vision of a social democracy. There is a frequently recurring idea, in his various works, that an efficient, responsible Christian society must be made up of "classes"—each with its special traditions and culture and its special contributions to make to the total culture of that society; and each, accordingly, with class and local as well as general, national, loyalties—all subordinate to the stabilizing force of Christian traditions of belief and behavior.

By the "idea" of a Christian society, Eliot has no notion of a society that ever was or ever would be; he was, he explained, using the word "idea" in its classical sense of "the conception of a thing which is given by the knowledge of its ultimate aim." The Christian social goal may, he feared, seem undesirable to most of the present-day intelligentsia, perhaps "intolerable" to "the liberal mind." Neutral societies may persist indefinitely. But, he believes, "if the present-day peoples are to develop any positive culture of their own"—in other words, if they are to have any culture at all—they "must proceed in the direction of a pagan or of a Christian society." In either event, he believes, liberalism has spent its force, played out its historic role. Its distinctive attitudes and beliefs "belong to an age of free exploitation which has disappeared; and our danger now is that the term may come to signify for us only the disorder the fruits of which we inherit, and not the permanent value of the negative element." Whether religion or paganism prevails, liberalism, Eliot believes, is "destined to disappear."

Professor Hallowell finds confirmation for his own views on the futility, or the positive evils, inherent in modern liberalism, in the writings of various representatives of "Protestant Neo-Orthodoxy," chiefly Niebuhr. He restates, with emphasis, the view that liberalism's basic defect is its ignorance or repudiation of the essential Christian doctrine of original sin.[20] He attributes to traditional liberalism the extreme view that, since man has natural inclinations to deal reasonably and amicably with his fellows, progress is "automatic," "inevitable," and "irreversible." And then, through a special application of the familiar argument that extreme affirmations lead to extreme contradictions, he assigns to present-day liberals a large share of responsibility for the irrationality and violence of the mid-twentieth-century totalitarian regimes. Overconfidence in man's reasonableness and goodness becomes an exaltation of will over reason, which leads to the triumph of evil over good; trust in the strength of the normal man's natural desire for freedom ensures the victory of the abnormal, power-seeking man.

Professor Hallowell cites two sorts of examples of this fateful transition from liberalism to totalitarianism: the legal theory of some German jurists, setting forth their explanations of "positive" law (as distinguished from natural law and moral law); and some public statements by prominent men who, in the mid-nineteen-thirties, spoke in praise, defense, or extenuation of Hitler's acts.

The legal positivist defines "law" (the law of a state, that is, which is what the jurists are talking about) as consisting of commands issuing, directly or indirectly, from the "sovereign" in a state—that is, from the person or body or bodies of persons formally designated as having final authority to make the laws to be enforced by the government of that state. The dangerous fallacy in this legal doctrine, Hallowell says, is that it treats as law every formally proper command issuing from such a source, however unreasonable or unjust the command may be. Thus the legal positivist, typical representative or product of the modern liberal mind, ignores, or leads others to ignore, all distinctions between good and evil, reason and unreason. The legal positivists thereby, Hallowell declares, "teach that might makes right." [21]

The defenders of "Hitler's terror," cited by Hallowell as examples of liberalism's baneful influence, are James W. Gerard, Hans Rothfels, and Winston Churchill. Gerard said that Hitler unified the German people, improved the education of German youth, rid the country of communism, curbed parliamentary government (a form of government not suitable for Germans) and created a "Spartan state"; Gerard described these achievements as "all good." The burden of Rothfels' defense or apology was that anyone was "pharisaic" and "self-righteous" in passing judgment on Germany's "mistakes" without having experienced the hardships the Germans had suffered. Churchill, praising Hitler's "courage" and "perseverance," said he had always hoped that if England were ever defeated in a war, the English people would "find a Hitler to lead us back to our rightful position among the nations." [22]

Professor Hallowell believes that our political ideas should be founded in the spiritual and moral principles revealed generally in the Greek-Hebraic-Christian tradition. He finds those principles set forth best by St. Thomas Aquinas and St. Augustine, and he follows Niebuhr in urging liberals to acknowledge their sins and proclaim their repentance. He summarizes his own version of essential Christian principles, upon which our political beliefs and policies should be based, as follows, in the last sentence of his book:

Only if we are concerned about the salvation of our souls shall we be of much use in saving the world, only if our eyes are focussed on the Kingdom of God shall we see with clearer vision what needs to be done here and now, only if we surrender our wills, as completely as men can to the will of God, will we be enabled by the power of God to make the self-sacrifice which the salvation of the world demands—in short, only by aiming above the world shall we succeed in mastering the world.

Hallowell had explained that he did not mean to exclude consideration of necessary reforms in the structure of our economic and political life. He means rather that no institutional reforms are likely to achieve anything of essential value unless they are undertaken with the perspective and principles provided by Christianity. We cannot obtain peace, security, and happiness in this world unless we seek "first the Kingdom of God and his righteousness."

Professor Hallowell's somewhat more specific statement of the proper principles upon which to found a Christian social order consists chiefly of quotations from the late William Temple, Archbishop of Canterbury. Temple summarized his basic principles as follows: Man is not "wholly" ruled by reason, and we cannot remove social injustices merely by reforming our social institutions; yet "civic action" is necessary in the social application of moral principles; recognition of the need for "social fellowship" must be reconciled with a respect for the worth of every person, "absolutely independent of all usefulness to society"; and society must be organized in such a way as to give to every individual "the widest extension of personal responsibility." [23] These views, approved by Hallowell, do not seem essentially different from the views of the liberals criticized by Hallowell.

Professor De Grazia regards "toleration" and "the absence of community" as the characteristic maladies of modern civilization. Under the final triumph of the "notion of the Individual," which "has agitated the Western world since the deaths of Alexander and Aristotle," we have lost all sense of the need for "common belief systems" and the "religious and political bonds" that create a community and hold it together.[24] We have now sunk to that condition in which people feel united with their fellows only in "war and crisis"; for only in such tragic situations do most of the people gain a "feeling of community." To make this feeling a normal part of life we must restore the political community to its rightful place and function. We must shift the center of our political interests from "individuals and classes and their mutual antagonisms" to the people united in "the Great Community"—"the state," which "embraces all other communities." This community must be sustained by a body of common values, with "moral authority," and by a recognition of "the close psychological connection and mutual support of religious and political ideologies." The state is "the highest secular association because like its counterpart, the religious community, it exists to protect man from his greatest fear—isolation."

De Grazia assails modern liberalism for its advocacy of toleration, which he describes as the enemy of morality as well as of community.[25] He lists, as representatives of this immoral doctrine of tolerance, outstanding names in the Anglo-American liberal tradition—from Milton, Roger Williams, and Locke to J. S. Mill. He regards Mill as the worst of the lot, since Mill (De Grazia says) advocated complete tolerance of every kind of thought and pursuit. De Grazia calls tolerance a "radical immoral force" and (borrowing a name from Martin Luther) "a sly whore." Tolerance, he continues, "working silently," has "turned the tolerator into a twilight man and the tolerated into a pale disbeliever," reducing "communal moral standards to a burnt-out hulk." He believes that Mill's ideas foster a "forced variety"; and he states his own belief that "it is always better to be right than to be different."

De Grazia's alternative to tolerance is not intolerance (which he regards as, like tolerance, a "counterfeit"), but "forgiveness," which he defines as "the promise and act of receiving the errant person back into the community." The "right to forgive" must be the special prerogative of "those who have the authority to lead, to guide, to watch over the community." The rest of the community should demonstrate their disapproval of bad ideas and pursuits by communicating their "moral disfavor" through "ridicule, rebuff, irony, contempt, avoidance, cold silence," and other "bloodless forms of moral expression."

Comment on the religious critics. Mill did not (the present writer believes) belittle the value of consensus. He said: "As mankind improve[s], the number of doctrines which are no longer disputed or doubted will be constantly on the increase; and the well-being of mankind may almost be measured by the number and gravity of the truths which have reached the point of being uncontested." He did warn against an overemphasis on consensus and against the dangers in governmental coercion as a means of securing agreement. And he did put a high value on individuality and originality. There will always, he said, be the need for persons who can "discover new truths . . . and set the example of more enlightened conduct and better taste and sense in human life. This cannot well be gainsaid by anybody who does not believe that the world has already attained perfection in all its ways and practices." And Mill did not advocate toleration of every sort of speech or action. Like De Grazia, he preferred bloodless forms of opposing the speech and action he considered immoral or unreasonable. For "moral vices" and "irrational behavior," he advocated such methods as "remonstrating," "reasoning," "persuading," "entreaty," and (in words strikingly similar to De Grazia's) such forms of "moral retribution" as "reprobation," "expression of distaste," "avoidance," "contempt," and (in extreme cases) "abhorrence." [26] Since Mill advocated free discussion as an essential means of discovering truth and securing clear agreement and strong convictions about what is true and right, he would (it would seem) readily accept De Grazia's aphorism that it is better to be right than to be different; as De Grazia would probably agree that it is better to be right than to be alike, and better to be different than to be wrong.

It is difficult to see why either the theorizing of the legal positivists or the praises of Hitler sung by some misguided commentators should be taken as indicative of typical liberal views or as typical products of liberal doctrine. Some legal positivists have been liberal in their general political theory, some have not. There is nothing in the positivist's theory of law (of the sort of law he is talking about) that should make it difficult for him to distinguish bad laws from good laws, and jurists of that school have not hesitated to make the distinction. Certainly, on the one hand, a Christian can recognize his obligation to obey the laws of a state, even those laws embodying commands which seem to him essentially immoral. No state could exist in a Christian community whose Christian citizens acted on the assumption that they were obligated to obey only those laws which their Christian consciences approved. And certainly, on the other hand, there is nothing in the positivist's definition and discussion of law that implies any unusual limitation on the right of a citizen to express his moral condemnation of a law, or any unusual limitation on his right to disobey or resist rulers who rule unrighteously.

It is difficult also to see why liberals should be blamed for the misguided utterances of Messrs. Gerard, Churchill, and Rothfels. Mr. Churchill seemed (to the present writer and to other ordinary liberals) wrong in his praise of Hitler, and wrong ten years earlier in his more emphatic praise of Mussolini; and Archbishop Temple (whom Hallowell commends for basing his political views on secure Christian foundations) seemed wrong in his pleas for cooperation with the Nazi regime and wrong in his warm commendation of Mr. Chamberlain's pact with Hitler.[27] The most charitable excuse for such utterances is that the speakers were badly informed as to Hitler's designs. If they had listened to warnings from the liberals they might have been more promptly alert to the signs of Mussolini's and Hitler's terrorism.

Professor Hallowell, in his various charges against the liberals, applies some of his specific criticisms to special sorts of liberals. Thus, he says, "bourgeois" liberals "consider only the material individual"; "extreme" liberalism "denies the existence of divine authority and thus in effect makes every man a law unto himself"; "some" liberals hold "that freedom of speech is unlimited"; and "degenerate" liberalism is "congenial to the rise of tyranny." Yet in many other passages Hallowell appears to regard his extreme characterizations as properly applicable to liberals generally. Thus, he declares, "It was the liberals who taught that might makes right." [28]

It can be said of any doctrine that it has its degenerate forms. What Hallowell says of some degenerate liberals can be said of some degenerate Christians. There is utility in pointing out the differences between the pure and the perverted forms of a doctrine. But it is difficult to see wherein there is any more justification for saying that liberals teach that might makes right than for saying that Christians teach that illiberal, un-Christian, doctrine.

Literary critics who claim T. S. Eliot as a special teacher and guide have differing opinions as to what Eliot means, or as to how far he intends to speak clearly, or whether his meanings are merely "too subtle for the intellect." Other readers should, therefore, be cautious in stating their own opinions. To some readers Eliot's description of a Christian society and a Christian life seems (in some passages) over-intellectual; too unemotional; preoccupied with structure and ritual, and ignoring experience; callous in its attitudes towards the ordinary lives of ordinary individuals. In some passages he is explicit in ranking thought above feeling, "truth" above experience, Christian "observances" above Christian conduct or a Christian spirit. "The spirit killeth," he says in one place, "but the letter giveth life." [29] Here, and in some other places, he appears deliberately supercilious in his comments on equality, tolerance, popular education, and any sort of merely humane public policy. His conception of "sin" as some sort of mystical entity, independent of human behavior, seems to make him indifferent to such secular qualities as kindness, honesty, and diligence. "What is worst," Eliot says, "is to advocate Christianity not because it is true, but because it might be beneficial." His Christian ideal would be realized in "a community of men and women not individually better than they are now, except for the capital difference of holding to the Christian faith." [30]

Yet in other passages there are (or appear to be) valid admonitions to liberals and democrats; as in his warnings against both a "slovenly," irresponsible, individuality, and the superficiality and short-sightedness in many of our attempts at economic equalization and mass education. In some passages also Eliot shows great respect for individuality and "the rights of personal life." He points out the various economic and social pressures that "steadily diminish the concrete reality of the individual." He opposes any "censorship," political or moral, of art and literature. Although he would provide for public support of the Christian religion, he recognizes the vagueness and irresponsibility in the use of the term "Christian." Many who call themselves Christian, do not, he says, understand or try to understand what the word means. Some who "vigorously repudiate Christianity are more Christian than many who maintain it." And although he would withhold any sort of positive encouragement of dissenters and sceptics, he would let them argue at will. Moreover, he says (somewhat surprisingly), "The Spirit descends in different ways" and "perhaps there will always be individuals who, with great gifts of value to mankind, and the sensibility which such gifts imply, will remain blind, indifferent, or even hostile. That must not disqualify them from exercising the talents they have been given." [31]

Thus Eliot warns against any sort of "totalitarian" democracy, with its insistence on "conformity without respect to the needs of the individual." He is no advocate of the sort of unlimited political authority insisted on by some of the critics of liberalism.

Niebuhr's belief that "nothing that is worth doing can be achieved in our lifetime" seems as much of an exaggeration, and as much of a contradiction of Christian doctrine, as the belief, attributed to liberals, that man can successfully act independently of his history, his environment, and the limitations of his own nature. Liberals have not imagined that man is solely a reasoning creature or always sound in his reasoning or right in his moral judgments; and they do not believe that we can ever find perfect solutions or always achieve partial solutions. They do believe that we can learn something from our failures and from our partial successes, in efforts to remove some of the economic, political, and psychological obstacles to partial successes. They see no good reason why such attitudes should be called "fantastic" or rejected as the useless products of eighteenth-century "enlightenment," "nineteenth-century rationalism," and the "pretentious social science" of the twentieth century. [32]

Niebuhr and the liberals he criticizes do not, however, seem very far apart in their positions on public policy. They should not object to his warnings against self-righteousness in appraising their intentions and against over-optimism in their expectations. In some passages he seems to be urging a sort of mystic pessimism that might lead to despair of any sort of action. But he does urge action. When fortified by a proper understanding of our imperfections, we should act, vigorously, realistically; we should not wait until we are at some never reachable vantage point of guiltlessness. Niebuhr recognizes fully the powerful part we have to play in preserving our civilization from communism, fascism, and our own selfish nationalism and inept liberalism. We must resist Russia's "demonry" as well as our own vanities and frailties.[33] Niebuhr stands with other liberals in urging vigorous action at home in support of religious freedom, free speech, fair law-enforcement, equal protection of the laws, and greater equality of economic opportunity.

IV. CONCLUSION

Liberalism needs criticism. A liberal may have exaggerated notions of man's capacity and disposition to think and act justly and intelligently. Optimism may obscure the need for creative thought and imagination. Tolerance may degenerate into indifference and irresponsibility. Confidence in institutional reforms may divert attention from reforms of the mind and spirit. The problem of maintaining intellectual and moral freedom and vigor is not merely a matter of bills of rights and checks and balances. Liberalism, which began with strong moral convictions, has no less need for them now, and moral convictions about rights imply moral convictions about obligations. As the right to property is conditioned by an obligation not to use property exploitatively, so the right to speak is conditioned by the obligation to speak honestly and fairly. "There are no costless rights." [34] Liberals should also recognize that in their openmindedness they may have exaggerated notions of the possibilities of freedom and variety. They may under-rate the individual's need for participation with others in a community in which there is some basic intellectual consensus and some common devotion to common causes. Philosophers and scientists have reminded us that an individual is the sort of person he is, not solely by virtue of his natural endowment and his physical environment, but also by virtue of the sort of conventional relationships in which he finds himself. The standards of conduct and opinions which these conventions express go far towards determining his character and achievement.

The views of some of the critics seem extreme; there are anti-liberal as well as liberal "stereotypes." Few of the criticisms require the liberal to abandon essential ideas in his political theory. He has no reason to object to the characterization of his theory as "mixed" and "middle-of-the-road." It is a Christian doctrine that man is a creature of "competing" dispositions and faculties and that good and evil are "curiously intertwined" in human history.³⁵ Anthropologists tell us that man is subordinate to his society, yet in essential ways independent of it. Political philosophers have shown how governments exercising unlimited power become incompetent and impotent governments.

The liberal does not ignore the pervasiveness and stubbornness of evil in human history. The fact that he may be an earnest advocate of secular reforms is no sign that he feels sure that his reforms will be adopted or that if adopted they will fully or finally solve any problem. It seems an exaggeration to say that there ever was a typically "liberal" belief in "inevitable," "automatic," and "irreversible" progress. In traditional liberal as in traditional Christian political doctrine, the chief reason for the existence of government is found in the need to prevent men from dealing unreasonably or unjustly with one another. Yet it is no contradiction of these beliefs to believe also that normal men know (in Locke's words) that they "should not destroy one another" or "harm another in his life, health, liberty or possessions." And not all Christian theologians make a virtue of exalting doubt and despair above faith and hope. Even Niebuhr agrees that man "is not involved in guilt merely by asserting his creative faculties." ³⁶

In all societies, we are told by anthropologists, conformity and dependence are combined with individuality and independence. Societies, Professor Ralph Linton says, "work as wholes"; the interests of each individual are subordinate to those of the group; a "community of ideas . . . values . . . habits" holds the group together. "It is this psychological and emotional unity, the *esprit de corps*, which ensures common emotional reactions and makes the individual willing to sacrifice his own interests to those of the whole and to do the things which need to be done even when there is no one watching him." Yet also: "No matter how thoroughly the persons who compose a society may have been trained, they remain individuals, distinct psychological entities," who "retain the capacity for independent thought, feeling, and action"; and these "alternatives," in thought, feeling, and action tend to become more "plentiful" and "varied" in the evolution from primitive to civilized societies. "All life in society is a compromise between the needs of the individual and the needs of the group, and it has the indefiniteness and instability of all compromise situations." ³⁷

There are special difficulties in the compromises that have to be made between the need of a government for power and the need of the citizen for freedom. "The *via media*," T. S. Eliot says, "is of all ways the most difficult to follow. It requires discipline and self-control, both imagination and a hold on reality. In a period of debility like our own, few men have the energy to follow the middle way in government." ³⁸ Whatever utility there may be in the bare logic of the argument that there can be no sensible combination of majority rule with limitations on majority rule—i.e., you either have unlimited rule by bare majorities or you do not have a democratic form of government—attempts at the combination are made in countries having governments called democratic, according to the proper definition of that word. Professor Latham discusses the lack of "logic" and "precision" in the opinions of our Supreme Court in applying to acts of Congress the Constitutional command that "Congress shall make no law . . . abridging freedom of speech"; and he believes we "win no real victories in the courts" in such matters. He proposes, as a better way to protect our liberties, that we instruct our legislators "in the limitations upon their powers" and that we vote out of office the "rascals" who violate the limitations. This seems certainly better than instructing our legislators, or the people who elect them, that their powers are not limited and that individuals who denounce the rascals show thereby their misunderstanding of the nature of democracy. The liberal believes that there is moral and political wisdom in the constitutional declarations naming "rights" and "freedoms" that "shall not be violated" and "shall be preserved," and that majorities do not necessarily act irrationally in setting up devices against "absolute" and "unlimited" majority rule. He is in agreement with Latham in the belief that "In the struggle to preserve civil liberty, no protection, however slight, should be discarded." [39]

The liberal, of the sort considered in this paper, believes in inviolable rights—in freedoms inviolable in the sense that men ought to possess them, not only as means for the realization of other values, but as values in themselves. He regards the rights as natural to man, as a being distinguished from other animals by his faculties of reason, speech, a sense of justice, and a capacity for independent thought and action. He believes that the rights are inalienable in a political community in the sense that a citizen will not disclaim them if he is to retain his character as a citizen; and inalienable in the sense that the community will not take them away if it is to retain its character as a political community. He believes that order and agreement are goods that may be sought extravagantly, by means that confuse or destroy the sort of consensus upon which the security and strength of a democracy depend.

NOTES

1. *Politics*, Ernest Barker trans. (Oxford, 1946), Bk. I, Chs. ii and v; Bk. III, Ch. xi; Bk. IV, Ch. iv.

2. For general descriptions and appraisals of traditional liberal ideas, see Frederick Watkins, *The Political Tradition of the West* (Cambridge, Mass., 1948); Lionel Trilling, *The Liberal Imagination* (New York, 1950); Crane Brinton, *Ideas and Men: The Story of Western Thought* (New York, 1950), esp. pp. 373-550; John J. Saunders, *The Age of Revolution; the Rise and Decline of Liberalism in Europe since 1815* (New York, 1949); Eduard Heimann, *Freedom and Order* (New York, 1947), Chs. 1, 8, 10, 12; John H. Hallowell, *Main Currents in Modern Political Thought* (New York, 1950), pp. 84-367 and *passim*.

3. Oswald Spengler, *The Hour of Decision* (New York, 1934, translated from the German by Charles Francis Atkins), pp. 14, 109, 119; Nicolai Lenin, *What Is to Be Done* (London and New York, 1929), and *Proletarian Revolution and Kautsky the Renegade* (London, 1929).

4. On liberalism as a doctrine of human rights, see: Carl L. Becker, *Freedom and Responsibility in the American Way of Life* (New York, 1945); Robert M. MacIver, *The Ramparts We Guard* (New York, 1950); J. Roland Pennock, *Liberal Democracy: Its Merits and Prospects* (New York, 1950); Denis W. Brogan, *The Free State, Some Considerations on Its Practical Value* (New York, 1945); Bertrand Russell, *Authority and the Individual* (New York, 1949); UNESCO ed., *Human Rights: Comments and Interpretations; A Symposium* (London, 1949); David Fellman. "What is Liberalism?", *Prairie Schooner* (Fall, 1945), pp. 204-18. See also Harold D. Lasswell, *National Security and Individual Freedom* (New York, 1950), esp. Chs. 2 and 7.

5. Willmoore Kendall, *John Locke and the Doctrine of Majority-Rule* (Urbana, 1940), and "Prolegomena to any Future Work on Majority Rule," *Journal of Politics*, Vol. 12, pp. 694-713 (Nov., 1950), written in reply to an article by Herbert McCloskey, "The Fallacy of Absolute Majority Rule," in the same journal, Vol. 11, pp. 637-54 (Nov., 1949) criticizing Kendall's views; J. Austin Ranney, "Toward a More Responsible Two-Party System: a Commentary," *American Political Science Review*, Vol. 45, pp. 488-99 (June, 1951); J. Austin Ranney and Willmoore Kendall, "Democracy: Confusion and Agreement," *Western Political Quarterly*, Vol. 4, pp. 430-39 (Sept., 1951). The quotations from Kendall alone are from the "Prolegomena" article, except where otherwise indicated.

6. For a discriminating criticism of our system of judicial review as it operates in the protection of civil liberties, see: Henry Steele Commager, *Majority Rule and Minority Rights* (New York, 1943); Fred V. Cahill, *Judicial Legislation* (New York, 1952); Earl Latham, "Theory of the Judicial Concept of Freedom of Speech," *Journal of Politics*, Vol. 12, pp. 637-51 (Nov., 1950).

7. *John Locke and the Doctrine of Majority Rule*, p. 129.

8. Aristotle, *Politics*, Bk. III, Chs. iv, vi, xi; Bk. IV, Chs. i, iv, xi, xiv; Bk. V, Ch. ix. Plato, *The Laws*, IV, 715.

9. For Locke, see the *Second Treatise of Government*, secs. 16, 22, 49, 87, 88, 95-99, 116, 131, 134-42, 222. For Jefferson, see the Declaration of Independence, his *Notes on the State of Virginia* (1789), and his first *Inaugural Address* (1801).

10. *Modern Democracies* (New York, 1921), Vol. 1, p. 59; Vol. 2, pp. 121, 521.

11. *Reflections on Government* (Oxford University Press, 1942), pp. 26, 175, 196.

12. *Modern Democracies*, Vol. 2, Ch. 64 and pp. 393-95.

13. *Modern Democracies*, Vol. 2, pp. 11, 27 84; and see Cyril John Radcliffe, *The Problem of Power* (London, 1952), pp. 61-64, 85-87.

14. *Modern Democracies*, Vol. 2, pp. 390-91.

15. *The Nature and Destiny of Man*, 2 vols. (New York, 1941-43), Vol. 1, p. 273. See also *Reflections on the End of an Era* (New York, 1934); *An Interpretation of Christian Ethics* (New York, 1935), pp. 140-50, 171-79; *Children of Light and Children of Darkness* (New York, 1944).

16. *Christianity and Power Politics* (New York, 1940), p. 156.

17. *The Irony of American History* (New York, 1952), p. 143.

18. T. S. Eliot, "Religion and Literature" and "Catholicism and International Order," in his *Essays, Ancient and Modern* (New York, 1936). The following account of Eliot's specific criticisms is based chiefly on *The Idea of a Christian Society* (New York, 1940), Ch. 1.

19. The following summary of Eliot's ideas on the structure and functions of a Christian society is based chiefly on *The Idea of a Christian Society*, pp. 23 ff. See also his *Notes Towards the Definition of Culture* (London, 1948), pp. 13-20, 28-34, Chs. 4-5, and pp. 122-24; *For Lancelot Andrewes: Essays on Style and Order* (London, 1928), Ch. 8.

20. Professor Hallowell's views on the moral and practical defects of modern liberalism and his proposed reforms are set forth in his *Main Currents in Modern Political Thought* (New York, 1950); see especially pp. 558-70, 612-24, 662-73.

21. *Ibid.*, p. 613.

22. *Ibid.*, pp. 614-15.

23. *Ibid.*, pp. 689-91, quoting from William Temple, *Christianity and the Social Order* (London, 1942).

24. Professor De Grazia's eloquent pleas for the restoration of the idea of community are set forth at length in his *The Political Community: A Study of Anomie* (Chicago, 1948). See especially his preface and pp. 176-90.

25. De Grazia's ideas on the evils of toleration and his proposed cure are emphatically set forth in an address on "Toleration and Forgiveness: the Ability to Judge Good from Evil," in *Vital Speeches*, Vol. 16, pp. 149-53 (Dec. 15, 1949).

26. John Stuart Mill, *On Liberty* (Modern Library ed.), pp. 47, 83, 91, 102.

27. London *Times*, May 24, 1935, p. 17, and October 5, 1938, p. 9.

28. *Main Currents in Modern Political Thought*, pp. 326, 613, 614, 678.

29. *For Lancelot Andrewes*, Ch. 5 and at p. 89.

30. *The Idea of a Christian Society*, p. 61.

31. *Ibid.*, p. 43.

32. *The Irony of American History*, pp. 25, 43, 45, 63, 80.

33. *Ibid.*, Ch. 6 and p. 174.

34. William E. Hocking, *What Man Can Make of Man* (New York and London, 1942), pp. 49-50.

35. Reinhold Niebuhr, *Irony of American History*, pp. 157-58.

36. Reinhold Niebuhr, *Irony of American History*, p. 156.

37. Ralph Linton, *The Cultural Background of Personality*, (New York, London, 1936), pp. 5, 15-16, 23-25, 36; *The Study of Man* (New York, London, 1945), pp. 91-96, 273-74. For similar views by a religious writer, see William Temple, *Christianity and the State* (London, 1928), pp. 99, 101-2, 108, 124-25.

38. T. S. Eliot, *For Lancelot Andrewes* (1928), p. 42.

39. Earl Latham, in article cited in note 6, above; and see generally Arthur Holcombe, "Natural Limits to the Power of Numerical Majorities" and "The Paramount Principle of the Political Mean" in his *Our More Perfect Union* (New York, 1950), pp. 23-36 and 400-7.

THE PRAGMATIC COURSE OF LIBERALISM

Alan P. Grimes

So much is being written extolling the virtues of conservatism today, so much is being stated that is derogatory of liberalism, that to present a case for liberalism now seems almost out of date, and certainly out of fashion. For in the present climate of opinion the word liberal seems

Reprinted from *Western Political Quarterly*, vol. IX, no. 3 (September, 1956), 633-640. By permission of the author and the publisher.

to be more of an epithet than a truly descriptive expression. The trend of much of the literature of today tends to give the impression that Burke was one of the Founding Fathers; that only the conservative tradition, as articulated by such antidemocratic figures as John C. Calhoun and Irving Babbitt, can save us from chaos; and that there is a little more of shame than glory to being a secular liberal or even a secular intellectual. Liberalism is clearly at another intellectual cross-road.

Liberal, and liberalism, have always presented problems in definition. When Morris Cohen talked of "the faith of a liberal" it is evident that he was referring to something different than the liberalism which John H. Hallowell said was declining as an ideology. The liberalism whose course and history in Europe Guido de Ruggiero has traced was of course essentially the same liberalism which Alfredo Rocco brought under attack in his plea for fascism, but it was clearly not the liberalism which L. T. Hobhouse advocated for England. The liberalism which Herbert Hoover advocated for the United States was not the liberalism associated with Franklin Roosevelt, nor was the liberalism which Ogden L. Mills found "fighting on" in 1936 the liberalism John Dewey was pleading for in 1935. Must we then despair of definition? Is a liberal nothing more than any man who calls himself one? Or is called one?

It seems to me that in spite of the obvious confusions associated with liberal and liberalism, we can at least attempt a definition which may be useful for classifying concepts and identifying ideas. There is certainly more to liberalism than the label. It represents a system of ideas that aims at the realization of the pluralistic society, favoring diversity in politics, economics, religion, and our cultural life. It is opposed to uniformity; it is opposed to conformity. It is, in the broadest sense of the word, antimonopolistic; for it favors the widest possible degree of self-determination. It denotes an attitude toward human problems as well as goals for human endeavor. It seeks in its simplest sense to advance the freedom of man. It is essentially antiauthoritarian, and represents the claims of those who are out of power and thus lacking in authority; but who, had they the power, would not impose authoritarian solutions on others. It seeks to increase the individuality of man by increasing his area of choice and decision. It is essentially humanitarian in its appeal and therefore endorses toleration and is motivated by a sense of compassion for mankind. Finally it is flexible in the method of its realization and, while a doctrine, is itself not doctrinaire. These are, I believe, the basic components of liberalism. Let me explain them further.

1. If liberalism seeks to advance the freedom of man it would seem to be implicit that the freedom of man, rather than his restraint, is a desirable end in itself. A truly liberal society would thus be a society of free men. The free man is thus the end product of the free society. Now, of course, the general issue of freedom always resolves itself into a specific question of whose freedom to do what. The diversity of our natures—of our temperaments, desires, and aversions—together with the organizational necessities of our social life, make impossible equal freedom to all

men. Thus the question of "whose freedom" is perhaps the most crucial issue in politics. The interdependence of modern society gives all "freedoms" consequences. The group nature of society, however, places men in often conflicting camps, in competition for freedom as they are for power. The issue of freedom is in fact directly related to the issue of power in society so that the question "whose freedom?" also involves the question "whose power?" Freedom, to be realized, must be translated into power while power is the expression of those in authority exercising their freedom. I should qualify this to note that power is, of course, reciprocal and not the possession solely of those in command of institutions; those who are governed control in some manner those who do the governing. Indeed the vitality of this interaction is the measure of a democracy. But the preponderance of power, and freedom, is with those who make and enforce decisions with social consequences.

When the liberal talks about free men in a free society he is usually referring to that vast majority of men who do not directly make enforceable decisions with social consequences. These are the people whose freedoms the liberal wishes to extend, those people whose sphere of meaningful choices is at the time restricted. For all the inherent conflicts in society liberalism does not suppose with Hobbes that by maximizing the areas of private judgment society would eventuate in a war of all against all. It rather supposes with Locke no socially destructive conflict between private choices and majority rule; that the majority is best able to determine the social conditions of the public good and that men capable of this judgment will doubtless respect the human dignity of the minority.

To extend the freedom of some to make socially consequential decisions often curtails the freedom of others to make opposing decisions on the same subject. But we must always ask whose freedom was curtailed and whose extended, and what was the conventional status in authority of the respective groups, and how great was their number of supporters. Does this measure at issue promote the freedom of the many or the few? To work in the direction of a free society we must therefore maximize the freedoms of the many. Implicit therefore in liberalism is the concept of human worth, of human dignity, of man as the end and social institutions as the means. Social institutions have thus no greater dignity than man; indeed, to the contrary, they exist only to achieve the dignity of man by implementing his individuality, by helping him fulfill himself. The reverence for the institutions of society, which in part characterizes the conservative, is thus opposed to liberalism.

2. Liberalism, as has been indicated, is antiauthoritarian and arises as a protest of those out of power against the uses of power to which those in authority are subjecting them. Thus liberalism arises as a protest against traditional forms of authority wherever found. Because those in possession of power seldom believe that they are acting in an authoritarian fashion, this decision must be made by those subject to authority. Liberalism is thus by and large the creed of the dispossessed,

the dissenter, of those who are subject to the decisions which others make. Because we live in a web of social relationships involving innumerable institutions, chains of command arising through prestige or power, man is continually brought under the control of authority possessed by others. The effort to remain free involves, as Jefferson said, "eternal vigilance." There is no final distribution of power which guarantees liberty for those not possessing authority. Using the analogy of Woodrow Wilson, we must be like the Red Queen constantly on the run in order even to maintain our present position. The freedoms of the past have a way of making possible the servitudes of the present. As social institutions change they present new problems in authority and restraint, and the zealous liberal finds that his struggle must take on new forms and new foes in order to preserve the liberties that now exist. Liberalism thus looks to those lacking in power in society for its test of the adequacies of present freedoms. And here again we may distinguish liberalism from conservatism, for the latter takes its cue from those traditionally in authority.

3. Liberalism seeks to increase the individuality of man by increasing his area of choice. This is, of course, closely allied with its antiauthoritarian impulse. It seeks to increase the individual's opportunity for making meaningful decisions. It seeks, in other words, a continuous revolution in decision-making in the direction of those individuals who will be most subject to the consequences of the decision. The area of choice can never be constant or static, but moves with social flux, responding to the felt necessities of the times. Today's most vital choices may not appear very significant tomorrow. The question of meaningfulness must then be determined by those who feel the consequences of past decisions or fear the consequences of future ones. Thus liberalism usually follows the path of protest. Implicit, of course, is the assumption of equality; positing man as an end in himself carries with it the belief that to each man choices are important. Each man must decide where restraints are most oppressive, where freedom is most desired. The logic of free choice for all men thus rests upon the assumption of the equality of all men, otherwise we should have to accept the elitist argument in favor of free choice for only the few. Individuality, freedom of choice, and equality are thus mutually dependent concepts. Again, we may distinguish the liberal from the conservative, for at heart, if not overtly, the conservative rejects the belief in equality and the legitimacy of freedom of choice for all men. For the conservative inevitably argues in favor of freedom of choice restricted to the aristocracy, the elite, or those who claim to possess superior talents or ability.

4. Another core concept of liberalism is humanitarianism. It seeks to support the weak and curb the strong. It seeks to redirect the flow of society's benefits—to prevent them from becoming the monopoly of the few—into the hands of the many. The privileges of the past thus through liberalism become the necessities of the present. In education, health, employment, and housing we think less of privilege and more of

necessity as the fruits of our co-operative living are distributed more widely. Without a sense of compassion for one's fellow man, a sense of social obligation, a sense of tolerance and good will that cuts through all the artificial distinctions that separate individuals, men would act like so many cats in a bag. The benefits of man's social experience would then fall to the predatory, the strong, and the cunning. It is the humanitarianism in liberalism which rejects the notion that benefits should accrue only to those who can take the most and which constantly pushes against social institutions to see that benefits get the widest distribution. Humanitarianism wages a constant warfare against conservatism. Conservatism is full of little mottos about not killing geese that lay golden eggs and endless other reasons why a wider distribution of the benefits of social experience is not possible in the present. The practice of humanitarianism inevitably displaces the existing power relationships; the status quo of superiors and subordinates is always disturbed a little as new groups gain the privileges of other groups. Liberalism pushes the frontier of privilege forward with the distant goal constantly in view that all men as men are privileged and entitled to all the necessities and some of the luxuries of civilized living. Conservatives love charity, as rewarding the giver as well as the receiver, but draw the line at a commitment to a social obligation that disturbs the existing power relationships. Liberals prefer obligation to charity as more in keeping with a belief in the dignity of all men.

5. Finally, liberalism is not a static creed or dogma, for dogmatism provides its own restraints. It is rather a tentative attitude toward social problems which stresses the role of reason and human ingenuity. Were it to settle for the conclusions of yesterday then it would be succumbing to the authoritarian restraint of past precept. In its efforts to free mankind liberalism seeks to free the mind as well as clothe the body. As social institutions change, new formulas for liberation must be devised based upon the felt necessities of the present. Liberalism indeed ceases to be liberal when it employs shibboleth in place of searching inquiry, when it becomes committed to yesterday's formulas as final answers. Herein, I believe, lies the sin of many "liberals" of the past. By equating classical economics with liberalism, Manchester liberals so abused the term that for nearly fifty years Americans had to resort to the word "progressive" to describe the attitude of liberals. So opprobrious did the term liberalism become, with its Manchester connotation, that it is difficult to realize that at one time it represented a genuinely liberal doctrine. Modern liberalism did not reach its final triumph with the policies of the New Deal or Fair Deal and a liberalism dependent upon such formulas might well go the way of Manchester liberalism, which was committed to free trade and civil service reform, for example, and judged all men by these tenets. Thus liberalism must continually look ahead. It must look to new ways of doing things, to new tentative and temporary expedients to perennial problems, to new ideas and new institutions. In a word it must be pragmatic. It must seek practical

answers to evident problems, but answers which work constantly in the direction of those without power, of those who lack the benefits, of those in other words who need the most help in order to fulfill the requirements of their individuality. Liberalism thus looks ahead, with a flexible approach, seeking to make the future better for more people; as conservatism looks back, aiming mainly to preserve the attainments of the past.

Now drawing together these five components of liberalism, we may define the term as follows: Liberalism denotes an attitude which seeks to make possible those social conditions in which the individuality of all men may best be realized. Because as a general rule those who possess authority enjoy a large measure of freedom, liberals, impelled by humanitarianism, seek to advance the freedom of those without authority, of those without special benefits. Liberalism is then the doctrine of the social and economic underdog. It is usually on the side of those who are neglected by the conventions of society, and thus it must eternally plead the unconventional cause.

With this approach to liberalism, I think we may fairly note its pragmatic course in modern times. And liberalism, as a social concept, like democracy which it informs and gives value to, is essentially a modern conception. Liberalism, perpetually seeking to free mankind from the authorities that restrain, establishes the goals which democracy implements. The methods of liberalism change as situations change but the goal of liberation remains constant. Thus liberalism follows a pragmatic course to realize constant ends. Without the constant ends there would be no continuity to liberalism and the term would possess no meaning beyond that of a temporary and convenient party label; yet without the pragmatic means liberalism would indicate nothing beyond vague aspirations, incapable of fulfillment.

The continuity of liberalism may be indicated by reference to its three most influential manifestations as they affected American thought: Lockean liberalism, Manchester liberalism, and the pragmatic liberalism of John Dewey. For all their disagreements over method the goals of Locke, John Stuart Mill and John Dewey were essentially the same. Notice the essential similarity of thought in three successive epochs of liberalism regarding the equality of men, toleration of ideas, majority rule, and social institutions as the servants of men. Each phase of liberalism marked a revolt against the existing form of authority and in a social sense sought to evaluate the class below the class which in that epoch was the traditional possessor of power. Each sought a displacement of those in power with a new, a broader group, and a new and more liberating ideology. Thus, in America, we think of the liberalism of Locke, interpreted by Jefferson, in contest with the traditional rule of the British. The success of this liberalism in America is attested to by the fact that following the Revolution more people were able to make more meaningful decisions affecting their lives then had heretofore been the case. In other words, the right of private judgment for more people was more fully realized.

Manchester liberalism in England, whether considered in the Bentham sense of utilitarianism, or in the Adam Smith economic sense, was originally a liberating movement. The reform of penal codes, the extension of the suffrage, and the abolition of the Corn Laws were in their day motivated by a liberal impulse in the direction of equality, humanitarianism, and a greater degree of private choice. Clearly the rising bourgeoisie was favored over the landed aristocracy—but the latter were at that time the traditional holders of power. To legislate or avoid legislation to the advantage of the bourgeoisie was thus to seek to accomplish Bentham's "greatest good of the greatest number." That this was not good enough for later generations is no criticism of the proposal, given the circumstances, at the time it was offered, but only points up the pragmatic necessity for liberalism to alter its content to meet new requirements if it wishes to stay liberal. Jacksonian democracy, the American counterpart of the English liberal movement of that age, turned fervently to classical economics, antislavery, women's rights, extension of the suffrage, prison reform, etc. Why do we think of this as a liberal movement? It is, I think, because Jacksonian democracy sought in its time to grant more freedom in a more humane setting to more people than had heretofore been the case. Conventional lines of authority, conventional institutions, and conventional beliefs were brought under attack at every turn in the effort to extend the area of choice and control to those who had previously been subject to the authority of others.

The economics of a Jacksonian liberal constituted the tenets of economic conservatism in the late nineteenth century, and of reaction in the twentieth. This did not make Jackson less a liberal in 1832; but it made those illiberal who attempted to apply his economic principles to the conditions of 1932. For Jackson's economics were intended to liberate a new mass of people; while those who employed this economic theory a century later were intending to retain in power an old established hierarchy. Manchester liberalism had thus ceased to be liberal.

Pragmatic liberalism in the United States, arising out of the progressive ferment of the late nineteenth and early twentieth century, turned the liberal crusade back in the direction of those out of power, of those without privilege. Again humanitarianism, equality, and a respect for man regardless of his economic plight were recognized. In the jurisprudence of Holmes and Pound and the philosophy of Dewey and Cohen the limitations of absolutes, the final truths of the classical economists, were challenged in an effort to find workable solutions to social problems. In education, law, politics, and economics the assumed necessities of the past were brought into question, and a wider vision of meaningful choice was offered to more people. It was again the liberal spirit of Jacksonian democracy employing new techniques to achieve however the same ends. Flexible and non-doctrinaire, it shattered innumerable precedents to the great distress of conservatives. Rejecting final answers, it seeks, as Niebuhr has observed, approximate answers to insoluble problems. To find such answers it seeks to keep open the doorways to ideas. And it has a faith in the good judgment of man in a free society to arrive at humane and intelligent decisions. Thus it opposes guardians of thought who would protect the majority from themselves. Rather it respects the ability of the majority to know when the shoe pinches and where relief and liberation are most sorely needed.

In conclusion then, it is my thesis that there is continuity to liberalism; that the term is basically descriptive and may be used in an operational sense. It establishes goals of social policy which, though perhaps never fully realizable in a human society, are constantly in the process of realization. The goals of liberalism—dignity and individuality and liberty, equally for all men—give special meaning to democracy, for democracy I would contend is a method of realizing liberalism, of maximizing the areas of meaningful choice. It matters little that Locke employed the contract theory and was a rationalist or that his conception of toleration left something to be desired. Or that Bentham's social views were conservative, Smith preferred *laissez faire,* and Ricardo's labor theory was abominable. Or that Holmes' "clear and present danger" test is not so clear after all, and Dewey's educational theories have fallen somewhat into disrepute and New Deal Democrats made some egregious errors. What does matter is that the social direction of these forms of liberalism was always in favor of new groups, new masses of men not then in power who were quite conscious of the arbitrariness and inhumanity of old forms of restraint. Because liberalism is pragmatic in method its specific content or program has changed to meet the repressions of new institutions. But liberalism denotes far more than a desire for change; it denotes purposeful, reasoned change that would elevate the status and increase the liberty of what we would today call the common man. As conservatives often seek to protect the liberty of those in authority by defending the existing social conventions and institutions, liberals seek through changing means to increase the liberty of those lacking in authority. With constant goals and changing means liberalism seeks today, as in the past, to refashion social institutions to better realize the equal individuality and dignity of man.

MODERN LIBERALISM

Ernst Bieri

With a certain condescending pride the political competitors of Liberalism like to point out that the Liberals constitute but a small minority in the democratic countries today—a group that "hardly counts." They also take pleasure in recalling the glorious past of liberalism, in order to then speak of the "regression" and "decline" of liberal influence. The role of the Liberals—so they argue—has been taken over by the forces which determine the fate of democracies in our day: mass movements of a Socialist or Christian-Democratic character. These, they hold, constitute the true bulwark against totalitarian Communism, it is in *their* hands that the freedom of Europe and of the Atlantic world is safe. More than that: they not only guarantee freedom, but the "social gains" that Liberalism has failed to provide. These mass movements, they say, are far more "progressive" than the Liberals, since they provide not only "formal," but "integral" democracy—the democracy of the modern welfare state. The new mass organizations are said to have taken over the heritage of Liberalism and in the process to have made valuable additions to it. Everything that the heart of the people desires—from political institutions to security to individual and collective happiness —they are said to supply from their horn of plenty.

WHY NO MASS ORGANIZATION?

The idea of a "decline" of Liberalism, as allegedly manifested by the external transformation from a mass to a cadre party without rank and file, is based on an error. *Liberalism never was a mass movement in the modern sense of the word.* These mass movements are of much more recent date, and sociologically belong to the age of totalitarianism. Its precursor was the political organization of the fourth estate, that is a movement deliberately running counter to the liberal epoch. Liberalism appeals to the individual, whom it wants to emphasize as a responsible

Reprinted from the *Swiss Review of World Affairs*, vol. IX, no. 12 (March, 1960), 13-16. By permission of the author and the publisher.

citizen. The modern political organizations, however, use the individual primarily as a means to an end, as a quantity desired to increase the number of voters. The individual's personal conviction and the level of his political knowledge play a much smaller role with them than his function as an element of political competition—he is to help make the party "strong," i.e., large. The modern mass parties are built on a concept of democracy that differs from that of the Liberals. To the former, the techniques of democracy are of primary interest. They want to gather the largest possible number of voters in order to increase their influence, and, wherever possible, to move into office. The gathering of votes by any and all possible means of propaganda and moral pressure (such as appeals to class consciousness or to religious duty) is more important to them than the capture of members endowed with independent judgment.

It is evident that Liberalism cannot approve of this form of "organized democracy." Liberals do not consider the quantitative principle of democracy—the rule of the majority—as an ultimate aim. They rather want to know just what principles this majority practices, and just what is the fate of the individual where the majority rules. In brief, they look for the content of democracy and not for its form alone—and they demand that democracy be liberal and not authoritarian.

The large parties to the right and the left that consider themselves superior to the numerically weaker Liberals, incidentally, do not live on their substance and strength. They owe their position to definite social entities located beyond the properly political sphere of life: the Church in the one case, and the unions in the other. Without the powerful help of these institutions the large parties would not be able to get any masses of people to the polling booths. To a high degree the large parties are representative or executive organs of outside social organizations. For this reason alone the Liberals find themselves handicapped in political competition: they draw their followers from all classes of the society and on an individual basis: they cannot sit back and rely on compact organizations, based on specific interests or denominations to do the work for them.

THE INDIRECT TRIUMPH OF LIBERALISM

An examination of the percentages of the electorate controlled by the various parties does not tell the whole story, and frequently does not tell anything of decisive importance on the content and orientation of their respective politics. The parties, to be sure, do compete for votes, and in this respect the Liberals, for the reasons described, seem to be inferior, although—the fondest hopes of their opponents notwithstanding—they do not simply disappear from the picture, but with a proportion of 10 to 20 per cent of the electorate continue to constitute a factor of some importance especially with a view to the formation of strong government majorities in the Parliaments. *It is not the voters, after all, that "make" politics, it is their representatives:* in the parliamentary democracy, which is the prevalent form of government in the Western world today, the effective levers of power are in the hands of the parliamentary groupings, of the leaders of these groupings and of the Government with its administration. The question, therefore, is whether any constellation emerging in an election campaign will necessarily repeat itself in the legislature that follows, and whether the influence of the political forces corresponds exactly to the percentage of the electorate represented.

This question must be answered in the negative. To begin with, most electoral laws provide a correction of purely representative representation. Above all, however, the factor of individual personality—so largely suppressed in the very act of voting in the system of quantitative democracy—asserts itself more strongly in the Parliament and in the Government. It is not sufficient for the conduct of the affairs of state to belong to the "right," i.e. momentarily governing party: it is in addition necessary to possess the ability required to satisfy the demands of office.

On the level on which the *weight of personality* begins to play a role, the Liberal parties need not fear competition with the mass organizations. Their reliance on individuality—in the voting process often a handicap to them—now begins to pay off. This explains why in Parliament and in public administration the influence of the Liberals is frequently larger than their percentage of the electorate would make one expect. A traditional field of activity for Liberal leaders, moreover, is that of the *law* and the *courts*—a consequence of the historic struggle of Liberalism for the establishment of the rule of law. Particularly outstanding, however, is the role of Liberals in the field of *economic policy*. Although in Germany, France and Italy the Liberal parties do not play an influential part in the Governments—in the election campaigns, as a matter of fact, they usually combat the governing parties—Liberal economists have been charged with the drawing up and carrying out of these countries' economic programs and policies. Ludwig Erhard in West Germany, Einaudi in Italy and Rueff in France testify to this striking phenomenon. The economic development of Europe was, and is, being realized along Liberal principles, and the non-Liberal Governments do not hesitate *to call Liberal leaders to the pertinent posts,* because they have more confidence in realistic Liberal doctrine than in the immature schemes of their own party ideologists. . . .

The "indirect triumph of Liberalism," however, far exceeds the role of individually eminent exponents of Liberal thought within certain "alien" party environments. The large parties to the right and the left have themselves taken over—whether by lip service only or by real adoption—important elements of the Liberal creed. Socialism calls itself "democratic socialism" today and proclaims itself the heir of the Liberal era. And it would be presumptuous for the Liberals not to acknowledge that Western socialism has largely detached itself from the

Marxist foundation and integrated itself into the democratic state. No wonder that in the course of this evolution *socialism discovered the fundamental importance of Liberal thought for the protection of freedom and of democracy.* In the somewhat fuzzy doctrine of "Christian Democracy," too, some of the diamond-hard elements of Liberal thought are now embodied. Friedrich Heer, a Catholic historian, pointed to the intimate kinship of present-day Catholic politics with the once severely condemned Liberalism in the following words: "The defamation of the whole of Enlightenment . . . both within and without Catholicism, in which the reactionaries and the romantics, rightist Catholicism of the Restoration and its literature ever since 1800 to date have indulged, overlooks the fact *that in newer European Catholicism there is hardly anything that does not derive from that very Enlightenment.* Only the heirs have largely forgotten that today they are living in word, slogan and reality on what 20, 50, 100 years ago was severely condemned as 'leftist Catholic' heresy. Today, Church meetings are being held under the motto: 'A free Church in a free state!'—it was on this very principle that Italian left-wing Catholicism arose in the 19th and 20th centuries."

Without a doubt: a more direct line leads from the constitutional struggles of the Liberals in the last century to all the democratic parties of today than from Marxism or orthodox Conservatism. The principal postulates of the Liberal movement—individual freedom, human rights, political rights, the rule of law—are today, at least nominally, the accepted common ground of all democratic forces. No large party dares attack the positions of the state governed by the rule of law, as achieved by the Liberal movement. It is *communis opinio* that the inescapable alternative to the Liberal rule of law is totalitarian government, against the grasping reach of which all true democrats must join forces today as in a primary concern. In the far-reaching reception of its concrete political creed by the former severe opponents of the "bourgeois" and "godless" state, Liberalism has achieved its true victory. To protect this victory, and to preserve its partners from once again forsaking the salutary osmosis of thought is the aim of contemporary Liberal politics, and for this purpose vital Liberal parties must be present. Not only and primarily to achieve power and office, but to strengthen their former opponents' frequently superficial adherence to the Liberal concept of government and economics, is the Liberals' mission.

DELIMITATION TOWARD SOCIALISM

Democratic Socialism at first defined itself negatively as a differentiation of Communism, with which it shared the historical roots and for a long time also the ultimate aim. Socialism's detachment from the Marxist pattern of thinking had not been successful everywhere. In Italy, a large Socialist party is in close communion with the Communists, and in many

Social Democratic parties a left wing flirts with Gomulka and Tito, i.e., a Socialism independent of Moscow, but yet simon pure.

This new form of Socialism recommends itself not only as a proved bulwark against the Communists, but also as an "expansion" and "fulfillment" of democracy as a principle. The fulfillment is to consist in supplementing the "merely political" by economic and social democracy. The desire to make democracy a real home for people merits the fullest support: the Liberals know as well as the Socialists do that hungry and unemployed masses have but a limited interest in individual freedom, and provide but a poor support and poor propaganda for democracy. The question, however, is that of the methods employed to give democracy a firm social foundation.

The Socialists continue to be deeply distrustful of everything private and individual. They do not believe that the Liberal call for separation of political from economic power, for free enterprise and for a limitation of government control are sound. They believe that only a collective organization of the whole economic life can solve social problems. For them, "just distribution," not maximum growth of the economy, is the primary aim. Dissatisfaction with the so-called profit economy and love of egalitarianism seem to be so pronounced with them that they would rather put up with a stagnating or regressing economy than relinquish collectivist methods and institutions. The unions, to be sure, have acquired and proclaimed the realization that social gains are a result of an increase of productivity rather than of an increase of laws; but the *dream of a "complete organization"* of economic processes lingers.

An outstanding American businessman refutes the Socialist faith in the omnipotence of state intervention in these simple words: "Reformers, politicians, and others frequently claim credit for the shorter workweek and other social gains. While their contributions are considerable, it is nevertheless true that social gains are only made possible by abundance, *and abundance has never been created by law.*" The restriction of government intervention to the general framework of the economy and to special cases is a consequence of this realistic appraisal of the circumscribed role of legislation. Not even a Socialist state can overthrow this fundamental rule: "abundance has never been created by law." A controlled economy may lead to respectable production in selected sectors—usually in the heavy and the armaments industries—but it does not increase the prosperity of the individual, so that at the end both freedom and prosperity are lost at the same time. According to rich and varied experience the competitive enterprise economy is the only system to guarantee maximum prosperity with maximum freedom.

The chief Liberal argument against Socialist "integralism" of democracy, however, is not only the certainty that the limitation and, finally, elimination of private economic freedom harms the general welfare and freezes the standard of living in a static system of government controls. It is, above all, the combination of economic and political power that gives rise to the most serious apprehensions. In a Liberal democracy economic power—or whatever is described as such "power"—is distributed to many shoulders, large and small; competition in the market takes place among private individuals. But if the leading functions are entrusted to the state, economic competition on the one hand is changed into a *politicum*, and the rule of law, on the other hand, is covered over by a presumptuous entrepreneur activity on the part of the state. The *cumulation of political and economic power* radically alters the relationship between citizen and state to the citizen's disadvantage. The broad masses of salary and wage earners may in a first phase not feel any great change with respect to their freedom, because the shift of control at the top does not touch their level immediately (the shift, on the other hand, does by no means give them an increased measure of freedom, in the direction of increased influence on management, for example). But their opportunities for contradiction and resistance, control and criticism are at once decisively curtailed—for now, resistance is no longer directed against a politically equal private entrepreneur, but against the "general welfare," any violation of which is a mortal sin in collective democracy. In practice, the leading organs of a Socialist economy will possess a fullness of power such as no private enterprise ever had: to the concrete power of management is added that of political rule, since these organs exercise the double function of entrepreneur and representative of the people.

The absorption of economic and social life into the political, i.e. government sphere, will, therefore, not produce the fervently desired growth of prosperity, but limit freedom and replace the pluralist society with a monistic, in the final analysis, totalitarian society. The more ground private law must yield to expanding public law, the smaller the individual's real freedom—however beautiful the references made in the countless new laws to the "interest of the people" and the "liberation of the working class."

Democratic Socialism differs from the Liberal concept less by its formulations than by the practical consequences of its formulations. It, perhaps unintentionally, leads away from the open to a *closed society,* in which the initiated and the high priests of the doctrine silence every criticism by conjuring up the general welfare which they pretend to stand for. The well-meant "fulfillment" and "completion" of democracy ends in its own destruction.

While the demarcation line between Liberals and Socialists is derived from a critical appraisal of economic and social doctrine and policy, the area of controversy with the Christian Democrats is less clearly defined.

THE CHRISTIAN DEMOCRATS' CHALLENGE

This is a result of the fact primarily *that Christian Democratic doctrine lacks clarity and precision.* It is a mixture of old Conservative and new Socialist ideas, a combination of patriarchalism and reformatory zeal, of democratic and authoritarian elements, in short, of "right-wing" and "left-wing" Catholicism and all their nuances. A further difficulty results from the circumstance that the actual politics of the Christian Democratic parties bear the imprint less of any particular doctrine than of particular leaders. The Liberal appraisal of the Christian Democrats accordingly is subject to the reservation of the *hic et nunc*. Because Christian Democratic politics are subject to change, the Liberal appraisal of it is always *ad hoc*. For example, Liberal opinion on a regime like Chancellor Adenauer's or Premier De Gasperi's cannot be the same as that on Fanfani's, although all three call themselves Christian Democrats.

Of course, the Liberals *reject the authoritarian component* of Christian Democratic doctrine. While they agree with the Christian Democrats in evaluating the rule by majority, they do not expect salvation from the principle of authority, about the legitimation of which an endless quarrel would have to be carried on; rather they propose to consolidate democracy and to protect it against its own potential excesses by the postulates of respect for the individual and for the minority, in the spirit of Lord Acton's, a Catholic's, words: "The most certain test by which we judge whether a country is really free is the amount of security enjoyed by minorities." (It is hardly necessary to point out that this principle is not to be construed to provide shelter for forces whose open or hidden aim it is to destroy freedom and the rule of law.) The unfortunate application of the hierarchical structure and teaching authority of the Church to the state—an application actually not authorized by the Church—arouses the Liberals' determined resistance. They invoke the *freedom of conscience*—acknowledged and proclaimed by the Church!—and the autonomy of the state. Certain currents among the Christian Democrats reject this separation of powers as "pernicious laicism." Their ideal is a clerical, monolithic organization of life on earth. Liberalism's *No* to such tendencies is a matter of principle—based on the tenet of the freedom of conscience and the autonomous sphere of the state.

Closely connected with the authoritarian components is the Socialist, more accurately, collectivist, trend of the Christian Democrat movement. Economic doctrine and policy within this trend is distinctly anti-Liberal and largely identical with that of the Socialists, however different the intellectual background. The dream here, as in the case of the Socialists, is a closed society, the model of a completely organized democracy; and the source of this dream is the fear of "destructive individualism," of "arbitrariness" in social relations. This philosophy, well-known from history past and present, is in sharp contradiction to the assurance given simultaneously that freedom no longer needs the protection and vigilance of the Liberals, because it is well taken care of now by the Christian Democrats. Those who take a negative view of individualism, and thus condemn the open and pluralist society and want to "overcome" it by a collective organization of all existence, depart from the foundation of free democracy.

Usually the Christian Democrat polemics attack Liberalism with philosophical and theological arguments. In so doing they fight against the imaginary windmills of an atheist, morally and spiritually indifferent Liberalism. Such accusations can no longer be raised against Liberalism. Actually they are raised only to distract discussion from the *really crucial question, which is acceptance or rejection of individual freedom, acceptance or rejection of the open society*. The Liberals should, therefore, not enter into any sterile debates on their alleged or real philosophical errors of yesterday, but attack both the Socialists and the Christian Democrats with the demand that freedom be transformed from postulate to reality, and to let their social and economic plans be judged by the criteria of tangible individual liberty.

Men—and that is the chief assertion of modern Liberalism—desire concrete freedom and choice in their intellectual, moral, spiritual and material life. These values, to be achieved and preserved in the process of a continuous struggle, cannot be replaced by any artificially constructed society of the future, however attractively pictured. More than that: parties relying on the drawing up and carrying out of such constructions will be missing the immediate task, which is to make life worth living here and now for the individual and for the society.

PART FIVE

NATIONALISM

INTRODUCTORY NOTE

Nationalism is a separate political current, yet it is curiously inter-mingled with the major ideologies. After all, political ideologies operate within national milieux. Is nationalism an ideology? It covers a broad range of moods from mere sentiment to a political creed, a substitute for religion of which modern totalitarian systems can make good use.

At one time regarded as the other side of the democratic coin, nationalism has also appeared as a distemper of democracy; although its role as a basis of modern totalitarian ideologies is irrefutable, the alliance between the two "isms" has not proved satisfactory. The Soviet Union, for example, has difficulties in coming to terms with nationalistic forces.

Broad dividing lines separate political from economic and cultural, primary from secondary, old from new nationalism. An analysis of modern nationalism reveals its many forms, all shaped and conditioned by specific circumstances. One speaks of the various phases of nation-alism: the liberating phase (which Rupert Emerson sees as "youthful and exuberant"), the authoritarian phase, and the aggressive phase, (the second taking place within the state, the third without), according to Morris Ginsberg.

Apart from being subject to change, nationalism is highly relative and subjective. In his paper, "Nationalism—A Reappraisal," Ginsberg speaks of its ambiguity: "Among the subject peoples nationalism is the enemy of imperialism . . . among the ruling peoples nationalism and imperialism tend to appear as allied." An ubiquitous political current, nationalism is not confined to any single part of the world; it flourishes in countries of varied political persuasion; it serves many masters and many causes. It is also a prism which reflects and distorts both Western and Communist ideas. William G. Carleton observes in his article, "The New Nationalism," that "the antithesis between bourgeois nationalism and proletarian internationalism is no longer so clearly drawn." Nation-alism has become more ambiguous, its contours more blurred.

The main difference between nineteenth-century nationalism and the new version is that while the former was bourgeois and democratic, the latter has both democratic and nondemocratic components and shows a marked trend toward collectivism. In both cases the nation is a central point of reference; but while in the older version the national purpose was the end toward which the political process was directed, now the nation-state may serve as an end and also as a means to a higher universalistic purpose achieved through expansion and conquest.

What are the present links between nationalism and democracy—which were so strong in the movements of national liberation before the First World War? Nationalism and democracy are no longer regarded as equivalents, although it is true that democracy may provide a fertile ground for nationalism by approving the principle of national self-determination. Still, there is no reason why democracy should result from nationalism. (One may add that democratic institutions tend to be confined within national limits and develop on the national level, a qualification that reveals the broad dimensions of nationalism, which has to be defined in terms of "nation," "nationality," and "nation-state.")

What links nationalism and totalitarianism, the communist variety of totalitarianism in particular? Historically, nationalism has been recognized as a basis of modern totalitarian ideology. In his *Conservatism Revisited*, Viereck writes: "Future historians will see the national socialism of Hitler and the national bolshevism of Stalin as variations on a single historical theme: the totalitarian mass-man." Nationalism provides a climate in which totalitarian seeds may find it possible to grow even in a democratic soil.

Today, communism and nationalism have become comrades-in-arms fighting the wars of national liberation. The relationship is more complicated than that which existed between nationalism and democracy in the past. Thus Soviet communism uses Afro-Asian nationalism as a weapon to undermine the colonial powers and produce antagonism toward the West. Communism makes temporary compromises with national bourgeoisies in order to achieve its long-run objectives. Through coexistence and infiltration it hopes to convert "nationalists" to its own cause. In an article on "Coexistence and Nationalism" (*The Listener*, February 1, 1962), Walter Kolarz, a keen observer of the international scene, said that "a good nationalist, in the eyes of the communists, is one who ceases to pay allegiance to his own nation, and looks upon the world primarily from the viewpoint of the communist bloc."

Soviet communism, to repeat, finds nationalism a rather untrustworthy instrument; it is troubled by nationalist stirrings inside the communist bloc. Irredentist movements take the form of a new "national socialism" rather than of "national communism." Nationalism is at the base of communist polycentrism. "Should Communism grow and spread," William Carleton predicted more than a decade ago, "should the opposition shrink and grow weaker, undoubtedly national rifts inside the Communist world would sharpen and multiply."

THE NEW NATIONALISM

William G. Carleton

In spite of strong indications of the persistence of nationalism, there is a general notion, part belief and part hope, that nationalism is gradually diminishing, that little by little it is being replaced by internationalism. This notion was particularly strong near the close of World War II, and was fed by the collapse of Fascist nationalism, by the enthusiasm of victory won by a widely inclusive international coalition, and by the high hopes entertained for the germinating United Nations. During the past five years the world situation has become clearer, and we are in a better position to appraise future trends in international relations.

It now seems fairly certain that nationalism will again dominate the twentieth century as it did the nineteenth century. True, in Western Europe, where modern nationalism first developed and grew to maturity, it seems to be weakening. A number of factors are here at work to produce this result: a drastic decline in strength due to the frightful losses involved in bearing the brunt of two great nationalistic wars; the collapse of old-fashioned imperialism, the loss of overseas colonies, and the withering of foreign investments; the distressing realization that national power is passing from the nations of Western Europe to nations in other parts of the world. Still, even in Western Europe, in spite of notable advocacy and the immense practical advantages to be gained, no really effective steps have been taken toward the formation of a federal state. And in Eastern Europe, in Africa, in the Americas, and in Asia nationalism seems to be definitely on the rise. Indeed, the coming of the twentieth-century industrial revolutions to the backward areas of the world threatens to build and intensify nationalism in those areas in much the same way that nineteenth-century industrial revolutions built and intensified nationalism in the older industrial countries.

There is a facile and an uncritical assumption that as cultural barriers are broken down, as the various parts of our planet come to be more and more alike, as the industrial and technological and scientific

Reprinted from the *Virginia Quarterly Review*, vol. 26, no. 3 (Summer, 1950), 431-440. By permission of the author and the publisher.

revolutions increase commonalities, as more peoples come to be urban and metropolitan, the world will move toward political unification. This may be the ultimate result, but progress toward political unification may not be much greater in the twentieth century than it was in the nineteenth century. Indeed, since the breakup of the medieval order the world has been getting closer and closer physically and culturally. The commercial revolution, the rise of capitalism, imperialism, the scientific revolution, and the industrial revolution have all contributed to the eroding of cultural diversities. But, paradoxically enough, as cultural diversities diminished, political nationalism increased. The industrial revolutions, coming to different countries at different times, were developed within national patterns, and consequently national unity and the feeling of national self-interest were increased. And this process of breaking down cultural diversities while at the same time intensifying nationalism—this process characteristic of the sixteenth, seventeenth, eighteenth, and nineteenth centuries—now shows definite signs of continuing through the twentieth century.

Liberal thinkers of the nineteenth century thought that nationalism could be curbed by law and by an international organization based upon contract. These conceptions suffered a severe set-back when the League of Nations foundered on nationalistic difficulties and fierce ideological conflict. They are now being tested in the United Nations, and again national difficulties and fierce ideological conflict threaten disaster. Another unfavorable portent is the failure of functional group alliances to cross national frontiers and to co-operate with similar groups abroad and against dissimilar groups at home; and thus apply the process of group conflict and compromise of domestic politics to international politics, disrupt national unities, and build a going international society. Delegations in the United Nations still operate as solid national fronts, and the United Nations is thus largely an arena for the playing of national balance-of-power politics. There are, of course, some signs that leftists are crossing national frontiers to co-operate with leftists, centrists with centrists, rightists with rightists; but this tendency is still too weak to counteract in any effective way the forces making for a continuation of national solidarity. Besides, this process, even if it developed appreciably, could operate for all groups only among democratic countries; dictatorships would not allow it, except for the particular ideological groups the dictatorships represented.

And this brings us to Marxism. The Marxists have claimed that when one group—the class-conscious proletariat organized as a Marxist party—came to power it would cross national boundaries and join hands with similar groups that had come to power in other countries, and thus the international proletariat would end the national state and create the international state. The Marxists contended that the national state was the creation of the bourgeoisie, that the national state was a broad cloak to disguise bourgeois interests, that through nationalistic imperialism and nationalistic wars the owners of production and their parasites exploited the masses and served their own class interests. Therefore, predicted the Marxists, when the workers came to power in old national states they would destroy those national states and establish an international workers' state.

This Marxist conception of nationalism has fooled and is fooling non-Marxists of the West today. Many non-Marxists of the West think that this Marxist concept is historically true; and more, that Communists today subscribe to it in the old literal, orthodox Marxist-Leninist sense and always operate on it in the realm of practical politics. Hence many in the West who have had a hand in American foreign policy have fondly believed that the non-Communists had a monopoly on nationalism; that the wars of national liberation in Asia would have to be non-Communist revolutions because Communism by its very nature could not be nationalist; that nationalist revolutions would be bourgeois simply because they were nationalist.

The truth is that contemporary Communism does not conform strictly to the Marxist-Leninist dogma with respect to nationalism and internationalism. Stalinism at home is more national than the Marx-Lenin formula contemplates, and it makes allowances for social revolutions waged as wars of national liberation. In actual practice Communist revolutions more and more take on the nature of nationalist revolutions, particularly in Asia. And as a matter of fact, the whole Marxian conception of nationalism as the mere creature of the bourgeoisie is much too simple and is not borne out by anthropology and history.

The essential characteristics of nationalism are older than modern nationalism, older than capitalism. To date nationalism from the commercial revolution, from the rising power of the modern bourgeoisie, is inaccurate. Men have always made a marked distinction between the in-group and out-groups, and loyalty to the in-group, whether it be tribe or city-state or nation, has been universal and persistent. (There has been, too, a continuing historical process of combining out-groups with in-groups to form larger in-groups, and it is this process that gives the adherents of internationalism their hope of ultimately breaking down nationalism.) Imperialism, too, is older than modern nationalism, older than capitalism. Indeed, imperialism was one of the most prominent aspects of antiquity. It is true, of course, that every great movement of modern times—the commercial revolution, the Protestant Reformation, the French Revolution, the rise of democracy, the industrial revolution—has intensified nationalism. And paradoxically enough, the modern socialist and Communist movements, by bringing direct government services to the mass of peoples, may also result in strengthening nationalism in spite of the hopes, the predictions, and the dialectical demonstrations of their prophets.

National differences represent more than the mere rivalries of conflicting business men. Different nations *do* have different needs and different cultures. They represent different geographies, different economic necessities, different stages of historical development. They are "culture-bound" in different ways. Even the coming of machine civilization does not break down all cultural differences, and it tends to lessen power differentials and thereby to intensify the power conflict.

Both in Europe and in Asia, the patent truth is that today Communist revolutions are taking place within the framework of individual countries and are being established and consolidated along national lines. These revolutions are not so much international as they are national; the people look for work, and social services, and consumer goods not to an international Communist state, which is mythical, but to individual national governments, which are real.

A genuine international revolution creating a genuine international state was expected at least four different times in this century: at the outbreak of World War I, at the time of the Bolshevik Revolution, at the end of World War I, and in the concluding days of World War II. Each time these expectations miscarried, and as a result Communist revolutions have been forced to develop within national patterns.

When the truly international revolution failed to materialize in 1919 and the early 1920's, following World War I, Russian Communism itself became more national and developed Stalinism as distinguished from Marx-Leninism. The sacred texts, of course, were not repudiated, but in practice they have been watered down considerably. In Russia a totalitarian Soviet patriotism has been evolving. For purposes of fomenting revolution abroad, the antithesis between bourgeois nationalism and proletarian internationalism is no longer so clearly drawn; national and social liberation are viewed as one and the same process to be achieved under the leadership of the Communist party. But even this watered-down version does not go far enough to meet nationalist realities, and increasingly Communism seems to divide between those who follow Moscow rather closely and those who would take a more independent national course, as for example Tito in Yugoslavia. Today the Communists, like the socialists in the period around World War I, seem to be dividing between the internationalists (whose internationalism already has been watered down) and the nationalists.

It is probable that we have been thinking of socialism and Communism too much as complete social systems and not enough as mere economic systems. Perhaps it would be nearer the truth to think of them as mere economic systems capable of being democratic or totalitarian, international or national, peaceful or imperialistic, depending upon the larger cultural milieus within which they work. Today they are working within national milieus and hence cannot escape national expression.

It is even possible that in Asia modern nationalism will emerge for the first time with the Communist revolutions, just as in Europe modern nationalism emerged for the first time with the capitalist revolutions. Communism and nationalism are being linked together in wars of national liberation, just as democracy and nationalism were linked together in Europe's nineteenth-century wars of national liberation. For instance, the Chinese Communists are making the political unification of China one of their primary goals. Real nationalism in China may come to be as inseparably connected with the Communists as in its formative stages real nationalism in Europe was inseparably connected with the rise of the bourgeoisie. In Asia, Communism may be the maker of nationalism, not its destroyer. Under Communism, the mass of Asiatics in some countries may come into close contact with their governments for the first time in their history, and this contact, because of the many functions exercised by Communist governments, will be far more intimate than the contact of the mass of Europeans with their national governments in the days when European nationalism was emerging. And the industrial revolutions engineered today by the Communists are being worked out within national patterns, just as were the industrial revolutions led by the bourgeoisie in the nineteenth century.

What of the solidarity of the proletariat? Even as a revolutionary force it has been exaggerated, particularly in its international role. And after a successful Communist revolution within a nation, will it survive? Or will not the successful revolutionaries re-emerge as different and proliferating groups and classes? Will not the new Communist societies develop new groups and classes? Will not managers, directors, engineers, technicians, professional classes, skilled workers, unskilled workers, and farmers evolve within the Communist states, breaking the so-called solidarity of the international proletariat and making impossible any real international action by an international proletariat—in the inclusive sense of the old Marx-Lenin formula—across national boundaries? Will not the old international proletariat then become a revolutionary myth rather than a reality for practical international co-operation and action? In short, will not the so-called international proletariat inside Communist states turn out in fact to be neither international nor even proletarian?

It is probable that today the Communist world owes much of the co-operation that does exist among its various national parts to its own feeling of precariousness and to its fear of the non-Communist world. Should Communism grow and spread, should the opposition shrink and grow weaker, undoubtedly national rifts inside the Communist world would sharpen and multiply.

Nationalism is growing among the backward peoples everywhere not only because it is an instrument to drive out ruling colonial powers but also because only centralized state machinery can satisfy the mass demand for modern technology, heavy industries, and the rising standard of living these make possible. The backward peoples, led by their native intellectuals, want the industrial revolution, and they want it now—in this generation. They have no native capitalist class or middle class sufficiently large to finance modern technology, and they do not want the increased wealth produced by industrialization to be siphoned off as profits for foreign capitalists. They want industrialization; they want it now; and they want its benefits conserved for their own societies.

Only centralized state power, only collectivist organization in some form, only government financing can bring in this generation so gigantic an economic transformation. Every vital revolutionary movement among backward peoples envisages industrialization and a great increase in centralized national power; every vital revolutionary movement is both social and national. This is true whether the leader is Sun Yat-sen or Mustafa Kemal or Nehru or Tito or Mao Tse-tung. The revolutionary movements in backward countries differ only in degree of socialization, centralization, and freedom; in the allocation they propose to make of the new national wealth; in their various attitudes toward Soviet Russia.

Nationalism, then, under different names, is on the march among the backward peoples. But it is not bourgeois nationalism. Indeed, its primary urge comes from the *absence* of a bourgeoisie. It is because the native middle classes are insufficient to finance industrial revolutions that all these movements are under compulsions to increase and socialize national power. (In this connection it is also significant that even in the West the strongest proponents of nationalism are no longer the bourgeoisie. For instance, in the United States during the nineteenth century it was the bourgeoisie who spearheaded centralized national power, whereas in the twentieth century it has been the labor groups who have spearheaded it.)

The very nature of the situation in backward countries gives the Communists certain advantages. The Communist fatherland, Russia, is the example inspiring all backward peoples. These people see in Russia a once backward people who in one generation lifted themselves from medievalism to a degree of modernity. The Communists, too, are better organized, assert a ruthlessness over even workers and peasants which facilitates change and the accomplishment of specific goals, and are fired by the proletarian myth. But the Communists suffer some disadvantages, too. There is the fear of becoming an appendage of Russia. There is the conflict of native nationalism and the old myth of proletarian internationalism, still not modified enough to suit the views of many nationalists. Nehru, for instance, is reputed to hold the opinion that the Communists are still not nationalist enough to satisfy the growing nationalism of Asiatic peoples. The Communists are in somewhat of a dilemma. If they do not espouse the cause of nationalism they will not get into power in the backward countries; if they do espouse it they endanger still further Communist internationalism (or Russian imperialism). But no matter what the original intentions of the Communists, when Communists acquire national power they do not seem able to escape going more and more national.

Americans must awaken to the fact that non-Communists have no monopoly on nationalism. The Communists, too, may use that weapon and use it against us. And if in playing for the high stakes of international politics we sponsor nationalist revolutions in Asia and in other backward areas, we must reconcile ourselves to the fact that these revolutions will be in large measure socialist revolutions and not bourgeois or status-quo revolutions. For today nationalism and socialism and nationalism and Communism are not incompatible; indeed, the great wars of national liberation in our times are not only nationalist but also socialist (as in India and Burma) and Communist (as in China and Indo-China).

If nationalism is rising over those extensive areas of the earth we have hitherto called "backward," then the implication of this for future international relations is most significant. The ultimate effect may well be to halt the Soviet-American polarization of power and to revive the old multiple balance-of-power system. Also, internationalism by way of long-time American or Soviet empire, and internationalism by way of socialist or Communist international solidarity may have to be discarded as probabilities for the future. Our hopes for political internationalim may have to center around the United Nations, frail reed as this may appear to be in a world of old bourgeois nationalism and of spreading and intensifying collectivist nationalism.

NATIONALISM AND DEMOCRACY: BACKGROUND AND FOREGROUND

Rupert Emerson

Nationalism has in its time been variously acclaimed as an integral and necessary part of democracy and denounced as the open gateway to autocracy and dictatorship. In fact, to assign it any particular political coloration is presumably impossible since it has been associated in one or another time and country with almost every conceivable political regime and attitude. Even though an impressive case can be made for the proposition that any true nationalism contains a strong strain of fundamentally democratic elements, there are many ardent and unmistakable nationalisms in which democracy is either virtually nonexistent or is no more than a façade of outward conformity with current political fashions. Where the general constellation of forces has been such as to promote democracy, as most notably in Western Europe and the countries which it has settled overseas, nationalism has maintained a predominantly democratic cast; where the underpinnings of democracy have been weak, as in much of the rest of the world, nationalism has betrayed the democratic promise which the nineteenth-century liberal saw in it and has become an instrument of the established ruling groups or of totalitarianism. Everywhere it is the champion of self-government in the sense of national as opposed to alien rule, but it is only accidentally self-government in the sense of rule by the many as opposed to rule by the few. Reduced to its bare bones, nationalism is no more than the assertion of a particular "we" arrayed against the "they" of the rest of mankind, by itself giving no clue as to how the "we" may choose to manage its own affairs.

The themes of nationalism and democracy cross and recross each other at so many vital points that it is essential to seek some understanding of their intricate interrelations. In some instances nationalism and democracy have been so intimately associated with each other as to be almost indistinguishable; in a number of others, for example the colonies of the Western powers, the nationalist movements have regarded themselves as the bearers of a democratic structure of state and society; but there remain a substantial number of important cases, among which Japan would head the list, in which democracy was at the best an afterthought. Furthermore, one strand of logical development inherent in nationalism, happily more frequently recessive than dominant, leads directly down the path of totalitarianism. The issue to be explored is whether any general principles can be discerned which suggest the circumstances under which nationalism does or does not take the democratic path.

At a time when nationalism in the West has often drifted in reactionary or militarist directions and when the most dangerous and abhorrent elements in it have so recently been arrogantly paraded by the Fascists and Nazis, it may appear paradoxical, or even outrageous folly, to suggest the existence of an essential bond between nationalism and democracy; yet both in idea and in actual historical development this bond has been of central importance. Hans Kohn has put the matter in the extreme form of saying that "nationalism is inconceivable without the ideas of popular sovereignty preceding—without a complete revision of the position of ruler and ruled, of classes and castes." [1] On the face of the historical record no statement as uncompromisingly sweeping as this can be sustained . . . and yet it has more than a germ of fundamental truth.

Once full-fledged nationalism has appeared, a transformation of deep and lasting importance in the relations of people, rulers, and state tends to occur. Even in the Fascist variants the role which the people play is

sharply distinguished from their role in the earlier type of dictatorship
or monarchy, as witness the efforts of Fuehrer and Duce to carry the
masses with them, to give the appearance of popular consultation
through plebiscitary techniques, and to spread the tentacles of the
Party down into every cranny of the society. This, certainly, is not
democracy, and yet it is equally certainly a perverse offshoot from
democratic roots, a post-democratic phenomenon. The Leader and the
Party put themselves forward as emanations of the popular will, as a
truer distillation of the national *volonté générale* than the people themselves can produce.

To reduce the question to its most basic terms, the argument linking democracy and nationalism would run something as follows. Nationalism is peculiarly a product of the distinctive forces which have gone
into the shaping of the modern world. Those forces are inherently and
inevitably "democratic" in the sense that they mobilize formerly submerged elements and classes of society into new social roles, eat away
at traditional relationships, and work toward the building of a new
great society into which, in principle, all men are actively drawn. Obviously what is involved here is by no means necessarily a democratic
constitutional structure nor even an immediate approximation of a
society striving toward egalitarianism, although both of these are likely
to be present at least as active aspirations. Far more, it is the general
conception, derived from the changing social scene, that the people,
the mass of ordinary human beings, are of consequence, that they are
achieving a sense both of their own worth and of their right and
ability to do something about it, and that the leaders must speak in
their name. The national era comes to be an era of mass communications
and mass production, inescapably headed toward mass politics.

The heart of the argument is the proposition that the rise of nationalism is normally associated with deep-running social ferment and change
which disrupt the old order of society and speed the processes of social
mobilization. On this basis nationalism is seen as one of the major
manifestations of what Karl Mannheim has spoken of as "the fundamental democratization of society," the stirring "into action of those
classes who formerly played a passive part in political life." [2] As the
peoples begin to come of age and to a new consciousness of themselves,
they demand a new place in a society in process of transformation. One
of the characteristic forms which this demand has taken is insistence
upon the centrality of the national community and upon the latter's
right to make the state the sovereign organ of its identity and will. The
people, after all, compose the nation, and it is thus not beyond the
bounds of reason to suggest that the revolutionary importance of
the fact that the social-political community which has come to occupy the
center of the contemporary stage—taking over the state in its own name
and establishing a new criterion of legitimacy—should, therefore, be
defined in terms of the people. In the new dispensation the state could
no longer be seen as made up of the ruler and those who happened to

be his subjects, but became in principle the emanation and instrument of the nation. The forward thrust of the bourgeoisie in Europe and, in due course, of the masses, had its close overseas parallel in the awakening of colonial peoples, in roughly similar circumstances and similarly under middle class leadership, to the struggle against their alien masters.[3]

At the next remove it might be contended that the only true nationalism is one which has deep popular roots. "Genuinely nationalist movements," Harold Lasswell has written, "are not to be confused with separatist demands which may be made in nationalistic vocabularies but with which the masses are not identified. A ruling elite may buttress its own demands by adopting a nationalistic phraseology, although the community remains aloof, which was true of some of the secessions from the Spanish and Turkish empires."[4] Those who would give full credence to the democratic thesis are tempted to settle the troublesome problem of nondemocratic nationalisms in this abrupt fashion, and possibly something can be made of it; but the easy course of cutting Gordian knots with the paper sword of definitions is one to be resisted. There is an element of obvious absurdity in any scheme of analysis whose premises lead on to a denial that nationalism existed in, say, Japan at one or another period since the Meiji Restoration or in Iran in the twentieth century. However demonstrably it may be that democracy in all or some of its aspects was missing from these countries, and that nationalism preceded rather than followed social-economic change, common sense will not permit the ruling out of what all the world has regarded as nationalism. But, even though the common term of nationalism be applied across the board it remains necessary to distinguish between different types of nationalisms and to examine their very diverse relationship to democratic assumptions and practices.

That the national and democratic principles were for many purposes to be regarded as opposite sides of the same coin was a commonplace in much of the political thinking of nineteenth-century Europe, although quite a few commentators stood out against such an interpretation and a number of contemporary developments belied it. As it was a part of the basic beliefs of the liberal publicists and statesmen of the period that democracy was on the march and that the people must come to a constantly growing share in power, so was it also an article of faith that mankind was divinely or naturally divided into nations and that these nations set the territorial and demographic boundaries within which democracy would operate. Increasingly it was taken for granted that if men were set free to choose for themselves, they would organize their societies on national lines. Woodrow Wilson, as the heir of nineteenth-century liberalism, made national self-determination an integral part of his democratic remedy for the world's ills. "By 1918 nationalism and democracy were generally taken as synonymous in the thought of the Western nations. The nation-state was regarded as the political expression of the democratic will of the people."[5] In the tortuous United Nations debates on human rights the presumption has from time to time been vigorously asserted that national self-determination is the starting point and indispensable condition of all the other rights and freedoms associated with a democratic society.[6]

This thrusting of the nation into a central position in relation to the concept of democracy meant a striking and significant innovation when contrasted with the democratically inclined political thought of preceding centuries. Where the latter, as most notably in the variants on the theme of the social contract, had appeared to assume that any chance assemblage of men might lay the foundations of a state, the nineteenth century moved to the conclusion that a viable state and particularly a viable democracy required the firmer foundation of an already existing community of sentiment, culture, and tradition. The social contract theorists may have implicitly taken for granted that the rational beings who were contractually establishing political obligations and institutions would have a prior bond among them; but, if they so believed, they for the most part signally failed to say so. Though Montesquieu had earlier pointed to the role of environment, only with Rousseau, in this school, are the elements of emotion, custom, and social milieu brought significantly into the picture, leading on through romanticism to the national age. For the dominant rationalism and individualism of the seventeenth and eighteenth centuries, the nineteenth century tended to substitute a Burkean return to history and a sociological approach which stressed the traditionally shaped communities of men. To the natural rights of individuals were added the natural rights of nations.

By the middle of the nineteenth century the new outlook had consolidated its hold to the point where its basic propositions could be asserted almost as truisms. It would be difficult to find anywhere a calmer statement of the issue, assuming as self-evident matters which are in fact open to grave dispute, than that of John Stuart Mill in his *Representative Government*.[7] Setting off from his definition of a nationality as a portion of mankind united among themselves by common sympathies, desiring to be under the same government and a government by themselves, he continued on to affirm that where such a national sentiment existed in any force there was a prima facie case for the establishment of a separate national state. This proposition he linked to fundamental democratic conceptions by suggesting that it "is merely saying that the question of government ought to be decided by the governed." While this statement may appear to be a commonplace expression of the democratic creed, he added to it the truly surprising assertion that: "One hardly knows what any division of the human race should be free to do if not to determine with which of the various collective bodies of human beings they choose to associate themselves"; whereas in fact it is far more plausible to contend that this is one of the last, most difficult, and most precarious of the freedoms to which human beings may lay claim. It deserves notice that the book in which this tranquil judgment appeared was published in 1861, at the start of four years of warfare in which the South sought to assert its right to associate with itself and not with the North in the United States.

For Mill, as for many other thinkers of his own day and since, the relation between democracy and the national principle went well beyond the proposition that if peoples were left free to choose they would sort themselves out on national lines and that they should be given an opportunity to do so. The claim was frequently made that democracy required a national setting, or at least that it flourished best where the people concerned were knit together by emotional and traditional bonds. As Mill put it, "it is in general a necessary condition of free institutions that the boundaries of governments should coincide in the main with those of nationalities." Such institutions he saw as being "next to impossible in a country made up of different nationalities," because of the lack of a united public opinion, of common sources of information, and of leaders having the confidence of an undivided public. Pointing to the Habsburg Monarchy he emphasized the danger to liberty in a multinational state in which the rulers could play off the antipathies of one element in the population against another and could rule "with the iron rod of conquerors" through the instrumentality of an army lacking both national attachment and sympathy with the people.

Here there was, perhaps, a far too easy transition from the accepted principle of the rights and freedoms of individuals to the rights and freedoms of nations with little awareness that the insatiable appetite of the latter might come to consume the former. That the transition was confidently made by Mill and many others of his day and later is beyond dispute. The English social philosopher, L. T. Hobhouse, summed the matter up some decades later in his confident claim that "national and personal freedom are growths of the same root, and their historical connection rests on no accident, but on ultimate identity of idea." [8]

In its youthful exuberance nationalism has at least the appearance of being a movement of liberation which embraces all other good things, including the freeing of the individual to pursue his own destiny in the democratic company of his fellow citizens. Only as nationalism progresses does it become evident that the claims of the individual may be subordinated to the drive for national unity and independence and that liberal democracy may give way to an authoritarianism in which the actual and diverse wills of the people of the nation are replaced by a leader or an elite supposed in some mystical fashion to express the national ethos. The French Revolution itself drifted into the hands of Napoleon; a number of thinkers, such as Bonald and De Maistre, stressed the conservative and traditionalist aspects, finding the nation embodied in its aristocracy rather than in the newly rising elements; in Germany Bismarck, and not the liberals of 1848, accomplished national unification; and in southeastern Europe the achievement of the national goals, under whatever auspices, took priority over the implementation of liberal ideals. Despite these and many other nondemocratic manifestations of nationalism, including its turn in militarist and imperialist directions, faith in the identification of nationalism and democracy remained widespread until Fascism, Nazism, and the shortcomings of Wilsonian self-determination made inescapable the doubts which Lord Acton and others had expressed. The young nationalisms of Asia and Africa are still disinclined to take such doubts significantly into account.

On the historical record two items may be cited as buttressing the democratic thesis. One concerns the regularity with which the loosening of the forces of the Western revolution has served as a stimulant to national sentiment, and the other, the fact that democracy in the modern world has appeared to flourish at its best in a national setting.

Wherever the characteristically modern processes of social mobilization, of fundamental democratization, have been set in motion they have with a striking degree of consistency operated on men to heighten or to create a sense of identification with national communities.[9] To whatever corner of the world one may turn, whether it be Europe or America, Asia or Africa, a central fact of modern times is that the encroachment of the new upon the earlier patterns of society has brought peoples to an increasingly vivid consciousness of their national distinctiveness (even though the nations concerned may still be in process of creation) and urged them on to nationalist self-assertion. Later developments have worked both to sustain the assumptions of Marx and Engels as to the national attachments of the bourgeoisie and to override their contrary assumptions as to the essentially unnational character of the proletariat. The masses no less than the classes have been drawn into the national stream once the modern ferment has been introduced.

On the second score, whether it be because the nation furnishes that "common understanding and sense of belonging together" without which "successful democracy is not really possible," [10] or for other reasons, the record shows that democracy in the modern world has worked best within the nation-state. If the existence of an opposition as an integral part of the governmental system may be accepted as a touchstone of political democracy, then one may suggest that an overriding sense of national unity has been a key element in transforming it into a *loyal* opposition. The rise of democracy as a political phenomenon has coincided too closely with the emergence of nations as conscious entities to allow of an explanation in terms of random chance. This is not to say either that all emergent nations have taken the democratic path or that some other form of social cement may not be discoverable to serve as a substitute for the social solidarity of the nation. What does appear evident is that the reason of man, on which the social contract theorists had generally placed primary reliance, needed to be supplemented by some other bond of unity, and it was nationality which came to the aid of rationality. Perhaps the next turn of events will see the emergence of larger supranational entities, as, for example, in a unification of Western Europe. To date, however, democratic institutions have not moved significantly beyond the national level.

The experience of the modern world suggests that national unity has been a necessary condition for democracy, but that it is far from being a sufficient one. The classic Western European models indicate that democracy has been at its best where history has shaped homogeneous peoples who managed to dispose at a relatively early stage of some of the more urgent issues of national identity. Contrasting the fortunate position of Britain with that of other European countries, R. H. S. Crossman has written:

British democracy evolved within the firm framework of national unity, and British Liberals could demand freedom without any fear of disrupting the nation into nationalistic minorities. . . . They could speculatively atomize English society precisely because it was not atomistic, but a community inspired by the deepest of common feelings—patriotism.[11]

In Britain, national unity was already solidly established by the time the nineteenth century presented a host of new economic and social challenges. In less happily situated countries the emphasis was a very different one. The experience of Eastern Europe and the Balkans indicates that democracy has not fared well in a multinational setting or when the drive for national unity and independence came at a late stage and took precedence over the issues of social, economic, and political reform which were simultaneously beginning to crowd in on peoples whose national destinies were still unresolved.

No simple and straight-line theory of cause and effect, however, can hope to embrace the actual historical diversity. The pitfalls into which one may all too easily stumble can be illustrated, for example, by the failure of old-established Spain and Portugal, both reasonably well-consolidated nations, to develop on democratic lines and by the contrary situation of an ethnically divided Czechoslovakia which achieved national statehood only late in the day and yet was certainly to be counted among the successful democracies. It must also be said immediately that the characteristic forces of the modern world, with the concomitant rise of the middle class, had penetrated deeply into at least the Bohemian portion of Czechoslovakia whereas they had impinged only lightly and in passing on the countries of the Iberian Peninsula.

To the positive proposition that democracy has taken firm root and flourished best in consolidated nations can be added the obverse contention that democratic institutions have shown little or no ability to cope with the problems of the multinational state. One can, indeed, argue that where deep-running ethnic diversity exists the introduction of democratic institutions is likely to have the effect of intensifying national distinctions and antagonisms since such institutions work to force a reconsideration of the definition of the "we" into whose hands power is passing. In the European setting two obvious instances are the dissolution of the Habsburg Monarchy into its component nationalities and the failure of the British parliamentary system to meet the needs of militantly nationalist Irishmen. In Asia the splitting off of Pakistan from India is the most striking example.

Such generalizations would carry a firmer ring of conviction if, as with every generalization about nationalism, there were not so many borderline cases and exceptions. Democracy has indeed flourished where national unity established the emotional framework of basic consent within which political disagreement could be tolerated. Yet, among the small number of European or European-descended nations clearly to be counted in the democratic camp, a surprising number deviate markedly from the classic model of across-the-board national homogeneity. One need only suggest the familiar examples of Belgium, Switzerland, and Canada, each divided in language and culture. The British nation embraces English, Welsh, Scotch, and some Irish. The United States and, in varying degree, other "overseas" democracies settled primarily by Europeans have been melting pots for peoples of many tongues, creeds, and races. In these instances it is certainly not stretching the known facts to surmise that the existence of democratic institutions aided in the process of welding national unity from original diversity.

The problems involved in the relations between nationalism and democracy are adequately complex if they are examined solely within the confines of Europe. They take on a different magnitude and emphasis as they are pursued into the vast areas of Asia and Africa. In many of the newly rising Asian and African countries a good case can be made for the proposition that the association between nationalism and democracy has been as intimate and the democratic character of the nationalist movements as unmistakable as in the earlier Western European models. Particularly countries with a considerably European colonial experience, such as India, Burma, Indonesia, the Philippines, and Ghana, took a full-scale and immediate leap into democratic institutions not only in constitutional structure but also in the extension of the franchise and on a universal basis. However problematical their political future may be, the record shows clearly that the nationalist movements saw themselves also as the champions of democracy.

On the other side of the fence, in a number of countries, such as Japan, Thailand, Iran, Ethiopia, and various of the Arab states, not to mention many Latin American examples, nationalism has had no more than a bowing acquaintance with democracy in any of its forms. In most instances, to be sure, a *pro forma* compliance with the mode of the day has been made through the adoption of constitutions of a nominally democratic variety. The working reality, however, has been the exercise of power by a small clique of insiders who have often not even bothered themselves seriously to take cover behind their constitutional façade, although postwar Japan may be taking its democracy more to heart.

If there is validity in the general proposition that the rise of nationalism is to be seen essentially as a phase of the expanding Western revolution, then it seems plausible to look for at least part of the explanation of the difference between democratic and nondemocratic nationalisms in the diverse circumstances under which that revolution has developed or been transmitted. This revolution has by now penetrated in varying degree to every corner of the earth, and every people has been forced to make some sort of response to the challenge which it imposed. The nature of the response is conditioned by the way in which the challenge was presented as well as by the character of the society undertaking the response.

One line of analysis which appears worthy of exploration is to draw a distinction between nationalisms which are original or primary in character, and those which are imitative or secondary and which, through their customary failure to draw in the broader masses of the nation, may properly be regarded as premature or incomplete in development. In the first category would fall those nationalisms which are the product of the challenging and new-modeling forces operating *within* the society concerned, while the second would embrace those cases in which nationalism, at all events in its early phases, appears to be primarily a reaction to the *external* impact of forces which have not yet significantly affected the inner structure of the society itself.

An immediate objection to such an approach is that, from one standpoint, only the Western European initiators of the new era can legitimately be held to have produced a primary or original nationalism. For all others, and perhaps peculiarly for the non-European peoples, it could be contended that their nationalisms must be of a secondary or imitative variety since they are followers in a second, third, or fourth generation and are all reacting to forces which came into being elsewhere. This is so evidently true as not to require more than statement, but one can argue that it obscures as much as it reveals. The forces brought into play by the revolution which spread out from Western Europe have operated in different ways in different countries and have had widely varying effects, even though the over-all results have been similar. The nature of the difference which is most characteristically involved can be illustrated by pointing to the contrast between, say, the Philippines and India on one side and Saudi Arabia and Ethiopia on the other. In the first pair of countries there has been a substantial penetration of the traditional order of society by the new. Westernized elements have emerged which are prepared and eager to push forward with further social transformations. This new-style elite has adopted democratic assumptions and practices, and the populace at large has a growing awareness of its own democratic claims and potentialities. In the second pair the traditional order has remained largely intact. The internal forces for change are still relatively undeveloped, the older dominant elites have in great part maintained their hold, and there has been both an avoidance of measures and appeals which would stir up the masses and a minimum of active popular participation, even by such middle class elements as have come into being. That the two pairs are already moving toward a greater resemblance to each other does not impair the fact that their experience of the age of European imperialism has been different in significant respects and that they have emerged from it with characteristic dissimilarities. The difference could be most concisely stated as involving the degree to which the *ancien régime* has been undermined and displaced.

Every kind and gradation of relationship to the imperial powers can be found at one or another point on the globe. Everywhere in greater or less degree the West has penetrated and disturbed the old order, although a few countries, such as Mongolia, Tibet, and Nepal, were sufficiently remote to limit Western contact to a minimum. The established ruling groups have almost everywhere been under some measure of attack, and only rarely have they been able to hold on to substantially unimpaired power and privilege. The term "quasi-colonial," applicable to, say, China, Thailand, Iran, and Liberia, points to the extent of imperial penetration under very different circumstances in four countries which never experienced colonialism. Again to suggest markedly divergent examples, Laos and Libya have both been influenced by their temporary subjection to European rule, and yet they could hardly be regarded as having had "long and intensive" colonial experience. The facts of the case establish a no-man's land in which the colonial shades off into the noncolonial with no clear line of demarcation to separate them. Political reality is diverse and recalcitrant, but colonialism has placed a distinctive stamp on those peoples whose destinies it has ruled.

NOTES

1. *The Idea of Nationalism*, p. 3.

2. *Man and Society in an Age of Reconstruction* (London: Kegan, Paul, Trench, Trubner & Co., Ltd., 1940), p. 44.

3. Maurice Duverger suggests that paternalist policies in the colonies have produced results comparable to those which shook Europe in the nineteenth century: "Les transformations économiques entraînent des transformations sociales, lesquelles conduisent à un bouleversement politique. Que la classe moyenne soit créée par le progrès technique ou par la colonisation, les résultats sont les mêmes au point de vue des structures politiques." "Une Course contre la Montre," *La Nef: Ou va l'Union Française?*, vol. XII, cahier no. 9, nouvelle série (June 1955), p. 216.

4. *World Politics and Personal Insecurity* (New York, London: McGraw-Hill Book Co., Inc., 1935), p. 97.

5. Alfred Cobban, *National Self-Determination* (London, New York, Toronto: Oxford University Press, 1945), p. 6. This view reached far beyond the liberal camp. Speaking of the period around the turn of the century, Richard Pipes states: "The principle of 'national self-determination' was generally recognized by socialists in Europe and Russia as a basic democratic right, like, for instance, the principles of equality of the sexes or freedom of speech." *The Formation of the Soviet Union* (Cambridge, Mass.: Harvard University Press, 1954), p. 33.

6. The Asian-African Conference at Bandung adopted this position in its final Communiqué of April 24, 1955: "The Conference declared its full support of the principles of self-determination of peoples and nations as set forth in the Charter of the United Nations and took note of the United Nations resolutions on the rights of peoples and nations to self-determination, which is a pre-requisite of the full

enjoyment of all fundamental Human Rights." *The New York Times*, April 25, 1955. The latter part of this statement repeats the words of the first "Whereas" of the General Assembly Resolution 637 A(VII) of 1952.

7. The material in this and the succeeding paragraph is drawn from the opening pages of chapter xvi, "Of Nationality, as Connected with Representative Government."

8. *Liberalism* (London, New York, Toronto: Oxford University Press, 1945), pp. 135-136. See also his *Democracy and Reaction* (New York: G. P. Putnam's Sons, 1905), pp. 157 ff. Cobban comes to precisely the contrary conclusion: "We are bound to conclude that the association between nationalism and democracy and therefore the theory of self-determination itself, may have been the result, not of their innate interdependence, but of historical accident." *National Self-Determination*, p. 7.

9. "The rise of nationalism accompanied the growth of democratic sentiments and of democratic instrumentalities." R. M. MacIver, *The Web of Government* (New York: The Macmillan Co., 1947), p.169.

10. Alexander Dunlop Lindsay, *The Essentials of Democracy*, 2nd ed. (London, New York, Toronto: Oxford University Press, 1935), p. 45. He added that "it is a commonplace that successful political democracy on a large scale implies something that we call nationality."

11. *Government and the Governed* (London: Christophers, 1939), p. 169. "Englishmen thought nationalism a subordinate manifestation of liberalism." Raymond J. Sontag, *Germany and England* (New York: Appleton-Century Co., Inc., 1938), p. ix.

NATIONALISM: A REAPPRAISAL

Morris Ginsberg

. . . The term nationalism is emotionally highly charged and it is used in different senses. It may denote, first, consciousness of nationality, that is, of belonging to a nation involving a sentiment of attachment akin to patriotism. It may mean, secondly, the belief in national self-determination or the "principle of nationality," that is, the principle that nations should have their own governments, that nation and states should be co-extensive. It may mean, thirdly, an intensified consciousness of nationality, characterized by the striving for prestige, power, domination. In practice the notion of self-determination has been used in a

---

Reprinted from Morris Ginsberg, *Nationalism: A Reappraisal* (Leeds: Leeds University Press, 1961), pp. 24-33. By permission of the author and the publisher.

self-contradictory manner to justify the inclusion within the nation of subject peoples not belonging to it. "Nationalism" then passed into "imperialism." This term, again, is notoriously ambiguous. In this context it is important to distinguish between the imperialism of a "superior" national group claiming the right to rule over subject groups within its state territory, and the imperialism which consists in the efforts made by states to extend their power, wealth and prestige by appropriating less advanced countries. This distinction helps us to understand the complicated relations between nationalism and imperialism. Among the subject peoples nationalism is the enemy of imperialism. On the other hand, among the ruling peoples nationalism and imperialism tend to appear as allied, the sentiment of nationality being used to provide the energy and enthusiasm needed for policies of expansion.

There is a somewhat similar ambiguity in the relations between democracy and nationalism. In the nineteenth century nationalist movements were on the whole liberative. Hence it was natural to regard them as based on the principles of liberal democracy. But the connexion is not a necessary connexion. For though democracy favours nationalism in the sense of national self-determination (the *droit des peuples à disposer d'eux-mêmes* of the French Revolution), nationalism in the other senses distinguished above does not necessarily imply democracy, and, historically, movements which have begun as liberative have in their later phases passed into phases of authoritarianism within and aggression without.

We are now in a position to consider the widely current feeling of disillusion concerning nationalism. This can be traced back, I think, to three or four main sources. First in importance is the experience the world has had of the aggressive nationalism of Germany, Italy and Japan. Next there are the disappointments with the attempts made to apply the principle of self-determination in the treaties of 1919. To this must be added the growing conviction, based on the experience of the second World War, that the independence of small nations is illusory, that in asserting their independence they are liable to become "danger-spots." Finally, there is the growing realization that in the conditions of the modern world wider forms of political organization are needed than those provided by nation-states, and that the independence, not only of small states but of most large ones as well, is illusory.

These are all matters of great complexity. The problem is to determine to what extent the difficulties involved are to be attributed to nationalism as such, what to the association of nationalism with the claim to absolute sovereignty, and what to the rivalries of the great powers. It is obvious enough that nationalism, in the sense of consciousness of nationality, may be raised to an intensity which can be used both for good and evil. It can provide the energy needed in a struggle for freedom and independence or for defence against external attack. It can also be used in wars of aggression and expansion. As we have seen, it readily passes into imperialism. It is thus not surprising that recent writers have tended to interpret nationalism as a function of imperialism. Sulzbach has argued that modern nationalism is in essentials the taking over by peoples of ambitions formerly pursued by kings and aristocracies. When sovereignty passed from the hands of kings to peoples, he suggests, the nations inherited the mystical qualities attaching to kings and at the same time their striving for power. "Modern nations are the democratic versions of kingship; they have a hunger for land and power and they consider themselves as superhuman beings for whom their members can on occasion be rightly expected to sacrifice their lives." [1]

Arguments such as these are made plausible by the ambiguities of both "nationalism" and "imperialism." It is true, of course, that there are few nations which have not at one time or another sought to expand their territory. But this does not show that wars of expansion are necessarily due to nationalism. Clearly, there have been wars of expansion in the era before modern nationalism and, on the other hand, the sentiment of national solidarity may exist among peoples who have no ambitions of territorial aggrandizement. Some wars may perhaps be correctly described as wars of nationality, as, for example, when it is said that the war of 1914 had its origin in the rivalries of Slav, Magyar and German nationalism. But in such cases it is the failure to generalize nationality rather than nationality itself which is the cause of the trouble. As Norman Angell once put it: "It is not the desire of nationality, but the desire to destroy nationality, which makes the wars of nationality." [2]

We are thus brought back to a further consideration of the "principle of nationality," that is, the principle that nation and state should be co-extensive. This principle was formulated with his usual moderation by J. S. Mill. "It is," he says, "in general a necessary condition of free government that the boundaries of governments should coincide in the main with those of nationalities." But he adds immediately that in practice the principle is subject to various qualifications. There are areas in which nationalities are so intermixed that separate governments are not possible or desirable. Recent defenders of the principle have not always been so cautious. Thus, for example, Ernest Barker, stout defender of freedom as he was, committed himself to the statement that in "some form a nation must be a state and a state a nation." [3] I do not see how this can be defended, either in point of fact or of right. It is true that states must be able to rely on the political loyalty of their citizens. But it does not follow that there can be no such loyalty without cultural homogeneity. Thus in modern societies political solidarity has been found to be quite compatible with religious diversity, not only in the forms of church organization but of beliefs considered fundamental by their adherents. The experience of Switzerland and of other countries shows that in certain conditions differences of language present no insoluble administrative difficulties and that it is not impossible to find ways of dealing with divergent cultural needs. In any case it is perfectly clear that in many areas of the world cultural plurality must be accepted as as inescapable datum. On the ethical issues involved the verdict of Acton stands:

The greatest adversary of the rights of nationality is the modern theory of nationality. By making the state and the nation commensurate with each other in theory, it reduces practically to a subject condition all other nationalities within the frontier. . . . The best states are those which include various distinct nationalities without oppressing them.[4]

It does not follow that nothing remains of the principle of nationality. It retains its value (a) as asserting the right of peoples to freedom from alien domination; (b) in stressing the importance for mankind of a diversity of cultures; and (c) of providing peoples in those areas of the world which are in the process of freeing themselves from foreign rule with the energy and vitality needed in the struggle for liberation, and with sufficient community of feeling and outlook to enable them to build up viable states. (a) needs no further comment. As to (b), the world would surely be the poorer if small states like Holland or the Scandinavian states were to lose their distinctive identity. It should be remembered that the principle of nationality does not exclude the possibility of the union of several small nations in a single state, providing such unions are voluntary and not imposed on the rest by one of the nations or by an external power. As to (c), it is plain that many of the areas of the world, such as China, India or Africa, are now testing the national ideals cherished in Europe towards the end of the nineteenth century. They are in the stage in which nationalism plays a liberative role. Nationalism in these areas, however, has peculiar characteristics. In the West, nation states are units within the larger unit of Western civilization. China and India, on the other hand, are themselves entire civilizations. On the analogy of what happened in Western societies they might be expected to subdivide into national units, as medieval Europe did in the effort to overcome local particularisms. On the other hand, the close connexion between nationalism and economic planning and the advanced technology which they have learnt from the West may make it possible for large units to remain in being without going through the process of unifying previously formed smaller units. In Africa the situation is different. States are arising on the basis of the administrative units established by the colonizing powers. These states will eventually create nations; they need nationalism, in the sense of community of feeling and will, if they are to weld the diverse elements of which they are composed into working units. The more inclusive organizations may follow later by way of federation, regrouping or otherwise. In all these cases nationalism is having a revivifying effect. There is everywhere evidence that the spirit of independence is quickening men's lives and giving their actions an energy and *élan* hitherto unknown.

It is true that we have come increasingly to realize that in the conditions of the modern world organizations on a larger scale are needed than states uni-national or multi-national. But different types of organization may well be required for different purposes. Thus to secure peace a world organization is now necessary. For economic purposes, on the other hand, regional groupings are needed and are indeed coming into being. Cultural needs again may be served by different organizations. This has an important bearing on the problems of nationality. These problems would be completely transformed if matters of military security were taken out of the hands of sovereign states. There would then be less reason for states, large or small, to strive for economic self-sufficiency, and there would be a greater readiness to form supra-national economic organizations. The claims of cultural nationalism would then be seen in their proper perspective. Various possibilities are open and have indeed been tried. Witness the different ways in which democratic countries have dealt with the relations between church and state or with the problem of reconciling the need for universal education with the need for variety and experimentation. Variety in educational systems need have no disturbing political significance. Thus no one feels that Britain is endangered by the fact that Scotland has retained its own educational system.

The future of nationalism depends on the future of large-scale organization. If the larger units are to be centralized sovereign states, they will have to develop among their citizens a common feeling differing from nationalism as we have known it hitherto merely in the scale by which it operates. The minor nationalities are then likely to be submerged despite ostensible rights of cultural autonomy. If, on the other hand, different types of organization are adopted for different purposes, if, in particular, military control is transferred to a world authority and states abandon the idea that their sovereignty includes the right of pursuing an independent economic policy, then cultural pluralism will not have the political significance it has at present and the specific culture of peoples large or small will have a greater chance of survival. Meanwhile the forces which made for nationalism in the past continue to operate and to find fresh worlds to conquer. So long as alien rule remains anywhere, the peoples, suffering from it will feel that their economic and cultural development alike will not be furthered without political independence. Whether the new areas to which nationalism is now spreading will follow the familiar sequence of liberation, unification and aggression remains to be seen. But for good or evil, nationalism is far from being a spent force.

NOTES

1. W. Sulzbach, *Imperialismus und Nationalbewusstsein* (1959), p. 167.
2. *War and the Essential Realities*, p. 51.
3. *National Character*, pp. 16-17.
4. *History of Freedom*, p. 292.

POSTSCRIPT

NEEDED: NEW POLITICAL LABELS

Kenneth K. Krogh

Of all the political ideas that have gone into shaping our modern world, none has gained wider usage or wielded greater influence than the left-right concept of political relationships. This is the concept that visualizes our political world as a spectrum stretching between two polar extremes, the extreme left denoting revolutionary radicalism, and the extreme right denoting revolutionary reactionism. The various political schools of thought are ranged in between like the colors of a spectrum according to the intensity of their respective tendencies.

This concept of political relationships stands as the common denominator of political thought throughout the modern world. The terms "left-wing" and "right-wing," derived from this concept, are the most common of all political labels. They reflect the scale by which we evaluate the political thinking of ourselves and others. They also reflect the attitudes with which we look upon change, whether in regard to laws, customs, ideals, cultures, economic arrangements, class structures, educational systems, religious institutions and creeds, or any of the other relations of man to man. In short, it is this left-right concept of political relationships that provides the sense of political direction by which men steer themselves in the troubled waters of our world.

But what if the sense of political direction it imparts is wrong? What if it confuses and distorts, so that man is directed into the very conflicts and pitfalls he wants most to avoid? What if our whole system of political relationships can be realistically explained only on the basis of a very different concept?

Despite its wide acceptance, the left-right concept is vague and ill-defined. No complete agreement exists as to the number of categories to be included in the spectrum. Furthermore, the division between any two categories is not a precise line but an imperceptible gradation. And people generally do not fall neatly into one category so much as they are mixed between them in their various views. The spectrum as out-

Reprinted from *Saturday Review* (December 3, 1960), 17-19, 63-64. By permission of the author and the publisher.

lined below, however, would seem to represent the most widely held view of the concept.

The left is generally understood to include those parties and movements that demand wider popular participation in government, push actively for reform, and draw particular support from the disinherited, dislocated, and disgruntled. The right is generally understood to include those parties and movements that are skeptical of popular government, oppose the bright plans of reformers and do-gooders, and draw particular support from men with a sizable stake in the established order.

This general concept provides the master frame of reference in which is cast the bulk of all our thinking about political phenomena, both past and present. But is it accurate? Is it realistic? Does it truly represent our world of political relationships?

The major premise of the concept is the existence of two political extremes which are thought to be a world apart in their fundamental principles. Thus Communism on the left and fascism on the right are thought to be opposites—the most divergent of all political beliefs. Yet we know from the experiences of recent decades that they actually share important features. Their commitment to the totalitarian state structure, the single party, the leader, the secret police; their image of the political world as a struggle between morally irreconcilable forces; their belief that all their opponents are secretly leagued against them; their own aspirations for concentrated and total power; their common recognition of war as a tool in their growth and development—all of these show that the two "extremes" are more like each other than they are like anything that is found in between.

Indeed, Communism and fascism are so much alike that most people are unable to observe any real differences between them. There is a general awareness that they have different names, fly different flags, and use abusive language toward each other, but beyond this most people are unable to recognize distinguishing features. The more discerning may point out that under Communism the means of production belong to the people while under fascism they belong to wealthy capitalists. But this distinction pales in significance beside the fact that in both cases the means of production are in reality under the control of an unchallengeable dictatorship wielding unlimited power. And it is this primary similarity rather than the secondary distinction that most significantly characterizes the relationships between the two.

Thus, although the concept says they are complete opposites, reality tells us they are much like twins. And the result is an explosion of the left-right concept as a reliable guide to political relationships. We cannot accept it except by pretending that vast differences exist between fascism and Communism which, in fact, do not exist at all.

The error of the two "opposites" is of no less magnitude than Ptolemy's error of an earth-centered universe. And just as Ptolemy's concept required a series of assumed epicycles to make it work, so does the left-right concept require certain assumed trends to make it work. If the concept is to hold together and make sense, for example, it must be assumed that any trend in the direction of liberalism and socialism will lead toward Communism. But what is the reality of the situation?

The reality is that no nation which has achieved a liberal or socialist government has ever become Communist of its own volition. Instead, it is precisely those nations that are the most advanced along the line of liberal and socialist policies (notably England and the Scandinavian countries) which stand among the strongest and most effective opponents of Communism. The strongest evidence of fact thus indicates that, if anything, a move toward liberalism and socialism really is a move *away* from Communism.

A companion assumption, which also must be believed if the left-right concept is to work, is that any trend in the directions of conservatism and reactionism will lead *away* from Communism. But reality tells us that Communism has come to power as an indigenous movement only in those countries that have been characterized by reactionary governments (notably Czarist Russia and Nationalist China). And today Communism enjoys its most powerful following in precisely those countries which are still laboring under the effects of conservative and reactionary rule. The strongest evidence of fact therefore indicates that, if anything, a move to conservatism and reactionism really is a move *toward* Communism.

The error in assumed trends thus adds further to the explosion of the left-right theory as a reliable guide to political relationships. Further, there is the fact that the left-right concept is forever shifting its ground. As political and economic conditions change, the left-wing position of yesterday tends to become the right-wing position of today. Thus, as early as the French Revolution, the left of the National Assembly became the right of the Legislative Assembly and the left of the Legislative Assembly became the right of the National Convention, and so on down to the present day, when "right-wing" politicians are to be found embracing as moral certitudes the very measures their predecessors denounced as the epitome of wickedness.

Inevitably, the question arises: How can a world that has attained such fantastic precision in the physical sciences continue to fumble along with such inaccuracies in political science?

How did it come to believe in a system of political relationships which is clearly shot through with error and which shifts ground with every passing decade?

To understand this situation we need to go back to the very origins of the left-right concept.

The terms "left" and "right" as used in the political sense appear to have originated during the French Revolution. In the National Assembly, which met in the summer of 1789, three parties were represented. One party was of a conservative type, opposed to any changes in the powers of the monarchy or the privileges of the nobility. A second was of a more liberal type, favoring limited reforms which would have introduced some form of representative government without unleashing the fury of the oppressed people at the expense of the nobility. The third was viewed as a radical party which, although at first not opposed to the monarchy as such, demanded a constitution to limit and regulate the powers of the monarch and insisted on such other reforms as equal taxation, freedom of speech and press, trial by jury, and abolition of feudal dues. The meeting place for the assembly in Paris was a large hall with a horseshoe-shaped amphitheater. The conservatives sat to the right of the speaker, the radicals to the left, and the liberals in the center, and it was this seating arrangement that is said to have given rise to the use of directional terms in politics.

The French Revolution, however, was only one part of the growing democratic movement. The British Bill of Rights and the American Revolution had preceded the French Revolution, and all three developments served to give impetus to the belief in the inevitability of democracy and progress. Here Western civilization saw itself progressing out of the tyrannies and oppressive traditions of old along a path which pointed in the direction of democracy and expanded human freedom.

At this stage of the democratic movement, the left-right concept was adequate to the political complexities of the day. The right simply stood for those who wished to preserve the existing order, while the left stood for those who wished to change it in the direction of expanded democratic freedoms.

But then something happened which has left its imprint on man's political thinking to this day.

Looking back from a perspective of more than a century and a half, we can see that two diverging lines of political development emerged from these early beginnings. In England and the United States, the democratic movement followed a way of progress in liberal constitutional democracy. In France, however, the movement veered off along what Walter Lippmann has described as "a morbid course of development into totalitarian conditions."

If we follow the political development of England we see, as did de Tocqueville, that the English aristocracy had a way of accommodating itself to the pressures and demands of the growing democratic movement. As a result, the aristocracy retained its place in the government, and the government and its constitution continued to grow ever more representative of the people as a whole and ever more responsive to their needs. Here was "government by discussion," following a course which was steadily to broaden the base of decision-making power among the English people. A similar tradition was developing in the United States.

In France, however, the reverse was true. The nobility of France proved unable to merge and mix with other social groups. On the eve of the revolution, the nobility closed ranks and resisted every attempt toward reform. The result was a virtual impasse which led to the formation of the Jacobin Clubs and a clamor for the head of the king. The Jacobins, who eventually came to power, believed that the principle of the revolution itself was at stake and proceeded to guillotine not only Louis XVI but all others suspected of conspiring or wishing to conspire against the revolution and the new republic. The Jacobin policy of Terror was to claim the lives of thousands from all ranks of life. Even the head of Robespierre, key instigator of the Terror, was to fall under the guillotine before a reaction to the slaughter set in. And so great was the reaction that many Frenchmen turned about to favor a restoration of the monarchy.

Here a movement toward government by discussion had turned into government by terror. A movement toward government by assimilation had turned into government by liquidation. A historic issue of *progress* had turned back upon itself to become a historic issue of *excess*. And the stain of excess was to be indelibly imprinted on the left-right concept.

What is significant here is that the left-right concept did not evolve from the successful movement toward democratic progress in England and the United States, but from the unsuccessful attempt in France. Thus the left retained the distinction of its democratic aspirations, but it tended to take on the coloration of excess as experienced in France. And the issuance of the "Communist Manifesto" in 1848 was to give further impetus to this tendency.

With the issuance of the "Manifesto" there was need for accommodating the Communist approach to politics within the left-right system. But this posed a dilemma. In theory, the Communists were committed to the high goals of the withering away of the state and the liberation of individuals—goals in keeping with the democratic ideals of leftists everywhere. But in practice, Marx and Engels used the same formula as the Jacobins had used a half-century earlier. They championed liquidation of the ruling class through force and violence and committed themselves to a concentration of decision-making power in the hands of a dictatorship. Significantly, the elements of force and violence and the concentration of decision-making power in the hands of a single individual were precisely the characteristics of power exercised by European monarchs from feudal times. Thus the Communists, like the Jacobins before them, sought to fight fire with fire. But fire is fire, and force is force, and tyranny is tyranny, no matter what other labels they bear. In their practical approach to politics, therefore, the Communists committed themselves to a position on the political right. But in the end, theory won out over practice. With their Utopian goals, the Communists did not *seem* to belong to the right or center. So they were given a position on the far left, solidifying the belief that the democratic movement is inherently addicted to excesses of the most objectionable sort.

In 1925 Hitler issued his "Mein Kampf," and there was need for accommodating the fascist approach to politics. The fascists were hardly conservative, since they did not wish to preserve the existing order. They were revolutionaries in every sense of the word, purposefully planning to transform the existing order into an all-absorbing authoritarianism that would overcome the frustrations of modern industrialism. Yet their totalitarian ideal did not fit the left's Utopian goals of freedom, so they were given the position on the far right.

Thus we have the left-right concept in its present form. It is a concept that started out to mirror the outlines of the world's democratic movement. But when that movement split into two diverging lines, the left-right concept stuck with its parent body, the French Revolution. As a result, the concept reflects the logic of the French Revolution and insists that pursuit of the democratic ideal leads to and requires government by terror and measures of class *liquidation*. It utterly fails to reflect the logic of the English and American experiments, which prove that pursuit of the democratic ideal through "government by discussion" leads to measures of class *assimilation* in which all classes gain representation and a voice in the decision-making power.

The tragedy of political thinking over the past century and a half is the fact that the devotees of class assimilation have never put the devotees of class liquidation in their proper place. Instead of developing a concept that could comprehend the success of assimilation and the futility of liquidation, the entire democratic movement has succumbed to and suffered from the left-right concept.

Consider the devastating effects of the catastrophic default on the fortunes of the democratic movement. Conceptually, its first effect was to trap the democratic movement between two forms of dictatorship. Gone was the promising democratic horizon and its new vistas of "verifiable progress" which beckoned to Bagehot and other advocates of "government by discussion." Astride the path stood a new political specter, Communism, which spat on "government by discussion" as a decadent "bourgeois" institution and which championed instead a "dictatorship of the proletariat" as extreme as any known to history. To the rear, in league with all tyrannies of old, stood the other modern specter of dictatorship, fascism.

Outflanked by the arbitrary placement of Communism in the left-right concept, the freedom movement split asunder. Part of it tried to come to terms with Communism, with the tortured results now becoming evident in the writings of those who have emerged, shaken to the very core, from their involvement in "dictatorship of the proletariat." Another segment, composed of the traditional socialists, has tried to go ahead as if Communism might not be an inevitable end to the freedom movement after all. But it has itself been confused in part by the Communist apparition on the far left and has been dogged at every step by fusillades of opposition from fore and aft. The relentless tenets of the left-right concept have allowed the Communists to brand them as "running dogs of capitalism" and as "capitalist lackeys," while the conservatives and reactionaries have responded to the confusion in the socialist ranks by throwing charges of "fellow travelers," "pinks," and "Communist-fronters" at the group as a whole. A third segment, the liberal group, has all but halted and turned back upon itself to join a large segment of the world's body politic in a desperate attempt to find new facets of the middle-of-the-road approach which might solve the world dilemma.

Thus we see that what started out as a clearheaded approach to progress through the enlargement of human freedom has today become a splintered, dazed, demoralized effort characterized by indecision and defeatism. Beset from left and right, and yet finding the center position intolerable in the face of world conditions, the democratic movement has no place to go.

In the midst of these developments, man has become increasingly preoccupied with a different basic question. With the advent of the left-right concept he has gradually switched from "What is progressive?" to "What is excessive?" as his chief political concern. And it is this basic question which now grips the political thinking of the world. With despotism prevailing at either end of the political spectrum, the center and *status quo* have been glorified as the only safe realm of political life. Conformity has become the ruling consideration, and departures from traditions have become the greatest causes of political heat. "What is excessive?" is the characteristic question of the left-right concept and the age which it dominates.

Our intellectual world is thus in a state of crisis today over the meaning and possibility of human progress for the very reason that its basic concept of politics does not admit of progress. The left-right concept is an anti-progress concept. The full import of its logic is to discourage new approaches of any kind. What progress may be made toward greater freedoms in our modern world must be made on the basis of a blind faith in human nature so moving as to override the influences of this villain concept.

Can the situation yet be saved?

Can we replace the left-right concept with a more realistic theory of political relationships, one that can comprehend the opportunities and promises of the democratic movement as well as its failures?

Voltaire has underlined the urgency of our need for such a concept with his dictum that "men will continue to commit atrocities so long as they believe absurdities." Fortunately, the clues to a new concept are already at hand as a result of the accumulated knowledge of recent decades. The next forward step in political theory will be to piece these clues together in a meaningful fashion and relate them to the chaotic situation in which we now find ourselves.

INDEX

INDEX